THE SHORT OXFORD HISTORY
OF THE MODERN WORLD

General Editor: J. M. ROBERTS

THE SHORT OXFORD HISTORY OF THE MODERN WORLD

General Editor: J. M. ROBERTS

THE CRISIS OF PARLIAMENTS: ENGLISH HISTORY 1509–1660
Conrad Russell

EMPIRE, WELFARE STATE, EUROPE: ENGLISH HISTORY 1906–1992
Fourth Edition
T. O. Lloyd

THE OLD EUROPEAN ORDER 1660–1800
Second Edition
William Doyle

THE LIMITS OF LIBERTY: AMERICAN HISTORY 1607–1980
Maldwyn A. Jones

THE BRITISH EMPIRE 1558–1983
T. O. Lloyd

ENDURANCE AND ENDEAVOUR: RUSSIAN HISTORY 1812–1992
Fourth Edition
J. N. Westwood

BARRICADES AND BORDERS: EUROPE 1800–1914
Robert Gildea

REBELLIONS AND REVOLUTIONS: CHINA FROM THE 1800s TO THE 1980s
Jack Gray

BRITISH HISTORY 1815–1906
Norman McCord

THE EUROPEAN DYNASTIC STATES 1494–1660
Richard Bonney

MODERN INDIA

The Origins of an Asian Democracy

SECOND EDITION

JUDITH M. BROWN

OXFORD UNIVERSITY PRESS
1994

Oxford University Press, Walton Street, Oxford OX2 6DP

Oxford New York

Athens Auckland Bangkok Bombay
Calcutta Cape Town Dar es Salaam Delhi
Florence Hong Kong Istanbul Karachi
Kuala Lumpur Madras Madrid Melbourne
Mexico City Nairobi Paris Singapore
Taipei Tokyo Toronto
and associated companies in
Berlin Ibadan

Oxford is a trade mark of Oxford University Press

Published in the United States
by Oxford University Press Inc., New York

First published 1994
Paperback reprinted 1994

British Library Cataloguing in Publication Data
Data available

Library of Congress Cataloging in Publication Data
Brown, Judith M. (Judith Margaret), 1944–
Modern India: the origins of Asian democracy / Judith M. Brown. —
2nd ed.
p.   cm.—(The Short Oxford history of the modern world)
Includes bibliographical references and index.
1. India—History—19th century. 2. India—History—20th century.
I. Title. II. Series. DS475.B79 1994
954—dc20   93–31405Ï
ISBN 0–19–873112–4
ISBN 0–19–873113–2 (pbk)

Printed in Great Britain
on acid-free paper by
Bookcraft Ltd, Midsomer Norton, Bath

In piam memoriam

Eric Thomas Stokes
1924–1981

Atque inter silvas Academi quaerere verum

CONTENTS

TABLES

MAPS AND FIGURES

ABBREVIATIONS

AICC	All-India Congress Committee
CID	Criminal Investigation Department
CP	Central Provinces
CSP	Congress Socialist Party
CW	*The Collected Works of Mahatma Gandhi*
DCC	District Congress Committee
DMK	Dravida Munnetra Kazhagam
IAS	Indian Administrative Service
ICS	Indian Civil Service
IESHR	*Indian Economic and Social History Review*
IOL	India Office Library
JAS	*Journal of Asian Studies*
JP	Justice of the Peace
MAS	*Modern Asian Studies*
MISA	Maintenance of Internal Security Act (1971)
MLA	Member of Legislative Assembly
MP	Member of Parliament
NAI	National Archives of India
NMML	Nehru Memorial Museum and Library
NWFP	North-West Frontier Province
NWP and O	North West Provinces and Oudh (this became UP after 1902)
PCC	Provincial Congress Committee
P. & O.	Peninsular and Orient (Shipping Line)
PSS	Poona Sarvajanik Sabha
Rs.	Rupees
RSS	Rashtriya Swayamsevak Sangh
UL	University Library
UP	United Provinces (Uttar Pradesh since independence)

GLOSSARY

ahimsa	non-violence
Ahirs	cultivating caste
ashram	religious retreat; religious community round a *guru*
babu	clerk; used by British to describe western-educated Indians
bhadralok	'respectable folk' in Bengal
bhakti	devotion
brahmacharya	celibacy
Brahmin	priestly caste
Chamars	Untouchable caste
charkha	spinning-wheel
chaukidar	watchman
crore	10,000,000
dar ul-Islam	land where Islam is secure
dharma	duty
diwani	revenue-collecting right
durbar	ruler's open court for his subjects
Gounders	dominant agricultural caste
Gujars	agricultural caste
guru	teacher; religious guide
gurudwara	Sikh temple
hartal	stoppage of work as sign of mourning or protest
hijrat	Muslim flight from place where Islam is unprotected
hundi	bill of exchange
hookah	pipe
imam	officiating priest at mosque
izzat	prestige
jagir	grant of land in return for service
jagirdar	holder of jagir
jati	local caste group
Jats	peasant farming caste
jihad	Muslim holy war

Kammas	dominant agricultural caste
karma	law of ethical causation
Kayasthas	writer caste
khadi	hand-spun cloth
Khalifah	spiritual head of all Muslims; Sultan of Turkey
Khatri	caste name
Kshatriya	warrior caste
lakh	100,000
Lingayats	agricultural group; sect within Hinduism worshipping Shiva
Lok Sabha	lower house of Indian Parliament
mahajan	money lender and changer
mahalwari	adjective describing village land settlement, cf. *zamindari* or *ryotwari* settlements
Mahatma	honorific title meaning 'Great Soul'
malguzar	revenue-farmers given land in CP
malik	village notable
Marwaris	trading community originating in western India
maulvi	Muslim theologian
maund	measurement of weight, *c.* 82 lbs.
maya	illusion; veil of matter over reality
memsahib (fem. of sahib)	British woman in India
mofussil	hinterland
mohulla	urban neighbourhood
moksha	salvation; liberation
Moplahs	Muslim peasant community in Malabar
nabob	Englishman returned to England with fortune made in India
Nagas	tribal group on north-east frontier of India
nawab	title of Indian ruler
panchayat	court; caste council
Panchayati raj	post-independence form of rural self-government
Paravas	South Indian fishing community
Pathan	North-West Frontier tribal group
Patidars	agricultural caste in Gujarat
Pir	Muslim spiritual leader
pundit	Hindu scholar, teacher
rais	urban notable

raj	rule; particularly used of British rule in India
raja	ruler, king
Rajputs	warrior caste or clan
Rajya Sabha	upper house of Indian Parliament
Rani	Queen
Reddis	dominant agricultural caste
Rohillas	descendants of Muslim Afghan warriors who established Kingdoms in north and central India in the seventeenth and eighteenth centuries
ryot	peasant
ryotwari	adjective describing land settlement with peasant proprietors, *ryots*
sabha	association
satyagraha	'truth-force'; 'soul-force'; non-violent resistance to injustice or evil (word created by Gandhi out of Gujarati words)
sepoy	Indian soldier
Shariah	Islamic law
Sheristadar	senior Indian revenue official
shetia	commercial magnate
Shudra	labouring caste
Shroff	money-lender and changer
suttee	widow's self-immolation on husband's funeral pyre
swadeshi	use of things belonging to one's own country
Swaraj	self-rule
taluka	administrative division of a district for land revenue purposes
taluqdar	landowner (particularly in UP)
Thakurs	dominant agricultural caste
ulema (pl. of *alim*)	Muslim clerisy
Vaishya	trading caste
varna	one of the four theoretical divisions of Hindu society
zamindar	landowner
zamindari	adjective describing land settlement with large landholders, *zamindars*

India c. 1980

India *c*. 1930

Introduction

India's recent historical experience and development have been remarkable. Events in the subcontinent have been significant not just for those whose home India now is, who number between 800 and 900 million. They concern us all because they mirror many of the critical issues facing the whole world of the later twentieth century—a world marked by increasing interaction of peoples and continents, wracked by political and social turbulence within nations and major international conflicts, yet a world concerned with the dignity of human life and the worth of the earth's resources. India also reflects many of the forces which have created this world. For example, it was the first non-white nation to emerge from colonial control, and its independence from Britain in 1947 undermined the whole fabric of the British empire which had dominated world affairs in the preceding decades. Standing at a sensitive juncture of the Middle East, Europe, and Asia, it has not only retained its territorial integrity, but has in contrast to most African ex-colonies proved politically stable. Moreover it has become adept at organizing its government and politics through democratic institutions and a civil service built, somewhat ironically, on foundations left by its imperial rulers. Yet it has still to solve major economic and human problems, as its population soars and the fabric of its political, social, and economic infrastructure creaks and threatens to crack as it is sorely strained in an environment of scarcity and social conflict.

This book introduces some of the major themes in modern Indian history. It investigates the origins of India's independence and democratic political system, which lie in the historical processes of interaction between a stable society and venerable culture and forces of change created both within India and brought to bear on it from beyond its borders in the circumstances of British rule. Although the main focus of the study is political it sets its analysis of changing political patterns in a broad socio-economic context. The structure and economic base of society are fundamental. We need to know who lived on the subcontinent, how they earned their living, how authority and power were distributed among them, in what groups people felt they belonged, and the strength both of the linkages and the divisions between them. For these are the very stuff of politics, and stability or change here will have fundamental repercussions in political life. We

1

need also to inquire into matters of belief, of unvoiced assumptions and of overt ideologies. The observer must try to understand how people remote in space, time, and culture have interpreted good and evil, how they have understood the good and desirable life, how they have evaluated different forms of social organization and structures of government, and what worth they have ascribed to public action to further such goals. More prosaically, the inquirer must also be concerned with institutions through which social, ideological, and economic forces are channelled. Modes of administration, ways of consulting opinion, strategies for making public decisions, frameworks of law, and the organization of force—all these are the outer shell of political life, but also profoundly influence it.

These three themes—institutions, ideas, and the nature of society—are essential to understanding the origins and viability of any political system. They will appear and re-appear, interwoven, through this book, though its main thrust is chronological. For history is about movement in time, and the degree, patterns, and sequences of change are central to the historian's viewpoint. This is an introduction to modern India, for non-specialists and those beginning to study the subcontinent. Comprehensiveness is neither intended nor possible, given the time-scale, the country's great regional diversity and numerous local patterns of change, and the British dimension to Indian history for much of the period under discussion. I shall point out the main areas for consideration in trying to understand the dynamics and tensions of modern India. This will mean indicating where there is historical controversy and acknowledging where there are gaps in our evidence. Consequently there will be some loose ends, unanswered questions, and ambiguous evidence, rather than simple arguments and possibly facile answers. But this is in the nature of historical reality, particularly when observers and observed live through times of unprecedented change.

This new edition is necessary for several reasons, even though it is less than a decade since the book first appeared. It incorporates or discusses new work which has appeared since the first edition, where this illuminates little-known or misunderstood aspects of Indian history; and it points to significant departures and trends in historiography, of describing and conceptualizing the country's recent past. One of the excitements of a field of study comparatively recently released from the intellectual grip and periodizations of 'imperial history' is the constant opening of new lines of enquiry, asking of new questions, and realization of the significance of forces previously underestimated or ignored. For example, where historians of late eighteenth-century India once concentrated on political and military initiatives and weaknesses, now it is recognized that longer-term socio-economic changes profoundly affected Indian rulers and polities, the role of European traders, and interactions between the two, enabling the political as well as economic intrusion of the British and their eventual construction of a new Indian 'imperium'. Or again, the work of the 'Subaltern School' of historians has further illuminated the presence of many varieties of Indian political awareness and activity, and their often ambiguous and turbulent connections, despite the predominance often given to 'nationalist politics' and its spokesmen, in accounts of late nineteenth-century and early twentieth-century political change. While work on woman and social reform has not only opened up a world of experience and contested identities closed to historians who focused on high politics and the male public domain, but has disclosed the many subtly gendered dimensions of Indo-British encounters. Yet another reason for a new edition is India's experience in the last decade. By contrast with the first thirty years of independence, the recent past has been turbulent and unpredictable. Two prime ministers have been assassinated, and there has been an unprecedented level of public violence. Established political institutions have been weakened. Powerful politico-religious movements have threatened to tear apart polity and society and undermine the state's secular foundations. And India has encountered its most severe economic crisis since 1947, leaving the state within weeks of bankruptcy in 1991, and thus necessitating major economic policy re-orientation. Such dramatic experiences can easily be oversimplified, particularly in foreign reporting, and can encourage the reconstruction of 'neo-colonial' images of the subcontinent. It is hoped that the changes in the Epilogue which permit some discussion of these developments will invite deeper and more sensitive interest in India's recent experience, and encourage readers to progress to some of the excellent new studies of late twentieth-century Indian politics now available.

Oxford
Spring 1993

CHAPTER I

The Indian Subcontinent: Land, People, and Power

The Indian subcontinent has long exerted a fascination over people from other lands. Writers in the classical Mediterranean world as early as Horace and Herodotus commented on its supposed wealth and wonders—its gold, precious stones, and ivory, and its allegedly fabulous beasts such as eels 300 feet long, dogs capable of combat with lions, and one-horned horses. But then, as now, what people of different races and cultures knew or thought they knew of each other often took the form of a stereotype: a single image or stylized picture drawn from myth, fancy, and scanty knowledge, rather than true familiarity and accurate observation. This is not surprising, since India is 7,000 miles distant from western Europe and the journey had to be made by land or sea until the coming of commercial air travel in the mid twentieth century. Before steam replaced sail in the last century at sea and substituted railways for horses as the fastest mode of overland travel, visitors to India from Europe could spend at least three months on the way, facing considerable hazards from climate and disease. Moreover, those who made the perilous journey east were not trained observers of society and government; but diplomats, traders, and sailors, interested in profit and survival rather than in accurate reporting of the land and its people.

The image of India in European eyes has changed markedly over the centuries. Whereas it was once seen as a land of marvels, by the nineteenth century European Christians, scandalized by stories of customs such as child marriage and widow-burning, viewed its people as benighted heathen, fit subjects for conversion, good government and reforming education. But as western scholars began to learn Sanskrit, so the wealth of India's religious literature in that sacred language became apparent to them, and gradually India came to be seen not just as a 'white man's burden' but as the source of ancient wisdom and enlightenment on which Europeans and Americans, locked in the profit-making materialism of industrial society, could meditate and from which they could draw fresh inspiration. Later still, in the twentieth century, the image of a 'spiritual India' was reinforced by those westerners who were captivated by the preaching of non-violence by M. K. Gandhi during the nationalist movement; and by those discontented men and women who 'dropped out' of western society to search for Indian spiritual teachers and techniques of self-realization. Indians, too, have had their images of the west. The red-faced, beef-eating Englishman of imperial days was one element in their image-making. Another, which still persists, is of Europe and America as materialistic and immoral societies, whose people have rejected God and all the moral values which make for stability and sobriety in human relations. As Gandhi himself said after a visit to England in 1909,

> Looking at this land, I at any rate have grown disillusioned with Western civilization. The people whom you meet on the way seem half-crazy. They spend their days in luxury or in making a bare living and retire at night thoroughly exhausted. In this state of affairs, I cannot understand when they can devote themselves to prayers.[1]

Even though we now know much about the mental pictures people paint of unfamiliar races and cultures, it is tempting for an author beginning an introduction to modern India to sketch an outline of 'traditional society' at about the end of the eighteenth century, when the forces of European commercial and political intrusion, and then of imperial government, began to set in motion significant changes in the subcontinent. Scholars have hotly disputed whether such a concept as 'traditional society' is legitimate in any context, not just that of India; and whether it is merely a crude and distorting intellectual construct rather than an accurate reflection of an actual society or historical state of affairs. But comparatively recently people have still written of 'unchanging India' and of 'timeless Hinduism'. Yet historical study shows without doubt that India's economy and society were never static, and that certainly in the later seventeenth and eighteenth centuries major economic and social changes were occurring which provided the basis for the more obvious and rapid changes of later years. Society on the subcontinent provided mechanisms and sanctions for social change. Moreover, the religious traditions of Indians proved remarkably accommodating, absorbing new ideas and practices, and adapting to changing situations. Without contributing to an image of a changeless, traditional society, it is important to indicate some basic features of the Indian environment and social order which have been slow to change or are natural 'givens', such as geography. For these have been part of the context within which successive governments have had to operate, the raw materials with which they have had to work; whether they were Mogul emperors, British administrators, or Indian politicians in an independent, democratic state. But a further warning is essential. The subcontinent is very large—the size of Europe without Russia, or about half the area of the USA. (From north Kashmir down to Cape Comorin on the southern tip is 2,000 miles; and at its broadest in the north the distance is even further.) Within this land mass are major regional areas with their own geography, climate, language, customs, and even food. Over time different experiences of government, economic change, and politics produced varied local power structures and patterns of political behaviour. Nonetheless, certain natural, social, and political aspects of the lives of most of the subcontinent's inhabitants are central to our understanding of India's recent past and present experience.

i   The natural and material framework of life

Our first concern must be the most basic 'raw materials' of life on the subcontinent: what nature provides as a framework for human life, and what men have made of and within the natural order. Geography and ecology are crucial in the historical experience of any people, and consequently to the historian who pieces together the record of that experience. They determine, for example, where settled cultivation is possible, and where a profit can be gained from agriculture above the inhabitants' subsistence needs. Such a surplus can fund centres of stable power, sophisticated government, and expanding circles of conquest, and possibly the blossoming of cultural activity. Great civilizations, the glories of artistic endeavour, intellectual creativity, and the pursuit of luxury and leisure all require a secure economic base. Geography dictates the barriers of land and sea which may isolate peoples from a wider world. It also provides the natural transit routes which can be used for migration, invasion, and trade. Furthermore, the nature of a region's terrain and its productive capacity does much to mould the social organization viable in that area. Different ecological situations throw up different styles of production, and of economic and social control—the great landed estates of South America, for example, the sturdy small-holders of parts of western Europe, or the form so remarkable in parts of northern India, the tough and enterprising peasant brotherhood.

The traveller by air over India senses vividly both the unity and the diverse panorama of the subcontinent. In two or three hours he jets over stupendous snow-capped peaks, lush agricultural plains, and brown semi-desert land: he sees the magnificent course of great rivers and the long, snaking coast lines on the east and west of the great land mass. Two hundred years earlier few Indians would have travelled beyond a small group of villages which formed their economic community and provided their social network, built on marriage ties. Consequently they would never have grasped the idea of the subcontinent 'whole'. But even without the aid of modern communications and maps those merchants, courtiers, soldiers, and holy men who did travel for professional reasons would quickly have realized something of India's size and diversity. The Indian troops from Bengal in the east, who served the British in the early nineteenth century, were given foreign service allowances when they fought in western India, so far from their native places was it and so culturally different from their homes.

The subcontinent is, however, a distinctive geographical entity, bounded and thus united by mountains to the north and great oceans to west, east, and south. The outsider could only reach India by sea or by the passes in the north west. (It was not until 1942 that invasion was launched by the north east; as then the Japanese attempted after their conquest of South East Asia in the Second World War.) Such natural barriers have not only protected India. Their presence has also meant that those peoples who *did* migrate or invade through the north west had to become 'Indianized' to a significant degree. Not until the advent of swift sea travel in the nineteenth century was it possible for invaders to retain easy links with their place of origin. Even the British, with their command of the seas, and latterly with advanced systems of postal, telegraphic, and air communication, were in a real sense prisoners of the subcontinent they had conquered—perhaps a strange-sounding assertion, but one which indicates a historical reality which will be a major theme of this study. But though India was an entity in itself it was never isolated from the rest of the world, as China tended to be. Coasts can mean contact: and India was at the centre of a great arc of maritime trade and travel, stretching west to the Persian Gulf, the Red Sea, and Africa, and east deep into South East Asia.

Within India there are marked geographical areas. First, in the extreme north and west there are the great mountain ranges, including the Himalayas, three of whose peaks rise above 28,000 feet. They have a crucial effect on northern India's climate, soil, and river systems. They also capture the imagination of those who are subject to their influence. Not surprisingly they are seen as some of the holiest places of the subcontinent by Hindus, and beckon thousands of pilgrims, mendicants, and hermits in search of salvation and solitude. The second geographical region as one moves south is the Indo-Gangetic Plain, formed by the three rivers, the Indus, Ganges, and Brahmaputra. This is the expanse of flat land where there are great extremes of heat and cold at different times of year, so often called 'the heartland of India', or simply 'the plains' by the British who fled from its fierce sun to the hills in an annual exodus celebrated by Kipling and countless other literary portrayers of Anglo-India. Here the British made their capital, in Calcutta and then in Delhi, as did the Mogul rulers before them. Here agriculture has been long established, where adequate water makes the land extremely fertile. It is the home of a large proportion of the subcontinent's people. After 1947 part of it became Pakistan. Moving still further south, as the land mass thins down like an upturned cone, a range of hills much lower than the northern mountains separates off the southern two-thirds of the subcontinent. This hill region has its own distinctive economy and is peopled by India's tribal population. While to the south there are again settled areas whose economy and society are formed by the pattern of coast and river system. Parts are rich agricultural regions, such as the coastal plains of east and west. Elsewhere agriculture can be a back-breaking and heart-rending occupation with scanty water supplies, as on the Deccan Plateau.

Water is crucial to agriculture. Before the coming of widespread, scientific irrigation in the later nineteenth century most Indian farmers relied on rivers and the monsoon rain. The aftermath of the rare, dry summer in temperate north-west Europe can only begin to hint at the vital importance of an adequate monsoon and the disastrous consequences of its failure for hundreds of thousands of ordinary people. On it depends not just the fertility of different regions, but the level of prosperity each year and the very survival of much of the population. Its pattern also helps determine the type of crops which can be grown. The name 'monsoon' comes from the Arabic word for season, and denotes the climatic pattern caused in South Asia by an annual rhythm of winds: as the air warms in April–June and cools again later in the year. When the warm air moves inland and meets the land mass it causes rain: the rain is showery, but can be torrential while it lasts, or it can 'fail' almost completely. Southern India has rather more even rainfall throughout the year than the west coast or the north. To the north comes the powerful 'hot weather' from mid-March to mid-June, when temperatures can rise to 120°F in the sun and well over 100°F in the shade. The rains cool down the air and land if they come on time late in June; and they should last until September. Then, until the climate heats up the following year there is the 'cold weather', pleasantly temperate for the British for whom it was the time of social festivities and visitors from Europe. For centuries before their rule, however, the rhythm of climate had determined the pattern of Indian economic and social life—the cycle of sowing and harvest, and linked to that the pattern of religious festivals, the marriage season, and the time for military campaigns.

Even such a brief note on the natural framework of life suggests some of the forces underlying the major patterns of political and social relationships in the subcontinent's long history. Geography and ecology show us where for millenia it has been possible for people to cluster and build up bases of power and civilization. India's history is in part the story of the interaction of the peoples of such areas with those of other zones less favoured by natural resources. These long-standing centres of orderly and cultured life are river basins and plain areas—in the north the Ganges valley, for example, and in the south the rich agricultural river deltas and coastal plains. Founded on settled agriculture, growing either rice or grain, they became centres of permanent settlement and stable government, generated trade links and developed distinctive and often rich cultural patterns. Here have been based the major political powers which over centuries have dominated India. Compared with these have been areas of relative isolation, insulated from wider contacts by barriers of mountain or desert. The Kashmir valley set jewel-like in the northern hills is an example; as is the hilly central part of the subcontinent. The peoples of such regions have lived in ambivalent relationship with their remote but more powerful and organized neigh-bours, who with differing degrees of success at different times have tried to extend their authority into the more isolated areas. The post-1947 contro-versy between India and Pakistan over Kashmir can be seen as part of such a long-term cycle of interaction, as well as an aspect of border conflict between two independent nations. Yet other areas have become distinctive because they are like transit camps, route areas, through which migration, conquest, and contacts take place, rather than by virtue of their own natural features or endowments. The dry tableland of the Malwa plateau connects north India with the west coast and stable settlements further south: while on the far eastern side of the country the Orissa coast links south India with Bengal.

Fertile land has for thousands of years been the single most vital resource which men could control in India. It was, and still is, the major source of wealth and basis of occupation in the subcontinent. Even in 1980, 70 per cent of the working population depended for their livelihood on agriculture and food production. The man who has land, depending of course on the amount and its fertility, can not only feed himself and his family. He can sell his crops and on the proceeds buy both necessities and luxuries, including labour, either to work his land or to perform domestic service. He can also give credit to the less fortunate or the less prudent, in the form of seeds or cash; credit being a major source of influence in a land where the seasonal variations and climactic hazards can produce not just serious 'cash-flow' problems but even threaten the survival of farming families. Consequently the history of land usage in India, the grant of power over land to different groups by successive political regimes, is not just part of a specialized economic or administrative history. It is a vital component of the changing patterns of social influence and political control. We shall return to it constantly in our study, whether we are trying to understand social struc-ture, tension between groups, rural unrest, political ambition, or the undergirding of state power.

In later chapters we shall observe these patterns over time: but at the outset a few general observations are essential. First of all, statistics relating to land are extremely unreliable. The impossibility of accurate quantifica-tion over extended periods of time is a major drawback with which histori-ans have to work. Figures for land ownership, for example, are hazardous before the mid-nineteenth century because of the lack of accurate records, and even more because of problems involved in defining 'ownership', as we shall shortly see. Figures for crop yields are also unreliable—until well into the present century. Often they do not exist for pre-British times; and even after the British started compiling records of agricultural yields it was immensely difficult to collect accurate figures, given the type of village official or notable who was entrusted with the task. Often statistics were really only estimates. Moreover, regional variations in crops and productivity made all-India generalizations almost meaningless. (One analyst working in the 1950s and 1960s actually produced three different estimates of all-India crop yields!)

Although the details of India's agrarian history will probably never be accurately known, there is no doubt that agriculture was the heart of the economy. The actual crops varied from area to area, according to soil and climate. Where rainfall permitted, rice was the basic crop, as in Bengal or near the southern coasts. In the drier areas wheat, barley, millet and maize were staple crops and staple diet. (Even in the twentieth century Indians are still classified in times of shortage for ration purposes as rice or wheat eaters.) Before the improvement in transport in the last century and a half it is probable that many farmers still grew for their immediate needs or for limited barter within the vicinity in exchange for basic necessities such as cloth or cooking pots. However, there is evidence at least from the eighteenth century that there was a significant amount of cash cropping, in some areas, and a widespread exchange network of agricultural goods, well before the more modern development of valuable cash crops for internal and international trade. To take one region only as an example: we know that a large volume of trade in agricultural products passed through Bengal in the eighteenth century, including food grains, sugar cane, poppies, indigo, betel nut and tobacco.[2] A further impetus to the monetization of the rural economy was the payment in cash of the Mogul revenue demand; and the silver which fed the Mogul revenue system came from the New World via European trading companies or through middle men, in return for India's raw materials and manufactures such as fine cloth and silk.

Access to the resources of land was a major determinant of social and political power. But what was the nature of this 'access'? When the British began to grapple with the question at the end of the eighteenth century they brought with them mental baggage from Europe which in fact confused them when they looked at the Indian scene, and vitiated much of what they tried to do when they had the authority to settle land with groups or individuals in return for payment of annual revenue. It is all too easy for the modern reader, like earlier British administrators, to bring to his picture of Indian rural society the notion of a single 'right' to land: as if land were property which could like a house, a horse or a piece of jewellery be bought, sold, mortgaged, and taxed. The early British assumed that land in India should belong in this outright way to a clearly discernible owner in return for the payment of revenue. It was an assumption rooted partly in Roman law and its definitions of property and ownership which has moulded European thinking; and partly in Britain's historical experience of land ownership and government. However such notions of land ownership were probably rare in India, although there are some indications that the idea of proprietory right was developing in parts of the subcontinent in the seventeenth and particularly in the eighteenth centuries as Mogul power weakened and local men began to transform 'prebendal' holdings (temporary holdings for service rendered) into 'patrimonial' ones which were more like outright, hereditary rights.[3] It is more realistic to visualize various layers of people and groups who had an interest in land and different access to its resources, rather than any group of outright owners of land. For example, the top layer would be those who paid the revenue to the dominant political power. Beneath them would be those who actually controlled the land, made decisions about its use, employed labour and disposed of the produce. Because of religious taboos many of these would have felt demeaned or polluted had they actually ploughed and harvested themselves. Consequently beneath them were the actual tillers of the soil, who despite their low status had a recognized 'right' to a part of the produce in return for their labour. Furthermore, there were others like potters, barbers, scavengers, and midwives who performed essential services in the rural community: they, too, had a recognized interest in land and access to part of the produce in return for their work.

This hierarchy of interests meant that change could occur at one level without necessarily affecting other levels. Those who were required by government to pay the revenue might change, but life at village level might go on much as before, with the land being tilled and managed by the same people. In practice there were wide regional variations in this structure of interests in land. In some areas the revenue payers might be powerful warriors and their descendants, or people whom the British with their alien assumptions took to be 'large landlords'. Elsewhere they could be brotherhoods of farmers, or even comparatively uninfluential individuals. It was also possible 'to wear different hats' at the same time, to be responsible for revenue for one plot of land, while organizing the cultivation of another for which someone else paid the revenue. Not only was the structure complex; it was also flexible. Conquest or other political upheaval could bring new people into the status of revenue-payers: and at lower levels peasants could migrate to virgin land or flee from oppressive revenue-collectors. Although we do not have accurate population statistics until the nineteenth century, it seems that there was not great pressure on the land as there was from late in the nineteenth century—a change in land-man balance which then constricted rural movement and helped to solidify the pattern of land control.[4]

Even though land was the major source of wealth and influence, we must not underestimate the complexity of India's economy and society, or ignore the other resources provided by nature or contrived by man within this natural framework. The rivers and coast offered rich fishing opportunities, and this natural source of wealth was often exploited by hereditary groups who made fishing their speciality. Some made a bare living from it, while others did very well indeed. The Paravas of the southern Tamilnadu coast, for example, were specialist pearl fishers and prospered on their skill. Later they used their maritime knowledge to branch into other sea-linked occupations such as piloting, dockhandling and even ship-owning. Although India is rich in minerals the absence of a modern extractive technology meant that only some of them could be procured and processed before the last century. Particularly important were salt and saltpetre. For example, in the eighteenth century salt was manufactured along the coast of the Bay of Bengal, by boiling sea water in pans.

Industrial production as it developed in modern Europe was unknown in India until the first cotton mills were opened in Bombay in the mid-nineteenth century. Only then was part of the subcontinent's economy markedly influenced by the system of large-scale production which gathers together large numbers of wage workers and uproots them from a rural environment to work at machines in factories, controlled by owners who have made major capital investment in plant and raw material. In India secondary production of material goods tended to be cottage based i.e. carried on at home, generally in the framework of village life. The economy was not divided as sharply into different sectors as are modern, industrial economies. Many people did a variety of jobs, particularly in the slack times in the agricultural cycle. Often the women in a household would be involved in small-scale, home-based production, particularly spinning yarn or weaving cloth, both for family use and for wider sale. Furthermore there were specialist artisan groups—potters, jewellers, blacksmiths, weavers—who provided for the needs of the village community, and were paid locally in a mixture of cash and kind, rather than selling their skills and wares in a wider market. Cloth is the most obvious example of early Indian manufacture which was produced in large quantities but not in an industrial factory framework with the aid of power machinery. Made in a host of different qualities and varieties, it was essential at home, and much in demand abroad. Often it was produced on a form of 'putting-out' system, which linked merchant, middle-man and village-based weaver, the first in this chain advancing the necessary money. Some luxury 'industry' also existed, to service the courts and other wealthy groups, and to satisfy the eager Europeans who marvelled at the beauty of Indian silks and muslins, for example. This production was also a specialized and highly skilled handicraft, as was jewellery manufacture.

Clearly, although India's economy and society were predominantly rural, by the seventeenth and eighteenth centuries there was considerable commercialization and mobility of goods. There is evidence of internal trade by land and the great river arteries of the subcontinent, a thriving coastal trade, and a developed international trading network. All three types of trade were interconnected. Foodstuffs, such as grain and sugar, and cloth were among the main commodities of internal trade. Cloth, silk, indigo, saltpetre, and opium all travelled in significant quantities to the coasts, either for shipment to other parts of the subcontinent, or for export in exchange for bullion and foreign goods. India had long been an element in the long-range trading networks of the Islamic world, both as importer and exporter. But even when these networks declined by the eighteenth century, and with them some of their key commercial centres such as Ahmedabad or Dacca, other internal and international trading routes developed or increased in significance, producing new centres of commerce such as Mirzapur, Kanpur, or Calcutta. Europeans had begun to involve themselves in this complex web of 'country' and international trade, at least from the seventeenth century, alongside a wide spectrum of Asian operators—traders, bankers, political magnates, and those who made a living from military and revenue entrepreneurship. The Europeans, indeed, came to perform a vital function in the working of India's economic and political structures, because they imported the bullion on which the coinage system rested—coinage which enabled commodities to be turned into cash and surpluses to be exchanged and transmitted, and which also permitted the smooth functioning of the revenue system. Within a hundred years they were the most powerful group involved in importing and exporting; but they were still only a part of a whole Asian trading network, dealing alongside Hindus, Parsis, Jews, and Arabs.

Scholars are now unravelling the details of this trade for certain areas from the ledgers of European trading companies, shipping lists, and private papers. Calcutta, for example, was in the eighteenth century the entrepôt for a substantial trade linking the Bengal hinterland with other parts of India, with South East Asia, and with Europe. Textiles were the most valuable items of its trade with Europe and other parts of Asia. In Bengal there was also a large volume of trade in agricultural produce. Some of it, too, was exported—rice to South East Asia and Indonesia, and to south India, sugar to western India and the Middle East, indigo to Europe, and opium to Malaya, Java, and China. India's western coast also had a strong trading tradition, carried on by Indians, Arabs, and Chinese, to be joined in the sixteenth century by the Portuguese, and in the seventeenth century by the Dutch and English. Surat and then much later Bombay were the major western ports. As a modern student of Surat and its merchants in the early eighteenth century observes, their multifarious activities 'hung together, and were all directed to the end of gathering the production of northern and western India at the port of Surat and then exporting it to other Asian ports and to Europe, as also to the importing of a considerable amount of bullion from abroad and some . . . spices, silk and other items and distributing these through other networks into the interior of Gujarat and northern India.'[5] In Surat in the early 1720s the Dutch had the largest foreign trading post with a non-Indian staff of 57. In their store sheds they had spices, sugar, Japanese copper, tin from Malacca and Siam, all to be exchanged for locally hand-woven cotton goods which they would sell in Europe and Asia. About 45 larger trading ships came here annually: only 7 or 8 were 'Europe' rather than 'country' ships, and at least two-thirds of the latter were owned by non-Europeans.

Such enterprises needed finance. A sophisticated system of mercantile credit and transference of funds had developed to service this complex trading network, although a modern 'banking system', such as developed a little later in Europe, did not exist. Surat, for example, had its group of *shroffs*, who converted currency, lent money, bought and sold bills of exchange on distant places, and even undertook marine insurance. Bengal's trading finance was dominated by a great banking house based in the royal city of Murshidabad. It dated back to the late seventeenth century and was founded by a western Indian family. They not only went into business themselves; they lent money to Indian princes and European traders, and controlled the Bengal mint. Large banks in Banares, deep in the heart of north India further up the trade lines which supplied Calcutta, also did business in Bengal. These were the big-timers; trader bankers whose services maintained the long-distance trade of India, and oiled the wheels of revenue payments and political power, who became both prestigious and politically influential. They took the high risks, and they could make great profits. Regional trade was serviced by lowlier, local money-lenders, money-changers and bankers, known as *shroffs* or *mahajans*. They worked the local currency system, advanced money, and arranged remittances between places with *hundis* or bills of exchange.[6] (Agricultural in contrast to mercantile credit, however, tended to be a far more local affair, in the hands of many small-time grain dealers, pawn-brokers, and more substantial agriculturalists. They catered for the perennial credit needs of farmers caught without sufficient seed at planting time, without cash when revenue payment fell due, or needing the crippling capital outlay to provide a socially acceptable dowry and suitable marriage celebrations for a daughter.)

Such are the broad outlines of the natural framework of life on the subcontinent, and the ways men contrived to use natural resources for subsistence and profit. There were other means of earning a living. 'Scribal groups' serviced the Mogul courts and their successors, for example; others made livelihoods through military service and enterprise; while yet others lived as religious professionals within India's several religious traditions.

But far fewer people were supported by 'professions' which concerned organizing and controlling people rather than crops or goods, as in the civil service or the army. As in the case of land and crop yields, so for population and its distribution, accurate statistics are unobtainable for this earlier time. One economist has 'guesstimated' that under 20 per cent of the working population were supported by a 'non-village' economy, while 72 per cent of the labour force were village based and 10 per cent were tribal folk.[7] Then as now India was a land of villages. This was the environment in which the vast majority lived, worked and developed their views of human community and the meaning of life.

Some significant urban centres also existed, though we do not know the size of the urban population until the 1872 Census, when town-dwellers accounted for somewhat under 10 per cent of the population. Estimates of townsfolk under the Moguls vary from 15 to 7 per cent, or even lower. Towns and cities were generally built for defence, or round a court with its administrative structures, social and economic needs, on a natural point for exchange of goods, or to express religious aspirations and enable ritual performances. They often combined military, administrative, economic, and religious functions. Centres of administration and cultured living, such as Delhi, Lucknow or Hyderabad, were predominantly court-centred. Forts like Calcutta or internal marts such as Allahabad were major commercial centres, while Banares on the sacred river Ganges was both a city of temples and mercantile enterprise.

Despite urban centres and the economic influence they exerted through their services and requirements, and despite the networks of trade, India's economy well into the nineteenth century was both rural and segmented into regional economies rather than integrated as a single economic entity in the way modern national economies are. A villager in the hinterland might well live most of his life little touched by what occurred in Bombay or Calcutta in terms of economic activity, his needs met by locally grown crops and local handicrafts, whose availability and price were determined by local forces. Gradually this became less true under the pressure of political as well as economic change. But India's earlier economy should be visualized as a cluster of regional economies, some of which, like Bengal, were not only internally more integrated but also linked into wider economic networks by virtue of their natural position, resources, and communications. The local nature of much Indian economic and social experience becomes even clearer when we consider some of the main features of social life on the subcontinent.

Before we turn in more detail to the structure of society and its underlying assumptions, one further aspect of the natural framework of life must concern us—namely, language. It is a clear link between the two. Language is in one sense a natural 'given', part of the framework within which men are born and have to live. Yet it deeply affects how people perceive themselves and others, and how they relate to them. Moreover language is a natural resource which, as much as fields or fisheries, can be consciously exploited, and even manipulated to influence individuals and groups. Its influence in group relations is particularly significant. For language is a means of communication, a potent means of linking people together—and so, of course, dividing them off from others. It also bears powerful emotional overtones and transmits shared culture, as it conjures up the myths and shared historical experiences it records and celebrates in song and story, whether in written or oral form. It can define who is friend and foe in relations between language groups. Within a group which speaks the same language, differences in accent or dialect can also be divisive, marking status, for example.

India is a land of many languages. Their presence underscores regional divisions which, as we have seen, were often created by geography and climate. The distribution of languages also demonstrates the lengthy interaction of peoples and the patterns of migration which have helped to create India's rich and complex culture. Figures for the distribution of language are available for this century. But languages live. They change, they lose or attract speakers. So it is impossible to extrapolate from contemporary statistics to present an accurate account of the linguistic state of India two centuries ago. But broad patterns can be traced. India's languages fall into four main families. There are the Indo-Aryan languages, spoken in north and central India; Dravidian languages spoken in the southern third of the subcontinent; Tibeto-Chinese surviving in the north-east mountain area, where there must have been long-standing connection with people of Tibet and South East Asia; and the Austro-Asiatic tongues of the tribal people in India's central hill regions. The tribal languages may well have been spoken more widely in prehistoric times. Their present distribution reflects the interaction of different zones—the more settled agriculturalists pushing the more primitive people up into the less fertile regions. Dravidian was probably the language of the settled cultivators throughout India until halfway through the second millenium BC, when the Aryans began to migrate from the north west, bringing with them Sanskrit, an Indo-European language. This is now a 'dead language'—the sacred language of the Hindu scriptures, known only by those who actually learn it for religious or academic reasons. But it forms the basis of the script and grammar of India's northern languages, such as Gujarati, Bengali and Hindi. The southern languages are completely different—in sound, shape, and script. Within these language families, however, there are different languages. And even within one language area there are numerous dialects. From the eighteenth century with the introduction of printing and the spread of education differences of dialect have to some extent been ironed out and languages have been standardized. But even in this century, for example, in the Hindi-speaking areas of the north there are local dialects extending over groups of villages. Very often women will speak only this; their men and children, with the benefit and demands of schooling and wider travel beyond the home village, will also know 'standard' Hindi, though they will revert to village speech in the privacy of the home.

For this study two points about language need stressing. Firstly, language differences are a highly significant aspect of the diversity of India. They are part of regional identity, helping to perpetuate regional distinctiveness and loyalty. From the later nineteenth century, as society and the distribution of power began to change, language became an explosive political issue. It has remained a sensitive problem for independent Indian governments. Secondly, the British brought their language to the subcontinent. As they achieved political dominion English became the language of administration and higher education. So the potential was born for a new unity among Indians who had no other shared language. English, too, was a cultural carrier. It not only crossed India's regional boundaries as an efficient mode of communication. It carried with it to Asia new ideas and ideals, nurtured in the culture of Europe with its roots deep in classical Greece and Rome and the Christian tradition, and in the British historical experience of stable government, gradual change, and developing democracy.

ii Society—structure and assumptions

Our focus now shifts to aspects of life, some of which, like the natural and material framework, are clearly visible and even measurable, but of which others are subjective, belonging to the realms of human perception and unvoiced assumptions. We must ask what sort of society developed within this framework, how people organized themselves in relation to their resources, and what sort of groups emerged within which people felt shared bonds or between which they perceived deep divisions. We must examine values—what was seen as good and desirable, and conversely what was evil and to be shunned. In academic language this means investigating social structures and their underlying beliefs and assumptions.

There are formidable problems in such an enterprise of understanding for students of India brought up in a different continent at a different period. Most modern observers will have experienced life in societies structured largely in classes, where a person's place in society is largely determined by occupation, and particularly by the individual's relation to the means of production; where relations between people are based on contract rather than time-honoured conventions. Moreover in contemporary industrial societies there is considerable mobility between classes, and individuals can change and achieve status by their own efforts. In India we see a society where until the twentieth century class was a concept and a force of little significance. Most people's place in the social order depended on ascribed rather than achieved status, and was determined by the accident of birth. Social relations—between men and women, different generations, relatives, neighbours, employers and employed—were ordered according to long-standing conventions learned from childhood onwards. In most pre-industrial societies ascribed rather than achieved position has been usual. What is distinctive on the Indian subcontinent is the *basis* of ascription and the comparative rigidity of the society to which this gave rise through the mechanism of caste. This word was Portuguese for breed or type. It is now used to describe the closed social groups of which Indian society is composed. Caste lies at the heart of the Hindu's religious and social experience. Therefore some appreciation of its function and strength is fundamental to an understanding of public and private life on the subcontinent.

The very existence of caste highlights another problem in understanding: namely, that in contrast to many late twentieth-century societies, in India religion was, and still is to a significant extent, a vital bonding and dividing force between people and groups, and a major bearer of values in social, economic, and political life, as well as personal belief. It is difficult for the western inquirer, accustomed to a world in which religion tends to be each individual's private affair and does not distinguish him overtly from his neighbours, to appreciate that in India religious community has been essential to daily life and self-perception. It is an enfolding framework; and dress, diet, social customs as well as rituals and beliefs are ordered by it. It is therefore not surprising that it became a force of great power and often a matter of deep anguish as India began to move into more rapid change in the later nineteenth and twentieth centuries—change which altered the environment in which the different communities lived and the terms of the relations between them.

India is a religiously plural society. The majority of its people are Hindu, and were so when Europeans first encountered India. Their world view and social order emerged over several thousand years from the interaction of the Aryan migrants and the earlier inhabitants of the land. But there are also distinct religious minorities. The surviving tribal people in hill regions have persisted in forms of animism and have not been integrated into the Hindu social order or imbued with its values. Other religious minorities originated in waves of migration, in movements of reform or conversion. Some tiny groups fled centuries ago from persecution or wandered in search of prosperity and arrived in the subcontinent: India's Jews and Parsis are such. The largest minority are the Muslims. Although they are a minority in the subcontinent as a whole, in certain areas they became a majority, particularly in the north west and north east. In the north west they were the politically and economically powerful descendants of central Asian invaders and migrants from the eleventh to the eighteenth centuries, who ultimately built up the Mogul empire, while in the extreme east in Bengal they tended to be humbler, agricultural groups who were converted to Islam partly as a device for hitching themselves to the rising star of Muslim political power. Fewer Muslims were found in the south, except as a ruling élite based on Hyderabad, an outpost of Mogul influence; or as notoriously unruly labourers on the Malabar coast who were descended from Arab traders. The last significant religious minorities to emerge in India were the Sikhs and the Christians. The latter were scattered groups who responded to European missionary activity; though there was a far older Christian group, the 'Syrians', deep in the south, whose origins were claimed to lie in the preaching of one of the apostles, St. Thomas. The Sikhs were a sixteenth-century reform group, born of the interaction of Muslims and Hindus in the route land of the Punjab in the north west; and they remained a highly localized group, clustered in that region.[8] Such minorities tended to be separate social units, following their own social customs and marrying strictly within their own community. But they were integrated into the regional social order rather like vast castes, separate and closed groups yet interdependent with the rest of society. Within the minorities there were social gradations which looked like castes: the Syrian Christians or the Bengali Muslims were cases in point. But these gradations did not have the ritual and ideological undergirding peculiar to the Hindu caste system. It was that distinctive social order which was the context of life for the vast majority of Indians.

Caste society as an ideal form is a hierarchical ordering of closed groups. It ranks in order, from high to low, whole groups rather than individuals. Each person is born into a caste, cannot leave it unless literally out-caste (in which case he is left with no place in society), or by voluntary renunciation of normal society for the life of a religious ascetic. No one can change caste for another. Marriage is within the caste, but outside the immediate kin-group. A basic cluster of assumptions on which this order rests relate to purity and pollution. Certain substances (such as human and animal waste, dead bodies, leather) are considered religiously polluting. Consequently groups are ranked according to their connection with such substances. Everybody is at some stage in their lives temporarily polluted, as in the case of a woman in childbirth, and elaborate ceremonial procedures exist to purify those affected in such situations. But some people by virtue of their occupations are more permanently in contact with such substances and are never completely purified. Therefore the protection of the purity of those above them in the hierarchy demands that they be kept separate as far as possible.

The rules for permissible marriages are a powerful means for maintaining social separation. But it is contrived in many other ways: as, for example, in the clothes worn by each group and therefore demonstrative of its status, and in the elaborate conventions prescribing who can give to or receive food from whom. There is prohibition, too, on physical touch between those at the top of the hierarchy and those at its base. Those right at the bottom because they do the most polluting jobs of all, like scavenging, are considered literally untouchable. In some areas even their shadow is felt to pollute and they have in the past had to draw attention to their threatening presence by calling out, or they have been denied access to streets frequented by higher castes. Denial of access to the village well has been a widespread phenomenon. Castes tend to live in clearly distinguishable separate areas of the village, with Untouchables often inhabiting a ramshackle hamlet beyond its bounds. Even in the 1990s in the city of Jodhpur in Rajasthan, the houses of Brahmins are painted blue to distinguish them. In some parts of India these distinctions and separating devices were more rigidly maintained than in others, the south being particularly formidable in this respect. It is difficult for contemporaries to grasp the power of caste conventions in the past, although they operated well into this century. A novel such as M. R. Anand's *Untouchable*, the outcaste's autobiography by Hazari, or a village study can best bring the social order to life. The separation between groups was and to some extent still is demonstrated, and the criteria of worth which underpin it and the whole hierarchical order, when villages gather for rituals, festivals, and feasts. Each caste has its allotted task and physical place in the communal celebration and festivity.

The sight of a village enjoying a Hindu festival, feasting or producing a dramatic performance of a scriptural story or folk tale shows clearly that *separation* also means *interdependence*. Each group needs the skills of others if the community is to survive, perform tasks essential to its social and religious life, and exploit its natural resources efficiently. The landed need those who will labour for them, make pots, ploughs, and jewellery, fetch water, make clothes, act as barbers, midwives, and scavengers. People with skills to sell, however lowly, need employment and protection. From mutual needs has emerged a system of patron–client relationships between families over many generations. The more prosperous and higher-ranking families will have clients who perform vital services for them in return for an assurance of grain at harvest time, and often loans or gifts in kind at times of natural shortage or disaster, or family crisis. Each group is therefore vital to the whole village as an economic, social, and ritual unit. By such means natural resources can be used, labour organized, and an elementary type of social security created for the economically weaker. Consequently for each person the immediate kin, the caste, and the village were important social units, experienced as powerfully supportive while to some extent restrictive. It must of course be remembered that hierarchical separation and interdependence is the ideal. In practice prevailing socio-economic conditions have produced considerable variations and deviations. When rural society was less settled and labour scarce as in the eighteenth century, the social order seems to have been more fluid and flexible, and people were not locked into immutable communities or socio-economic roles, but had considerable bargaining power to change their situations.

Some confusion is also often caused, and considerable unreality injected into descriptions of caste, if a distinction is not made between *varna* and *jati*. *Varna* refers to the simple, four-fold caste hierarchy described in Hindu scripture; an *ideal* which seems to have formed by the third century BC of Priests (Brahmins), Warriors (Kshatriyas), Traders (Vaishyas) and Cultivators (Shudras). In practice caste as experienced by Indians means the *jati*, or the caste group which enfolds many small kin-groups. The latter are exogamous while the former are generally endogamous. *Jatis* are essentially local groups with a known local order of hierarchy which is far more complex and also more fluid than the four-fold division in literary descriptions. Brahmins and Shudras will always be just what their name implies. But in between these groups there will be as many as ten or more *jatis* with a variety of jobs, which are locally ranked in order, though there may well be some dissension about the precise placings of some of them. *Jatis* are normally named after an occupation—goldsmith, potter, weaver, herdsman and so forth. Although this may once have helped to determine their status it is clear that *jati* members have not always been confined to that occupation but could do other jobs, provided that these were not defiling or someone else's ritual duty. For example, Brahmins often became administrators or held land, as these occupations were compatible with their high ritual status: only some actually earned their living solely by performing priestly functions. Many castes also combined their hereditary occupations with agriculture.

The origins of this elaborate, hierarchical system of social stratification have long been debated. Many different theories have been advanced as to why and how it developed in later Hindu society. One of the most common is that of racial prejudice by the incoming Aryans who wished to preserve their racial purity from intimate contact with darker-skinned indigenous peoples. None has been proved as a satisfactory single explanation. What is amply clear is that there emerged over centuries a complex and sophisticated social order of a kind markedly different from that prevailing elsewhere, in Christian Europe, for example, both in its divisions and its assumptions. It proved over centuries to be tough and resilient: so much so that no ruling power—Muslim, British or 'secular'—has cracked it. All have accommodated themselves to it.

Generations of Indians have been born into this system and socialized within it. Children quite naturally and very early in life absorb the often unvoiced values underlying distinctions between groups. Childhood training in watching and obeying the separating devices also helps to build up within people deep internal controls against deviant and socially disruptive behaviour. External forms of control are not lacking. The head of each family (almost always the senior male) has a firm grip on its members. The immediate kin-group, often including a joint family network in which several brothers, their wives and children live with the parents and various close, single relatives, is a vital source of affection, support, and social interaction, as well as an economic unit. Few risk the displeasure of such an indispensable group as there is virtually no escape from it by personal physical mobility or independence. The caste itself through its *panchayat* or governing group of elders can also back up the authority of the family head or act if he fails to exercise a proper discipline. Its sanctions are carefully graded in relation to the gravity of the offence against the caste or the contravention of its rules; ranging from warnings to fines, public penance and ritual reconciliation, through to the ultimate sanction of outcasting. Furthermore, other castes can enforce the system by diverse means, including social boycott and physical violence. The small-scale, 'face-to-face' society is often more stern and efficient in dealing with its members and regulating their behaviour than any modern, large-scale society which relies on state sanctions and law-enforcement mechanisms.[9]

The scholar trying to understand India's social order from scriptural texts or Hindu law books (as many attempted to do until the later twentieth century) can draw an elegant picture of a static hierarchy, moulded by religious values. But this would be a stylized picture: actuality is more messy and confusing. Life in Indian society has always been infinitely more complex than text and law suggest. Certainly religious values, and particularly the powerfully emotive ideas of purity and pollution, lie deep within the caste system. But other forces influence social ranking, demography, economic factors, and the practice of politics, for example. Indians have long used social categories which denote economic difference combined with ritual status, such as *bhadralok* to denote 'gentry', and could encompass in that category people of different castes. Moreover, on closer observation there appear to be various means of adjusting the caste system in practice to the exigencies of secular power, of keeping ritual status and worldly power in tolerable equilibrium.

For example, in each area there will in practice be one or more 'dominant' castes: those which actually control local life. 'Dominance' is created by a variety of factors, only one of which is high ritual standing. Physical numbers, access to land or other resources, connection with the ruling authority, may all have an influence. Generally the locally dominant caste will be of fairly high ritual standing but it must also have the material and numerical resources to act as patron to client families. Brahmins, for example, though always ritually superior to all others, will only be dominant if they also own land. If they are poor they may be in client relationship to a ritually inferior but actually dominant caste: although in strictly ritual matters they will always be deferred to. Another aspect of flexibility in the system has been the possibility of movement. It is true that until the later twentieth century there has not been any real avenue for, or social acceptance of, individual mobility in social status. As we have seen, the individual has little value or status: his worth and position depend on the groups to which he belongs, and is ascribed rather than achieved. However, forces could put actual power and influence out of step with ritual position. Famine, natural disaster or impoverishment from having to dower too many daughters could undermine a group's prosperity. Conquest, a change of ruler, or access to new economic wealth, such as previously unsettled land, could boost a group's resources. In such cases *group* mobility up or down the hierarchy often over a considerable period of time was possible. A *jati* attempting to raise its ritual status would often indulge in a ritual 'keeping-up-with-the-Joneses'; imitating the life-style and rituals of a locally prestigious caste and publicizing stories about their exalted origins. Scholars call this process 'Sanskritization', because it involves imitation of castes whose norms are closer to that of the classical texts, though they may not be Brahmins if there are high castes whose local position makes them more suitable objects for imitation. Furthermore, whole new *jatis* could emerge from patterns of migration and the splitting up of older groups. Because such mobility was group mobility, validated according to the conventions of the system, it never threatened the system itself. Indeed it made the system more resilient because it proved it could accommodate change in the way a hierarchical order based solely on ritual criteria could never have done.[10]

Anthropologists, sociologists and historians from their particular disciplines have recently contributed to a deeper understanding of Hindu society by studying small communities in detail. The student can best learn to sympathize with the social order, grasp something of its rationale and understand its power by immersing himself in some of these. (See the guide to further reading, pp. 432–3.)

Several further general points deserve notice. Forces for change were working in Indian society long before western influence and the imposition of British rule, and society had contrived ways of absorbing and adjusting to change. 'Unchanging India' is a myth. Acceptance of it not only implies little understanding of the internal dynamics of Indian society and culture; it also encourages an unrealistic assessment of the effects of the British presence on the subcontinent. What can be said, and will become clear in our investigations, is that in the last hundred years at least the *pace* of change quickened remarkably, with major implications for the functioning of society and the economy, and the stability of the political order. Secondly, the observer must not expect to find a homogeneous social order throughout the subcontinent. Though the assumptions and social relations sketched here operate in principle among all India's Hindus in practice each region has over time produced its own variations in social hierarchy and the local distribution of power, depending on the interweaving of economic and political forces and natural resources. In some areas Brahmins are dominant, in others not. Sometimes several castes will vie for dominance. Some villages are single-caste, particularly if they have a special ecological position, as in the case of a village of fisher-folk. Others are the more usual multi-caste villages, dominated by a single family or a large group. Such local and regional variations were important factors in the response of an area and its inhabitants to political change. This has been evident in circumstances as diverse as the great upheaval and rebellion in northern India in 1857, and later during the nationalist movement in the nature of rural support for Congress and its politicians. Caste, of course, was not just a rural phenomenon, though we have concentrated on the rural context as most Indians were and are country people. But caste was equally the context of urban social life. The resources of an urban economy provided means of patronage, just as landed wealth did in villages. There were still services to be performed and to receive, according to ritual status. Small areas of each town, known as *mohullas*, produced face-to-face communities with their potential for community feeling and discipline; and there tended to be residential segregation according to caste, as in the village setting. Until late in the nineteenth century there was no clear or rigid distinction between town and countryside. Kin ties linked groups in towns and nearby villages, and much urban life was rural both in occupation and setting.

The nature of caste and Hindu society suggests that the Hindu religious experience is very different from that of people in environments where articulated beliefs, unvoiced perceptions of religion, as well as institutions, have been moulded by the world's great monotheisms—Judaism, Christianity, and Islam. To note some of the most striking differences: in the Hindu context religion is not basically something 'to be believed' but 'to be done'. There is no central revelation of the nature of God to which each individual must respond, and on which response his temporal and eternal destiny depends. Rather, religion is concerned with *dharma*; the fundamental laws of existence, to which men and women must conform through performance of their own *dharma* or religious duty. The context of this conformity is the whole community; and the precise prescriptions of personal *dharma* are known to individuals through the norms of their particular caste's behaviour. One should therefore be wary of using the word 'Hinduism' until late in the nineteenth century when some Hindus began to perceive of and present in India and abroad their religious experience as 'a faith' which could be transported, and accepted by anyone who was convinced of its truths.[11] Despite this development, it is, as it has always been, almost impossible for one not born a Hindu 'to be converted to Hinduism'.

(In such a case what is one's *dharma* if one has no caste? What is one's place in society where entry into caste is by birth alone?) By contrast Jews, Christians, and Muslims welcome converts and provide for their instruction in their new-found faith.

A further striking aspect of the Hindu context—and a natural result of the absence of a fundamental creed—is that there is no organized church with centrally trained and authorized priests to maintain orthodoxy and to conduct public, communal services at which attendance is obligatory for 'believers'. The social framework rather than a specific institution is the guardian and mediator of religious values. Brahmins are the priestly caste. Their authority stems from birth into a position of ritual purity, although they need to learn Sanskrit and the technicalities of rituals if they are to act as priests. They are not essentially educators or defenders of right belief. They assist families at times of crisis in family members' life-cycles—birth, puberty, marriage, death, or some major occasion of pollution which demands elaborate ritual purification. Their ministrations act out the assumptions of much Hindu life, but this is not their main purpose. Religious authority is widely diffused in the Hindu world; in contrast to its concentration in churches and their ministers in the Christian context, for example. Many different individuals and groups have distinct religious roles, and authority in different contexts: the father in ordering the family's life, the mother in some family forms of prayer, the guardian of a shrine who tends the images and performs worship, the *guru* or teacher in relation to his disciples, and the wandering ascetic who renounces normal social life. Brahmins are ritual and textual experts with authority in a restricted though vital area. The Hindu's religious life is centred on the family and the caste. Its manifestations are not just the conventions and disciplines already noted; but also the family rituals and the communal observation of the great festivals of the Hindu year, marking spring, harvest, and the birthdays of various deities. The church, synagogue, and mosque have no real Hindu parallel as a focus of worship and religious education. Only in pilgrimage centres in the north, like Banares, and in the south with its great temples, are buildings major centres of worship. Even in the south with its distinctive temple-orientated tradition, family and community are indispensable contexts for the religious experience.

Every religion makes explicit or implies a particular understanding of the fundamental nature of reality, man's relation to that reality, and the value of the visible, material world in the context of this central perception of what is 'really real' and of true significance. Despite the absence of an explicit Hindu creed some core assumptions of the Hindu world view can be teased out from the evidence of the Hindu scriptures, particularly the Veda which are the oldest and most authoritative; from the great mythological stories of the later Epics, from the accumulated wisdom of Hindu thinkers and lawyers; and from the careful conventions of social life. But it must be stressed that there is no theological commitment or orthodoxy obligatory for the Hindu. Within the many traditions which make up the Hindu environment of thought there are many different philosophical views and ways of understanding divinity and reality. Even atheism is an option! Hindus would tell the inquirer that the Hindu vision of reality and the meaning of life has emerged over a long period of time, as new truths became apparent, and new comprehensions were integrated into a living tradition. Scripture, epic accounts of gods and goddesses disporting themselves on earth with men and women, the teaching of sages past and present, are all partial pointers to deep truths about the nature of human existence in relation to the total order of life, the reality beyond all things.

In Hindu thought the material world as known by men is the product of vast cycles of creation, decay, destruction and re-creation: not as the result of accident or a divine whim, but in deep harmony with fundamental laws of existence. When expressed as the actions of deities the gods in their various reflections of the actions of the supreme power both create and destroy. Shiva, the destroyer, Brahman, the creative power, are apparently opposing forces interwoven in a mysterious whole. Like so many other apparent contradictions they are resolved by the Hindu awareness that mystery lies at the heart of being. Following from this is the conviction that matter veils reality. This is the concept of *maya*; too often translated as 'illusion' implying a crude misunderstanding that Hindus believe that material things are illusory. It is rather that what is tangible and visible is not the last word about what is real: beyond and beneath it, often obscured by it, is the mystery of meaning. Hindu thought has for thousands of years been haunted by the desire for *moksha* (salvation); which means liberation from the clutches of the unreal into perception of the real. In less philosophical terms *moksha* also means release from the weary cycle of rebirths to which all creatures are condemned. The dynamic of this cycle is the law of *karma*, or ethical causation, by which actions receive their appropriate reward both in the present life and in subsequent incarnations.

In Hindu tradition there is not one path to salvation, but many ways by which men can seek the coveted prize of *moksha*. For most the way will be the humdrum path of *dharma*; performing the duties peculiar to one's caste, age, and sex, in the belief that such personal *dharma* links the individual into the central *dharma* of existence, the way things really are. More dramatically there is the arduous and often harsh path of renunciation, of loosing all ties with ordinary social life in pursuit of reality. This can be chosen at any point in life by anyone: hence the hermits who seek enlightenment in the mountains, or the wandering ascetics whose austerities and eccentricities amaze and attract the ordinary people whom they encounter. There is also a conviction that every Hindu passes through distinctive phases of life—child, student, householder, eventually reaching the point of retirement and increasing detachment from worldly cares and ties, which can shade into total withdrawal from family and social life. We have no means of quantifying this phenomenon; either now or in the past. But even in the late twentieth century there are elderly Hindu men and women who deliberately undertake this process of detachment after fifty or sixty years of ordinary life. Another way of salvation is that of knowledge—not meaning accumulation of facts or much study of books, but a disciplined waiting, often at the feet of a *guru*, for enlightenment, true vision of the real, at a depth of experience beyond the rational mind. In total contrast there is also the way of devotion, *bhakti*; of love for a particular deity, like the glamorous god, Krishna, and joyous abandonment to his worship in a group of devotees.

The variety of beliefs, practices, and emphases within Hindu tradition is immense. The most widespread practices are those forming the cluster of domestic and public rituals which compose a total ceremonial framework for the life of each person. It is colourful, sociable, and often highly enjoyable: and it provides for every eventuality of life. The family is the basic unit of observance. It is also central in the religious education of each succeeding generation. There are no formal instruction classes in religion, no equivalent of Sunday Schools. Each child brought up in the extended family setting hears the great stories of Hindu mythology from mothers, aunts, and grandmothers, sees the village community or travelling players perform them at certain seasons; just as he or she rapidly learns what is proper behaviour within the caste group, and watches the Brahmin priest presiding over the mysteries of purity and pollution. Culture, daily life, and religious experience are an indivisible whole.

What we have so far seen of conventions, rituals, and ideas belong to what scholars call the 'Great Tradition', because its roots are in textual religious sources and in the laws of such classical Hindu writers as Manu. It is pre-eminently the religious idiom and style of the higher castes. However, interwoven with the 'Great Tradition' are numerous 'Little Traditions' of religious understanding, compulsion and practice. Particularly in village life there are elements in the religious experience which are far less sophisticated. They help men and women to deal with the multifarious hazards of daily life in a world where man and nature often seem hostile; and many of the forces impinging on people seem explicable only in terms of demonic possession, haunting or varieties of witchcraft. Consequently there are 'specialists' and ceremonies which deal with such apparently supernatural forces, and have a vital religious significance; though they have no place in the 'Great Tradition', just as the forces they deal with are not part of the great Hindu pantheon of deities. This is particularly true of the experience of lower caste people with their less 'sanskritic' life style. But higher castes are also involved: for who would despise help in times of crisis, when illness afflicts the family, or crops mysteriously fail? Village studies have shown how naturally elements of 'Great' and 'Little Traditions' intermingle. Precautions against 'the evil eye', placation of ghosts, shrines honouring local goddesses, coexist with more 'orthodox' practices in Gujarat, for example. While in central India the local healer/exorcist has a place in the religious life of the village as clear as that of the Brahmin priest. Each caters for different religious and social needs. The one is an intermediary between villagers and malevolent local powers and village deities: the other has dealings with the upper levels of the pantheon and has a religious sphere by virtue not of character, proven wisdom or 'success', but of ritual purity and ritual knowledge.[12]

Variations within the Hindu experience are not only those of 'level', of caste and culture. There are also distinctive regional variations, even at the level of the 'Great Tradition'. Areas may have their particular cults and devotions towards certain deities, as in the worship of the fearsome Mother Goddess, Kali, in Bengal. Or there may be local traditions of spirituality, such as the western Indian one in Maharashtra which stems from a long line of outstanding, saintly figures. The temple orientation of much south Indian religion is another regional variation. However, such differences are being partially ironed out by the development of communications; starting with the eighteenth-century development of printing, and then the spread of literacy in the last 150 years. Religious art sold in bazaars, cheap books and tracts telling the great Hindu stories and reproducing some of the more popular scriptural texts, such as the *Bhagavad Gita*, became available and helped to popularize the 'Great Tradition'. (More recently radio, television, film, and even children's comic strips have quickened this popularization.) The spread of roads and railways, for military and economic purposes, also enabled interregional travel and easier pilgrimage to major all-India religious sites. But despite this democratization of a formerly high-caste religious idiom, it would be a distortion of the Hindu world view and experience to describe it even now solely in sanskritic terms. India's 'Little Traditions' are still very strong.

Among the subcontinent's Muslims there are also religious variations. There are sectarian differences; and in parts of north-western India a distinctively devotional form of Islam, fostered by the Sufi orders and focused on *Pirs* and their followers. In some places there has also occurred a transfer of many originally Hindu and 'Little Tradition' beliefs and observances into the Muslim experience, particularly among the Bengali Muslims with their low-caste Hindu origins. Western and northern Indian Muslims, tracing a more exalted ancestry, often consider their Bengali co-religionists to be 'degraded'. But to a far greater extent than Hindus, Muslims all live within a well-formulated and powerful belief structure. For them theology, right belief about God, is vital for the correct response of man to fundamental reality. On right belief and its fruits, right actions, depend men's present fortunes and eternal fate. Muslims are passionate monotheists: the heart of reality is Allah, one God who is creator and arbiter of all things. Islam means 'obedience to the will of God'; and this is the core of the Muslim religion. Each individual must strive to obey that will, but he can only fully do so in the context of a society based on acceptance of that will as its central value. God's will is known through revelation and law. Revelation has come to man over centuries in scriptures shared with Jews and Christians: but the final and decisive revelation came through the seventh-century prophet, Muhammad, and is preserved for his followers in the holy Koran. God's will is also manifested in Muslim law, the *Shariah*. This is the structure for community life which supports the individual in his obedience to God, and it regulates all aspects of life. It is expounded and interpreted by the Muslim clerisy, the *ulema*, who receive seminary training for this purpose. So they are unlike Brahmins, whose religious authority and role rests ultimately on birth. They are also unlike Christian ministers because they have no sacramental powers, nor do they even have to lead the Muslim congregations in prayer.

It is not only the fierce monotheism, the belief in a decisive historical revelation and the clerical structure to preach and protect orthodoxy in belief and behaviour which distinguishes Indian Muslims from their Hindu neighbours. Muslims lay great stress on congregational worship, and each Friday Muslim men gather for prayer in mosques. All Muslims aspire to go on pilgrimage to the holy places of Islam in the Middle East, particularly Mecca. So by faith, worship, and hope the community is bound together, and also bound to other Muslims throughout the world. The extra-Indian orientation and dimension of Indian Islam is crucial, and is unparalleled in the Hindu experience. Furthermore, Islam has a distinctive political theory, stemming from its foreign origins. Its ideal is a theocratic state, where God rules in practice because his ministers and law order life. Although this lasted briefly in practice the ideal remains, enshrined in the notion that a Muslim cannot live under an infidel ruler. If he finds himself in such a predicament he must either flee to a Muslim land (*hijrat*) or fight a holy war (*jihad*) for the establishment of an Islamic state. Observation of Indian society shows that, despite the absence of caste among Muslims, Islam regulates Muslim social behaviour in many ways as firmly and in as great detail as do the conventions of caste. Food and drink, dress, marriage, burial rather than cremation (the Hindu custom), the veiling of women and their subordination to men are a few of the many aspects of life which are ordered by convention and law to enable men and women to respond correctly to ultimate reality, which is Allah.

Although Muslims and Hindus have often lived as neighbours in harmony and indeed have sometimes shared patterns and places of worship, there was a gulf between them. The bonds which joined them to members of their own community separated Hindus from Muslims in social practice and the values on which this was based. Marriage across the religious divide was very rare, even in places where some blend of Hindu and Muslim life style and values developed, as in the old court cities of the north such as Lucknow. Further, the different beliefs and customs produced perennial flash-points in their relations. To take the most extreme examples; to the Hindu the cow was sacred, while Muslims on great festivals such as *Id* might sacrifice it. Muslims hold their mosques sacred places and their communal mosque prayers occasions of great significance and solemnity: there was thus opportunity for desecration, or disturbance at times of prayer.

The way *potential* points of communal discord became *actual* occasions of communal conflict and violence, and were woven into the development of political life is a sombre theme in political change in the later nineteenth and twentieth centuries. Before leaving our observation of Indian society we must note where its structures and values have political implications, not just for Indians' relations with their neighbours, but with their rulers.[13]

In the realm of values we must ask whether religion teaches that history and its events are of consequence, whether the ordering of society is crucial, and whether there is a traditional linkage between the exercise of political and religious authority. The Muslim answer to these questions is already clear. History is the context in which Allah makes himself known and demands obedience: so the ordering of society as well as the preservation of pure belief are of supreme importance. The fusion from the outset in Islamic tradition of religious and political authority as two sides of the same coin is thus entirely explicable. But as a result there are potential problems for Muslims if they find themselves a religious minority, or if they are compelled to live under non-Muslim rulers. Hindus have a less serious view of the significance of historical events and the nature of the political order, as radically affecting man's understanding of reality or his quest for salvation. What matters is that society should operate in such a way as to permit each person to follow his *dharma*. Within Hindu tradition religious and secular authority have been separated, as symbolized by the Brahmin and the Kshatriya, the priest and the warrior, each with his separate *dharma*. The King was never expected to perform priestly functions, nor the Brahmin to usurp temporal power. However, the King was expected to use his Kshatriya's power to protect the social order, in particular to prevent the 'confusion of castes'. Hindu society has proved it can coexist with different types of political regime, some dominated by non-Hindus, provided that political authorities allowed society to function without interference. The massive Hindu majority on the subcontinent is also a guarantee of society's integrity and security. This has helped to produce a rather more relaxed attitude to political power, in contrast to the fears of India's religious minorities. The Sikhs are an example. From its origins their reformist movement had to battle for existence against Muslim power; and early in this conflict it had acquired martyred leaders. An acute sensitivity to the exercise of political power was thus built into Sikh self identity and was heightened by their minority status.

Actual religious structures can exert political influence. No European historian can ignore the entanglement of churches, ecclesiastical dignitaries and material resources as well as actual beliefs in politics even in the twentieth century. In the Hindu environment the structures to watch are caste groups, their understanding of their identity and security, their attitude to other castes, and their ability to organize themselves and mobilize their members for political action. (For example, dominant castes will later concern us as they learnt the conventions of new styles of politics; and we shall also see new political activity among aspiring castes who wished to raise their status in a changing society and exploit new sources of wealth, and even among Untouchables who began to glimpse a vision of a new polity whose citizens would be equal.) Hindu temples could also be a focus for political awareness and organization, because of their material resources. In the Muslim community the *ulema* obviously have great political potential as a network of prominent and respected men down to village level, speaking in the name of Islam. They might have considerable capacity for local organization and mass appeal if they preached that Islam was in danger. In Sind, where the Sufi tradition was so strong, *Pirs* combined religious leadership with control over land, and became central to the politics of the region. Among the Sikhs, in contrast, there was a deep commitment to the idea of the Sikh brotherhood, and the short dagger was one of the Sikh's distinguishing marks—like the more obvious turban. This long-established identity of Sikhs as a band of brothers in arms was one which might be politically significant in new ways if the political process seemed to threaten Sikh identity. Sikh *gurudwaras*, or places of worship, had considerable resources at their disposal, control of which might become of far more than religious significance.

iii   Authority and power: government and politics

Society and the material frame of life were the continuing context of Indian politics. They have deliberately been considered first because of the complex reality behind the word 'politics'—namely, the way men perceive and act in relation to the exercise of public power. This broad definition applies whatever the context—pre-industrial kingdom or empire, modern dictatorship or democracy, business corporation, university, even a church or voluntary organization. In each power is at stake, to be used and its use controlled. Students of politics may start with the narrative, often partial record of transactions producing decisions, actions or inaction. To comprehend the reasons for these transactions and their particular patterns at a certain time in a specific context they must probe deeper. What material and ideological resources are available: what is there to be shared out, what can be mobilized and what value system moulds the rules for the use of resources? How do men actually experience the significance of public power, and what value do they ascribe to political action? (For many avoid politics or are not equipped for political activism.) What individuals, groups, and organizations are interested in politics? Is their awareness prompted by fear, ambition or altruism: or like kings and others whose birth gives political status, do they have no choice about involvement? What are the institutions of government—the formal mechanisms for the exercise of public power: and what mechanisms exist for controlling government, whether formal (elections, Parliament, Ombudsman) or informal (rebellion, strikes, and varieties of peaceful non-co-operation)?

Such questions indicate that in any country there will be many levels of politics, geared to the exercise of particular sorts of power. Each level will have the style or political idiom which is functional at that level in that it fits the participants' capacities and 'delivers the goods' they want. (In Britain, for example, as well as the level of parliamentary politics there are the politics of city and district councils, trade unions, business corporations and educational structures. Each level has its area of concern, and often participants in one will not have the expertise or motivation to operate at other levels. But they all impinge on each other. Parliamentarians must consider what trade unionists are doing: city fathers cannot ignore the policies, finances, and values of government in London.) Interconnections between levels are crucial both to the functioning and the understanding of politics. The same is true in India although the levels of political life, participants, their values and resources are very different. A major theme of our study will therefore be the variety of political levels and their styles, and the relationships between them.

It is particularly important to make this wide definition of politics in the Indian setting, not just because, as in every country, politics are inexplicable in isolation, by narrative of events and description of formal institutions, and must be seen in their total social context of values and structures as well as the material framework of life. In India there is a distinctive ecology of political life which underlies so many of the basic political continuities whether we look at the eighteenth or twentieth century. Indeed, at times that environment has seemed like a prison both to Indian and British rulers. This broad view should also prevent facile assumptions that certain dates or phases marked dramatic or clear points of change. Historians are now profoundly sceptical of any argument that European political involvement in India was immediately a major turning-point or the trigger for radical change, and are aware of the longer and deeper trends in society and the economy which enabled and moulded that involvement and continued to be of formative significance. Or again it may seem easy to talk of a 'new politics' when nationalism became an important political force. But this ignores the many continuities in public life simultaneous to this development; the interweaving of 'nationalism' into many pre-existing levels of political aspiration and action, and the activities of many 'nationalist' politicians at different levels in the appropriate political style. Even 1947, when India became independent, was not a radical break with past politics (see chapter VI).

India's 'political ecology' raises basic problems for anyone attempting to exercise power on the subcontinent. Certain themes recur over centuries, whether the all-India rulers were Mogul, British or independent India's politicians. The subcontinent's sheer size and diversity mean that it will always be difficult to administer from an all-India centre enforcing rules and regulations applicable to the whole of India. Particularly was this true before swift communications between government and its servants, by metalled road, railway, telegraph, telephone, and air travel. The old saying, 'Delhi is far off', referred to the Mogul government and its capital. It can still apply. The fate of locally unpopular legislation after 1947 demonstrates this—as in the case of the legal abolition of Untouchability or limitations on holding of land (See chapter VII). Efficient and uniform administration demands thousands of civil servants, who must be paid. It also rests on efficient 'intelligence', the gathering of information about local conditions and attitudes. There has been a long series of intelligence catastrophes—from the Moguls' failure as their strength ebbed in the eighteenth century, to the British incapacity to predict the communal carnage which accompanied their departure in the Punjab, and Indira Gandhi's miscalculation in holding a general election in 1977, at which the electorate swept her and her 'Emergency rule' away.

India's geography means that there will always be a problematic relationship between the centre and the periphery. Governments have also been constrained by the existence of tough local societies, with their integrated structures of dominance and control, and their firm value systems. This has made the local units of public life, substantial villages or clusters of villages, capable of running their own affairs, whoever came and went in the regional centres of power, let alone all-India government. It also made them extremely hostile to outside interference in any way which seemed likely to upset the local balance of power and interests, or to threaten the value system which undergirded it. India's governments have also faced the continuous hazard of bankruptcy. Where land provides most wealth, land tax is the most important source of government revenue. But, given the problems of size and local community strength, how is it to be collected? Even if it could be reasonably efficiently drawn into central coffers, it was unlikely to be enough to fund a massive civil service, army, and police force. Pre-industrial societies have rarely generated sufficient wealth to produce a surplus which through tax has financed more than minimal government.

In such circumstances it has proved essential for aspiring all-India governments to persuade people to act as go-betweens or intermediaries between central authority and local society. 'Persuasion' takes many forms—concessions in revenue, the right to 'farm' revenue and keep part while remitting the remainder to the centre; grants of land or local administrative power, largely uncontrolled by the centre; conferment of honours, titles, and status. Governments tended to look for substantial local men with independent local resources who would collaborate in a working system of producing money and information, and guaranteeing local loyalty—to provide in effect an administrative system on the cheap. British colonial rulers in Africa were by no means the first to discover the political and financial advantages of varieties of 'indirect rule'. Authority and power on the subcontinent has therefore hinged on these key intermediaries, the inducements offered to them and their dependability, for only on such foundations could all-India control be built. Consequently the practice of government has often proved very different from government as perceived only through the work of formal structures and recognized officials. The reality behind the formal facade will show the interweaving of many of the different levels of politics.

In visualizing the structure of government before the political intrusion of Europeans it is helpful to recognize the differentiated nature of political power and to distinguish between four different levels through the interaction of which control was exercised, finance raised for governmental functions and docility secured.[14] On each level were focused different styles of political behaviour functional in relation to the type of power at stake. At the apex was the all-India regime. In the seventeenth and eighteenth centuries this was the Mogul empire which ruled the greater part of India. It had an all-India administrative structure; and we shall consider this later because its strains and weaknesses were the context of European political intrusion, and are also an example of the general problems of governing India which reappeared in the succeeding two centuries.

Beneath the all-India regime were regional structures of authority; for example, the Rajas of Banares in northern India, or the Nawabs of Bengal. Such regional figures might be of ancient lineage and venerable local standing. But often possession of power at this level was unstable, and politics in pursuit of it offered potentially great prizes. Mansa Ram, Raja of Banares in the mid-eighteenth century, for example, started his career as a Mogul tax collector, and through the status of land-controller ended up as a local ruler under the emperor, with his own administration and military resources. The third tier was the more local administrative level, controlled by individuals, or lineages. Persons of this status of authority were known in different areas by diverse names—*rajas, jagirdars, taluqdars* and large *zamindars*. They exercised little formal administration but were instrumental in extracting revenue from those beneath them who actually directed the use of village land, the locally dominant castes. This third level was also a profitable hunting-ground for the ambitious. In Bengal at the time of British occupation in the later eighteenth century nearly 60 per cent of the region's revenue was paid by fifteen large *zamindars*. Only four of these were of ancient family. Many of the others had, like the Raja of Banares, gained new power earlier in the century, using the profits of office and official patronage.

The life histories of such political entrepreneurs confirm other evidence that there was no such political reality as 'unchanging India', and that at least in the eighteenth century polity-building was in a considerable state of flux, and a range of new regional kingdoms and states were in the making within the structure of the Mogul empire at the hands of expanding warrior groups such as the Rajputs and Afghans, or of revenue farmers of whom Mansa Ram was only one egregious example. Only at the bottom level was there stability and, indeed, often a stubborn resistance to change. Villages or clusters of villages virtually ran themselves, under their dominant families, who in return for controlling land acted as local patrons and were crucial intermediaries between the village and higher authority, remitting what revenue was necessary, but also maintaining village interests and prosperity. There was little direct contact between most country folk and the higher political authorities. Their village notables dealt with authority for them: with these notables outsiders, whether imperial agent or local raja, had to come to terms. (It should also be remembered that all-India and regional polities alike tended to rest on the surplus of the valleys and plains. There were still areas of north, central, and western India, mostly hilly regions, where society was not settled and the 'political' unit was little more than a nomadic or hunting group. Nomads, hunters, and slash-and-burn farmers would remain outside the range of settled agriculture and formal polities often well into the nineteenth century, despite economic changes and the efforts of British administrators to tame and control such wandering groups who were thought to threaten civilized life and government.)

The Mogul empire is a fascinating quarry for students of India's government and politics. The case of Muslim, foreign, conquerors building up a structure capable of controlling most of the subcontinent and then losing that control, highlights the fundamental and persistent problems of any all-India authority with its periphery, and with local society, most acutely in times of social and economic change; particularly the enterprise of maintaining a working system of intermediaries. Although there are many gaps in the evidence, what scholars have ferreted out hints that the delicate balance between the various levels of politics was critical in imperial stability. This is also ground for an intriguing comparison with the nature and eventual fate of British *raj* (rule) in India, for similar patterns recur, though in circumstances moulded by different economic and international forces, as well as different ideas and levels of technical skill.

A teenage Turk who ransacked Samarkhand at the end of the fifteenth century was the founder of the Mogul empire. He turned his attentions to India in 1519, and from being a foreign marauder transformed himself into the deposer of the Afghan and Hindu rulers of a wide area round Delhi. His successors maintained effective rule over much of India until 1748; though the last Mogul, a feeble, defeated old man, was only deposed in 1858 by the British, the fiction of his 'imperium' at last cast off. The key figure in the stable ordering of this empire was Akbar (1556–1605): he came to terms with the 'raw materials' of India's natural and material resources and social framework, and contrived out of them a remarkable political edifice.

The hallmark of Akbar's empire was perhaps its political realism, though often its historical image has been projected in terms of its military ethos, its elegant court culture, or its bureaucratic tendencies which are emphasized as pre-figuring the steel administrative frame of later British rule.[15] What Akbar did was to create a framework of control which though innovative in some respects was grounded in a canny appreciation of the dynamics of India's society and economy. While it functioned it proved able to remit a flow of revenue from the fields up to the court, and secure considerable peace and order. Its success lay in its capacity to attract key intermediaries to help in these processes. At its base were the *zamindars*—a word which covers a bewildering variety of local notables who controlled land and were accustomed to collecting revenue and despatching a part of it (generally as little as possible) to higher political authority. Such were now recognized and some attempt made to survey their resources and regularize their revenue liabilities to the state—a formal process now documented by historians, at least in the Deccan and Hyderabad. It is significant that such low-level intermediaries with rural society (the third tier described earlier) were not only expected to remit taxes, in return for status, tax-free land, and a percentage of their remittance. They also had to send in periodic reports—an intelligence function vital to any continental authority. But the *zamindars* were also controlled from above by imperial officials.

It was the group of officials who were the most obvious intermediaries on whom the empire rested. (If a business analogy were considered, one might say they were both investors and managers in a massive undertaking.) Their origins were varied; relatives and associates of the Moguls who followed them into India, other foreign Muslims who migrated into India to jump on this imperial band-waggon, and local men, both Hindu and Muslim, who were recruited into the system, the former often because they were local magnates in their own right. Honoured service and alliance could sweeten the pill of conquest: or it could provide an economical alternative. (Rajasthan's Hindu Rajput chieftains were incorporated into the official-nobility group in prudent recognition of their local power base in the sensitive transit area west of Delhi. Marathas were recruited in the seventeenth century for similar reasons.)

The duties of noble officials included administration, which was closely connected with their duty to remit revenue collected from the *zamindars*, and the provision of military contingents for imperial service. The inducements for them to collaborate in the imperial structure were diverse. In return for their services they probably seldom received hard cash. Normally the emperor gave them a *jagir* or grant of land (hence the name *jagirdar*), from whose resources they financed themselves and their soldiers. Although *jagirs* were temporary grants, some officials clearly managed to dig themselves in and become powerful magnates, though this was not the official intention. Prestige, personal loyalty to the emperor, and ambition, were also reasons for a man to join himself to the Mogul train. They were a select—and selected—band, under 2,000 in Akbar's time. There were checks on their actions, however. They were frequently transferred from post to post, officials' authority overlapped each other, and there were also imperial intelligence gatherers who kept watch on their actions, among other things. Moreover the emperor in person kept his eye on them: they were required to attend regularly at court, and the imperial court itself was remarkably peripatetic. (It has been calculated that the emperors spent nearly 40 per cent of their reigns on tour.) The personal connection between emperor and noble official was highly significant, to both parties in that relationship. Indeed, the empire was run not so much as a bureaucracy but as a blend of a bureaucratic and patrimonial regime.

This brief description is intended to show how the empire at its most successful took account of the circumstances the Moguls found in India and worked within them: in particular how it constructed a network of allies from key figures in local or regional life with whom it had to come to terms since it could not obliterate them and replace them with salaried officials. Central, too, in this process of accommodation with society was Mogul religious tolerance. Hindus were welcomed into the collaborative enterprise, and no attempt was made to undermine caste or restrict Hindu religious observances.

Yet this imperial edifice built on accommodation weakened in the eighteenth century, allowing the emergence of new, more localized polities within its formal shell. Considerable scholastic controversy rages over the thorny problem of 'Mogul decline'.[16] Some date it from the reign of Aurangzeb (1658–1707) and his southward expansion. Others believe that there was no inevitable process of decline which could not have been halted, given other decisions and strategies. Not only is the timing at issue: so are the causes. Most of the simple theories are closely connected with Aurangzeb's southward thrust and unsuccessful attempt to subdue the attacking Maratha warrior bands. They stress such phenomena as peasant revolt because of high tax demands to meet military expenditure, leading to short-fall in tax collections and the consequent inability of officials and emperor to pay troops; or a shortage of *jagirs* as new nobles were hastily recruited because they could not be defeated; or even demoralization of the nobility because of the empire's persistent military defeats by the Marathas and the emperor's subsequent inability to provide them with status in a successful concern or security in the areas where they drew their resources.

More recently scholars have recognized that concentration on a short-term alleged 'decline' distorts the broad historical reality, tends to divorce 'high politics' from longer-term socio-economic change, and perpetuates a view of Indian history held by older imperial historians who contrasted supposed social and political decline under the later Moguls with the enterprise and initiative of British traders and administrators, and saw in the former a simple explanation for the expansion of European dominion. It now seems that the erosion of continental Mogul power was the culmination of several long processes of political and socio-economic change, some of which reflected the very succeess of Mogul rulers in bringing a modicum of peace to the subcontinent and encouraging its long-range trading networks as well as the commercialization of the domestic economy. Within the Mogul empire there had gradually occurred a process of 'decentralization', whereby local social groups consolidated their strength and autonomy at the expense of the imperial centre, building their new influence on a range of developments including commercialization, revenue-farming and the emergence of clusters of patrimonial landed holdings. Provincial societies became less easy to control, and earlier systems of central control began to break down; and this in turn weakened the empire against external invasion and internal subordination. Without the alliances of provincial leaderships and the regular transmission of revenue from the provinces to Delhi, Mogul strength quickly disintegrated.

The precise details of this process varied from region to region, but it is already clear that in many places vital intermediaries ceased to co-operate with imperial authority and so maintain its support-system and infrastructure. In the Deccan, an area for which there is detailed evidence, the lowest level of intermediaries, the *zamindars*, clearly began to reassess their position in the light of persistent military attacks. Some did not make their full tax returns even in Aurangzeb's last years; but it was not until after his death that local insecurity made them cut their losses, sever their links with the empire, refuse to remit revenue, take to plunder and eventually to open revolt. The provincial administration went bankrupt, could not pay troops to pacify the area, and the chaos was compounded by imperial troops mutinying for pay. More dramatic and better known is the defection of the upper echelon of intermediaries, the noble–officials, or at least their inaction against outside raiders. They, like notables viewing the British rulers in 1857 or nearly a century later, were wondering if their alliance was worth it, as imperial authority proved decreasingly capable of guaranteeing either their local resources or their prestige. As they failed to provide soldiers and remit revenue, so the imperial structure was enfeebled, its links with the periphery of its empire and local society snapped. Or again in Bengal, provincial governors had begun in the early eighteenth century to establish an independent regional polity only tenuously connected to the centre at Delhi. They appointed to administrative office, controlled military force, and increasingly failed to remit revenue to Delhi—a failure which was to be as disastrous for Mogul power as it was to be a source of strength for the British, for Bengal was one of the richest areas of the subcontinent on the proceeds of which to build political authority.

There is a further reason why historians should be wary of the notion of Mogul 'decline'. Mogul culture still had a profound influence in the successor regimes, whether Indian or European. The emperor was still seen as the legitimation of political authority even in the late eighteenth century and the British themselves maintained the forms of imperial grants and the ritual of Mogul authority into the new century. Even more important was the way in which Mogul administrative culture continued to shape the reality of Indian governance, including the central function of the collection of land revenue.

iv   Authority and power: the European political intrusion

The erosion of Mogul authority permitted the political intrusion of Europeans into Indian life. By the third quarter of the eighteenth century the East India Company, operating out of London, was in the novel and highly ambiguous position of collecting revenue and so administering a large and prosperous part of eastern India. Its servants were part of the structure of authority and power on the subcontinent. This was the start of the British *raj*. But until the closing years of the century the British, like other Europeans, were more influenced by India than influencing it. Indeed another heading for this section could well be 'Europeans as Asians': for this is what they were. Whether in commerce, or in eventual political intrigue and achievement, it was Indian people, finance, products, political culture and above all circumstances which were dominant influences on Europeans. These created the framework in which they operated, and according to whose conventions and expectations they acted. Europeans had no particular superiority as traders or as soldiers. Only at sea were they achieving a marked dominance over Asians; a fact which was finally to influence their political relations with Indians and to enable the British to shatter French political ambitions in India.

Furthermore, most European governments had no wish to involve themselves in massive landed empire in Asia, which would be hard to control and might become a financial and political liability. Where Europeans had achieved political dominion in Asia their objective had been spices grown in islands. The Dutch found the East Indies' spice islands relatively easy to control and defend with sea power, and the small-quantity, high-value product required close supervision and monopoly access. Indian products and geographical conditions could hardly have been more different. (The only parallel to the expansion of British rule in India was Spanish domination of South America. There, climate, Catholic missionary zeal and Spanish willingness to settle and manage landed estates all favoured such a land empire. Disease disastrously weakened the potential resistance of the local people, as did the blow to communal morale dealt by the death of their leaders who were the embodiment of their religious and political community.) In the face of such an extraordinary political development as the British *raj* in India it is partly understandable why some later narrators, popularizing the story, spoke of the British acquiring an Indian empire in a fit of absence of mind. In fact the British in Asia, like other Europeans, were mostly hard-headed, tough-minded merchants. They had to be to survive. Survival and profit were their main preoccupations, even when their actions ended in the acquisition of political power. Contemporaries were uneasily aware that European political intrusion into India was novel and possibly undesirable. In 1767 the East India Company's secretary specifically denied to the House of Commons that the Company was interested in conquest and power: 'it is commercial interest we look for'. Ten years later the Secretary to the Treasury noted that the spectacle of the Company exercising political power in India was patently 'absurd and preposterous'.[17]

India's value to various English people as well as other Europeans explains why Mogul weakness and the nature of the resulting regional states so altered the terms of European connections with the subcontinent. Four main European national groups were involved in trade based on India—the Portuguese, Dutch, French, and British, though by the mid-eighteenth century the total British interest was by far the largest, and the smaller-scale activities of such groups as the Danes were really British operations under a flag of convenience. Each of the four main trading companies was financed from Europe: the Dutch and English companies depended on private finance, and the other two on government investment. Ships annually took bullion and goods such as wool and metals from Europe to India to company 'factories' or fortified trading stations, almost all on the coast. There company officials used them for exchange in the three interlocking aspects of India's trade—the country trade, the inter-Asian trade, and the Europe–Asia trade. In the early days of European involvement, until the end of the seventeenth century, spices were the main commodity shipped back to Europe from different parts of Asia, bought in exchange for Indian textiles, which in turn had been bought with the bullion and goods exported from Europe. By the eighteenth century Indian textiles had overtaken spices in importance in the long haul back to Europe.

The East India Company, based in Leadenhall Street in the City of London, was in the eighteenth century governed by a charter of 1698 which protected its Asian trading monopoly but also imposed restrictions on its operations (in such matters as goods carried and modes of finance), and enabled Parliament to watch its actions and debate them, in times of concern or when the charter came up for renewal. The Company raised its money by issuing bonds which proved popular short-term investments among the more prosperous of the British public. Its annual sales in India averaged £240,000 in the middle of the century; but that was not enough to pay for its investment in Asian goods, and nearly three times as much had to be shipped in bullion to India to make up the difference. The Company also traded in China, principally in tea. There it was forced to deal on stringent terms with a small monopoly ring of Chinese merchants. The problem of what to exchange for tea grew acute, as the Chinese were by natural endowment and political choice economically self-sufficient. This problem was only 'solved' from the British point of view late in the century when the Company's expanding political power in eastern India enabled it to monopolize local production of opium for illegal exchange in China—an unsavoury transaction which proved essential for British financial stability in India. So in the mid-eighteenth century the Company was a venerable institution, part of the fabric of English economic and political life, making stable but unspectacular profits in Asia of about £500,000 annually, and satisfying its stock-holders with 7 or 8 per cent interest. It handled about 13 per cent of British imports and 5.5 per cent of the nation's exports.

The Company's servants abroad lived a strange and hazardous life. 'Nabobs', or men returned from India with fortunes which enabled them to live in style and exert considerable public influence, were the exceptions. Many died on the journey to India: European graveyards in such settlements as Calcutta, Bombay or Madras witness poignantly to the brevity of European life and the ravages of disease and climate, in an age when tropical clothes and medicine were unknown. The 'factories' were sternly ruled by a President or Governor, and beneath him were the most senior merchants who composed his Council. It was a highly stratified community, each knowing his place. Beneath the Councillors were the Senior Merchants, the Junior Merchants, then the Factors; and at the base of the hierarchy of Company officials the Writers, young men of at least sixteen, 'to be trayned up in our business' and encouraged 'in hopes of preferment, to be sober, industrious and faithful.'[18] Membership of this hierarchy was much prized among England's professional and commercial families, but the aspiring Writer needed a Director in England as patron, since entry was by Directors' nomination. Each one who made it into this commercial and social élite among the British in India entered into a covenant with the Company which bound him to good behaviour and fair commercial dealings. This gave rise to the name 'Covenanted Service' which later referred to the élite Indian Civil Service under the crown, somewhat ironically since by that time the administrators had severed all links with trade, and British commercial men were looked down on disparagingly as 'box-wallahs'. In the Company's eighteenth-century settlements also lived the Company's European soldiers, its surgeons and chaplains. There were also some 'free' merchants and mariners permitted by the Company, and a motley selection of other Europeans who got in by stealth but were tolerated if they kept the peace. Among the Europeans living under British protection in Calcutta in 1766 were merchants, shopkeepers, watchmakers, jewellers, lawyers, undertakers, and even a teacher of the French horn. From this list and contemporary descriptions of British life in India it is evident that those of means and sound constitution lived in considerable style, and despite local climate and custom indulged in dancing, parties, gambling, and copious drinking.

The records of Company trade and settlement only indicate the 'official' value of India and its wide-branching trade to the British. What recent research has made clear is the complex 'private' trade and profiteering carried on under the Company's wing and benefiting from its presence and protection, by Company servants themselves in an unofficial capacity, and by 'free' merchants, often in partnership with Indians who provided not only local knowledge and management skills but considerable capital. By the eighteenth century there was a private merchant fleet based on Calcutta, and private British involvement in sea-borne trade, at first west from Calcutta round India's coast, then later in the eighteenth century east to China. Company servants also plunged into Bengal's internal trade particularly as the Company's influence expanded, often using the Company name and privileges to cover their activities, and jealously excluding 'free' merchants from this sphere. Opium, salt, tobacco, and betel nut were all commodities they tried to lay hands on, in defiance of the still existent Indian Nawab. By 1763 this private involvement in Bengal's trade was probably worth well over £500,000—more than the Company's annual profit! The Company did not pay its servants enough to live on, so they had to make money by other means. Trade in their private capacities was not their only recourse. Office in the Company itself proved profitable in relations with Indians; and present-taking and other perks reached staggering proportions as Company political influence increased in the 1760s. A House of Commons Select Committee identified well over £2 million distributed in presents in Bengal between 1757 and 1765, which was probably a substantial underrating of the true magnitude of the custom. Undoubtedly the risks were high—both of death and bankruptcy. But at certain times the hope of spectacular profit was also considerable. In Bengal the boom years were 1757–69, after the assertion of Company power in regional politics at the battle of Plassey. Then for just over a decade, it was virtually certain that anyone in Company service who survived would return to England with a fortune.[19]

Both 'official' and 'private' aspects of British involvement in India contributed to the subcontinent's value to the British by the mid-eighteenth century. The result was a honeycomb of groups with a stake in the survival of this whole Asian trading network. It was in different ways the life-blood of the Company's servants. London-based Directors who never ventured east gained profit and power by controlling Company patronage. (This has been calculated to have been worth £7–8,000 a year to each Director.) Hundreds of stockholders in England's towns and shires also had personal stakes in the Company's operations. So did a substantial shipping interest. This was composed of owners and builders of the great sailing ships which took the Company's goods to and from India, and the ships' masters who could use in person or sell their permanent master's positions, which included free space for goods traded on their own account. All those connected with shipping had extracted highly favourable monopoly terms from the Company for their services.

'The British' were not a monolithic group with a firm structure of command and centrally-determined policies. (This was truer of the French.) Different elements or cells within the honeycomb of interests interacted with each other, with Asian circumstances, and with politics in Britain. The result of this interaction was 'policy' of a sort, but was often ignored or modified in the process of enactment in India. British political intrusion should be understood in this context rather than as the outcome of any official imperial design by Company or Parliament. (The complexity of interacting interest groups, confusingly referred to *en bloc* as 'the British' is an abiding feature of the British connection with India, although the interests and groupings changed in subsequent centuries, as did the structure within which they operated. This will become clear when we observe strains and contradictions within the formal *raj* itself.)

In the Indian polities and culture within which European traders had so long been operating there was a constant interpenetration of political authority and commercial enterprise, stemming from rulers' needs to ensure revenue flows, and the activities of a wide range of commercial, revenue, and military entrepreneurs who used political offices and connections as sources of profit. However, overt and direct European political as opposed to commercial involvement in India occurred in the mid-eighteenth century because of two interlocking sets of circumstances. The first was the gradual erosion of Mogul authority. As control slipped from their hands, particularly on the empire's periphery, so Indian claimants to their power warred with each other at the regional level of politics and government. Political instability is generally bad for trade. It disrupts trade routes, can cut off supplies at source, or even threaten the physical safety of commercial men. Europeans discovered this to their cost in Bengal as a provincial Nawabi regime established itself at the expense of Mogul authority. Although at first they were able to operate in satisfactory conditions, the new Nawab, Siraj-ud-Daula, who succeeded in 1756, challenged the interests of many local élites and also the terms of English trade, to the extent of attacking the English base in Calcutta. Political instability proved even more threatening to the British stake in India because it coincided with the outbreak of a series of European wars which locked French and British against each other—opposition which spilled over into Asia, where indigenous political rivalries consequent on Mogul weakness provided fertile ground for the furtherance of intra-European conflict. Both sides found willing local allies in rival Indian princes and their factions, and so were drawn into the subcontinent's internecine struggles. Open Anglo-French conflict erupted in India in 1744, its main theatre being southern India, where the famous Frenchman, Dupleix, built up a significant power-base, but was eventually dislodged by the East India Company's Robert Clive, who had started as a Writer but turned out to be an astute general, puppeteer of Indian rulers he helped to elevate, fortune-hunter and administrator. It was he, too, who extricated the British settlement in Calcutta from its conflict with Siraj-ud-Daula, the Nawab of Bengal, who captured and sacked Calcutta in 1756. Clive's victory at Plassey in 1757 not only marked the beginning of his own astonishing accumulation of wealth: it established the British as a major political influence on the subcontinent. But it did not end the threat to the British stake in India, either from the French or from intra-Indian rivalries. Indeed European involvement in Indian politics in support of rival nawabs only de-stabilized the situation still further; as did overt exploitation of the Bengali economy by 'private' English interests after the battle of Plassey. When Clive returned to India in 1765 to govern Bengal he took the decisive step of accepting formal political power at regional level in preference to propping up puppet nawabs. So the East India Company slipped into the remnants of the Mogul imperial network of intermediaries, taking up the *diwani* or revenue administration for Bengal, the richest province in India.

Four years earlier renewed Anglo-French conflict further south had ended in French capitulation when they attacked British settlements, once a force was sent south from Bengal to confront them.[20] Despite the drama of political intervention, there had been no obvious increase in the English commercial stake in India, nor any pressure from London to intervene. It was rather that the combination of political circumstances had given the English a compelling interest in securing a stable and well-disposed regime in Bengal which in turn led by stages of involvement in domestic politics to overt political control. Once secure in Bengal, and immeasurably empowered by its revenue as well as its commerce, they were able to stabilize their other trading posts in the south and west. So the protection of English interests led traders to a political intrusion which was to be crucial for their subsequent relations with the whole subcontinent.

Older textbooks whose focus was imperial history devoted pages to the complexities of Indian factionalism, European rivalries, feats of bravery and generalship. In retrospect of course these middle decades of the eighteenth century did prove seminal in the making of modern India. But *at the time* there was no indication that this European political intrusion was to be the start of a process of interaction between India and the West of such significance. Indeed, those English and their Indian allies who combined to defeat Siraj-ud-Daula were essentially conservative in their intentions, hoping to restore an earlier equilibrium and accommodation of interests in Bengal, rather than trigger major and widespread political change. The British defeated the French because of their superior naval power and their ability to deploy the resources of Bengal. But they did not 'conquer India'—or even Bengal. They won certain battles, and came out top in political intrigues because of Indian divisions, and with Indian allies. In 1765 they became part of an existing regional power structure: but they had no influence either at the all-India or the local levels of power. Nor was there any indication that they might have a decisive effect on Indian society or ideology. Indian circumstances permitted them a limited political intrusion only at this stage. The constrictions of Indian geography, society, and political structures remained, and the newcomers would have to work within these just as their predecessors had done.

CHAPTER II

The Consolidation of Dominion:
Illusion and Reality

Earlier historians whose framework of study was imperial history had little difficulty in seeing distinct phases in Indian history and marking clear dividing points in it. Their Eurocentric vision led them to chop up India's experience into segments suggested by British politics, institutions, and decisions: for example, the gaining of empire, 1757–1818, or the subsequent 'Age of Reform' inaugurated by Lord Bentinck's Governor-Generalship. But such clear periodization disappears when the observer shifts his focus to actual practice in India rather than proclaimed policy, whether the issue is the creation of a clear administrative system, the settlement of land rights and revenue obligations, or aspects of social reform. Nor does older periodization help if the historian's main interest lies in the historical experience of India's people in their own right, in Indian society's own dynamics and resources, and in interaction between that society and western influences, rather than in attempting to discern any simple impact of imperial rulers and their policies. Recognition of the interactive nature of this relationship and of its unevenness and diversity is a hallmark of recent historical study of India. It stems from detailed research by scholars exploring particular questions and the varied experiences of different regions, and drawing on Indian source materials unavailable to their predecessors. These reveal more fundamental patterns of stability and change than those discernable from the bare and often superficial record of imperial decisions; and underline the importance of Indian ideas, solidarities, and initiatives in the fashioning of a new regime and a new order.

This chapter will cover nearly a century of this interactive relationship, from 1765 to 1857/8—a century which was in a real sense a unity. These were years in which British political intrusion developed into full-scale imperial dominion: 1857/8 marked a significant challenge to this dominion, which was defeated, and the British position subsequently symbolized by the removal of the last Mogul emperor from his throne in Delhi. In the decades since acquiring the *diwani* in Bengal an all-India imperial structure had been consolidated. In this process of constructing institutions and networks of allies, the diverse British interest groups had been forced into new relations with each other, and constrained to face the complexities and dilemmas of peace and government rather than trade and war. Priorities

46

and principles of empire were discussed, and then subjected in India to the tests of viability and necessity in the context of local society. These decades are also an entity in terms of India's society and economy, and the degree to which the British were influenced by them or able to exert influence over them. This was certainly a time of new rulers at the upper levels of political power; a time of much talk and brave policy-making on paper. But it was also a period characterized by British ignorance of the subcontinent they were attempting to control, and by the physical and financial weakness of the new 'imperialists', as well as their lack of technical knowledge and skill to effect major, intentional change. Dominion was both reality and illusion. The chapter concludes with the 1857 rebellion. This was not a decisive break-point in Indian history. (Such decisive breaks are rare: continuity and evolution are the most usual modes of historical experience.) 1857 does give the historian something like a geological cross-section to examine, however, for events in that year make it possible to see the trends of interaction between Indian society and the influences which accompanied British administration, and to perceive both the reality and illusion of British power in the subcontinent.

i   The expansion and stabilization of territorial dominion

The most dramatic and obvious change in the relationship of India and the British in the century following British intrusion into Bengal occurred at the upper levels of politics and government. The East India Company expanded its control to cover the whole subcontinent: in so doing it had to transform its servants from traders into administrators, and it was in turn more rigorously controlled by Parliament in London, though India was not ruled directly under the crown until after the Mutiny. Territorial expansion was erratic and piecemeal. The early intrusion into Bengal was followed at the end of the century by annexations in southern India, and then early in the nineteenth century by the extension of Company rule in western India. By 1818 British dominion had expanded over the whole subcontinent south of the river Sutlej. Actual control was extended both by direct rule and by alliances with Indian rulers who were allowed to retain their territories as subsidiary allies, their relationship with the all-India power partially regulated by treaties permitting different degrees of British intervention. Such intervention was no remote possibility: in the first half of the nineteenth century several princes had parts of their territory lopped off, and some had their states obliterated as political entities and amalgamated into areas directly administered by the British. By the middle of the century, after the northern and western areas of Punjab and Sind had been annexed, the princely states formed about one-third of the Indian empire. Some were large, strategically situated and politically significant, such as Mysore and Hyderabad in the south. Others were minor chiefdoms scarcely bigger than a large country estate, like those scattered across western India in a complicated mosaic in between large areas directly ruled from Bombay.

The reasons why the Company was able to achieve this position lie partly in its resources, but even more in the weaknesses of its competitors. At the basic military level British fighting strength and skills were no greater than those of other warring groups in India. All the armies which ranged over the subcontinent, whether 'European' or 'Indian', were largely composed of Indian troops. Some Indian rulers had also had their forces trained by Europeans or had adopted European military techniques. Where the British scored over their rivals was first in their resource base in wealthy Bengal, which yielded up to their disposal Rs. 30 million in land revenue alone and bolstered British settlements and armies in other parts of India; and ultimately in their sea power which enabled back-up from England. But it was the weakness and disunity of its rivals which constituted the Company's real strength. The French were not serious contenders for power from the last two decades of the eighteenth century onwards, despite the British fear of a 'French threat' under Napoleon. In the aftermath of crumbling Mogul power the contending Indian successors warred with each other, or at least failed to support each other instead of combining against the foreigner. The Maratha warring bands and the southern Indian princes who most gravely threatened British interests repeated on a continental scale the process which had enabled the growth of British political power in Bengal. This is crucial to an understanding of the subsequent British position in India. They never conquered or dominated Indian society; nor in these early years the lower levels of political life. They were permitted to intrude at the higher levels of political power only by Indian weakness and divisions. This meant that their imperial dominion was for years both reality and illusion. The circumstances of their acquisition of political power continued to influence and cramp their ability deeply to affect India's peoples, their society and economy.

The deeper reasons of intention and motive for the Company's acquisition of vast areas of territory are more obscure, particularly as the Company remained officially hostile to any overt policy of expansion. Company directors saw that military campaigns were expensive, and often embroiled their trading organization in long-term administrative commitment; and it evoked hostile criticism in Britain. It would be simplistic to look for a single determinant of the expansion of British power in India, to expect one motive, intention or interest to be dominant. For that expansion occurred in such different parts of India at different times. In each particular situation the precise British interests at stake varied, and the perceived danger to them; as did the relative weight in decision-making of different British groups concerned in Indian affairs.

Several aspects of the British presence were always important, whatever the immediate circumstances of any particular territorial thrust. Given the distance from England, and the voyage of up to three months which separated the Company's servants in India from Westminster and Leadenhall Street, it was normally the man on the spot who made the key political and military decisions. Men such as Clive, Warren Hastings or Lord Wellesley had far more opportunity for initiative and manoeuvre than their successors who could not ignore the fast mail and telegraph. However, they in turn depended on information received from lowlier Company servants, sometimes far from Calcutta, who had substantial interests at stake in India in their private capacities. Private interests were another significant element in the British presence, often inextricable from official Company interest: they were a continuing part of the context in which dominion was extended and often had a marked influence on that process. Between the middle of the eighteenth century and the 1780s a commercial revolution occurred in Asia's country trade. At its heart lay India, a point of trans-shipment and exchange between Persia, Arabia, and East Africa to its west, and China to the east: it was the producer of goods vital to this inter-Asian trading network, particularly to pay in China for the increasing quantities of tea which were being shipped to England. In this 'country trade' British traders had become dominant by the late eighteenth century. The private profits made in this trade kept the East India Company solvent,[1] and the delicate balance between private trade and Company survival thus gave private British interests considerable weight in decision-making in India, though private interest and the use to which it was put varied with time and place.

The extension of political dominion was primarily driven on by the requirements of the Company: as both trading company needing to extract Indian goods, and as Indian ruler needing to stabilize its internal frontiers and pay for the growing army with which it protected its Indian interests. (By 1805 the Company's army numbered 155,000, one of the largest European standing armies in the world, and far better equipped and supplied than in the previous century.) This dual mercantilist and military thrust produced an increasingly fraught relationship with those local Indian regimes which were consolidating themselves in place of the Mogul empire. Wherever possible the Company entered into subsidiary alliances with amenable regimes, providing 'protection' in return for alliances and payment for Company troops, as a cheap means of defending the borders of its territory. But Company pressure and financial demands inexorably destabilized those regimes, often driving their subjects into open revolt, thus necessitating further British intervention and eventually annexation. The

extension of dominion was thus almost always pragmatic, rather than ideologically motivated. Occasional worries of a 'French threat' served to reinforce pragmatism; but it was perhaps only under Lord Wellesley in the early
nineteenth century that a more ideological commitment to imperial expansion emerged, and his aspirations did not find favour in London.

The blend of interests and pressures which led to the extension of Company rule varied from area to area.[2] For example, in Bengal the pursuit of
private profit by Company servants in particular was a provocative factor
which led to the clash between the Company and the Nawab in 1756: while
the enormous private profiteering after Plassey destabilized the political
order still further and so helped to draw the Company into overt political
control. In the case of Oudh, inland up the Ganges valley, European private
interests were increasing, and were deeply involved in local trade, the more
so as the East India Company extended its monopoly over goods produced
in Bengal. However, there is no evidence that commercial considerations
influenced Wellesley's decision to annexe large parts of the Wazir of
Oudh's dominions in 1801. Indeed, it was not at all certain that formal
Company rule would actually benefit private interests in this particular
situation, since those in private trade would then face competition from
Company purchases and the implementation of Company monopolies.
Here, rather, was a classic case of Company financial pressure on a subsidiary ally destablizing the regime it sought to prop, generating internal
revolt, and eventually leading to outright annexation as the way to secure a
dangerous western frontier.

Further west the pattern was different yet again; and here the interlocking commercial interests of Company and private traders can clearly be
seen as dominant in the drive towards formal imperial control. In Malabar
and Gujarat Company and private traders were deeply and profitably entrenched; only to find their trade lines or sources of supply of such raw
materials as pepper or cotton for the country trade with China threatened
by the political instability which followed the breakdown of Mogul authority. They were determined to see effective authority established, to enable
the cultivation of cash crops and their unharassed collection and transpor-
tation. Pressure from these groups, and the information they retailed to the
Company authorities, was a peristent and crucial exercise in local
'subimperialism'. By contrast the British clash with Mysore and the
Marathas was little influenced by trading interests in any simple sense.
Rather, it was a political confrontation with Indian polities in the process of
reconstruction as successors to the Moguls whose very success and military
power threatened British dominance, and enabled them to attempt to break
away from the clutches of a subsidiary alliance and all that that seemed
increasingly to entail for Indian rulers and their states.

The precise blend of intentions, hopes, and fears, within the honeycomb of interest groups comprising the British presence in India which led to territorial dominion varied in each region according to local circumstances. The overall result of such uneven and unplanned territorial acquisition was a political frontier which did not coincide with an economic frontier. It far outreached the limits of actual British trade and economic influence. Moreover, it was a frontier determined in India, not by decisions made in London. Both Westminster and Leadenhall Street on occasion opposed these expansive trends: neither had much option but to acquiesce in their results. By the second decade of the new century India was in effect under the direct sway of a military despotism disguised as a commercial company. In search of revenue to pay its army and goods to remit to Britain, it had increasingly become unable to accommodate itself to the politics of the Moguls' Indian successors; and had consistently undermined or confronted them, thereby implicating itself in a new style of dominion which was often at first more illusory than substantial.

As Company territory expanded two important processes developed and ultimately succeeded in stabilizing the new territorial dominion and regulating its use of political power. One was the construction of a system whereby the Company's administration in India could be controlled by the British government. The other was the transformation of profiteering merchants into responsible administrators, by regulating their recruitment and training, and establishing rules of administrative procedure.

The East India Company had never been isolated from British political life. Its wealth and weight in London's city politics involved it with the government of the day in Westminster. But the expansion of its Indian territories radically altered the terms of that involvement, and the issues at stake. The changing relations between Westminster and Leadenhall Street belong to the intricacies of British public life. They also concern the student of the Indian subcontinent because they were an important means whereby British opinion and western values were brought to bear on India, and began to interact with Indian society and values. Although India was never effectively governed from London, what happened in London helped to shape the nature of British rule and ensured that those who administered India were accountable to an audience outside the subcontinent.

The conquest of Bengal created a range of new problems in the eyes of London politicians. It triggered a rush for lucrative offices under the Company, and the unedifying scramble for patronage disrupted internal Company politics and rent it into factions. Writerships were even offered publicly for sale, though this was rare! Reports of fortune-hunting, rapacity and corruption in Bengal itself in the decades after Plassey were too numerous and well-founded to be ignored. Not only did they offend consciences in London: such actions threatened to impoverish the Company's richest Indian possession.[3] Furthermore, Indian fortunes had implications in British political life. Contemporaries were apprehensive of the Nabobs who invested in English acres, and used their Indian wealth to buy political influence, including Parliamentary seats, at a time when 'rotten boroughs' were easy game for men with money but no established political base. But it was the Company's acute financial disarray which precipitated government intervention—as the price for bailing it out of its financial crises, as in 1772–3 and 1782–4. However, other considerations made politicians in London wary of interfering in Company affairs. It was a Chartered Company; and chartered rights were seen by contemporaries as a powerful defence of the liberties of the subject. To tamper with them in this case might be a perilous precedent. Money and patronage in the hands of the Company and its servants might be disquieting. Infinitely more so was the prospect of Indian wealth and places being at the disposal of the Crown and the government of the day. The considerable number of members in Parliament who had either served in India or had interests in the Company also inhibited radical interference with the Company's position.[4]

The foundation of the East India Company was its two to three thousand shareholders. Many were individuals living in or near London, who saw their shares as the safest investment they could acquire. Those owning £500 of stock were entitled to vote in the Court of Proprietors, or General Court, which was the ultimate authority in the Company's affairs. The General Court elected from those of its own ranks who had at least a £2,000 stake in the Company twenty-four Directors, who actually ran the Company. By the early nineteenth century an increasing number of Directors had actually served in India, though many were still London merchants for whom the Company was only one of a large range of financial interests, and who knew little of India. Given ignorance, distance, and the disruption of internal Company politics caused by the scramble for patronage, it was little wonder that the Company should appear inadequate to meet its growing political obligations in India.

When Parliament and Government did intervene the occasions were generally Company financial crises and/or controversies, and personal vendettas relating to prominent Company servants in India.[5] The first significant intervention culminated in the Regulating Act of 1773, carried through by Lord North's administration, despite considerable hostility from the Company's shareholders in alliance with the Parliamentary opposition. It aimed to stabilize the Company's London structure, and to increase London's control of events and officials in India. The Court of Directors was strengthened in various ways, including the lengthening of the members' tenure of office from one to four years, while in India a new over-all authority was vested in a Governor-General with four advisors, who formed a Supreme Council in Calcutta. They were to hold office for five years, and were appointed by Parliament; moreover three of the original members were not Company men. North's government was determined that so important an area as India should not be left to the Company alone, though control of the Company and through it of India seemed the only viable mechanism in the circumstances of contemporary politics, rather than so radical a step as replacing the Company. This measure did not stop rumours of abuses in India, or the financial drain on the Company from Indian warfare; and the Supreme Council proved woefully inadequate in providing the authoritative supervision hoped of it. Nor did the Act's provisions prevent the General Court from defying both Directors and government, and pursuing the immediate interests of stockholders, their relatives, and connections.

A solution to these problems emerged after various abortive attempts at more rigorous control, in the 1784 India Act brought to Parliament by the government of the younger Pitt. It remained the legal basis of the Company's relations with the state until 1858, although the Company's commercial privileges were whittled away long before, in subsequent renewals of its Charter in 1793 and 1813. The 1784 measure deprived the General Court of any power to intervene in Indian administration, and provided for a system of 'double government'; whereby the Court of Directors (now supreme within the Company structure) was counterbalanced by a Board of Control, composed of six Privy Councillors, including a Secretary of State and the Chancellor of the Exchequer. Trade and patronage remained in the charge of the Directors but the Board of Control supervised matters relating to Indian revenue, administration, war, and diplomacy. Its members, however, could not communicate directly with Company servants in India, though they could amend Directors' instructions. This constraint could be avoided in various ways—as with so-called 'private' correspondence between the President of the Board of Control and the Governor-General. Surprisingly few conflicts erupted between the two halves of this double government apparatus, and compromises were generally arranged whenever conflict threatened. A strong President of the Board of Control backed by a stable home government could not be defied; and no government in London was prepared to leave the most important Indian political appointments, such as the Governor-Generalship, to the Company alone. Governments either made their wishes known in advance, or used their power to recall Company servants. Within India the Governor-General's powers were strengthened, over the area beyond Bengal, and over his Supreme Council colleagues.

So was state control of the Company formally established, and with it the principle of public responsibility for the government of India, though the Company remained intact. British public opinion and influence outside those groups with specific Indian interests was brought to bear on the subcontinent in the formal framework of control created by the state, and was supplemented by other pragmatic procedures. Parliament did not as a rule concern itself greatly with India; but on occasion its Select and Secret Committees could be formidable engines of enquiry into alleged malpractices of Company servants in India. It also had the weapon of prosecution—impeachment—as Clive, Warren Hastings, and Wellesley discovered. In such cases personal vendettas against prominent men were obviously rampant. But the process of impeachment provided set-piece occasions for the public justification of actions in India and the rehearsal of the principles which were at stake in an alien government of the subcontinent. The audience was the central, most articulate segment of Britain's limited 'political nation'. Day to day policy making and administration rested, however, with the Court of Directors and the Board of Control. Or, more precisely, it was available within that interlocking mechanism to whoever had the impetus and energy to master the correspondence with India which the process of government generated. A strong President of the Board, an ideologically zealous Director, or a competent Company civil servant with distinct views could therefore exert a decisive influence over policy towards India.

A second process essential to the stabilization of British dominion was the creation of an administrative structure on the subcontinent. It intertwined with the extension of London's control over the Company in several ways. No policy made in London was worth more than the paper it was minuted on unless it could be carried out in India: a dependable machinery for so doing had been conspicuously lacking for the first three-quarters of the eighteenth century. Furthermore, supervision of the Company's servants, and regulation of their recruitment, training, and terms of service, eased the scramble for patronage which had so disrupted Company politics in the 1770s and 1780s when a Company passage to India seemed entry into the land of the pagoda tree which none could fail to shake to personal profit unless death cut him down. The business of turning profiteering servants of a trading concern into sober, dependable civil servants responsible for an expanding state was a huge and novel enterprise. The creation of a regular civil service, recruited on known criteria of qualifications and integrity, trained and well paid so that members did not have to resort to surreptitious perquisites, and with a clear ladder of promotion, was a phenomenon of the later nineteenth-century even in Britain. Moreover the customs and actions which had produced such problems and scandal in Bengal—patronage, placing, considerations, presents, and the profits of office—were all part of public life in Britain in the eighteenth century. What distinguished the Indian case was the scale of such operations; and the fact that they had such dire repercussions on the political and economic stability of Bengal, and such potential implications in British politics.

The primary and most glaring target for reform and regulation were the British servants of the East India Company, its 'covenanted' servants who were the precursors of the prestigious covenanted Indian Civil Service, commonly known as the ICS. The emergence of this service is not just a dry page of administrative history. It proved vital in the interactive process between Britain and India because its members became part of the chain of intermediaries between government and Indian subject on which the British *raj*, like the Mogul empire, depended. In the countryside ICS men were the last British link in the chain: and in many cases their capacities and relations with local Indians largely determined whether what was decreed by policy-makers in London or Calcutta actually got done. (Even in the twentieth century there were instances of ICS men cheerfully disregarding orders from superior authority which they considered locally inappropriate, with wry and ribald humour.) The ICS did not even die in 1947 at independence. Its ethos, characteristics, and traditions have been powerful in independent India (see chapter VI).

Lord Cornwallis was the Governor-General (1786–1793) despatched from London with the brief to regulate efficient administration in the Company's territories.[6] He had not only the expanded powers noted earlier, but also strong backing from Parliament and the Court of Directors. Both these circumstances boded well for his success in contrast to his predecessor, Warren Hastings. Cornwallis was convinced that Indians were dishonest and incapable of ruling India in their own best interests, but he was also an English Whig who conceived of good government as light government rather than major administrative interference in or management of society and the economy. With this dual orientation an administrative system was developed which, despite later modifications, was the framework of Indian government for nearly two centuries. Its ground plan was Cornwallis's 1793 Code of Regulations.

The land was divided into districts, each under a Collector. This title reflects the centrality of land revenue collection to government in India: it was government's primary function and it moulded the institutions and patterns of administration. Under Cornwallis's regulations landholders were settled with rights in land, in return for a fixed revenue liability. (In so doing the British joined together two types of property right which had previously been separate in India—the right to collect revenue and the right of proprietorship—a conjuncture which would be the prelude to major change in the socio-economic order, as land could now be sold if proprietors failed to pay their revenue.) This was the 'Permanent Settlement', and under it the Collector had only a supervisory role: he in turn was supervised by the Board of Revenue in Calcutta. Quite separate was the administration of law. This was in the hands of a local civil judge and magistrate, who in turn were supervised by provincial courts of appeal. However, as more territory came under British direct rule this system was modified substantially in the new areas, most of which were not 'permanently settled' in

Bengal fashion. In these other districts the constantly changing revenue liabilities of greater numbers of lesser village folk settled with land generated far more assessment and collection work for civil servants, while changing attitudes to the potentially positive role of government, stemming from Britain, also led to the assumption by district officers of more judicial functions.[7] Bengal always remained lightly governed compared with many other parts of British India. Elsewhere the paternalistic and more powerful district officer liked to see himself as the 'mother and father' of the villagers under his care, supervising their revenue obligations, listening to their complaints, and exercising justice; whether in his district headquarters office, or 'on tour' in the cooler weather in a peripatetic tent encampment. Out of the experience of ruling different parts of India, the nature of Indian society, and the ideas injected from Britain about the nature and role of government, there emerged a definite *system* of administration, founded on the geographical division of India into districts which were grouped into provinces—often the size of a small European country. In each province a clear hierarchy of civil administration and a legal structure developed, stretching from provincial capital down to district, manned by British civil servants. Beneath the district officer was the network of Indian subordinates who were crucial to the working of the system's upper levels.

However, at the close of the eighteenth century those who aimed to stabilize British rule concerned themselves primarily with the British who were to administer the expanding dominion. While a known system of government and supervision of Company servants was developed, a parallel development concerned the selection, training, and promotion of those who were to man it. Without changes here no structural reform would bear fruit. Patronage remained the door into the Indian Civil Service until 1853, when open competition was introduced. Until that date the Company Directors nominated writers, cadets, surgeons and chaplains. This was laid down, with rules for promotion within the service, in the 1784 India Act and the 1793 Charter Act. By the end of the eighteenth century the Directors had worked out the distribution of patronage between themselves, according to their seniority; the Chairman and Deputy Chairman of the Court having a double share, while the President of the Board of Control had an allocation matching the Chairman's. (In an average year an ordinary Director had about eleven places at his disposal.) Once in the service, promotion was by seniority, and those important Company posts carrying high salaries (up to £4,000 a year) had to be filled by men with substantial service in India behind them. Only the highest civilian positions—the Governor-Generalship and provincial governorships—and high army commands could be filled directly from Britain by prominent men. So a clear career structure was established and men given good salaries and prospects of promotion, in place of the old lucky-dip, get-rich-quick nature of former Company service.

Research into the type of young man attracted by these more sober but certain prospects and nominated by Directors shows that they were often related to Directors by blood or friendship, and many had relatives who had already served in India. From the 1830s almost all the Directors themselves had served in India. They tended to live in or near London and formed a close-knit, restricted segment of upper-class society, distinct from the aristocracy, but separate, too, from small-scale businessmen and artisans, and from the newer industrial and commercial entrepreneurs. Their nominees to Indian service almost certainly belonged to this distinctive banking and commercial world, with a sprinking of sons of clergy and land-owners. This is confirmed by the education of these young men before they received a semblance of Company training at Haileybury College, founded in 1805 by the Company's Directors. Well under a third entering Haileybury between 1809 and 1850 had been to public schools: most had attended special crammers, grammar schools, and academies, or had been privately educated by clergymen. Well over a quarter of Haileybury students at this time were from London; while just under a quarter had actually been born in India, though sent home for English education.

Once nominated for Company service recruits received a rudimentary preparation for their Indian work. Wellesley laid great plans for a Company training college in Calcutta in 1800, where Indian law, history and languages would be taught, beside more general elements of education. All this was to be in the context of building in the students such 'solid foundations of industry, prudence, integrity and religion, as should effectually guard them against those temptations, with which the nature of this climate, and peculiar depravity of the people of India, will surround and assail them in every station, especially upon their first arrival in India.' But these plans did not come to fruition; and the College became an important language school for new arrivals in the Company's service. While studying Indian languages they were also introduced to the flourishing, if rather formal, social life of Calcutta, and often drawn into debt in order to keep up their social position, in a manner quite contrary to Wellesley's intentions!

However, the Company did feel that it should instil Christian principles into its recruits as well as preparing them more technically for Indian service—hence the foundation of Haileybury in England. It was certainly not renowned for demanding hard work, and despite the elevated intentions of the Directors the only real teaching about India seems to have been the language classes. These stressed Indian classical languages, Sanskrit, Persian, and Arabic, whereas Fort William College in Calcutta concentrated on the living vernaculars. Probably far more important than any moral or specialist Indian training given at Haileybury was the sense of community which these young recruits developed and then carried to India to sustain them in their strange and often isolated lives. Continuing features of the ICS were to be this sense of belonging to a chosen élite which must support each other; and a belief that the best civilian was not a technical expert but a broadly educated man who could cope with any situation or problem because of his 'character', background, and general competence.

It is very difficult to assess actual performance in India of these newly-recruited and semi-trained civil servants, particularly where they were out on their own in their districts. Certainly the worst abuses of the 'pagoda tree' period were stamped out, as British civil servants were properly paid, forbidden to take presents or to trade privately. Their whole orientation now was to government as a career proposition, in which the rules were known, and corruption discovered would be the end of the road; though this rooting out of old habits doubtless took time. But this was only part of the problem of stabilizing British rule and ensuring that administrators actually carried out what was required of them. From the few local studies[8] of district level administration and the fate of British policies and civil servants it would appear that administration on the spot was a hand-to-mouth opera-tion, making the best of a job beset by practical difficulties, with results which often bore little relation to orders issued from provincial secretariats or policies planned by idealistic Directors or Company administrators in London. Given the system of recruitment and training, many of the British who arrived in India were in fact mediocre administrators. One Collector of Surat district for nearly twenty years in the early nineteenth century had left Fort William College knowing no Indian language: another Collector in western India appointed in 1817 had previously been a court registrar and assistant warehouse-keeper, and was after several years considered by his Bombay superiors to be ignorant of the local language and 'backward in all points of his duty'. Some tended to be ignorant of or confused about the actual policies they were meant to be implementing—not a surprising fact given the complex economic theory and calculations behind some later land settlements and the scant economic training civilians had received. Far more were profoundly ignorant of local conditions in their districts. This could result from failure to understand the local language and/or a constant shunting of officers between districts, giving no individual time to study the local situation in depth. It was also the inevitable result of limited local records of land holding and crop yields, and of very primitive techniques of assessing yields, surveying and measuring land. As late as 1863 a Chief Justice in Bombay observed that 'the Chief administrators of our vast Indian Empire . . . are often, if not habitually, in complete ignorance of the most patent facts . . . around them'. District officers were constantly under pressure from their superiors to remit the revenue as fully and promptly as possible. This was a sure way to find favour and an upward passage through the service career structure. So understandably they were generally prag-matic in their approach to their job, doing what seemed possible and least likely to stir up trouble, given the local circumstances, particularly the local Indian power structure in the village setting and the stance of their Indian subordinates in government service.

Arguably the real problem besetting the performance of the British civilians lay here. There were far too few of them to govern India without a substantial base of Indian officials below the level of the Covenanted Service. (Even at the beginning of the twentieth century there were only about 1300 ICS men.) At the start of the nineteenth century Indians were excluded from the Covenanted Service; but beneath that level they were in government service the key intermediaries between the British and village society. As revenue collectors, record keepers, accountants, and clerks they were not just the lowest level of policy implementation: they were also the key source of information about local conditions, on which policy implementation had to rest. If they distorted or withheld information, if they falsified accounts, if they failed to collect the revenue, if they intrigued with the dominant castes in the village to mitigate their revenue burden, then the British officer was literally stranded in a sea of ignorance and impotence, whatever was said or demanded in his provincial capital, or in Calcutta, let alone in London. Control of the Company's lowly Indian servants was not part of the great reforms launched late in the eighteenth century to stabilize the expanding British dominion. But it is here the historian must look if he is to understand how stabilization of British rule at the upper levels of political authority rested on fragile local foundations, how dominion was both all-India reality and local illusion.

The titles of Indians who manned the lowest levels of government varied according to region. In the villages they performed such tasks as keeping village records and accounts, and collecting the revenue. Others worked in the Collector's offices at the headquarters of the district, as revenue officers and clerks. The headquarters office was the nerve-centre of fiscal, police, and general administration for the district, and the senior Indian officials under the Collector were very influential men indeed. Without their co-operation the Collector was ignorant and powerless.[9] We know far less about their recruitment and training than we do of British civil servants. But in the early nineteenth century they entered service with the new rulers not by passing examinations but by the operation of 'connections' and personal knowledge: many came from families and caste groups who had long traditions of government service, whatever the current political power in the land. This was particularly true of the so-called 'writer castes', such as Brahmins and Kayasthas, who, at the apex of the ritual hierarchy, would be polluted by physical labour. In Guntur District in Madras, for example, in 1855, 154 out of 305 senior Indian posts were manned by Maratha Brahmins: 17/21 Head *Sheristadars* (head Indian revenue officers) were from this group which had a long tradition of local administrative dominance. In this region young lads would start work as volunteers in offices where friends and relatives worked; here they received a rudimentary in-service training in writing, accounting, and practices of government, under the eagle eye of their protectors, until they found a niche in the government payroll. From then promotion in government service depended on patronage, nepotism, manipulating financial and other sorts of influence, intrigue, and attracting the notice and confidence of British officers. Only those who rose the highest were well paid. The rest, particularly out in the villages, had to supplement their poor pay by much the same expedients as British Company servants had done a generation earlier. Many would also have had connections with land, as they were often members or clients of dominant local caste groups. But this meant that their loyalties were divided. They owed as much, and probably more, to their Indian patrons and relatives than to their British superiors: they acted accordingly.

British officials complained loud and long of the corruption and low quality of their Indian subordinates. Existing studies confirm that such complaints were often justified, and that Collectors were trapped in local webs of intrigue, false or inadequate information, and outright bribery. But, given the patterns of recruitment and the conflicting financial, political, and social pressures to which their Indian subordinates were subjected, this is totally explicable. It should also be remembered that a 'public service ethos' certainly did not dominate English public life at the time; and was alien to Indian thinking in a context where ties to family, patron, and caste were paramount in the functioning of the social and political order. In the districts of Gorakhpur and Saharanpur in northern India in the 1820s and 1830s Collectors discovered 'scandalous and daring mutilations' of village records, record-keepers falsifying records and taking presents from village headmen, *sheristadars* allowing newly cultivated lands to evade revenue payment, and a large-scale embezzlement operation by a number of Indian officials. In Guntur district a massive Desastha (Maratha) Brahmin conspiracy came to light, in which this dominant administrative group distorted, falsified, and suppressed information to feather its own nest and defraud government—to the despair of Collectors who received little help from Madras in combating it. (To make matters worse, the Desastha Brahmins were split into two factions, each of which jockeyed for position and tried to get the ear of the Collector and the Madras administration.) Only when revenue from the district began to dry up completely did Company authorities in Madras launch a major enquiry and subsequent revolution in district administration and its personnel. Such cases suggest that though reforms in the late eighteenth and early nineteenth centuries stabilized the administration of the Company's extended dominions at the higher levels, at the local level of the village and its dominant groups politics continued much as before, now using the resources of British employment and revenue structures in old power games. The new rulers were imprisoned by the forces of Indian society: their local weakness and ignorance was the reverse face of their dramatic territorial expansion.

ii The buttresses of dominion

Descriptions of government structures only scratch the surface of the reality of any regime's authority and effectiveness. To understand the underlying nature of the British *raj* historians must investigate its foundations as well as its superstructure, and must ask what were the buttresses of its dominion. Money in government coffers and Indians' political acceptance of the legitimacy of the British rulers were both vital. To some extent they interacted on each other, as the bankrupt Moguls found when they ceased to be able to reward their friends and servants, and saw their loyalty crumbling under the strain of counter political attractions.

Our obvious starting point is the hope of Englishmen in the late eighteenth century that India, once under more regular Company rule, would be for Britain a goose laying golden eggs of surplus revenue and expanding trade.[10] Clive had anticipated a surplus revenue from Bengal of £1½ million, while others made wilder prophesies of many millions. Such assessments were explicable because political dominion had been acquired largely to protect profitable trading lines; while the resources of the Bengal revenues paid for the protection of the smaller and poorer British settlements and financed much of the subsequent expansion of British rule deeper into India. However, hopes of surplus revenue which the East India Company could then return to England via its 'investment' in trade were quickly dashed. As the area under British rule expanded, so administration costs rose, particularly the cost of maintaining the large standing army deemed necessary for the protection of British interests. When expansion involved war the drain on Company resources was catastrophic. So when a House of Commons Committee looked at the years 1792 to 1809 it saw that far from producing surpluses, Company *raj* had generated a deficit of £8 million.

Particularly disquieting was the accumulating evidence as the eighteenth century closed that the venerable Company, once a solid if unspectacular commercial success, was ceasing to be a going commercial concern. Not only did it have little or no surplus to use for the purchase of goods for export. Britain's own emerging cotton industry also eroded its once profitable home market for Indian piece goods, while the American War of Independence, European conflicts, and then Napoleon's continental system permanently disrupted the important foreign markets for Indian piece goods re-exported from Britain. Other raw materials from India could not compensate for this changing commercial pattern. Moreover, the

Company's trading practices proved too conservative in novel trading conditions where cheap bulk transport was crucial for profitability instead of the traditional high-value goods which could support expensive shipping and trading establishments. Its critics plunged into the attack—private traders in India goaded by the Company's monopoly of trade between the subcontinent and Britain, followed by British manufacturers wanting free access to Indian markets for their goods and to supplies of India's raw materials. In 1813 they triumphed. The Act renewing the Company's charter broke its India monopoly and allowed all British ships to trade freely with India.

There was, however, one area of the East India Company's financial operations which was spectacularly successful, and was in various ways a powerful buttress of the Company's viability as ruler of India. This was the China tea trade.[11] The Company had in China nothing like the string of fortified factories it had built in India, but traded through Canton, and a small officially authorized body of Chinese merchants. Through this narrow funnel poured tea, which was drunk in increasing quantities in Britain, particularly after the 1784 Commutation Act which drastically reduced the customs duty on tea as it entered Britain. As a result Company sales of tea rose, and with it British government revenue, as tea smuggling was curtailed. Between 1793 and 1810 the Company's China trade probably made a profit of £17 million. But the intricacies of commercial and financial exchange behind the China–Britain tea traffic meant that the tea trade was far more significant than just a means of keeping the Company's finances afloat. The Chinese economy was so insulated from outside influence, by imperial decree and its actual self-sufficiency, that in the later eighteenth century there was little the Company could exchange for tea except bullion. The answer to this problem emerged in the shape of Bengal opium, whose production and sale the Company monopolized after it took control of Bengal. As opium was a prohibited import into China the Company sold the drug to English 'private' traders, who smuggled it into China with the Company's connivance, and then paid their illegal proceeds into the Company treasury at Canton where the money was used to buy tea for shipment to England. The trader-smugglers recouped themselves by drawing on the Company in Bengal or London.

As a result of this devious manoeuvre a range of powerful British interests was satisfied. The British government got its revenue from tea: and this amounted to one-tenth of total government revenue in the early nineteenth century. The Company also gained a large revenue from its opium monopoly—nearly one seventh of its total revenue at that time. It also financed its tea business, and contrived a method of transmitting money to London for pensions and other 'home charges' generated by government in India; while the private traders found a way to send their profits home. Little wonder that a contemporary could enthuse in 1839 about the benefits to the British of the opium trade:

From the opium trade the Honourable Company have derived for years an immense revenue and through them the British Government and the nation have also reaped an incalculable amount of political and financial advantage. The turn of the balance of trade between Great Britain and China in favour of the former has enabled India to increase tenfold her consumption of British manufacture; contributed directly to support the vast fabric of British dominion in the East, to defray the expenses of His Majesty's establishment in India, and by the operation of exchanges and remittances in teas, to pour an abundant revenue into the British Exchequer and benefit the nation to an extent of £6 million yearly without impoverishing India.[12]

The Company's security in its monopoly of the China trade was in jeopardy, however, from attacks by private English traders in Asia and from British manufacturers who increasingly felt that even this limited monopoly remaining to the Company restrained their access to Asian markets and raw materials. The Company was eventually forced to bow to their campaign and in 1834 lost its China monopoly, too. Thereafter it stood out starkly in India not as a trading enterprise but as an instrument of government in all but name. It still retained its monopoly control of Bengal opium, however, and even in 1858–9 opium still contributed 17 per cent of the Government of India's revenue: though by this time the Opium Wars with China had forcibly opened China to Britain's traders and opium no longer had to be smuggled in.

If the East India Company was to finance its rule in India without subsidy from Britain—a subsidy which the British taxpayers and their representatives in Parliament had no intention of giving—it had to look elsewhere than commercial profit for financial buttresses. Taxation of income, possessions, and services finances most modern governments. But India provided little scope for such taxation: because the economy was only partially monetized and much agricultural production was for subsistence rather than profit; because trade was limited, and spare cash tended to be converted into silver for security or jewellery for social prestige rather than invested to create income. Furthermore, government had only limited facilities for enquiring into people's incomes and possessions, compared with the battery of men and administrative machinery at the disposal of twentieth-century governments. Much of India's internal and international trade which *could* be measured avoided taxation for ideological reasons. The nineteenth century was the heyday of free trade in Britain; and it was axiomatic among manufacturers, merchants, and governments that British goods should be allowed free passage into foreign markets without fiscal barriers or burdens. Consequently despite the financial embarrassment of the Company's *raj*,

from 1814 to 1859 British exports entered India almost free of taxation—
5 per cent on piece goods, for example, and $3\frac{1}{2}$ per cent on cotton
yarn. Similarly, raw cotton left India at a nominal duty to supply British
manufacturers.

Consequently the Company's government looked to land for revenue, a
tangible asset which could be measured and assessed for tax. Land revenue
had been the financial foundation of Mogul *raj*: it was to be crucial to the
British *raj* well into the twentieth century. Drawing revenue from land
necessitated some recognition and record of those who were thought to
own or control land; and this made the 'settlement' of land with individuals
or groups in return for payment of revenue a political and ideological
decision as well as a financial arrangement. It brought into play British ideas
of legal rights in land, their perception of existing Indian society, which they
imperfectly understood, and their vision of what Indian society ought to be.
More pragmatically it demonstrated their need to find or create influential
groups at village level to guarantee local quiesence and so act as allies in the
imperial enterprise. Land settlements could have significant repercussions
on the distribution of land—and on the distribution of power in society
because land was the most valuable economic resource in the absence of
modern industry.

British land settlements in India varied from area to area.[13] The variations depended partly on timing—how early or late in the process of expansion an area was annexed, and the consequent mental baggage the British
brought with them to the task from Britain. Settlements were tempered by
previous British experience (or lack of it) of Indian society, and by what was
actually possible given particular local circumstances and pressures. The
first great experiment occurred in Bengal. This took final shape in 1793
under Lord Cornwallis, who imported into India Whig notions that the
functions of government were minimal, namely to ensure the security of
person and property; and that the main agents of rural order and improvement should be substantial landlords. Working on these assumptions his
administrators 'settled' the land on those local controllers of land or
zamindars who seemed most likely to fulfil this role. They also fixed the
revenue demand in perpetuity; to curb the influence of the government in
the area and provide an incentive to the hoped-for 'improving landlords'.
As Cornwallis wrote, 'I am on this point really an enthusiast, from a perfect
conviction that the future happiness of this country depends on a fixed and
unalterable assessment of the land revenue without which it cannot prosper.'[14] No detailed survey of land and its productivity was carried out, so no
one knew what share of the region's wealth the government was getting;
and, moreover, government revenue remained static when land and produce values rose. The region was also very lightly governed compared with
other parts of India—a spin-off from Cornwallis's enthusiasm which had

dire results for the British in the twentieth century when Bengal became the scene of radical politics and political terrorism which were scarcely controllable by the forces locally available to the administration. The aspect of Cornwallis's policy which profoundly disquieted his immediate successors was the failure of the Bengali *zamindars* to become improving landlords, and the rapid turn-over in possession of revenue-paying rights which ensued.

A number of formidable administrators early in the nineteenth century consciously resolved to avoid the Cornwallis pattern of settlement and its repercussions. They hoped for practical and ideological reasons to protect the existing social order as far as possible, in particular to avoid creating a non-productive *rentier* class, and to allow for revised revenue assessments in the future should economic conditions permit the government to increase its revenue. Their techniques included distinctive, simple modes of government, and conservation of existing institutions. In land settlement their goal was the prosperous peasant cultivator rather than the improving landlord. This vision became a powerful force in Madras wherever a Bengal-type settlement had not already been made, under the aegis of Thomas Munro. He was profoundly aware that the British were ignorant of Indian society, customs, and institutions, and feared the consequences of importing into India 'fanciful theories founded on European models'. He saw in southern India many small proprietors and recognized their value as a source of rural stability; commenting in 1824 that in relation to 'the distribution of landed property . . . we ought to take it as we find it, and not attempt upon idle notions of improvement, to force a distribution of it into larger properties where every local circumstance is adverse to its continuance in that state.'[15] The resulting *ryotwari* settlement (i.e. with the *ryot* or peasant) demanded far more government inquiry and management than did the Bengal *zamindari* settlement, because records of land had to be made, and the revenue demand was not permanently fixed but set for a number of years and could be reassessed according to the value of land and crops. It also meant that government could increase its revenue from this source; although Munro himself insisted on the value of moderate revenue demands to encourage peasant enterprise. Despite the conscious pragmatism of *ryotwari* settlement in the face of south Indian society, theory and practice often remained far apart, and the actuality of land settlement reflected very specific local conditions in particular areas. In some places, village headmen retained their dominance, while in others there was not even a monetized settlement. Rural society had its continuities and constraints, whatever the ideals and plans of the new rulers.

Ryotwari settlements under Munro's hand were essentially conservative. They re-appeared to perform a different function soon after, as a result of Utilitarian influence in London on the Company's policy-makers, and on the young ICS men of the next generation who imbibed it at Haileybury. Utilitarian philosophy, associated with the names of Jeremy Bentham and the two Mills (who actually worked in the Company's London headquarters), was one of the most powerful innovatory strands in early nineteenth-century British attitudes to India. Its adherents looked to the reformation of society and the liberation of individual potential and energy, particularly through the operations of government and law. India seemed a convenient testing-ground for their theories, and they envisaged a radical transformation of Indian society and the release of its people from the thraldom of superstition and tradition as a result of firm government, sound law, and the application of scientific principles of political economy. This last was a central part of their plan; and at its heart lay a particular theory of 'rent'. This theory informed the thinking of James Mill, who was responsible for all the despatches relating to Indian revenue which left London between 1819 and 1830. He believed that government was the ultimate lord of the soil and should not renounce its right to 'rent', i.e. the profit left over on richer soil when wages and other working expenses had been settled. 'Rent' as thus understood was a particularly suitable object for taxation, because its absorption by government would not hinder efficient agriculture; whereas, if it was left untapped by government it would merely enable the emergence of a parasitic, landlord class. Consequently he argued for *ryotwari* settlement involving government measurement and assessment of individual plots, lasting for 20 to 30 years, whereby government would tax according to the differential fertility of the soil and syphon off a carefully calculated proportion of the supposed 'rent'. (This proportion was about nine-tenths in the early nineteenth century, gradually falling thereafter.)

This remained official land revenue theory for well over a century, and was the rationale behind the peasant settlements in western, northern, and central India, which were in stark contrast to the Cornwallis-type settlements with an intermediate body of landlords, made in perpetuity. In some areas the land was actually settled with peasant *groups*, particularly brotherhoods of cultivators, rather than with individuals, where this seemed the most practicable course: this was known as *mahalwari* settlement. But the ideas of 'rent', regular settlement revision, and direct relations between government and peasant cultivators remained. The theory advanced by Mill was elegant, and convincing to contemporaries; but it was complicated to understand and calculate in detail, and almost impossible to enact in its pure form since government in India had neither the man-power nor the machinery to gather the information necessary to calculate 'rent' and extract it. Studies of particular areas, however, show that huge gaps yawned between theory and practice, as they had done in Madras after Munro. ICS men used Utilitarian *language*. But often their actions owed more to pragmatism than doctrine, in the light of their local situation, the people who would contract to pay revenue, the information made available to them by their Indian subordinates (who generally had local vested interests), and the constant need to remit money to the provincial headquarters.[16]

Land settlements, however far in practice from theories emanating from idealistic enthusiasts, were perhaps the major administrative enterprise ever undertaken by nineteenth-century British governments in India. Except in the permanently settled areas, land settlement involved continually repeated processes of measuring land, assessing fertility, recording rights. It occupied much of the time of district officers, brought them constantly into touch with rural life; and after the Company lost its trading role and ability to influence the economy through its powers of purchase and production, was the major means by which government intruded in local society to any depth. In purely financial terms it was vital—land revenue was the single most significant source of government revenue, producing over half in the middle of the nineteenth century. (In contrast, customs produced only 8 per cent.) But even in spite of the flow of land revenue, government often found itself in severe financial straits; and in the 45 years between 1814 and 1859 the Government of India incurred deficits in 33 years. The financial buttresses of the apparently awesome *raj* were in reality distinctly shaky. Even in good years when there was no deficit, there was only enough revenue to pay for a thinly spread and non-interventionist administration, a skeleton and poorly-paid police force which was almost useless, and the army. Though large in numbers (the Bengal army for example still had 150,000 men in 1857) the army would have been totally inadequate to cope with wholesale rebellion or a major invasion. Imperialists on a tight budget recognized that such financial constraints made it imperative for them to construct effective *political* buttresses of their *raj*, in particular to secure a web of intermediaries with local society who could be sub-agents in securing order, and ensuring Indian acquiescence if not positive loyalty to the foreign rulers.

The single most important political buttress of the *raj*, looking at the subcontinent as a whole, were those Indian princes who were permitted to retain their territories as subsidiary allies of the British. In the early nineteenth century they accounted for over one-third of India (and one-third even in the final decades of the *raj*). Some were little more than larger landholders. Others, like the rulers of Mysore and Hyderabad in the south, controlled areas as large as provinces in British India: their size and strategic position made them both valuable and potentially disturbing to British security.

The British had never annexed territory for its own sake, but for political, strategic or commercial reasons, or a complex blend of these. Consequently, where an Indian ruler was prepared to enter into alliance and seemed able to secure his territory the British welcomed him as part of a cheap method of indirect rule, involving them in none of the expense of direct administration or the problems of gaining the acquiescence of alien subjects. They undertook to defend such subordinate allies, and treated them with traditional respect and marks of honour. But they also sent a political officer as 'resident' to each princely court to keep a watching brief on events and to tender advice, to control the succession and educate heirs, and eliminate undesirable influences at court: or at times to remonstrate with the prince if his administration seemed through corruption or inattention to threaten a minimum degree of order and local content. In the early part of the nineteenth century considerable intervention did sometimes occur, as in the case of Mysore. But even when a British administrator temporarily took over Mysore in 1834 his aim was to restore the traditional form of princely rule rather than to innovate or reform.[17] Some, however, came to view the princes with distaste as relics of a despotic, unscientific age, particularly those who, under Utilitarian influence, saw government as a positive engine of change. But it was not until Dalhousie became Governor-General at the close of the 1840s that the political buttress of princely rule was jeopardized by British policy itself. Dalhousie determined to take 'advantage of every just opportunity which presents itself' for consolidating British territory and absorbing princely states which he felt could never add to British strength, and whose governments were in his estimation inferior to that of direct British administration.[18] In seven years his government annexed seven states, by the procedure of refusing to allow Hindu rulers to adopt heirs when their natural line died out, so that their states 'lapsed' to British rule.

In areas under direct British control the new rulers had to make far more complex political choices about those who might be desirable and effective collaborators; who would help interpret and relate the government to its subjects and *vice versa*. Some imperial powers have found that communities of expatriate settlers could fill this role, as in East Africa or Spanish South America. Not so the British in India: for India never became a colony of large white settlement, partly for reasons of climate and the nature of economic opportunity. There was throughout the nineteenth and twentieth centuries a small group of British businessmen, tea and indigo planters, and managers of jute factories, clustered largely in eastern India. Late in the nineteenth century they were tied into the structure of British rule through the provision of special seats in the new legislatures; but they were too tiny a group to be a substantial political prop. Moreover, their tendency to overt racialism and, occasionally, ill-treatment of their Indian employees was often counter-productive to imperial tranquillity, and helped besmirch the intended image of a tolerant empire in the eyes of educated Indians. For different reasons government also had an ambivalent relationship with British and other European missionaries who were allowed into India only from 1813. Socially they were often inferior to those recruited into Company service, and this tended to separate them from their compatriots. But they were also suspect in some official eyes because their educational work and more specifically their preaching and attempts to obtain converts threatened to stir up strife within Hindu society; as, occasionally, did their own sectarian conflicts.

Far more important were those groups of Indians who could be recruited into active co-operation with their rulers. Munro from Madras argued this firmly in 1817 when he pleaded for a strong establishment of Indian officials at village level, to fill the gap between the European district officer and the peasant proprietors.

Where there is no village establishment, we have no hold upon the people, no means of acting upon them, none of establishing confidence. Our situation, as foreigners, renders a regular village establishment more important to us than to a native Government: our inexperience, and our ignorance of the circumstances of the people, make it more necessary for us to seek the aid of regular establishments to direct the internal affairs of the country, and our security requires that we should have a body of head men of villages interested in supporting our dominion.[19]

As the structures of Company rule expanded in the early nineteenth century and became more regularized, so they came to rest on those thousands of Indians who were attracted into Company service. The attraction was not so much the salary, which was meagre; but the status thereby confirmed on those who for ritual reasons could not labour with their hands and had traditionally looked for employment in government service. Office also meant the opportunity for perquisites and the wielding of influence on behalf of patrons, clients, and relatives. This group of 'paid collaborators' often overlapped with dominant social groups whom the British tried to weld into their imperial structure through the grant of revenue-paying rights in land. Sometimes at least in the early days of their *raj* the British found it hard to find such potential revenue-paying allies. Sometimes their experiments in attracting and supporting landed groups went sadly awry, as in Bengal. But throughout the existence of the *raj* it was assumed that the proprietorial groups in villages and commercial notables in towns were essential allies of government. Gradually the connections with them were confirmed and elaborated; sometimes through the grant of administrative duties as well as revenue rights, but always through the informal grant of personal *access* to local British officials. This has sometimes been seen as a form of 'neo-durbari politics', reminiscent of former Indian rulers who had held *durbar*, or open court, at least to their more influential subjects, in order to receive information and to grant redress of grievances as well as to display their authority in public. Informal links with the locally influential, designed to cement their loyalty, later reached a high degree of refinement in the honours system, whereby at New Year and the Sovereign's birthday those who had proved themselves loyal could expect their rewards, alongside many others who had spent years in administration or dedicated themselves to genuine public service.

Probing even deeper into the buttresses of British rule involves asking how the new rulers were able to gain 'legitimacy' in the eyes of their Indian subjects. In government as in many other spheres of life 'possession is nine-tenths of the law': and many Indians barely thought about the legitimacy of the new regime. It was accepted because it was there and apparently successful: just as—in reverse—the Moguls had lost credibility as they lost power. The British were always acutely sensitive to this problem of their public image, of the visible and ritual demonstration of authority: hence insistence on what was known as *izzat* or prestige, their meticulous attention to rank and precedence and its public display, and their adaptation of older rituals of authority to legitimize their exercise of power. Furthermore, when prominent local men were prepared to 'play along' with the new regime and its conventions, the British could assume that the clients and social inferiors of such men would follow suit.

However, there were sensitive areas of social and public life where the British trod with extreme delicacy in order to gain recognition as acceptable and legitimate rulers; particularly where Hindu and Muslim religious beliefs and customs were involved. Although Muslims were a minority in the subcontinent as a whole they were in certain northern areas a proud and influential minority, mindful of the fact that within living memory the imperial *raj* had been Muslim. Moreover, Islam is particularly sensitive to the operations of law and government (see chapter I). The British responded to this situation by refraining from deposition of the Mogul imperial family until after 1857; and in those areas where they ruled directly they took care not to invade those aspects of life governed in Muslim eyes by the *shariah*. Until 1790 the *shariah* procedures of Aurangzeb's time regulated penal justice in Bengal; and from 1792 it was laid down by regulation that in cases of family law and custom involving Muslims the Koran should be adhered to. Right up to 1864 British magistrates were assisted by Muslim legal advisers whenever Muslim law was being applied.

Similarly in relation to Hindu family matters, social convention, and caste in particular, the British respected Hindu law and tradition, and were exceedingly reluctant to undertake any social reform without the assurance of public Hindu support. Even more interesting, and indeed galling to those Evangelicals who felt that the Company should extend more support to missionary activity, was the Company's willingness to incorporate existing Hindu institutions into its system, and even to reinforce them, as political buttresses of the *raj*. This was clearest in south India where Hindus were a massive majority, and observance of caste particularly rigorous. The Madras Board of Revenue, for example, became responsible for the financing and regulation of Hindu temples, and festivals. The army continued to observe regimental worship in Hindu style, paraded at and guarded over great southern Hindu festivals, while many temples and Brahmins were supported by land which was free of revenue. One author has gone so far as to call the Company's 'civil religion' Hindu; commenting that 'the Company raj in south India was a Hindu empire.'[20]

Investigation of the *raj*'s political buttresses, the Company's financial straits and its meagre administration poses a fundamental question. To what extent were the British free agents, able to make coherent policy decisions which stood a reasonable chance of enactment? Or were the buttresses of their rule to become restraints like iron shackles? The evidence also suggests that the loyalty of active allies and a more generalized acceptance of their legitimacy were crucial in the construction of the new *raj*. They would also be central to its disintegration in the following century.

iii   India and the new raj: change and continuity

Our focus now shifts to the experience of Indian society during the first three-quarters of a century of British *raj*. It is important to stress the extent to which Indian society had its own strength, internal rationale, and its own resources and dynamics for development and change, for it was no static, traditional society on which the new rulers could make any dramatic impact. 'Interaction' rather than 'impact' best suggests the relationship between the British presence and the society over which the British ruled. To focus on Indian society weakens an older, simple periodization related to British ideas and intentions, which depicted the early nineteenth century as an age of reform. Certainly Lord Bentinck, arriving as Governor-General in 1828, perceived himself as a herald of reform, writing to Jeremy Bentham, 'I shall govern in name, but it will be you who govern in fact.' Not only Bentinck and his contemporaries, imbued with ebullient reformist idealism, saw in prospect India's transformation at the hands of the British. So austere a critic as Karl Marx writing in mid-century also thought that British rule was working a radical social revolution on the subcontinent.[21] But ideas and influences emanating from Britain were often much transmuted by the realities of India: and the boldest of policies could become little more than aspirations inscribed on paper when imperialists tried to enact them.

Nonetheless we begin with British hopes for India in the early nineteenth century. However, 'the British' in India were never a monolithic group with a single 'imperialist' policy. They were a honeycomb of interest groups, including civil servants, army personnel, international traders, small-scale entrepreneurs, missionaries, and the home connections of these various groups. Even different elements within the governmental structure had different priorities and points of vulnerability. This engendered strain in intra-governmental relationships—London *vis-à-vis* Calcutta, or civilians in the districts in relation to their masters in Calcutta or the provincial capitals. Exactly the same was true on a vastly magnified scale of different groups of Indians who were forced to reassess their attitudes to their compatriots in the light of the new *raj*. So the interaction of Britain and India involved shifting relationships *across* the racial divide, and simultaneously *within* each racial group, between British and British, between Indian and Indian.

The third and fourth decades of the century saw a remarkable convergence of different strands of reforming zeal emanating from Britain towards India, in contrast to the earlier caution and deliberate conservatism of a Cornwallis or a Munro. The most articulate and intellectual was that of Utilitarian philosophy. A generation of men imbibed the teachings of Bentham and the Mills, not only in formal study at Haileybury but in the general intellectual ambience of contemporary England. They saw all men, of whatever race and background, as potentially similar in energy, enterprise, and understanding, if once they were liberated from deadening and constricting tradition by a combination of good government, sound law, and the framework of a proper political economy. Consequently theirs was an authoritarian reformism, bent on imposing on India what was in their eyes best for Indians' ultimate good and happiness.

Similarly inspired with the vision of a transformed India were those increasing numbers who were influenced by Britain's Evangelical revival. Its influence in British society was deep and pervasive, and through the Clapham Sect it had a marked influence on the ethos of British politics. Two of its main objectives were the abolition of the slave trade and the opening of India to missionaries. Evangelicals, basing their faith on a simple biblical gospel, saw man's ultimate good not as happiness, as did the Utilitarians, but salvation from sin through Jesus Christ. General moral improvement was a penultimate goal and an essential concomitant to the preaching of the gospel and the spread of civilization. Consequently in the Indian context they crusaded against a range of 'moral evils' such as *suttee*, the self-immolation of widows on their husbands' funeral pyres; supported missionary work, and education in particular which would not only open Indians' eyes to a new morality but also to the text of the Bible, a necessary precursor to individual salvation. Their broad social concern rather than any narrow pietistic zeal shines through a typical observation by Charles Grant, member of the Clapham Sect and also a director of the East India Company.

It is not . . . the introduction of a new set of ceremonies, nor even a new creed, that is the ultimate object here. Those who conceive religion to be conversant merely about forms and speculative notions, may well think that the world need not be much troubled concerning it. No, the ultimate object is moral improvement. The preeminent excellence of the morality which the Gospel teaches, and the superior efficacy of this divine system, taken in all its parts, in meliorating the condition of human society, cannot be denied by those who are unwilling to admit its higher claims; and on this ground only, the dissemination of it must be beneficial to mankind.[22]

Evangelical influence bore down on India through such men and groups prominent in Parliament and British public life, and through civilians and army officers who went to India in pursuit of their careers, carrying with them an evangelical faith. However, in the structure of the Company's government there was considerable tension between the overt Evangelicals and those who feared the repercussions of such religious enthusiasm on Indian society. Offical ambivalence on this score was even clearer in the relations between government and the wave of Protestant missionaries who entered India after 1813. The missions with their preaching and their schools were the most dramatic sign of the new evangelical zeal in India.

The third strand of reforming enthusiasm was that embodied in Britain's Free Traders; although the strands were inextricably interwoven— Evangelicals, for example, being convinced that commerce like education was the work of the Lord in India, as well as being beneficial for Britain. To quote Grant again:

In considering the affairs of the world as under the control of the Supreme Disposer, and those distant territories . . . providentially put into our hands . . . is it not necessary to conclude that they were given to us, not merely that we might draw an annual profit from them, but that we might diffuse among their inhabitants, long sunk in darkness, vice and misery, the light and benign influence of the truth, the blessings of well-regulated society, the improvements and comforts of active industry? . . . In every progressive step of this work, we shall also serve the original design with which we visited India, that design still so important to this country—the extension of our commerce.[23]

In a sense the Free Traders' interest in reform was an ironic twist of their principles. Though free trade was their cry and pride in the British context, and the platform on which they had fought the Company's monopoly, when it came to carrying through their principles in India they found that Indian conditions so hampered the free operation of commerce that they needed government intervention to 'liberate' trade. Whether it was official guarantees for railway-building, the construction of roads and irrigation systems, it was government which in their eyes had to initiate and finance economic reform. The famous 'Manchester School' might inveigh against formal imperial rule in India: in practice their wish to open up the cotton districts and to improve communications led them to support deeper governmental intervention and closer imperial ties between Britain and the subcontinent.[24]

By the end of the 1830s the strength of this triple tide of reform was beginning to ebb. Bentham and James Mill both died in that decade; and prominent men who had carried the Utilitarian and Evangelical banners in India, such as Macaulay and C. Trevelyan, retired. In India frontier wars limited already overstrained government finances and checked zeal; as did the fact that whatever British ideals, Indian society proved stable, not to say intractable. When Hardinge became Governor-General in 1844 his instructions reflected a recoil from the enthusiasm of the previous decades. However, there was no radical shift of policy in the 1840s. On the one hand, the ebb of zeal was gentle and some remained in post who retained their enthusiasm for transformation, such as James Thomason, Lt.-Governor of the North-Western Provinces from 1843 to 1853, and William Muir, Secretary of the same local government from the mid-1840s to 1857, who were both deeply committed Evangelicals. On the other hand, reformist plans, even at their height, had in practice been tempered by persistent and necessary pragmatism. Even Bentinck's commitment to governmental reform originated partly in the need for economy and efficiency; and was understood by many contemporaries primarily as 'economical reform'. Indeed, his major achievment was the dramatic pruning of government's civil and military expenditure, between 1829 and 1835 turning a large budget deficit into a modest surplus.[25]

Both the reformers and the earlier conservatives had pinned much of their hopes for Indian society on the new land settlements, although their ignorance of local conditions and their physical weakness meant that the settlements were actually far more pragmatic than reflective of ideals. The British were not equipped to enforce a social revolution, even where they wished to: and everywhere their plans were modified or even distorted by forces operating deep within Indian society. This rapidly became obvious and caused much official concern, particularly as evidence began to accumulate showing that as a result of revenue and sales laws and the operations of the courts, land was changing hands at a rapid rate. In the Banares region, for example, by the mid-nineteenth century about 40 per cent of land had changed hands in the first half century of British rule: a total reversal of the vision of aristocratic stability which lay behind the Permanent Settlement. Further west in Rohilkhand cultivated land was also being transferred at a considerable rate—7.5 per cent between 1848–9 and 1853–4, and probably at an even higher rate in the previous two decades.[26]

However, the bare record of land sales does not tell us about the social reality. What was actually happening on the spot varied from area to area (and even from district to district within one region); but we can draw some general conclusions from those areas where detailed research has been done. The evidence suggests that often local society before the arrival of the

British experienced major flux in the distribution of land and its attendant influence. There was often no static rural order with landholding families continuing over many generations; particularly where changes in local political control in the wake of Mogul imperial decay gave ample opportunities for men and families to make and break their fortunes. When the British occupied Bengal, for example, nearly 60 per cent of land revenue was paid by fifteen large *zamindars*. Only four of these were of really ancient landholding families, and many of the others had mushroomed in the early eighteenth century on the profits of official patronage or the use of office. Thirty years later when the British took control of Rohilkhand they could not locate well-established proprietorial families. As a Board of Commissioners noted in 1808, 'It will be difficult to determine who are at present best entitled to the lands . . . for the old Hindoo proprietors were generally excluded by the Pathan Government, and there are few individuals who have continued in the situation [of established landholders] . . .'[27]

Where titles to land *did* change hands there was no simple pattern of transfer from old to new landholders. Some landholding families acquired more land, while some 'aristocrats' who emerged in the eighteenth century consolidated their gains, as in the case of the Raja of Banares. Other buyers were of commercial origin. A significant number were men who had profited by taking service with the East India Company and now used their connections and knowledge of the new legal system to their advantage. In caste terms this often meant that Rajputs were losing their titles to Brahmins and Kayasthas, the 'writer castes'. However, even where 'new' men bought rights in land and became responsible for the revenue payment, in practice this often did not mean that older landed families were physically dispossessed or lost all local influence. Often the new revenue-payers became just another layer in the complicated structure of rights and interests in land; while the older, dominant families remained *in situ*, cultivating land and wielding considerable local power, particularly if they retained some of their land as home farm and only became tenants of new purchasers for part of what they had once controlled.

Another factor in the complicated interaction of Indian society and the new regime was the high pitch of the British land revenue demand. Although the British denied this and attributed cultivators' distress and high levels of land transfer to natural disasters and supposed traits of laziness in the Indian character, administrators were under pressure from their superiors to remit as much revenue from their districts as possible. No clear and uniform pattern of social change occurred in rural India. The pitch of revenue, the fate of harvests and the changing distribution of rights in land varied from district to district as each area responded in its own particular experience to the pressures and opportunities presented by the new *raj*. But the Cornwallis vision of Indian society remained vision rather than reality:

equally, Utilitarian hopes for social liberation and reconstruction were dashed on the rocks of Indian society and ecology and official ignorance of the implications of government policies.

Although the various plans of imperial reformers worked no rapid rural social revolution on the subcontinent, over a longer period, between the mid-eighteenth and mid-nineteenth centuries, significant and long-lasting change did occur, as the result of 'pre-British' trends in economy and society as well as of the influence and interests of the new regime. Perhaps the most important of these was the growing 'settlement' of rural people into a more stable and homogeneous peasant society, at the expense of those who had previously had a more wandering life-style—whether as nomads, slash-and-burn cultivators, herdsmen, or cattle and horse breeders. The expansion of permanent agriculture and settled agricultural communities also markedly altered the terrain and ecology of many parts of India: as forests were cut down to make way for roads for soldiers, administrators, and traders, to enable farming on new soil, and to provide timber for fuel, boats, and railways; and as new crops were grown for export—sugar, indigo, and cotton for example. The impetus behind this long-term change stretched back into the commercialization and growing monetization of the economy in the eighteenth century, and the slow processes whereby India's local economies became more integrated with each other and linked to an international market in agricultural produce. The British political and economic presence deepened and strengthened these trends, particularly the growth of commercial agriculture, adding to them the greater peace of the nineteenth century, the need for regular revenue from settled agriculture, and a bureaucratic distaste for the untamed and nomadic, who all too easily became classified as criminals, subversive of imperial order and control. As communities became more stable and deeply rooted, so it seems likely that the Hindu hierarchies of caste also became more pervasive and constraining in rural life, at the expense of older, more fluid and egalitarian communities. Although it is probable that at least until mid-century there was not the population pressure on land which later reduced the bargaining power of rural labourers, and tied them more firmly as subordinates into the hierarchy of the village.

Another means by which nineteenth-century reformers hoped to effect major change in India was the framework of law and administration. In 1813 Parliament had publicly recognized that the East India Company had a duty to amend the 'moral condition' of its Indian subjects; and Utilitarian doctrine prescribed good laws and sound administration as the medicine for what to zealous Western eyes seemed morally base in personal life and public relations. Under Bentinck's guidance the 1830s saw considerable change in the mechanics of the *raj*, though Utilitarian beliefs in clear legal codes, a simplified judicial structure and a strong executive were only partially enacted. In the localities the Collectors' powers were strengthened as they took on the roles of magistrate and controller of police functions beside their existing duties of revenue collection and general administration. Provincial appeal courts were abolished and their duties handed over to civil judges. Indian judges were also employed more widely. At the centre the principles of a supreme legislative authority and the non-division of legal and executive authority were implemented in the remodelling of the Supreme Council, which was henceforth composed of the Governor-General, the Commander-in-Chief, three ordinary members and one Law Member, whose expertise would be particularly valuable when the Council sat in its capacity as Legislative Council. This put an end to much of the previous confusion of authorities arising from the relations between the Company courts, the supreme courts in the three Presidency towns (Calcutta, Bombay, and Madras) and the local governments. Steps were also taken towards uniformity in law and its codification with the arrival of Macaulay as Law Member (1834–8) and the appointment of a commission of enquiry into the law. The fruits of its labours and of Macaulay's work appeared much later, however, with the Indian Penal Code of 1860.

Controversy and compromise within the structures of the *raj*, pressure of time, money, and ill-health all impeded the imposition on India of laws and governmental structures as instruments of social reformation as Utilitarians had wished. Moreover, officials in India were reluctant to use law or executive power to intervene directly in the functioning of society and the delicate interplay of social relations, so deeply embedded were they in religious belief and economic conditions. Although in 1833 all Indians were declared eligible for public office, regardless of religion, class or caste, there was no frontal attack on social structure and its inequalities, no attempt directly to undermine caste or end the practice of Untouchability. Only hesitantly and under pressure from missionaries and their home supporters, and from some Indians newly educated in western style, did the Company move towards the legal suppression of certain social 'abuses' and an end to official support for Hindu practices.

One example was the Pilgrim Tax, which the Company continued to collect. Not only did it finance the upkeep of Hindu shrines: it also made a profit for the government. (In Gaya, for example, in sixteen years the Company gained almost £446,000 from it.) Few Company officials felt disturbed in conscience by this. Even the reforming Bentinck assumed that he should preserve those Hindu rites which were harmless. Only a concerted campaign by missionaries in India and at home, particularly through the literary campaign of the Church Missionary Society, backed by Bishop Heber of Calcutta, convinced the Board of Control that it must overrule the Court of Directors. In 1833 the policy was laid down in an official despatch that strict religious neutrality should be observed and the Pilgrim Tax abolished. Missionaries and others involved in this campaign similarly bent their efforts against a range of Hindu customs which they felt to be inhuman; particularly *suttee*, the self-immolation of a widow on her husband's funeral pyre. (This reflected Hindu belief in the sanctity of the marriage bond, the spiritual worthlessness of an unmarried woman and the impossibility of widow re-marriage: it was also a practical response to the drain on a family's resources of having to support an unproductive woman. It was not, however, geographically widespread or practised among the lower castes.) In this case Parliament, the Board of Control, and the Court of Directors all agreed that something should be done; and in India some officials were veering to the same opinion. But it was not until educated Indians began to support the idea of abolition that the Company felt it was safe to depart from its former policy of tolerating the practice. In 1829/30 it was prohibited. But legal prohibition did not mean that *suttee* ceased. Often it was hushed up or adequate proof for prosecution was lacking. (Even in the twentieth century cases are still reported: one occurred in 1980.) The inability of the law radically to change social relations and habits deeply rooted in religion and/or economic necessity was even clearer in the case of slavery. This, too, varied in intensity from area to area, depending on the nature of local society and its economic base. Where slavery was an integral part of a region's life, as in areas of southern India, officials like Munro were extremely cautious about interfering. In 1833 Parliament directed that the position of slaves in India should be eased, and the status abolished as soon as possible. The Company did not free its own slaves in Malabar, for example, until 1836, and did not begin to act against the institution itself until ten years after Parliament's demand. Even then it did not confront slavery head on, but merely made it unenforceable in the courts. Not surprisingly serfdom persisted, even into the twentieth century.[28]

Far more significant in the long term for the shape of Indian society and the quality of social relations than changes which government tried to 'engineer' were areas of interaction between Indian society and new educational and economic influences which accompanied British rule. These were more diffuse than changes in law or government mechanisms: but both were agents which different groups hoped would be strong enough to blow up the old society and herald a new era for the peoples of the subcontinent.

Evangelicals set their sights on education as the primary means of spreading enlightenment and new faith in India; and their pressure contributed significantly to the act of 1813 which renewed the Company's charter and for the first time set aside an annual sum for the provision of education in India. The sum was paltry—£10,000. But the way in which it was to be spent provoked a spectacular debate which became known as the Orientalist–Anglicist controversy.[29] Both groups realized that their limited resources could only assist advanced education, that mass education was beyond government means and must be in vernacular languages. They joined issue on the language and content of higher education. The Orientalists believed that the money should support Oriental learning in India's traditional literary languages, Sanskrit and Arabic: while the Anglicists favoured English as the medium and English literature and western scientific knowledge as the content of higher education. The Anglicists' contempt for Indian learning was evident in the famous 1835 Minute on Education by Macaulay, who was not only the new Law Member but also President of the Committee of Public Instruction. To him 'a single shelf of a good European library was worth the whole native literature of India and Arabia'.[30] Macaulay and his allies hoped by this means to raise up a class—'Indian in blood and colour, but English in taste, in opinions, in morals, and in intellect'—who could act as interpreters between the British and their alien subjects: men whose new learning would also revitalize vernacular languages and raise up vernacular literature. They believed that the new education would weaken Indian tradition, caste, and the social dominance of the Brahmins. In the words of one official, C. E. Trevelyan, traditional Indian systems of learning 'have been weighed in the balance, and have been found wanting. To perpetuate them, is to perpetuate the degradation and misery of the people. Our duty is not to teach, but to unteach them,—not to rivet the shackles which have for ages bound down the minds of our subjects, but to allow them to drop off by the lapse of time and the progress of events.' At a more mundane level the Anglicists wished to train Indians as cheap and efficient government servants, and candidates for the modern professions. While in the extreme distance they visualized a future in which Indians might be able to rule themselves, achieving such independence not by revolution but after a long apprenticeship in close partnership with their rulers.

The Anglicists won the policy battle, partly because the flood tide of Utilitarian and Evangelical opinion was flowing in their favour in India and England. There was evidence that some Indians also supported the change to western education, because of the material benefits it offered, and, as in the case of the eminent Bengali, Raja Ram Mohan Roy, because they were genuinely moved by their contacts with the West towards the reform of their own society. Government's need to reduce administrative costs and employ more Indians who knew English also affected the outcome of the controversy. Thereafter English medium higher education of the sort experienced by students in England boomed; on the triple initiative of government, missionaries, and Hindus who wanted such education for their sons but hesitated to send them to secular or overtly Christian institutions. Although the figures for growth are impressive they must be seen in the context of the vast mass of Indian humanity to whom English education, and indeed education of any formal kind, remained a closed book. Exact statistics are not available for this early period, but by mid-century there were probably under two hundred English educational institutions with about 30,000 pupils in attendance. Official expenditure on education was less then 1 per cent of government revenue; and this total includes institutions dependent on missionary enterprise.

The new policy produced so curious and explosive a blend of what the British had envisaged and results which they regretted, that within twenty-five years they were re-thinking their educational priorities and within three-quarters of a century some officials were bitterly regretting what their predecessors had set in motion. The spread of English did help to prompt remarkable linguistic and literary renaissances in some Indian vernaculars later in the nineteenth and twentieth centuries. But the western-educated never acted as downward filters through whom education passed to the masses. Instead the secondary schools and colleges remained a prestigious, arts-orientated educational sector vastly overbalancing the weak primary sector. They produced a small educated élite, while mass illiteracy remained the norm. Those educated in the new style and the new language were not a 'new' social group or a 'middle class'. They tended to come from higher Hindu castes with traditions of literacy and government service but without great wealth. The very wealthy, prospering either on business or land, saw little profit from the new education, at least until the twentieth century. The poorer and lower castes, and all women, had little chance of access to western-style education. So in social terms education did not work a revolution in society. It did not break the power of the Brahmins or the dominance of the higher castes, or the power of men in relation to women, either by virtue of its content or its distribution. Those who in British eyes needed 'liberating' from traditional social shackles did not benefit from it; instead it tended to reinforce existing lines of social division.

The new education, however, had ideological and political implications and repercussions which were of almost immeasurable consequence in the making of modern India. It stimulated radical consideration of Hindu tradition and society among a few, as western religious and secular values became available as a source of comparison. Equality of all because of their basic humanity, the status and significance of women in their own right, charity, and liberty were but a few of the ideals which challenged much of what was accepted in India, together with the specifically religious stress on monotheism and Christian morals preached by the missionaries. The result was a commitment to social reform among a small group of educated Indians, centred on Calcutta where opportunities for the new education were most prolific. Some were as outspoken about what they saw as evils in their own society as were the critical outsiders who felt they had a moral duty to promote India's uplift. Ram Mohan Roy was one of the Calcutta group's leading figures; and *suttee* was one of the main objects of his condemnation. Slightly later I. C. Vidyasagar, also Bengali, concentrated on

ameliorating the plight of widows, and was important in persuading government that it was safe and right to pass an act enabling widow-remarriage
(1856). He had just published a major book, *Marriage of Hindu Widows*,
which argued that widow re-marriage could be justified by reference to
Hindu teaching, not just to reason. Roy was an important religious figure,
too, a founder of the Brahmo Samaj, a monotheistic Hindu reform movement which ultimately became a separate Hindu sect, but which in its early
days was one of the first signs that Hindus would reassess their religious
heritage as part of their interaction with the West. Roy was deeply influenced by Christianity. He wrote, 'I have found the doctrines of Christ more
conducive to moral principles, and better adapted for the use of rational
beings, than any other which have come to my knowledge.'[31] But he also
abhorred dogmatism, and felt that Hindu scriptures contained all fundamental religious truths; and he never left his natal religious tradition.

Educated Indians' political perceptions and sense of identity also began
to change. Like Victorian schoolboys and students in England they were
introduced to the great political theorists of the West, to European and
English history, taught in a way which assumed and glorified 'progress' not
just in material standards but in politics and morals. Liberty and equality
enshrined in Parliamentary government were held up as ideals, while the
nation was assumed to be the natural form of political identity demanding
man's supreme public loyalty. It was little wonder that educated Indians
began to apply these ideals to their own country: to think for the first time
in terms of an Indian nation transcending old barriers of creed, caste, and
region. This new sense of identity was enabled and powerfully reinforced by
the possibility of all-India contacts in the new common language, English,
both spoken and written in the press which began to emerge in the first half
of the nineteenth century. A growing sense of frustration at their subservient role in public life, particularly in government service, encouraged the
educated to join together in common religious and secular interests, the
latter including education, the spread of 'useful learning' as well as problems of discrimination against Indians. Voluntary association in pursuit of
shared and non-ascriptive interests was a vital step along the road to a
recognizably modern form of political organization and activity.

A further strand in the tangled results of the new education demonstrated the unpredictable nature of the interaction between Indian society
and western influence. This was the uneven spread of education. At first
only those areas where the British were longest established, the three
Presidencies, offered opportunities for western education. Within these
regions only certain social groups had access to the opportunities. So rural
Indians and lower caste groups in those regions, together with most of those
who lived in the rest of the subcontinent, were deprived—in relation to the
material benefits of the new education as well as its ideological influence.

Among these were many of India's Muslims, who were either of lowly social origin as in Bengal, and like their Hindu counterparts could not afford the new learning; or they were, as in parts of north and west India, a powerful social minority but living where little chance of western education was available to anyone, of whatever community. This unevenness later had important repercussions on Indians' relations with each other, as education became not only a source of material advantage but a vital qualification for certain types of political activity.

Education produced willing recruits into government service and some modern professions such as law, medicine, and teaching. As a result small groups of adaptable Indians did very well out of the 'service' opportunities available under the new imperial regime. Prominent among these were the Bengali writer castes, who followed their new rulers in their expansion westwards from Bengal, and were in the nineteenth century to be found throughout northern India as administrators and professionals in the imperial train; or the southern Tamil and Telugu Brahmins who similarly entrenched themselves under the aegis of the British state in administration, law, and education in the south and even overseas in Ceylon and south-east Asia. But the social and cultural results of English education were limited in the early nineteenth century to small urban enclaves. The changes initiated by the Anglicists and their missionary allies produced no social revolution and barely touched the shape of Indian society or its underlying values.

Nor did economic change work a revolution, despite the hopes of the Free Traders. Much controversy surrounds the economic effects on India of the British presence. Accusations of British 'draining' wealth from India and destroying indigenous industry by imports of cheap Lancashire textiles have become part of nationalist historiography, merging into later twentieth-century attempts to explain India's continuing poverty. Academic controversy has also erupted over the nature of the evidence and its interpretation. The blunt truth is that accurate statistics are not available, and that scholars are only just beginning to discern what was happening to economic relations, levels of production, lines of trade, crops, prices, and population.[32] Furthermore, all-India generalizations are likely to suggest only a bare outline given the localized nature of the economy before the development of continental communications networks.

Clearly, however, there were powerful physical barriers to major change, whether the development of a significant industrial sector or the expansion of commercial agriculture. As late as 1817 there was no main road on which wheeled vehicles could be used; nor were there any railways. But the Company, running its empire on a tight budget, was unlikely to be able to afford investment in the necessary infrastructure for economic growth. Bentinck tried to improve the roads, but his successor, Lord Auckland, abandoned the attempt on financial grounds; and it was not until Dalhousie became Governor-General (1848–56) that a programme of road-building was put in hand. Free Traders and railway companies pressed the Company's government to improve communications within India by rail, and with Britain by steamship. In 1840 out of a welter of conflicting interests and pressures emerged a regular P. & O. service between Britain and India subsidized by the British government and the East India Company. But it was not until 1849 that the mercantile and railway interests won the crucial battle with the Company for an official guarantee of the interest on British capital invested in Indian railway construction. By 1854 only 34 miles had been constructed. More obviously successful was Dalhousie's reform of the post office, and under his impetus the completion of 4,000 miles of telegraph lines. Where developments in public works did occur the official motive was often security. Commercial interests were primarily interested in private profit, though they argued their case in terms of imperial security and moral benefit to India. In 1848, for example, the East India Railway Company urged the Prime Minister that railway building could deeply influence for good the lives of all Indians. 'This is a matter of extreme importance in India, where the energy of individual thought has long been cramped by submission to despotic governments, to irresponsible and venal subordinates, to the ceremonies and priesthood of a highly irrational religion, and to a public opinion founded not on investigation, but on traditional usages and observances.'[33]

The absence of government commitment to dramatic economic intervention and official development enterprise is not surprising, given the acute problems of financing even a minimal government in India in the early nineteenth century, and also the intellectual ambience of the period. Only later in the twentieth century did imperial and then indigenous governments begin to perceive their role as active instigators of economic change or acquire the financial resources and technical skill for this role. However, such initiative has proved essential to economic transformation in Asia and Africa: Japan at the end of the nineteenth century is an obvious example and clear contrast to India's experience. For without government investment, and fiscal policies designed to transfer resources between different sectors of the economy, the capital to finance economic expansion and industrialization has been lacking.

In India there was no major inflow of private foreign capital in the first half of the nineteenth century. The railway companies were the first importers of capital, for earlier British investment in the subcontinent had consisted of savings made by East India Company servants in India or profits made by European business houses re-invested in India, and British investment in internal trade and production remained what it had been in the previous century—a mechanism for returning profit to England, and therefore liable to dramatic fluctuations. Nor did Indians' own economic activity generate sufficient surplus to finance significant economic development. India remained a poor society, with many of its agriculturalists still producing for subsistence: while its social and economic networks remained fragile and vulnerable to climatic disaster and famine until the second half of the century when marked progress in communications by road, rail, and sea opened up wider internal and international markets, made commercial agriculture more viable and secure, and enabled famine relief.

Free Traders had hoped that the end of the Company's commercial monopoly would open up a new economic era for India. Undeniably there was commercial expansion. Between 1814 and 1858 the volume and value of Indian exports and imports more than quadrupled, and over time India became an exporter of primary goods (indigo, cotton, opium, sugar, and—decreasingly—piece goods and raw silk) and an importer of manufactured goods. But in this first half of the century long-distance trade and the commercial agriculture on which it was founded was unstable and subject to violent fluctuations. The consequences were different in different parts of India, but could result in rapid changes of fortune in particular areas. In northern India, for example, the first four decades of the new century were marked by stagnation and probably decline, after successful early penetration of the rural economy by European and Indian traders, and the resulting growth of commercial crops. The period of down-turn was the result of complex interactions between international trading patterns and external demand, local patterns of bad weather, and blockages inherent in Indian systems of production and credit. (In one sense the precariousness of agriculture and trade lay in the very limitations of European economic penetration of the countryside, and their inability to control production, credit, and transport, while opening the rural economy to the fluctuations of international trade.) When profits were made they went into the hands of European Agency Houses with their wide economic interests, or of the growing number of substantial Indian trading families: but both groups were vulnerable to the unstable economic environment and could suffer dramatic collapses. Consequently, commercial agriculture and long-distance trade did not at this time provide the basis for sustained and widespread economic growth. European imports, by contrast with Indian exports, sharply inceased in volume and value from the 1830s despite the difficulties and depression encountered by Indian consumers. The import of European finished textile goods, twist, and yarn clearly dislocated the lives of whole artisan communities in some areas, and probably lessened the income of some families some of whose members spun and wove. But again, such effects were localized and uneven, and it would be wrong to see them as indicating a general 'de-industrialization' of the Indian economy. By mid-century little had occurred to change the basic modes of peasant agriculture, or to alter the structures of rural society. Urban life also seems to have been subject to fluctuations and cycles of decline and growth as a result both of political change and variations in patterns of trade. No new major urban industry had emerged, and where sustained more modern commercial activity developed in such cities as Calcutta and Bombay it was too insulated from the rest of the economy, or too monopolized by Europeans, to undermine the foundations of the old order.

Although the evidence of so little purposive or structural change in India's economy erodes any simple assumptions that India experienced the beginnings of 'modernization' or of a new capitalism in the first half of the nineteenth century, it is important to remember the disruptive socio-economic implications of the British political assault on the Indian polities which had emerged in the shell of the older Mogul empire. Linked to those polities and the aristocracies they sustained were a wide range of economic functions and opportunities—for soldiers, civil 'service groups', and artisans who produced luxury goods central to courtly culture. With the British political advance, Indian princes and courts ceased to be such prolific patrons and consumers, higher and regular revenue demands reduced the disposable income of larger landholders, and of course soldiering communities lost many of their openings for employment. Spending for military, political, and ritual reasons by those with political power had given bouyancy to many small towns and rural communities. But the British did not step into this pattern or fulfil expected roles of patronage and consumption—and their more frugal style of government was intensified by their own need to cut civil and military expenditure. Yet gradually as one ruling élite declined, another emerged: and in time Indians who became the new courtiers, taking service with the British, developed more western tastes, following their rulers' patterns of dress and consumption, and so generated other economic opportunities for craftsmen and service groups who could satisfy their cultural needs.

An age of reform existed in the minds of many of the British concerned with India: whether it ever existed in Indians' experience is doubtful. Continuity, not radical change, was the dominant feature of Indian society in the first half of the nineteenth century. What change occurred was often unintended and unforeseen, while its incidence was extremely uneven geographically and socially. The events of 1857 show many of these themes in the interactive process in microcosm.

iv   1857

1857 remains a highly emotive date in Indian history. No historian can ignore the military mutiny and social upheavals of that year, although their significance remains debatable. The events of 1857 became part of an overtly ideological, nationalist interpretation of the subcontinent's recent past; flamboyantly stressed in V. D. Sarvarkar's *The Indian War of Independence*, published in 1909. This view of the 1857 disturbances as an early manifestation of nationalism was still receiving scholarly acceptance as late as 1957, in the work of S. B. Chaudhuri. Early Marxist analysis also confirmed the understanding of 1857 as a national war of liberation. At the time many British people preferred to see the events largely as a military mutiny—understandably, as any wider interpretation would have cast doubts on the nature of their *raj*. But the occurrences of that year, particularly the much publicized massacres of English women and children, bit hard into British communal consciousness, generating a deep, irrational fear. It is notoriously difficult to document racial and imperial attitudes and to do justice to their complexity; but a 'mutiny complex' does seem to have become part of the British picture of India, and to have surfaced at times of disturbance. How an event can become an idea and a symbol, and can influence relationships between peoples, is a fascinating phenomenon of intellectual and emotional history. Here 1857 is important for what it can tell us about the British *raj* and the interaction between western influences and Indian society, with its distinctive values and structures of influence, a century after Plassey. What follows is not a narrative of events or analysis of causes and effects. It uses evidence of the catastrophe as a geologist uses a cross section—to look at India under British rule at a specific point in time, to pinpoint areas of change and continuity, sources of unease and tension, in the experience of Indians under their new rulers.

However, the events of 1857 must be seen in their true context—that of persistent resistance to British authority in many parts of India in the preceding years. Although the British had established their rule by the early part of the century, a whole range of revolts and dissidences were endemic in India. Former princes, ruling groups and their allies rebelled against the imposition of British nominees, or against the centralizing revenue system of the new imperial authority, village leaderships resisted changes in tenurial rights and revenue obligations, townsmen resisted taxes. Indians also often became involved in conflict with each other as a result of the pressures and changes which accompanied the new regime—landords against their tenants, nomads against settled people, consumers against grain dealers, for example. There were also revolts of Company soldiers well before 1857, the most serious being in Vellore in 1806. The year 1857 was peculiar because of the scale of the disturbances, the conjuncture of military and civilian revolt, and the threat it posed for British power throughout northern India.[34] The storm broke on 10 May in Meerut, a small military station forty miles from Delhi, where the sepoys, or ordinary soldiers, of the Bengal army mutinied, set fire to the station, and marched to Delhi, the old Mogul capital, where they compelled the last Mogul, the feeble Bahadur Shah then aged 82, to stand as their leader. Mutiny spread quickly throughout the Bengal army, and within weeks most of the major stations in the North-West Provinces and Oudh were in rebel hands, their English officers and residents dead or beleaguered, where they had not fled for their lives. Civilian rebellion spread rapidly across the Gangetic plain, and in whole tracts British authority collapsed suddenly and catastrophically. As one senior ICS officer, M. Gubbins, noted, the recently annexed princely state of Oudh remained quiet until the end of May: but in the first ten days of June the end of British control there was sudden and total.

When . . . the troops at the capital had set the example, all the rest soon followed, and the fabric of civil government fell to pieces like a house made of cards. As the regiments mutinied at each station, the civilians fled, or were destroyed: the offices were burnt; the police and revenue out-stations, and officials left without a head, broke up; the people were left to themselves, and anarchy ensued.[35]

Lord Canning, the Governor-General who had followed Dalhousie, began to collect troops in Calcutta to march 'up country' to restore control. By October they were reinforced by sea from Britain. The spring of 1858 saw the advancing imperial forces re-establishing British rule, though Oudh remained rebel country until the end of the year. A reporter for *The Times* described the situation in April: 'At present all Oudh may be regarded as an enemy's country . . . All our machinery of government is broken and destroyed. Our revenue is collected by rebels. Our police has disappeared utterly. Oudh is to be conquered. Before it was only "annexed".'[36] Beyond the Gangetic plain and parts of central India there was little or no disturbance at any time in 1857–8. There was quiet in Bengal, Madras, and Bombay, where the British presence was longest established. While the more recently acquired Punjab became a bastion of British strength, where Sikh princes collaborated with their imperial overlords to rally forces for the reimposition of British authority in the disaffected areas to the east.

Recent research suggests the complexity of the causes and character of the 1857 disturbances, though from then onwards people have sought simple, often mono-causal explanations. The *military* mutiny is the easiest aspect to explain. Only one of the Company's three armies mutinied—the Bengal army—not those based on Madras and Bombay. The Bengal army had a distinctive pattern of recruitment. A large number of its sepoys were of high caste and therefore likely to be peculiarly watchful for potential threats to their religion and caste. Moreover, nearly one-third of them came from Oudh and were closely connected by bonds of family and neighbourhood as well as caste. They were likely to be sensitive about events in Oudh, and as a group to be fertile ground for rumours. The backdrop to their revolt and its dramatic wider repercussions was the weakness of the British military presence in the Bengal army. Only 23,000 out of the army's 150,000 men were British, partly because European troops had been withdrawn to serve in the Crimean and Persian Wars. Europeans were concentrated in Bengal and Punjab, and this meant that the Gangetic plain, including its key towns, was virtually denuded of British troops. In the opinion of one contemporary this 'was the one, great, capital error.'[37] It was also true that compounding British weakness was the decline of discipline in the army, and the generally poor standard of British officers.

Specific grievances actually precipitated the sepoy mutiny. Some observers have stressed the anxiety felt by the sepoys at the annexation of Oudh in 1856 as a result of princely misgovernment, noting that the sepoys lost their special privileges in Oudh courts thereby. They may also have feared that annexation presaged higher revenue demands on the village land holding groups from which so many of them came. Others have suggested that by 1857 the Indian soldiers were becoming convinced that the British were determined to attack their religion. One senior sepoy told Henry Lawrence, Chief Commissioner of Oudh who was killed in 1857, that 'for ten years past the Government has been engaged in measures for the forcible or rather fraudulent conversion of all the natives.'[38] The presence of missionaries was misinterpreted as a sign of official attempts to convert Indians to Christianity; while some evangelical army officers such as Colonel Wheeler in Barrackpore openly preached the Christian gospel. There is, however, little evidence that particular reforms such as the abolition of *suttee* had any marked effect on sepoys' loyalty. Far more significant were grievances relating to their terms of professional service. As the territory under British dominion expanded and far-flung areas of India ceased to be alien territory, so the Bengal sepoy found himself committed to service far outside his home region, in areas strange to him though part of the subcontinent, but now without the incentive of the extra field allowance for foreign service which had originally been offered if he agreed to serve 'abroad'. In the 1840s several regiments had mutinied when they were expected to serve in newly-annexed Sind and Punjab. In 1856 the General Enlistment Order brought the Bengal army's terms of service into the line with those of the Bombay and Madras armies, and all sepoys were automatically expected to serve outside Company territory, even overseas if necessary. Sea travel was considered polluting to high caste Hindus. But the real threat to caste appeared to come from the cartridges issued for use with the new Enfield Rifle early in 1857. These were greased with beef and pork fat, contaminating to Hindus and Muslims respectively; and they had to be bitten before insertion into the rifle. When the government realized its gross error it allowed sepoys to use their own grease and to break rather than bite open their cartridges. But the damage was done. Rumours of ritual defilement could not be easily hushed; and it was the punishment of eighty-five sepoys who refused to use the cartridges in Meerut which sparked the mutiny of their fellow soldiers.

Civilian rebellion was more complex in origin. It was essentially élitist— not initiated or supported by the really poor or landless, but by some of the dominant castes and notables in the countryside. Those at the base of society were caught up in a conflict which they neither chose nor understood; in which they were victims or only followed their traditional master and patrons. *The Times* correspondent noted compassionately, 'What a life must be that of the Oudh peasant! Which ever side wins, *he* is sure to lose; and in the operations which determine the conquest, he is harassed and maltreated by both parties.'[39] Civilian rebellion was also extraordinarily patchy, even in areas where the British lost general control. In the Aligarh district of the North-West Provinces, for example, there were local disturbances, some settling of old scores between Indians; but no general revolt. Further west in Muzaffarnagar district, bordering Meerut where the sepoy mutiny started, there was comparative tranquillity, particularly in the prosperous upland area irrigated by the Ganges Canal.

The local incidence of civil disorder demonstrates that simple theories positing a single cause just do not work. Take, for example, the idea that the North-West Provinces and Oudh were disturbed by fear of a threat to religion from particular reforms and from the spread of the new education. Certainly when leaders such as the Mogul Emperor or Khan Bahadur Khan of Bareilly made political appeals they stressed the danger to religion. But the force of such appeals was muted by the leaders' awareness that they must try to unite Hindus and Muslims against the British. Furthermore these were essentially political appeals, evidence of an attempt to construct a common front, not indications of real grass-roots fear. Evidence from the localities does not suggest that fears of an attack on religion were a prominent cause of disaffection. Etawah district, where a school tax had recently been levied and nearly 200 schools opened in two years remained, in the words of the District Magistrate and Collector, 'pre-eminent for loyalty'.

... not only have the schools remained open in many instances through all these troubles, but in some cases the zamindars have themselves paid the masters, saying they would take credit for the amount when they next paid up the school cess, and long before I thought it safe to collect the revenue, the little lads were everywhere humming away at their lessons, as if all was quiet, and the fate of empires was not quivering in the scale.[40]

Those areas of India where education had penetrated most deeply remained conspicuously unmoved by rebellion, whereas those areas where British authority was most threatened were markedly backward in educational standards and opportunities. In Bengal, for example, educated Indians at once expressed their loyalty, and their associations presented addresses of support at Government House in Calcutta. Their response was hardly surprising. Such men had material interests in the new order, and often a deep, ideological commitment to new ideas. They would have been uneasy bed-fellows with the rural rebels and disgruntled sepoys who attempted to revive older loyalties.

Another explanation, much favoured at the time, was that of a Muslim conspiracy to restore the Mogul empire. But there is no proof of such a conspiracy. The rebels were notoriously divided in loyalty and intention, and the elderly Mogul was completely surprised by his sudden elevation by Meerut's Hindu sepoys. At a local level all castes and communities were fractured in their response to events—including the Muslims. Only in Rohilkhand were Muslims the prime movers and supporters of wide-spread civil disaffection. That area had been ceded to the British by the Nawab of Oudh in 1801; and it was the Muslim Rohillas who, nursing their ancient grievance, led and organized the revolt half a century later. Hindus were locally the victims of revolt. Rajput villages were burnt, cows were slaughtered in temples—a hideous sacrilege to Hindus—, and at the entrance to some towns Hindu heads were set up on poles. It was little wonder that when a Hindu leader of revolt, the Nana Saheb, attempted to persuade Rohilkhand Hindus to join the rebel Muslims in opposition to the British he had little success. Many Rohillas for their part found his arrival offensive. In other areas Hindus and Muslims could be found both in the rebel camp and among British supporters.

An explanation which merits further consideration is that which notes the working of British land settlements and courts, and suggests that heavy assessment often led to established landed families losing land and/or becoming intolerably indebted to money-lenders. 1857 is then seen as the despairing gestures of losers under the new order against their rulers and the money-lenders who were able to foreclose on debts and acquire land through the new courts. The Collector of one Rohilkhand district had no doubt about this connection.

To the large number of these [land] sales during the past twelve or fifteen years, and the operation of our revenue system, which has had the result of destroying the gentry of the country . . . I attribute solely the disorganization of this and the neighbouring districts in these provinces. By fraud or chicanery, a vast number of the estates of families of rank and influence have been alienated, either wholly or in part, and have been purchased by new men . . . without character or influence over their tenantry . . . I am fully satisfied that the rural classes would never have joined in rebelling with the sepoys . . . had not these causes of discontent already existed.[41]

Such contemporary opinions as this and the evidence of land sales in northern India have convinced some later commentators such as T. R. Metcalf that over-assessment and the operation of the British legal system were at the root of rural rebellion.

Yet there does not seem to be any simple or automatic correlation between high assessment, recent poverty and land loss, indebtedness, and the incidence of rebellion. In Rohilkhand under recently-established British dominion there was undoubtedly a high rate of land alienation and a stiffly-pitched revenue assessment. But it was *not* 'traditional' landed families who lost their land under the British and then revolted in 1857. The Rohillas in the eighteenth century had obliterated the ancient landed groups by leasing villages for ten years to those who bid highest at auctions: and when the British took Rohilkhand they could not find the well-established owners with whom they hoped to settle the land and revenue obligation. They too had to adopt the device of selling to the highest bidders, who were often Indian government servants. Those who lost land under the British tended to be Hindus, mainly Rajputs and Jats, while the major gainers were Rohillas and Brahmins. So 1857 cannot here be seen as the desperate throw of those who had lost out. Further, the Rohillas were branching out into commercial money-lending in the years before 1857, and buying land on their profits. The anti-money-lender theory collapses too for this region. In the districts of Saharanpur and Muzaffarnagar plundering of money-lenders was certainly a symptom of civil disturbance. But those who rebelled were not those who had lost most land. The rebels were cohesive clan groups who had managed to keep money-lenders at bay; and where rebellion erupted in Muzaffarnagar district it was in an advanced and productive agricultural region. Further east in Oudh the theory of rebellion by the dispossessed at first sight seems plausible. Here the British had in an act of conscious policy begun to dismantle the power of the *taluqdars*, a group of magnates peculiar to the region, who controlled two-thirds of the land, but also owned forts from which they exercised lordship over the countryside. They were the leaders of revolt in Oudh; and their ex-tenants and clients, whom the British had hoped to establish as a proprietorial peasantry, followed their old masters into rebellion—much to the chagrin of the British. But on closer inspection even here land loss and rebellion did not always coincide. In fact under the British settlement of Oudh in 1856 the *taluqdars* who lost land were generously compensated; and much land remained under their control—62 per cent of the area settled at the time. In 1857–8 not all those who lost land rebelled. Raja Harwent Singh lost 200 of his 322 villages in 1856–7, yet gave refuge to British officers during disturbances. Others bided their time before siding with the rebels. As substantial men they had most to lose if they made an ill-judged decision. Raja Man Singh, for example, havered until August 1857 before 'rebelling' to safeguard his future when it seemed that British power had been irreparably demolished. He had lost all but six of his villages: but rebellion for him was a political calculation rather than an automatic response to dispossession.

Single explanations of civilian revolt do not work. Historical reality appears to have been a confused patchwork. The degree of rebellion and disorder varied greatly from area to area: so did its promptings. In some places high revenue demands were a cause of rebellion. In others it was not so much *objective* loss, poverty or indebtedness but a sense of *relative* hardship or loss of status by comparison with neighbours or kin groups which prompted revolt. In Muzaffarnagar district, as an example, the Jat brotherhoods had a real grievance in a punitive land revenue demand; but they seem to have felt it to be intolerable because their caste fellows of the eastern part of the district had a lower demand. In parts of Saharanpur district the trouble lay in heavy assessment, but more significantly in the lack of irrigation; so that the Gujar clans felt that they were doing less well out of the new order than their caste fellows in irrigated parts of the district. Often, too, once order had broken down Indians began to settle old scores with each other; and the way was open for indiscriminate plunder. What appears to have been vital was the presence or absence of a thriving local group of notables who were prospering under British rule, wanted its continuation, and were prepared to use their local influence to maintain order. Such men were present in Mathura and Aligarh districts, and they not only maintained a local peace but forwarded valuable sums of revenue to the British besieged in Agra. Elsewhere aggrieved aristocrats who for various economic and political reasons were unable to prosper in the new environment were prepared to rebel as a desperate measure of defiance and protest. The Rajas of Etah and Mainpuri were such: traditional leaders who not only lost land under British settlements but held land in poorer areas where there was little commercial agriculture and therefore little opportunity for retrieving their fortunes.

Such magnates were crucial if revolt was to be anything but a series of ill-co-ordinated rural outbursts, for only men of standing could generalize revolt and weld the different groups of disaffected together. Similarly those who had been dispossessed at an even higher level of political authority became leaders, or at least were used as figure-heads, helping to bond the movements of sepoy and civilian groups. Among the most prominent were the last Mogul emperor, and the Rani of Jhansi in Central India, who under Dalhousie's policy of 'lapse' had been deprived of her state, though it was one of the foremost of the Maratha principalities. But even such people were often unable to control the events in which they became embroiled. The Rani, for example, only rebelled and resumed the administration of her state when the sepoys revolted in Jhansi, giving her little option if she was to save her own life and prevent conflict in her region. A lesser rebel notable, Nawab Walidad Khan (whose family had lost land under the British and who was also connected by marriage to the Mogul royal family), also had trouble attempting to 'lead' local rebels in Bulandshahr, whence he was sent by the Delhi regime to establish its authority. He was totally unable to control the district because local clan groups either resisted him or were unstable allies, and because local landowners would have no truck with him—though in this area few of the landholders actively collaborated with the British either. His failure demonstrates widespread patterns of civilian disturbance—the lack of unity among the disparate rebel groups, each with their particular sense of grievance, and the absence of any coherent vision of the future. Although the British were a central focus for discontent, this was no simple anti-foreigner rebellion. Other Indians, whether neighbouring Hindus or money-lenders, were attacked as symbols of forces making for loss and deprivation. Even loyalty to the Mogul family and its restoration was an ideal which prompted a very few.

The complexities of 1857 may disconcert those who look for simple patterns of grievance and revolt: but they are a rich source of insight into the nature and results of interaction between Indian society and influences stemming from British rule. At the simplest level, 1857 demonstrated that in the century since Plassey the erstwhile merchants had successfully consolidated a new political dominion over the subcontinent. They might lose control over a limited area, but there were no other contenders for the role of continental rulers. They proved in the months of local but bitter conflict, and painful re-consolidation following May 1857, that if rebellion was geographically confined and their military strength was reinforced from Britain they could re-establish their authority. But the breakdown of their authority in parts of northern India also demonstrated their fundamental reliance on a network of Indian subordinates and sympathizers prepared to collaborate with their regime. Where that network held firm, as in Bengal or in the princely allies from Punjab, their dominion was secure. It was extremely vulnerable when these layers of loyalty proved untrustworthy. The British collapse in Oudh and parts of the North-West Provinces was presaged by the mutiny of their military collaborators, the sepoys. It was total and catastrophic where this defection was followed by the non-co-operation or active hostility of the rural élites and those Indians recruited into the administrative and revenue services. (The latter particularly were often pushed into this position if they wished to save their skins, let alone salvage some prospects for their future.)

It is also clear from the evidence thrown up by the disturbances of 1857 how *uneven* was the nature of British–Indian interaction; and how different were the responses of different groups and regions to the experience of British *raj*. Russell of *The Times* put this dramatically in his diary for February 1858, when he attended a military ball in Calcutta!

The arrangements were admirable. The rooms—curious, quaint, old, barrack chambers—were well lighted, decorated with flags, flowers and fire-arms; bowers and pleasant arcades were improvised in the open. Dancing vigorous, music good. The supper-rooms gave one an exalted notion of the resources of Calcutta, and one could not help asking himself, 'Has there been a mutiny at all? Is this a delusion? Do the enemy still hold Oudh, Rohilkhand, Jhansi, Kalpi, and vast tracts of Central India?'[42]

Not only whole regions but far smaller areas within regions responded according to the timing of their experience of new influences, according to the specific local nature of these influences, as well as the nature of local society. It is clear that the differences in the interactive process depended not just on British policies as these were modified over time and adapted according to region—types of land settlement, levels of revenue demand, provision of irrigation, educational facilities, and reform programmes. Pre-existing patterns of power and authority among Indians, the natural economic environment, bonds and divisions in local society, as well as conscious ideologies, were vital in the relationship. India was no *tabula rasa* on which new rulers could write at will. It had its own motors for action, its own areas of tension and change, its distinctive patterns of commitment and belief. These often distorted the policies of alien rulers, conceived as they so often were in partial ignorance, and brought to birth in weakness.

Although Indian initiatives and priorities were so central in the experience of change there was no national revolt in 1857. The discontented were fractured in loyalty and intention, often looking back to a society and polity which were no longer viable. They generated no coherent ideology or programme on which to build a new order. While those who did visualize India as a nation, or at least a nation in making, remained aloof, seeing India's future in more change and more connection with people, ideas, and forces coming from the newer world of the West.

CHAPTER III

The Dilemmas of Dominion

The half century between the suppression of revolt in 1857 and the First World War was arguably one of the most decisive in India's history: a time critical for India's emergence as Asia's first democracy, with all its strengths and contradictions. It lacks the drama or towering personalities of the Mutiny or later nationalist movement, for Indian history in these years largely concerns the more mundane experiences of those, rulers and ruled, who lived and worked in the subcontinent. Both faced dilemmas posed by the new dominion. The new rulers faced problems generated by different and often conflicting interest groups among themselves—Whitehall in ambivalent relationship with Calcutta, British industrialists pressurizing the Government of India over its financial policies, expatriate planters and missionaries in uneasy political and social relationship with the civil and military officials who composed the *raj*'s 'establishment'. More fundamental still were the dilemmas of administering India and financing the British structure of control; and, interwoven, the issues of British attitudes to and relations with different groups of Indians. Behind these obvious problems lay questions of India's worth to the British, and their duty to India and its peoples—questions to which answers were more often taken for granted than articulated. Indians also had to adjust their relationships with each other in the new context. Some long-established perceptions of identity, bonds, divisions, and patterns of dominance remained, others were eroded, and some new ones emerged in response to the British presence and its ramifications. Subjects had to react to their rulers: to decide whether to oppose or co-operate with them, to despise or copy them, or adopt different strategies in different areas of life. They also had to come to terms with the new influences and opportunities which accompanied British rule.

Such issues were posed at a time when India was experiencing unprecedented economic and political and, to a lesser extent, social change. Consequently they were not clear cut or static. India's history is therefore difficult to analyse as a whole. Under the surface of policy-making, routine administration, and the emergence of new political groups, interwoven changes were occurring in ideas, institutions, society, and the economy. By 1914–18 the British were consequently engaged in a much changed dominion, and having to fashion very different political strategies compared with the nineteenth century. In 1857 the British were challenged by armed revolt, which they mastered with bayonets and guns; sixty years later they faced political pressure in a recognizably western style and responded with careful political calculation.

i 'High Noon of Empire'

The last half of the nineteenth century is sometimes referred to as the 'high noon' of Britain's Indian empire. In those years it seemed at its most secure. Its external appearance was prestigious, sometimes flamboyantly powerful: while its structures solidified into a heavy, bureaucratic machine. Immediately after the Mutiny it became a government under the British Crown rather than of a commercial company, its supreme representative henceforth known as the Viceroy. The abolition of the East India Company had been a possibility for some time before 1858. Contemporaries realized that it was a commercial fiction; yet liberals feared to hand over its considerable powers of patronage to whichever of Britain's political parties was in power at home, and believed that the Company was a buffer, protecting India from the despotism of a Minister of the Crown or from Parliamentary meddling and 'the selfishness and rapacity' which might emanate from Britain's representative government.[1] However, the Mutiny took British lives, tales of its horrors deeply scarred British public opinion, and its suppression cost £36 million. It was little wonder that one result was the Company's abolition by Parliament in 1858.

In many ways little changed. Numerous officials remained at their posts despite the change from Company to Crown rule. A Viceroy now ruled in India, while in London a Secretary of State for India, responsible to Parliament, inherited the duties of the Court of Directors and the Board of Control. He in turn was assisted and supposedly checked by a fifteen-member Council of India, though in emergency he could act without it, provided he recorded his decisions, and in matters of war, peace, and high diplomacy could use his own authority. The Councillors were generally 'old India hands' who had close if often outdated knowledge of the subcontinent. In its early days most of the Council's members were former Company Directors or officials. Despite the continuities, India now lay open to the gaze and greater influence of Parliament. Its peoples were therefore exposed to the force of British racial and political sentiment to an unprecedented degree. As India's own public became more literate and sensitive, so British Parliamentary reactions to Indian affairs could and did become sources of political disquiet in India. Furthermore, all programmes for constitutional reform in India had to go through Parliament where there was often a strategic and vociferous Conservative minority even when a

Liberal or (later) Labour government was in power. Another source of friction built into this system of government was the relationship of Calcutta and Whitehall. The Secretary of State faced a Parliamentary audience and a Treasury concerned with balancing Britain's own books, while the Viceroy had to consider Indian opinion and the interests and ideas of his own officials. As the man on the spot he was often better informed than his London colleague, and on many issues his opinion prevailed though he was technically subordinate to the Secretary of State and the British government. There was constant ebb and flow in the balance of power between Calcutta and Whitehall; depending on the personalities of the two senior officials, on the questions at issue, and on the Parliamentary situation.

In India government by civil service assumed the form for which the Indian empire became renowned, and which served as the pattern for other parts of the British empire. In 1853 patronage ceased to be the route of entry into the ICS, the élite of bureaucrats often nicknamed 'the heaven-born'. In place of patronage came the competitive examination, the first of which was held two years later. Haileybury was closed down, and after various experiments in training in subsequent years, successful recruits went to Oxford, Cambridge or London Universities for a year's study, and thereafter received 'in-service' training in an Indian district, apprenticed, as it were, to an experienced district officer. In contrast to the early nineteenth century the ICS drew more heavily on the sons of professional rather than commercial families, and more of them came from public schools. However, throughout the later part of the century the ICS was increasingly unpopular as a profession, partly because of widening opportunities at home, professional grievances in India, and the health hazards, uprooting, and family disruption which an Indian career demanded. As a result there was persistent official concern that the quality and numbers of recruits were declining. Changes in the age at which young men could sit the examination were partly strategies to attract the largest number of able recruits of good social standing.[2] It was considered particularly important that they should have a 'natural' sense of leadership and responsibility, because in their early twenties they were charged with authority over thousands of Indian lives. Intellectual achievement was valued and fostered rather less than 'good all-round intelligence', as the ICS was pre-eminently the field for the talented amateur who could turn his mind and hand to virtually anything: from land revenue assessment to criminal law, from fraternization with dignified Indian notables to giving school prizes, inspecting slaughter-houses or mediating in village squabbles.

The district officer spent much time in the open air, seeing and being seen in his district. But increasingly as the years passed the pioneering independent qualities of service life were edged out by the demands of the study and paper-work often generated by the demands of the local officer's superiors. Effective British government of India became possible with the expansion of roads, railways, telegraphic and telephone communications. It was also intensely bureaucratic; and particularly in the secretariats in Calcutta and the provincial capitals it was dominated by file-pushing and regulations in a formidable, desk-bound hierarchy. Lord Curzon, Viceroy at the turn of the century, waged war against red tape and endless minuting; and during his term of office the 18,000 pages of reports printed annually came down to 8,000, and statistics from 35,000 to 20,000! He had been warned at the outset of the stone-walling powers of the top bureaucrats, for they had been described to him as '. . . the Augurs of India, who smile at one another when a Viceroy tries to introduce reforms, or a District Officer is bold enough to utter a new idea. . . . It is an accursed system and is sapping the usefulness and individuality of the Civil Service.'[3] Such an administrative structure not only tended to stolid conservatism and blocked innovation; it generated friction between its component parts, particularly between men in the districts who valued their individuality and freedom (and could be distinctly eccentric) and their superiors in the secretariats, as Curzon's informant, himself a senior ICS man, had indicated. Others were of course anxious to rise rapidly out of the districts and into the urban milieu of the central and provincial governments, where professional achievement was rewarded with higher pay and eventually with a place in the Honours Lists.

Not only did the structure of British rule solidify. In the later nineteenth century a distinctive imperial life-style also developed among the British in India. The new rulers exported and re-created, even in the most isolated parts of India, a culture and life-style fashioned in upper middle-class Britain. It was a life free of manual exertion, dependent on Indian servants for its smooth functioning. It was meticulous in its codes of dress and manners, of elaborate social courtesy, and of appropriate behaviour in relations between dominant and subordinate, male and female. It surrounded itself as far as possible with all the domestic trappings of British life at home, even to the extent of dressing for dinner in the jungle. From this domestic and social world Indians were very largely excluded, by convention and by the spatial segregation of British homes from areas where Indians lived, both in town and countryside. So the British separated themselves from their subjects—a far cry from the social life of their eighteenth-century ancestors, some of whom had Indian wives and mistresses, and had delighted in Indian culture and habits, from the exquisite achievements of Indian art and literature to the earthier pleasures of dancing girls or the *hookah*, the 'hubble-bubble' pipe companionably shared among friends. Instead the P. & O. liner service permitted some European family life in India, bearing children to and from boarding school and the famous 'fishing fleet' of young women who visited India in the cold weather, more eager to land a husband than to see the glories of India or to visit relatives. British people became in a real sense a separate caste in an already segmented society.

Their social style found one of its greatest observers and commentators in Rudyard Kipling, who gained first-hand experience of his subjects as a journalist on a provincial paper in north India. His fiction and poetry depict the formal, assured social world which revolved round the bungalow in the district with its bevy of servants, the European club, the Secretariat and its hierarchy transported socially to Government House and its satellites, the Regimental Mess and Officers' Quarters; and of course the hill stations to which expatriate families and much of the government repaired in the hottest months of the year. Of these the most famous was Simla, in the Himalayan foothills, the Summer Capital where Viceroy and entourage took refuge in as gentle and as English an environment as possible, escaping the burning sun and baking earth of the plains. Within the British community there was extreme stratification, depending largely on seniority and actual job, which in themselves depended heavily on membership of the right social group 'at home'. Every civil and military official and every official's wife knew exactly where he or she stood in the social hierarchy. Social conventions hallowing the hierarchical order were minutely observed, long after wars and education had eroded them in Britain.

European women, the 'Memsahibs', have been criticized for their supposed role in undermining the empire, being variously castigated as frivolous, as snobbish and insular, and as increasing racial separation by frowning on Indo-British sexual liaisons and creating an atmosphere of sexual fear and competition between European and Indian men. Some women did conform to the idle, gossipy stereotype: but the image does less than justice to those who supported their husbands at great personal cost of health and separation from children, or those who engaged in welfare and educational work for Indians. More importantly, this judgement fails to see that the memsahib and her expected role were quite central to the later nineteenth-century imperial self-image and ethos, rather than being destructive of it. Specific gender expectations and identities fashioned in Britain were implicit in British imperial self-perception; and in British eyes the role and treatment of women in their own society marked them and their social order as 'superior' to Indians and Indian society, where women's roles were circumscribed in different ways, and their relationship with men was more blatantly unequal. As Indian and British patriarchies encountered each other in the imperial context, women's place was a crucial point of mutual judgement and criticism, in the British case contributing to a gendered dimension of their own justification for the *raj*. In practical ways, memsahibs were similarly crucial for the preservation and reproduction of the imperial social order carefully separated from the Indian society in which it was set: by providing sexual partnership for the men whose world it was, rearing children, and presiding over and moulding British homes on the subcontinent. Moreover, they were essential in the ruling caste's own processes of internal social stratification—maintaining the conventions of status based on seniority and socializing new recruits, male and female, into imperial society.[4]

Some British people remained on the periphery of this charmed circle; particularly missionaries and businessmen, whose social origins and political 'soundness' were suspect. Eurasians of mixed descent (known as Anglo-Indians, though, confusingly this could also mean pure British people and families who had lived a long time in India or had extensive Indian career connections) had no place in the polite society of the *raj*; except in the lowlier church pews or as the recipients of charitable interest in such forms as children's Christmas parties. In the early twentieth century they numbered over 110,000. This unhappy but enterprising community, often born of marriages or illicit unions between Indian women and British private soldiers, lived in a social limbo. They identified with the British, referring to Britain as 'home' though many had never been there; while their women wore European clothes and used make-up to disguise their tell-tale complexions. They were accepted neither by Indians nor by the British. To the rulers they were, nonetheless, an invaluable source of man-power in such strategic and technical positions as the railway and telegraph services. Until 1878 the Indian Telegraph Office was entirely manned by Anglo-Indians and domiciled Europeans.

India, however, meant far more to the British than a chance to live in a life-style many of them could never have afforded at home. It was also of immense significance in Britain's total world position. By the later nineteenth century India's value to Britain differed markedly from the worth of interests in India whose protection had entangled the East India Company in territorial dominion three-quarters of a century earlier. This value was rarely discussed at all overtly. It is for the historian to disentangle the interests and connections which contemporaries assumed as self-evident.

The subcontinent provided employment for those British men who went into the ICS and other civilian services, such as forestry, education, medicine, and engineering for public works and irrigation. Almost all expatriate employees of government retired to Britain and received pensions at India's expense, which were one of the main 'home charges' on the Indian revenue. The number of expatriates was always small. At the beginning of the twentieth century about 3,500 were employed in the all-India services taken together, the ICS accounting for over a quarter of these. (In 1921 the whole European population including women was only about 156,500.) India also gave careers to British soldiers who officered the Indian army. (There were no Indian officers until after the First World War, other than those holding the Viceroy's—not the King's—Commission: and they were lower in rank than even new British subalterns, however long their service.) British 'other ranks' were also recruited to balance the sepoys. A major result of the Mutiny was a drastic reduction in the Indian element in the army. It dropped from 238,000 in 1857 to 140,000 in 1863; while the European forces rose from 45,000 to 65,000. By 1880 there were 66,000 British and 130,000 Indian troops in the Indian army. The army was far more than a career structure or wage-payer. At no cost to the British tax-payer it was a large force which could be widely deployed to protect imperial interests over and above its role in India's own defence and internal security; and its presence in the subcontinent helped to safeguard imperial trade and communications between Europe and Australasia. The value of this 'English barrack in the Oriental Seas' (as Lord Salisbury called it in 1882) was indicated by the areas in which India's army was used in the second half of the nineteenth century—China, Persia, Ethiopia, Singapore, Hong Kong, Afghanistan, Egypt, Burma, Nyasa, Sudan, and Uganda. Its potential manpower was also great in times of grand emergency; and India made a momentous military contribution in 1914–18 as far west as France, producing for Britain's war effort men, animals, stores, and money.[5] (See below, p. 195.)

Less dramatic but as vital a foundation of Britain's position as a world power was India's economic role. The subcontinent exported to Britain, and to Europe, North America, and South East Asia, a variety of raw materials and foodstuffs—cotton, jute, rice, tea, oil-seeds, wheat, and hides—as well as some manufactured goods such as cotton yarn and piece-goods. Continental Europe was in fact a larger consumer of India's exports than Britain. The imperial homeland, however, dominated India's import trade. She supplied over 60 per cent of India's imports in 1913; while India was the largest single market for British exports, and particularly significant to certain staple British industries, cotton, iron, steel, and engineering. (See Tables A and B.) The subcontinent was also a large importer of British capital. In the later nineteenth century nearly one-fifth of Britain's overseas investment was in India—around £270 million. By the beginning of the twentieth century India and Ceylon together were the fifth largest recipient of British capital, just over one-tenth of British overseas investment. In 1910 this amounted to £365 million; nearly half in government loans, 37 per cent in railways and 5 per cent in tea and coffee plantations. This estimate is probably too low, as it deals only with public companies registered in Britain. Certainly a great deal more unrecorded expatriate capital was tied up in the subcontinent. India's economic importance to Britain is evident from these direct trade and investment links. But India's exports to other parts of the world while importing heavily from Britain, enabled Britain to use India's surplus and so balance her international trade books with other

Table A. *UK Imports from India, 1854–1934 (in £1,000)*

Commodity	1854	1876	1900	1913	1929	1934
Cotton, raw	1,642	5,875	657	1,226	3,826	3,153
Indigo, natural	1,546	1,809	457	48	8	2
Rice	884	2,639	1,625	1,281	492	444
Linseed, flax and Rapeseed	735	4,115	2,080	1,785	1,922	1,769
Jute, raw	510	2,799	4,101	9,182	6,413	2,860
Wool, raw	404	987	828	1,659	2,992	1,031
Hides, raw	382	1,064	1,334	351	107	158
Rubber and Resins	146	552	444	32	1,488	2,120
Tea	24	2,429	5,576	7,839	20,083	15,007
Leather	18	444	2,820	2,839	5,111	3,307
Wheat	—	1,647	2	7,999	78	60
Jute goods	—	—	1,979	2,430	2,798	1,512
Oil-seeds	—	—	50	398	1,106	1,340
Other goods e.g. sugar, silk	4,382	5,665	5,435	11,351	16,465	9,392
Total	10,673	30,025	27,388	48,420	62,889	42,155

Source: W. Schlote, *British Overseas Trade From 1700 to the 1930s* (Oxford, 1952), p. 170.

parts of the world with which she as an isolated unit had a deficit. This was true of Britain's economic relations with Europe and North America. The British connection with India therefore enabled Britain to perform as an economy with a world-wide balance of payments surplus when her own trading position had declined.[6]

Such were both the obvious and less visible 'nuts and bolts' of India's worth to Britain and her people. But the subcontinent also had a peculiar place in Britons' self-image and their perception of Britain's role in the world. This was true to some extent of the mass of the British public, but more particularly of that small but influential segment of British society who through family traditions and contacts, and education in the reformed public schools, increasingly came to dominate 'service' in India. The way India entwined itself into the imaginations and spirits of many British people can be discerned from such scattered and amorphous pieces of evidence as the Indian words which have become part of ordinary English (bungalow, gymkhana, and verandah, pyjamas and jodphurs, chintz and chit, for example); from the India bric-à-brac which cluttered the homes of those with Indian connections; and from the popular literature of the time. It is difficult to discern any overt imperial ideology, because British people assumed that they shared attitudes to India and rarely talked about or

Table B. UK Exports to India, 1854–1934 (in £1,000)

Commodity	1854	1876	1900	1913	1929	1934
Manufactured textiles	7,191	15,961	19,069	40,729	32,340	11,373
Iron and steel goods	584	1,864	3,280	9,801	10,099	4,070
Other metals	203	799	713	1,733	1,701	1,343
Arms, munitions	33	53	120	200	810	497
Tobacco, liquor, sugar	308	501	626	914	3,034	1,007
Leather and leather goods	37	101	200	632	476	235
Books	33	80	131	309	397	305
Machinery	101	724	1,529	4,558	9,182	5,689
Chemicals	67	232	683	1,309	2,559	2,424
Coal, coke etc.	36	298	129	177	25	2
Locomotives, railway carriages	10	155	867	2,200	3,429	515
Paper, paper goods	1	110	167	513	988	537
Electrical Eng. products	—	145	76	362	1,347	1,071
Soap	—	22	114	433	1,010	444
Instruments, tools	—	13	219	504	791	562
Rubber goods	—	13	67	95	200	125
Cement	—	8	52	242	255	89
Ships	—	—	288	260	125	37
Motor vehicles and parts	—	—	—	679	1,945	1,745
Other goods	524	1,326	1,786	4,623	7,595	4,639
Total	9,128	22,405	30,116	70,273	78,308	36,729

Source: W. Schlote, *British Overseas Trade From 1700 to the 1930s* (Oxford, 1952), p. 172.

analysed them. Unlike some other Europeans, they created little conscious imperial theory. Discussions of Britain's imperial role and position only occurred under the impetus of particular Indian events or problems, when the forum for debate would be Parliament or intellectual journals such as *The Nineteenth Century*.[7]

British imperialism was a pragmatic exercise, the response to current pressures, threats, and opportunities. But always in the later nineteenth century an underlying assumption was that the British were a superior nation whose duty was to spread the benefits—material and moral—of trade with them and to propagate their own styles of education, law, and manners to the benighted of the earth, simultaneously making a profit for the imperial metropolis. In this imperial mission and destiny India had a vital role. Without India the varieties of British control and influence in Africa, the Middle East, and Asia would have been impossible. In turn the need to guard the routes to India made these diverse strategies of power essential. Consequently there was virtually no dissent from Britain's fundamental commitment to open imperial domination in India, however skilfully Whitehall men tried to contrive other less expensive forms of control elsewhere, knowing that British public opinion would decry another India in the Dark Continent, for example, and that the British taxpayers would rend any party which involved them in such expense as suppression of the Mutiny had incurred. It mattered comparatively little which political party was in power. The raw materials of the imperial equation were patent.

Furthermore, all thinking people had been influenced by changes in Britain's intellectual climate since the early nineteenth century. The ebullient confidence that change could be effected in foreign lands had been sapped by the waning of pristine Utilitarian philosophy and Evangelical zeal, and by the emergence of pseudo-scientific racial theories which stressed actual and potential differences between races at the expense of earlier, more sanguine assertions of similar human potential given the right conditions. India's Mutiny only confirmed the suspicions lurking in British minds even in the late 1840s and early 1850s that progress and reform would be long and tedious processes. Moreover, the mythology of 1857, in particular of supposed British heroism contrasted with Indian barbarism and violence, served to confirm assumptions of British racial superiority, and undergirded the racial separation and arrogance which increasingly marked the imperial ethos and style in India. Such attitudes bred an elaboration of stereotypes of Indians which helped to justify imperial rule, stereotypes in which assumptions about race, class, and gender peculiar to a section of British society were subtly blended. Indians, were, for example, often described as weak and effeminate, deceitful and deficient in character, and incapable of leadership: and thus needing and benefiting from rule by Anglo-Saxons displaying opposite and desirable qualities. Certain groups of Indians were seen as superior, however: the princes and larger landowners who could be equated with 'English gentlemen', or those social groups like Rajputs or Sikhs who were seen as upstanding 'martial races' who made good military material.[8]

Among the men who ruled India in the later nineteenth century there was a general consensus about their role, despite the vagaries and doubts of individuals and the different emphases of those working in particular provinces. (For linguistic reasons ICS men tended to spend their careers in one province and became deeply attached to and influenced by 'their' region and its people. The men in the Punjab, for example, became notable for a stern but compassionate paternalism reflective of their image of the Punjabi agriculturalist; an approach to India in marked comparison with that of Bengal ICS men who faced a very different society which much earlier was marked by the growth of English education and the professions.) All assumed that the British ought to be in India as imperial rulers. They believed they were there by the dispensation of a wise providence: to quit would be unthinkable for it would mean shuffling off a burden of moral responsibility, abandoning India to certain commercial chaos and probable political and social tyranny, as well as abandoning a fair field of profit for their compatriots. To them the obverse of privilege and material gain on the *raj*'s imperial coin was a serious obligation, seen in almost mystical terms. As Sir Walter Lawrence, who joined the ICS in 1879, put it in 1932, ruling India was 'splendid happy slavery . . . Looking back it seems a divine drudgery, and we all felt that the work was good. We were proud of it; we were knights errant.'[9]

The concept of obligation held by these self-styled knights errant was, however, limited. Although few now believed in the possibility or desirability of rapid change in India they persisted in the belief that political stability and gradual social, economic, and political reform would result if they concentrated on providing sound government and a stable framework for a natural rather than forced dissemination of European civilization. As Lord Lytton, Viceroy in the 1870s, remarked, 'able and experienced Indian officials' maintained 'that we can hold India securely by what they call good government: that is to say, by improving the condition of the ryot, strictly administering justice, spending immense sums on irrigation works, etc.' Fitzjames Stephen, Law Member from 1869 to 1872, demonstrated how even those in the Liberal tradition, steeped in Utilitarian philosophy, now rejected older notions of rapid transformation and were more concerned with making the system of government work, in a spirit of authoritarian paternalism. He saw the British task in India as promoting the welfare of its peoples through 'the introduction of the essential parts of European civilization into a country densely peopled, grossly ignorant, steeped in idolatrous superstition, unenergetic, fatalistic . . .' But this turned out to be a much circumscribed programme when he explained,

Now the essential parts of European civilization are peace, order, the supremacy of law, the prevention of crime, the redress of wrong, the enforcement of contracts, the development and concentration of the military force of the state, the construction of public works, the collection and expenditure of the revenue required for these objects in such a way as to promote to the utmost the public interest, interfering as little as possible with the comfort or wealth of the inhabitants, and improvement of the people.[10]

The men of the bureaucracy saw their government's economic role in strictly limited terms. (This was true in Britain as well, of course.) It should tax as little as possible, gathering revenue sufficient only to pay interest on government loans and meet the costs of the 'home charges' and the army. It should help provide the basic infrastructure—primarily communications and irrigation—for the free play of private agricultural, industrial, and commercial enterprise. But it should not instigate major economic development. Nor did the bureaucrats see government's role as the protection of private British economic interests, whether of northern England's cotton industry or of expatriates engaged in planting and business in India. Their main concern was levels of taxation and rates of exchange between the pound and the rupee, as both affected the tight financial margins within which they had to manoeuvre to meet even these minimal commitments. They had neither the ideological motivation nor the financial and political freedom to become prototype developmental economists.

Similarly in political matters officials had no sense of any duty to become innovators or engineers, moulding Indian political opinion and activity in a conscious, modernizing design. They admitted that the *raj* was a government with a naked sword in hand; but recognized that both moral and financial considerations made it necessary for the *raj* to rest on a combination of active alliances with particular groups of its subjects and the acquiesence of the vast majority. Their role was to provide stability and order, to attract allies and in the process to engage in some cautious political education; but certainly not to make drastic political changes. An independent India, the vision of Macaulay and the Anglicists, was too far off to be considered seriously. Even the most liberal of Viceroys, Lord Ripon, whose essay in local self-government was partly a measure of political education, demonstrated this realism and extreme caution of the later part of the nineteenth century. He wrote in 1881: 'I hold as strongly as any man that we must be careful to maintain our military strength; but, whatever may have been the case in the past, we cannot now rely upon military force alone; and policy as well as justice, ought to prompt us to endeavour to govern more and more by means of, and in accordance with, that growing public opinion, which is beginning to show itself throughout the country.'[11]

It was Lord Curzon who as Viceroy at the end of the century was the embodiment of many of these strands of authoritarian paternalism in British imperial attitudes to India. He took some to their extremes, not least perhaps because he more than many of his contemporaries was a consciously ideological imperialist rather than a pragmatist. He cared passionately about India, its land, cultural heritage, and its peoples, and bore a heavy sense of obligation to the subcontinent whose sovereign he represented, a sense of calling which alienated both Indians and his own compatriots. He had supreme confidence in, and almost missionary zeal for, the task of efficient government. In 1905 he commented, 'If I were asked to sum it up in a single word, I would say 'efficiency'. That has been our gospel, the keynote of our administration.'[12] But he lacked the sensitivity and compassion which softened the paternalism and rigorous efficiency of some of his contemporaries. As we shall see, unlike the more perspicacious Ripon, he had a sublime contempt for any Indian presumptions or aspirations to challenge his vision of the British mission in India.

ii The changing context of the imperial relationship

The attitudes of India's rulers and the structures for handling power which they created were obviously important factors in their relations with their subjects and in the ordinary experiences of India's peoples. But of more long-term significance for the subcontinent were changes in the Indian context of the imperial relationship, over which the British had little or no control, although their presence and policies were sometimes responsible for setting change in motion.

It was in the realm of communications that the most obvious developments occurred which proved fundamental to the making of modern India—in terms of the physical environment, the economy, as well as the more subtle perceptions of peoples and groups. Outside the subcontinent the opening of the Suez Canal in 1869 did more than anything to weld India into the world economy and bring closer contact with all aspects of western life and culture. In India already in the 1840s a real start had been made on the construction of a system of major roads linking the main cities and regions, with feeder roads to open up the hinterland. The most famous Indian highway which was started in 1839, was the Grand Trunk Road: 1,400 miles from Calcutta west across to Delhi, and thence up to Peshawar on the rugged north-west frontier.

Railways soon followed, when government guaranteed interest on private capital invested in railway-building, in the belief that railways were not only vital for military purposes but would inevitably trigger economic and social development.[13] Even the financial crisis caused by the Mutiny did not lessen the government's commitment to railway expansion, and in the late 1860s the government itself began to build lines, particularly where these were considered necessary for political rather than commercial considerations. By 1880 the state had built over 2,500 miles of track and private enterprise just over 6,000. In that year the guarantee system was abandoned and replaced with arrangements to divide railway earnings between government and the private companies; while government systematically took over company lines whenever it could. The relief of famine was now a further reason for government involvement in increasing the country's

Table C. *Rail freight carried in India (in millions of tons)*

1873	4.75
1880	10.5
1890	22.25
1900	43
1905	54
1910	65
1914–15	81

Source: D.H. Buchanan, *The Development of Capitalistic Enterprise In India* (New York, 1934, London, 1966), p. 190.

railway system. By 1900 under this joint government and company enter-prise 25,000 miles of track had been built, and a total of 35,000 by 1914. (The maximum was reached just before the Second World War—43,000 miles.) The railways became profitable in 1899, as the number of passengers and the amount of freight carried rose rapidly. (See Table C.) They were also the largest employer of organized labour in the subcontinent: the total number of railway staff was over 80,000 a decade after the First World War. There were drawbacks, however, to this piecemeal development—not least the fact that different companies used different gauges, which involved transhipment from one set of rolling stock to another at certain main junctions! The lines had not been built to a plan. Nor were they designed to integrate India into a single economic unit; but rather to enable military control, to alleviate famine, and to open India to foreign trade. Many lines were therefore built to link hinterland to coast rather than region to region. Freight charges, too, reflected the preoccupation with facilitating foreign trade, and the rates were lower on the hauls between the interior and the ports than between internal entreports. This tended to hurt industrial cen-tres inland, and to result in industrial concentration on the coast. There were, too, unforeseen ecological effects of railway building which have since posed serious problems, such as interference with natural drainage lines and deforestation where wood was used as fuel instead of the more expensive coal. The hazards to human health and the soil's productivity are only now beginning to be understood, as the dark side of the much-hailed 'progress' of the previous century. The other developments in internal communications of momentous consequence for both the creation of a modern state and the emergence of new patterns of politics were the postal and telegraph services. By 1880 there were 20,000 miles of telegraph wires.

British railway enthusiasts envisaging a multitude of benefits flowing from a revolution in communications were not mistaken in thinking that they presaged a wide range of developments in Indian life. Rapid travel within the subcontinent enabled new senses of identity which caused both unity and disunity. For the first time a substantial number of quite ordinary people could travel long distances, and in doing so could learn to perceive the distinctiveness of the region in which they lived, and might realize too that the subcontinent was a geographical, political, and to some extent a cultural unit. On such fresh perceptions were later built new senses of identity which were both cultural and political: of belonging to a nation, a region or a community, whereas earlier the cluster of villages interlocked by marriage and exchange of material goods and services was the widest extent of most Indians' public experience and perceptions. Such widened horizons and the actual necessity for travellers to touch and talk to people of different castes and creeds not only began to erode some of the entrenched orthodox Hindu hostility to secular contacts outside the precisely ordered relationships of a local caste society; it also expanded many people's social range in ways of wider significance—as, for example, in the formation of caste associations tying together many local *jatis*, and, longer term, in the emergence of new perceptions of identity based on shared interests such as professional skill and status, and economic position. Government could also be seen rather differently. Delhi might still be far away: but it could now spread its tentacles far deeper into the land and into the lives of its subjects. This in turn proved a fresh bond of experience, and sometimes of shared grievance, among those subjects. Such changes in ways of looking at oneself and other people became part of the raw materials of new types of politics. At an even more basic level trains, telegrams, and letters were the physical infrastructure of new patterns of political behaviour, because they enabled wide-scale voluntary association, organization, and contact. The economic repercussions of this revolution in communications are even clearer. Without the new roads and railways there could be no escape from the economic patterns of the early nineteenth century: no access to expanded internal and foreign markets, no motivation or outlets for commercial agriculture, no chance of industrial growth. But impressive statistics for all these developments should not blind us to the limited extent to which they broke down the isolation of India's hinterland and its peoples. Well into the twentieth century many villages remained untouched by metalled roads or railways, post offices were many miles apart, and telegraph offices even more scattered.

The breakthrough to a process of industrialization, however limited in comparison with Europe's experience, was one of the most marked economic changes which occurred in the later nineteenth century context of the imperial relationship.[14] The leading industries were cotton and jute. Mills processing both these raw materials were started in the 1850s. The cotton industry developed mainly in western India, in the Bombay Presidency. By 1892–3 there were already 120 mills employing 113,003 operatives: by 1912–13 there were 241 mills with a work force of 224,000. Jute mills clustered in

Bengal close to their raw product, over which India had a virtual monopoly. In 1892–3 there were 26 mills employing 66,000 workers; in 1912 63 mills with 201,000 operatives. Plantation industries also started. Their spectacular success story was tea, which virtually displaced China tea from the British market—somewhat ironically, considering the crucial role China tea had played in Britain's relationship with India at the start of the century. Tea flourished in Assam, Bengal, and Madras, with Assam outstripping the other areas by a long way. In 1875–9 about 173,000 acres were planted with tea. By 1915 this area had risen to 594,000 acres. Mining began, too: for coal (predominantly in Bengal, Bihar and Orissa, and Assam), mica (Madras, Bihar and Orissa), and manganese (Bombay, Central Provinces). The first steel mill was built in 1911 by the Tata Company in Bihar. By 1914 Indian coal output had reached 15.7 million tons, and largely met the needs of the railways.

Tables D–G set out in statistical form the extent of change such developments wrought in the living and working experiences of Indians. Thousands more lived in towns, many of them in urban agglomerations far larger than any previously known in India. Thousands now worked in the totally novel environment of the factory, using new manual and technical skills, having to co-operate with people in ways totally alien to village patterns of interdependence. But though industrialization and urbanization occurred, they were relatively limited in terms of India's economy as a whole, and they were 'encapsulated', confined to certain locations on the coast or close to raw materials. Most of India remained deeply agrarian: and the vast majority of Indians still earned their living through agriculture and its related

Table D. *Urbanization in India, 1872–1951*

Year	Number of towns	Urban population (millions)	Urban population (as % of total)
1872	n.a.	n.a.	8.7
1881	n.a.	n.a.	9.3
1891	1,999	26.7	9.4
1901	2,093	28.2	10.0
1911	2,087	28.6	9.4
1921	2,234	31.1	10.2
1931	2,483	37.5	11.1
1941	2,703	49.7	12.8
1951	2,682	69.7	16.1

Note: 'urban' and 'towns' denote places of 5,000+.

Source: L. and P. Vinaria, 'Population (1757–1947)', ch. v of D. Kumar and M. Desai (eds.), *The Cambridge Economic History of India, Volume 2: c. 1757–c. 1970* (Cambridge, 1983), p. 519.

Table E. *Urbanization in India: The fifteen largest cities in India in 1941 and their rank, 1891–1941*

City	1891 Population	1891 Rank	1901 Population	1901 Rank	1911 Population	1911 Rank	1921 Population	1921 Rank	1931 Population	1931 Rank	1941 Population	1941 Rank
Calcutta, Bengal	744,249	2	921,380	1	1,013,143	1	1,046,300	2	1,163,771	1	2,108,891	1
Bombay, Bombay	821,764	1	776,006	2	979,445	2	1,175,914	1	1,161,383	2	1,489,883	2
Madras, Madras	452,518	3	509,346	3	518,660	3	526,911	3	647,230	3	777,481	3
Hyderabad, Hyd.	415,039	4	448,466	4	500,623	4	404,187	4	466,894	4	739,159	4
Lahore, Punjab	176,854	9	202,964	8	228,687	7	281,781	5	429,747	5	671,659	5
Ahmedabad, Bombay	144,451	14	181,774	11	214,000	8	270,775	6	310,000	7	591,267	6
Delhi, Delhi	189,648	8	206,534	7	229,144	6	248,259	7	347,539	6	521,849	7
Cawnpore, United Provs.	194,048	7	202,797	9	178,557	12	216,436	9	243,755	11	487,324	8
Amritsar, Punjab	136,766	15	162,429	14	152,756	14	160,218	15	264,840	9	391,010	9
Lucknow, United Provs.	264,953	5	256,239	5	252,114	5	240,566	8	274,659	8	387,177	10
Howrah, Bengal	116,606	22	157,594	15	179,006	11	195,301	12	224,873	13	397,292	11
Karachi, Sind	98,195	25	108,644	24	140,511	16	201,691	10	247,791	10	359,492	12
Nagpur, Cent. Provs.	117,014	21	127,734	19	101,415	25	145,193	17	215,165	14	301,957	13
Agra, United Provs.	168,662	11	188,022	10	185,449	10	185,532	13	229,764	12	284,149	14
Banares, United Provs.	223,375	6	213,079	6	203,804	9	198,447	11	205,315	15	263,100	15

Source: K. Davis, *The Population Of India And Pakistan* (Princeton, New Jersey, 1951), p. 132.

The Dilemmas of Dominion

Table F. *Industrialization in India: average daily number of operatives employed in factories*

Year	Number	Total Population (in millions):	
1892	316,816	282.1	(1891)
1897	421,545		
1902	541,634	285.3	(1901)
1907	729,663		
1912	869,643	303.0	(1911)
1917	1,076,201		

Note: 'factory' here indicates concerns employing 50+ hands. Some of these workers would only have been seasonally employed in factories, e.g. in tea and jute concerns.

Source: D.H. Buchanan, *The Development Of Capitalistic Enterprise In India* (New York, 1934, London, 1966), p. 139.

K. Davis, *The Population Of India And Pakistan* (Princeton, New Jersey, 1951), p. 27.

Table G. *Industrialization in India: origin of net domestic product in Rs. billion*

Year	Agriculture, forestry, and fishing	Mining, manufacturing, and small enterprises	Other	Net domestic product
1900	13.1	2.7	6.9	22.7
1905	13.9	3.0	7.2	24.1
1910	16.3	3.0	7.7	26.9
1915	16.3	3.0	7.8	27.1

Source: A. Maddison, *Class Structure and Economic Growth. India and Pakistan since the Moghuls* (London, 1971), p. 167.

services, while their life experiences were moulded by traditional values and patterns of relationship. At the beginning of the twentieth century about 72 per cent of the male work force were engaged in agricultural and allied rural activities; with only 9.5 per cent in manufacturing and 5.8 per cent in trade and commerce. Statistics can at best only mark the bald outlines and extent of change in society. We need to enquire deeper if the evidence permits, to discover who were the new urban men, both factory labourers and industrial magnates. Were they foreigners or Indians, men launching into new fields or modifying traditional working patterns?

Much misunderstanding, almost amounting to historical myth, surrounds the emergence of India's early industrial labour force. It is often said that recruitment of factory labour was difficult because Indians' mobility was inhibited by their caste occupations and reluctance to leave their place of birth; that recruits were rural migrants who never felt committed to town life or factory work, and would return to their family fields for planting and harvesting. Some have argued that the problems of attracting and organizing a reliable work force were so great that they were a real barrier to industrial growth. Our evidence for migration from countryside to town is unfortunately unreliable, as the decennial census figures tend to distort the true picture for a number of reasons. But for 26 cities figures are available for inhabitants who were born outside the city—figures which give some idea of the influx of workers. In 1931 the average for these 26 cities was 37.3 per cent of their population born elsewhere. Bombay, one of the major new industrial cities, had an even more striking figure for its migrants: by 1921 84 per cent of its people had been born outside the city.[15]

Studies of several industrial centres confirm this picture of migration to towns for factory work. In Bombay City, for example, most of the mill-hands came from the surrounding Presidency, many from quite long distances; and in time some even came from the United Provinces. The chief city of Gujarat, Ahmedabad, in the north of Bombay Presidency, was another industrial centre, which became known as the Manchester of India. There, too, mill-hands were mainly migrants. In 1926 only 20 per cent of them had been born in the city itself; but three years later the owners reckoned that 80 per cent of their labour was drawn from within fifty miles of the city. Many of them had no land, occupation or prospects in village life. In Bengal's jute mills by the early twentieth century migrant labourers from UP, Bihar, Orissa, Madras, and CP outnumbered Bengalis: and most came from social groups with few resources and prospects in their villages. The Bombay evidence, too, suggests that many of those who left for the city had no land. Contrary to the conventional view, they appear to have had a real commitment to their new life and homes, spent much of their working lives in the cotton industry, and did not return seasonally to their villages or prove a particularly unstable work force. Nor does the evidence suggest that caste in the sense of *jati* divisions inhibited labour recruitment or the willingness of the new factory hands to work alongside men from a wide range of castes. The exception was the Untouchable work-force who appear in both places to have been excluded from the weaving processes in deference to caste weavers' fears of pollution. Those above the Untouchability line were prepared to work together; though it is improbable that such tolerance extended to the home situation, or broke down patterns of acceptance and avoidance in eating, drinking, social contact and supremely, marriage. The degree of social change involved in the creation of an industrial work-force was therefore limited. But a sizeable, permanent urban proletariat was emerging; though often its members appear merely to have exchanged membership of a rural proletariat for that of an urban one.[16]

The evidence is as complex when we investigate the owners and financiers of these industrial developments. But here there is a clear distinction between western and eastern India, to take two of the main centres of industrialization.[17] (Regional patterns of recent economic change can be as varied as regional patterns of landholding and caste distribution: and in all cases continental generalization is difficult, particularly where evidence from case studies is not available.) On the Bengal side a large proportion of the new enterprises were owned and managed by Europeans. A few examples from 1911 show this. In Bengal and Assam together, 652 tea plantations were owned by Europeans and only 30 by Indians. In Bengal 49 jute mills were owned by Europeans and none by Indians; while 53 collieries were owned by European companies, 21 by companies whose directors were Indian and European, and 6 by Indian companies. Englishmen and a large contingent of Scots controlled the main industries and financed them, and minimized competition among themselves; through their Chambers of Commerce and trade associations, but particularly through the system of Managing Agency Houses. By this contrivance of business organization which developed to meet the particular business needs and problems of Europeans in India, an Agency House provided not only part of the capital but also management services for many separate companies straddling a wide range of industries and foreign trade. At the beginning of the twentieth century seven such Houses controlled 55 per cent of the jute companies, 61 per cent of the tea companies and 46 per cent of the coal companies in India. It seems to have been this tight expatriate grip which effectively hindered Indians in eastern India from moving into these main industrial concerns, rather than barriers of caste or traditional ideas of status tied to landowning. In other parts of the subcontinent Indians had no hesitation in breaking into new fields of economic enterprise. Even in the Bengali hinterland, where the Agency Houses had little interest or influence, there were Indian entrepreneurs who displayed acute financial sense and skill in exploiting new opportunities and diversifying their activities beyond any single 'traditional role'. One rural family whose fortunes have been traced over several generations combined landholding, money-lending, shopkeeping, warehousing, road and building contracting for government, and in the late nineteenth century mica and coal mining.[18] Other larger landowners were also investing in such ventures as pottery works and sugar factories. But it was not until the First World War and its economic aftermath that the expatriate hold over Calcutta's industry and eastern India's main foreign trade was loosened and Indians moved in in strength.

In western India Indians and expatriates had from the beginnings of the new industries worked in collaboration; and Europeans never had such an exclusive hold either in industrial or foreign trading ventures as they did in the east. In 1911, for example, in Bombay Presidency, of the factories in which different stages of cotton processing took place, 25 were owned by Europeans, 184 by Indians, and 38 by companies directed by Indians and Europeans. Indians predominated in flour and rice mills, and only in railway workshops were Europeans in total control. But even this Indian involvement did not imply radical social change through the movement of erstwhile agriculturalists into industry, or the dramatic rise to wealth of new groups. For those Indians who turned to the new opportunities tended to be groups with long traditions of business enterprise. In Bombay Presidency the main groups were Parsis and Vanias, though some Brahmins and men from agricultural castes also owned and managed industrial ventures, particularly those connected with cotton. The Parsis of Bombay City, for example, had a long connection with ship-building, ship-owning, and trade, and close ties with the British. In Ahmedabad there was a Vania élite of families with generations of experience in trade and financial operations: and it was they who invested in Ahmedabad's mill industry. In so doing they felt no sense of cultural strain, nor did they dislodge the old urban society. As a recent observer commented, 'They were men who remained within their castes, faithful to their religious obligations and generous in their charities.'[19] They continue in such cultural and economic dominance of Ahmedabad even in the late twentieth century.

The limits of India's industrialization in the late nineteenth century and the slow entry of Indians in many regions into industrial enterprise have become the subjects of a historiographical controversy. In the later stages of the imperial relationship they also became a political brickbat thrown by Indians who held the imperial government and its policies responsible for the limited economic change. In particular it is alleged that government purchase of stores favoured British firms and goods, and that tariffs protected British industries while strangling infant Indian industries which might have competed with them. From 1883 onwards government rules on buying stores encouraged the purchase of locally made goods, not least because it was cheaper than buying in London when the rupee was weak against the pound. But most of the manufactured stores ordered did come from abroad—to the tune of Rs. 13.9 million in 1917–18; and practically all these from Britain. Iron and steel goods, for example, were still bought from Britain, as were railway locomotives. Moreover, major government contracts tended to go within India to European rather than Indian firms. Government tariff policy was determined by a wide range of considerations, including the need to encourage imports, because customs duties were a more popular source of revenue than direct taxation. Officials certainly did not believe it was their duty to foster and cosset Indian industry: but nor did they think they should favour British business at the expense of its potential Indian rivals, although this is often alleged. However, one very substantial British group, the Lancashire cotton industry, did manage to secure preferential treatment in 1894 by means of a countervailing excise on Indian cotton manufactures when a general tariff of 5 per cent was imposed. They seem to have succeeded because of their peculiar leverage in British political life just at a time when the Secretary of State for India was increasing his power in relation to the Viceroy and the Government of India. Lancashire's success should not be seen as evidence of general Government of India discrimination in favour of British interests. This particular decision did not favour other sections of British commercial life, such as the manufacturers of textile machinery who needed their Indian market, or the British who were heavily involved in Bombay's cotton industry. Government did not see its role as a positive one of engineering India's industrialization. But without such action any major economic transformation of the subcontinent was unlikely. The one Asian country which did achieve such a breakthrough was Japan, where the government was the prime mover by means of direct intervention, tariff, and taxation policies.[20]

Other 'explanations' for India's limited industrial growth rest on interpretations of Indian society which emphasize, for example, caste and the joint family as inhibiting factors, traditional ideas of status, or belief in *karma*. But the evidence already quoted in this chapter suggests the contrary. Where urban work appeared profitable labour was forthcoming. Where profits were to be made in new fields Indian entrepreneurs were found, unless Europeans were clearly blocking their way. Studies of those who moved into new enterprises suggest that neither Hindu values nor family structure nor caste status inhibited innovation and keen business sense.[21] We must look deeper than simplistic theories which 'blame' particular ideas or institutions, and ask more fundamental questions about the workings of India's economy and its potential for self-generated and self-sustaining change. The availability of capital and the level of consumer demand were of crucial importance. India was a poor society and its people could ill afford many manufactured goods. Moreover, traditional financial institutions in the agrarian and trading sectors of the economy seldom seem to have been willing or efficient agents for transfer of capital to new industrial enterprise, not least because existing patterns of investment still yielded substantial profits. Indeed, changes in India's vast rural economy made some of these even more attractive prospects.

In discerning trends in rural economic changes it is tempting but hazardous to make all-India generalizations. Change certainly occurred in places like the Punjab quite dramatically; but some areas remained isolated, barely touched by new influences, locked in a subsistence economy where the exchange of goods and services was still not monetized. Whatever developments took place India remained extremely poor in absolute and relative terms. It was estimated that in 1895 the *per capita* income in India was £2.65, compared with a figure of £36.94 in Great Britain.

Yet extraordinarily powerful forces were at work, disrupting many of the old balances and patterns of rural society. The expansion in communications made possible production for markets far wider than a localized cluster of villages; and this in turn enabled specialization in the growth of particular products and the spread of money exchange. The new markets might be other rural areas, the growing towns whose inhabitants needed feeding, or the wider markets of Europe and America.

But nothing could grow without water. The lack of rivers and wells, and the unpredictability of the monsoon might make it impossible for Indian farmers to feed themselves, let alone provide for other people. Irrigation was the remedy: it could provide an area with a predictable, constant water supply, and in places could increase productivity by making double-cropping possible. For centuries India's people and rulers had seen the significance of irrigation, and had invested in wells, artificial lakes known as 'tanks', and some large-scale works. In the early nineteenth century the British had attempted to remodel some of these older irrigation works with the benefit of more modern scientific expertise; and in the middle years of the century they embarked on new projects, either under the aegis of government and the direct expenditure of official revenue, or by private companies. Disastrous famines and the financial failures of private companies which undertook works led in 1867 to a new policy—that productive irrigation works should be financed by public loans. Thereafter irrigation forged ahead, the spectre and actuality of famine being an added impetus to the official recognition that a stable and prosperous Indian dominion could only rest on secure agriculture. At the end of the century the most ambitious enterprise was undertaken. Previously irrigation had been designed to improve existing agricultural areas. Now in the Punjab arid tracts were watered by a network of canals, and canal colonies created to be farmed by migrants of proven agricultural background and repute. By 1903 about 19.5 per cent of cultivated land in British India was irrigated; 10.9 per cent in the areas under princely rule. Canals were by now the major source of irrigation, followed by wells, then tanks. By 1914 virtually all the northern Indian rivers had been tapped by canals. In 1940 roughly one-fifth of the cultivated land of British India was irrigated—50 to 60 million acres. In places the results were spectacular—Punjab being the show-piece. Elsewhere, as in UP, there was a steady rise in the prosperity and security of those involved in agriculture where canal water was available. Nor does it seem that the resulting expansion of commercial crops occurred at the expense of basic food grains. As with railway construction, canal building, too, had unforeseen ecological repercussions—disturbances of water levels leading to the destruction of wells, flooding and swamping, and an increase in malaria spread by mosquitoes breeding in stagnant water. Canal irrigation could also precipitate surface salinity, rendering soil infertile. But such side effects were not uniform: and over all canal irrigation led to marked agricultural growth.[22]

Another major force making for change was the rise in population. The first general census took place in 1871 and figures for population before then are informed 'guesstimates'. In 1600 the population may have numbered about 100 million, and in the mid-nineteenth century somewhere nearer 200 million. Thereafter the figure rose to 305.7 million in 1921.[23] The most dramatic upswing only occurred after 1920; a result of a falling death rate combined with a high birth rate. Before 1920 the death rate was very high particularly because of the incidence of famine, and the ravages of epidemics of such killer diseases as cholera, smallpox, malaria, and influenza. Life expectancy very low: throughout the later nineteenth century an Indian's expectation of life at birth was under 25 years. The growth of population began to affect relationships within rural society by altering the man–land ratio. Even taking into account the use of land which was previously waste or unirrigated, acreage per head began to fall. As this happened not only was there the problem of actually feeding the larger numbers. Rural relations were thrown out of balance in different ways according to the ecology of each particular area. Sometimes labouring and service castes were squeezed out of rural work and thrown on the unpredictable and insecure urban job market. Often tenants found their ties with their landlords increasingly restrictive, as their masters attempted to capitalize on rising agricultural prices, and as the absence of vacant land closed the path of literal escape via migration which had often been a peasant option in earlier centuries. It is hard to quantify this change in the balance between men and land, and of course an all-India figure tells us little about the fortunes of a particular region or village. But between 1891–2 and 1939–40 the number of acres per person engaged in agriculture fell by 15 per cent from 2.23 to 1.90. In one Punjabi village studied from 1848 to 1968 increasing population led to a *per capita* decrease in agricultural land and a decline in the size of holdings. In 1848 the *per capita* acreage was 0.95: by 1891 it had dropped to 0.59. In Bombay Presidency however, increases in land under cultivation kept ahead of population growth until *c.* 1930.[24]

The working of such motors of change in the countryside produced some clear trends. But over one basic trend there is major academic controversy and little likelihood of its resolution until much more research has been done—that is, whether agricultural output grew substantially or was keeping pace with the rising population. One scholar hazarded successively estimates of a 3 per cent increase, a 16.6 per cent increase, and a 28.9 per cent increase in crop output between 1893 and 1946; and this was a period when population increased by 46 per cent. If this was true Indians' food resources would have been cut dramatically. In the absence of evidence of such a drastic cut perhaps a more realistic estimate is that in the early twentieth century at least, when the population explosion really began, agricultural output rose roughly in line with population.[25]

The sobering fact for historians is that the apparently impressive statistics on agriculture collected for the Government of India are suspect until at least the third decade of the twentieth century. Records of the actual *areas* under crops probably underestimated acreage because the Indian officials who did the local reporting were ill-paid, poorly supervised, and were often subject to the influence of substantial agriculturalists whose interest was frequently to disguise the extent of their income. Furthermore, it was impossible to assess *yields* from crops until there was scientific measurement and sampling. These skills were only introduced by Sir John Hubback, Bihar's Director of Land Records, 1923–4; and his methods were neither used nor fully understood for several decades. In the 1860s one official in the Punjab admitted that the statistics for areas and yields were 'so manifestly erroneous, that it has been thought advisable to omit the return on the present occasion.' Yet another hazard of continental statistics is that they mask considerable local variations: the poverty of Bihar or Bengal, for example, being masked by great developments in Punjab. Indeed, even within one province there could be major variations; and, moreover, regions could suffer marked fluctuations in economic well-being. Only regional and local studies can tell us what actually happened in the countryside.[26]

One marked trend in many areas, however, was the growth of commercial agriculture. Farmers responded keenly to the prospect of wider markets, rising prices for their products, and the light burden of taxation on rural incomes. In the Punjab village of Vilyatpur, for example, the dramatic shift in crops happened between 1895 and 1915, when the pulses which formed the villagers' daily diet began to disappear from the fields, to be replaced by wheat, sugar cane, and maize, for both local consumption and sale. Thereafter pulses had to be bought at the market. In neighbouring UP a similar pattern occurred even earlier. Agricultural production increased with the help of canal water; but the increase was in commercial crops (cotton, indigo, sugar cane, and wheat) not in the staple food grains of ordinary people, because farmers were reluctant to use the canal water for which they had to pay on any but the most profitable crops. Further south in Central Provinces the stimulus to commercial agriculture came primarily from the new railway links, in the 1870s between Jubbulpur and Bombay, and in the 1890s between CP and Bengal. The acreage under wheat rose markedly in the 1870s and a very substantial portion of the wheat crop (nearly one-quarter) was exported in peak years. Rice was another crop with which farmers responded to new markets; and in the century's last decade much of the rice went to different parts of India and became a more important commercial crop than wheat. Non-food crops were also grown

more widely except in times of bad weather. In 1871–6 they covered about
12.2 per cent of the province's total cultivated area, and 17.2 per cent in
1911–16. Oil seeds were a dramatic example of the changes new communications could precipitate. Instead of being an importer of oil seeds CP
began to export them, and particularly the bulk of the linseed crop, to
Europe's Mediterranean ports. Cotton, too, was always an important export crop and an increasing proportion of it went abroad—over 90 per cent
in the early twentieth century. But even within the province certain areas
took advantage of new opportunities to specialize in crops particularly
suited to their terrain and climate, and, for example, invested in wheat crops
rather than cotton.

However it was rare that such new agricultural opportunities benefited
those at the base of rural society, or markedly affected older patterns of
social stratification. The case studies of certain rural areas which are available make this clear, particularly the evidence they give of rural dominance
and the availability of credit in rural society. For without capital or credit
farmers could not take advantage of new supplies of water or risk investing
in commercial crops; let alone pay their revenue dues or meet their inevitable expenses at times like marriages. Indebtedness was a feature of much
Indian peasant life which greatly concerned the British. But it was almost
inescapable for the majority, given the hazards of weather and disease, the
inexorably regular revenue demand, and the social pressure for expenditure
on certain ritual occasions, all of which occurred in the context of a basically
poor economy. Sources of credit were diverse. Some caste groups specialized in money-lending, often using the profits of trade for this purpose. Such
professionals disliked having to foreclose on land and actually work it, as
they were not agriculturalists, and because the combined social pressure of
a village and its leaders could make life extremely difficult for an unwel-
come outsider. Far more important were the wide range of wealthier farmers who lent money to poorer villagers both for profit and for such social
considerations as building up a village following. Often lending was the only
way of investing small sums in the nineteenth century, for there was no
stock market, and no building societies, post office savings accounts or
modern banks where country folk could put spare cash on deposit. Lending
could be very profitable; the high rates of interest reflected the intention of
the creditors to acquire income rather than secure repayment of the original
loan. In such circumstances there was little incentive for countrymen to
seek out new patterns of investment, least of all in towns where they had no
kinsmen and no control over the way their money might be used. Government itself provided some credit, through loans, advances of cash for the
purchase of seed, plough cattle, and the construction of wells. But the rules
governing loans were tight; they only went to those with impeccable security, and they were consequently useless to the poorest peasants whose need

was often sudden and pressing. Even the Co-operative Societies, which began a halting progress in the later nineteenth century with official blessing, did not challenge existing professional and side-line lending as the main sources of credit. As late as 1930 Bombay's Co-operatives probably only met about 4 per cent of the Presidency's rural credit needs.[27]

With such scant new provision for credit poor peasants could not break out of the vicious circle of poverty and indebtedness, and were forced to rely on their social and economic superiors in the village. It was often these groups with established positions of rural dominance who did best from the new opportunities in rural life. They not only profited from lending 'downwards' in village society. They also had the security on which to borrow from professionals, government, and Co-operative Societies; and they were able to take the risks and make the investments necessary in exploiting the expanding field of commercial agriculture. This trend emerged in parts of Madras, for example, between 1878 and the late 1920s. Rising grain prices and growing demand for cash crops increased the wealth and social leverage of the dominant families who combined agriculture and money-lending. Eventually such men became a regional élite, drawn by these forces into wider economic, social, and religious connections throughout the Presidency. In Maharashtra, too, the last twenty years of the nineteenth century seem to have been a crucial time for the sharpening of existing social divisions; as the richer peasants profited from cash cropping, better communications, and irrigation. They then had the freedom to manoeuvre in response to the market, in stark contrast to the heavily indebted. Maharashtrian evidence suggested that some achieved new wealth from a position of comparative poverty and weakness. This happened to a Poona caste of gardeners who prospered on the profits of sugar cane at the turn of the century, because they cultivated and leased land watered by new canals. But evidence from UP suggested yet again that in the later nineteenth century it was not the ordinary cultivators who profited from canals and commercial agriculture, but the various *maliks*, or village notables, who in turn further dominated the poorer in the villages with their loans and their customary, if illegal, dues and perks.[28] Overall the picture of India's countryside by the end of the century showed some marked technical and agricultural changes. But the many were still trapped in deep poverty, struggling to subsist and feed their families, while the few prospered and increased their social and economic dominance in their local communities.

The poverty of so many and the profits to be made in the countryside by those who had cash or access to credit go a long way to explaining why there was so little transfer of capital from rural to urban sectors, from agriculture to industry. We know very little about the working of India's networks of trade and finance in the late nineteenth century. But evidence so far available suggests that where trade and finance were not in foreign hands they ran along traditional grooves, benefiting established groups who responded to the potential of the new situation. The most sophisticated level of banking and trade rested on overseas shipping, and was mainly in European hands, particularly the most lucrative trades in jute, tea, opium, and later in coal. In western India Indians owned some ships; and there trade in cotton, yarn, and locally produced opium was in Indian hands. Overseas shipping was mainly financed by exchange banks which had head offices outside India and were in European hands. Most of the capital in these institutions came from outside India, but some Indian money was also deposited with them. The next tier was composed of the major import/export firms and the Joint Stock Banks which until the first decade of the new century were also run by expatriates. Of these the Presidency Banks of Bengal, Bombay, and Madras were the most prominent. They did not deal overseas, and drew most of their money from within India. It is unclear how far such banks had penetrated deeper into the economy and begun to help finance internal trade. But beneath them was a third level, the indigenous banking system, which provided the bulk of credit for India's expanding internal trade in food and non-food stuffs. *Shroffs*, Indian bankers, organized far more loosely than the western-style banks, lent to cultivators and up-country traders using their own internal trade bills, in much the same way as they had done for centuries. Through their networks much of the profit made in rural trade and marketing was kept within the traditional investment and financial sector, and never found its way into westernized financial institutions or was deployed in the modern, industrial enclaves of the economy. From the point of view of economic development India's economy and traditional financial institutions fitted *too well* into the new economic scene. India provided the raw materials other parts of the world required, and herself needed foreign manufacturered imports. Existing financial institutions topped with a sophisticated superstructure manned by foreigners enabled and serviced this exchange and the domestic production and exchange on which it rested. Consequently there was little need or impetus for radical change.

Nor did the expansion of internal and overseas trade in this framework significantly alter the distribution of power, wealth, and status in Indian society. Much of the profit from overseas trade went into British pockets: while those Indians who did well were almost certainly the numerous middlemen who handled the commercial crops as they passed between regions or from the fields to the ports, as well as the small groups of dominant cultivators. 'New' groups do not appear to have broken into trade and financing. Instead, established families and caste groups with generations of financial experience, resulting in expertise, capital, and 'good standing' among those they dealt with, adjusted to the new opportunities. Each region had its own groups of this kind, and there were some all-India communities who spanned the subcontinent with their closely linked members. Most visible of these were the Marwaris, originally money-lenders and traders from Rajputana, who fanned out through the country as merchants, bankers, and small industrialists in enterprises which complemented their trade in agricultural products, like cotton processing. But they did not invest in modern large-scale industry until the twentieth century. Traditional social structure, and established patterns of economic relations, production, and exchange proved capable of adapting to new opportunities. So the economic changes of the later nineteenth century were *accommodated*, rather than wrenching Indian society up by its roots or radically disturbing the economy.

Far more obvious to contemporaries as a source of far-reaching change, and of consequent disturbance in the context of the imperial relationship, were the emerging patterns of education and the employment of those who received it. Government was deeply concerned about Indian education, for obvious economic and political as well as 'social' reasons. But its resources were painfully limited, given the sheer numbers of Indian children and a starting base of mass illiteracy. Education policy therefore required careful decisions on spending strategy. Until mid-century the 'downward filtration' theory was the mainspring of official thinking; but by then the failure of the Anglicists' hopes and the fading of the more sanguine reformers' vision of a transformed India led to a re-direction of official effort. Sir Charles Wood's Education Despatch of 1854 indicated that government was now abandoning the strategy of providing *only* higher education, and had realized that it must actively promote mass education using vernaculars as the medium of instruction. It saw its duty as the creation of a total system of education from primary school to university. The key to financing this was to enter into co-operation with private educational enterprise by means of grants-in-aid. Consequently Departments of Education were established in all provinces, and in 1871 they came under the control of provincial governments, but with a fixed assignment from the central revenues. Although government increasingly saw the need for help to mass education it did not cease in its concern for the growth and regulation of higher education; and in the same year as the Mutiny it founded India's first three universities, in Calcutta, Madras, and Bombay.[29]

The pattern of educational development did not, however, differ significantly from that which had emerged since the Anglicists' triumph in 1835. Educational facilities and the numbers attending them certainly expanded more rapidly. But still the trends were towards marked growth in higher education, atop a base of primary and secondary schools which was not only weak in proportion to the population but expanded more slowly than the college sector. Figures indicating this uneven expansion and the resulting literacy rates are given in Tables H–K. The number of India's highly edu-

The Dilemmas of Dominion

Table H. *Percentage of population in British India being educated in recognized institutions, 1917*

	Population: (1921)	% being educated: (1917)
Total	247,333,423	2.96
Males	127,044,953	4.85
Females	120,288,470	0.97

Source: 1929 Interim Report on Education, p. 22.

cated is further indicated by the statistics for those who passed and failed university entrance and university examinations. In the period 1864–85, 48,251 passed the university entrance examination and 79,509 failed: 12,518 got through the First Arts Examination but 18,902 failed. Just over 5,000 achieved a BA degree, and rather more failed; while 708 attained MA status and 464 failed. By the beginning of the twentieth century there were nearly 30,000 Indian graduates, roughly 1 to every 10,000 of the population.[30]

India's educated were drawn from distinctive segments of society, and predominantly from those areas where the British had been longest established and educational provision had accompanied the growth of administrative and commercial cities. Table K shows how far ahead the Presidencies of Madras, Bombay, and Bengal were, when compared with India's other provinces, in rates of literacy; and Table I shows the greater proportion of children of school age actually at school in those three areas. Tables

Table I. *Percentage of population of school age receiving primary education in British India, 1917*

	Boys	Girls
British India	30.3	6.7
Madras	39.2	10.1
Bombay	37.2	9.7
Bengal	39.8	9.2
UP	19.2	1.9
Punjab	20.5	2.4
Bihar and Orissa	25.7	4.1
CP	29.1	3.7
Assam	36.5	6.0

Source: 1929 Interim Report on Education, p. 43.

Table J. *Growth of education in Arts Colleges in British India, 1870–91*

	1870–1		1881–2		1886–7		1891–2	
	Colleges	Pupils	Colleges	Pupils	Colleges	Pupils	Colleges	Pupils
Bengal	16	1,374	21	2,738	27	3,215	34	5,225
Bombay	5	297	6	475	9	955	9	1,332
Madras	11	418	24	1,669	31	2,979	35	3,818
NWP & O	8	165	6	349	12	478	12	1,311
Punjab	2	102	1	103	3	319	6	462
CP	—	—	1	65	3	100	3	232

Source: A. Seal, *The Emergence Of Indian Nationalism. Competition and Collaboration in the Later Nineteenth Century* (Cambridge, 1968), p. 19.

I and K also indicate how backward women were in education, even in the three Presidencies.

Other social distinctions of marked significance in relation to education were caste and religious community. Those whose families saw the worth of the new education and could afford it tended to come from the higher castes with traditions of literacy and learning. Neither the very wealthy nor the very poor sent their sons to the new schools and colleges: the former because they had no need of the fruits of education, the latter because they could not afford it, and needed their children to labour in the fields or help in the fathers' craft or service. In 1881–2, for example, in 15 Bengal colleges 159 out of 1,870 pupils came from the wealthiest Presidency families: the

Table K. *Literacy in British India in the early twentieth century*

	Percentage of literates			
	1911		1921	
	Men	Women	Men	Women
British India	11.3	1.1	13.0	1.8
Madras	13.8	1.35	15.2	2.1
Bombay	12.1	1.5	14.1	2.5
Bengal	14.0	1.1	15.9	1.8
UP	6.1	0.5	6.5	0.6
Punjab	6.5	0.6	6.7	0.8
Bihar and Orissa	8.0	0.4	8.8	0.6
CP	6.8	0.3	8.4	0.7
Assam	8.8	0.6	11.0	1.3

Source: *1929 Interim Report on Education*, p. 145.

Table L. *Education among the Depressed Classes (1922)*

	Population of depressed classes (in millions)	No. of depressed classes receiving education
Madras	6.53	157,113
Bombay	1.46	36,543
Bengal	6.64	96,552
UP	7.89	39,873
Punjab	1.70	3,732
Bihar and Orissa	2.53	15,096
CP	3.01	28,919

Source: *1929 Interim Report on Education*, p. 218.

rest came from families with middle-size incomes, but not from the labouring and agricultural families who were the vast majority of the population. In the same decade an Indian from CP commented, 'If the history of our smartest graduates and public men were enquired into, it would be found that they were, with very few exceptions, children of persons who had struggled hard to make the little savings which obtained high education for their sons.'[31] The extreme educational deprivation of the Untouchables or 'depressed classes', as they were officially known, was clear. (See Table L.) Not only poverty but the risk of polluting high-caste children kept them outside the doors of schools and colleges. Even well into the twentieth century higher caste parents withdrew their children from one village school in UP when an Untouchable child was admitted. Where such despised children did manage to attend school their drop-out rate was very high; and few reached college level.

Indian Muslims were also backward in terms of western education; a fact which concerned both the community and the government. It gave rise to various explanatory theories such as the one that Muslims by virtue of their beliefs and political background were specially hostile to the new education. In the 1880s just under 4 per cent of college students were Muslims, though they were over 22 per cent of the population. Nearly 90 per cent of students were Hindus, though Hindus were only just over 73 per cent of the population. The disproportion between Hindus and Muslims was marked at lower levels in the educational system, though not as much as at college level. By the start of the twentieth century Muslims were also less literate than Hindus—6 per cent of Muslim men compared with 10.2 per cent of Hindu men. Muslims, however, were not a homogeneous community: in some areas they were a minority, in others a majority; some groups were low caste converts, while others had established political and economic status in their localities. Their educational position varied accordingly, rather than being any uniform continental phenomenon explicable in terms

Table M. *Regional variations in Muslim access to education (1917)*

	% of Muslims to total population	% of Muslim students to total students
British India	23.5	23.2
Madras	6.6	11.1
Bombay	20.4	19.2
Bengal	52.7	45.0
UP	14.1	18.2
Punjab	54.8	40.8
Bihar and Orissa	10.6	13.0
CP	4.1	9.2
Assam	28.1	23.8

Source: *1929 Interim Report on Education*, p. 187.

solely of religion. In Bengal, for example, where they had been converted from the lower ranks of Hindu society they shared educational deprivation with the lower Hindu castes who remained. In UP, where they had considerable local standing, their educational position was far in advance of their numbers. But it must also be remembered that in northern India where Muslims had a strong position there was less provision for education than in the Presidencies, where Muslims were not a significant élite. This fact helped to depress their all-India educational performance. Table M shows the regional variations in Muslim educational achievement, showing the proportion of Muslims to total pupils and of Muslims to the whole population.

The fruits which Indian students and their parents hoped to pluck from the tree of education were gainful and prestigious employment. Most of them had no entrée into the indigenous world of business, nor the talent and capital to break into new business enterprises. In many areas they had few connections with land, or were rentiers whose rents were insufficient for a livelihood, and many would have considered farming ritually polluting. So they looked to government service and expanding modern professions, law, medicine, teaching, and journalism, for their livelihood. Of the 1,712 Indian graduates of Calcutta University between 1857 and 1882 over one third went into government service. Law was the best organized of the professions. It attracted many members, and offered both prestige and to the successful high monetary reward. In the same period, 1857–82, over one third of Calcutta University graduates went into various branches of the legal profession, slightly more than those who opted for an administrative career. The hurdles and pitfalls, however, between the aspirant graduate and a successful career were many. The antipathies and frustrations generated, among those who had access to the new education, were as much part of the changing context of Indians' relationship with the British and each other as was the new education itself and its uneven spread over regions and social groups.

The clearest case of the frustrated were those who failed the university entrance examinations, and those who failed somewhere within the university system. Poor teaching at every level, lack of fluent English, and a tendency to cram answers for examinations was partly responsible for the high failure rates. Our evidence has already hinted at the magnitude of the problem between 1864 and 1885. Thirty years later BA and BSc passes were running at 62 per cent in Madras, 72 per cent in Bombay, 60 per cent in Bengal, 43 per cent in UP and 35 per cent in Punjab.[32] Yet these lads considered themselves educated. They had passed through school and college, had set their hopes on status and employment befitting the educated, and now found themselves without qualifications and jobs. (So desperate was their plight that 'failed BA' was a 'qualification' paraded by those in search of work even in the twentieth century.) Unemployment began to be a real problem even for those who had passed their examinations. The Lieutenant-Governor of Bengal wrote in 1877, 'It is melancholy to see men who once appeared to receive their honours in the university convocation, now applying for some lowly-paid appointment, almost begging from office to office, from department to department, or struggling for the practice of a petty practitioner, and after all this returning baffled and disheartened to a poverty-stricken home . . .' The following year a Calcutta paper noted the thousands of educated men coming on to the job market annually, only to find that government service and the professions were becoming over-crowded. 'What are they to do is the question of the hour.'[33] Indians were vital in the lower echelons of the bureaucracy and were not debarred from the ICS. But in practice Europeans predominated in the Covenanted Service as well as in other well paid government posts. By 1887 only a dozen Indians had entered the ICS through open competition; and from 1904 to 1913 only 5 per cent of the new entrants were Indian—27 compared with 501 Europeans. Access to the poorer-paid government posts was fiercely competitive. Similarly in law, the most profitable and prestigious of the professions, the doors began to close in the last quarter of the century, as the universities produced more lawyers than could earn a reasonable living. The Anglicists' dream of the 'educated native' who would man the administration cheaply and come to share his rulers' sentiments was becoming a nightmare for rulers and ruled. Many of India's western-educated found themselves in the later nineteenth century in an economic strait-jacket, caught between rising prices and badly-paid employment or unemployment. They were fired with a new sense of their indentity and capacity to participate in the government of their country. Yet sharing of ideas and their implementation, which Macaulay and his supporters had anticipated as the natural outcome of the new education, was discouraged by their successors in the later nineteenth century; and the *babu* or Indian clerk became a figure of fun and scorn among many of the British. Yet it was the 'babu explosion' which most obviously altered the context of the imperial relationship, and changed the nature and dimensions of the problem their Indian dominion posed the British, in striking contrast to the comparative simplicity of 1857.

iii Some British and Indian dilemmas

Although we may refer to 'the British', they were not a monolithic group. Indian problems appeared somewhat differently to different interests among them—expatriate businessmen compared with Government of India officials, for example. A factor in all policy-making was the potential and often actual divergence of views and priorities held by men in Calcutta and Whitehall. The fate of the flamboyant Curzon demonstrates such tension within the British ranks. He resigned after bitter conflict with his Commander-in-Chief and with the London government. Equally, if more quietly, indicative of cross-currents among the British was the careful manoeuvring of John Morley, who, as a Liberal Secretary of State, piloted the 1909 scheme of constitutional reform through a Parliament where Tories dominated the House of Lords.

It has been suggested that the events of 1857 radically changed British policies and attitudes towards India across a broad spectrum of issues, including race relations, land settlements, the role of the landed and of Indian princes, peasant indebtedness and social reform. The rulers are depicted as withdrawing, bewildered and disillusioned, into racialism and conservatism; now leaning heavily on India's aristocratic groups and forgetting their earlier zeal for reform of Indian society and manners. But this is much too simple. Policy-making was complex, and influenced by many considerations both in India and Britain. The evidence in this chapter has already suggested that there was much continuity, in people and plans, throughout the 1850s, while some of the most important plans for modernizing reform and education were speeded up and expanded in the later nineteenth century.[34] British relations with the landed in the area of the worst disturbances in 1857 did come under close scrutiny and changed as a result, as we shall note later. But the most pressing problems specifically caused by 1857 were more mundane—the army and government finance. The sepoy mutiny of the Bengal army was so complete and shattering that subsequent army reform was inevitable. As Wood told the Viceroy, Lord Canning, 'I never wish to see again a great Army, very much the same in its feelings and prejudices and connections, confident in its strength, and so disposed to unite in rebellion *together*. If one regiment mutinies, I should like to have the next regiment so alien that it would be ready to fire into it.'[35] Thereafter the number of Indian soldiers was cut drastically—from 238,000 in 1857 to 140,000 in 1863; and the European element was strengthened, from 45,000 to 65,000. The three Presidency armies remained separated, as a strategy of balance. New recruits were drawn from groups who had remained loyal in 1857 and whom the British liked to think of as 'martial races', such as the Punjabi Sikhs or the Gurkhas from Nepal. (The latter still formed part of the British army in the last quarter of the twentieth century; while Sikhs are a dominant group in the army of independent India.) Moreover, new soldiers were put into units on the basis of caste and community, reflecting Wood's fears of another united military revolt. All artillery was henceforth in European hands, and all important military posts were manned by Europeans and Indians.

The Mutiny was also a formidable financial blow, largely because of the vast increase in military expenditure necessary for its suppression. It piled up a debt of over £38 million, increased the government's loan charge by £2 million a year, on top of a deficit on income which in the three years from 1857 to 1859 came to over £30 million. A new Finance Member for the Government of India was imported to reform government finance and retrieve this financial disaster—James Wilson, former businessman, MP, Treasury official, Secretary to the Board of Control, and founder-editor of the financial paper, *The Economist*. One of his favourite expressions was 'economical efficiency'; and though he died within a year of reaching India he started the remodelling of the government's financial system which his successor, Samuel Laing, continued. Its main features were proper annual budgets, a new system of audit and accounts, and the re-organization of the Finance Department, combined with a marked centralization of control over government finance. Another innovation was the introduction of income tax in 1860, to tap incomes unrelated to land, particularly those generated or increased by economic change, those of the businessman, the money-lender or the newly-prosperous lawyer. By 1863 Indian accounts showed a surplus.[36] Yet throughout the later nineteenth century the Government of India relied heavily on land revenue as a source of income, as it and its predecessors had done for centuries: land revenue produced over 40 per cent of its revenue. Opium, salt, customs and excise were significant but less important; and direct income tax made a minute contribution to public funds when compared with the direct demands of modern governments on their citizens. (See Table N.) But imperial dominion as constituted was an expensive mode of government, not least because of the well-paid and pensioned Europeans at the apex of administration, the government's use of the army outside India, and its obligations in London. The main calls on the government's purse were the army (about one third of expenditure),

Table N. *Principal constituent items of Government of India revenue*

	1858–9 %	1860–1 %	1865–6 %	1869–70 %	1870–1 %
Land revenue	50.03	43.1	41.8	41.4	40.1
Opium	17	16.6	17.4	15.6	15.7
Salt	7.2	8.9	10.9	11.6	11.9
Customs	8	9.7	4.7	4.8	5.1
Excise	4.1	4.1	5.3	5.4	5.5
Income/License tax	0.3	2.6	1.4	2.2	4
Stamps	1.6	2.8	4.1	4.7	4.9
Post Office	1.6	1.4	0.8	1.4	1.6
Public Works receipts	1.8	2	1.9	1.9	1.8
Tribute	1.6	1.8	1.5	1.5	1.4
Other heads	6.5	8	10.2	9.5	8

Source: S. Bhattacharyya, *Financial Foundations Of The Raj* (Simla, 1971), p. 292.

civil administration (about one third), public works (about 15 per cent) and interest charges (about one tenth). (See Table O.) Some of this money had to be paid in sterling in London as 'Home Charges' over and above interest payments on the government's sterling debt. At the turn of the century the London bill was about £17 million annually.

Wilson's reforms did not solve the government's long-term financial problems. These continued and were exacerbated by rising prices and, ironically, by the growing efficiency of the administration, staffed by better educated men, including Indians, who expected higher salaries. As govern-

Table O. *Principal constituent items of public expenditure*

	1863–4 %	1865–6 %	1869–70 %	1871–2 %
Army	32.6	36.3	30.06	32.3
Revenue collection charges	21.1	18.5	17.3	17.5
Law and Justice	4.8	5.3	5.4	4.7
General administration	2.2	2.7	2.7	3.7
Superannuation allowance	2.1	2	2.5	2.9
Furlough allowance	0.2	0.2	0.3	0.4
Public Works (ordinary)	12	10.9	10	5.3
Political agencies	0.5	0.5	0.8	0.7
Debt charges	11.2	11.1	11.5	12.3
Other heads	13.3	12.5	18.9	20.2

Source: S. Bhattacharyya, *Financial Foundations Of The Raj* (Simla, 1971), p. 293.

ment strove to make ends meet its policies had major implications for its relations with its subjects—quite apart from the disquiet of educated Indians at the large expenditure on the army and Home Charges, compared with education and economic development. Government's quest for revenue led it deep into the lives of ordinary people in novel ways, making them more conscious of the presence and character of imperial dominion, and often generating discontent which might be channelled into new sorts of anti-government politics. Decreasingly could men believe that government was 'far away'. Land revenue was a case in point. In the 1860s official thinking still favoured a permanent settlement of the revenue demand. It was cheap to administer, was thought likely to attach landholders to government, to encourage agricultural improvement and investment. By the next decade the idea of permanence was abandoned, to enable the *raj* to tap rising values of land and agricultural produce. Periodic re-surveys of land and re-assessment of revenue liabilities were major occasions for rural folk to feel the tightening grip of government, in the physical presence of the survey teams, and sometimes in substantial rises in the revenue demand. But officials were sensitive to tensions within rural society and aware that they must be judicious in exerting pressure on agricultural groups. So they looked elsewhere for revenue; but in so doing they drove deeper into the pockets of other groups of their subjects. Direct taxation was one answer, but it proved highly unpopular. Income tax lasted initially until 1865, and was abandoned so soon because of its unpopularity and comparatively small return. Government tried other direct taxes, such as Licence and Certificate taxes, and in 1869 reverted to income tax. Not surprisingly these and similar imposts goaded a wide range of urban groups into novel political action in protest in the later part of the century, in big cities such as Bombay but also in provincial towns like UP's Allahabad. Similarly when local governments tried to increase the efficiency of their servants, contractors and licencees in the search for economy, they provoked outcry and agitation.[37]

Another tactic in the struggle for solvency was to reverse Wilson's financial centralization and to make local levels of administration responsible for their expenditure. This led in the 1870s to the devolution of some financial power to provincial governments, which then received fixed assignments from the central revenues. The devolution tactic drew the government on to even more local departures in self-government, as power to make local taxes and spend the proceeds was given to municipal and rural boards which included Indians, chosen at first by nomination but increasingly by election. If Indians at this level could be induced to tax themselves it would lighten the load on government and draw the fire of anti-British criticism. It would simultaneously be a means of political education and articulation for Indians which would not endanger the foundations of the *raj*. Such thinking lay behind the development of local self-government by measures such as the UP Municipalities Act of 1868, and the Government of India Resolution on Local Self-Government in 1882 for which the Viceroy of the day, Lord Ripon, has become famous. As his Finance Member baldly noted, 'We shall not subvert the British Empire by allowing the Bengali Baboo to discuss his own schools and drains. Rather shall we afford him a safety-valve if we can turn his attention to such innocuous subjects.'[38] However, even such limited devolution and wider Indian participation in and election to municipal and rural boards embroiled the government still further in its subjects' lives. It *invited* the growth of Indians' concern with a new arena of political action. It also raised the issue of which Indians would be acceptable, both to their compatriots and to their rulers, as 'representative'. In these new political structures British perceptions of Indian society, and the categories such as caste and community they assumed as significant in Indian public life were to become increasingly important, as Indians adapted to the patterns they believed their rulers would accept.

Because so much revenue was spent on the army, finance and external security were inextricable. Earlier in the century the quest for boundary security had led the British into a pragmatic policy of annexation and alliance with Indian princes. In the second half of the century they had dominion throughout the subcontinent south of the Himalayan ranges, and security took on a new meaning. Now the problem was to defend this natural boundary and ensure that the Asian kingdoms bordering India to the north were either friendly or subordinate to British interests. Afghanistan, Tibet, and Burma became the key areas of concern: concern intensified by the persistent fear of Russian influence penetrating south and constricting their freedom in Asia or even threatening their dominion of a subcontinent which was a crucial part of their total imperial enterprise. At this stage China was not an element in the calculations of India's rulers. In the later nineteenth century China was comparatively isolated from the rest of the world by its own choice, and showed neither wish nor capacity to threaten India's north-eastern border. Otherwise the lineaments of India's external security problem as it was to persist beyond independence were emerging, though as yet uncomplicated by more sophisticated military technology, air power and road-building, which made the interference of distant great powers a real possibility rather than an imperialist's fearful fantasy, or by the division of the subcontinent and the emergence of Pakistan.

British frontier policy oscillated between aggression towards these neighbouring states and a diplomatic securing of friendship without troop movements. It depended on the perceptions and style of the current Viceroy, and on the party in power in London. Mayo was the first Viceroy chosen by a Tory government (in 1869), but as he soon had to co-operate with a Liberal government his policies did not demonstrate Conservative predelictions. He pursued a delicate policy of friendship with and non-intervention in Afghanistan. Both he and his successor, Northbrook, made little of potential Russian menace. But when Lytton arrived in 1875 the full force of Conservatism was let loose on India; and on the North-West Frontier led to an attempt to cage the Russian bear back in central Asia by force of arms against Afghanistan. In 1878–9 British force met humiliating disaster when the Resident in Kabul and his entire staff were wiped out. Imperial forces marched north to recompense the Afghans with like brutality. News of the expense and atrocities of this second Afghan war brought down Disraeli's government in 1880. The incoming Liberals withdrew British forces from Afghanistan, and under Ripon and Dufferin reinstated a policy of non-interference and friendship as the best strategy to secure the frontier. Even the Tory Curzon at the close of the century did not revert to the extravagant aggression of Lytton, though he was determined to build a ring-fence round India against Russia. Rather than keep 10,000 troops on the North-West Frontier, as he found in 1899, he planned a controlled 'no man's land' north of the British-administered territory. There tribesmen were paid to police their own areas, their quiescence also secured by the possibility of British lightning swoops from frontier forts, should they forget their obligations.

In the north east security was not so urgent a problem, and India's neighbours were weaker and less belligerent. Despite the massive costs, Burma was swallowed up in 1886 and thereafter administered from India. Tibet escaped the rigours of full conquest and annexation. But after Curzon decided that it, too, must become part of India's ring-fence it received an 'expedition' followed by an 'invasion' in 1903–4; and thereafter was firmly under British influence. Curzon's comments on Tibet in 1901 illuminate his perception of the dilemmas of frontier security.

> It is really the most grotesque and indefensible thing that, at a distance of little more than 200 miles from our frontier, this community of unarmed monks should set us perpetually at defiance; that we should have no means of knowing what is going on there; and that a Russian protectorate may, at no distant date, be declared without our having an inkling of what was passing.
>
> Of course we do not want their country. It would be madness for us to cross the Himalayas and to occupy it. But it is important that no one else should seize it; and that it should be turned into a sort of buffer state between the Russian and Indian Empires. If Russia were to come down to the big mountains, she would at once begin intriguing with Nepal: and we should have a second Afghanistan on the north ... Tibet itself, and not Nepal, must be the buffer that we endeavour to create.[39]

Britain's quest for security on the northern Indian borders succeeded if judged by the simple criterion of maintaining imperial dominion and terri-

torial integrity. But her strategies were often ruinously expensive and consequently attracted Indian criticism. So at a deeper level they increased
British dilemmas within their secured borders; and constricted still further
their ability to meet growing Indian expectations of generous expenditure
on productive projects or education, and to respond with political sensitivity to their subjects.

Increasingly the British found that their dominion in India was no simple
matter of external security and sound administration. As the context of
their rule changed so they were forced to modify their relations with their
subjects, and to face afresh fundamental questions about their role and
obligations in India. Race relations themselves became an issue in an unprecedented way. It is easy to say that social relations between Indians and
Britons deteriorated as a result of the barbarous behaviour of both racial
groups in the course of 1857–8. In 1861 one official commented, 'the sympathy which Englishmen, whether long resident or fresh to India, felt for the
natives has changed to a general feeling of repugnance if not of antipathy';
he felt that his compatriots were now 'disinclined to remain here, or to care
for India, and disposed to look at things in any but an Indian light'.[40] But as
we have seen a far more complex alchemy than a simple reaction to the
Mutiny was at work, distancing the races from each other and generating
some violent conflicts. Racial theories emerging in Europe, the growth of
the English community in India with its distinctive life-style played a part.
So did the arrival of less well-educated expatriates who came to India as
planters or ordinary soldiers but lacked the sense of duty and vocation
which softened the sense of superiority in many ICS men. The racial arrogance and discourtesy of such people was explosive when mixed with the
expectations of western educated Indians who knew their Shakespeare,
Mill, and Carlyle, and who in growing numbers had actually been to England, where they certainly found life strange but rarely experienced the
attitudes which greeted Asian migrants a century later. Discourtesy was
particularly galling to men whose own culture regulated social relations,
even between men of different status, with considerable decorum.

Most Indians did not have much public and professional contact with
British people, and Indian caste conventions as much as British aloofness
meant that social contact was minimal. The foreigner was polluting to the
caste Hindu, at least in the home setting; and the latter would have felt ill at
ease in an English club with its chairs and tables, knives and forks, non-
vegetarian food, alchohol, and the club atmosphere peculiar to the Anglo-
Saxon male. When ICS men met villagers in the pursuit of duty or sport
they tended to respond with a protective warmth: these were their 'charges'
who confirmed rather than threatened their position. To Indian princes and
large landholders they showed elaborate courtesy, out of deliberate policy
as well as deep rooted respect for landed gentry. Racial tension tended to

erupt in relations between educated Indians and non-official British. Sometimes these eruptions were of continental and political significance; as in the case of the controversy and agitation surrounding the Ilbert Bill in 1883. This bill would have done away with the right of Europeans in country areas not to be tried by an Indian judge. As more Indians went into the civil and judicial services this anomaly became a live problem. The bill provoked vituperative and hysterical language and a major publicity campaign in India and Britain from the Anglo-Indian community, particularly the expatriate planters in Bengal whom it would mainly affect. Even European women became involved in the opposition, and their presence and the arguments used showed how understandings of gender were intertwined with assumptions about racial identity. It was said that Indian men were effeminate and therefore unfit to try Europeans; and that Indian men were lustful and therefore a potential threat to European women if given new rights. Yet to give Indian judges inferior status in relation to British offenders was offensive to Ripon, as a dedicated Liberal. It also flew in the face of the 1858 Royal Proclamation which included the pronouncement that all Queen Victoria's subjects, 'of whatever race or creed, be freely and impartially admitted to offices in our service, the duties of which they may be qualified, by their education, ability, and integrity, duly to discharge.'[41] The 'White Mutiny' demonstrated not only racial prejudice, but deep-seated fear which is often at the root of prejudice; in this case not only that English men and women would be subject to the jurisdiction of men with very different codes of social behaviour and honour, but also that these same newly-educated Indians were squeezing them out of positions in the lower echelons of the administration. Ripon's government was forced to compromise, and allow Europeans the privilege of a jury, at least half composed of Europeans, when they were tried by district magistrates or sessions judges.

Racial incidents occurred not infrequently, often as assaults on Indians by European soldiers or planters, who then were acquitted by European judges and juries, although Indians found guilty of assaulting Britons were severely punished. The Queen herself was anxious that relations should be improved, and when considering Curzon's appointment as Viceroy put this point to Salisbury, noting 'the *snobbish* and vulgar overbearing and offensive behaviour' even of officials. Curzon waged war on this front, sickened by European violence against Indians in a country under British rule. In 1899 when a European jury acquitted men of the Royal West Kent Regiment of the rape of a Burmese woman, after evidence likely to lead to conviction had been witheld by the men's superiors in the regiment, Curzon discharged the men from the army, censured their officers, the local police, and magistrates. Even before the trial he had transferred the regiment to Aden (the most unpleasant station available) and cancelled all leave and amenities. For Curzon such cases were of supreme imperial importance, because he believed that one way to neutralize the growing discontent of the educated was 'to be perpetually building bridges over that racial chasm that yawns eternally in our midst, and which, if it becomes wider . . . will one day split the Empire asunder.' Racial violence must be checked, he felt, lest it boil over into rebellion and the time come when 'the English may be in danger of losing their command of India, because they have not learned to command themselves.'[42]

However, the political dilemmas of continuing British *raj* were more complex than Curzon perhaps perceived: and it became increasingly clear to officials that their position in India would have to be secured by political strategies of considerable subtlety and flexibility. Slender finance and manpower had always made them dependent on Indian allies, linked informally to them by interest or formally by ties of employment. These constraints persisted. But the changing context forced the rulers to reconsider who among their Indian subjects would make the most stable collaborators in the imperial enterprise, who would be most efficient in providing finance and acting as nodules of loyalty deep within Indian society, where alien rulers could not reach and which they so little understood. The growth of towns, new pressures in the countryside, and above all the emergence of a highly articulate western-educated group threw their earlier alliance structure into question. But to attract allies meant consultation and possibly concessions: to weigh the gains and losses involved and secure support would be one strategy of imperial control. Of course the British possessed considerable resources and techniques for overt control of their subjects. They could imprison without trial, under a regulation of 1818, but they avoided this as far as possible. The criminal code backed by the courts helped to keep public violence and disorder at bay—but only just. Considerable violence was endemic in India, despite Gandhi's glorification in the following century of the supposed non-violence of village society, where he believed mutual inter-dependence and respect moulded social and economic relations. Internal village conflicts between individuals, families, factions, and castes, outbursts against money-lenders, religious strife, and grain riots common to any poor, rural society, were so much part of daily experience that they were rarely commented on, and only reached the status of an official 'problem' if they occurred too frequently in one place or coincided with other sources of disruption. The British also had the power to legislate and in emergency to rule by ordinance. Consequently they could respond to situations as they arose with new definitions of what was permissible behaviour. Notable examples in the later nineteenth century were the 1878 Vernacular Press Act (which Lytton described as 'a very stringent gagging Bill') and the Arms Act of the same year which introduced a licensing system for fire-arms but exempted Europeans.

The extent to which the rules laid down by the rulers were *obeyed* depended partly on the degree to which they were acceptable to Indians, and partly on the means to enforce obedience which the rulers possessed. Virtual collapse of control of the civilian population in certain areas in Gandhi's civil disobedience campaigns in the twentieth century showed what could happen when subjects declined to obey the law. As the British realized, they could not have contained India-wide rebellion or serious non-co-operation with their regime: mass acquiescence was vital, and it was due in some measure to Indian awareness of the *raj*'s monopoly of organized force. In the last resort the British had the army. One of its functions was internal security. Troops could be encamped in disturbed areas, despatched on route marches to remind subjects of the power of the sword, and actually sent 'to the aid of the civil power' in official parlance, even to the extent of firing when riot or rebellion appeared otherwise uncontrollable. But troops were limited in numbers, and their deployment was expensive and unpopular, both in India and Britain. The rulers, though painfully aware after 1857 that soldiers were their ultimate sanction, took to India a dislike of this mode of controlling civilians which was deeply rooted in their own historical experience.

Consequently they tried to rely on civil police forces; and in the later nineteenth century took seriously the problem of creating an efficient police service since the piecemeal attempts of the previous half century had failed conspicuously. The Company Directors had stated in 1856 that the police were disorganized and 'all but useless for the prevention and sadly inefficient for the detection of crime', and furthermore often 'unscrupulous' and reputed for 'corruption and oppression'.[43] A Police Commission in 1860 laid down the lines for reform which were incorporated in an enabling act the next year. Policing was to be rationalized and reorganized into one civil police force in every province under an Inspector-General. Each district was to have its Superintendent of Police subordinate to the Inspector-General yet closely co-operating with the local ICS man. To this level the police would be European. Below them would be Indian constables and the existing village watchmen. The police should be trained in the use of arms, but should normally carry only a baton or stave. Their pay should be sufficient to attract men of quality and ensure their integrity. However another Commission, in 1902, indicated that there had been little improvement in performance, recruitment, training, and pay: and everywhere the Commissioners went they heard complaints of corruption. Effective police organization was only developed in the twentieth century. Simultaneously, further steps were taken to strengthen the police as agents of imperial control—the creation of small armed reserves which could be used as mobile trouble-shooters within each province, and the development of a central and provincial Criminal Intelligence Departments from 1904. The government had found that the ordinary police were often deaf ears and blind eyes; and prior intelligence was crucial to government control, particularly as political life became more complex and terrorism and communal conflict erupted. Consequently CIDs rapidly became absorbed in political surveillance and reporting.

The need for CIDs indicated the way the problems of imperial control were changing. So did the gradual development of techniques to monitor and contain the vernacular press.[44] Ripon's government had abandoned Lytton's 'gagging' act; and the new Viceroy told a group of grateful editors that he felt a free press wisely conducted was an important help to government, particularly as representative institutions were so limited. Yet the expansion of the vernacular press in the later nineteenth century, and its often critical if not inflammatory tone, forced the British to modify their ideal of a free press in the Indian context. In 1905 there were 1,359 newspapers in English and the vernaculars, and they were thought to reach two million subscribers and an innumerable number who received them at second hand or heard them being read aloud. Gradually the government evolved means to survey the press, intercept and confiscate material, demand security from editors, and ban objectionable publications. Piecemeal measures of control were made coherent in the 1910 Press Act. In this controlling process the new CIDs played a vital surveillance role. However, the coercive powers were used with a restraint which reflected British ambivalence towards restriction of press freedom. During the years 1910–13 most securities demanded were minimal, less than 15 per cent of new presses and papers were asked for deposits, 272 existing presses and 158 newspapers were required to make deposits, only 15 were actually forfeited, and not a single press was seized. In the period 1910–12 only 20 prosecutions were launched.

Far more important as the *raj*'s working basis than possession of coercive powers and techniques was the construction of a network of alliances among influential groups of Indians. Most visible among the chosen friends of the British were India's remaining princes. The loyalty of many of them in 1857 and the remarkable capacity of the few rebel rulers to generalize and lead revolt made the imperial overlords accord them a new value in the second half of the century. A Government of India despatch of 1860 described them as 'breakwaters to the storm which would otherwise have swept over us in one great wave.'[45] Rewards of money and land were dispensed to the loyal princes after the Mutiny; and Queen Victoria's 1858 Proclamation promised respect for their rights, dignity, and honour. A new honour, the Star of India, was created—intended to be an honour in the sovereign's gift, to bind co-operative princes more closely to their royal suzerain, though it also became a reward for a successful ICS career. This was only part of a complex elaboration and orientalization of the ritual display of the imperial authority of the British monarch after 1857. Now the

Queen was to be the focus of Indian allegiance in place of the deposed Mogul emperor, the fiction and conventions of whose authority the British had so long maintained. This new loyalty was formalized in 1876 when the Queen assumed the title of Empress of India; and was symbolically enacted in the Imperial Assemblage in Delhi at New Year, 1877, when the Indian princes led India in homage to the Empress, binding themselves to her in a Victorian 'feudalism'. Most significant for the princes was the British decision in 1860 to grant them the right to adopt heirs. This would safeguard them against the 'lapse' of their states to British rule as had occurred to childless princes under Dalhousie. The British still had—and used—the power to intervene and even temporarily to administer a state if they felt there was misgovernment under its Indian ruler. Although they valued their princely allies they never believed such native rule was as efficient or beneficial as their own, and felt it their duty to guard the princes' subjects as far as they could. In the twentieth century the alliance with the princes become entangled with the politics of British India. Only then did the pressures of politicians in areas under direct British rule force the *raj* to insist on reform of princely government in order to cover itself against the charge of conniving at despotism and corruption, and to prevent the possibility of insurrection in the princely states. The main mechanism for controlling the princes was the Political Service, manned by Britons who were often ex-army officers. They were sent as 'Residents' to native courts to keep a watching brief for the Government of India. Although the princes were treated with elaborate courtesies, and given a central ceremonial role in the public representations of imperial authority, their position was that of the most prestigious of imperial subjects, and they could never forget that the British were not equal allies, as in the days of John Company. Now they were the Paramount Power, which protected and buttressed, but also regulated princely possession of arms, and monitored the princes' relations with their subjects, their public image and their private lives.

It would be elegantly simple to argue that just as the British reconsidered the value of their princely allies in the half century after the Mutiny so they tended to lean heavily on landowners of substance in British India and forget the vision of a prosperous yeoman peasantry which had inspired their Utilitarian predecessors and provided a rationale for the *ryotwari* land settlements. But after 1857 the British rarely had the option of totally revising their land settlements: owners and tenants were in lawful occupation. The one *tabula rasa* was Oudh where the majority of *taluqdars* had eventually joined the mutineers, followed by their former peasant clients and tenants, even those who had received new rights to land in the immediate pre-Mutiny settlements. As the Commissioner of Oudh noted later, 'This voluntary return to the *status quo ante* showed clearly what the feeling of the people was, and on this ground, as well as because the Talookdars if they chose could materially assist in the re-establishment of authority and the restoration of tranquillity, it was determined . . . that the settlement of the land revenue should be made with the Talookdars.'[46]

As a result of this deliberate political calculation that the ex-rebel notables would make the best allies the British not only restored to many of them their lands, but also confirmed them in a new and protected landlord status. They drew up a definitive list of *taluqdars*, made them observe primogeniture to prevent splintering of estates, and were prepared to take estates under direct control if *taluqdari* incompetence or profligacy made them insolvent and then to hand them back when they were a going concern. Another aspect of this strategy of using the newly elevated landlords as allies in imperial control was to grant them certain revenue and magisterial powers, in part reflecting British experience at home of landed gentry as Justices of the Peace. *Taluqdars* were also allowed direct access to district officers rather than having to deal with minor Indian officialdom: and ICS men were instructed to show them courtesy befitting the dignified status and privileged role envisaged for them. The British also set up the British Indian Association in an attempt to generate among them a cohesive spirit; and through it engineered the founding of Canning College with a view to imparting western education to the rising generation of *taluqdars*. But the *taluqdars* saw little point in the new education for their sons; and, secure in the support of government, they often blatantly squeezed their tenants rather than interesting themselves in improving agriculture or securing peaceful rural relations.

Elsewhere it proved almost impossible to find landholding groups who could be similarly 'restored', or to overturn existing village and peasant settlements. In Punjab there was a group of Sikh Sirdars who, contrary to earlier policy, were now encouraged to consolidate their estates—despite hostility from the London end of the government. In CP the *malguzars*, a very mixed bunch of revenue farmers who had been permitted to take short leases on lands, were now given full proprietory titles to the land and judicial powers. In Sind, where the landed, including Sufi Pirs, were seen as necessary local allies even before 1857, the system of local control via their allegiance as a favoured group of notables was further formalized and developed. Elsewhere the government had to be content with giving JP powers and duties to existing gentry, though it was sometimes difficult (as in the North-West Provinces, where for twenty years there had been village settlements) to find men who were of sufficient local eminence. Although Oudh was a special case, throughout India the rulers were keenly aware of the value of the landed as allies in maintaining stability and order. As the numbers of the western-educated grew and articulated novel ambitions and claims, so the British clung to their landed friends and argued that they represented more real and substantial interests at stake in India than did the

educated. When they created advisory and then legislative councils to assist
the Viceroy and the provincial governments they ensured by such mechanisms as reserved seats and franchises linked to property that the landed
were prominent among those chosen to 'represent' India in the new institutions. Typical of this attitude was the comment of the Lieutenant-Governor
of the United Provinces (which included Agra region and Oudh) in 1909:

I sincerely trust that in the elections about to take place for our enlarged councils the
landlords will obtain an adequate representation. To my mind they are the one force
on which we can rely at present among the leaders of Indian politics. We shall want
their support before long . . . In the present state of the political world in India it
would be the height of folly to alienate the landholding community by any attempt
to curtail their rights, and I have no such intention of making any such attempt in my
time.[47]

Yet alliance with substantial landed men did not ensure rural peace and
prosperity. The British had unwittingly allied with a group whose socio-
economic position was fast changing and who could decreasingly perform
the rural political roles their mentors had anticipated and relied on. The
growing commercialization of the rural economy, the regular revenue demand, and the grant of proprietary rights over land injected a starker
economic element into the relationship of the landed and their subordinates
and clients, eroding older semi-feudal ties. As prices and population rose,
landlords and money-lenders (and they could combine the roles) pressed
their clients, debtors, and under-tenants harder, both legally and with the
subtle economic and social forces common in small-scale communities. In
some areas one result seems to have been a definite increase in riots.
Government also became seriously worried by evidence of peasant indebtedness, and land loss to money-lenders. In the 1860s in Oudh, for example,
government noted a steady rise in rents and an increase of about 25 per cent
each year in the number of suits brought to the courts to enhance rents or
oust recalcitrant tenants. Consequently the rulers attempted in various
ways to protect peasant cultivators, sometimes even against the very dominant landed men they themselves cosseted as imperial allies.

In many provinces legislation was passed to protect sub-tenants; but each
measure caused controversy in the British ranks, not just on the nature of
the problem but because British ideals of *laissez-faire* and an aristocratic
rural order clashed with concern for the peasantry in which Utilitarian
doctrines and paternalism combined. The first tenancy legislation was
passed in Bengal in 1859; but it was not until 1885 that the *zamindars'*
powers were curbed by the award of occupancy right to *ryots* who had held
land in the same village or on the same estate continuously for twelve years.
In Oudh the government eventually felt constrained to help tenants against

the *taluqdars*, and contrived a compromise in 1866–8, whereby *taluqdars* agreed to recognize the occupancy rights of specified groups in order to prevent any similar rights accruing in the future. They then lost no time in forcing up the rents of the vast majority of their peasant tenants left unprotected; and their victims' position was worsened because pressure on land left them no chance of escape. At last in 1886 ordinary tenants were given some protection in terms of their right to land and freedom from arbitrary and annual rent rises. In Punjab peasants gained a much greater security on the land and protection against large rent increases under a Rent Act of 1868.

Further signs that government was anxious about the political repercussions of changing rural relations were the first moves to soften the harsher workings of the courts; in particular to prevent peasant landholders in areas without substantial landlords from losing their land to money-lenders when they defaulted on debts. The Deccan riots in 1875, whatever their actual cause, confirmed official fears about peasant indebtedness and possible social dislocation. They resulted in the 1879 Deccan Agriculturalists' Relief Act which was the first attempt to prevent the transfer of land from agriculturalist to non-agriculturalist hands. It required the civil courts to investigate the nature and circumstances of a debt before permitting sale of land to liquidate the debt. The 1900 Punjab Land Alienation Act went much further and actually prohibited all transfer of land to non-agriculturalists. A note on land transfer from established agricultural groups in the Punjab by the Government of India Revenue Department five years before showed the link in official thinking between economic change and the availability of a secure network of rural allies able to wield their local influence on the government's behalf.

The agency by which the executive has ensured the interior of the villages and the means of control over the masses which were previously at the disposal of Government have materially suffered in strength. It is essential on the one hand that the management of the villages should be in the hands of men who possess the confidence of the villagers, and it is equally essential on the other that if the executive is to be obeyed and its objects rightly understood, there should be a class of men intermediate between the Government and the mass of people who, while trusted by Government, should have influence over their neighbours. In this respect the money-lender can never take the place of the large ancestral landlord or the substantial yeoman whom he dispossesses . . .[48]

Punjab was an area in which the British had invested heavily in irrigation, and prized the rural communities they had created in the canal colonies. It was also a key centre of recruitment for the army. So great was official concern for the contentment and quiescence of its vital rural and military collaborators that the Government of India was prepared to overrule the provincial government in 1907 when the latter planned a law to tighten conditions of landholding in the canal colonies which generated real rural discontent and a rash of agitation. The Viceroy, Lord Minto, justified his veto thus: 'the appearance of surrender to agitation . . . would in my opinion be far less dangerous than to insist upon enforcing the unfortunate legislation proposed upon a warlike and loyal section of the Indian community.'[49] Incidentally this episode also shows how faulty official channels of communication were, and the inadequacy of the police and infant CID in discovering the state of Indian opinion.

In towns the British likewise needed to strengthen ties of friendship and support with notable Indians who could perform the same function for them in an urban setting as the rural gentry. Urban violence could be even more savage and disruptive than rural disturbances; and only local men of influence could help control it and mediate in local disputes. Urban peace was particularly important to the British because 1857 had shown that their authority disintegrated when they lost control simultaneously of town and neighbouring countryside. Grant of JP status, honours, places on the new municipal boards, and open access to ICS men were means of attracting effective allies. In small towns where rajas and landed men exercised influence as patrons they were the natural recipients of British favours in return for the services of local control and mediation they could render. In larger towns, such as Allahabad in UP, there were generally magnates who controlled house-property, were often heads of powerful trading and banking families, prominent in local credit mechanisms, and renowned for their charitable patronage. Commanding such resources they exercised considerable influence in town political life. Immediately after the Mutiny the Viceroy realized that they were as important in his programme of reconstructing imperial alliances as were the landed. In 1861 he wrote of those who could be given magisterial powers in Lucknow, 'They are, of course, men of a class quite different from that of the Talookdars—Bankers, Merchants, Contractors etc.—but scarcely less influential in their way.' Such magnates, or *raises*, gained from the establishment of the new municipal boards. In these they found a more formal political arena in which they rapidly became prominent. Then as municipal councillors they had access to official funds, and patronage in relation to municipal contracts and employment. Their intermediary role between government and people was enhanced as government made them honorary magistrates, consulted them on the regulation of income tax and religious festivals, and further confirmed their special position by exempting them from such restrictive legislation as the Arms Act.[50]

Yet this style of urban control was jeopardized as the century drew on: not by the emergence of new businessmen or an urban proletariat over which the *raises* had no influence, but by the growth of a group of educated

Indians with new publicity skills who became increasingly forceful in urban politics. They were drawn into municipal politics as the franchise was extended to include them; and as the incidence of taxation and the potential of municipality seats as springboards to places on provincial legislatures convinced them of the importance of entering the arena where the *raises* with their old 'connections' had held sway. Government was forced to consider its response to western-educated Indians who could not be allies and intermediaries with local societies in the same way as the urban and rural notables in established positions of traditional influence. The major British political dilemma of dominion lay here. What were they to make of the educated? Should they treat them as a significant interest group which merited recognition? Should they attempt to incorporate them, too, into the network of alliances buttressing the *raj*; or would that alienate existing and more valuable allies? In one sense they had no option. They had to employ educated Indians for lack of anyone else. Only men with these new skills and knowledge of English could man the increasingly complex infrastructure of the *raj*—as minor officials, lawyers, doctors, teachers, and journalists. But British responses to their *political* demands for more opportunities in high administration and increased influence in public affairs, and their claim to 'represent' India, were far more varied. Here imperialists had choice: they could calculate the gains and losses of alliance with and concessions to such men, knowing that some balance between different groups of allies was crucial for the stability of their rule.

At one extreme British response to the changing counters on the political board was articulated by the Tories, Lytton as Viceroy, and Lord Salisbury as Secretary of State in London. They thought the educated were a tiny minority making inordinate and unjustifiable demands, representing neither the 'real India' of the peasant, nor any substantial interest in the subcontinent. Salisbury wrote to Lytton in 1876,

The literary class—a deadly legacy from Metcalf and Macaulay—are politically alive enough; but under the most favourable circumstances they never give any political strength to a state, whatever other benefits they confer: they seldom go further in the affirmative direction than to tolerate the existing order of things. In India they cannot be anything else than opposition in quiet times, rebels in time of trouble. There remains the aristocracy; . . . if they are with us, we can hardly be upset . . .'

Lytton agreed, noting acidly the following year, 'As for the Babus, I thought it necessary to tell them plainly that the encouragement of natives does not mean the supremacy of Baboodom.'[51]

Thirty years later Curzon felt much the same about the educated and the appropriate imperial response; even though by his time as Viceroy their claims were far more sharply articulated by the first recognizably modern all-India political association, the Indian National Congress. (For its origins and development see below, pp. 183–90.) In his view they were totally unrepresentative, and to make concessions to them would be dereliction of imperial duty. He expressed this view before he became Viceroy: but his term of office did not change it.

The people of India are the voiceless millions who can neither read nor write . . . The people of India are the ryots and the peasants whose life is not one of political aspiration but of mute penury and toil. The plans and policy of the Congress Party . . . would leave this vast amorphous residuum absolutely untouched. That party contains a number of intelligent, liberal-minded and public-spirited men . . . but as to their relationship with the people of India, the constituency which the Congress Party represents cannot be described as otherwise than a microscopic minority of the total population.[52]

Yet even Curzon realized that one of the greatest changes in India in the century's closing years was the growth of public opinion. Many of his colleagues shared his assessment but drew different political conclusions. Ripon was sure that British rule must increasingly be in accordance with public opinion, consciously using its potential. In his judgement educated Indians had begun to shape that opinion in the 1870s, and their influence over their compatriots would inevitably grow. He felt it would be folly to alienate them by ignoring their aspirations and ambitions, and so create dangerous and influential enemies from men who might become friends of imperial rule. He chose to befriend them and capitalize on them as a *resource* of the *raj*. The repeal of Lytton's Press Act and the moves towards local self-government were partly measures to this end. Ripon would have liked to push further ahead and permit the larger municipalities to elect Indians to the Imperial and Provincial Legislative Councils, hoping that this would lead to further steps 'along the same road of extended self-government . . . but then according to my way of thinking that is the road along which we ought to travel.' He felt himself becoming more radical daily, despite what he called his despotic power. Not so the India Office, where the Secretary of State was influenced by the 'old India hands' on the India Council, who thought Ripon was radical to the point of being dangerous! Ripon was told his plan was premature. Even before this rebuff he was complaining bitterly of the frustration of being tied by the Council, a set of aged and well-paid gentlemen whose pastime was obstructing those who really knew what was happening in India and bore the responsibility of imperial rule.[53] His dilemmas of dominion lay in relations with his compatriots as much as with Indians, as he also discovered during the Ilbert Bill fracas.

Despite this polarization of views, over the later years of the century there was among the men who ruled India a gradual accommodation to the emergence of western-educated Indians with new ideals and ambitions; and a growing recognition that even if they could never 'represent' the whole of India's complex society, yet they were a legitimate section of public opinion, and an interest group whose claims must be treated seriously. By the 1890s Lansdowne as Viceroy was describing the emergence of Congress as an inevitable development, but one which was currently as innocuous as it could possibly be, making demands which were not only reasonable but moderate in tone. A Tory Secretary of State took comfort from his belief that Congress was a movement against Anglo-Indian bureaucracy, not against the *raj* itself. Lord Minto, a Tory Viceroy, in a letter to Morley, the Liberal Secretary of State, showed how far even the conservative wing of British opinion had moved in its perception of the value of educated Indians as potential allies.

The truth is that by far the most important factor we have to deal with in the political life of India is not impossible Congress ambitions, but the growing strength of an educated class, perfectly loyal and moderate in its views, but which, I think quite justly, considers itself entitled to a greater share in the government of India. I believe we shall derive much assistance from this class if we recognise its existence, and that if we do not, we shall drive it into the arms of Congress leaders to whom it will be forced to look for salvation.[54]

British reluctance to welcome educated Indians into their alliance network can be seen more precisely in their policies on two matters which aroused deep concern among the educated. In each case the issue was the degree to which the educated should be incorporated into the formal infrastructure of dominion. The admission of Indians to the highest posts in the administration, particularly the ICS, was a constant theme in educated Indian discontent at their position under the British. It was the issue behind one of the first major political agitations of this group, initiated by the Bengali, Surendranath Banerjea, in 1877–8. (He was an ICS recruit who had been dismissed in his first year.) It became a problem to which Congress addressed itself persistently from the 1880s. Because the ICS entrance examination was held in London it was hard for any Indians to compete except the more affluent: and few educated boys came from wealthy families. The age limit was also a barrier, as it was lowered from 23 to 22 in 1859, to 21 in 1866, to 19 in 1876. The rationale of this was to ensure that successful English candidates could then have a university education before going to India. But it effectively excluded anyone who had not been at school in England from about the age of 15. Not surprisingly, few Indians succeeded. Between 1868 and 1875, 14 Indians sat the examination and 11 passed: from 1876 to 1883 there were 28 Indian candidates and 1 succeeded. Lytton wished to exclude Indians from the ICS but this would have meant the impossible—overturning the 1858 Royal Proclamation. He was left with his plan for a Statutory Civil Service which came into being in 1879. It was an alternative route into high administration, open only to Indians, entry being by nomination. This was, however, a device to attract *aristocrats* into government, not the educated; and because few of the wealthy and landed had either qualifications for or interest in high administrative posts the scheme petered out. Only 69 appointments were made under it. Ripon, despite his radicalism, could do little to improve the chances of the educated except for raising the examination age limit to 21. He also set in motion the Public Services (Aitchison) Commission to review the whole question of the civil service. It recommended the end of the Statutory Service, raising the age limit for examination entry to 23, but rejected the idea of simultaneous examinations in London and India. Indian successes increased after the age was raised in 1892, but even by 1909 there were only about 60 Indians out of around 1,142 ICS officers. What became known in the twentieth century as the *raj*'s 'steel frame' was still made predominantly of the steel of British manpower.

There was rather more flexibility in British policy towards incorporating Indians into mechanisms of consultation. Shocked by their ignorance of the tensions which exploded in 1857, the rulers immediately began constructing consultative councils which would give them 'ears to the ground'. But as they expanded these councils they were reluctant to give them real power (for example, over finance), and they took care that councillors should be their nominees or, later, elected under franchise regulations which ensured that they would be men of substance. In 1861 under the Indian Councils' Act the Viceroy's Legislative Council was reconstructed and provision was made for provincial legislatures. Non-official members (some of whom could be expatriates like planters and businessmen if they were a substantial local interest as in Bengal) were given a minority of places: and they were chosen by government, not elected. These bodies could only discuss legislation, so their role was very restricted. Even so, Sir Charles Wood considered the Act was one of his most important Indian measures. He judged it 'a great experiment . . . That everything is changing in India is obvious enough, & that the old autocratic government cannot stand unmodified is indisputable.'[55] In subsequent decades educated Indians in their associations and the press urged further reform, including election of councillors. But not until 1892 did a further Councils' Act introduce an indirect form of election. In the case of the provincial councils the 'recommending' bodies for the additional members were often municipalities and district boards. Although the representational base of these councils was still very restricted this reform gave the first real opportunity for educated Indians to enter the formal consultative processes of the *raj*. Yet councils were still only consultative, although they were now permitted to discuss government finance and to address questions to the executive. Officials still formed the majority.

In 1909 the Morley–Minto reforms abandoned the official majority in the provincial legislatures as well as enlarging them, and provided that most of the non-official members should be elected either directly, for Muslims and landholders, or indirectly by recognized local interest groups such as trade associations and universities. The Viceroy's Legislative Council was also enlarged, though officials remained a majority on it. Election of the non-official members was again by a combination of direct and indirect election. Although this marked a considerable liberalization of the consultative process the executive still controlled legislative functions. Furthermore the rationale behind this method of election remained the representation of distinctive interests rather than the right of all citizens to be represented as in a simple territorial franchise. Morley seems, according to recent research, to have been the driving force behind this package, concerned to rally behind government not only existing allies but moderate-minded educated Indians, too. He was deeply influenced by one of the most able and attractive educated men of his generation, G. K. Gokhale, from western India. Their frank discussions helped him appreciate the difficulty of moderate men such as Gokhale if the British did not respond to their stance with a proposal which would enable them to convince their educated compatriots that moderation, quiet and reasoned argument, rather than violence or extreme verbal opposition to imperial dominion bore political fruit. Morley may well have realized how significant a step towards a form of colonial self-government his reforms might be. But as he had to deal with a Tory Viceroy and House of Lords, and a conservative India Council, he played down this prospect, actually denying in the Lords in 1908 that he intended to set up a parliamentary system in India. He was content to let Minto take much of the credit for the reforms, perhaps calculating that Minto's name would ease its acceptance in conservative British circles. Yet even Minto's government in Calcutta had realized the need for incorporating a wider span of Indians permanently into the decision-making structures of the *raj*; though they saw reforms to this end as a defensive measure, whereas Morley viewed reform as a natural step in the direction of political education and progress. A Government of India despatch at an early stage in the reform plans, when they were far less radical than the eventual product, suggested how far British thinking had moved since the Mutiny in appreciation of the groups which would make effective allies. The proposals were

An attempt to give to India something that may be called a constitution framed on sufficiently liberal lines to satisfy the legitimate aspirations of all but the most advanced Indians, whilst at the same time enlisting the support of the conservative elements of native society . . . not an experimental makeshift, but a working machine representing all interests that are capable of being represented and providing an adequate expression of the sentiments and requirements of the masses of the people . . . We anticipate that the aristocratic elements in society and the moderate men, for whom at present there is no place in Indian politics, will range themselves on the side of the Government and will oppose any further shifting of the balance of power and any attempt to democratise Indian institutions.[56]

The Morley–Minto Reforms provided separate electorates for Muslims—a new continental departure, though the device had operated locally, in Punjab for example in elections to municipalities. Much controversy surrounds British policy towards Indian Muslims, and imperial responsibility for the growth of communal hostility which ultimately could not be contained within democratic political structures and ended in the partition of the subcontinent along religious lines. Were the British playing the dangerous game of 'divide and rule', as Indian nationalists and some historians have claimed, and were they turning to Muslims as conservative allies of their *raj*? Immediately after 1857 there was real hostility between the British and their Muslim subjects, not least because many of the rulers firmly, but erroneously, believed that the Mutiny was the result of a Muslim conspiracy. However, this hostility ebbed away in just over a decade. Prominent Muslims began to lead their co-religionists towards religious acceptance of the legitimacy of British rule despite its alien faith, and to urge on them co-operation with their rulers in the educational and administrative opportunities their rule provided. The British simultaneously began to realize the importance of loyal Muslim subjects, the more so as educated Hindus became vocal critics of the *raj*. The Government of India declared publicly its concern for the low educational standards of Muslims in 1871, and in 1885 resolved that more Muslims should be employed in government service. (Impressions among contemporaries and later observers of alleged Muslim 'backwardness' in education and possession of administrative posts tended to rest on evidence from Bengal, where Muslims were poor and of low social standing. Elsewhere in the north and west they did well on both counts in proportion to their numbers.) Yet Dufferin as Viceroy stoutly denied any deliberate government contrivance of religious disunity as a means of promoting British power.

The diversity of races in India, and the presence of a powerful Mahomedan community, are undoubtedly circumstances favourable to the maintenance of our rule; but these circumstances we found and did not create, nor had they been non-existent, would we have been justified in establishing them by artificial means. It would have been a diabolical policy on the part of any Government to endeavour to emphasize or exacerbate race hatred among the Queen's Indian subjects for a political object.[57]

Any district officer faced with the horrors of communal violence would have echoed the Viceroy's words.

It is as difficult to talk about 'British policy towards Muslims' as about 'Indian Muslims'. Just as Muslims differed in characteristics and needs according to locality, so provincial governments related to Muslims according to local problems and opportunities. In UP, where Muslims were a prestigious élite, the provincial government consolidated an alliance with some of them, in the hope of reconciling them to the *raj* after the strained years following 1857. It encouraged the prominent writer and educationalist, Sir Syed Ahmed Khan, who was urging a positive Muslim response to British rule; and gave patronage and verbal support to the Aligarh College (of which he was the prime mover) which became the premier modern Muslim educational centre of northern India. In neighbouring Punjab, where the numbers of Muslims, Hindus, and Sikhs were precariously balanced and where religious strife was a constant danger, the local government was concerned to damp down communal conflict and to observe strict religious neutrality where this was compatible with quieting conflict and maintaining a balance between the communities. Communal representation in local elections was one strategy the Punjab administration tried: so was the decision to bring Muslim employment in government service more into line with the Muslim proportion of the wealthier and educated Punjabi population.[58]

When the Morley–Minto Reforms were being hammered out there was no significant change of British policy, nor any novel attempt to 'divide and rule'. The principles governing representation were still that legitimate interests should be voiced, and that minority groups should have representation in proportion to their proportion of the population. What gave Morley little room to manoeuvre in the *mechanics* of Muslim representation was the Viceroy's sweeping assurance to a Muslim deputation that he would safeguard Muslim political rights and interests. Yet again the diversity of opinion *among the British* generated policy dilemmas. In this instance Minto's intentions seem to have been to boost his viceregal influence at the expense of Whitehall, rather than to court Muslim support at the expense of Hindus. Nor is there any evidence that he engineered the Muslim deputation to which he gave this assurance.[59]

Although it would be too simple to see British policy towards India's religious groups either as monolithic or as deliberately divisive, yet the way the British saw Indian society, particularly in assessing what were legitimate interests meriting representation, was a crucial influence on Indian responses to the imperial order. Indians saw in the language, categories and labels their rulers used, something they, too, could use profitably, whether they referred to caste, religious identity or economic position. So in the changing context of imperial dominion there was constant interaction between British understanding of their own political dilemmas as rulers of a diverse society, and Indians' political response. Furthermore, the British creation of distinctive consultative structures, particularly the local, provincial, and central councils, whose entrances were patronage and election, generated and encouraged distinctive and novel styles of politics. Imperial structures and categories not only influenced Indian responses to their rulers, but became a significant factor in Indians' relationships with each other. They were therefore a major determinant of the dilemmas which British dominion posed for Indians.

Immediately one focuses on Indian dilemmas there is a problem over sources of evidence. The British side of the complex interaction is well documented in official material generated as policies were made, in parliamentary debates, and in the prolific semi-official and private correspondence passing between men in government. For Indian feelings and responses to British dominion there are some written sources—petitions to government, the Indian press, records of policy discussion in the emerging voluntary associations of the later nineteenth century, and some private letters and autobiographical writing. Such 'private' Indian source material is more readily available for the twentieth century. However, these tell us most about the reaction of educated Indians, particularly those literate in English. To understand a deeper and wider range of Indian perceptions of the problems posed by the British presence we need more knowledge of the vernacular press and also fiction in Indian languages. We must also look at varieties of actions which were responses to the changing situation, including religious movements and even riots. Clearly, by comparison with the earlier part of the century, the *raj*'s presence was stirring up Indian society in new ways and at new depths, with the result that many established bonds and divisions in society were strained and opened to radical questioning.

The starkest dilemma for Indians was the legitimacy of British rule: whether the foreign rulers were considered as having a right to their new dominion, or were seen as usurpers meriting only disaffection or overt rebellion. Most Indians did not think about this issue. They accepted British *raj* as they had accepted Mogul *raj*—because it was there. At a more sophisticated intellectual level of response Hindus had comparatively little difficulty in accepting British rule. Hindu political theory did not envisage a theocracy, and any king was accorded legitimacy who protected caste society. The 1858 Royal Proclamation was the public declaration of British religious tolerance, and the new courts never interfered with the workings of caste society or tried to undermine its hierarchical structure. Where legislative reform occurred it was almost always in the form of enabling acts (for example, enabling widow remarriage or inheritance by converts to other faiths), unless there had been strong Indian pressure for change. For the Muslim intellectual and religious élites, however, there was an ideological problem because of the interrelationship in Muslim thought between political power and the right ordering of society according to Allah's will, and because of the actual experience of Muslim rule in India. The problem of legitimacy was revived by the experiences of 1857 and the consequent, though short-term, deterioration in relations between the Muslims and the British. Muslim religious leaders, the *ulema*, did not agree on the correct stance by their co-religionists. But in the later years of the century many *ulema* did encourage Muslims to accept British rule and consider India under the *raj* as *dar ul-Islam*, where Muslims might pursue their religious duties and social obligations unhindered. Others such as the educationalist and politician, Sir Syed Ahmed Khan, went so far as to deny that the Koran contained and undergirded a divinely-ordained code of law. He argued that devout Muslims could remain so even if they altered their customs; provided they treated the Koran as a source of reflection and guidance, though not as a comprehensive blueprint for living in a changing world.[60]

A far wider problem which deeply concerned many more Indians was their perception of their own identity under British rule, particularly in relation to their foreign rulers. Major pressures generated by new experiences forced them to consider such questions as 'Who are we?' 'Are we a nation?' 'Are we just diverse regions, castes, and religious groups?' (Many British observers of India constantly asked this last question and gave the answer 'yes' in justification of their rule.) Most significant in forcing these questions into conscious articulation was the very presence of the *raj* and the unifying forces resulting from it—one government for the whole subcontinent, the spread of communications linking the regions more closely, the growing economic integration of the country, and the increasing use of English as a common language of higher administration, education, and communication. English medium education and English-style curricula also introduced some Indians to ideas which were a radical challenge to the old social order, and an invitation to new senses of common belonging and public identity. European history glorified the nineteenth-century flowering of nationalism as a spiritual renewal and political endeavour; and posited the nation state as the highest and natural form of political order. English political theory examined the nature of representative government and underlined the assumption that all men were equal. Familiarity with such ideals and examples, and a deepening appreciation of English literature, not only bound together in intellectual community those who received the new education. It also made them aware of standards and skills they now shared with their rulers. One Indian in 1878 spoke eloquently in public of the disruption this caused in Indians' awareness of themselves and their environment.

English education tells us that we live under tyrannies more numerous and more radically mischievous than those which produced the great political revolution of '89. It tells us that, here in India, we have a social tyranny, a domestic tyranny, a tyranny of caste, a tyranny of custom, a religious tyranny, a clerical tyranny, a tyranny of thought over thought, of sentiment over sentiment. And it not only tells of all these tyrannies, but makes us feel them with terrific intensity.

It was hardly surprising that Curzon's government was deeply concerned with the textbooks available to Indian school children, and suspected the influence of Burke, Carlyle, Byron, and Macaulay, to name just a few. (In 1900 local governments were authorized to proscribe undesirable books: in future all government-aided schools were to use only authorized books, and candidates for public examinations or government scholarships from un-aided schools could be excluded if their schools used books under official disapproval.)[61]

Yet a further disruptive influence on accepted ideas and patterns of behaviour was the presence of Christian missionaries. British evangelical bodies who had dominated early missionary activity in India were now joined by other British, American, and European missionary groups, in-cluding Roman Catholic orders. No part of British India was left untouched by their evangelism, educational work, and medical care. When judged in numbers of converts Christian missionary influence was limited, and region-ally patchy (see Table P). Furthermore, converts tended to be from the depressed classes and tribal people, who were the lowest in Hindu society or had not been fully assimilated into it. The only prestigious Indian Chris-

Table P. Christians in India, 1881–1911

Area	Numbers of Christians				% of Christians to population, 1911
	1911	1901	1891	1881	
India	3,876,203	2,923,241	2,284,380	1,862,634	1.24
British India	2,601,761	1,935,358	1,516,356	1,175,738	1.02
Assam	66,562	35,969	16,844	7,093	0.99
Bengal	129,746	106,596	82,339	72,289	0.29
Bihar and Orissa	268,265	172,340	110,360	55,943	0.67
Bombay	244,392	220,087*	170,009*	145,154*	1.19
CP and Berar	73,401	27,252	14,451	13,174	0.25
Delhi and Punjab	199,751	66,591	48,472	28,054	0.99
Madras	1,208,515	1,038,863	879,438	711,117	2.88
NWFP	6,718	5,273	5,437	5,645	0.30
UP	179,694	102,955	58,518	47,673	0.38

*Includes figures for Western India States

Source: *Census of India, 1931. Vol. I India. Part I Report* (Delhi, 1933), pp. 420–1, 424.

tians were the Syrian Christians of the south who had existed long before the nineteenth-century Christian outreach from Europe: who, indeed, were accepted and valued by their Hindu neighbours because their religious style and value-system so closely approximated to their own, unlike the recent converts who were sometimes 'de-Indianized' by their missionary preceptors, and even gathered into separate villages to emphasize and protect their new identity. Yet conversions, however few and despised, showed that the existing social order was not immutable. Christian preaching also challenged Hinduism and Islam at the religious level—questioning beliefs, and posing new and critical problems, such as the nature of religious revelation and the authority and authenticity of scripture, or the relationship of reason to belief and practice. Christianity also underscored secular philosophies of equality by its insistence on men's equality before God, both in the matter of sin and in freely bestowed rather than earned salvation. The missionary presence placed question marks beside existing customs not only by missionaries' words but by their actions; particularly in the compassion showed in medical and educational work among the most deprived, including women.[62]

In response to these interlocking pressures on Indians' ways of looking at themselves and their country, there erupted intense questioning as to why the British had been able to assert political control over Indian society, what was the essential nature of Indian society and civilization, its strengths and weaknesses; and whether India was in any sense a nation or could become one. Out of the intellectual turmoil emerged a sense of nationality which could not have existed or been articulated before the later nineteenth century because the means for an experience of belonging to the whole of India were not present, neither was there any political concept of nationhood. As one Bengali nationlist put it, 'Our language has ... no word corresponding to the English word nation ... And the reason is that our social synthesis practically stopped with the race-idea ... We never had, therefore, this nationalist aspiration before.'[63] Yet Indians' understanding of nationhood and its origins varied.

One strand in the growth of the new sense of identity was the belief that India was a nation in the process of being made. The early nationalist politician, Surendranath Banerjea, called his autobiography *A Nation in Making*. Men like him were steeped in the British Liberal traditon: and they saw Britain's role in India as fundamentally creative. India in their eyes had formerly been a mere collection of diverse regions, races, religious and linguistic groupings, and it was the British presence which was welding these into a new national unity. A sense of nationhood could not rest on geography, religion or language, as it so often seemed to in Europe. In India's circumstances it must be forged consciously out of a commitment to political liberalism which would unite Indians and transcend these earlier

divisions and loyalties. The British connection, and above all the new education, were seen as divinely-ordained preconditions for this growth of
nationality and the reconstruction of a new, cohesive Indian society. Consequently those who held these ideas did not seek to overthrow British *raj*,
but to amend it, to make it more responsive to educated opinion, and to
enable Indians to participate more fully in it. In a sense they wished to make
it conform more closely to what they saw as true British political principles.
In 1880 Lal Mohan Ghose voiced these aspirations in a speech in Bombay,
putting clearly both the acceptance of British rule and the potential for
disquiet if the British successors of Macaulay were less liberal in action than
the Anglicists in their hope for fruitful co-operation between the rulers and
the western educated.

You [the British] have for a long time past given us the blessings of a liberal
education. Our minds are expanded under the generous influence of Western culture. We are deeply grateful to you for all these benefits. But remember, as our
intellectual faculties are developed, so are our aspirations, both personal and national, sharpened and stimulated. . . . Remember that the study of European history, and particularly of the history of England and of English political institutions,
is not calculated to deaden, but on the contrary to rouse and fire those instincts of
patriotism, which have slumbered in the national breast of India for centuries. Open
up a career for those whom you yourselves have fitted for a high and useful career,
and remember, above all, that the surest way to make the people of this country
disloyal and to array them in bitter opposition to the British Government, is to close
and shut up every avenue for the legitimate vent and gratification of their ambition
and aspirations.[64]

Other Indians saw the British presence and influence in India as basically
destructive. Another distinctive strand in the emerging sense of national
identity was an emphasis on the supposed glories of the Hindu nation
before the arrival of the British. Foreign rule, alien literature, science and
art, western customs and religious teachings, were all seen as eating at the
heart of Hindu culture, which was in turn visualized as the heart of Indian
nationhood. An *Indian Mirror* editorial in 1884 under the heading, 'The
denationalization of the Indian people', declaimed,

With the loss of our country we have lost our national religion, our national literature, our national science and philosophy, and our national traditions. It is not
surprising that under such circumstances, the growth and progress of the Indian
people as a nation should be in abeyance. . . . In our present denationalized condition, we are neither fish nor flesh, neither Indian nor English.[65]

For Indians who thought thus, India was 'a fallen nation' (to use the phrase
of Keshub Chundra Sen): it could only be revived by a cultural regeneration

drawing inspiration from the Aryan past and Sanskrit culture, which worked for the re-establishment of traditional Hindu morality and religious principles. India was described as the Motherland, symbolized powerfully in the figures of some of the great goddesses of the Hindu pantheon, to whom the highest devotion was due, even to the point of death. A further variant on the theme of the destruction wreaked by foreign dominion was the claim that the British had de-industrialized a previously thriving commercial and industrial nation. Such economic criticism of the *raj* was not confined to those who saw the Hindu heritage as the core of Indian nationhood. It spread far more widely among the educated, including those who spoke of the providential nature of British rule.

All who wrestled with the problem of India's national identity, whether it was seen as belonging to the past, being created in the present, or as possible in the future, had to consider the place of India's religious minorities within the nation. Liberal nationalists understood all religious groups as integral to the new nation, and denied that religion determined nationality. But to many Hindu thinkers, and not only those who harked back to an Aryan past, the main Indian religious minority, the Muslims, were a destructive force, whose time of political dominance in India had fatally weakened Indian culture and society. (It was a historical view confirmed by some of the earliest British historians of India who looked back on the Muslim era as equivalent to Europe's 'Dark Ages'.) Not surprisingly Muslims began to question their identity, and to discuss the nature of the Islamic community of believers. Because there were comparatively few educated Muslims at this juncture their ferment was not as widespread and articulate as that of educated Hindus. Some Muslim intellectuals were beginning to question the possibility of belonging to an Indian nation. Sir Syed wrote in a private letter in 1888, 'I object to every Congress in any shape or form which regards India as one nation . . .'[66] Among educated Muslims a more general assumption was that Muslims were a particular and separate interest group which needed special protection in the changing environment where Hindus seemed to be succeeding in education and employment. The theory that India's Muslims and Hindus were two nations was only fully developed in the 1930s, as Muslims faced for the first time the real possibility of a British transfer of power to an independent Indian government elected on the basis of numbers. A further dimension of Muslims' sense of identity was their membership of an international body of believers whose spiritual, though not political, leader was the Khalifah, the Sultan of Turkey; who were linked across political boundaries by faith and a veneration for certain holy places in the Middle East connected with the origins of Islam. There are signs that in the later nineteenth century this Pan-Islamic dimension became increasingly significant for Indian Muslims. It actively increased their sense of separation from Indian Hindus: but simultaneously it joined them with Muslims outside India and so inhibited the growth of a specifically Indian Muslim sense of nationhood.

The dilemmas of Indians' status and identity in relation to their rulers thus inevitably raised further dilemmas of Indians' relations *with each other*. The nature and significance of group identities within the subcontinent became live issues late in the century because it was only then that British dominion began to stir up Indian society at any depth. This stirring process occurred at many levels, as a result of various mechanisms of change. Some we have already seen. Population growth, price rises, and the expansion of a wider money economy began to sharpen divisions in rural society and to create new connections between people and groups based on achievement and contract, rather than on ascriptive and more traditional bonds. Some began to question the significance of caste in their new situation, and occasionally to feel ties with people of similar economic status—though modern 'class consciousness' was rare until later in the twentieth century. The uneven spread of the new education and access to the jobs for which it was the doorway made those who felt they were lagging behind increasingly aware of the group identity of those who were more successful and those who shared with them in comparative weakness and failure. Communities such as Muslims, lower caste groups, and even regions where education was not widely available, came to a new sense of identity through the shared experience of deprivation.

Such dislocation of existing relationships and sharpening awareness of the linkages and differences in society stemmed from influences the British had unleashed on the subcontinent, but whose precise effects they neither foresaw nor intended. In other ways deliberate actions by the government began to generate tension and a heightened sense of particularity. Towards the end of the century the British, concerned to know what was happening in the country lest tension should erupt as unpredictably and savagely as in 1857, and anxious to make the best use of limited resources, began to make a wide range of inquiries into such matters as educational standards, access to administrative posts, or the transfer of land between social groups. The actual process of inquiry involved the use of categories such as caste and religion, and this inevitably increased the significance of those categories and sharpened their outlines. The decennial census from 1871, for example, made different communities aware of their numerical position in each province, and the relative fluctuations in it. If they saw a decline in their numbers this generated anxiety lest they should thereafter be considered a less significant local interest group in the distribution of benefits, seats on municipal boards and in the new legislative councils. This reaction was evident among Punjabi Hindus; and official enumerations were not a little responsible for the emergence of novel conversion campaigns to reclaim to the Hindu fold those who had been converted to Christianity and so redress

the Hindus' numerical decline.[67] Commissions on education and employment in the public services similarly heightened Punjabis' senses of communal identity and generated keen concern about the language of local
administration when one alternative would obviously benefit one community, as Urdu would the Muslims of northern India. Similarly the government's creation of new political arenas in the municipalities and legislatures
invited a new style of competitive politics in which the aspirants had to
demonstrate their standing by eliciting Indian support and by slotting into
the categories of interests the rulers were prepared to recognize.

A more direct provocation to Indians to consider the nature of their
social ties, conventions, and responsibilities, was the missionary presence.
The Christian challenge often triggered religious and social movements for
revival and reform: these in turn set off a chain reaction of fear and change
among other Indians. In combination these varied influences produced
turmoil in Indians' self awareness and their perception of significant corporate identities.

One of the earliest signs of change was the Hindu movement for social
reform which was almost coeval with the new education and in part owed its
inspiration to it. As more Indians encountered new social ideals in western
literature and philosophy, heard the harsh criticisms levelled at Hindu
society both by Christian missionaries and their rulers, and saw how these
were welded into justifications for imperial rule, so they began to question
a wide range of social practices such as *suttee*, the prohibition of widow re-
marriage, the treatment of widows, the age of marriage, mechanisms of
social avoidance, and abhorrence of foreign travel as polluting. Underlining
this self-questioning in response to external challenges were the arguments
of social efficiency—responding to the internal needs of a changing society.
Many were deeply perturbed that economic and social change were threatening Indian society, and they were concerned to re-establish it on a sound
basis. For example, educated men were now more likely to be occupation-
ally mobile, and needed more mature and educated wives who could be
companions in the new environment.[68] At first the social reformers were
prominent individuals or small, separated provincial groups, who responded piecemeal to particular problems which made them feel acutely
the tension between the society in which they lived and the values to which
they were exposed by their contacts with the West. Among the early nineteenth-century reformers were Ram Mohan Roy, whose crusade against
suttee encouraged the British to legislate against it; and I. C. Vidyasagar,
famous for his pleas for marriage reform and the enabling of widow re-
marriage. It should be stressed that neither of them, nor indeed other
advocates of reform, wanted to overturn Hindu society or abandon their
religious heritage. Rather, they argued that Hindu scripture and 'pure
tradition' sanctioned reform; while the injustices and abuses they con-

demned were signs of degraded Hindu manners and corrupt accretions which could be abandoned without endangering the pure core of the Hindu heritage.

From the 1880s there was more continental co-operation in reform, largely because an issue emerged which touched the hearts and lives of educated Indians in all regions—namely, the age of marriage of Hindu girls. Early marriage, even before puberty, was favoured among higher castes; and this practice caused further problems of marriages where the groom was far older than the bride, the 'sale' of young girls to older men, physical mistreatment of child brides, and of course the likelihood of young widows who were neither permitted to re-marry nor sufficiently educated to be self-supporting. Bitter controversy erupted over a bill to raise the age of consent to twelve years for married and unmarried girls. Although the British insisted that this was a measure to protect young girls, the debate raised far deeper issues as the age of consent was central to Indian (and particularly Bengali) male perceptions and control of female sexuality. Here British and Bengali assumptions about gender clashed, and for many Indians the question became a perceived imperial attack on Indian masculinity by a legislative change which would mean that the husband who consummated his marriage with a girl under that age would be guilty of rape though following religious convention.[69] The ensuing furore publicized the social reform movement and united reformers across regional boundaries. It also demonstrated how deeply divided Indians were in their reaction to western standards and to government interference in the working of Hindu society. Reformers were under acute social pressure, whatever their ideas, to conform their personal lives to traditional standards for the sake of their families' reputation, and in deference to the cherished beliefs and observations of older relatives. Verbal abuse and social avoidance made life even more difficult for the reformer who practised what he preached. M. G. Ranade, a western Indian Brahmin who graduated from Bombay University in 1859 and became a prominent reformer, married a girl aged eleven, after his first wife died, out of deference to his father's wishes; and he later did penance for a breach of caste rules when he was accused of taking food with Christians. Reform was so divisive that when the Indian National Congress came into being it declined to discuss questions of reform, and relegated them to the National Social Conference which met after Congress had concluded its annual meeting. Those who were striving towards a new national identity were not prepared to wreck it on the rocks of controversy about the nature of Hindu identity, and the propriety of the existing Hindu social order. But the problem was shelved, not solved: it continued to erupt and plague both the nationalist movement and independent India's governments.

But beneath the controversies, there emerged a slow but steady transition in the social lives of many educated Indians, particularly in the realm of familial relations and the role of women. In areas such as Bengal and Bombay where the new education was most easily available, small groups of women began to receive education in and outside the home. Gradually they began to take on new roles within the house and in the public domain; though there was no major break with older assumptions about what constituted a 'good woman' but rather an expansion and modification of it to suit changing times and needs. In line with arguments for social efficiency, women of educated families were encouraged to become competent housewives and mothers, thus sustaining the home as the core of Indian culture and society in a time of change. Athough there was no equality between male and female, increasingly educated couples perceived themselves as companions within the marriage bond, and developed new personal expectations of the marital relationship. Outside the home women expanded their accepted domestic and nurturent role, and tended to develop an extended female sphere of women's organizations and institutions, rather than challenging men or the fundamentals of patriarchy.[70]

Social reform raised critical questions about the essentials of Hindu tradition, the status of different kinds of scripture, the source of religious authority and the applicability of human reason to religious matters.[71] In essence it demanded conscious definition of 'Hindu-ness', whereas earlier generations had lived out the main assumptions of their Hindu inheritance with little need for credal definition. Reform posed the new question, 'What does it mean to be a Hindu in a changing world?' Indeed, all India's religious traditions were forced into self-questioning and reformulation by a wide range of pressures in the nineteenth century—socio-economic change, western criticism and intellectual traditions of scholarship, the example of missionary religious organization and charitable activities, as well as the growth of printing and literacy which in different circumstances had had such a profound effect in Reformation Europe. Three of the central issues on which debate focused were boundaries (who belonged and who did not: who were authentic believers and adherents); the nature and authority of scripture and of religious specialists such as Brahmins; and the relationship of religion to society, particularly religious sanction for particular customs and relationships, and the treatment of the vulnerable.

The process and results of this questioning of Hindu identity can be seen in a wide range of religious movements of Hindu revivalism and reform, or blends of the two.[72] The earliest were small and appealed to western-educated men who wished to explore the intellectual and spiritual world opened to them by contact with the West, without ceasing to be Hindus. The Brahmo Samaj, founded by Ram Mohan Roy, was the first and perhaps the most famous. It drew deeply on Christian faith and practice as well as on Hindu tradition. Its members were theists, and opposed idol-worship, em-

phasizing spiritual devotion to God rather than elaborate external ceremonial. Ultimately the Brahmos, as the Samaj's members became known,
separated from the main stream of Hindu society and practice, and developed into a distinct community of faith governed by its own marriage laws,
and famous for its activities in the field of social reform. In western India a
religious reform body inspired by Bengal's Brahmo Samaj was the
Prarthana (prayer) Samaj (1867). Its adherents, too, were firm theists,
preached salvation through the worship of God, opposed idolatry and the
authority of Brahmin priests, and such beliefs as *karma* and transmigration.
Unlike the Brahmos they did not separate themselves from the rest of
Hindu society; and felt that personal religious adaptation and wider social
reform could take place within the embrace of Hindu tradition. M. G.
Ranade, for example, was one of its earliest members.

Rather different in emphasis and wider in appeal was the Arya Samaj,
founded in 1875 by Dayananda Saraswati. Its strength was in northern
India, outside the early heartlands of weatern education, in regions where
communal relations were more tense, and Hindus were under religious and
secular pressure from Muslims, Sikhs, and Christians. But again its appeal
was to men who felt religiously ill at ease in the changing intellectual and
social environment, and needed new and appropriate answers to problems
of Hindu identity, the relevance of caste, the nature of scriptural authority
and the right response to modern knowledge, including experimental science. Compared with the earlier religious reform movements the Arya
Samaj was far less western in inspiration, and blended reform with revivalism. Dayananda certainly preached theism and denounced the current practice of caste and Brahminical authority. (In vernacular Arya literature
Brahmins were denounced with the English word 'pope', i.e. as alleged
mediators between God and men: an interesting linguistic spin-off of Protestant missions!) But he accepted *karma* and transmigration, and drew his
main inspiration from what he accepted as Vedic texts. About these he was
fiercely fundamentalist, seeing them as the source of pure Vedic religion
which he must revive. Later Hindu scriptures such as the Puranas were not
in his estimation authoritative. This gave broad scope for religious and
social reformation because beliefs and customs could be abandoned if they
were only sanctioned by these later, 'degenerate', texts. Dayananda believed in the total separation of God and the human soul, and in so doing
placed great emphasis on the moral stature and responsibility of man—
hence the Arya stress on personal virtue and the performance of good
works. (Some of the latter also had a more mundane rationale: as in the case
of care for orphans, lest they fall into the hands of missionaries and become
lost to the Hindu fold.)

Dayananda's philosophical position as a dualist ran counter to another
strand in the contemporary Hindu agonizing over religious belief and iden-

tity. Advaita Vedanta, the non-dualist conception of the one divine spirit flowing into all men, was another philosophical approach which enabled many educated Hindus to remain Hindus in a changing world, to tackle new social and intellectual problems, and to take pride in their heritage as a 'faith' rather than a mere cultural tradition. Ramakrishna Paramahansa, a Bengali ascetic born in 1834, inspired a vital religious revival which is still strong in later twentieth-century India. A messianic figure, he preached the realization of 'God-consciousness' within each individual through devotion rather than works or ritual. His followers, especially Vivekananda who organized the Ramakrishna Mission to perpetuate the Master's work and teachings, and the monastic members of the Mission, almost certainly emphasized their master's commitment to Advaita Vedanta in order to make his teachings into a far more systematic and coherent 'faith' than he had ever espoused or preached. It was a faith which could be presented, as Vivekananda did at the World Parliament of Religions in 1893 in America, as an equal to the world's great monotheisms, as a viable religious option for modern man, whatever his culture or race. Vivekananda also stressed the religious duty of social service, and this became one of the hallmarks of the Ramakrishna Mission. Here was a compassionate religion with a clearly defined and intellectually defensible doctrinal heart which claimed to be 'Hinduism' but in reality was the reworking of one strand among the many which have over time contributed to the infinite variety of the Hindu heritage. But it has appealed to thousands of Hindus who could no longer accept many of the practices and ideas of that heritage and craved a new religious identity which involved no radical break with their social and cultural roots.

However, not all Hindus felt a need for reform, or saw adequate grounds for change. In tradition was all they needed for their religious identity; and new ideas were a threat rather than an invitation to deeper understanding of truth. Revivalist movements designed to defend orthodoxy rather than re-work tradition in the light of change, were consequently a powerful force in Indians' relations with each other. Among the bodies founded to defend orthodox beliefs and practices against western influence and Indian reform were the Dharma Sabha (1830), the Sanatana Dharma Rakshini Sabha (Society for the Defence of the Eternal Religion—1873), and the Sanatana Dharma Sabha (1895). Some defensive groups also emerged as a result of particular issues, such as an association in the 1860s to oppose widow re-marriage. But the most strident upsurge of orthodox opposition to change was in response to the proposed alteration in the age of consent; for this highlighted the threat of change in a religiously sensitive area of personal relationships, and also the spectre of change at the hands of a foreign and non-Hindu government.

There were other more diffuse signs of Hindu fears about the security of their religious inheritance in the changing environment, which in turn generated fear among non-Hindus and sharpened existing tensions and lines of division in society. One such was the movement to prevent the slaughter of cows—these animals being sacred to Hindus, but the material for sacrifice by Muslims at certain festivals such as Bakr-Id, which commemorates Abraham's sacrifice. This movement reached a peak in the later nineteenth century. It was highly emotive, and reached a wider range of Hindus in northern India than had been touched by revivalist societies or agitation against reform legislation. The movement was supported by the Arya Samaj and many local societies for the protection of Hindu orthodoxy. Special cow protection societies mushroomed, cow protection lectures occurred in rural areas, and itinerant Hindu ascetics appear to have been key agents in the movement. The worst repercussions were a series of Hindu–Muslim riots in 1893, in which over 100 people were killed. Another distinctive movement blending fear of Hindu weakness and revivalism was the development of martial activities to demonstrate Hindu courage and to protect Hindu interests. These included the development of gymnasia and student societies; and disciplined groups to accompany Hindu festival processions, as in Maharashtra. At their most dangerous martial bands took the form of terrorist societies which combined virulent nationalist and Hindu convictions. In the later nineteenth century this more sinister aspect of Hindu paramilitary activity seems to have found little favour with most Hindu politicians and leaders of religious reform.

Such diversity of reponses to change indicates a widespread Hindu unease, and a conviction that 'Hindu-ness' must be both defined and protected. It is therefore not surprising that for the first time the Hindu experience generated missionary movements; in marked contrast to its traditional tolerance of a wide range of beliefs, and acquiescence in the coexistence of several religions in India. The Ramakrishna Mission became an international missionary body while seeking to reconvince Indian Hindus of the vitality and relevance of their religious heritage in the changed world. Within the subcontinent the *Shuddhi* movement emerged, to reconvert the lapsed, where Hindu numbers seemed endangered by the missions of other religions, as in Punjab.

As Hindus began publicly to sharpen their sense of religious identity, so Muslims reacted in fear, and were forced into a heightened sense of their specifically Muslim identity. Cow protection, reconversion movements, martial displays and the championship of orthodox Hindu values and customs made Muslims aware that they were a vulnerable minority. Some like Sir Syed and the sophisticated products of Aligarh sought identity and protection in a 'modernized' Islam, much as some of the Hindu reformers did. Others turned increasingly to orthodoxy. In 1885 a society for the defence of Islam (Anjuman-i-Himayet-i-Islam) was founded in Lahore. It invested much importance in the religious education of Muslim children, and rescuing Muslim orphans 'so as to save them from falling into the hands of the followers of other religions', as the society's prospectus put it. It also took counter-publicity measures against Christian missionary work. A Muslim Defence Association was founded in UP in 1894. In the same province various major Muslim seminaries also developed, ranging from the deeply conservative at Deoband to the more modern Nadwat al-'Ulama in Lucknow (1894).

Religious identity was not the only cluster of linkages which came under scrutiny and strain. Among Hindus caste itself was a structure of self-awareness which took on new significance in the changing context of British dominion. Few reformers considered attacking caste outright; nor, of course, did government. There are scant signs of caste weakening in the later part of the century. However, changes in the economy combined with official enquiries through the census into social structure, including local caste ranking, made many *jatis* eager to claim higher status in the hierarchy, often to bring new prosperity and ritual ranking into line. 'Sanskritization' of *jati* life-style and ceremonial, a pattern of group mobility within the existing social order which had been visible for centuries, became more possible in the context of expanding opportunities; and the decennial census gave aspirant *jatis* a splendid new way of publicizing and gaining some public ratification of their claims. The Census Officer for Bengal in 1911 described the strain this unforeseen result of government enquiry put on the whole operation of which he had charge.

No part of the census aroused so much excitement as the return of castes. There was a general idea in Bengal that the object of the census is not to show the number of persons belonging to each caste, but to fix the relative status of different castes and to deal with questions of social superiority. Some frankly regard the census as an opportunity that might fairly be taken to obliterate caste distinctions. The feeling on the subject was very largely the result of castes having been classified in the last census report in order of social precedence. This 'warrant of precedence' gave rise to considerable agitation at the time and proved a legacy of trouble. The agitation was renewed when the census operations of 1911 were instituted. Hundreds of petitions were received from different castes—their weight alone amounts to $1\frac{1}{2}$ maunds—requesting that they might be known by new names, be placed higher in the order of precedence, be recognised as Kshattriyas, Vaisyas, etc.[73]

The same process was visible a decade later. Generally it involved low to middle rank *jatis* who were claiming higher *varna* status. One group (Rawani Kahars) tried to claim Rajput status in Bihar and Orissa: while in a district of neighbouring UP their caste fellows claimed to be Brahmins! Such claims were both signs of dislocation in local group relations, and in their turn a source of local tension.

Linked to movements for sanskritization, but of wider significance in changing group identity and enabling experience of new types of voluntary association was the formation of caste *sabhas*, a process visible from the later nineteenth century. *Jatis* are locally circumscribed groups into which one is born. These new *sabhas* were voluntary associations, and often spanned several *jatis* of similar names and standing across wider, contiguous regions. Their objectives were to strengthen sanskritization trends among their component parts, to reinforce the new identity by means of journals and meetings, and often to raise their members' educational standards by provision of student hostels. In the twentieth century they were to become active in politics, and to demand recognition in the legislatures and official employment as particular 'interests' worthy of representation. One major *sabha* was the Ahir Sabha which came into being in 1912. It included members from the whole of north India, held annual sessions which were attended by several thousands, published a monthly journal, and literature supporting the Ahirs' claim to Kshatriya origin. They were also engaged in sanskritizing their funeral rites in support of their claim to higher status; and some had even assumed the sacred thread of the twice-born castes. Not surprisingly some Rajputs and Brahmins resisted this ritual impertinence. In north Bihar tension led to violence and cases in the criminal courts.[74]

Although manipulation of the census, sanskritization and new forms of association were often attempts to change status in the existing hierarchy, signifying acceptance of ritual norms, the differential spread of education and consequent access to prestigious jobs and new political power gradually began to convince some lower castes that they must pursue secular rather than ritual ends; and exploit modern rather than traditional resources for influence. Non-Brahmin movements emerged, for example, in southern and western India, where the distance between the Brahmins and the middle to lower castes was most keenly felt, and where high castes had disproportionate and early access to the new education and its fruits. These movements became marked in the early twentieth century, when opportunities for the educated were expanded by British policies of administrative and political reform. British perceptions of castes as interest groups then made caste labels more attractive and productive; though the men who wore them often represented only a small segment of a *jati* or group of *jatis*. This seems to have been true of the Madras movement which claimed to represent 'Non-Brahmins'. But over all, changes had begun to sharpen felt distances between castes, to give caste identity new social and political salience, and to begin the process of prizing caste identity away from its origins, namely in the relationships of mutual dependence in a hierarchical society. As the social and economic order built on group interdependence began gradually to give place to a society where achievement and competition were significant, so the way opened for caste to signify modified senses of group identity; and for men to become aware of class position in relation to economic resources. A sense of identity akin to western class consciousness was still rare in the nineteenth century. Older identities were more significant for most Indians, however much these were being re-assessed and invested with new meaning.

The presence of the *raj* and the wide range of changes it triggered in India's society and in Indians' thinking ultimately posed new political dilemmas for the ruled. In their perception and resolution of these dilemmas came together their diverse problems of identity; in conjunction with the problems of dominion experienced by the British. Indians' political responses to the *raj* changed in the later nineteenth century. At any point in time they depended on the political opportunities made available by the rulers and by imperial choices of the interests they were prepared to countenance as legitimate. They also varied according to the political level at which Indians were politically involved: whether they were caught up in the rural politics of a changing economy, the bargaining and expanded patronage of the new municipalities, invited into or aspiring to the heady atmosphere of the new legislatures. Moreover, Indians' political relations with their rulers were bound up with their relationships with other Indians. Intricate new patterns of interaction began to appear.

However, the *raj* as constructed in the later part of the century offered three basic political options to its subjects. They could collaborate with its structures and conform themselves to its expectations; with the result that some would reap the not insubstantial rewards of co-operation. They could engage in guarded co-operation with their rulers, simultaneously manoeuvring for change in the structures, the rewards offered through them, and the rules of acceptable political action which the British overtly or covertly laid down. Or they could ignore the political conventions accepted by the *raj* and take to violent rebellion, with the intention of overthrowing rather than changing and then engaging in the system. 1857 had suggested that this was a barren enterprise. Not until Gandhi refined a tactic of non-violent, non-co-operation in the aftermath of the Great War was the range of political responses Indians could make to British rule expanded with a method of peaceful but overt resistance to the fundamental structure of the *raj*.

iv Patterns of politics

Studies of Indian politics written before the 1970s tended to have a narrow focus. They described British policies, the work of the legislatures, the emergence of political groups (particularly the Indian National Congress), and the development of anti-British agitation. Dominant themes in political change were seen as the ideals and techniques of imperialism, and the growth of all-India nationalism. This approach was understandable. British historians concentrated on imperialism in India as a key part of British world-wide expansion: consequently their main interest was in British policies and achievements, and the challenges to them. The emphasis on nationalism by Indian and foreign historians was equally predictable: because nationalism was one of the major forces re-shaping the world of the nineteenth and twentieth centuries, and India's was the first of the Afro-Asian nationalist movements which shattered the established international order. In this unprecedented situation Indian historians were under particular pressure to build up a mythology of nationalism, to laud its heroes and martyrs, to 'prove' the existence of Indian nationhood, and to mask the tensions which threatened to rend the movement and undermine the nationalists' claims. Furthermore, academic analysis of India's situation was based on the way English speakers studied history and political science— concentrating on institutions, parties, pressure groups—because these were the main forms of political change in recent western experience. Even when any simplistic notion of a mass national upheaval against the *raj* was discarded in favour of a more sophisticated study of élites who led political change, that, too, reflected western political theory.

However, this study has assumed as a starting-point a much broader definition of politics; in order to demonstrate the depth and complexity of political change on the subcontinent and to help readers see the Indian experience in its own terms rather than forcing an understanding of that experience into exclusively western categories. If politics is the way people perceive and act in relation to the exercise of power in the public domain, then it follows that in the changing environment of the later nineteenth century there would be a great variety of concerns for power at different but interconnected levels of public life, each viewed in its own moral and ideological famework, each generating styles of action deemed appropriate and effective by those engaging at that level. Such an approach uncovers some of the richness and diversity of changing political patterns, whereas concentration on imperialism and nationalism as the main modes and motors of politics can blinker the historian or become a distorting lens. Recent regional and local studies have done much to illuminate the diversities of politics in India even within restricted areas. While the 'Subaltern School' of historians have helped to give a voice to those who rarely found a mention in histories of the high politics of imperialism and nationalism, and have underlined the vitality and autonomy of politics among non-élite groups, and their profoundly ambiguous relationship with the politics of the articulate and dominant in society.

This section does not provide a chronological account of Indian politics. It explores emerging political patterns, by using the categories of different levels or arenas, particularly the locality, the province, and the subcontinent. This choice rests partly on the objective facts of the structure of government. Because that structure was so important in determining the power available at each level, access to it and permissible Indian political activity, it deeply influenced the nature of political awareness and action. Looking at these three levels also makes it clear that 'traditional' and 'modern' political perceptions and modes meshed in each, and thus prevents any simple assumption that any one level was particularly modern or traditional. (For example, the politics of educated Indians, so often seen as modern, on closer inspection turn out to be a blend of old and new.) Finally, this angle of vision highlights the business of making or failing to make links between different levels. This hinge-making, brokerage, activity between people with varied concerns about power in a changing context determined the larger patterns of Indian politics. It complemented the structures and actions of the *raj* which also built political bridges and beckoned Indians into political diversity. Indian fashioning of new political links among themselves occurred in various ways—by party organization, factional alignments, personal linkages, and shared ideological commitments—and became crucial in the twentieth century when all-India leaders tried to construct a broad-based national movement, to bring into synchromesh political awareness and actions which had very different origins, priorities, and time-scales.

The locality was the most geographically restricted of these three arenas; much smaller than the provincial unit of government. In rural areas it was the district or a distinctive group of villages. In the urban context it was any urban agglomeration ranging from the market town to the great city like Calcutta or Bombay. In rural politics at local level the crucial sources of power were land, water, credit, and influence through the patron–client network of relationships, dovetailing with local caste structure. The framework within which people perceived and contested for power was this social order, the distinctive local pattern of landholding, and from the end of the century, the rural boards which, like the municipalities, were part of the government's strategy of devolving power to attract allies and shift the burden of expenditure. There was also a profound sense of moral order in this deeply rooted world: a perceived rightness in certain relationships and actions, and expected limits on types of behaviour which could undermine the moral and social world. This, too, moulded perceptions of power and political activity. A wide range of issues was at stake, including the revenue obligation, irrigation dues, grazing regulations, legal and illegal cesses and modes of pressure by the dominant and landed, the availability and mechanisms of credit. Obviously the specific patterns of rural politics varied from district to district, depending on the local distribution of power, and particularly on the structure of landholding and the balance of numbers and influence between castes. But work has been done in depth on sufficient rather different localities for us to see some of the emerging patterns.

Peasant violence, ranging from grain riots to outbursts on specific occasions in response to particular pressures, was one of the most familiar political patterns: it continued through the nineteenth and twentieth centuries. In Bengal and parts of Bihar, for example, where European planters exercised tight control over the *ryots* who grew indigo, there was persistent unrest, erupting at times into open turbulence. In neighbouring UP relations between *ryots* and *taluqdars* were often strained to breaking point, and the latter were not scrupulous about using their bully-boys as well as their more formal powers to subdue their restless tenants. In the south on the Malabar coast the Moplah community of Muslim peasants was locked in an uneasy relationship with Hindu landlords; and government recognized it as an area of endemic rural violence in which economic and communal tension coalesced. Elsewhere peasant violence was less predictable and could be quietened by measures to ease specific problems, as in the Deccan in the 1870s. Other more sophisticated rural agitations involved substantial cultivators, and were directed at government rather than landlords and creditors. These were new political departures: evidence of changing economic conditions and expanding political horizons among rural groups who for the first time saw the significance of trying to influence government, and actually had the means other than violence to do so. One example was the disturbance in the Punjab canal colonies in 1907 when legislation tightening access to land coincided with increased charges for canal water. Its manifestations included mass meetings, petitions, and press publicity. Its leadership consisted of peasant landowners, helped by western-educated Punjabis who were themselves landholders as well as having a profession such as law.[75] In neighbouring UP there was growing hostility to another aspect of the changing countryside and man's relationship with it—the commercial use of forests and increasing restriction by the government on local people's entry into and use of the forests. Here economic grievance blended with a sense that the moral order was being disturbed by the imperial rulers; and it bred a variety of political protests, including refusal to co-operate with forest regulations and deliberate incendiarism.[76]

Not all rural politics were crisis responses to particular situations, or symptoms of chronic rural strains. Nor was violence the only rural political mode. Many had much to lose in times of turbulence, and it is important to distinguish between different socio-economic segments in rural society, and appreciate the different political interests and styles of action particular to each, even in one locality. One study from South India has shown the ordinary, day to day political interests and operations of a group of dominant peasants in areas of Madras Presidency organized for 'dry' grain cultivation.[77] We see them profiting from cash cropping and rising grain prices, tightening their hold on the local economy; and simultaneously increasing their political power as local bosses, through their position as village headmen which was sanctioned and utilized by the government which recognized that it needed their alliance in controlling the area. Such local bosses engaged in conflicts with men of similar standing for local dominance. Rural faction fights among the peasant élite sometimes broke into open vendetta or used the mechanisms of the courts rather than fists and sticks. Early in the twentieth century the development of district boards gave such men a further and more sophisticated arena in which to engage for control of local resources and prestige. The district boards in Madras actually increased locally available resources and so made politics related to them an essential activity for men with local aspirations or positions to maintain. The district boards disposed of considerable funds, and some could even afford to build railways. It was no wonder that local bosses rapidly realized their potential and sought access to the new funds and patronage available through them in order to build up their followings. The committees to which the British delegated management of southern India's temples in the later part of the century were similar local arenas where significant resources were at stake, and local leaders sparred for control of land, money, and patronage.

Of course similar local patterns did not emerge in all regions, because the resources and power structures of localities varied greatly. Even in the nearby 'wet' cultivation regions of Madras the economy, patterns of social change and of politics took a very different course from those of the 'dry' areas. In districts where there was a landlord class yet other patterns emerged. In the northern province of UP, for example, landlords had to maintain delicate political links with their estate managers and rudimentary 'bureaucracies' and with the dominant groups in the villages within their estates, if they wished to collect revenue and control the area peaceably. This political necessity stemmed from the nature of landed estates. These were often geographically split and scattered, while villages were sometimes divided between different landlords. Few estates were economic and social frameworks bound by traditional allegiance and deference. Consequently they were a political arena for village leaders, estate 'bureaucrats' and the landlords themselves, who simultaneously were engaging in the politics of collaboration with the British.[78]

In towns newer patterns of local politics were more evident; partly because of greater changes in the economy and expanded opportunities for education and new careers which modified the resources of power available in local public life, and partly because the British deliberately institutionalized part of the urban political arena by introducing elected municipalities. However, older political patterns of urban *raises* and their 'connections', engaged in bargaining and informal alliance with the rulers were only gradually replaced, or were integrated into newer modes of politics. The earliest of the new developments in urban public life were often as little recognized as part of the infrastructure of Indian politics as were the varieties of rural manoeuvrings for power and status. Both escaped the notice of historians who fixed their gaze on all-India Congresses and official political structures. But in India's towns from the middle of the century there flourished a wide range of voluntary associations and actions in which men were bound together by choice and the perception of shared interests rather than ascribed status. Those interests might be educational, recreational, religious or overtly political. But all were the means by which participants were educated in new forms of co-operative action, on which were later founded more sophisticated and clearly political associations and activities.

A few examples from different types of towns indicate the spread of this development and the span of people involved. It was not, as has sometimes been suggested, the pastime of an educated élite in cities with universities and an overproduction of matriculates. But it was in the great cities where western influence was earliest felt that the new associations first appeared. In Calcutta from the 1820s there were various student clubs, such as the Society for the Acquisition of General Knowledge, founded in 1838, which had 200 members by 1843. In 1851 the British Indian Association was founded, and dominated urban political life for two decades. Most of its members were rich *zamindars*, joined by some commercial men and western-educated Bengalis. Government recognized its role in forming and expressing an important part of public opinion, by nominating its leaders to the Viceroy's Council and the Bengal Legislative Council. But the Association lost its appeal for the growing numbers of educated and professional men, not least because it seemed to represent little but the landlord interest. It was eventually superseded by the Indian Association (1876), which was dominated by highly educated young men. (Of the twenty six members of its first executive committee, ten had Calcutta degrees and one— Surendranath Banerjea—a Cambridge degree.) Other interest groups which organized themselves included European business men; Indian merchants, in the Bengal National Chamber of Commerce; and the migrant Marwari community of bankers and traders, in their own Marwari Association. The activities in which these new groups engaged ranged from their own meetings, public meetings, memorials to government, tentative links with similar groups in other towns, to an attempt by the Indian Association to attract support from educated men in the districts of Bengal. They concerned themselves with a wide span of public issues, including Indian entry into the Civil Service, reform of the legislatures, tenancy legislation and, closer to home, the administration of Calcutta.

Extension of representative local government to Calcutta in the 1870s roused concern among many of these groups, but they were divided in their hopes for the future of the city's administration, the divisions reflecting the divergent interests of Europeans, the British Indian Association, and the educated ratepayers who campaigned for a broader-based elected government. Eventually three-quarters of the Calcutta Corporation's commissioners were elected by ratepayers—a development which opened up a whole new and valuable political arena in the city. (Just as southern Indian peasant bosses rapidly learned the value of the district boards, so even the most ardent Bengali nationalists in the twentieth century declined to withdraw from the Calcutta Corporation when they agreed to Gandhi's plan of non-co-operation with the legislatures.) The new Corporation was vulnerable to public pressure in unprecedented ways, now that its members had an electorate to consider. A ratepayers' agitation against enhanced rents in the 1890s indicated the range of landed, property-owning, and professional residents who were prepared to engage publicly in new styles of political behaviour. The agitation took the form of public meetings (at which even a few respectable property-owning ladies were present), a court case, as well as action within the Corporation. All of this was duly reported in the expanding English and vernacular press which, as the British had realized with concern, was a powerful generator of a growing and increasingly articulate body of public opinion on political matters.[79]

Bombay, too, had its new associations creating links between men of business and men of letters. But the heavy involvement of some of the city's Indian communities in industry and trade pulled the new associations towards concern for business issues. Bombay's early politicians were far more moderate and aloof from the populace both of the city and the surrounding districts than their Bengali counterparts. As a contemporary remembered of the 1860s, when Bombay was enjoying a cotton boom, 'All Bombay and its wife was too busy amassing handsome fortunes . . . to manage its domestic affairs'.[80] The first of Bombay's new secular associations was the Bombay Association (1852), the offspring of some of the Presidency's first graduates and a group of liberal *shetias*, wealthy heads of business communities. Just as Calcutta's British Indian Association came to represent a distinctive, privileged economic group, so the Bombay Association increasingly became the organ of *shetia* interest. The educated, professional men found outlets for their views in new papers like *Rast Goftar* (1851), *Indu Prakash* (1862) and *Native Opinion* (1864). One of their complaints was the financial mismanagement of the Bombay municipality, and the increasing burden of local taxation. In the early 1870s they launched a ratepayers' reform campaign. The battle for reform raged between *shetias* and ratepayers inside the Bombay Legislative Council, in public halls and private houses; and in 1872 the Bombay Municipal Act gave the ratepayers power to elect half the members of the reformed corporation, though the franchise qualification was so high that the educated were still at a disadvantage in city politics.

1888 saw further reform when the qualifying tax was drastically reduced, and all graduates were given the vote at ward elections. Political organization faltered after the conflicts of the ratepayers' campaign until the foundation in 1885 of the Bombay Presidency Association by three lawyers. Thanks to their energy it quickly became a significant political force in the locality, airing local problems and making demands of the Government of India on a range of matters, by telegram and memorial.

Two other smaller towns which exemplify the expanding range and changing styles of local politics are Poona in western India and Allahabad in UP. Both were very different from the cosmopolitan Presidency capitals just considered. Poona was a long-established religious and cultural centre in the Deccan, an area dominated by a Brahmin élite (the Chitpavan Brahmins), who increased their influence by flocking into western education and the modern professions. It was they who organized new schools and colleges in Poona, and new associations to protect their interests. Like the Bombay educated and business men they had little contact with the peasantry of the countryside surrounding their urban bastions. The Chitpavans' élite position actually aroused non-Brahmin suspicion and counter claims to places under the British in education and administration. Chitpavan Brahmins dominated the Poona Sarvajanik Sabha, the most prominent of the new associations. Founded in 1870 it organized meetings, and sent petitions to government on a wide range of matters indicative of the questions about the use of public power which were at issue in local politics—Lytton's notorious Press Act, Bombay's regulations governing access to and use of forest land, the Licence Tax, the Ilbert Bill, reforms of the legislatures, and that running sore, Indian recruitment to the Civil Service. But Poona's politics were bedevilled by feuds within the Brahmin élite: they rent asunder the Poona Sarvajanik Sabha and the Deccan Education Society which had been founded in Poona in 1884. The chief protagonists were B. G. Tilak, and Gokhale who later became Morley's confidante in the matter of reform. These two highly educated Chitpavans actually shared far more in background and interest than the issues which prevented their co-operation. These were partly personal, but also ideological in that they disagreed over the extent to which Maharashtrian (and Indian) regeneration rested on a return to strict orthodoxy aligned with overt hostility to the *raj*. When Tilak was defeated by the more liberal in the two associations he turned to a wider public and exploited an orthodox appeal in his newspapers, *Mahratta* and *Kesari*; and by organizing festivals in honour of the god, Ganpati, and the Maharashtrian hero, Shivaji, both of which played on Hindu and regional sentiment. His style of hostility to the more liberal social reformers paid dividends when in 1895 he was able to recapture the PSS; though he remained unable to appeal to the Maratha population of the Deccan by such devices redolent of Brahminical orthodoxy.[81]

In Allahabad there was no dominant Brahmin élite; nor was western education so available or significant for those who wished for local influence. Consequently the voluntary associations which emerged encompassed a great variety of interests, from the overtly religious to those more obviously angled towards the power generated in the new town government. But none was as influential as Poona's PSS, for example. The emergence of Hindu associations was noted previously as a sign of changing understanding of Hindu identity and the dangers to it. Another yoking of new patterns of association and action to the defence of long-standing interests was the co-operation of Allahabad's Hindu *raises* and educated, professional men, in attempts to control the famous Magh Mela, a religious fair held annually at the confluence of the holy rivers Ganga and Jumna. This was an important concern of the Prayag Hindu Samaj founded in 1880; but the Samaj was also active in educational matters, including the controversy over the use of Hindi or Urdu. Allahabad also sprouted an Institute in the 1860s, which probably represented the interests of educated Bengalis working in the town. Just as western India's Marwaris migrated east creating a vast web of business connections; so educated Bengalis fanned west, following the expansion of British administration, taking with them not only their administrative expertise but their political ideas, aspirations, and organizational experience, all of which served as a political catalyst in the towns where they settled. They were at first predominant in Allahabad's most significant new association intended to influence municipal government—the Allahabad People's Association—though local businessmen were also active in it.[82] Such a proliferation of temporary and longer-term associations, interested in such a diversity of local resources for influence, was evidence of the vitality of local politics in a changing environment. They were the stuff of which more modern political movements would later be made.

These examples suggest that municipal reform increased political awareness and generated new patterns of organization in urban localities. This was hardly surprising considering the new resources the municipalities offered to those who gained seats on them. Councillors raised significant amounts of money, and the incidence of taxation could be shifted to benefit or disadvantage certain social and religious groups. They had their hands on patronage in municipal contracts and employment. They could make regulations on religiously sensitive matters such as the management of slaughter houses. Service on municipalities also brought Indians into range of the official Honours Lists; and from 1892 opened the door to membership of the provincial legislatures. The municipalities themselves became an important arena of political action with its own stylized behaviour reminiscent of the rituals of British local government. Indians quickly learnt the ropes of debate in the council meetings, of manoeuvres in council to create consensus or sharpen issues and divisions. They managed the synchronizing of debate within councils and external pressure campaigns through the local press and public meetings. Local studies suggest that different types of linkage came into play in the alignment of groups in the municipalities, long-established patronage connections, personal factions, caste groupings and religious alignments—depending on each town's specific political ecology. In one eastern UP municipality the main dividing lines in council politics were caste ones, there being clear Kayastha and Khatri 'parties'. Between them was no significant ideological division, nor any distinctive class opposition, since both 'championed to some extent the rights and interests of the new taxpaying classes of merchants and professionals as against traditional landlord and aristocratic groups whom the British had tended to favour exclusively in the past. Both advocated more and better education, more and better municipal facilities.'[83] In the west of the province cross-communal alliances between Hindus and Muslims based on landed interest and trade were rare. Municipal politics increasingly reflected communal hostility and Muslim fears for their local position, which sprang from the particular patterns of economic change in the western compared with eastern UP. Their local experience rapidly came to be projected into the provincial and all-India arenas of politics.

The province was in one sense a natural level and context of political awareness and behaviour. Often its boundaries coincided with linguistic regions, creating among its inhabitants ties of verbal expression, culture, and historical experience. Often a province was a distinctive geographical area or cluster of areas, with particular problems or potential. Provincial distributions of caste, community and relative educational standards varied markedly from province to province, thus creating particular patterns of competition and co-operation between groups. However, this arena which was in so many respects a natural one only became so in practice in the later nineteenth and early twentieth centuries. As communications developed and agrarian change made viable whole regional economies, so new ties of interest were created, spanning older local boundaries; and new provincial resources were opened up and became a focus for competition. The province was also the middle tier in the *raj*'s framework: and the provincial government demanded the attention of men who were concerned with the implications of provincial administration as it touched their employment prospects, their careers or businesses, and even their religious sensitivities. Furthermore, new political resources, in terms of access to influence and benefits through new institutions, became available for distribution at this level as the British moved haltingly towards constitutional reforms. Not until 1919 did the provincial arena become crucially significant. Then the Montagu–Chelmsford Reforms did for provincial government what local government reforms had done for the localities from the 1870s, giving elected Indians wide powers of decision-making, raising and distribution of funds. In the previous half century the province was still a political arena in the making. But it was one where educated men, skilled in the political language and style of the rulers, were to become increasingly important in creating links with men whose base and expertise rested in the localities, who needed new political education if they were to enter and exploit the potential of provincial politics.

In the later years of the century a range of actions developed which indicate the people and material out of which provincial politics were made. Even brief examination of some of them suggests the potential and actual bonds and divisions between Indians within provinces and across provincial boundaries, and hints at the complex interplay between different political levels. At one end of the spectrum were movements which at first look far more cultural than political, but in which concern for culture and tradition blended with a keen appreciation of the changing nature of provincial resources. Literary renaissances in many of India's vernaculars are an obvious example. The Anglicists had hoped that infusion of western learning into Indian culture would reinvigorate vernacular literature: and in this they were proved right, despite the failure of their educational policy of 'downward filtration'. The Bengali renaissance was the earliest and most famous. Its fruits reached the West in translations of such works as the poetry of Rabindranath Tagore. But lesser-known flowering of vernacular languages occurred among speakers of Oriya, Tamil, Telugu and Marathi, for example. These renaissances created new bonds of sentiment, artistic and intellectual experience among vernacular literates; and, furthermore, stimulated some of them to a new awareness of their political position as linguistic minorities with low standards of education compared with other linguistic groups. Linguistic regionalism became a marked phenomenon of provincial public life in some parts of India. It bonded speakers of the same vernacular, and generated hostility towards other Indian groups who appeared to 'colonize' areas outside their own linguistic regions because of their education and consequent access to administrative employment. The Bengalis left a trail of hostility as they fanned out across northern India as junior civil servants, clerks, and lawyers. The Biharis whose area was actually part of the Bengal administration until the early twentieth century were particularly strident in their anti-Bengali feeling; and they began to demand a separate province where Biharis would have the monopoly of provincial administrative posts. Oriya speakers down the east coast from Bengal had the misfortune to be administered by Bengalis, Telugu speakers from Madras Presidency, and Hindi speakers in the areas nearer the Hindi regions in the north and west. Their linguistic revival began in the 1870s and generated from 1903 a political demand for a separate Oriya province where local vernacular speakers would be free of these 'foreign' Indian administrators who were intermediaries between them and the British. Telugu speakers in their turn resented the influence of Tamil speakers from areas close to Madras where educational opportunities were greater. The Telugu renaissance of the later nineteenth century fed into a demand for a separate Andhra province for Telugu speakers in the opening years of the new century. By the outbreak of the Great War there was in existence an Andhra Mahasabha which met annually and made this separatist demand.[84]

More evidence of the entangling of cultural, religious, and political awareness at provincial level, often in response to particular provincial situations, is found in the north Indian cow protection movements. Here old ideas of the sacred and traditional religious leaderships were yoked with new senses of religious identity and threats to it, and new modes of publicity and organization. The limited terrorist movements similarly reflected particular provincial strains. The terrorists themselves were a curious product of Hindu orthodoxy and western education. Among the earliest outbreaks were those in Poona in the late 1890s, which included the murder of two British officials. Violence was directed primarily against the British because of their alleged disruption of Hindu society and morals (in this case during the enforcement of stringent anti-plague regulations): but Indians who preached or practised social reform also became its targets. The terrorist society responsible, run by the Chapekar brothers, never had more than a handful of members. Its leader, Damodar Chapekar, was a young Brahmin outside the educated Brahmin élite which dominated Poona public life. His family were poor: he was only partially educated. A sense of deprivation combined with a profound conviction of imminent danger to Hindu orthodoxy generated in him and his associates a reckless extremism which took him far beyond the approval or control of his fellow caste men and co-religionists who were learning more subtle political adaptations to the changing environment. Across the country in Bengal a decade later, a larger terrorist movement emerged, but with many similar characteristics. Terrorist actions there ranged from theft to murder. Those involved were comparatively few and almost all were of student age and came from the three highest castes in the Presidency. They hoped romantically and unrealistically to overthrow the government. But their driving passions were economic insecurity, as an educated and prestigious group under severe pressure in a time of rising prices and professional unemployment, and a devotion to the goddess Kali, bloodthirsty and demanding symbol of the holy motherland. These young fanatics were organized in secret societies, which were bound by rigorous training, religious vows, and iron discipline. Revolvers and bombs were countenanced by few established provincial politicians. Yet this strand of political and religious violence continued for decades in the politics of Bengal, in highly ambiguous relationship with the open politics related to new provincial institutions in which substantial power was offered to those who accorded them legitimacy and abided by their political rules.[85]

In certain provinces the distribution of communities and castes, and their relative access to new sources of influence, produced distinctive political patterns reflective of particular provincial strains, and generated new senses of regional identity. The non-Brahmin movements of Madras and Bombay Presidencies were reactions to high caste access to education and its fruits, sharpening long-standing strains in provincial society. In the southern part of Bombay, for example, Maharashtrian society had a cultural tradition of anti-Brahmin feeling and lower castes' attempts to free themselves from Brahmin ritual dominance. Economic and educational changes intensified rather than softened such trends. In 1873 Jotirao Phule, a non-Brahmin who had been educated at a mission school, harnessed his expertise to this old cause and founded the Satya Shodak Samaj (Society of Truth Seekers). At the level of religious discourse he tried to disprove the need for Brahminical mediation between men and God, and to prove the equality of all men. He also encouraged non-Brahmins to improve their educational standards. It was a short step for non-Brahmins to call for an end to Brahmin employment by government until non-Brahmins equalled them in their share of provincial administration.[86]

Communal rather than caste tensions were predominant in other provinces, and gave rise to distinctive alignments in concern over particular provincial grievances. In Punjab and UP, for example, changing and sharpening senses of religious identity gave birth to new organizations and political styles. In Punjab there had been for centuries extreme religious diversity because of the area's geographical position as the gateway from the north where Muslim invaders met Hindu culture. It was not inevitable that religious differences would become crucial in Punjabis' views of themselves in the changing world of the later nineteenth century. That community rather than caste or class became a major determinant of loyalties within the province, the distinctive group identity people assumed when considering the nature and distribution of sources of power in Punjabi public life, was due to various forces. The balance of communal numbers was the background. But hostility between Muslims, Hindus, and Sikhs was generated by the work of the Arya Samaj, the presence of Christian missionaries, and the emergence of religious conversion movements; as well as the framework of government and the competitive style of politics the *raj*'s changing structures encouraged, and the growing dominance of high and trading Hindu castes in education and provincial administration. Each community began to organize in specifically religious bodies—Anjumans, Singh Sabhas, and Hindu Sabhas respectively—with a view to protecting their communal interests on as broad a front as possible. Across the border in UP Muslims were rapidly becoming aware of particular threats to their local position. Against a backdrop of Hindu revivalism which threatened the élite provincial culture, which had been moulded over centuries by the Urdu language and the presence of an urbane and powerful Muslim group with traditions of political and administrative expertise, the provincial government seemed to be undercutting the Muslim position—by its educational policy, its bureaucratic reforms and the expansion of local self-government on the elective principle. Simultaneously in the western part of UP Muslims began to lose land to Hindu commercial men. Muslim anxiety about their provincial position in relation to varied sources of power generated new province-wide defence movements; of which the most significant were the unsuccessful campaign to retain Urdu, the language of the Muslim élite, rather than Hindi written in the Nagri script as the language of provincial administration, and demands for special representation in provincial elected bodies. These spawned such new organizations as the Muhammadan Anglo-Oriental Defence Association of Upper India (1893) reorganized in 1900 as the Urdu Defence Association, which attracted an unusually wide band of support from among the province's Muslims, including landlords, lawyers, and *ulema*. In 1906 the Muslim League came into being, an all-India body heavily influenced by UP men and their particular problems, which connected the provincial and all-India political arenas.[87]

This broad range of provincial activity indicates that there was no clear division between traditional and modern politics. Educated men fostered traditional values with new skills; long-established leaderships were willing to use new methods and make new allies in the changing context. However, when western educated Indians tried to gain provincial support in pursuit of their concern for new sources of power in the *raj*'s changing structures or for redress of grievances which affected them particularly as a western educated group, then they found it extremely hard to attract allies, unless they could dovetail their specific concerns with other, more popular grievances. The fate of some of their political associations shows the enormous problems of creating public bonds of alliance across social barriers.

The Poona Sarvajanik Sabha at first steered clear of divisive issues; but in the 1890s it became involved in communal issues which showed up its Hindu and high caste complexion. When Tilak 'captured' it he tried to generate a popular following by techniques redolent of Maharashtrian chauvinism, and by sending 'famine agents' and students into the villages to create links with agricultural communities. But government cut this tactical ground from under Tilak's feet by refusing to recognize the Sabha as a body which could address government on public matters. The *raj* after all ordered the ground rules of the political game, constricting certain styles of politics, even non-violent ones, thereby reinforcing the constraints of social divisions on aspiring 'popular' leaders among the educated. In Bengal the

Indian Association tried to reach beyond Calcutta. From 1879 its agents travelled the Presidency, attempting to establish new branches and affiliate existing associations. In this they had considerable success: by 1887–8 the Association had 124 branch associations, most of which were composed of educated men. But the Indian Association also attempted to generate support in the villages on issues such as tenant right, and reduced its subscriptions to attract lower social and economic groups. However, the communal composition of Bengal was eventually to dash hopes of a broad-based political movement led by the Presidency's educated men. For most of them were of the three highest Hindu castes, the *bhadralok* ('respectable folk'), and they had little in common with their province's Muslim peasantry.

The problems of the Bengali *bhadralok* in extending their political connections and popularizing their political style were plain in the great upsurge of provincial political agitation which followed Curzon's decision to partition the vast and unwieldy Presidency in 1905.[88] This was primarily an administrative and economic measure; plans to rationalize the administration had been mooted in the 1890s. However, in its final form it raised a storm of protest from educated Bengali Hindus who clustered in Calcutta and in the Presidency's eastern districts. They believed that their separation from Calcutta by the creation of a province of East Bengal and Assam would dry up their career opportunities, and give more chance to Muslims and Assamese in the new province; while in the contracted Bengal more jobs would go to men from Bihar and Orissa. As the scheme matured, the government saw further political value in redrawing boundaries in a way which would actively help the locally backward Muslim community and neutralize the political influence of the '*babu* agitators' as they called the educated Bengalis who frequented the new political associations and supported the national Congress. The anti-partition agitation was led by such men; but it took far more popularist and direct forms of protest than the decorous style of petition and public meeting which had hitherto characterized the *babus*' provincial politics. Meetings and petitions were now backed up by a campaign to boycott English cloth and develop indigenous industries—the *swadeshi* movement (meaning use of things 'belonging to one's own country'). The campaign was taken out of Calcutta into the districts by lawyers, students, and schoolboys, *zamindars* and their agents. Even Hindu learned men, *pundits*, were roped in to give religious backing to *swadeshi*. However the blunt facts of provincial political life rapidly became apparent. These political and economic issues concerned only educated Hindus, particularly in Calcutta and eastern Bengal, and the Hindu landowners of the east (who were often one and the same or linked by kinship). Muslims, whether tenants of Hindu landlords in the east, or aspirants to education and administrative employment, would have no truck with the campaign. Communal hostility, blending religious and economic fear, erupted—into open violence in some districts. Ultimately the big Hindu *zamindars* also ditched the campaign, being more interested in retaining the political advantages of collaboration with the *raj*, particularly as constitutional reform was in the offing. Even the educated were caught in a cleft stick; unwilling to retract their overtly critical stance against the British on the partition issue, yet painfully aware of their long-term loss if they stood aloof from the processes of reform.

Problems experienced by provincial politicians in creating a broad front for political action were magnified at an all-India level. How were aspiring continental leaders to construct broad geographical co-operation except among men of similar interests? Interests which united some Indians were almost certain to divide them from others. Even where similar economic or professional concerns might join men across provincial boundaries, their attitudes would be coloured by the provincial and local infrastructure of politics in their different provinces. Indians active at each level faced several ways and had to consider several 'constituencies'. They had to weigh the resources and reactions of the *raj* at its different tiers of authority; and to look to the interests of their compatriots in locality, province, and subcontinent. Their freedom of action was tightly constrained by their interlocking relationships.

Despite the difficulties of operating in the all-India arena, it proved an increasingly significant and at times essential level of political action for certain groups. Here was the apex of the *raj*. Certain issues had to be tackled here because policy was made in Calcutta, consulting with London, which affected the whole country. Almost all the professional and political issues of specific concern to the educated were decided at this level—ICS recruitment and constitutional reform, for example. Furthermore, the British were prepared to admit into new central structures of collaborative consultation a few Indians who could claim some degree of continental status or expertise. Reform of the Viceroy's Legislative Council offered little real power to its Indian members because the official majority remained into the twentieth century. The prestige of membership, however, was a political resource which Indian members could exploit in all-India and provincial politics. Moving in the charmed circles of Calcutta, Simla, and even London, gave them the ear of very senior officials and British politicians which could, as in Gokhale's case, be more important than membership of a legislature. Yet other considerations drew Indians into continental alliances and actions. They needed to 'prove' their continental standing to reinforce their claims to be taken seriously by the British. Otherwise they laid themselves open to the charge that they spoke only for a restricted interest or a microscopic minority. Some provincial politicians also reached across provincial barriers to strengthen their local position, and draw on the resources of one arena to bolster them in another where their standing was weak. (Tilak was a fascinating example of a politician who tried to cement alliances in local, provincial, and continental politics at different times, reaching beyond his Poona 'home base' when he was under threat there.) All-India politics was therefore a delicate enterprise, fraught with difficulties; but one which could be immensely creative if pursued by men of broad vision, and compassion for their compatriots.

Educated Indians in the secular associations of the three Presidencies had seen the benefits of a common stance even before the Mutiny, on such issues as the renewal of the East India Company's charter. If they had need of further proof of the efficacy of concerted action in relation to government, the Europeans' example in the Ilbert Bill agitation provided it. It was no coincidence that so soon afterwards Indians' halting attempts towards unity came to fruition in 1885 in the first meeting of the Indian National Congress. Thereafter it met annually and became the one really significant all-India political body representing Indian opinion, demanding the attention of Indians and their rulers in the years leading up to the Great War.[89]

Congress was not a political party in the modern sense, or like political parties in late nineteenth-century Britain. It was a loose confederation of local men interested in the distribution, use, and abuse of public power, who found it mutually profitable to meet at Christmas time to air their fears and aspirations, and possibly to make demands of government, and to plan joint action. In fact the annual sessions were often a major social event as well, as eagerly anticipated as weddings. The fluid nature of Congress is clear from the almost total absence of institutional organization. It had no formal constitution until 1899. Participants in the December gatherings were 'elected' from a wide range of local groups or selected themselves; and the local Congress committees either did not exist for most of the year, or were other bodies which used the Congress name temporarily, when convenient. Even the annual sessions were *ad hoc* arrangements, organized by a temporary local committee in the place which had been chosen the previous year, often because it was the 'home base' of a group who wished to make a particular point, or because it was a centre in which a meeting could be 'packed' with local delegates. (Table S shows the predominance of local delegates at each session.) Furthermore, Congress had little permanent financial support. Most of the money it managed to raise in India was sent to England to support the publicity work of a British Committee. Only Bombay Presidency seems to have had no difficulties in collecting money. There the Congress politicians drew material support from some Indian princes, Hindu and Parsi industrialists, and, in the Deccan, from money-lenders, bankers, and merchants. Lack of organization and funds obviously hindered strong and sustained political action. Yet this weakness also helped Congress to survive. It gave it flexibility in response to changes in the political situation, and enabled it to absorb multifarious local groups and different opinions. It protected it against the factional strife which might well have developed among its disparate components if there had been obvious material and institutional resources and positions within it worth capturing.

In the absence of a formal constitution Congress tended to be dominated by a few major political figures. There was at first and pre-eminently a retired ICS man, A. O. Hume, who played a leading role in its foundation, guided its deliberations, and gave generous support from his own pocket. Indians who had met in London while studying for the Bar and the ICS, and might never have become friends or aware of common interests had they stayed in India, became the first generation of Indian leaders of Congress— for example, Pherozeshah Mehta, Badruddin Tyabji, W. C. Bonnerjee, Manmohan Ghose, Surendranath Banerjea and Romeschandra Dutt. All of these had while in London been influenced by a grand old Parsi, Dadabhai Naoroji, who lived in the imperial capital and from the 1860s attempted to form a London base to foster a sense of Indian national identity and co-ordinate action back in India in order to pressurize the British rulers and attract British public sympathy. Most of these early leaders inevitably came from the three Presidencies where western education was earliest available. The composition of the Congress sessions also suggests that support came from limited segments of the population. Tables Q, R, and S show the small numbers who attended, and the overwhelming majority of Hindu delegates, while among Hindus Brahmins attended in numbers out of proportion to their strength of the Hindu population. Lawyers were the single most significant occupational group among delegates: not surprisingly, as they knew English and could operate easily in the context of a constitutional framework ordered by the British, and could take a Christmas vacation more easily than many! However, landowning and commercial men were a substantial minority. This underlines the fact that all-India politics was not solely the preserve of an educated élite, nor were modern styles of politics insulated from men who were concerned about long-established sources of power in society. In geographical terms the Presidencies tended to produce most Congress delegates. However on the rare occasions in these early years when Congress met in other provinces, as in 1888, 1891, 1892, 1897 or 1900, men from the host province attended in considerable strength.

Certain religious and caste groups clearly had little influence in Congress; and some regions, such as CP, Bihar, Punjab, and UP, were commonly considered 'backward' in Congress politics. As late as 1917 a Lahore newspaper reported that 'the Punjab considers it an act of heresy to take part in politics.' As we have seen, there was plenty of political awareness and action in Punjab well before that date. But Punjabis found local and provincial politics more relevant to their particular concerns over public power than involvement in the all-India arena.[90] Regional disparities in continen-

Table Q. Religious and Caste groupings in the Congress 1892–1909

Year	Place	Total number of delegates	Brahmins	Non Brahmin Hindus	Muslims	Parsis	Christians	Others
1892	Allahabad	625	261	254	91	1	10	8
1893	Lahore	867	207	523	65	20	12	40
1894	Madras	1163	744	371	23	6	12	7
1895	Poona	1584	996	494	25	16	10	43
1896	Calcutta	784	282	427	54	4	15	2
1897	Amraoti	692	287	327	57	8	8	5
1898	Madras	614	401	192	10	8	7	2
1899	Lucknow	739	135	280	313	2	6	3
1900	Lahore	567	65	400	56	4	4	38
1901	Calcutta	896	268	533	74	2	7	12
1902	Ahmedabad	471	115	306	20	22	6	2
1903	Madras	538	336	180	9	5	2	6
1904	Bombay	1010	189	715	35	65	1	5
1905	Banares	757	268	437	20	6	2	24
1906	Calcutta	1663	523	1046	45	25	8	16
1908	Madras	626	383	206	10	20	5	2
1909	Lahore	243	63	169	5	2	2	2
Total		13,839	5,523	6,860	912	210	117	217

Source: P. C. Ghosh, *The Development Of The Indian National Congress 1892–1909* (Calcutta, 1960), p. 23.

Table R. *Professional, Social, and Occupational Groups in the Congress, 1892–1909*

Year	Place	Total no. of delegates	Legal Profession	Landed Gentry	Commercial Classes	Journalists and Newspapermen	Medical Profession	Teaching Profession
1892	Allahabad	625	237	161	70	39	22	21
1893	Lahore	867	305	134	152	51	22	28
1894	Madras	1163	544	211	158	36	12	61
1895	Poona	1584	457	149	437	26	38	50
1896	Calcutta	784	312	224	88	23	58	32
1897	Amraoti	692	135	257	160	20	8	16
1898	Madras	614	259	102	65	23	12	40
1899	Lucknow	739	176	112	100	21	17	18
1900	Lahore	567	245	32	77	23	23	20
1901	Calcutta	896	370	241	73	39	33	32
1902	Ahmedabad	471	168	162	23	12	13	4
1903	Madras	538	295	92	52	15	13	11
1904	Bombay	1010	362	110	219	27	34	12
1905	Banares	757	372	134	100	9	35	26
1906	Calcutta	1663	705	394	230	50	53	50
1908	Madras	626	369	95	60	17	11	12
1909	Lahore	243	131	19	27	10	4	5
Total		13,839	5,422	2,629	2,901	441	408	438

Source: P. C. Ghosh, *The Development Of The Indian National Congress 1892–1909* (Calcutta, 1960), p. 24.

Table 5. The number of delegates from the different provinces attending the Congress, 1885–1909

Year	Place	Bengal and Assam	NWP and Oudh	Punjab	Bombay and Sindh	CP and Berar	Madras	Total No. of Delegates
1885	Bombay	3	7	3	37	...	22	72
1886	Calcutta	238	74	17	48	10	47	434
1887	Madras	79	45	9	99	13	362	607
1888	Allahabad	254	583	80	163	73	95	1248
1889	Bombay	165	261	62	821	214	366	1889
1890	Calcutta	377	148	18	47	29	58	702
		NB 25 delegates were without certificates						
1891	Nagpur	73	56	5	137	480	61	812
1892	Allahabad	105	323	19	77	63	38	625
1893	Lahore	59	133	481	124	39	31	867
1894	Madras	30	13	4	132	37	947	1163
1895	Poona	51	24	3	1257	131	118	1584
1896	Calcutta	605	60	7	52	31	28	784
		NB W.S. Caine attended as member of British Committee of the Congress						
1897	Amraoti	33	10	1	17	593	38	692
1898	Madras	38	11	1	27	18	519	614
1899	Lucknow	57	603	26	36	6	12	740
1900	Lahore	38	39	421	57	3	9	567
1901	Calcutta	580	89	30	51	44	102	896
1902	Ahmedabad	20	5	0	418	16	12	471
1903	Madras	47	8	5	76	18	383	538
		NB 1 delegate came from Burma						
1904	Bombay	102	54	28	618	104	104	1010
1905	Banares	290	203	105	110	64	65	758
		NB 2 delegates came from Burma						
1906	Calcutta	686	187	139	262	160	221	1663
		NB 8 delegates came from Burma						
1908	Madras	36	23	7	134	18	404	626
		NB 4 delegates came from Burma						
1909	Lahore	20	64	76	57	6	20	243
Total		3,905	3,023	1,547	4,857	2,170	4,062	19,605

Source: P. C. Ghosh, The Development Of The Indian National Congress 1892–1909 (Calcutta, 1960), pp. 25–6.

tal political participation partly reflected the unequal spread of education across India, because the issues on which Congress concentrated tended to be those of immediate concern to the educated. However, Congress could become at least temporarily more popular in appeal and its range of support, if in a province or locality significant concerns or movements were linked with the Congress name or given support by all-India leaders. Quite clearly this happened in Allahabad in 'backward' UP between 1885 and 1892. Many wealthy business men were prepared to support Congress at this time, as were some *zamindars* and village leaders. Economic change and more particularly hostility to graded income tax was partly responsible for this influx of support from men outside the circle of educated and professional men. But the broad-based support evaporated in the 1890s, for equally local reasons.[91] Such evidence of fluctuating local support in the early years of Congress foreshadows one constant theme in the later fortunes of Congress—the complex relationship between continental and more local political movements and leaderships, and the need to create bonds between them if the strength of different parts of India was to be channelled into anything approaching national movement. In this enterprise leaders with a wide range of skills in publicity, communication, and brokerage would be essential: without such, local interests would threaten to rend rather than reinforce a continental political movement.

Early Congressmen were quick to see the sorts of issues and interests which would destroy their fragile and hard-won unity. To preserve it they deliberately limited Congress consideration to issues of a high level of general concern particularly to those who shared western education and professional expertise. Entry into the Civil Service, expansion of the legislatures, reform of judicial administration, Cotton Duties, and general levels of Indian poverty dominated Congress discussions and resolutions. By contrast it avoided many problems which were the really powerful motors of local and provincial politics, thereby preserving itself but limiting its ability to draw on a wider and deeper reservoir of public support. Questions of religion and social reform were excluded because of their divisive potential. Congress refused in 1887 to discuss a resolution on cow-killing, for example, although some Congressmen and important Congress patrons were involved in the cow protection movement. Such a self-denying ordinance cut Congress off from the roots of political action in northern India; though its rationale was to strengthen Congress at the national level by preventing dissension on this issue among Hindus and more crucially between Hindus and Muslims. Congressmen were ambivalent about specific economic problems, too; such as landlord and peasant rights, and the alienation of land. Behind this lay the fear of alienating actual or potential supporters. It was easier to protest about the 'drain' of resources to Britain and the high pitch of land revenue, for which the *raj* could be held responsible, than to delve into Indians' economic and social relations as a possible cause of poverty and rural distress. On occasion Congress did take a stand on a divisive issue, as in its opposition to government attempts to stop the alienation of land to non-agriculturalists in Punjab at the turn of the century. Its opposition by implication supported the interests of Punjabi Hindu money-lenders who were most active in the provincial Congress; though its argument was that the government's high and inflexible revenue demand was the root of the problem. This stand alienated Punjabi Muslims because the intended Act would benefit the Muslim peasantry. In 1900 Congress abandoned the whole question out of deference to Muslim feeling. The price of unity was high.

By 1914 Congress had established itself as a permanent and significant element in Indian political life. It had no power to force government to bow to its wishes. Yet government in its perpetual search for influential allies listened to it, and was increasingly mindful of its more moderate spokesmen. It was not in itself a political power base for aspirant Indian politicians: these remained in locality and province where material resources were available. Yet it was an embryonic structure and a powerful name invested with national prestige which politicians were increasingly reluctant to ignore, or from which they found it paid to be divorced. For a few it became their main arena of action and influence, if they were skilled in fostering cross-regional alliances, wording conciliatory resolutions which bonded rather than divided different groups, arranging compromises, and representing Indian views to the British in terminology and a style which their rulers countenanced as politically legitimate.

Furthermore in the interplay of men from different regions with each other and the *raj*, Congress had as a movement advanced its accepted goals beyond the polite demands of the early liberal nationalists and was now prepared to countenance novel forms of political action. In Bombay Tilak chafed at the restraints placed on him by government and the faction personified by Mehta and Gokhale. While in Bengal in the turmoil of the anti-partition agitation there were men who wished to dislodge the long-standing Bengali leader, Surendranath Banerjea. In 1906 these provincial groups of dissidents who were locally weak joined forces and the result was the injection of a far more radical temper into the resolutions of that year's session held in Calcutta. These included an endorsement of *swadeshi*, acknowledgement that boycott was a legitimate tactic in the special conditions of Bengal at the time, and a call for the extension to India of self-government like that enjoyed by the self-governing colonies of the British Empire. In the aftermath of this meeting Tilak tried to create a 'New Party', devoted to Indian self-help rather than petition to the British. Speaking in Calcutta after the Congress he spelt out a new political alternative for those who felt that violence was unacceptable and unproductive, but saw petitioning as equally useless. That alternative was boycott, or non-co-operation, in the vital functions of the *raj*—in defence, administration, and the payment of taxes. Since the *raj* depended on Indian allies and Indian co-operation, the obvious political response to this apparent immobility was to withdraw its key allies. Divisions between the opposing groups who became known as 'moderates' and 'extremists' lay partly in ideology and choice of tactics, but also in regional factionalism and personal animosities which were clothed in 'ideological' form to make them more respectable—and exportable beyond their regions of origin. They erupted at the 1907 Congress session, held at Surat, for which both groups had been carefully manoeuvring in advance. The session disintegrated in chaos. But Tilak's bid for leadership failed. It became abundantly clear how few supporters he had, how non-existent his 'New Party'. Most Congressmen realized the importance of all-India unity just when they needed to cajole the eagerly welcomed Liberal government into as generous reforms as possible. Reconciliation became unnecessary as the 'extremist' leadership disintegrated. Tilak was removed from the scene by a government deportation order. Others of his friends retired from politics or joined the majority. This left the 'moderates' in control: but ironically in control of a Congress which owed much to the preceding conflict. It was now a more vocal continental movement; better known as a result of the press publicity given to the dramatic factionalism which had rocked it; and better placed to deal with the government which now appreciated its moderation.[92]

However splits within Congress in 1906–7 were far less significant than the absence of a strong Muslim presence in this federation of local politicians who claimed to speak for India. The Muslim reluctance to participate in Congress and assertion of separate political identity was the other crucial development in the continental political arena before the 1914–18 War. Here, too, as in the emergence of Congress, the *raj*'s presence and changing structures, economic, educational, and social change, and shifts in Indians' senses of identity were in complex interaction, eventually producing an awareness among some Muslims of the need for all-India political action of a new style with new types of organization. When the All-India Muslim League came into being it faced many problems parallel to those confronting Congressmen—problems of masking or containing regional and social differences, arranging compromises, creating constructive rather than destructive links between political levels, and deciding on the most productive stance in relation to the British and their institutions.

By 1888 it was clear that Congress could count on little Muslim support. This was not because of any simple Muslim hostility to Hindus, or any machiavellian British plot to divide and rule. Rather, it was the end product of distinctive regional responses of the social and economic groups which composed India's very disparate Muslim community. In the three Presidencies there were comparatively few western-educated Muslims: Muslims were in business (as in Bombay and Madras) or were tenants of Hindu landowners (as in Bengal). Consequently they had little sympathy or common interests with the sort of people who saw value in Congress politics. In upper India, where there *was* a Muslim élite, we have seen how economic and educational change, Hindu revivalism, and government action made them anxious about their future and suspicious of Hindu intentions. Syed Ahmed Khan noted in the *Gazette* of the Aligarh Institute his reactions to the topics debated at the 1887 Congress: 'Can any Bengali honestly say that the resolutions passed . . . will be beneficial to any class of natives except Bengalis and Mahratta Brahmins . . . the Congress is nothing more or less than a civil war without the use of arms.'[93] One of the only prominent Muslims who supported the infant Congress was the Bombay lawyer, Badruddin Tyabji, who was already important in local politics where he had found it possible to co-operate with Hindus and Parsis of similar standing. He actually chaired the third Congress, projecting his local experience of cross-communal alliances into the continental political arena. Not surprisingly Congress was eager to have him in a prominent position as a symbol of the communal unity they claimed lay behind Congress, but which was disintegrating beneath them. Congressmen's need of 'token Muslims' was a persistent problem, stretching into the politics of twentieth-century nationalism, and even into the political choices of Presidents for independent India. It was to give those Muslims who could fulfil such a role particular leverage over their Hindu allies.

On the rebound from Congress Muslims in various regions founded their own associations, and Syed Ahmed Khan's Aligarh men toured India pursuading Muslims to repudiate Congress. However, an all-India Muslim political association did not emerge until 1906.[94] That year saw the Muslim deputation to Minto in anticipation of constitutional reform, and in December the creation of the All-India Muslim League at a meeting in Dacca of the Mohammedan Educational Conference. Both the deputation to Minto and the League ironically displayed in relation to Indian Muslims many of the limitations and weaknesses of Congress in relation to India as a whole. Yet this was hardly surprising, given the disparate nature of India's Muslims and the constraints inherent in political action at the all-India level.

The Muslims who waited on Minto and formed the League were in no sense 'representative' of the whole Muslim population. They selected themselves, and came mainly from northern India, and UP in particular, although Muslims were far less numerous there than in Bengal. Their demands reflected the very specific interests of educated and wealthy members of UP's Muslim élite. UP men ignored their Bengali co-religionists' wish to plead for the maintenance of a divided Bengal in their address to the

Viceroy. The demands for a strong Muslim position in the new legislatures reflected UP Muslims' experience in their local and provincial politics, particularly in the Municipal and District Boards. A large number of UP Muslims travelled to Bengal for the Dacca meeting, and came away having captured two joint secretaryships of a provisional committee of the new body, and nearly 40 per cent of its membership. Just as factional divisions and disputes drove Congress on to larger claims and more coherent organization, so among Muslims divisions were partly responsible for this departure into all-India petition and organization. It seems that some of the established UP leaders trained in the Aligarh school of Sir Syed realized the risk of a challenge to their leadership from a 'Young Party' as it came to be called—a younger generation of Aligarh men with fewer landed connections who saw little benefit from moderation and alliance with government, and more mileage in the politics of protest. Some even talked of joining Congress, as in May 1906 when the Aligarh College Students' Union advocated joint action with Hindus. To re-establish their position and head off such a dissident plan, Mohsin-ul-Mulk, S. H. Bilgrami and others acted swiftly, in drafting the memorial to Minto and travelling to Dacca to help found—and capture—the new all-India Muslim association. Membership was restricted to people over 25, who were literate and had a substantial income. So, like Congress, it drew on a restricted socio-economic as well as a regional clientele. Like Congress the League was also weak in funds and organization. Provincial Leagues were set up in all the major provinces, though the all-India body had no control over them, nor they over it; and each provincial league varied in political complexion, chameleon-like, according to the local pattern of Muslim interests. In 1910 when the first elections were held under the Morley–Minto Reforms the League failed to act as an organization and had no all-India appeal or platform. Financially it depended on the generosity of such Muslim princes as the Aga Khan and Nawab of Arcot.

The Muslim League was to have a far more chequered career than Congress, and its status in relation to Muslims was more dubious than Congress's position at the apex of Indian politics. Not until the late 1930s could the League even claim to be in any sense popular: nor did it represent Muslims of all regions until the 1940s. Many Muslim politicians made their careers and pursued their local or provincial interests in total disregard of it: and government listened and responded to many other Muslim groups in its search for collaborators. The League's appearance demonstrated the growing significance of the continental political arena. Yet its persistent weakness for so long after 1906 underlined the continuing importance of provincial and local politics; and the fact that there was no inevitable channelling of the forces generated in locality and province into an all-India movement even when it restricted itself to one community.

Examination of the political dilemmas and patterns emerging in India by the turn of the century has brought together the themes discussed earlier in the chapter—the nature of the *raj* and British attitudes to India, the changing context of British rule and Indo-British relations as well as interactions between Indians, and the development of new Indian senses of public identity. The half century after the Mutiny was a distinct and significant phase in the experience of those who lived in the subcontinent. Yet the evidence suggests that political change cannot be understood just in such terms as 'the emergence of the modern politics of a western educated élite' or 'the growth of nationalism'. Instead there was an immensely complex process of political response to the changing environment, which generated actions at different political levels in a range of political styles appropriate to each level, the power at stake within it and the perceptions and capabilities of those involved. Most of these were autonomous political developments, and often there were few or no linkages between them, or the connections were ambiguous and strained. But such were the building-blocks of India's political future. At the opening of the new century it was unclear whether new and more permanant linkages would be constructed, and whether all-India Indian politicians or British officials would securely weld together these disparate elements and by appeal, concession, promise, or threat, construct out of such political material either a cohesive new nation or a long-lasting colonial state. However, the lineaments of twentieth-century India were becoming visible. By 1914 there existed at least in immature form the governmental structures for administration, consultation, and the association of crucial allies with the *raj*; as also the political movements and styles which were to be central to the Indian experience throughout the twentieth century. Both British and Indians were making political responses to changes in the economy and society, in ideas and perceptions of identity. These changes were of radical importance compared to the previous half century when the new rulers had inserted themselves into the subcontinent's political structures and then been imprisoned by it, rather than triggering wide-ranging change which demanded reaction from British and Indian alike.

CHAPTER IV

War and the Search for a New Order

Change began to bite deeply into many areas of India's experience for the first time in the later nineteenth century. The subcontinent's exposure to the First World War not only quickened the pace of change and deepened its inroads: it elicited new initiatives from many of those interested in the future shape of India's society and polity. The *raj* began to re-think its relationship with its subjects and adapt its consultative and administrative framework accordingly; in the short term to win the war and mobilize India's resources, in the longer, to stabilize India in the economic and political aftermath of the war. The Indian National Congress was still a fragmented body. Composed of allies who co-operated for limited pur-poses, its capacity to take initiatives was consequently much restricted by its need to maintain a semblance of continental unity. But Indians were emerg-ing in the continental political arena, some of them within Congress, who were not just political pragmatists, but engaged in that arena with a vision of the future as well as an eye to their own personal or group interests. Among them were some convinced of the need for and viability of an Indian nation state, some communalist Hindus and Muslims whose vision was of a new order resting on religious ideals and identity, some Commu-nists who pinned their faith in redistribution of economic resources. But towering above them all was M. K. Gandhi, popularly known as the *Mahatma*, or Great Soul. Between 1914 and 1930 Gandhi and the British were consciously searching for a new way of ordering the raw materials of the Indian experience; a new framework, rationale and heart for public life. The official experiment took the form of tentative moves towards a more radical constitutional reconstruction and devolution of power, somewhat similar to the processes seen before only in white colonies. It was a design of careful, controlled change, in the hope of finding a medium-term solution to the problem of governing a changing India and channelling productively some of the new forces at work in public life. Gandhi embarked on the visionary enterprise of *creating* a new India which could achieve *swaraj*, self rule. Unlike the official design, concerned with re-forging alliance linkages, redistributing power and reforming institutions, Gandhi was attempting a spiritual and material reconstruction of society and polity on the subconti-nent, from the roots upwards, starting with the transformation of the hearts

194

and minds of Indians, rather than asking for political concessions from their rulers. The comparative power and appeal of these parallel strategies can be traced through three chronological phases: war-time consultation, post-war confrontation, and then the fragmented co-operation of Indians and the British in the later 1920s.

i   The catalyst of war and the official design

Historians rightly recognize that wars can make or precipitate radical change in economic, social, and political relations, and in attitudes and beliefs. This is particularly true of modern wars which necessitate major government interference in the lives of a state's subjects, and the expansion of administrative power in order to mobilize manpower and material resources for conflict. The effects of war became even deeper and more permanent once combat involved conscript or large volunteer armies, and civilian back-up forces as well as creating civilian casualties and hardship on the home front. It is tempting to argue that India emerged from its involvement in the 1914–18 War radically changed, and to point in proof to the economic developments accompanying the war, the reformed constitution which followed it, and the eruption of a new style of agitational politics under Gandhi's leadership. Yet there was far more continuity than change on the subcontinent, particularly in rural areas, although the war had significant repercussions on rulers and ruled, both in India itself and in the wider international context in which the Indian empire was set.

India became a crucial source of supply to the allied cause. Its resources of men, materials, and money were poured into the war effort. By the end of December 1919 nearly 1½ million Indians had been recruited into combatant and non-combatant services, nearly 1,400,000 British and Indians had actually been sent overseas. So had 184,350 animals! By the end of 1919–20 Indian revenues had provided over £146 million to the war effort, War Loans contributing significantly to this by raising £35½ million (1917) and £38 million (1918). The Government of India's military expenditure had risen dramatically; it had to raise its revenue demands by 16 per cent in 1916–17, 14 per cent in 1917–18 and a further 10 per cent in 1918–19. Most ordinary people felt the war's effects in higher taxes, shortages of essentials such as kerosene, and in rising prices in both domestic and foreign products, caused by disruption of international and domestic transport, exchange problems and increasing military demands (See Table A). The situation was aggravated by profiteering and speculation, despite government attempts to control prices: it was compounded by the monsoon failure of 1918–19. An official survey of Indian affairs accepted that during the war prices of foodgrains had risen by 93 per cent, of imported goods by 190 per cent and

Table A. *Prices in India, 1910–20*

Year	Index no.
1910	112
1911	129
1912	137
1913	143
1914	147
1915	152
1916	184
1917	196
1918	225
1919	276
1920	281

100-base in 1873

Source: *Statistical Abstract for British India 1917–18 to 1926–27*, Cmd. 3291, Table no. 297, p. 628.

by just over 60 per cent in the case of Indian-made goods. War-time controls and transport shortages also inhibited India's foreign trade and suppressed the export boom which would have occurred had India been able to take full advantage of the massive international demand for her raw materials. Yet the war benefited some—and not just the speculators with their dubious methods for exploiting official regulations and mass need. Industrial manufacture expanded, to replace goods normally imported by India—for example, in cotton, iron and steel, sugar, engineering, and chemicals. In Bombay dividends from cloth mills jumped from 6 per cent in 1914 to over 30 per cent in 1917. In Ahmedabad, India's Manchester, one leading mill owner told the Collector that in many cases mills there had trebled their profits in 1917–18 because of the temporary disappearance of foreign competition, which far outweighed problems of fuel, transport, and spare parts for their machinery.[1]

Economic change and disruption of such magnitude perturbed all levels of government, from the Viceroy concerned with mobilizing India's resources to satisfy the demands of his London colleagues, down to the district officer who watched prices spiralling out of his control, creating distress and disturbance. The economic effects of war quickly had political repercussions. By 1918 provincial governments were reporting regularly to Delhi the distress caused by high prices, and the consequent danger of violent outbreaks, grain riots, petty looting and other manifestations of lawlessness. In some areas groups of Indian officials went on strike, and the provincial administration feared lest the crucial local buttresses of the *raj* should be undermined by 'the almost desperate position to which many of

the lower-paid Government servants in the mofussil [hinterland] are reduced by the present high prices'.[2] Fortunately for the British local disorder
was never generalized; nor was there an all-India campaign against increased taxation. Had there been more than sporadic, local outbreaks they
would have had their backs to the wall, because of the withdrawal of troops
from India to the Middle East and Western Front, and the departure of
many expatriate civilians, including ICS men, for Europe and combat.
Hardinge as Viceroy wrote in 1914 of 'the risks involved in denuding India
of troops', and admitted 'there is no disguising the fact that our position in
India is a bit of a gamble at the present time.' By March 1915 there was not
a single British batallion, except Territorials, in the subcontinent, apart
from eight on the northern frontier which could not be moved.[3]

The political problem posed by the war became infinitely more complex
than local distress and dissidence when it created issues which were fo-
cussed in the all-India political arena and could only be dealt with there
because they concerned the nature and goal of Britain's relationship with
India. The presence of Indian soldiers fighting alongside British and white
colonial troops strengthened Indian self-esteem and Indian politicians' arguments that the war should be a turning point in the imperial relationship.
As the allies in Europe and later in America spoke of the war as one to
defend the rights of nations, the sanctity of treaties and charters, so Indians
began to apply these aims to their own situation. As early as 1915 the
Congress demanded an advance towards self-government and its President
asked the British to declare approval for this goal. Surendranath Banerjea,
speaking on the self-government issue, spelt out the connection with allied
propaganda and stated war aims.

Brother delegates, the idea of re-adjustment is in the air, not only here in India but
all the world over. The heart of the Empire is set upon it: it is the problem of
problems upon which humanity is engaged. What is this war for? Why are these
numerous sufferings endured? Because, it is a war of re-adjustment, a war that will
set right the claims of minor nationalities, uphold and vindicate the sanctity of
treaties, proclamations—ours is one (applause)—charters and similar 'scraps of
paper.' (laughter). They are talking about what will happen after the war in Canada,
in Australia; they are talking about it from the floor of the House of Commons and
in the gatherings of public men and ministers of the State. May we not also talk
about it a little from our standpoint? Are we to be charged with embarassing the
Government when we follow the examples of illustrious public men, men weighted
with a sense of responsibility as least as onerous as that felt by our critics and our
candid friends?[4]

Meanwhile Indian political activity began to give some substance to their
demands. By the end of 1916 the British were faced with a united front,
in Congress and between Congress and League, which would have been

unthinkable less than a decade earlier when the Congress split at Surat and
the League emerged to stake Muslim claims to special status. The initiative
towards Congress reunification came from Tilak, on his release from jail in
1914, and from Annie Besant, an English Theosophist who had made her
mark in India as a religious leader as Theosophy gained in popularity
among Hindus who were uneasy with their religious inheritance, and who
now embarked on an erratic political career on the subcontinent. Both had
their share of personal ambition and realized the importance of a voice in
Congress when all-India issues were at stake, though Annie Besant also
seems to have felt that reuniting and revitalizing Congress would convince
some younger Indians that terrorism did not pay. However, old animosities
died hard. Not until Tilak's long-standing opponents, Gokhale and Mehta,
had both died in 1915 was a formula reached whereby Tilak's men could re-
enter Congress. In each province men calculated that this might mark a
significant change of balance in Congress deliberations, strengthening those
like Tilak who wanted to push the British to radical concessions, and
weakening those who had co-operated with the Bombay 'moderates' who
had held out against his re-entry. When Congress met at Lucknow in 1916
Tilak clearly scored a personal triumph. Furthermore, his adherents were
elected to the Subjects Committee which steered proceedings, and the
resolutions passed indicated that the British would have to treat Congress
claims with a new seriousness, as it had emerged from its comparative
quiescence in the years since 1907. Among the resolutions was the claim
that the time had now come for the British to issue 'a proclamation that it
is the aim and intention of British policy to confer self-government on India
at an early date.' The British were pushed to consideration of their aims in
India by demands within the very collaborative structures they had set up.
In the Imperial Legislative Council itself the UP politician and Congressman, Madan Mohan Malaviya, spoke early in 1917 of the difference the war
had made in Indian politics.

I need hardly say that the question of reforms is a much larger one now than it was
before the war. As Mr. Lloyd George said the other day, the war has changed us
very much. It has changed the angle of vision in India as well [as] in England. I
venture to say that the war has put the clock . . . fifty years forward, and I
hope . . . that India will achieve in the next few years what she might not have done
in fifty years. Some persons are frightened at the use . . . of the term 'Home Rule';
some cannot bear to hear even 'Self-Government on Colonial lines.' But all will
have to recognise that the reforms after the war will have to be such as will meet the
requirements of India today and of tomorrow, such as will satisfy the aspirations of
her people to take their legitimate part in the administration·of their own country.[5]

New political moves were also afoot in the country at large to publicize
and back up the politicians' claims, in the form of two Home Rule leagues.

These were the brainchildren of Tilak and Annie Besant who, independently of each other, in 1915 planned new and more popular political organizations; designed to spread the idea of Home Rule and generate public pressure for it, and also to organize support for themselves to strengthen their hand in Congress. The two leagues were founded in 1916, complementing each other geographically as Tilak confined his efforts to his home base in western India, while Mrs Besant took on the rest of the subcontinent, fortified by her existing contacts in branches of the Theosophical Society. By the beginning of 1918 Tilak's league had 32,000 members, drawn mainly from the Karnatak, Maharashtra, and Bombay. At the end of 1917 the Besant league had 27,000 members, many of them in Madras, but some also coming from groups and regions which had previously had little connection with Congress, such as trading castes in Sind and Gujarat.

Both leagues broke new ground in publicity methods, to the dismay of provincial governments and some established politicians like D. E. Wacha who felt threatened by the support and ideas they were stirring up. Tilak and Besant both had newspapers at their command. The later's *New India* was so cheap that in Madras it had a very wide circulation among English speakers, even in rural areas; and had a specially large readership among the lower ranks of government servants. League publicity also took the form of vernacular pamphlets, posters, illustrated post-cards, missionary-style preachers, religious songs adapted for a political message, a drama society, reading rooms, discussion groups as well as mass meetings. Of course this did not amount to a mass movement. But the numbers actually involved in organizations with India-wide connections, concerned with continental issues, were remarkable when compared with attendance at early Congress sessions. So were the type of participants: for they included non-Brahmins, traders and agriculturalists, students, and lower government officials, and some men from regions which like Sind and Gujarat in the north of the Bombay Presidency would have been called 'politically backward' by those like Wacha who were skilled operators in the all-India political arena. The leagues' significance lay in this deepening and widening of a national political appeal and organization, in their novel style of agitation and propaganda, as well as in their actual demand for Home Rule. The pressure they put on the *raj* is clear from the official response—the banning of the two leaders from various provinces, the prohibition on students attending league meetings, and eventually the internment of Mrs Besant in June 1917.[6]

The Congress demand of 1916 was given weight by the backing it received from the Muslim League, in the 'Lucknow Pact' of that year which, for the first time, drew League and Congress together on a shared political platform. Such unexpected co-operation was a repercussion of Turkey's alliance with Germany, which had worried British administrators in India as early as November 1914. Pan-Islamic sentiment was ambiguous. It could divide India's Muslims further from their Hindu compatriots, as well as creating a tension of loyalties if the King-Emperor was seen to be in conflict with the Turkish Sultan, the Khalifah or spiritual head of the Islamic brotherhood. But events had conspired in the early twentieth century to increase Muslim doubts about the religious neutrality of the British and their allies, and to generate fears about the secular power of the Sultan to maintain his international position and safeguard Muslim possession of the Islamic holy places of Mecca, Medina, and Jerusalem. In India there was the evidence of the reunification of Bengal (whose partition had benefited Muslims), and the riots which followed a road-widening scheme which impinged on a mosque in Cawnpore, in the UP. Abroad, the British remained neutral when Italy and Turkey were in conflict, and during the Balkan War. Not all Muslims in India were deeply touched by these events, nor were all their religious leaders unanimous in their atitude to the Khalifah and his rightful status in relation to Indian Muslims: But by the outbreak of the war there were a number of *ulema* prepared to co-operate with a group of 'Young Party' Muslims from northern India on a Pan-Islamic ticket. Ironically it took them into alliance with Congress at Lucknow in 1916.[7]

The Congress–League pact was emphatically not an agreement between Congress and the whole Muslim community; any more than the foundation of the League had signified the emergence of a unified Muslim community with a single political voice. At the time of the pact the League probably had between 500 and 800 members, and the Lucknow agreement did not even represent all of them because the negotiations were carried on by a clique led by UP 'Young Party' Muslims. Under its terms Congress and the League put forward a scheme of constitutional reform. Congress gained at least token Muslim backing, vital if it was to put real pressure on the *raj*: while the Muslims' *quid pro quo* was Congress acceptance of their claim to separate political status which should be safeguarded by separate electorates for the provincial and all-India legislatures. In each province Muslims were to have a fixed proportion of seats: where they were a minority they would have extra seats as a further safeguard, as would Hindus where they were a minority. However when the political arithmetic was done it was clear that the minority Muslim élites in UP and Bihar did particularly well out of the bargain, while Muslim majorities in Punjab and Bengal were by comparison disadvantaged. (In Bihar and Orissa Muslims were 10.5 per cent of the population but under the pact gained 25 per cent of the seats in the legislature: in UP where Muslims were 14 per cent of the population they gained 50 per cent of the legislature seats. Whereas in Punjab the Muslim majority of 54.8 per cent gained 50 per cent of seats; and in Bengal the Muslim majority of 52.6 per cent were only allocated 40 per cent of seats.) Understandably there was Muslim hostility to the pact in many quarters—in the Muslim majority provinces as well as from more conservative public men, even in favoured UP, who disliked this new venture and the League's new allies. In Punjab the provincial league split on the issue; and in Bengal Muslim protests and defections forced the local league to come out publicly against the pact as it applied to Bengal. Some Muslim landlords and older politicians in UP also muttered of schism.

Prominent among those who contrived the pact were two brothers from UP, Mahomed and Shaukat Ali, who deliberately rejected their European dress in favour of a Muslim sartorial style which emphasized their devotion to the Pan-Islamic cause, rejected the political stance of the Aligarh school, and in their actions and their new Urdu newspapers developed a new Muslim political style. A combination of religious passion and political ambition was to bring them into conflict with their rulers and into alliance with a Hindu *Mahatma*.

Such a combination of wider and deeper political agitation and a joint Congress–League demand at all-India level in the peculiar circumstances of the war persuaded the British that they must swiftly design a new framework for their relations with their subjects which would contain dissidence the war had generated or sharpened, and would ensure active co-operation from those politicians who seemed increasingly to be potentially important allies or dangerous enemies. There emerged from the corridors of power in Delhi and London a carefully balanced combination of reform and repression. As British strategies for control showed, they had no intention of making very radical concessions or of abandoning their power to set out the ground rules for political action. Yet they were concerned to conciliate as new allies more 'moderate' politicians, while retaining and expanding the constitutional role of their established collaborators. When the British began to discuss reform in earnest the war had not *actually* undermined the *raj*'s existing buttresses, though it had begun to strain the administrative framework. The effects of international conflict were felt most deeply in 1917–19. But the potential economic disruption and political challenge facing the British gave those the rulers saw as 'moderates' greater leverage in relation to government, at a very early stage in the war. Hardinge noted in August 1915 in relation to the choice of his viceregal successor, that 'if . . . all moderate concessions are refused, and the people realise that they have a Viceroy who is out of sympathy with them, there will undoubtedly be trouble; for then the trend will be for the Moderates to become Extremists, instead of, as at present, the Extremists becoming Moderates.' Eighteen months later, after the crucial Lucknow Congress, UP's Lieutenant-Governor put the point more forcibly. 'The vital question for us is, will the Moderates rally to the side of Government and show some political courage and power of resistance, if Government does disclose a policy which can be weighed, article for article, against the manifestos of the Extremists? Many of my Indian friends think that they will, but that no time should be lost in calling upon them.'[8]

The precondition of reform was wartime security: and before the government was prepared to 'call upon' amenable politicians it took steps to reinforce its coercive powers. There was no dramatic shift to a more coercive stance during the war, merely a sharpening of existing trends. The *raj* had power to intern without trial, censor and control the press before 1914. However, in 1915 it 'topped up' its executive powers to deal with those it considered politically dangerous without recourse to the ordinary courts, in the 1915 Defence of India Act. It was prepared to use these powers, as in the case of the Pan-Islamic journalist politicians, the Ali brothers, and Annie Besant, even though she was a European and a women. The measure was used most in Punjab and Bengal, provinces where there was an underlying strand of political violence. Elsewhere officials dealt with troublesome people and situations under the ordinary penal code. Their task was made comparatively easy by widespread public acquiescence, and even the most vocal politicians' reluctance to 'rock the boat' to the extent of endangering the war effort or evoking official violence. The 1915 Act also added to official powers of censorship. Officials used these and, with greater intensity, the provisions of the 1910 Press Act; though there was no 'all-India' policy in these matters, and local governments were free to do what seemed locally appropriate. The result was a patchwork. For example, a book banned in one province might circulate quite legitimately in a neighbouring province. Over 1,000 individual titles were banned between 1914 and 1918. Securities were demanded from 289 newspapers and 389 presses: securities were actually forfeited in the case of 11 papers and 33 presses. About 300 editors and publishers were also officially 'warned'.

The Government of India preferred the postive way of propaganda to the negative strategy of control wherever possible, and from the start of the war it was pressed by London to undertake propaganda. The war years consequently saw the development of a range of official publicity, from films and tracts to 'loyalty postcards'. In the closing months of the war Delhi went further and set up a Central Publicity Board which acted as a link in an information system stretching from Whitehall to the Indian district. It evaluated publicity ideas, co-ordinated and spread information. Its work covered audio-visual material, posters, tracts, provision of special lecturers, dealing with the progress of the war and related domestic issues such as the evils of hoarding coinage, and how to combat the influenza epidemic of 1918. Local governments, however, had the greatest influence on the style and intensity of propaganda, as the Central Board allowed considerable decentralization in initiative and execution of the publicity campaign. UP, for example, had its own Board of Publicity which included officials, journalists, lawyers, businessmen and landed notables. It also had district war committees, a weekly war journal which was its main item of publicity expenditure, and it seconded an officer of its Education Department to propaganda work. Throughout India nearly 4,000,000 leaflets were produced, 331,000 posters, 2,500,000 war journals or special war notes, and 275 communiqués.[9]

Yet the spectre of revolutionary violence continued to haunt the government, although in practice only a tiny minority of political activists were involved in or countenanced violence, and it was never generalized on a continental scale. The possibility of constitutional reform seemed to officials to make the control of political violence even more necessary, and they were concerned to have adequate powers in hand before any reform of the legislatures made the passage of 'coercive' legislation problematic. As early as 1916 they were considering how to retain some of their wartime powers when the war ended; and in 1917 a committee was appointed under a judge from Britain, Mr S. A. T. Rowlatt, 'to investigate revolutionary conspiracies'. Its report in July 1918 pointed to Bengal, Bombay Presidency, and Punjab as centres of dangerous conspiracy and recommended emergency powers to deal with areas officially proclaimed to be subversive. These recommended powers were close relatives of war-time controls. They included trial of seditious crimes by three judges without juries, demand of securities from suspects, control on places of residence or certain types of action by suspects, and arrest and imprisonment in non-penal custody. The Rowlatt Bills embodying these suggestions were sanctioned by the Liberal Secretary of State for India, E. S. Montagu, with great reluctance. He told the Viceroy they were 'most repugnant', and although he saw the need 'to stamp out rebellion and revolution' he wished this could be done by due legal processes: 'I loathe the suggestion at first sight of preserving the Defence of India Act in peace time to such an extent as Rowlatt and his friends think necessary.'[10] However, Delhi pushed ahead and used the official majority to get the vital parts of the legislation through the Imperial Legislative Council early in 1919—in the face of every Indian vote. The concession to the concerted hostility of the *raj*'s established Indian consultants in the legislature was that the powers were to last only for three years and to be used 'for the purpose of dealing with anarchical and revolutionary movements'; while the second bill which would have altered the Penal Code was dropped. In the event the new powers proved unnecessary and lapsed swiftly. But they alienated a wide range of public opinion, from Indian legislators to such lowly men as taxi-drivers, and they nearly wrecked the venture which the British produced as the cornerstone of their new design for India, but for which they erroneously believed the new powers were a necessary precondition.

The Government of India realized well before 1914 that the Morley–

Minto Reforms could not be a permanent framework for the organization of government and the attraction of influential allies. But its programme for change was limited to freeing Delhi from some of London's controls—witness to long-standing strains within the *raj*'s structure—and extending the principle of decentralizing power to the provinces, while increasing the number of Indians employed in the administration. Overarching any change was the assumed permanence of British rule. In a letter to London in 1912 Hardinge asserted, 'Consequently, holding as I do . . . that, in order to ensure proper progress and development in this country, there can be no question as to the permanency of British rule in India, Colonial *swaraj* on the lines of Colonial self-government in our Dominions must be absolutely ruled out.' With this Lord Crewe, Secretary of State for India, agreed profoundly, and called the idea of 'working for an ultimately self-governing India' a 'hallucination'. By mid-1915, however, Hardinge was convined that 'the old régime *must* be changed': though he still thought that the most urgent matter was the loosening of London's stranglehold over Delhi.[11] Under his successor, Lord Chelmsford, policy advanced rapidly; partly because of articulate political pressure in India and partly because evidence from the battlefields of the Somme and the bungled Mesopotamia campaign indicated that there would be no quick victory and cast doubts on the efficiency of the Government of India as currently organized.

Discussions between Delhi and the provincial administrations led to a despatch of November 1916 to London proposing that in recognition of India's war services the British should make a range of generous gestures. These should include rewards to Indian princes, the grant of commissions in the army to Indians, and the removal of certain existing grievances such as the cotton excise duties and European exemption from the Arms Act on purely racial grounds. But its most important suggestion was that Britain should announce its goal for India and take steps towards it. After an India Office Committee and the Cabinet had considered it, the Secretary of State, now E. S. Montagu who was known for his liberal views, made the momentous announcement of 20 August 1917 that the goal of British policy was 'increasing association of Indians in every branch of the administration, and the gradual development of self-governing institutions, with a view to the progressive realisation of responsible government in India as an integral part of the British Empire.' Here was no licence for independence, no intended relaxation of British control of the nature and pace of constitutional change. The wording was the result of compromise and misunderstanding as well as due deliberation. But it expanded so significantly any former ideas about Indian responsibility in government that it marked a real turning point in imperial policy. For the first time something like colonial self-government was envisaged, however remotely, for a non-white colony, though the first steps would clearly be at the provincial level.[12]

Predictably this pronouncement attracted conservative criticism in England: though—significantly—very few British officials in India thought it unwise or untimely.

The processes of reform were even more tortuous than the events leading up to the Declaration. They began with a progress round India by Chelmsford and Montagu in the cold weather of 1917–18, during which they listened to a bewildering variety of Indian and European individuals and groups who came to put their ideas, hopes, and fears for the future of India and themselves in particular. In July 1918 their report appeared proposing reforms which would enact the 1917 Declaration. For the next eighteen months this was in turn discussed by the different segments of the government, by Parliament and a Franchise and Functions Committee which toured India. The end product was the Government of India Act of 1919, the so-called Montagu–Chelmsford Reforms, even though they differed in some respects from the proposals the two men had made. By this Act the provincial and central legislative councils were enlarged, and freed from the constraint of an official majority, though provincial governors and Viceroy respectively kept reserved powers, for example to certify legislation, should deadlock occur between the legislative and executive branches of government. Certain topics remained the preserve of the Government of India (e.g. military matters, foreign affairs, income tax, currency, communications, criminal law), while other areas of government were to become provincial subjects (e.g. local self-government, public health, education, land revenue administration, and 'law and order'). No radical change occurred in the Government of India: but in the provincial administrations real change occurred. At that level under a system known as 'dyarchy' some topics were 'transferred' to Indian ministers responsible to the legislature and through it to the electorate; while 'reserved' subjects were dealt with directly by the Governor and his executive council. In the transferred category were agriculture, public works, education, local self-government and Indian education: the reserved areas included irrigation, land revenue administration, police, administration of justice, prisons, and control of newspapers, books, and presses. The provinces were freed from some of Delhi's control not only by the distribution of topics between centre and provinces, but by the allocation of certain sources of finance to the provinces, such as land revenue.

The franchise was overhauled and enlarged, but in general it was linked to the amount of tax of different kinds men paid: though, for example, all ex-soldiers were automatically enfranchised. About one tenth of the adult male population received the vote, but even in this small group many were illiterate. Figure i, a speciment ballot paper, shows the symbols used to help illiterate voters identify their candidate. Some of these symbols could be highly emotive. Different colour ballot boxes were also sometimes used.

Constituency—BOMBAY CITY—
(North)   Non-Muhammadan
Urban.

Name or Number of Polling Station.

Number of Elector
on Electoral Roll.

Ward.

Part of Roll.

Signature or Thumb Impression
of Elector.

NAME AND SYMBOL OF CANDIDATE उमेदवाराचें नांव व चिन्ह. उमेदवारनुं नाम तथा निशान.		CROSS कुली × खाडी ×
ANANDRAO NARAYAN SURVE आनंदराव नारायण सुर्वे आनंदराव नारायणु सुर्वे		
FRAMROZ JAMSHEDJI GINWALLA ... फ्रामरोज जमशेटजी गिनवाला फ्रामरोज जमशेडजी गिनवाला		
KHIMJI NATHU ... खिमजी नथू खीमजी नाथु		
MANAJI RAJUJI .. मानाजी राजूजी... मानाजी राजूजी		
MANCHERSHA DHUNJIBHAI GILDER. मनचरशा धनजीभाई गिल्डर मनचेरशा धनजभाई गिलडर		
MAVJI GOVINDJI SETH मावजी गोविंदजी शेठ मावजी गोविंदजी शेठ		
MORESHWAR CHINTAMAN JAVLE ... मोरेश्वर चिंतामण जावळे मोरेश्वर चिंतामण जावळे		
NARAYAN DAMODAR SAVARKAR ... नारायण दामोदर सावरकर... नारायण दामोदर सावरकर		
NISSIM, MEYER .. निसिम, मेयर निसिम, मेयर		
RAJARAM KESHAV VAIDYA ... राजाराम केशव वैद्य राजाराम केशव वैद्य		
RAMCHANDRA SANTURAM ASAVLE... रामचंद्र संतुराम आसवले रामचंद्र संतुराम आसवले		
REUBEN SOLOMON रूबेन सालोमन ... रूबेन सोलोमन ...		✓
........NOTE.—See Instructions printed on the reverse........ टीप.—मागील बाजूवर छापिलेल्या सूचना पहा. टीप—पाछळ छापेली सूचना जुओ.		

Fig. i. Specimen Ballot Paper as used under 1919 Reforms

Each province enfranchised a few women, though the Act did not specifically give women the vote and left it to the provincial legislatures to remove the sex barrier if they wished to. But in every province except Madras, where there were 116,000 women voters, the number was less than 1 per cent of the provincial adult female population.

Yet in the allocation of seats in the provincial legislatures it was clear that older strategies of imperial control were still at work, and in fact were being extended: the strategies of incorporating groups perceived as significant into the imperial consultative structure, making provision for the representation of important 'interests', and maintaining a balance among subjects to buttress British rule. So rural areas were given a dominant representation in the allocation of seats between urban and rural (see Table B), offering opportunities to well-trusted rural notables over against aspirant urban politicians. Special Communal Electorates linked to reserved seats were provided for Muslims, Punjab Sikhs, Indian Christians, Anglo-Indians and Europeans. Seats were 'reserved' for various other interests such as non-Brahmins; while certain socio-economic interest groups like landowners, businessmen and university graduates also had special electorates and reserved seats. Communal representation also operated in relation to the all-India legislative council in Delhi. So the fateful principle Minto and Morley had conceded in 1909 as a result of the importunities of one Muslim pressure group was retained and expanded. However much Montagu and Chelmsford disliked the idea of communal electorates as divisive they felt they could not abandon them because of past assurances and also the evidence of the Lucknow Pact. Many of their petitioners in 1917–18 clamoured for special positions in the legislatures, too. The reforms took the Lucknow Pact as guide in the distribution of Muslim seats: so Muslims in provinces where they were a minority benefited while the disadvantage written into the pact for provincial Muslim majorities was now officially sanctioned. Punjabi Sikhs also did well. Although they were only 11. 1 per cent of the provincial population they produced 24.1 per cent of voters and had 17.9 per cent of the communal seats.

So the British made their bid for a new order in India. By this plan they hoped to control dissent, defuse tension, and channel the obvious political potential being generated among Indians into constructive use of power, particularly at provincial level. The Montagu–Chelmsford Reforms were thus a very significant departure. They offered Indians substantial access to the *raj*'s consultative structures in Delhi and the provinces, and in each province both legislative and executive power on an unprecedented scale. The provincial arena of politics was greatly enriched by new resources, and its ground rules were changed by new institutions. Yet there were potentially serious limitations: financial restrictions, the small franchise, the weighting of each legislature with special interest and rural representation,

Table B. The Composition of the Provincial Legislative Councils, as Laid Down in the Electoral Rules

Province	Executive Councillors and nominated members (other than those nominated to represent specified classes or interests) (a)	Members nominated to represent the classes or interests specified (a)					Members returned by General Constituencies								Members returned by Special Constituencies			Total
		Depressed classes	Anglo-Indians	Indian Christians	Labour	Others	Non-Muhammadan Urban	Non-Muhammadan Rural	Muhammadan Urban	Muhammadan Rural	Sikhs	Anglo-Indians	Indian Christians	Europeans	Land-holders	University	Commerce and Industry, etc.	
Madras	23	10	—	—	—	1 (Backward tracts)	9 (3 reserved for non-Brahmins)	56 (25 reserved for non-Brahmins)	2	11	—	1	5	1	6	1	6 (5 Commerce and Industry and 1 Planting)	132
Bombay	20	2	1	1	3	1 (Cotton trade)	11 (1 reserved for Mahrattas)	35 (6 reserved for Mahrattas)	5	22	—	—	—	2	3	1	7	114
Bengal	22	1	—	—	2	—	11	35	6	33	—	2	—	5	5	2	15	140
United Provinces	20	1	1	1	1	—	8	52	4	25	—	—	—	1	6	1	3	123
Punjab	18	—	1	1	1	2 (1 European and 1 Military)	7	13	5	27	12 (1 Urban 11 Rural)	—	—	—	4	1	2	94
Bihar and Orissa	18	2	1	1	1	4 (2 Aborigines Industry other than Planting and Mining 1 Bengalis)	6	42	3	15	—	—	—	1	5	1	3 (Planting and Mining)	103
Central Provinces (including Berar)	11	4	1 (Anglo-Indian and European)	—	1	1 (Excluded Areas)	9	32	1	6	—	—	—	—	3	1	3 (2 Commerce and Industry, and 1 Mining)	73
Assam	12	—	—	—	1	1 (Backward tracts)	1 (this is a non-communal constituency)	20	—	12	—	—	—	—	—	—	6 (5 Planting and 1 Commerce and Industry)	53
Burma	22	—	—	—	1	—	General Urban 14 / Indian Urban 8	General Rural 44 / Karen Rural 5			—	1	—	1	—	1	6	103

(a) The number of officials included among the nominated members may not exceed the following Maxima: Madras 19, Bombay 16, Bengal 18, United Provinces 16, Punjab 14, Bihar and Orissa 18, Central Provinces 8, Assam 7, Burma 14.

Source: Report of the Indian Statutory Commission Volume I—Survey, Cmd. 3568, pp. 114–15.

the reserve powers of the executive. The British had placed their cards on the table—in a gamble for Indian co-operation. The anticipated benefits might not outweigh the drawbacks and limitations of the proposals in the eyes of men interested in politics at the provincial and continental levels. If 'moderate' politicians did not come forward to work the new system the British might find themselves in a worse state: with their older alliance structures weakened by the new constitution, yet having to resort to official executive action which would be more unpopular than ever in the light of their declared goal and the expectations aroused by lengthy public discussion of reform and their solicitation of public opinion, just when they opened themselves to informed criticism in the new legislatures. How Indians reacted to the official design depended not just on its merits as a constitution, but on their reactions to the coercive element in the design (including the Rowlatt Act), on external factors such as the Turkish problem, and on the thrusts and constraints of local politics. Furthermore, Indian responses became enmeshed with the rise to public prominence of M. K. Gandhi, who in a manner unprecedented among Indian public men had a clear and consuming vision of India's future.

ii *M. K. Gandhi and the enterprise of swaraj*

Such is the mythology now surrounding Gandhi that it is hard to realize how unlikely a candidate he was for all-India political prominence in the early twentieth century and, indeed, how strange and unprepossessing a figure he was to his contemporaries. He was born in 1869 into a western Indian family who were grocers by caste, though its men had for several generations been in the administrative service of minor Indian princes in Gujarat. The young Gandhi was awkward, shy, and barely able to follow English: but when as a teenager (but already married) he lost his father, his family decided to send him to England to become a lawyer. His English experience was an emotional and social ordeal; and he soon abandoned his early attempts at being a late-Victorian dandy and lived in London as quietly and cheaply as possible. His only 'public' venture was activity in the Vegetarian Society! Gandhi returned to India a barrister in name, but failed in practice in Bombay because he was too tongue-tied to speak in his first case. A year's legal contract with an Indian firm in South Africa was a welcome relief from professional failure and dependence on his family. He went in 1893 and stayed until 1914, becoming the main spokesman for Indians in their struggles against white settler racial policies. He had none of the advantages which helped to make the all-India leaders of his vintage. He was from an area undistinguished in Congress politics; he was not a Brahmin or even from a traditional 'writer' caste. Nor did he have the education the Presidency towns could provide, the professional status and expertise of a Surendranath Banerjea, a Pherozeshah Mehta or a Gokhale; nor the connections which such men had acquired by legal practice or educational work, and long involvement in politics and a range of voluntary associations. He had to make his mark in 1915 as a middle-aged stranger lacking powerful backers and allies, and without institutional standing in local, provincial or all-India politics.

South Africa was a crucial experience in fashioning Gandhi into a potential national leader.[14] It prepared him internally to take a public role in his homeland by giving him a new confidence in his ability to handle public issues, deal with large numbers of Indians, and both confront and co-operate with men in authority. As he tried to help Indians in Africa he taught himself the rudiments of political organisation and publicity, and launched his first journalistic venture, *Indian Opinion*, to publicize immediate political issues, rally support, and suggest strategies for coping with the situation. It also educated Indians in English and several vernaculars in a wide range of social and religious issues. It was the start of an immense literary outpouring. Papers, pamphlets, books, and a vast personal correspondence were one of the hallmarks and mechanisms of Gandhi's public influence in India. His championship of Indian rights also gave him a public reputation in his homeland, but as a social worker rather than as a potential political leader. The Government of India recognized his services to Indians abroad by awarding him a Kaiser-i-Hind Gold Medal in 1915. His name had become known in Congress circles, and he had forged a close friendship with Gokhale, who visited him in South Africa, and whom he called his political *guru*. It is significant that Gokhale, realizing how out of touch Gandhi would be with India, advised him to observe a year's silence on public matters when he returned.

Gandhi's South African experience enriched him in ways which were to give him a potential very different from that of men already established in the all-India political arena. The variety of Indians in Africa, ranging from Muslim traders to low-caste indentured labourers, and the diversity of their problems, drew him into contact with a wider range of his compatriots than his contemporaries in India would have had occasion to meet, let alone weld into a co-operating political group. They included men from southern and western India, Hindus and Muslims, people of very little education, traders and labourers; and women—whose marital and therefore moral status was threatened by a court judgment which would have invalidated all non-Christian Indian marriages. In helping them Gandhi learnt and experimented with different techniques for putting pressure on the authorities in Africa and London, and for binding Indians together. These included the conventional political methods of the public meeting, the petition, visits to government officials, including the Colonial Office in London, and press campaigns. But when it came to challenging registration laws and bans on entry into different provinces because of racial identity when such decorous methods had failed, Gandhi took Indians into direct but non-violent confrontation with authority; as when he organized bonfires of registration documents or an Indian march into prohibited territory. Yet this method of non-violent resistance which he used from 1907 was not just passive resistance as known to the English-speaking world. For him it was a moral force, a mode of conducting unavoidable conflict which was integral to his religious vision of life. He called it 'satyagraha' (truth-force or soul-force), to distinguish it from passive resistance, the pragmatic response of a weak group to a situation in which they had no other means of redress.

It is crucial to try to understand Gandhi's religious sense and to see something of his vision of the meaning of man and his world. Otherwise the historian can fall victim to a cynical analysis of Gandhi as 'using' religion to cloak political ambition and manoeuvre; an attitude common among British officials and even his Indian contemporaries, who found him at times exasperating and unpredictable, and could not conceive politics in the religious and moral language in which he frequently discussed it. This should not lead to unthinking acceptance of Gandhi's claims, and uncritical adulation, as occurred among some of his devotees. Gandhi's vision dawned on him gradually in Africa, particularly in the first decade of the century, though he continued to explore its ramifications in changing situations, and saw himself as a pilgrim in search of deeper truth.

Gandhi saw people as spiritual beings created to search for the abiding truth which was their own deepest nature and underlay the whole universe. He believed passionately that there were as many religions as there were individuals, because each person to be fully a person had to reach truth in his or her own way. In his autobiography he expounded this conviction.

... for me, truth is the sovereign principle. ... This truth is not only truthfulness in word, but truthfulness in thought also, and not only the relative truth of our conception, but the Absolute Truth, the Eternal Principle, that is God. There are innumerable definitions of God, because His manifestations are innumerable. They overwhelm me with wonder and awe and for a moment stun me. But I worship God as Truth only. I have not yet found Him, but I am seeking after Him. I am prepared to sacrifice the things dearest to me in pursuit of this quest. ... Often in my progress I have had faint glimpses of the Absolute Truth, God, and daily the conviction is growing upon me that He alone is real and all else is unreal.[15]

Later in his life he felt he could say not only that God was Truth but that Truth was God.

However, as each individual at a particular point in time would only have a partial or relative grasp of and relationship with truth, non-violence in all relations between people and groups was essential: in any situation of conflict only non-violence would safeguard the integrity of all those concerned, rather than forcing the weaker to accept the views of the stronger against his own deepest convictions. Gandhi's commitment to non-violence had deep roots in the Hindu and Jain heritage of his western Indian homeland. Just as *ahimsa*, non-violence, was a powerful strand in Indian religious tradition, so the wider Hindu understanding of truth and man's *dharma* or duty in relation to it undergirded Gandhi's conception of ultimate meaning.

The primacy of non-violence in relationships had wide implications in Gandhi's social and political concerns. It drove him in his later African years to total disillusion with western society as basically materialistic, indoctrinating false ideals of merit and wealth, and gripping its members in relations which were predominantly violent because they were competitive. In contrast, and as a remedy, he looked to what he perceived (though often inaccurately) as India's traditional society based on spiritual values. He preached a life of simplicity in which people worked not for conspicuous consumption and ever-improved status, but for the satisfaction of their essential needs. He spoke of the need to limit wants and desires, of the dignity of labour, of the trusteeship of wealth on behalf of all by those whose accident of birth had made them richer than their fellows. He felt that the one social framework where this was possible was the village, where interdependence and co-operation were the guiding principles of relationship. He shunned the idea of urban industrial society, fraught with opportunities for exploitation of man by man, and for conspicuous gain by some at others' expense.

Non-violence also shaped Gandhi's notion of the ideal polity—one with as little government as possible. He believed this would guard against the misuse of public power, and thought that truthful individuals leading a simple, co-operative life would need little outside regulation, and as truth-seekers would be able to manage their own affairs harmoniously. He seems to have visualized a loose linkage of independent village republics as the ideal form of the state. In a sense he can therefore properly be called an anarchist. Where conflict of opinions and interests occurred the right response was peaceful persuasion of the opponent of the rightness of one's cause, always being prepared to compromise except on vital principles, culminating as a last resort in action to rouse the opponent's conscience, to defend one's own integrity and suffer the consequences—that is, through satyagraha. This could take various forms, as it had in Africa. Its most extreme and dramatic form was civil resistance to unjust laws. Satyagraha was peculiar to Gandhi's total religious vision, although forms of self-suffering to convert an opponent had long been known in Gujarat;[16] just as passive resistance was well established in western political thinking. But Gandhi seems to have come to it without any conscious reflection on either tradition. For him satyagraha was the last resort of those strong enough in their commitment to truth to undergo suffering in its cause. It solved the perennial dilemma of ends and means, because it was both means and end: its operation created stronger, more dedicated followers of truth, while converting their opponents to a deeper vision of truth. Gandhi had an apocalyptic belief in its virtue, for in all situations of injustice and conflict he believed it could only generate truth and never evil or falsehood.

Gandhi worked out his ideals in the several communities he founded in Africa and in India. In his *ashrams* in Ahmedabad (Gujarat) and Wardha (CP) he trained his followers to practise and preach satyagraha, considering these community experiments to be perhaps his most significant work. For him a precondition of 'seeing truth' was self-purification from baser desires; while the preliminary to exercising 'truth-force' was to strengthen oneself through self-discipline and persistent adherence to non-violence. So men and women in his communities were dedicated by a series of vows to a highly disciplined life of labour and prayer, simplicity and non-violence. They performed all domestic chores without respect to personal status, and tried to produce their own food and spin the material for their clothes. They were also to refrain from sexual intercourse, even if married, following his example. Such restraint, *brahmacharya*, was deeply embedded in Hindu tradition as essential for anyone pursuing a course which demanded special energy and dedication. In his *ashrams* men and women had equal importance; and people of all religious, social and racial backgrounds were welcomed, conventional caste distinctions being disregarded.

Gandhi was therefore in the tradition of the *guru*, the Hindu holy man who taught the followers who clustered round him, attracted by his personal sanctity. Yet he denied this role and preferred to see himself as a fellow pilgrim rather than as one who had achieved superior religious status. He did not fall easily into any of the established categories of Hindu religious leadership, which was one reason why people came to call him by the unspecific but honoured title of 'Mahatma'. However, his relationship with Hindu tradition and current practice was highly ambiguous, reflecting his conception of religious truth and authority. Placing reason above scripture as authoritative where the two conflicted, and relying finally on his experience of an 'inner voice', he could advocated radical reform, as in his rejection of Untouchability which he considered an accretion on earlier and purer tradition and deforming blot on Hindus' religious heritage. Gandhi's attitude to authority set him at loggerheads with the orthodox who gave overwhelming significance to the ancient Sanskrit scriptural texts. His ignorance of Sanskrit and treatment of textual sources also set him apart from the traditional *pundits* who expounded scripture. Yet he followed the long-established Hindu pattern of syncretism, and 'imported' from the West the notions of the dignity of labour and equality of the sexes, without any sense that he was threatening the Hindu heritage, but rather believing that he was reinterpreting it as appropriate for the current age, and therefore enriching and strengthening it.[17]

Gandhi's return to India forced him to sharpen his perception of how his vision could be applied in practice. Before 1915 he had considered India's position and problems in the light of his changing ideas. It was clear from his pamphlet, *Hind Swaraj* (1909), that he did not envisage a westernized, industrialized India whose *swaraj* would be mere freedom from the British. He maintained that *swaraj* could never be granted to Indians by their rulers, however radical the constitutional reforms they could be induced to grant. It was a state of being which had to be created from the roots upwards, by the regeneration of individuals and their realization of their true spiritual being and goal. Like many others within the Hindu tradition he had wrestled with the implications of imperial rule for Indian civilization and society, and like them he had concluded that their present political subservience was the result of a profound social and moral crisis: and it was this which Indians would have to tackle first. Therefore to him *swaraj* was far wider than mere constitutional arrangements: indeed he argued that India would be in no better state if Indians merely replaced Britons in the existing seats of government. His *swaraj* bore three hall-marks—unity among Indians of all religions, but particularly between Hindus and Muslims; the eradication of Untouchability; and the practice of *swadeshi*. The first two would indicate that Indians recognized their equality and unity as spiritual beings and were tolerant, as befitted those who realized how partial was their own vision of truth. The practice of *swadeshi* would signify self-limitation of wants and simplicity of life-style, simultaneously eroding one of the benefits of India to Britain and thereby weakening the imperial commitment to the existing form of *raj*. It demonstrated the dignity of manual labour; and one of its elements, hand-spinning, became part of Gandhi's daily routine and that of his closest followers. It had other practical benefits, such as helping to alleviate rural poverty and under-employment, and uniting educated and uneducated in a shared experience.

One of India's great figures, Jawaharlal Nehru, remembered that Gandhi was 'delightfully vague' about the actual form of government to be aimed for. In *Hind Swaraj* Gandhi had harshly criticized Britain's parliamentary government, but back in India he was prepared to work for some form of parliamentary government as an interim measure until India was ready for radical self-rule at village level.[18] For most of his contemporaries the departure of the British was an essential part of self-rule as they saw it solely in terms of controlling the machinery of government; though they differed on the time-scale they envisaged for colonial withdrawal, and were often prepared (as a political strategy) to pitch their demands higher than they thought possible. At least until 1920 Gandhi does not seem to have seen any urgent need to eject the British. To him the personal transformation of Indians and the reconstruction of their society were far more pressing problems. He felt that despite the disadvantages of British rule as the bearer of corrupting civilization, despite the humiliation of being a subject nation, there were certain ideals in British imperialism such as justice and equality which were valuable for India, if only their rulers would rule in accordance with them. He was even prepared to recruit soldiers to defend the empire at war; partly to teach Indians courage and self-respect, essential qualities for potential adherents of satyagraha; but partly because he still felt that there was a future of Indians as equal partners in the British Empire.[19] Because Gandhi approached the problem of the right society and political order from his distinctive moral standpoint he was able quite consistently to say that he never hated British people, however much he disliked their *raj*; and he hoped for as radical a 'change of heart' among them as among Indians.

On his return to India Gandhi did not see himself as a potential rebel or as leader of a nationalist movement, but as a social worker in the tiny area of western India where he had family roots. Futhermore, he disliked the status of Mahatma which people increasingly accorded him, experiencing pain and embarrassment in its connotations and the outward veneration which began to accompany it. Yet despite his intention to limit his sphere of work, and his studied political silence in 1915, he became involved in political life, in Gujarat and other localities, and ultimately at the all-India level. Even then his inner compulsion seems to have been the religious conviction that if he was to follow truth he must serve his compatriots and right 'wrongs' wherever he saw them. He maintained that all his speaking and writing, all his 'ventures in the political field' were part of his striving after *moksha*, salvation; and that anyone who sought truth could not 'afford to keep out of any field of life.'

That is why my devotion to Truth has drawn me into the field of politics; and I can say without the slightest hesitation, and yet in all humility, that those who say that religion has nothing to do with politics do not know what religion means.[20]

Although Gandhi was deeply committed to political action he was never a career politician. He always retained great flexibility in his approach to his work, being prepared to 'opt in and out' of politics (as his contemporaries understood politics) whenever he felt there was a task for which his capacities fitted him and which was likely to further the cause of true *swaraj*. His vocation was not to a political career but to the building of a new India by a variety of means—personal contacts, writing, life in his *ashrams*, social work, prayer, as well as obviously political action and the use of satyagraha in a political context. Believing that satyagraha was the 'sovereign remedy' for India's ills he was committed not only to spreading its message and training exponents of it; but equally to preserving it from mis-use—and that meant being prepared not only to launch satyagraha campaigns but to end them if he felt satyagraha was being manipulated or prostituted by the weak or irreligious.

From 1915 to 1922 Gandhi began to grapple with the real India and its problems as distinct from the India of his imagination and limited experience. In 1922 he began his first term in an Indian jail following attempts to give his countrymen a radical alternative to the official design for a new order as offered in the 1919 reforms. The dramatic transition from social worker honoured by government to a jailed rebel, leader of a Congress campaign of non-co-operation, and preacher of *swaraj* within a year came in stages through involvement in different levels of political life.

Gandhi's first essays in public action were in three local areas, each with a distinct problem which he felt called to rectify through satyagraha. In Champaran district of Bihar he took up the cause of peasant tenants forced to grow indigo at disadvantageous terms by white planters who dominated the locality and harassed the recalcitrant by means which even the government admitted to be dubious and disruptive of rural peace. There satyagraha took the form of individual action by Gandhi when he refused to obey an order to leave the district. The next year (1918) he championed two groups in his home territory, Gujarat—the substantial owner-cultivators of Kaira district who disputed with the government the enhancement of their land revenue; and the workers in the Ahmedabad cotton mills whose problem was low pay. In Ahmedabad Gandhi fasted as a personal part of satyagraha, and organized a workers' strike against the Indian mill-owners. In Kaira satyagraha's form was refusal to pay land revenue. Only in Champaran and Ahmedabad did the campaigns achieve a real solution to the original problem: and though the opponents shifted their position it was not the result of a 'change of heart' or a new perception of truth, but because they were in some way vulnerable to pressure generated by Gandhi's campaign. In Bihar the planters were not converted, but pushed by the provincial government, which in turn agreed to an official enquiry because of pressure from Delhi where the Government of India's priority was war-time peace. In Kaira by contrast the Bombay administration and the Government of India saw eye to eye: satyagraha was not able to drive a wedge between them and so weaken the local government's hand in dealing with Gandhi. Although satyagraha may have generated real local enthusiasm and support, it did little to alter the basic structure of relationships between Indians, which for Gandhi was crucial to *swaraj*. In Champaran the campaign for village uplift and education soon ebbed; and his *ashram* followers imported from Gujarat were among the only ones to engage in rural reconstruction. In Kaira Gandhi's supporters among the locally prestigious Patidar farmers continued to treat their low caste neighbours and labourers with disdain.

Yet these local actions were important for Gandhi personally and for his public standing. They gave him a confidence that he could and should act beyond the restricted area he had at first envisaged for himself. They broadened his geographical experience of the subcontinent, and brought him into contact with social groups whom established provincial and national politicians had rarely touched. Such rural people were by no means 'unpolitical': they had their own political interests, visions, and styles, moulded largely by the structures of their local societies and economies. But before the second decade of the century their politics were rarely intergrated into a provincial or continental political programme. Gandhi's interest, his definition of *swaraj*, and his technique of satyagraha helped to change this, acting as a bridge between their world and the political world beyond. Moreover, in these three campaigns Gandhi worked with and encouraged men from regions which had carried little weight in Congress politics, but who now became his committed allies. As small-town lawyers, teachers or prosperous peasants they had little interest in existing all-India politics; but Gandhi's impassioned declaration of his vision of *swaraj* and his training of them in a new and more accessible political style opened for them new horizons in terms of perception and action. Rajendra Prasad from Bihar, and Vallabhbhai Patel from Gujarat, for example, were to work with him until the end of his life, giving him access to networks of local supporters and themselves achieving all-India political careers of distinction. Gandhi's satyagrahas also gave him a continental reputation though responses to him were ambivalent. Peasants in Champaran flocked to venerate him as a saviour, but educated Indians were disquieted by his 'primitive' habits such as sitting on the floor, his hostility to English as a medium of conversation and education, and by the potential disruption of established conventions of political action and the lawlessness which satyagraha seemed to threaten. Officials began to think that the religious enthusiast and social worker was becoming a dangerous agitator, capable of stirring up discontent precisely because of his unwestern style and his grass-roots contacts. Yet Gandhi was still politically isolated. He had found no permanent allies in the Home Rule leagues, nor even in the Servants of India Society founded by his political *guru*, Gokhale, whose death in 1915 deprived him of his closest friend in the political world. As late as mid-1919 he told an old friend that he felt lonelier in India than in Africa and lacked the depth of rapport which he had had with his co-workers there.[21]

By that time Gandhi had begun to make his mark in the all-India political arena, not consciously planning the expansion of his political connections and influence, but still taking up specific 'wrongs' which seemed rectifiable through satyagraha, and working to lay the foundation of true *swaraj*. In the

summer of 1917 he urged Mrs Besant's sympathizers to take up satyagraha
as a protest against her internment, suggesting the drama of a march from
Bombay to her place of restriction. Her release in September by a Delhi
government anxious to secure a co-operative atmosphere for Montagu's
tour of inquiry enabled Congressmen to shelve a decision over a strategy
which divided them bitterly. The following year Gandhi spent much energy
exhorting the government to release the Pan-Islamist politicians, the Ali
brothers. In their case he only advised that they should break their own
internment order when the government proved adamant, not contemplat-
ing any wider use of satyagraha. He made it clear that his championship of
them was integral to his pursuit of *swaraj*, one of its foundations being
Hindu–Muslim unity which he hoped to further by this concern. Late in
1918 he told Mahomed Ali, 'my interest in your release is quite selfish. We
have a common goal and I want to utilise your services to the uttermost, in
order to reach that goal. In the proper solution of the Mahomedan question
lies the realisation of Swarajya.'[22] But the brothers proved unstable allies,
willing only to accept Gandhi's advice and insistence on non-violence when
it was clear that they had no other viable option. Yet even their erratic co-
operation was highly significant for Gandhi and for the course of Indian
politics. It gave Gandhi the personal sense of leading and championing
Muslims, as he had done in Africa: this was to be a persistent pattern
throughout his Indian career—seeking for Muslims who could to some
extent represent and interpret Muslim aspirations and fears to him, and
enable him to be a leader across religious boundaries, enacting that unity he
considered essential for *swaraj*. The Alis' alliance also gave Gandhi leverage in Congress politics because he appeared to be a lynchpin between
Hindu politicians and those Muslims who because of their Pan-Islamic
concerns would be most likely to join across communal barriers in an anti-
government alliance. It also gave this small group of Muslims a hold over
Gandhi, as he sought occasions and issues to unite Muslims and Hindus.
Consequently it blinded him to the interests of millions of other Indian
Muslims, particularly those who were provincial majorities and saw
little profit in anti-British action when their local numerical weight would
advantage them under the reformed constitution.

Gandhi's breakthrough into all-India politics occurred in 1919 on the
issue of the Rowlatt Bills. When conventional political protest and the
unanimous Indian vote in the Imperial Legislative Council failed to stop the
Rowlatt Act Gandhi offered an escape from the politicians' impasse, with a
new method of direct action which did not take the terrorists' way of
violence. He himself felt the Act was unjust and oppressive, and believed
that satyagraha on this issue would 'purify the atmosphere and bring in real
swaraj'.[23] So for him this continental plan was novel only in scale, not in
basic motivation. But it forced him to tackle the problem of offering

satyagraha when there was not an 'unjust law' which could easily be broken. (Indians would have to be suspected conspirators and terrorists to fall foul of the actual provisions of the Rowlatt Act!) His solution in this case was to adapt to a new purpose a traditional demonstration of protest and mourning—the *hartal*, or stoppage of work. He advised all Indians on a specified day to stop work and devote themselves to fasting and prayer. Later he expanded satyagraha to include disobedience to the 1910 Press Act, because this would be peaceful and educative. (The banned books chosen for illegal sale included his own *Hind Swaraj*.)

The Rowlatt satyagraha failed in that it neither changed the government's policy nor began the radical reconstruction of Indian society which was Gandhi's goal. He called it off because in April it erupted into violence in his own Gujarat and in the Punjab. Yet it was a remarkable breakthrough for a middle-aged stranger in Indian politics. His campaign became known throughout India, and in all provinces *hartal* was at least partially observed, though observance tended to be urban rather than rural, and varied greatly from region to region. Bengal and Madras were at the 'quiescent' end of the spectrum. But there was dramatic response in Bombay city and parts of Gujarat where Gandhi had established local prestige and the beginnings of an organizational base in the local Home Rule league branches and in a Satyagraha Sabha he founded in February 1919. On 6 April, the *hartal* day, a large proportion of shops in Bombay city were shut, and local transport was much reduced; and the police admitted that the whole effect was a strategic success for Gandhi. But the enterprise also showed that Gandhi, like any other Indian politician before or since, found his plan for national action manipulated, distorted or even wrecked by the forces of provincial and local political life. The nature of the linkages between people operating in India's very different political worlds were clearly quite crucial to any person, organization, or programme aspiring to national status and dimensions.

Where there were particular economic and communal strains, as in Punjab, these generated support for agitation but undermined Gandhi's careful strategy of non-violence. Where established leaderships in provincial or local politics saw no future in Gandhi's style of protest, as in CP, satyagraha hardly happened. Without a powerful countrywide organization, having only a limited regional standing in western India, Gandhi was at the mercy of those who chose to collaborate with or ignore him. 1919 showed that many educated Indians were still wary of the Mahatma, unconvinced by his vision of *swaraj*, and drawn more to co-operation in the *raj*'s design for reordering public life. But just when Gandhi came hard up against the realities of Indian politics he became utterly convinced that he had a continental vocation which he could only pursue by permanent involvement in those politics. He dated his real entrance into Congress affairs from the annual session at Amritsar in 1919, and from then was prepared to challenge the established Congress politicians if he felt that their vested interests and their strategies were blocking the enterprise of true *swaraj*.

The Mahatma's challenge came in 1920, when he confronted the Indian public with a plan of non-co-operation with the *raj*, designed to achieve *swaraj* in one year. He posited the enterprise of *swaraj* in a year at the special Congress session in Calcutta in September 1920, and in a subsequent article in his newspaper, *Young India*, reminding his compatriots of the humiliating fact that so few British were able to rule so many Indians. If they could only co-operate they could dispense with the British, and he urged them to withdraw from government schools, courts, and councils as a preliminary to non-co-operation in government service and payment of taxes; and to practise *swadeshi* as a means of ending their 'economic slavery'. Such 'self-purification' rather than armed rebellion was for him the core of India's destiny and her mission to the world. 'All this means discipline, self-denial, self-sacrifice, organizing ability, confidence and courage . . . Our salvation and its time are solely dependent upon us.' On the precise form of government to be aimed at he was vague and apocalyptic: to him the details of a political programme still mattered little compared with a reformation of attitudes and relationships.[24]

Although *swaraj* had been Gandhi's ultimate goal for over a decade, his decision actually to launch the enterprise was a startling contrast to his position at the end of 1919. Then he had urged Indians to co-operate in the Montagu–Chelmsford Reforms, believing that in conjunction with a Royal Proclamation appealing for Indian co-operation they were a sign of British intentions to act justly towards India, and could be the basis of a new relationship between rulers and ruled. Gandhi moved to this new stance of overt disloyalty because in the intervening six months he felt he had proof that the supposed new order based on co-operation was a mirage and that the British would never live up to their imperial ideals in India. Proof to him lay in the treatment of defeated Turkey after the war by the British and their allies and British disregard for Indian Muslim fears for the Khalifah's status, and in British reactions to the Punjab violence during the Rowlatt satyagraha.

In 1919–20 a strident campaign on behalf of the Turkish Sultan developed among a small group of Indian Muslims; the activists were mostly younger politicians and some *ulema*, particularly in UP, Bihar, and Sind. Yet Muslim unease on the issue was widespread, and deepened and broadened as the *ulema* took up the cause. Gandhi concerned himself with the Khilafat question because he felt it was a 'wrong' done to Muslim religious sensibilities, and provided occasion for promoting various causes central to his vision of a transformed India, including the achievement of communal harmony and the demonstration of satyagraha as the perfect action in situations of conflict and injustice. Rapidly he became the most prominent protagonist of the Khilafat case, the master-mind behind a Khilafat Day when he again urged the tactic of *hartal*, and eventually the formulator of a plan of non-co-operation with the *raj* if Muslim wishes were not respected. (In March 1920 the plan held in reserve by the Central Khilafat Committee, of which Gandhi had been the main architect, included staged relinquishment of titles and honours, and withdrawal from the legislatures, from private and public service with the British, culminating in refusal to pay taxes.) However, such a specifically Muslim issue had little appeal for most Hindus; and many Hindu public men were seriously worried at the prospect of a Gandhi-style campaign and the possibility of violence if mass Muslim feeling was stirred up by religious and political leaders.

Fortuitously at Gandhi's disposal lay the problem of Punjab. His handling of this in conjunction with the Khilafat question enabled him to appeal to a real sense of outrage among moderate-minded politicians, and to Hindu and Muslim sentiment simultaneously. During the 1919 violence martial law had been declared in the Punjab city of Amritsar. On one occasion the British General Dyer had ordered his men to fire on a crowd which had gathered, despite the current prohibition on large gatherings, in Jallianwalla Bagh, a walled area with limited shelter and exits. Over 300 were killed and 1,000 injured; and London and Delhi both condemned Dyer's action, done more to display power than actually to control disorder. Nonetheless Indian politicians accused the British of 'whitewashing', and were outraged by public support for Dyer in England when he was required to resign from the Indian army. Gandhi became the key figure in a Congress counter-inquiry to the official investigation into the Punjab disturbances. By June 1920 he considered British policy in this matter to be 'an insufferable wrong'—to which Indians should respond with satyagraha. This and the Khilafat question made him proclaim in July 1920, 'to my amazement and dismay, I have discovered that the present representatives of the Empire have become dishonest and unscrupulous. They have no real regard for the wishes of the people of India and they count Indian honour as of little consequence . . . I can no longer retain affection for a Government so evilly manned as it is now-a-days.'[25]

These two issues changed Gandhi's assessment of and relation to British *raj*. His handling of them gave him access to new sources of support in politics and institutional political leverage which he had so far lacked. He now had the support of the Central Khilafat Committee, though he found his Muslim collaborators on it hard to control and convince of the necessity of non-violence and the sincerity of Hindu support. As the main author of Congress's report on the Punjab issue he acquired new standing in Congress itself. Furthermore, he had realized his need of institutional position if he was to advance the causes dear to him: for this reason he was prepared to accept office as President of the All-India Home Rule League in place of Annie Besant in April 1920, thus losing what he called his 'splendid isolation' in politics.[26]

It is less clear why Congressmen agreed to non-co-operation in the last quarter of 1920. In December 1919 Congress had promised to co-operate in the new constitution, though to conciliate those who wished for more radical steps it called the reforms 'disappointing'. Given the peculiar nature of the British *raj*—dependent as it was on Indian taxpayers' co-operation and on Indian allies inside and outside the formal structures of government—non-co-operation made good tactical sense. If thoroughly pursued by enough strategically placed Indians it could bring the British to their knees when petition or violence proved ineffective. But withdrawal from the reformed councils shut those interested in political power off from a wealth of new resources: and non-co-operation in law courts and schools threatened the position and purses of many of the educated, and the future of their children. There is no simple reason for the apparently dramatic change of Congress policy and Gandhi's dominance in its decision-making. Taking the evidence of the months August to December 1920 and the two crucial Congresses (at Calcutta in September and Nagpur in December) the one simple conclusion is that there was *no* large-scale conversion to Gandhi's vision or style; nor was there among Indians any real anticipation or hope of making a rapid end to the *raj*.[27] Rather, the eventual Congress support for non-co-operation seems to have been the outcome of calculations by a range of groups of its advantages, often in terms of local and provincial politics. (For example, whether the actual distribution of seats in a particular legislature made it worthwhile for Hindu groups to contest seats, or whether they would be outweighed by special interests with separate representation. Another consideration was whether in a given local situation one faction found it temporarily attractive to appear 'extreme' under Gandhi's banner.) Furthermore, decisions were not seen as final. Many politicians envisaged temporary withdrawal from legal practice, and counted that they could stand in the next legislative council elections even if they stood aside in 1920.

One reason for the success of Gandhi's challenge to existing Congress policy was the absence of any other major all-India political leader or group who could organize opposition to him or provide a dynamic alternative. Mehta and Gokhale had been dead five years, Annie Besant was already being seen as a tiresome old lady; and death removed Tilak on 1 August, the very day Gandhi launched non-co-operation. So divided were Congressmen by region and faction that they could not orchestrate their fears about the course Gandhi was proposing. Some accusations of 'packing' the two meetings with local men who supported him were hurled at Gandhi by the disgruntled after the voting at the two Congresses. As there was no limit to the number of delegates this was a common enough phenomenon and had for decades made the choice of Congress venue particularly significant. But Gandhi did not have the material resources for such a venture; and Calcutta in September was not a location in which he could have felt confident of local support. It soon became clear that much of his backing in Congress and the country was from areas, and from social and religious groups which had previously carried little weight in Congress. They now not only swayed the vote but altered the political environment in which existing political leaders and established groups had to decide on their response to Gandhi.

Particularly significant were the Muslims engaged in the Khilafat campaign who came in large numbers to Congress itself to vote for non-co-operation. This was clear at Calcutta, as was support for Gandhi from a bloc of Marwaris, those prosperous business men who were prominent in Calcutta's trade yet had no local roots. In terms of regional support Gandhi at Calcutta also drew on votes from areas which had been 'backward' in terms of Congress politics; not because they were 'unpolitical' but because the particular Congress style of all-India co-operation offered little to local men, except on rare occasions when local issues dovetailed neatly with a Congress session held locally, or with a particular continental issue. Among them were UP, Bihar and Punjab; and within the Presidencies themselves such areas as Sind and Gujarat (Bombay) and the Andhra region of Madras. At the Nagpur Congress there was similar evidence of Muslim support for Gandhi; voters for him from 'backward' regions including Gujarat and Central Provinces; and people whose social origins in previous decades would have confined them to local politics. The Government of India noted this change of style and participation compared with the decorum of earlier Congresses which only the western educated had attended, and was considerably alarmed by it. 'As regards the class of persons attending, whilst many of the prominent politicians were present, the Bengal contingent included hundreds of ex-detenus and the intelligentsia, which dominated earlier Congresses, seems to have been swamped in a mass of semi-educated persons swept up from all parts of India.'[28] The reasons for this wider social and geographical span of support for Gandhi varied according to the group involved. Gandhi's religious reputation was an element in his appeal. The Marwaris in Calcutta, for example, were drawn by this as well as his western Indian origins. Bur far more often men revered or followed Gandhi because he had personally conducted a local campaign in an area such as Gujarat or Bihar where they had come under his influence and seen what he could offer them, or because he had championed a particular cause of significance to a group such as the Muslim sympathizers of the Khalifah. Or his style and programme offered an opportunity for local and all-India influence to local leaders who had had little access to or interest in Congress because they came from areas where educational opportunities were limited.

The shift of a large segment of Indian opinion in Gandhi's favour created a crisis for the established political groups in provincial and all-India politics, particularly in the Presidencies. They were so divided among themselves that the appearance of Gandhi in Congress with country-wide support, coming partly from within their own regions, made those who hoped to appear the most extreme or nationalist consider that alliance with Gandhi, at least temporarily, was a better way of safeguarding their home bases as well as their repute in Congress, than coming to terms with their local opponents in joint hostility to this enigmatic new political force. This was true of the prominent Bengali, C. R. Das, and of Tilak's former followers in Bombay. It is also significant that Gandhi's policy victories in the Subjects Committee at the two sessions further increased their difficulties by producing the crucial resolutions put before the open Congress, and thus giving Gandhi's outright opponents no real chance to vote down his plans. At Calcutta he swayed the Subjects Committee by a very small margin; but that was enough to determine the pattern of the open Congress. By the Nagpur session his standing was such that most established leaders judged him a profitable ally and a formidable opponent and preferred to make early terms with him rather than be seen in open conflict with him. As the elections to the new legislatures were now over they were prepared to give non-co-operation a trial, provided that they could influence its pattern and timing. In this Gandhi agreed, wishing to achieve as great a unity as possible as the prelude both to satyagraha and *swaraj*. He had no other implement than Congress, no other 'party'; and collaborators who had their fingers on the pulse of local life were crucial to him (as they were to the government) if his enterprise of *swaraj* was not to founder as had the Rowlatt satyagraha.

Non-co-operation lasted from 1 August 1920 to February 1922, when Gandhi called off the campaign because of a vicious attack on a police station in UP. *Swaraj* within the year had not been achieved, either in Gandhi's terms or according to the limited political definition of most Indians. Furthermore government was well able to cope with the unprecedented attack on its framework and prestige; shrewdly combining firmness at local level and restraint at all-India level combined with delaying tactics before taking what could be interpreted as provocative steps, particularly ones which would alienate more moderate political opinion. It refrained from arresting Gandhi to avoid giving him a martyr's halo until 1922. The revenue never dried up (though several provincial governments were embarrassed when temperance movements cut their excise revenue): nor did governments' collaborators in the services and informal networks of support withdraw their co-operation. The *raj* only faced real crises of control in restricted areas at particular times, such as the outbreak of violence among the Moplah Muslims on the south-west coast, where rural disturbance was endemic, or in Calcutta and Bombay city in November 1921 when rioting erupted most disturbingly just before the goodwill visit of the Prince of Wales.[29]

Nonetheless, non-co-operation marked a major change in the depth and dimensions of concerted political hostility to the *raj*. Never before had the British faced a continental campaign against their rule, masterminded by Congress, drawing support from deep within the provinces. The campaign clearly affected the November 1920 elections to the new legislatures. The polls occurred peacefully, and only in six cases out of 637 was an election impossible because there was no candidate. But most of the prominent Congressmen who would naturally have stood withdrew. The polls also varied wildly, from over 50 per cent in parts of Madras, down to 8 per cent in Bombay city and even lower to 4.4 per cent among Bombay Presidency's urban Muslims. In one UP village where Gandhi had spoken the day before the election there were no voters at all.[30] Resignation of titles was the part of the 1921 plan which had the least success. By the end of January only 24 out of 5,186 Indian titleholders had resigned their honours. Few government servants withdrew their services: but in some places their work was hindered by passive public hostility, and their private lives made disagreeable by social harassment. Law courts continued to function normally, though nearly 200 lawyers gave up their practices—if only temporarily. A crop of informal courts, *panchayats*, sprouted early in 1921, but they soon withered, because of the curious justice they dispensed and their lack of sanctions apart from social boycott and violence. There was, however, a very marked and longer-lasting drop in attendance at government secondary schools and colleges, and the emergence of a range of 'national' educational institutions. But the educational boycott did not last because Indians realized that literacy and educational qualifications from recognized establishments meant profit, power, and prestige. Similarly they declined to cut themselves off from the resources available in the municipalities: and while boycotting *provincial* elections and legislatures they were anxious to stand in *local* elections and work the local government institutions whose value they had rapidly learnt in the previous decades. Later in 1921 Gandhi and the All-India Congress Committee emphasized the *swadeshi* campaign, and encouraged the use of *charkhas*, spinning-wheels, both as a propaganda symbol and an economic strategy against poverty and some of the economic interests behind the *raj*. Imports of cloth decreased dramatically in 1921–2, though the *swadeshi* campaign was fortuitously strengthened by the bleak facts of reduced Indian purchasing power and a fall in the exchange rate in the disturbed economic conditions following the war. Indian merchants showed themselves to be shrewd and level-headed in the context of economic dislocation; and many of those who actually traded in foreign cloth refused to give it up, including Gandhi's Marwari supporters in Calcutta.

Although the all-India plan of non-co-operation had limited effects, some of the most striking manifestations of political unrest and the worst challenges to order occurred where pre-existing local tensions found an outlet in the all-India campaign and moulded it locally into patterns quite unpremeditated—nor indeed welcomed—by those who had planned non-co-operation at Nagpur. In a sense non-co-operation 'succeeded' most where it was least planned or controlled. Ultimately it was such local variations and the tensions which created them which broke apart the movement and wrecked anything approaching an authentic Gandhian satyagraha. In south India, for example, four distinctive campaigns contributed to non-co-operation, though all had origins in local conditions predating Gandhi's national call for satyagraha. They included hostility to government's forest regulations; temperance campaigns which stemmed more from opposition to the government's organization of the liquor trade than Gandhian or even orthodox Hindu morality; a brief stoppage of land revenue collection because of the resignation of some Indian district officials who were uneasy about their diminishing local position; and urban demonstrations which similarly were manifestations of pre-existing local problems. Far off in Assam non-co-operation was fuelled by the economic distress of plantation labourers who had migrated to work in the tea-gardens. In UP it became interwoven with a peasant agitation against landlord pressure, to the embarrassment of the Congress leaders who could not control it and its wilder spokesmen, and found that it alienated some of Congress's members or allies, including some of the smaller Muslim *zamindars*. In Punjab many non-co-operators were Sikhs who latched on to the campaign as they battled for control of Sikh religious resources against a group of their co-religionists who had legal rights to religious property and were therefore supported by the government.[31] Ultimately these local conflicts, among Indians as much as against government and its institutions, led to increasing violence: and in February 1922 Gandhi advised that the campaign should be called off. The eruption of new groups and regions into national politics, and the new, if temporary, linkages between previously distinctive political enterprises, had turned out to be a double-edged weapon. Moreover it was becoming clear that Gandhi's Muslim allies were becoming restive and reluctant to observe his idosyncratic policies; while his uneasy colleagues among the Presidency politicians were re-thinking the value not only of the Mahatma but of his strategies which seemed to have produced so little permanent political benefit after the year which was supposed to bring in *swaraj*. When the government jailed Gandhi in March it saved him from recognizing that the bases of his dramatic influence in Congress affairs in 1920 had weakened to the point of collapse.

Yet this first national episode in Gandhi's presentation of a radical alternative for India was of considerable significance. Most obviously it demonstrated that Gandhi was now a national figure. British and Indians alike could no longer ignore or ridicule him: his saintly politics were proved to have powerful practical repercussions. Non-co-operation also elicited from the British a changed attitude to political agitation which posed them a new problem because it was non-violent and so wide-scale, and because it erupted just when they were playing for wider political co-operation in the reformed constitution. In response they demonstrated skill in achieving a delicate balance of control and continuing solicitation of collaboration. But conflicts of opinion within the government and the near-failure of the policy at certain junctures (as when they nearly lost 'Moderate' political support late in 1921) showed, too, how the preservation of the *raj* would require continual re-formulation of political strategy in a rapidly changing context. Gandhi's enterprise also demonstrated both the possibility of Hindu–Muslim co-operation in action against the government, and the ambivalence of such co-operation. But in the perspective of India's political development and eventual achievement of nationhood and democratic independence, perhaps the most significant aspect of non-co-operation is the way it displayed the unprecedented disturbance of interests and senses of identity at different levels of public life, the variety of distinct and autonomous political interests and actions this disturbance generated, and the potential for new linkages between them. The dislocation of older patterns was immensely complex in its origins. It resulted from the economic and ideological pressures of the war, from the actions of government, particularly its re-structuring of the official framework of collaboration with its subjects, and from the deliberate actions of those with diverse political interests who reached out across old barriers of region, district, and community to generate support and find allies.

The actual programme of satyagraha enabled changes in interaction between different types of politics. As a new and infinitely flexible mode of expressing grievances and pressurizing opponents it gave new political opportunities to people whose political vision and capacities had hitherto been restricted and localized. It enabled some temporary mobilization of people who had never before been involved in a 'national' campaign, as in the case of those who flocked to Gandhi's meetings or participated in *hartal*. It gave opportunities for new aggregations of political awareness and action, when specific or local problems found an outlet in an all-India campaign, as in southern India or UP, or the Punjab. Temporarily the politics of different provinces and smaller localities, of different communities, and of widely divergent socio-economic interests might be synchronized and welded into a campaign which was national in spread if not in its basic motivation. But the novelty of the situation lay in the synchronization rather than the actual content of those politics. Work on south India and on Allahabad, for example, has shown the degree of continuity in ideas, interests, and people, before, during, and after Gandhi's campaign. The problems of UP peasants and forest-dwellers, likewise, did not go away: nor did their attempts to ameliorate them. His plans and preaching did not change the components of more local politics, but permitted them to be re-expressed in conjunction with the politics of other regions, and to some extent permitted the integration of the actions of people with very different interests and visions of the future. His image as 'Mahatma' rather than as an urban western-educated politician, became the connecting link between many different styles of politics. Congressmen heard one message of the future when he spoke the language of nation and of *swaraj*. Many whose visions were moulded by more traditional ideals venerated him as a 'Mahatma', a holy man of miracles who would bring in a new age, a leader whom they invested with powers familiar in Hindu mythology. The Gandhi 'imagined' by the UP peasantry, for example, was thus very different from the Gandhi who in practice was wrestling with the problems of non-violent resistance, and attempting in his speeches and writings to publicize the ideological content of a new national identity.

Satyagraha was if only temporarily a new bonding action and ideology in Indian political life. Under its impetus Congress became in a new way a bonding institution compared with its older role as the informal talking-shop of local political notables from restricted areas and social backgrounds. Gandhi was determined that Congress, if it was to be an instrument of *swaraj*, must be representative of the whole nation in terms of geography and society, rather than of an educated minority whose politics he believed were de-nationalizing India. He also insisted on efficiency in any organization in which he was involved. These convictions found practical expression in the new constitution Congress accepted at the close of the Nagpur session, of which Gandhi was the main architect. Under it Congress was to have a permanent and small executive in its Working Committee, while the loose and ineffective AICC of previous decades was relegated to a secondary position. Congress was also reorganized at provincial level; the Provincial Congress Committees (PCCs) now representing language areas. Local organization was extended to subdivisional and *taluka* level, at least in theory. Both these developments were strategies to broaden Congress's geographical and social base. Furthermore, at annual sessions provinces were to send fixed numbers of delegates in proportion to their population, to guard against swamping or packing of sessions by men from one area. Some results of these changes can be seen in the expansion of Congress membership and the greater participation of rural men in the AICC immediately after Nagpur. Clearly, though changes threatened older modes of using and controlling Congress politics, they also made good sense in the context of wider agitational and electoral politics, when leaders needed to forge new links with potential voters and backers.

Thus reconstructed Congress became a far more significant organizational resource in politics. Despite violent fluctuations in membership and the actual operation at grass-roots of the organization prescribed for local units, it was becoming a regular political institution which those concerned with political influence could less easily ignore. Congress as a body also began to control more funds for political work in comparison with its earlier poverty. Between April and June 1921 Rs. 10 million were collected for a Tilak Memorial Fund; and from 1921–3 the total funds available to Congress exceeded Rs. 13 million. This enabled a wider range of political and allied activity; as, for example, the new *khadi* organizations to promote Gandhi's *swadeshi* plans, which were aligned with Congress. Expanded financial resources also heralded the rise of the permanent political worker who could make a living and a career within the Congress structures. It is noteworthy that areas such as Bihar, Sind, UP, Gujarat and Punjab, which would once have been called backward in Congress politics, were now prominent in their financial contributions, as were Gandhi's Marwari supporters, and a range of quite ordinary people who contributed to Congress collections in streets and cafés.[32] As Congress planned and helped to finance non-co-operation it gained in prestige as the major national political body which could take on the *raj*. Its repute further added to its importance at different levels of public life, and its name became an increasingly significant asset. This, combined with its finances and organization, gave it a new potential both as a structure enabling interaction between levels of politics and as an institution which could bond India's political diversities into a national unity.

However the 1920–2 non-co-operation movement demonstrated the difficulties in the way of creating a new sense of national awareness and mutual interest across the subcontinent, and co-ordinating a political campaign which was national even in simple geographical terms. The problems of unity which had confronted early Congressmen were deepened now, precisely because the different levels of political understanding and action had been drawn into new and closer contact, because different modes of politics were not so disaggregated, and because Congress was no longer dominated by the western educated. No all-India leader after the First World War could exercise continental influence in the same way as a Surendranath Banerjea or a Pherozeshah Mehta. All concerned with all-India political power, whether they were in the ranks of the *raj* or among Congressmen, needed deeper and wider networks of communications and alliances to achieve success in the changing political environment.

As non-co-operation generated new linkages between political arenas, regional differences became marked. There was growing hostility of men from some areas to India-wide strategies which appeared to conflict with their local interests or political style. The social élite among Bengali Hindus who had prospered in the new education and professions, for example, found the Mahatma's idiom uncongenial; while non-co-operation boded ill for them as a minority already politically threatened by Congress's all-India strategy at Lucknow in 1916 which had been written into the 1919 reforms. Strategic reasons led C. R. Das to make a pact with Gandhi at Nagpur in December 1920, but his hostility surfaced within the year when Gandhi refused to negotiate with the British who, late in 1921, offered a Round Table Conference in an attempt to prevent embarrassing demonstrations when the Prince of Wales arrived.[33] Non-co-operation could also underline caste hostilities where certain groups felt they were disadvantaged. The Justice Party in Madras, for example, claimed to represent non-Brahmin interests. It resolutely avoided non-co-operation, and formed a ministry under the new constitution after successfully contesting the 1920 elections. For its members the fruits of office were far more significant as a strategy for consolidating power locally than any allegedly national call for self-denial by a Gujarati who seemed to be aligned with the Madras Brahmins who managed the local branch of Congress.[34]

Even more destructive of non-co-operation as a mode of national action and regeneration were the communal and socio-economic strains which erupted under its banner, or were triggered by its propaganda. In the Punjab Hindu–Sikh relations deteriorated as the more puritan wing of the Sikh community attempted to wrest control of Sikh shrines from those Sikhs in actual possession whom they accused of being 'Hinduized'. In Bihar non-co-operation brought to prominence long-standing issues between Muslims and Hindus, particularly cow-killing. That specific rift widened and seriously hampered the recruitment of volunteers and collection of funds for non-co-operation, despite Gandhi's request to leaders to stop discussing the question. A Hindu picture of Gandhi as Krishna above a Muslim flag deeply disquieted Bengali Muslims, as a local paper explained. 'The manner in which Mr. Gandhi is being worshipped in the country makes it impossible for the Moslem community to pull on with him. We are ready to work with the Hindus as their brethren; we can even forgo *korbani* [cow-sacrifice] for their satisfaction, but we will never allow the holy crescent to lie low at the feet of Sri Krishna.'[35]

The worst communal outbreak occurred on the Malabar coast, where the latest in a succession of Muslim peasant uprisings against Hindu landlords broke out in the wake of non-co-operation propaganda. There communal strains and socio-economic differences reinforced each other, precipitating a conflict disastrous alike for government and for Congress. Elsewhere socio-economic tension within regions was exacerbated by non-co-operation's particular local pattern. UP's peasant movement, loosely and ambivalently linked to Congress's name and campaign, was the most obvious case. Here the potential for discord between Indians was so great that Gandhi tried to restrain peasant activity, and deflect it from anti-landlord violence: and ultimately Congress rejected a rural alliance which would have alienated the privileged in local society. Non-co-operation in action uncovered many of the building blocks out of which a new order for India would have to be constructed. But despite Gandhi's insistence on non-violence, communal and class harmony, his campaign gave little indication that the groups and interests it brought together in new relationships would actually reinforce each other in the attainment of *swaraj* or the building of a new nation.

iii Patterns of adjustment

By mid-1922 the drama of immediate post-war political initiatives and innovations was over. Indeed the standard descriptions of India in the 1920s emphasize failure, disillusion, and the simultaneous collapse of unity among Indians with the muted hostility of many of them towards their rulers. The political picture often drawn is one of stagnation. One biographer of Lord Irwin (Viceroy from 1926 to 1931) even wrote of politics 'in suspense';[36] though this is misleading because it suggests that 'politics' were confined to all-India agitations or constitutional campaigns in relation to the British, and ignores the broad range and intensity of political actions beneath the pan-Indian arena. Stress on stagnation is explicable if one's focus is on Gandhi's career as a political leader, on imperial experiments in constitutions which would attract Indian collaborators, or on the development of a consciously nationalistic movement against the *raj*. Gandhi was in jail until 1924, and thereafter a rather detached figure in public life, devoting himself to social work and spinning. Indian politicians were engaged in sporadic and often grudging co-operation with their rulers in the new constitutional structures; while those who had been allies in non-co-operation drifted apart. One of the elder statesmen of UP politics, the eminent lawyer, Motilal Nehru, wrote to his son, Jawaharlal, in 1927 of his despair at the contemporary scene in contrast to his high hopes of non-co-operation days.

In short conditions in India have never been worse. The reaction of the N. C. O. movement which set in in 1922–23 has since been slowly but surely undermining all public activity. There is not much of it left now but the rot is still proceeding—at a quicker pace now than before. The only education the masses are getting is in communal hatred. It is not true today as it certainly was a couple of years ago that communal strife was confined to cities and was not known in the village. The latter now are more frequently the scenes of communal riots than the former. The older people among the nationalists have given way to despair. The younger men are taking greater interest in their own advancement by whatever means & however reprehensible in their own opinion of 2 years ago. Imagine Congressmen in the Assembly & the Councils tumbling over each other to shake hands with officials, stealthily attending offical functions after taking care that their names are not reported to the press, actually applying for invitations to such functions . . .[37]

However, if one examines politics as the broad range of concerns and actions relating to the exercise of power in the public domain—whether of village or town, district or province, as well as subcontinent—and tries to discern the elements which went into the making of India as an independent and democratic state in the later twentieth century, there were visible in the 1920s highly significant patterns of adjustment—in the relations of Indians to each other and the British, in Indian perceptions of their identity and the right framework for their lives, and in India's connections with the world beyond her shores. Even a brief indication of some of the most important of these suggests that a new order was emerging in the subcontinent, though not according to the imperial plan of 1919 or in accord with the Mahatma's spiritual enterprise of *swaraj*.

The most obvious re-adjustment was the breakdown of Congress unity and the reorientation of its component groups to the political context following the failure of its agitational strategy. Congress's unity had at best been precarious: it was forged by a common leader with a clear goal, by the non-co-operation campaign, and by its newly constructed organization. These were now removed or shattered. Gandhi was physically removed by his jail sentence and then by illness. On his resumption of public activity he concentrated on 'constructive work' to create the spiritual roots of *swaraj*; and the heady goal he had preached—*swaraj* in a year—lay in ruins. He was not prepared to make any political initiatives and concentrated on his *ashram*, on personal influence, and the *khadi* movement, with its economic benefits and its potential both for mass contact and for broad-based organization. (He said that if a revival of cooking had the same organizational potential as *khadi* he would support that!)[38] Non-co-operation lay at least temporarily discredited; and, like its architect, was no longer a bond between Congressmen. Nor was the Congress organization itself. Membership slumped in the mid-1920s down to just over 18,000 in 1925; and the tiered structure of committees went into a state of paralysis. By early 1929 the PCCs of Bombay, Bengal, Bihar, Punjab, UP, Gujarat and Tamil Nad actually functioned with proper offices: but even there lower level organization was weak or non-existent. In UP, for example, local work virtually stopped, and district committees only stirred into life when members were to be elected to them. Each level from PCC downwards was rent by a provincial faction struggle—of such dimensions that for most of 1927 there existed two rival PCCs. This worked against Congress effectiveness: but it does illustrate how even in its weakness the Congress name and organization was a resource which local men were eager to control. Congress funds, too, became drastically depleted. By the end of the decade the AICC was living off much reduced capital, and was owed large amounts by PCCs and some individual Congressmen.

When Congress abandoned non-co-operation its members split on the issue of strategy into 'no-changers' and 'pro-changers'; and after considerable controversy those who favoured action within the reformed legislatures retained their membership of Congress yet formed central and local Swaraj parties, dedicated to making the new constitution unworkable from within. However the all-India Swarajist leaders, C. R. Das and Motilal Nehru, could not weld provincial Swarajists into a united party with a coherent policy, such was the strength of local political issues and opportunities. In mid-decade many of those who had been the most uneasy of the Mahatma's allies during non-co-operation, like the Maharashtrian followers of Tilak, now took to 'responsive co-operation', actually working the reforms and abandoning the muted obstructionism of the original Swarajist policy. Motilal's pained letter to his son in 1927 had reflected the lure of the legislatures and constructive contacts with officialdom to men who where concerned to use the new provincial resources to influence provincial public life, build up their own followings and prevent their opponents from monopolizing the new opportunities. The weakness of Congress among Punjabi Hindus was a warning of the provincial repercussions of calling on men to refrain from using the legislatures in a context where they felt their social and economic position was being undermined by people who *did* use them. In the Punjab the beneficiaries appeared to be Muslims; and many educated Hindus consequently preferred to adopt a 'Moderate' or 'Communalist' label than deny themselves local influence under the Congress banner.[39]

Splits among the Swarajists and the increasing numbers of Congressmen who opted for constitutional politics demonstrated a crucial pattern of readjustment in political life. A 'provincialization' of politics was occurring, ironically just at the time when opposition to the imperial regime was being voiced in the name of the Indian nation more powerfully than before. These were the two faces of the coin of political change. Economic and social change, and the *raj*'s devolution of power through the reformed constitutional structures, generated deeper and wider political ambition and fear, focusing much of it on the new provincial structures of power. The province increasingly became a crucial arena of political activity, such was the power now available within it. Because the gateway to that power was through elections to legislature seats, those interested in that power began to achieve new ways of attracting electoral support, created political linkages within the province, and began to generate a genuine provincial political life, on which ultimately the politics of the states within independent India would be founded. Simultaneously the need to extract concessions from the British drew men into cross-regional alliances, as did growing ideological awareness of their unity across the subcontinent and their potential as an independent national community. As the nation began—however haltingly—to claim men's hearts and minds, so the provincial level of politics demanded their immediate attention, as the 1919 reforms opened the way to control of those 'provincial' subjects delegated to elected Indians and their ministerial spokesmen in the provincial legislatures.[40]

In the 1970s historians tended to focus study less on India as a political unit than on particular provinces, looking at that lower level for the goals of political life, the ideals and interests which fired men, and the alliances they entered across the spectrum of local public life. This shift in focus resulted partly from the need to investigate the effects of the new political structures: but also from a wish to understand more deeply the unities and disunities which emerged at continental level, and the fluctuations in all-India politics between agitation and constitutional action. The proliferation of regional studies has shown how the 1919 reforms created the province as an arena of great political significance, and how attractive, even vital, was control of its resources for men interested in the use of public power through legislation, administration, and patronage. The details of provincial political life are beyond the scope of this book. Each provincial study tells its particular story of the way in which the new institutions became integrated with the local structure of society, how provincial groups made use of the new resources, and how provincial problems were tackled through the new channels of influence. In some instances a once dominant educated élite began to lose influence because of the power given to other groups through the vote and distribution of conciliar seats. Such was the case of Bengali Hindus who were faced with Muslim politicians elected by the Muslim majority in the region. Elsewhere, as in southern India, the dominant agricultural castes began to use the new structures just as they had the local self-government machinery two decades earlier. In the process they came to new and wider alliances amongst themselves; and forged new links with educated politicians who could help them articulate their interests in the new arena, though on occasion rural bosses did without the educated as political intermediaries and spokesmen. In UP the great landowners in contrast found it increasingly difficult to ally with local Congressmen, or to rally votes through older channels of landlord influence.

Whatever the details emerging from each province, it is clear that the long-standing issues and alignments of local politics were now working their way into and moulding the new provincial arena, and that those who worked at all-India level would be constrained by the pressures generated from below. Any 'national' party or aspiring all-India leader would have to tap this reservoir of provincial experience; and to achieve influence across the continent would have to come to terms with provincial leaderships and their interests, offering them a range of inducements or threatening them with real sanctions. This was evident in the Swarajists' turmoil and in Motilal Nehru's failure to weld them into a disciplined national group. It was a crucial dimension in all Gandhi's later attempts at national agitation, and in all Congress efforts to build itself into a party representing the whole of India. The growth of provincial interests among Muslims was also central to the fortunes of the Muslim League and the difficulties Jinnah encountered in achieving all-India leadership to which he aspired, or cohering an all-India Muslim political position. The pressures of provincial politics were to constrain governments, too. The imperial government in Delhi had to listen to its governors, who spoke out of their particular provincial situations each with their specific problems and relationship with their local politicians inside and beyond the legislature. Yet this 'provincialization' as a pattern of adjustment meant that the institutions which were to develop into part of independent India's democratic structures were laid on solid social foundations. To change the metaphor, they were being grafted successfully on to an Asian society though they were western in example and inspiration. Over several decades they proved capable of serving the political needs of that society, channelling its fears and ambitions, defusing its tensions and providing means for pursuit of its goals. This was a legacy both of institutions and of experience over time which was to be crucial for the stability and adaptability of India's governments and political system after 1947.

Yet this pattern of adjustment meant that local tensions were given new political significance, and had increased political potential for individuals and groups. The Madras Justice Party which claimed to speak for non-Brahmins was an early case. But the main demonstration of this trend in the disunity of former Congress allies after the collapse of non-co-operation was the emergence of a more strident and consciously political Hindu communalism. Hindu revivalism, religious networks of authority and patterns of patronage had long been elements in Indian politics, though often those concerned were in uneasy relationship with 'official' Congress organization and activity. Now, in response to the 1919 reforms and the changed political context such elements came together in new organizations. Distinct communal parties emerged among Hindus, particularly in regions where Hindus faced peculiar social and economic problems, because of the local distribution of religions and the communal balance of power created by numbers and access to local resources of influence. The All-India Hindu Mahasabha had been founded in 1915 to bring together the diverse local Hindu movements which had roots in north Indian public life reaching back into the previous century. Until 1922 it was more an informal link mechanism between groups in UP and Punjab than a real organization. But then it was revived by its old stalwarts, including UP's Pandit Malaviya, and remodelled much on Congress lines, with a Working Committee and linguistic provinces. Although it managed to establish branches in most parts of India, its strength lay in the north (Punjab, UP, Delhi and Bihar), in the heartland of Hindustan where Hindi was the common vernacular language. At first it stressed practical social and religious work among Hindus and Untouchables, the protection of cows and Hindi; in the latter cases pursuing old threads in public life. Its members did not take a distinctive political stance until 1925, when they—often reluctantly—separated themselves from Congress and the Swarajists, and allowed local branches to nominate election candidates. Yet it would be misleading to see this development as indicative of a new and rampant 'Communalism', making religious identity the sole determinant of political loyalty. The Hindu *sabhas* in the north drew on a long tradition of people, interests, and loose social, educational, and religious organizations; and they remained a holding structure for many diverse strands in public life. Consequently there was often no clear ideology or organization to separate them from local Congressmen. What concerned those who on occasion flew a Hindu communal banner was the preservation of a range of Hindu interests when these seemed to be endangered by Congress tactics, whether of non-co-operation or in the councils, and its courting of Muslim support.[41]

As Hindu politicians worked out their re-adjustments to the changed political context, so did Muslims—with consequences of grave proportions for the future shape of the Indian nation. The precarious alliance of Muslim League, Khilafat Committees, and Congress broke apart when non-co-operation ended. By 1923 only 3.6 per cent of Congress delegates were Muslims, compared with 10.9 per cent in 1921. The collapse of the old alliance was more dramatically demonstrated when Congress refused to ratify an electoral pact made in Bengal by C. R. Das for local co-operation with Muslims, on the basis of a package of concessions. By mid-decade there were few Muslims who were prepared to accept the Swarajist ticket.

One-time Muslim allies were divided among themselves when the Turks after an internal revolution abolished the Khaliphate in 1924: championship of the Sultan was thus removed as a ground of united action among Indian Muslims. Among them, too, there occurred a reorientation of political action towards the provinces. In December 1924 the Muslim League met separately from Congress for the first time since 1920. It planned a strategy geared to the opportunities and apparent dangers of the new political situation, its basis being an eventual federal structure for India in which provinces would be largely autonomous, and Muslims would continue to have separate electorates. Muslim security as an all-India minority guaranteed by increasing provincial autonomy and light intervention from the centre clearly suited Muslims admirably where they were locally a majority. Its benefits were less clear where they were minorities, and some of them began to toy with the idea of trading joint electorates for further safeguards, such as the creation of more Muslim provinces and one-third of seats in the central legislature. M. A. Jinnah, a Muslim lawyer from Bombay who had withdrawn from Congress politics in 1920 when Gandhi began to change its style, and had subsequently tried to rebuild an all-India leadership role, floated this plan in 1927 at an informal Muslim conference. He thereby precipitated a split in the Muslim League, one section following him to a meeting in Calcutta, and the Punjabis, secure in their provincial majority, going with their M. M. Shafi to a meeting in Lahore. Increasingly it was the Punjabi Muslims who made the running and achieved the strongest voice in the continental politics of Indian Muslims in the later 1920s, having gained strength and confidence and a strategy for the future from their experience in the Punjab of the benefits of the provincialization of politics.[42]

A further dimension of the disunity among Muslims was the small group who preferred not to operate under a specifically Muslim name but stayed in Congress. They became known as 'Nationalist Muslims' and included such prominent men as Dr. M. A. Ansari and A. K. Azad. Many of them came from UP. They not only shared cultural and personal bonds with prominent Congressmen such as the Nehrus, but realized that as a local minority a co-operative stance with a Congress leadership they knew well and could trust was the best option for themselves in public life, for their co-religionists, and for India as a nation. They were an isolated minority, however, often vilified by other Muslims for their position as traitors to a specifically Muslim cause.[43] But Congress's need to 'prove' its national status and Gandhi's personal need to have Muslims close to him as he had had in South Africa gave them a special relationship with the Congress leadership and leverage over Congress policy towards Muslims out of all proportion to their numbers or the degree to which they actually represented Muslim opinion.

The Muslims' political realignments among themselves and in relation to Hindu politicans occurred in the context of deepening communal tension at local level. A marked increase in communal riots and violence is some index of this trend. In one outburst in 1924 all the Hindus fled from the town of Kohat on the North-West Frontier. A serious communal riot occurred in Calcutta in April 1926, and in the succeeding twelve months there were 40 riots resulting in 197 deaths and injuries to nearly 1,600 people. In UP alone between 1923 and 1927 81 people were killed and 2,301 injured in 88 communal riots. Far too little is known about the deep-seated causes of this surge of communal antagonism at the level of village alley and city street, about the anatomy of communal riots, their flashpoints, leadership (if any), and the way news of them spread to ignite further conflagrations in neighbouring towns or villages. Certain issues such as cow-killing, music before mosques and the routes of religious processions were constant occasions for potential strife between local groups of Hindus and Muslims. But though the ingredients remained the same, their interaction changed in the 1920s as wider forces of change impinged upon them.

Violence and rumour of actual or suspected violence bred more retaliatory violence. But the decade saw increasing minority fears of the local use to which majority communities could put the resources of the new provincial political structures. In Punjab and Bengal Indian ministers clearly used their powers of legislation, administration, and patronage to improve the local Muslim position. The economic dislocations of the decade and the financial strait-jacket in which governments had to work further exacerbated rivalry for limited resources. Moreover, the specifically religious movements for reform, reclamation, and missionary outreach which had intensified concern over religious boundaries and the numerical strength of religious groups since the previous century developed in intensity, disrupting relations between groups and generating further fear of changes in the balance of numbers between the communities. Hindu *shuddhi* (purification) and *sangathan* (consolidation) movements, encouraged by the Hindu Mahasabha, had their Muslim ripostes in movements in which the *ulema* were involved—*tabligh* (education) and *tazim* (organization). However, leading provincial and all-India politicians of both communities were unable to control the local tensions which their actions and propaganda partially generated. Many of them were deeply worried by these violent manifestations. Gandhi tried to find solutions in personal friendship and example, his journalism, a unity conference, and even a fast. But by 1927 he had lapsed into despair at the crumbling of the communal unity he perceived as one of the pillars of true *swaraj*, and as his other methods failed he said that he could only try prayer and personal friendship.[44] The danger lay not just in the immediate violence but in the long-term hostility and legacy of bitterness, and the potential within this for a popular appeal and agitation which politicians might be tempted to tap in their desire to forward their careers or to safeguard the community's constitutional position as the British devolved more power to Indians. It is historically unproven to interpret the 1920s as a time of 'no return' in communal relations, as a final break in co-operation and coexistence which made the division of the subcontinent into Hindu and Muslim states inevitable in 1947. As is abundantly clear from the political identities and alignments emerging in the 1920s, there was no single 'Hindu' or 'Muslim' community. There were, rather, a multiplicity of identities which could be used and re-worked and reconstructed; and community like region or nation was an identity which was as yet by no means fixed, but in the making, and capable of change, intensification or decline and decay. But the patterns of hostility emerging at the different levels of public life suggest that the devolution of power in a religiously plural society could have explosively divisive repercussions. The soothing of hostility and fear would need vision, dedication and much creative work by leaders of opinion and political movements, and it was unclear whether that would be forthcoming, given the potential of a religious appeal as a political strategy and the needs of politicians to win elections and achieve followings and alliances at local, provincial and continental levels of politics.

Yet as significant for the future of India, and for independent India's ability to address some of the most fundamental problems of many of its least privileged people, was the way in which during the 1920s so many of the linkages between different levels and styles of politics forged in the process of non-co-operation snapped, in particular the link between a 'nationalist' demand and strategy, and the politics of many of the 'subaltern' in Indian society. Throughout the subsequent decade it became clear that many of the political activists who spoke in the name of the nation and were connected with Congress, who operated in and around the structures of constitutional and administrative action, had little connection with the politics of the poor in town and countryside, and indeed were profoundly ambivalent towards the potentially disruptive demands and activities of those beneath them in the socio-economic order. Though small landholders and prosperous peasants increasingly found Congress a useful political organization and mouthpiece, and came to form its middle ranks of leadership in many areas, Congress as an all-India body and as a provincial and local organization remained wary of championing the rural poor, and was conspicuous in its efforts to maintain as broad a socio-economic alliance in the countryside as possible, and to control any actions which threatend to disrupt the rural order and their own supporters.[45] In India's industrial towns a similar gulf between 'nationalist' politics and genuinely popular issues and strategies was apparent. Although the 1920s were a time of increasing industrial unrest and militancy, industrial workers found little support or leadership in the country's most articulate politicians. Theirs continued, by and large, to be a political world apart. This gulf was to some extent the product of the very nature of India's industrial communities and their cultures, with their particular loyalties and identities; and in part the methods of control used by owners and the colonial authorities. But it was also due to the ambivalent stance of Congress and its leaders to the needs and demands of particular sections of urban society when these threatened their embryonic alliance with some of India's own industrial magnates.[46]

Few of the patterns of adjustment between groups of Indians in the public arena discernible in the 1920s were precipitated by ideological commitment, or indeed generated radical thought among participants or observers.

This was the more remarkable because a growing number of educated Indians was exposed to a widening range of new ideas as a result of India's involvement in a war fought partly for ideological reasons, the spread of left-wing political ideologies in the West, Gandhi's preaching with its trenchant criticism of contemporary Indian society and manners, and the experience of deepening communal conflict.

Political identity drawn on overtly religious lines was hardly a considered ideological position in the 1920s. Almost the only serious thinkers, apart from Gandhi, grappling with the definition of nationhood and its relationship to India's diversity of religions and castes, were the Maharashtrian Hindus, V. Savarkar, who was deeply committed to the Hindu Mahasabha, and K. Hedgewar, who broke with the Mahasabha after founding the RSS (Rashtriya Swayamsevak Sangh) in 1925 as a militant, disciplined force to unite and protect Hindus. Far more often both Muslims and Hindus who engaged in 'communal' politics were reacting pragmatically from fear and a wish for protection rather than positive commitment to a clearly conceived ideal or a common political identity rooted in religion. There still occurred political alliances across communal boundaries where these appeared fruitful. Political ideas labelled 'left-wing' in the western context found some adherents in India. But they were a handful within the limited circle of the western educated. News of the Russian Revolution and the ideal of communism fired a few, like one of the founders of the Indian Communist Party, Muzaffar Ahmed, who later admitted how superficial was his knowledge of Marxism; or M. N. Roy, an ex-Bengali terrorist who became Moscow's India expert and tried in the early 1920s to influence Congress leaders and then to build up an Indian Communist party. Communist propaganda and organization were smothered by a conspiracy trial launched by a Government of India which saw in Moscow both the fount of revolutionary anti-colonialism and a resurgent Russian bear, fear of whose territorial designs had haunted British imperialists in the previous century. British Labour interest in India similarly yielded little ideological fruit on the subcontinent, not least because the party's members and sympathizers tended to share in wider British racial and political stereotypes of Indians, and Labour leaders when cast in the role of actual or potential rulers of India had no intention of allowing radical change in its relationship with Britain. Far more significant long-term for Congress's ideological stance were those of its members and potential leaders who, like Jawaharlal Nehru, were educated in Britain and deeply impressed by what they read and saw in Europe. Nehru became one of Congress's major thinkers, though he was never rigidly doctrinaire and recognized as he became more deeply involved in Indian life that there could be no simple transfer of European ideas and solutions to Asia, with its venerable cultures and agrarian societies. Yet the vision of equality among men and the more equitable re-distribution of wealth were for him essential aspects of liberation from imperialism.[47]

The privileged social position of India's western educated and the absence of a large or self-consciously articulate urban working class partly accounted for the poverty of radical thinking. Moreover, most of them accepted the interpretation of history and an understanding of politics enshrined and purveyed in colonial discourse, and were consequently committed to the project of the nation state as India's goal—a commitment which not only absolved them of radical analysis of Indian society, but prompted them to sacrifice other interests to that goal. Among the major politicians of the 1920s Gandhi was the most truly radical thinker, in the sense of considering the roots of society. Yet he was no social revolutionary as Communists or western Socialists understood the term. He believed that the rich and powerful held their goods in trust for their less privileged brothers and hoped they would use their resources accordingly: but he resisted ideas of dispossessing the rich and landed either by legislation and administration or by brute force. However sincere an ideal this was for the Mahatma, it was also undoubtedly a reassuring and convenient social ideology for many of those with considerable vested interests in the socio-economic order who, like the Marwaris, other industrialists, and smaller landed folk, supported Congress. They were content with this 'official' vision of an inclusive society which envisaged no radical or enforced change when *swaraj* came. Even though Gandhi did not threaten vested interests he converted few to his religious vision of the true shape for India's society and polity, and he started no new school of thought. People were drawn to him by a combination of personal response to his care for them and his considerable charm, of semi-religious veneration of him as a Mahatma, and of pragmatic evaluation of his capacity as a political strategist and intermediary between different groups of Indians, and between Indians and their rulers. Pragmatism rather than ideological enthusiasm was the hallmark of much political thinking and action, compared with the acute intellectual turmoil of so many in the previous century in response to their reading and personal experience of imperial rule. Even though commitment to an Indian nation gathered strength and attracted deeper and wider support in the early twentieth century, most political activists were prepared in the 1920s to temper their goals to the realities of the *raj* and its power. As Motilal Nehru noted in 1927, 'I don't think there is one man among the old or the new sort of Congressmen who will not go into a fainting fit on hearing the words complete independence for India'.[48]

Although Indians were not building the ideological pillars of a new order they were laying foundations of political experience which were to be vital in the making of a stable, independent India. Working the reforms, even obstructing the legislatures' work constitutionally according to Swarajist strategy, gave several generations a wealth of constitutional expertise as they learnt the procedures of parliamentary politics, the possibilities of influence and persuasion in open debate and behind-the-scenes negotiation, and explored the range of alliances possible among legislators.[49] No formal party system emerged—a fact lamented by the British, who felt that party organization made for stability and efficiency in the legislatures and assurance of support from the electorate. Given the context of Indian society and politics, and the reservation of so many seats for special interests in the legislatures it was not surprising that fluid and changing alliances on specific issues and for limited periods were the most frequent modes of co-operation. Madras's Justice Party and the National Unionist Party in Punjab, which was a cross-communal agricultural interest group, were the nearest approaches to western political parties the rulers could discern. Despite the lack of party organization, funds, and propaganda, politicians began to construct new connections with voters. Little permanent constituency work was done; and appeals were limited to brief election campaigns and to influential electors. As one provincial Governor noted in 1926: 'Of course no one tries to organise the electorate as such. All efforts are directed towards getting hold of the men with local influence who can tell the others how to vote.'[50] Yet a real process of political education was under way, for candidates and voters: and in the three provincial legislature elections held during the decade the percentage of voters who actually voted rose consistently, though women appeared to use their vote less than men (See Table C).

Equally important for the peaceful transfer of power from British to Indian hands, in the provinces in the 1930s and then at the centre in 1947, was the pattern of adjustment occurring between rulers and ruled—a mutual process of learning the limits and potential of co-operation and confrontation. India was the first non-white part of the empire to experience constitutional devolution of power: and neither Indians nor British knew how the process would work. It was an experiment and a risk for all involved. (Africans in the 1960s had the Indian pattern before them, and knew how far the British would probably go, in reform and repression.) A curious relationship developed, rather like learning a dance; a mutual probing of the steps the partner was able or prepared to take, and withdrawal if certain steps seemed likely to wreck the dance. Indians learnt to combine opposition and co-operation in sequence, as in the swing between constitutional co-operation and non-co-operation, and at different levels of public life—for example, collaboration in local boards and educational institutions while opposing government in the legislatures. Few except the terrorists wished to break the political system the *raj* was constructing: most of the politically active wanted to modify and inherit the system. Consequently the new constitution functioned. In the provinces and Delhi a range of constructive legislation was passed, and Indians began to exercise very real influence over government, indirectly as well as through direct participation in its structures and processes. Rarely did the Swarajists succeed in making

Table C. *Elections in the 1920s*

Province	Percentage of population enfranchised (1926)	Percentage of votes polled in the election of		
		1920	1923	1926
Madras	3.2	24.9	36.3 [11.4]	48.6 [19.2]
Bombay	3.9	16.2	38.4 [15.3]	39.0 [19.3]
Bengal	2.5	33.4	39.0	39.2 [13.0]
United Provinces	3.5	33.0	42.2 [2.8]	50.2 [10.0]
Punjab	3.4	32.0	49.3	52.4 [6.8]
Bihar and Orissa	1.1	41.0	52.0	61.0
Central Provinces	1.3	22.5	57.7	61.9
Assam	3.7	16.4	37.5	35.0 [not known]
The eight Provinces excluding Burma	2.8	29.0	39.9	42.6

Note: The figures given in brackets give the percentage of women voters who actually voted. Their low turn-out clearly brought down the over-all percentage of votes polled.

Source: *Report of the Indian Statutory Commission. Volume 1—Survey*, p. 197.

government impossible in the provinces: though in Bengal the Governor had on several occasions to use his emergency powers to administer the 'transferred' subjects when the legislature refused to vote money for Ministers' salaries, and in CP the Swarajists managed to wreck the Ministry after the second elections.

Yet the strains of co-operation in the reformed constitutional structures were considerable, even for those who opposed or abandoned Swarajist tactics of obstruction. Tension and disillusion generated by the experience of working the reforms convinced rulers and ruled that they could not last long as a collaborative structure. Because ministers could seldom rely on solid support in the legislatures they tended to lean heavily on the official bloc, and, in turn, to support government over 'reserved' matters. As they were often seen as 'government men' and government was not really divided as the reforms had intended, ministers were not truly responsible to the elected legislators or beyond them to the voters, for 'transferred' subjects. Governors still retained considerable powers, such as the restoration of funds for 'reserved' topics, the veto, and the certification of acts the legislature was unwilling to pass. Governors used these; though not uniformly across the provinces. Further friction was generated by the prevailing financial stringency which forced local and central governments to

retrench on expenditure and increase taxation. Until 1927–8 provinces had
to contribute to central government revenues, to make up for revenue lost
to Delhi under the reforms. This drain on provincial resources was a constant source of irritation to provincial politicians. In the provinces the
money available for the 'transferred' topics under Indian control actually
fell in the early 1920s. Starved of the resources which made the reforms
initially attractive, the devolution of power seemed a pale shadow well
before the decade ended.[51]

However tardy and restricted reform seemed to the politicians in British-
administered India, it created a new situation for India's princes. Their
adjustment to changes in British attitudes added a new dimension to politics
on the subcontinent. Until the 1920s the British had treated India's princes
in isolation from the rest of the subcontinent, content to countenance
different administrative standards in the states while their rulers proved
buttresses of the *raj*; though they were prepared to intervene if stability
seemed in danger, as in the case of a minority. They had also discouraged
consultation among the princes. Early in the twentieth century the princely
states seemed even more important as 'breakwaters'; not now against
armed rebellion, but against the new political challenge emerging in British-
administered India. Lord Minto in 1906 floated a plan for a Council of
Princes to act as a counterpoise to Congress. After the decision to make
major reforms in British India the imperial rulers took up this idea and
created a Chamber of Princes, both to reward the princes for their wartime
assistance, and to utilize more effectively princely co-operation in the enterprise of ruling a changing India. This decision suited those princes who saw
in the Montagu–Chelmsford Reforms and their declared goal a possible
threat to their position, and had lobbied Montagu and Chelmsford for new
mechanisms through which they could as a group discuss mutual concerns
with the British and possibly with Indian legislators. The Chamber of
Princes as actually set up in 1921 had a restricted role. It was a deliberative
and advisory body and had no executive power. It met annually in a special
hall built in the newly designed capital of New Delhi under construction
beside the old Mogul city in the 1920s. Despite the Chamber's limitations it
was a significant departure from the previous relationship of the princes
with each other and the Paramount Power. It gave the princes a focus of
political unity and a forum for joint discussion. It also symbolized the fact
that increasingly the princes would not be able to stand aside from the
changes occurring the British India: though at this stage Congress policy
was not to interfere in the states and to leave the princes' subjects to
experiment with ways of pressing their particular rulers into political
reform.[52]

Some princes were becoming more sharply aware of the implications for
them of moves towards 'responsible government' and of the radicalization

of political demand and action in British India; and consequently placed greater value on joint action among themselves to clarify and strengthen their position. Fears were brought to a head by a period of strain between Delhi and one of the greatest princes, the Nizam of Hyderabed, whose state was nearly as large as Great Britain. Friction developed over the Nizam's demand for the restoration to his control of the region of Berar. In the course of the ensuing correspondence between the Nizam and the Viceroy, the latter, Lord Reading, stated that no ruler could negotiate with the British government on an equal footing, and that the British as the Paramount Power had the right to decide all disputes that might arise between states, or between one of the states and itself. Alarmed by this and the question of their relations with a future self-governing India, the princes as a group called in 1927 for an inquiry into their relations with the British. In response the Secretary of State for India, Lord Birkenhead, appointed a three-man committee under Sir Harcourt Butler, who was a former Governor of UP, where he had had cordial relations with that province's great landlords, the *taluqdars*. His committee visited sixteen states, and heard submissions in London, including those from individual states and from the Standing Committee of the Chamber of Princes, who briefed a number of eminent lawyers, led by Sir Leslie Scott (at a fee of Rs. 1,500,000). The Butler Committee refused to define or limit Paramountcy but it held that the princes' relationship was essentially with the British crown and its representative in India, and that therefore the relationship should not be transferred without princely consent to a new government in British India responsible to an Indian legislature.[53] Although in the 1920s princely attempts to re-adjust their relations with the British had limited success, the Butler reassurance as to their future gave them some long-term leverage over the British and over Indian politicans. More immediately they were to become a new factor in the political calculation of imperial rulers and Indian politicians as both played for allies in the creation of a new order on the subcontinent.

Reading's dismissal of the Nizam's claim might suggest a Viceroy arguing from an impregnable position. But the British were themselves making, or being forced to make, significant adjustments in their relations with the subcontinent, beyond the obvious major policy shift incorporated in the Montagu–Chelmsford Reforms. The 1920s saw both the loosening of imperial control, and the erosion of imperial interests in India: trends which were to be marked in the subsequent decade but which clearly originated in the post-war political and financial turbulence.

In India itself the reforms showed the imperial regime withdrawing from direct involvement in a wide range of matters considered peripheral to imperial security. The British had always had limited influence at the base of society and the economy. Now they consciously withdrew some initiative and effort from the provinces, though this tactic did not reach its climax until the grant of full provincial autonomy in 1935. This made sense in a time of financial constraint and Indian political demand for increased control of resources; but it meant the fragmentation of policy and investment in crucial constructive fields. (For example, it destroyed the Government of India's new policy of encouraging industrialization which was stated in its mature form in the 1918 report of the Indian Industrial Commission; because under the reforms industrial policy was transferred to Indian ministers in the provinces.[54]) Simultaneously representatives of the *raj* had to contrive new ways of controlling and steering Indian opinion, just at the time when the reforms were eroding the patronage and influence of the ICS man in province and district alike. The changed context created by the reforms and the increasing exposure of Indian affairs to international comment as the news media expanded meant that it had never been so important for them to carry articulate Indian opinion with them. Yet their resources were scanty compared with those of governments in most democracies where debate, controlled opposition, and consent are deemed essential to healthy political life and good government. The British were in an uncomfortable half-way position between autocracy and parliamentary government, but as the official bloc in the legislatures was diminished they were stranded without a party in the councils to ensure passage of legislation, or in the country to secure support for government policy. Nor did they feel they could formally organize such a party as it would have undermined their stated commitment to allow Indians free electoral choice, and their proclaimed impartiality towards different communal and interest groups. Obviously much informal solicitation of support occurred, the wheels well oiled by the honours system, local and national variants of 'neo-durbari' politics, patronage and social exchange.[55] Government propaganda techniques were too weak to have significant results in a time of increasing literacy and articulation of opinion in an expanding vernacular press when they would have been particularly valuable. Given the financial constraints and political pressures of the 1920s it was little wonder that publicity departments in most provinces were short-lived. In Bombay the legislature threw out the department's grant in 1924; and later, to minimize opposition, the Governor amalgamated the Directorates of Labour and Information. Henceforth a good governor or civil servant had to be an able politician. Those who had been recruited before the Montagu–Chelmsford Reforms had not been trained for this; nor had they chosen their careers with this role in view. Understandably a significant number of ICS men accepted the provision for early retirement after the reforms for those who had joined the service before 1920: 54 retired early in 1922, 22 in 1923 and 21 in 1924.

This drain of senior Europeans weakened the *raj*'s administrative framework; but it was only part of a broader trend towards the Indianization of the services and the erosion of the career interests and expectations which had been a significant link between Britain and India. Most ordinary soldiers in the Indian army were Indians, and it was the officer's career which had been the main attraction of India for British soldiers. In 1918 for the first time Indians became eligible for the King's Commission, which put them on an equal footing with their British officer counterparts. But the pace of Indianization of the officer corps contemplated in the 1920s was slow, giving weighty consideration to military efficiency and seniority. The Skeen Committee on ways of improving the recruitment of Indian officers assumed when it reported in 1926 that under its recommendations half the officers in the Indian army would be Indian by 1952. By mid-1928 only 77 had actually been commissioned. Indianization of the Civil Service was a far thornier problem. Restricted Indian access had for decades been a political flashpoint in relations between the British and educated Indians. Now as ICS men were in an increasingly ambivalent position as upholders of the *raj* in a phase of controlled devolution of power to Indian politicians it became even more critical for the *raj* to have reliable men in the service. Yet increased Indianization was written into the preamble to the 1919 act of reform, and the Montagu–Chelmsford Report proposed that 33 per cent of ICS posts should be recruited for in India, the percentage rising annually. Early in 1929 the number of Europeans and Indians in the ICS was 894 and 367 respectively: and it was estimated that at the beginning of 1939 there would be 715 Europeans and 643 Indians. (On 1 January 1940 there were actually 588 Europeans and 597 Indians.) But it was not simply policy which hastened Indian recruitment into the ICS at the expense of Europeans. In the early 1920s it proved very difficult to recruit adequate numbers of Europeans. A Royal Commission on the higher services, the Lee Commission, whose recommendations were implemented in 1925 tackled the problems of ICS morale and conditions of service which had become acute since the war, and substantially removed the real financial problems of becoming an ICS man. In that year European candidates for the London examination jumped from 23 to 71; and for the rest of the decade European recruitment was no problem. However the Lee Commission also recommended that half the men selected by direct recruitment should be Indians and half should be Europeans, and constructed an elaborate mechanism of annual examinations in London and India by which this balance was to be achieved and quality maintained. It created immense headaches for the Secretary of State when European recruitment fell in the early 1930s.[56] Even in the final years of the *raj* the ICS never lost its appeal to some young Britons. But increasing Indianization of it and the army loosened links between Britain and its Indian empire, and changed India's role in the lives of those British families who had for generations assumed that it was for them a career and a solemn charge.

More striking patterns of adjustment in relations between Britain and India began to appear in the 1920s, eroding India's pivotal position in the world-wide structure of Britain's imperial power. Their origin lay in India's war-time strain in meeting imperial military and financial demands, and in a financial crisis in the early 1920s produced by a contraction in world trade, India's swing into trade deficit and a fall in the value of the rupee. The financial position of the Government of India deteriorated rapidly, as revenue fell and expenditure increased, and interest rates made borrowing impossible as a complete remedy. The government was faced with increasing its revenue and reducing its expenditure. But its options were curtailed in unprecedented ways because the crisis occurred just when the new constitution gave Indians a crucial forum in which they could criticize and delay taxations, and expenditure which they saw as peripheral or detrimental to Indian interests, and consequently put powerful pressure on the Delhi end of the imperial government.[57] So India's domestic politics began to compromise the Government of India's ability to meet London's expectations, and to modify India's role in sustaining Britain's world-wide power.

The most dramatic demonstration of this was the debate between London and Delhi in the early 1920s on the part the Indian army would play in imperial defence. London hoped that India could be relied on to maintain Britain's power in the Middle East: but by 1923 it was recognized that this was impossible in the context of India's domestic politics and finances. For the rest of the decade the Indian army was used according to the policy of the Viceroy backed by the Central Legislative Assembly. It was primarily for the defence of India's borders and the maintenance of internal tranquillity, and could only be used abroad for wider imperial purposes in grave emergency, after consultation with the Viceroy in Council, and—critically—at London's expense. India was *de facto* acting more as a close ally of Britain than as a dependent territory.

In financial matters India increasingly managed her affairs independently of Britain, and sometimes in direct opposition to certain British interests. This was clearest in her new fiscal autonomy, recognized by a convention between Delhi and London in 1919. It *was* only a convention; but during the 1920s no Secretary of State for India seriously challenged tariff proposals emanating from India. Accordingly Tariff Boards were set up to advise on Indian industries requesting tariff protection, 'discriminatory protection' was introduced, for iron, steel, and sugar, for example. (By 1931 imported sugar was being charged at 190 per cent.) The cotton excise was abolished in 1926. So India flouted old taboos and challenged accepted imperial assumptions about India's role as the hand-maiden of British economic interests. But the imperial link and the need to pay home charges and interest in London remained a constraint on the Government of India's currency policy, however much Delhi struggled during the decade to abdicate control and construct a self-regulating mechanism to fix the value of the rupee.

India had played a key economic role in Britain's imperial position as a trading partner and recipient of capital. This relationship was changing in the 1920s though the disengagement of India from her former role only became marked in the 1930s. India and Ceylon were by 1930 the second largest outlet for British overseas investment; but the place of such investment in Britain's national income was declining. Figures for public and private British investment are not very reliable for this decade, but it seems that private investment stagnated in 1921–38 compared with earlier decades, and in the 1920s most of it went into the western Indian cotton mills and the Bengal jute mills. British money was still significant in financing the Government of India's sterling debt: but at the end of the decade the rupee debt was far larger than the sterling one. The pattern of India's imports and exports remained fairly constant in the 1920s. Trade between India and Britain did not alter greatly—India was still the largest purchaser of British goods until the late 1930s, taking over 10 per cent of the total in the 1920s. But the Indian market was not adjusting to changes in British industry: it was still important to Lancashire's cotton industry, but absorbed little from the growth sectors of British industry, such as chemicals and electrical goods. India's own industrial growth under the new tariff protection also began to generate competition between British exports and Indian-produced goods. However, India still had a deficit on her trading account with Britain, and a surplus in her trade with most other parts of the world. This enabled her to maintain her crucial role in the imperial pattern of financial settlements on which British economic power rested. Britain still had a vital economic interest in India, whatever loosening of the pre-war economic ties and methods of control had occurred.

It is tempting to describe the Great War as a watershed in Indian life and in the subcontinent's relations with Britain. Change more than continuity generates historical evidence and attracts notice. But despite the economic upheavals of the war and its aftermath, despite the British bid for a new political order and Gandhi's visionary enterprise, much remained the same in the content of the subcontinent's interlocking political worlds, just as remarkably little changed in ordinary Indians' daily experience of work, family, and leisure. No striking or simple process of 'westernization' occurred as communications drew the subcontinent nearer to Europe, and as more Indians passed between the two. Changes in social habits, from eating with forks to playing cricket, an appreciation of western literature, art, and music, and intellectual engagement with western political and social thought were only possible for the few who could afford foreign travel or were exposed to western cultural and intellectual influences through the higher education curriculum and those expatriates who came to teach in India either in the government's Educational Service, or as missionaries; and for those who were drawn into contact with British official and social life in urban areas. But British social aloofness, particularly in the club and family setting, limited their informal influence on Indian lives. While from the Indian side barriers were erected because even western educated Indians felt uneasy about changing long-established patterns of family life and allowing their wives and children 'freedoms' which might lower the family's prestige. Furthermore the Gandhian idiom in political life made some consciously withdraw from western customs, including wearing foreign clothes, in an attempt to underline their distinctive 'Indianness' and its cultural value.[58]

Yet India by 1929 was different from India in 1910, in significant ways; the changes being produced by a subtle interaction of the stable and traditional with the novel and obviously disruptive. India's international standing by 1929 was far higher and more nearly approached that of a white colony after her participation in the war and the making of the 1918 peace, and her acquisition of fiscal autonomy. Within the subcontinent a wider and deeper range of social groups had become articulate in public life, and momentous adjustments were occurring in Indians' political relationships with each other and the British. In response to many of these trends the British had transformed their structures for consultation, the attraction of Indian allies, and the control of the disaffected. By so doing they activated, strengthened or redirected forces which were to bring about major changes in India in the subsequent decades, making the imperial enterprise infinitely more complex and ultimately unproductive, but simultaneously making the emergence of one independent Indian nation equally problematic.

CHAPTER V

A Critical Decade:
India—Empire or Nation?

Written into the Montagu–Chelmsford Reforms was provision for an inquiry into their operation after ten years: but in 1927 Britain's Tory government appointed a Commission of inquiry under Sir John Simon earlier than scheduled, to keep its composition out of the hands of the less conservative politicians who might replace them at the next General Election. The all-white Simon Commission provoked widespread political protest in India. Its members encountered hostile black-flag demonstrations as they perambulated the country taking evidence in the provinces. The work of the Commission, its reception and its report indicated that British and Indian alike recognized that the imperial bid for a new order on the subcontinent had failed. Although the 1939–45 war is commonly seen as the great upheaval out of which the subcontinent emerged politically independent yet agonizingly divided, the decade until India was engulfed in it was critical for the nature of British dominion, and for the development on the subcontinent of senses of public identity, particularly for a sense of Indian nationhood. The 1930s saw no sudden and dramatic change—in the strength or structure of the *raj*, in the economic base and social framework of Indian life, or in the daily life and attitudes of India's millions. Yet by 1940 it was clear that the decade had intensified trends and brought decisions crucial in the shaping of modern India. Many of these decisions were the result of drift and default, or of sheer pragmatism. There was never a clear 'point of no return'. But by 1940 the Indian empire was no longer viable in the long term, though it could be kept going in the short term as part of the allied war effort. Furthermore, the potential viability of an Indian nation incorporating British and princely India and the major religious communities was almost as dubious.

Certain themes of long-term significance stand out in the decade. One was a questioning of the legitimacy accorded to different types of authority, particularly that of the imperial government. Closely connected with it was the growth and articulation of public awareness. Those who were once described as the 'real India' for whom the district officer had to speak became vocal and demonstrative on a wide range of public concerns and became a significant component of 'public opinion'. Yet it was still unclear how Indians were coming to perceive themselves as participants on the public stage. Nation, community, caste, region, and kin group were loyalties which claimed allegiance; identities which were real in certain types of situations. Which would become politically privileged was a question whose answer was being discovered in interactions between rulers and ruled, and between fellow Indians. Parallel with such trends and questions were the increasing institutionalization of politics, the construction of a more formal political system, including legislatures and parties, regular patterns of recruitment and behavioural conventions, through which concern for public power was channelled.

This chapter is about these matters; it focuses on some underlying patterns of social and economic change, then on the political handling of the raw materials of public life in two distinctive phases, 1928–34 and 1935–40. The sequence of political events makes clear the dual crisis of empire and potential nation, in relations between the rulers and ruled, and in the relations of Indians with each other. Indians responded to one another not just in terms of the 'high politics' which dominate conventional accounts of the *raj*'s closing years—relations between the princes and the Congress politicians, between Hindu and Muslim political organizations—but through 'vertical' linkages or disjunctures between levels of political life, apparent in the fate of political groups and their varying success in creating grass-roots support, and in the careers of men who proved able to attract followers or who 'failed' as leaders in the changing context. The historian has to enter the land of village influence and discussion, of caste connections and landlord pressure, of the resentments and pressures built up in urban neighbourhoods and alleyways, where decisions were rarely recorded and 'connections' were seldom articulated. Recognition of ignorance must therefore counterbalance the knowledge culled from the weighty files of Indian politicians and British bureaucrats engaged in the recorded formalities of institutionalized politics.

i   Some underlying trends

India's history has been evolutionary rather than revolutionary. Short, crucial times of change are hard to find. But times of intensification of underlying patterns of change can sometimes be seen, and among them was the decade of the 1930s. Even where social and economic changes are patent, though, there is no easy historical link between them and political events: they mainly operate as context rather than cause. Urbanization, the entry of Indians into modern business and banking, and the expansion of an industrial labour force all affected political decisions, but those with new economic interests and connections were often politically ambivalent. Indian businessmen were politically divided: some backed both Congress and the government. The industrial labour force was conspicuously peripheral to the development of the nationalist movement. Even a major economic upheaval like the Depression does not explain the appearance of wider political awareness and allegiances, though it may partially account for many of the temporary recruits into agitational politics. Major British political concessions did not coincide with the greatest financial strains on the *raj*. Yet such pressures were continuously but indirectly at work, ultimately making politics more complex and the task of politicians more taxing. As identities diversified and there were subtle changes in the balance of social and economic influence, Congressmen and imperial rulers had to re-think their priorities and alliances. They had to find or widen channels of communication so that within a flexible political system grievances could be aired, tensions defused and aspirations pursued. Only sensitive responses to a changing world could guarantee political support and ensure that changes in society did not rend apart or undermine older political systems which had functioned effectively in a more stable environment.

Within India one fact which was to be of overwhelming importance after independence began to manifest itself. Population had been growing since the start of census-taking in the 1870s, but erratically. From 1921 growth became steady and sustained. In 1921 the population was just over 305,700,000; by 1931 it was 338,171,000; and in 1941 nearly 400,000,000. In the 1920s there was an increase of 10.6 per cent, and in the 1930s 15 per cent. By 1931–41 an Indian baby at birth had a life expectancy for the first time of nearly 32 years. The result was more pressure on natural resources, particularly land, both for actual food and for jobs, for there was comparatively little else to employ the adult labour force. In 1931 in British India 432 people depended on agriculture per square mile of cultivated land: the figure had risen to 535 by 1941—a density far higher than in European countries which were as economically dependent on agriculture as India. Over the previous fifty years the number of acres per person actually engaged in agriculture had dropped by 15 per cent from 2.23 in 1891–2 to 1.90 in 1939–40.[1] Growing numbers put pressure on man-made resources and services, such as housing, communications, medical care, and education. As the population became younger educational opportunities and expectations became areas of particular strain and frustration. A young, under-occupied, population could be expected to be increasingly volatile and 'available' for political recruitment. More people also meant greater concentrations of population. This implied fruitful prospects for agitators as well as even more difficulty in maintaining civil order with an inefficient, under-paid and under-staffed police force.

Towns grew markedly in this decade, but the country remained deeply rural, and most Indians were villagers. The rise in the number of townsfolk reflected the general population increase and a limited industrialization, rather than a decisive swing towards an urban economy. Town-dwellers were 10.2 per cent of the total population in 1921, 11.1 per cent in 1931 and 12.8 per cent in 1941 (See Chapter 3, Table D). More striking was the growth of the larger cities. By 1941 the cities of half a million inhabitants and over had 130 per cent more people, and four new cities (Hyderabad, Lahore, Ahmedabad and Delhi) had entered that category in the previous decade (See Chapter 3, Table E). In 1931 2.86 per cent of the population lived in cities of 100,000 and over; by 1941 only 4.25 per cent did, but that was an increase of nearly 50 per cent.[2] Industrial cities grew most rapidly in the 1920s and 1930s, attracting migrants in search of work. Between 1921 and 1931 the industrial work force grew annually at 1 per cent, but this quadrupled between 1932 and 1937. A range of other economic indicators, for output and investment, suggest that the 1930s saw a marked increase in industrial enterprise (See Tables A, B, and C). Yet the work force engaged in agriculture and related pursuits was still overwhelming and its proportion remained remarkably constant at just over 70 per cent right through the first half of the century.[3]

Modern industrial growth in India had been narrowly based. Mining, plantations, some metallurgical products, and light manufacturing accounted for most of it. Between the world wars these early bases continued to be important and to expand. (The number of cotton mills, for example, rose from 253 in 1920 to 365 in 1935, despite the industry's internal problems, compounded by the Depression and Japanese competition. Furthermore, the industry expanded geographically beyond the early heart-land of Bombay and Ahmedabad, breaking the old barriers between coast and hinterland which had encapsulated early industry within coastal enclaves.) Far more significant was the development of a wide range of manufactures often for domestic consumption rather than for export, as older industrial products had been, among them were sugar, paper, cement, and matches.

***Table A**. Indices of Indian industrial production*

1928	92.6	1933	116.7
1929	109.5	1934	132.4
1930	100.7	1935	143.0
1931	108.1	1936	150.7
1932	108.1	1937	163.5
		1938	166.8
	(1925–9 = 100)		

Source: B. R. Tomlinson, *The Political Economy Of The Raj 1914–1947*, p. 32.

Table B. *Net domestic product of India (including princely states) (in Rs. billion)*

Year	Agriculture, forestry, and fishing	Mining, manufacturing and small enterprises	Other	Net domestic product
1930	17.2	2.9	8.1	28.2
1931	16.8	2.9	8.0	27.7
1932	17.2	2.9	8.1	28.1
1933	17.8	2.9	8.2	28.8
1934	17.1	3.1	8.2	28.4
1935	17.1	3.3	8.2	28.6
1936	18.1	3.4	8.4	30.0
1937	17.9	3.7	8.5	30.0
1938	16.4	4.0	8.3	28.7
1939	17.7	4.1	8.7	30.4
1940	17.8	4.2	8.8	30.7

Source: A. Maddison, *Class Structure and Economic Growth*, pp. 167–8.

Their development was remarkable when compared with the sluggish performance of the established industries.[4]

This second phase of industrial development was undoubtedly assisted by government policy. There was greater official patronage of Indian products, but more importantly a helpful tariff policy, whether tariffs were raised for revenue purposes or because the Tariff Board recommended deliberate protection for particular industries against the competition of imports. The sugar, cement, and match industries were clear examples. The Depression disrupted foreign trade and credit, and encouraged industry to produce for

Table C. *Paid-up capital of companies registered in India*

1930–1	342.4
1931–2	357.5
1932–3	345.7
1933–4	369.2
1934–5	373.5
1935–6	369.9
1936–7	383.8
1937–8	372.2
1938–9	387.1
1939–40	404.8

(Base = 100 in 1914–15)

Source: Rajat K. Ray, *Industrialization in India. Growth and Conflict in the Private Corporate Sector 1914–47* (Delhi, 1979), p. 39.

the home market to replace foreign goods which were held back by the international economic disruption of the early 1930s. It thus provided a temporary barrier behind which Indian industries could become established, so reinforcing official policies of protection. Although the Depression damaged India's international trade and internal and external credit arrangements, the experience of contraction in established patterns of credit and exchange at the start of the decade actually helped to provide capital for industrial expansion. A complex economic mechanism triggered by the export of privately-held gold from India from later 1931 created an abundance of funds in the modern banking sector. This provided a reservoir of capital and credit throughout the decade. Moreover, it seems (though the details are still unclear) that the traditional money-lending 'banking' sector suffered a severe decline as a result of the Depression. In its wake came an expansion of modern commercial banking institutions at local level into which savings were channelled, and which were in turn more flexible than older money-lending networks, willing to invest their funds more widely through the economy, and to enable a demonstrable switch of internal investment from the old security of agriculture and trade into industry.

Even this second stage of industrial growth though, did not create an urban working class either large or selfconscious enough to change the structure of society, or the nature of Indian politics radically. The imperial rulers and aspiring Indian political leaders had recognized that the crucial groups whose loyalty and acquiescence were the foundation of political legitimacy and stability were the articulate educated, and (increasingly) the diverse group of smaller landholders and dominant peasant families who were enfranchised by the reforms of 1919 and 1935. The urban work force, however volatile its members and susceptible to the appeal of radical agitators or disadvantaged politicians in search of a platform, was by comparison politically insignificant. To the rulers they remained a little understood section of their imperial subjects, in need of control. The main nationalist leaders could not find an entrée into their local worlds: only Gandhi took the issue of industrial relations seriously; and his vision of 'trusteeship' found little practical outlet except in Ahmedabad, and tended to stress co-operation between owners and workers rather than encouraging sectional articulation and action.

In terms of investment and control of resources the industrial expansion marked the early stages of a major shift away from European dominance of modern business. This ultimately was to enable the Indian economy to sustain itself without expatriate capital and expertise, and weakened British economic interests in India well before political independence. Taking into account both sterling investment and the expatriate share in rupee capital, foreign interests still dominated the private sector, particularly the established industries such as jute, tea, and coal. European dominance was most marked in Calcutta, as it had been since the inception of modern business on the subcontinent. But even in that stronghold Indian capital began to make headway between the wars. In 1914 under 3 per cent of capital employed in Calcutta was Indian: during the Second World War that figure stood at nearly 17 per cent. Established expatriate Managing Agency Houses tended to be conservative in their operations, sticking to well-tried patterns of business and commodities. In contrast Indian firms moved rapidly into the new, consumer-orientated industries—cement, sugar, paper, chemicals, paints, and electrical goods. They also expanded far more rapidly than expatriate firms, though they were not dissimilar in structure. Some private British capital was repatriated in the decade. Little new foreign money was attracted into the Indian economy (except in government loans); and expatriate firms increasingly relied on Indian investors for share capital. By the 1930s many of them had also at least a minority of Indian directors.

The 'new' Indian entrepreneurs were generally men from communities with business experience. Their increasing success represented diversification of business interests and a redirecting of existing expertise rather than a breakthrough by 'new' social groups into business. A prominent example was the Marwari house of Birla which established itself in eastern and central India, in cotton and jute, and then in the 1930s in sugar and paper. An old banking family produced one of Delhi's major entrepreneurs, Lala Sri Ram, who based a business empire on the Delhi Cloth and General Mills. The Dalmia Jain family went into sugar, paper, and cement. Some of those who became modern commercial bankers also seem to have capitalized on their traditions. The Chettiar banking community in south India, for example, converted part of their older money-lending business into a joint-stock bank even before the Depression. Indian society proved highly adaptable: far-reaching economic change was not only contained within the existing social order but actively facilitated by its potential and existing skills and family networks.[5] In politics such men became significant financial backers of India-wide political causes and organizations, whereas earlier businessmen had tended to confine their patronage to local institutions and charities. Their co-operation and skill became important factors in the calculations of all who tried or aspired to govern India.

By contrast with industrial India, the rural sector had a rough passage through the Depression. World wide, prices of food and raw materials fell more than those of manufactured goods. World trade swung against India as an exporter of raw materials: growers of food found their profits from internal markets plummeting (See Table D). The problems for cash farmers began when their incomes dropped while their rent and revenue commitments persisted. Sources of credit dried up, too, because they could offer little security, and credit was crucial at certain times of the year for payment

Table D. Prices in India, 1920–1939

	1920–1	1923–4	1926–7	1929–30	1932–3	1935–6	1938–9
Wholesale Prices							
Calcutta	123	118	102	97	63	63	65
Bombay	136	124	102	99	75	68	69
Retail Price							
of Food	128	88	103	106	54	54	55
			1928–9 = 100				

Source: Tomlinson, *The Political Economy Of The Raj 1914–1947*, p. 35.

of revenue instalments and purchase of seed. Rent receivers began to put on pressure when they found their tenants reluctant or unable to pay, for they in turn had to pass on part of the rent to government in land revenue. Government, for its part, faced an acute financial crisis as its receipts declined. Not only land revenue, but taxes on a wide range of goods brought in less as prices and consumption fell. Although dislocation of credit relations and patterns of production was widespread in the early 1930s, the precise impact of the Depression varied from region to region and crop to crop and it is impossible to draw conclusions about long term trends. In UP the peasantry faced downward spiralling prices for their crops, landlords anxious to maintain their incomes, and government needing to collect revenue. Predictably such areas became politically turbulent. They had been so in the earlier post-war inflation, which had propelled many into the non-co-operation movement. But where farmers had a choice they seem to have responded keenly to market conditions. They switched crops or searched out alternative markets. Beneath the temporary dislocations the underlying trends towards increasing commercialization of agriculture, the broadening of economic linkages within India, and the slow erosion of subsistence village agriculture persisted, and with them went the loosening of patronage and dependence sanctioned by caste divisions and values.

One significant change resulted from the difficulties of profiting from agriculture in the early 1930s. In the past, rural profits tended to be reinvested in the rural sector, in land, money-lending, or tied up in jewellery. Now rural wealth began to flow into industry through the new joint-stock banks. In UP and Bihar, for example, prosperous proprietors helped to establish sugar mills. In Madras rural money moved into sugar and cotton. Some physical mobility from the countryside also occurred. Enterprising rural capitalists in Madras left their villages; so did service groups as disparate as potters and priests, who found their livelihood going and sought to earn cash wages rather than continue in traditional patronage relations eked out with farming of small plots. In UP, too, there was evidence of increasing movement from villages to towns. Rural employers could pay fewer labourers, and petty tenants were forced by the economic crisis to relinquish their lands.[6]

Besides the economic forces beginning to break down patterns of relationship, residence, and occupation, the continuing expansion of roads, railways, and the press and the beginning of radio broadcasting, encouraged mobility of people and ideas. A more truly all-India community was in the making. Governments could increasingly expect to face demands concerted by wider segments of the public. But aspiring 'national' political leaders also found that wider contacts between people could sharpen the particularist fears of regions and groups and give substance and strength to public identities other than an Indian 'nation'. Another of the underlying forces shaping a new India out of older, separate communities, was the spread of education. Educated people were needed to man the increasingly complex infrastructure of a modernizing state; growing literacy spread ideas and helped to generate new identities. But more and better-educated citizens meant rising expectations about employment and political rights, which could be disruptive if frustrated. Compared with the exploding fireworks of political agitation and concession the progress of education was unspectacular. Arguably it was just as crucial for the emergence of a later democratic India.

Under the 1919 reforms, education became a provincial subject transferred to the control of Indian Ministers. Consequently it suffered from the absence of a co-ordinated continental policy. It was also the victim of the economies required in the provinces by the post-reforms distribution of government revenues, as well as of the Depression, which not only limited government capacity to invest in education but that of parents to pay for tuition, books, and uniforms. Government expenditure on education actually dropped in the early 1930s, then levelled off in 1936–7 at a lower figure than at the start of the decade.[7] Even so, and in the face of an expanding population, there was a striking increase in the percentage of literate people in the decade, with English literacy rising faster than literacy in general (See Table E). There was still geographical imbalance in standards. More town dwellers could read and write than country folk; literacy rates rose in proportion to the size of the city. Since literacy was still expanding faster in towns than villages there seemed little prospect of an evening out of performance. But there was marked improvement among certain previously backward groups. By the end of the 1930s there were more Muslims being educated than the average for all communities. In 1936–7, 26.1 per cent of all pupils were Muslims, while Muslims formed only 24.7 per cent of the population. Even Muslim girls were benefiting; and 25.6 per cent of girl pupils were Muslim while Muslims were only 24.1 per cent of the total

Table E. Literacy, 1921–1941

Date	A Literacy			B Literacy in English
	% Literates age 10+ (Both sexes)	% Male Literates age 10+	% Female Literates age 10+	% of Literates who can read English
1921	8.3	14.2	1.9	12.9
1931	9.2	15.4	2.4	14.9
1941	15.1	27.4	6.9	18.9

Source: Davis, *The Population Of India And Pakistan*, pp. 15, 159.

female population.[8] By then Muslims as an all-India community could no longer be considered educationally backward, though in provinces where they were a majority their standards still lagged behind the Hindus. Indian women in general were still far less educated than men. In 1941 there were still about four literate men for every literate woman. But the number of educational institutions for women and (critically) actual attendance at them was expanding swiftly in the 1930s (See Table F). By 1941 the inequality between male and female literacy rates was rapidly evening out in the under-twenty age group. However, untouchable castes were still severely disadvantaged in education: despite efforts to help them, they were held back by their own self-image, dire poverty, and the need for children to work with their parents, as well as by social discrimination.[9]

Despite financial difficulties, education in general made considerable advances between the wars. The number of institutions at all levels increased, as did attendance at them (See Table G). Expansion, however, was no guarantee of good teaching or high standards of achievement. Nor did it provide for the long term needs of a developing country, as it proliferated

Table F. Progress in Women's Education, 1921–1937

Year	Arts Colleges		High Schools		Middle Schools		Primary Schools	
	No.	Enrolment	No.	Enrolment	No.	Enrolment	No.	Enrolment
1921–2	12	938	120	25,130	548	85,079	22,579	1,195,892
1926–7	18	1,624	145	39,858	656	123,892	26,621	1,545,963
1931–2	20	2,966	218	75,479	787	170,997	32,564	2,073,141
1936–7	31	6,039	297	114,481	978	216,965	32,273	2,607,086

Source: Nurullah & Naik, *A History Of Education In India*, pp. 712–13.

Table G. Education, 1921–1937 (Recognized institutions)

	No. of Institutions		No. enrolled	
	1921–2	1936–7	1921–2	1936–7
Universities	10	15	n.a.	9,697
Arts Colleges	165	271	45,418	86,273
Professional Colleges	64	75	13,662	20,645
Secondary Schools	7,530	13,056	1,106,803	2,287,872
Primary Schools	155,017	192,244	6,109,752	10,224,288

Source: Nurullah & Naik, *A History Of Education In India*, p. 619.

arts students rather than young people trained in business and management skills, in science and technology. Furthermore, the greater the numbers of educated or partially educated, the greater was the problem of unemployment among young people with expanded horizons and ambitions raised beyond any possibility of fulfilment. In terms of India's future perhaps the most significant development was the advance in *mass* education, which had been the weakest link in the educational chain since the early nineteenth century. In the first decade when Indians controlled education nearly every province passed legislation making primary education compulsory, at least for boys, though financial stringency prevented as great expansion as might have been hoped for.

These economic, educational, and demographic changes did not create major disturbance of the social order, or radically change existing identities and accepted values. The position of all but a tiny élite of women did not alter significantly, for example, despite increasing education; nor is there real evidence of any weakening of the family as a focus of identity, as the centre of a web of social relations, and often as the basic structure of working life in agriculture and business. Caste, too, remained as a social and ritual framework, though in certain contexts caste was probably becoming less significant as a source of authority and regulator of action. In towns, conditions of work, travel and greater anonymity made for less rigorous observance of ritual avoidance patterns and attention to purity. Occupational change out of traditional caste callings loosened patron–client ties and set work relations in the context of cash transactions rather than ritual exchange. In some *jatis* the *panchayat* of elders lost authority over *jati* members' behaviour, particularly where the group was geographically spread and its members were moving out of the close-knit world of the village. Against this tendency, though, must be set the evidence that where *jatis* were sanskritizing their behaviour and rituals this could give caste elders increased leverage in the enforcement of the new standards.[10] Outside the original context of interdependent, hierarchical *jati* relationships in a redistributive economy, an expanded notion of 'caste' (which was strictly speaking neither *varna* nor *jati*) was being carried across wider groups of similar ritual ranking, in the work of the numerous self-help associations, caste *sabhas*, which interested themselves in jobs, education, housing, and politics. Even though such developments cannot be seen as the working of caste society as it had existed in a more stable environment, it is significant that caste names and identities, not notions of class, could be brought into play in new contexts and enlisted in the service of new causes.[11]

The 1930s brought a far clearer and more abrupt transition in India's relations with the wider world. India's growing integration into a world economic community since the later nineteenth century had made her increasingly vulnerable to economic trends and forces beyond her borders. As an exporter of raw materials she suffered from collapsing prices for primary products in the Depression. (The index number for the price of jute fell from 100 in 1928 to 95 in 1929, 63 in 1930, 49 in 1931 and 39 in 1934.) On the other hand, because the Depression also helped to activate or re-orientate sectors of the Indian economy, it enabled the economy in the long term to shift in relation to other trading nations, becoming far less 'colonial' in the sense of supplying raw materials to a metropolitan economy and providing other economic services for the imperial mother country.

By 1939 India's economy was far less complementary to Britain's than even a decade previously. The weakening position of British capital on the subcontinent has already been noted. Indo-British trade relations changed too; India began to play a far less vital role in Britain's world-wide exchange and credit operations. Britain's share in India's total imports had fallen to 30.5 per cent by 1939—the decline being marked in cotton piece-goods, machinery, electrical goods, iron and steel manufactures. Only in chemicals was India an expanding market for British exports.[12] This changing pattern reflected both a shift in the British economy away from dependence on older export-orientated industries, and the trend of increased production in India of goods to replace imports. In relation to the world economic community as a whole, India was producing far more of her own consumer goods and importing instead more raw materials and capital goods. By 1936 she produced well over three-quarters of her cotton and paper needs, virtually all her own sugar and cement, and over 70 per cent of her steel and tin-plate. In 1919 she had produced a mere 12 per cent of her sugar, and in 1920 only 14 per cent of her steel. A further dimension of the loosening of the old economic relationship between the two countries in the 1930s was India's withdrawal from her former role in the international pattern of trade settlements. Whereas once India's visible trade surpluses with most of the world had met her deficit with Great Britain (and enabled Great Britain to settle *her* accounts with other trading partners) now India increasingly had and used her surplus with industrial nations (including Great Britain) to meet deficits with those areas of Africa, Asia, and the Middle East which supplied her raw materials. By the late 1930s India was thus rapidly ceasing to help the United Kingdom settle her deficits with the rest of the world.

As India's relationship with the wider world and Great Britain began to change the British government in London also found it increasingly difficult for political reasons to extract from India the services and compliance with imperial needs which had helped to make her so strong a foundation of Britain's total world position. In 1930–1, for example, Labour and National Governments in Britain both tried to argue the case of the Lancashire cotton industry when the Government of India proposed to raise the tariff on cotton goods. Despite the fiscal autonomy convention the Cabinet threatened the Viceroy with a countervailing excise if his government persisted in its plan; it gave in when the Viceroy explained that five of his Executive Councillors, including three Indians, would resign if the Cabinet pushed through its proposals. This, as London recognized, would have been politically suicidal for Delhi, engaged at that moment in constitutional negotiations and claiming legitimacy as a government ruling in India's interests. Thereafter Britain accepted that she could not manoeuvre Indian tariff policy in her interests or those of particular groups of British businessmen. This was formally ratified in the 1935 constitution, though even at the 1932 Imperial Economic Conference India was treated in practice like a white dominion. In currency matters the British Government overruled the Viceroy in the crisis of the early 1930s, preventing him from devaluing the rupee and forcing him to ignore Indian opinion. But thereafter constitutional reform meant that London gradually relinquished its grip; in 1934 the Central Legislative Assembly passed the bill setting up the Reserve Bank of India which was henceforward to conduct India's currency and exchange policy. In military matters, too, London recognized in the 1930s that the Indian taxpayer could no longer be expected to finance wide areas of imperial defence. When detailed plans were laid just before the outbreak of war it was agreed that London would foot the bill for the modernization of the Indian army and the initiation of an industrial programme for the production of ammunition and equipment in India. India was to pay a strictly limited amount over and above the peacetime cost of the Indian army, and the cost of any war measures taken exclusively in India's interest.[13]

By the end of the 1930s it was evident to some that the old Indian Empire was a thing of the past. Although it was seldom openly admitted, British 'interest' in India was declining. The subcontinent's value to the imperial heartland was contracting as a source of economic benefit to individuals and the British economy as a whole, and as a cheap military bastion and barrack. It was also decreasingly a place for careers for a small but significant section of the British public, as European recruitment to the ICS slumped in the early 1930s. Furthermore, the management of India in the imperial interest became increasingly problematic. Intensifying political demands in India, and the proper constitutional influence of Indian politicians through the legislatures meant that India's own interests had now to be weighed against imperial demands. Viceroys came to see themselves as the servants of the former, as in the matters of currency and defence. A further constraint on British ability to rule in the old ways was the embarrassing articulation of world opinion in favour of colonial nationalism, which was apparent in British left-wing circles and America, particularly when there was physical conflict between the *raj* and Indian politicians claiming to speak in the name of an Indian nation. The imperial role in India now demanded new political sensitivity and skill, new techniques of conciliation and public justification of policy, if it was to retain legitimacy in India and abroad. Older styles of *raj* were now actually counter productive; and not worth the price financially or politically, given ebbing British interests in the subcontinent. Whether the effort to construct a looser imperial relationship would be repaid by real advantage to Great Britain was also open to doubt.

ii   Crises of legitimacy: conflict and consultation, 1928–1934

Historians removed from the drama and pressure of the events they study can try to discern and assess the significance of long-term social and economic trends. Contemporaries tend to be more impressed by the importance of political decisions and emerging political alignments. In the early 1930s these seemed to be carrying the subcontinent into a new era. There were two striking sets of political events: a second continental satyagraha under Gandhi's guidance, which lasted from early 1930 to early 1934, with a ten months 'truce' in 1931; and three Round Table Conferences in London between 1930 and 1932 to which Indians were invited to discuss with British politicians the making of a new constitution, which took final shape in the 1935 Government of India Act. These two developments were genuinely dominant influences in political life. In their different ways both civil disobedience and the conferences affected then and later the interconnections between different levels of political life. Both helped to change relations between different religious groups and between Untouchables and caste Hindus. On the British side, conflict and consultation demanded radical scrutiny of the framework of the *raj* and the means of control imperialists could use without provoking disorder. Among Indians conflict and consultation recruited and trained a generation of young and able men, committed to the vision of a new India. Jawaharlal Nehru, Rajendra Prasad, and Vallabhbhai Patel, for example, were to become all-India leaders of the

1940s and 1950s; beneath them emerged the middle-rank politicians and party activists who were to become the backbone of state-level politics after 1947.

The turmoil of 1928–34 was at heart the compound of a number of crises of legitimacy. The British faced a major challenge to their position as the country's rightful rulers. Simultaneously Indian groups as varied as Congress, disparate Muslim bodies, and the princely order offered themselves as alternative focuses for Indian loyalty and as sources of political authority, but they achieved limited acceptance. Furthermore, the very appropriateness to India of the institutions of politics imported from the western experience, in however modified form, were both overtly and implicitly questioned by the processes of non-co-operation and constitutional discussion.

The prelude to civil disobedience and the London consultations was the Statutory Commission chaired by Sir John Simon. Appointed under the terms of the 1919 Government of India Act, it had to inquire into the working of the system of government and to report desirable changes. This it did in 1930; by which time its proposals (for constitutional advance towards complete self-government in the provinces in place of dyarchy, but for no substantial change at the centre) had been overtaken by British initiatives in late 1929. An impressive range of Indian political opinion was hostile from the outset. Composed solely of British members of the Houses of Lords and Commons, the Commission seemed a negation of imperial promises of consultation with Indians and their incorporation into the decision-making processes. Indians were only to give evidence to the Commission, for its members then to report their own conclusions to the British Parliament for its decisions, about India's future. A wide range of Congressmen, Hindu communal leaders and Liberals, as well as a section of the Muslim League led by Jinnah, decided to boycott the Commission. Muslims from provinces where they were a majority decided to help the Commission's inquiries; as did a range of smaller minority communities such as the Anglo-Indians and the Sikhs, and most of those elected to the reformed legislatures. The Simon Report which emerged remains a monument to a conservative strategy for imperial control which was abandoned before its publication; and—more usefully—as a mine of evidence about Indian public life and education.

However, when it came to going beyond opposition to a constructive alternative the boycotters were less united. They met in an All-Parties Conference, of which a sub-committee produced a report which was the first Indian draft of a constitution for an independent India. It was mainly the work of two eminent jurists from UP—T. B. Sapru, Liberal ex-Congressman and former Law Member of the Government of India, and Motilal Nehru, staunch Congressman now increasingly influenced by

Gandhi's visionary challenge to older patterns of politics and by his radical and secular son, Jawaharlal, just back from a European tour which had opened his eyes to new economic and political developments in Russia. Known as the Nehru Report, their proposal was for an India with the same status as the white self-governing dominions within the British empire, which would join princely and British India possibly in some form of federation. Devolution of power to provinces was *not* to be increased, and residual powers were to remain in the central government. (This of course would give ascendancy to the Hindu majority, by then presumably reinforced by the Hindu princely states.) The Nehru Report made a limited attempt to assuage Muslim fears, with the promise of liberty of conscience and religion, and provision for new Muslim majority provinces including Sind and the North-West Frontier. On the other hand, Muslims were to lose separate electorates, though seats would be reserved for them at the centre and in provinces where they were a minority.[14]

In the wake of the Nehru Report differences of opinion rapidly appeared. The crack between Hindus and Muslims widened into a chasm; even the Jinnah section of the League rejected the Report, demanding that residual powers should be vested in the *provinces* rather than the *centre*, as a guarantee of Muslim interests against a unitary, Hindu-dominated state. Jinnah, who shared so much from his Bombay background, western education and legal training with Congressmen, who for so long had advocated political co-operation between Hindus and Muslims, is said to have felt that late 1928 was the 'parting of the ways' between the two communities. Other Muslim groups joined in the opposition. In January 1929 an All Parties Muslim Conference met in Delhi under the Aga Khan's presidency in an attempt to protect Muslim interests. In fact there was as little Muslim accord about the precise nature of desired safeguards as there had been in the late 1920s. Muslim interests and fears varied from province to province according to their local situation. But from mid-1929 the only Muslims to stand firm by the Congress were the 'Muslim Nationalists' who formed themselves into the All-India Nationalist Muslim Party in July that year.[15] Its leaders, including A. K. Azad, R. A. Kidwai, Syed Mahmud, C. Khaliquzamman and M. A. Ansari, were to become increasingly important to Congress in its claim to speak for the whole Indian nation, and to Gandhi personally in his dishearteningly tortuous search for grounds for the communal harmony he saw as essential to *swaraj*, now that the Khilafat cause was dead.

Even within Congress there were divisions and threats of open discord late in 1928. A powerful faction favouring complete independence rather than dominionhood as envisaged in the Nehru Report, had built up round the southern Indian, Srinivasa Iyengar, and two radical younger men, Jawaharlal Nehru and Subhas Chandra Bose from Bengal, who had the backing of vocal student opinion and ex-terrorist or terrorist sympathizers. Motilal Nehru, as President of the Calcutta session of Congress at the end of 1928, hoped to avoid an overt split and to salvage his report. To this end he urged Gandhi to return to active Congress politics to help contrive a formula of reconciliation. This the Mahatma agreed to do, considering national unity vital to the achievement of *swaraj*, and its consolidation his 'sacred duty'. Ultimately Congress accepted the Nehru Report on the understanding that if the British had not accepted it by the end of 1929 then Congress would revert to non-co-operation, with the objective of complete independence. Gandhi's skills as mediator were called on later in the year as it became clear that within Congress ranks there were those who were most reluctant to cut themselves off from the official, institutional sources of power. In 1929 the issue of non-co-operation was limited to whether Congressmen should participate in the legislatures whose life was extended by the Viceroy in an attempt to curtail opportunities for anti-British propaganda during election campaigns. Motilal as President called on Congress legislators to abstain from work in them during their extended life, but so great was the outcry by local men who wanted to influence important provincial legislation and keep faith with their electors, that it fell to Gandhi to propose that Congress should maintain its unity by avoiding a decision until the end of 1929. This augured ill for Congress's capacity to challenge the *raj* and its institutions as legitimate sources of political authority. Congress by its Calcutta decision also began to reopen the gap between it and Liberal politicians which had seemed to close in their joint opposition to the Simon Commission and in their preparation of the Nehru Report.

The role and weakness of Congress as a potential counter-focus for Indian political allegiance is explicable if one turns from its public claims and decisions at the Christmas gathering to its actual nature in the localities throughout the year. One politician noted in his diary in May 1929 that to all 'practically minded people' Congress appeared 'a sham show of tall talk'. Gandhi castigated Congress for its squabbles, lethargy, and disorganization in private correspondence and in *Young India*. Harsh proof of the depths to which it had sunk came to light when he and Jawaharlal began to arrange for inspection and audit of Provincial Congress Committees (PCCs) early in the year.[16] It might be India's major political organization, with sufficient prestige and a venerable tradition as a mouthpiece of national aspirations to make it a valuable political resource. But it was still far more a fluctuating, loosely-structured association of locally-based allies than a political party with a recognized ideology, regular organization, funds, and recruitment mechanisms. Its central finances were in a perilous condition, even the richest provinces producing paltry contributions to central funds, and its provincial and local organization was either non-existent or paralyzed. In CP, one of the worst areas, the PCC of the Hindi-speaking part had no office or fixed headquarters, while the Marathi-speaking section had been so rent by faction that it had to organize from scratch. The auditors were unable to fathom what was going on at town and district level in some places; failing, for example, even to gain access to the books of the Jubbulpore and Nagpur town committees! Figures for membership were unreliable where there were no proper channels of communication and much 'informal belonging' Membership had definitely slumped in the late 1920s. It varied across the country and even within provinces. In May 1929 Jawaharlal reported to the AICC that total membership was around 56,000. After an intensive recruiting drive in mid-year membership was thought to be near 500,000.

With his known passion for efficient organization and sound finance, Gandhi threw himself into the revival of a Congress which could back up its claims with action. He reiterated his long-standing belief that Indians had to discipline themselves and work together to create a new political order. Grandiose claims at Congress sessions or in plans like the Nehru Report could earn nothing but ridicule unless buttressed with a real sanction and shown to be valid national aspirations. His commitment to construction of a new society and polity from the very roots had led Gandhi out of Congress activity in the 1920s into constructive work in villages, his *ashram* and *khadi* organizations. To him this was a vital part of political work: his sense of a peculiar vocation to lead India to *swaraj* was still firm despite the failure of the 1920–2 satyagraha to achieve that end, and the critical and uncomprehending response of so many Congressmen to him.[17] Gandhi's surprising re-entry into active Congress work and his reassertion of a central position of authority within it from late 1928 were partly the result of political appeals from Congressmen. They needed him to effect unity among them, and to provide both a figurehead and a strategy to enable them to deal with their domestic divisions and with a new relationship to the British, after the Simon Commission.

Pressure from such as Motilal would not alone have persuaded Gandhi to reimmerse himself in styles of politics he considered secondary to the main work of national regeneration. But he became convinced that the time was now ripe for him. At the Calcutta Congress he had stated that he would return to his *ashram* if Congressmen did not subject themselves to his discipline, and they had responded with dramatic displays of welcome and a commitment to constructive work of the sort Gandhi most valued—the removal of Untouchability, *khadi*, temperance, village reconstruction, and the lifting of women's disabilities. Another reason for his re-evaluation of his public role was his experience earlier in 1928 of a local satyagraha, organized by Vallabhbhai Patel under his guidance in the Bardoli district of Gujarat. The campaign of Patidar farmers against higher revenue assessment is significant in the analysis of many trends in Indian politics in the

1920s and 1930s. It was, for example, an indication of the weakening of British prestige in the countryside, and underlined the issue of land revenue as central in the legitimacy of government, on which battle would be joined between Congress and the British. Bardoli also demonstrated how in some areas the political interests of prospering groups of peasant farmers had become increasingly articulated through Congress and its village-level organizations. Yet it is also important in our context because of its effect on the Mahatma. It seems to have dissolved many of his doubts, born of the débâcle and violence of the early 1920s, about the viability of satyagraha in India when most of its exponents were unlikely to be true converts to satyagraha as a creed. It revived his faith in the power of non-violence and in the potential for a mass struggle if people could be educated to lose their fear of government. It also gave him the 'sanction' he felt to be so essential to Congress claims. Yet in retrospect the Bardoli campaign shows the limited types of circumstances in which satyagraha could 'succeed' in the sense of achieving specific goals, rather than in the Gandhian sense of morally refining those involved. The Patidar farmers were a compact group with good internal communications, and amenable to discipline by themselves and their leaders. They were campaigning on one restricted issue to which there could be a simple 'solution'. Furthermore, their opponent, the Bombay administration, was vulnerable to their pressure; not in the simple sense of being irrevocably weakened by satyagraha but because their support among Bombay politicians embarrassed the government when it needed those politicians' co-operation in the Simon Commission's inquiries. An impending change of Governor made a local settlement more pressing, to allow the new man to start his term of office in a peaceful situation. Bombay was also under pressure from the Government of India, which judged that Bombay had mismanaged the whole settlement problem. The issue at stake, the discipline and unity of the satyagrahis, the vulnerability of the opponent, were crucial variables affecting the outcome of satyagraha in any conflict. Despite Gandhi's hopes and the widespread publicity Bardoli gave to satyagraha as a successful way of extracting concessions from the *raj*, it was not clear that similar conditions could be repeated on an all-India scale.[18]

Faced with Congress demands, backed by the threat of civil disobedience after the 'deadline' of late 1929, and evidence of the growing morale of and support for Congress in the country, the British took steps to reassert their authority and to attract articulate political support. Both were aspects of the *raj*'s battle for legitimacy. It drew up plans for the firm use of existing law against potential civil disobedience, and sent round to local governments history notes on previous cases of no-tax, boycott, and volunteer movements. The Secretary of State in London was clear how vital such plans were, not least for their effects on the *raj*'s credibility. 'I attach great importance to this, because it is the claim of Swarajists that they can reduce us to submission by making government impossible. It will be our business to show conclusively that they cannot.'[19] But simultaneously Irwin, that most sensitive of Tory Viceroys, listened to the messages coming out of political India, from Congressmen, Liberals, and some of his own officials, who urged on him the importance of conciliating Congress and finding some escape from the collision course on which Congress and the *raj* seemed to be set.

In July Irwin returned to England for mid-term leave. He brought with him the twin ideas of a conference to discuss the impending reforms, to which representatives of Parliament, the princes, and British India would be invited, and of a gesture: a British declaration that their *raj*'s goal was Dominion status for India. He found allies in the Labour government which had come to power since his own Viceregal appointment. His plan for conciliation matured into the famous Irwin Declaration of 31 October 1929. It stated that the British Government held that Montagu's 1917 Declaration implied 'that the natural issue of India's constitutional progress, as there contemplated, is the attainment of Dominion status.' It also declared the plan for a Round Table Conference to discuss reforms, including the relationship between British and princely India; in the hope that 'by this means it may subsequently prove possible on these grave issues to submit proposals to Parliament which may command a wide measure of general assent.'[20]

Irwin's declaration was lucky to survive the cross-currents of British party politics, and the deep hostility to the gesture which emerged in Tory and Liberal ranks from internal party manoeuvres as well as conservative commitment to continuing British rule in India. Although Irwin and the Labour government insisted that the declaration marked no major change of policy, and that Dominion status was the goal envisaged in 1917 and in Irwin's own instructions on his appointment by the King, it was a momentous declaration because it occurred *after* Balfour had defined Dominionhood in 1926 as a status of complete autonomy in internal and external affairs, rather than signifying a continuing measure of subordination to the British Parliament. This distinguished the Irwin declaration from former occasions when dominionhood had been envisaged as India's goal: India was to be the first non-white dependency to be set on a path to complete independence within the Empire-Commonwealth. Of course there was no word of the timetable intended in Irwin's declaration; he did not anticipate rapid Indian attainment of Dominion status. Some later commentators have, therefore, suggested that he was deliberately deluding Indians with a meaningless gesture. But many Indians realized that a time-lag was inevitable and this did not detract from their wish for such a declaration. Having listened to Indians' pleas for this kind of gesture, Irwin made it in good faith, hoping that a clarification of the British goal would stabilize British authority, while recognizing the need for changing forms of government and linkage with Britain. He hoped also to elicit a wide span of Indian co-operation in discussion of those forms.

It was not clear for two months whether he would succeed in attracting Indian support and avoiding confrontation with Congress. The Liberal, Sapru, was overjoyed at the news, as was the 'Nationalist Muslim', Ansari. They among other politicians believed that Gandhi was cautiously favourable and would help ensure that Congress would take it as an adequate response to the challenge made at its Calcutta session. However, Gandhi was in an even more difficult position than Irwin. For the Viceroy the logic of peaceful discussion was clear, provided this could be obtained without conceding the foundations of the British position or its commitment to the welfare of all groups on the subcontinent. For Gandhi there were pressing arguments for co-operation *and* for conflict. He knew that Congressmen were grievously divided over civil disobedience, that Congress was hardly fit to launch a mass movement of any strength. He knew also that civil disobedience would further exacerbate communal tensions and would alienate 'Nationalist Muslims', moderate Congressmen, the Hindu Mahasabha, and Hindus in local minorities such as Punjab, and— critically—Liberals like Sapru whose alignment with Congress though not within it was so important for Congress's standing in British eyes and leverage over the *raj*. Yet there was evidence of a build-up of resentment and unrest among many younger Congressmen and their adherents in the districts, youth and trade union movements, and an increasing danger of political violence. (The Viceregal train was bombed, for example, in December.) Controlled conflict with the *raj* might reintegrate the more militant into Congress politics and defuse violence by providing a non-violent mode of direct action.

Gandhi was, as always, willing to talk—with Congressmen, with the Liberals and with Irwin; he manoeuvred for an interpretation of Irwin's declaration to enable him to conciliate those who were for conflict with the *raj*, and to assure himself of Cabinet backing in London to buttress Congress claims at any conference. (He asked, for example, that the Round Table Conference would actually frame a Dominion constitution for India, that Congress should have the largest representation of the political groups at it, and that meantime there should be an amnesty for political prisoners.) But, having failed to extract any helpful gloss on the declaration, Gandhi eventually came down on the side of Jawaharlal Nehru and those who favoured rejecting Irwin's gesture. He seems by this stage to have concluded that co-operation would only weaken Congress further by exposing its own divisions, and would send its representatives to London with a poor negotiating hand, their position compounded by evidence of hostility from the religious minorities, and by the weakness of the Labour government as its British political ally. In the deeply divided Congress session at Lahore a policy decision could no longer be shelved. Gandhi made his position plain by moving the main resolution that the Congress goal of *swaraj* must now be understood as complete independence, and that the means to it were civil disobedience rather than co-operation in the Round Table Conference.[21] He steered his policy through a timid Subjects Committee but had to give way on certain elements such as the boycott of schools and courts, and non-co-operation in municipal government, which threatened the interests of many Congressmen. It passed almost unanimously through a more militant open session, and he also secured a Working Committee of his own choice for the forthcoming months when civil disobedience would be on the anvil. As at Calcutta, he had engineered at least a semblance of Congress unity—but at a price. Not only communal minorities, but many Hindus within and on the periphery of Congress, were alienated by the decision. The issue of legitimacy remained unresolved. Neither Gandhi nor Irwin were secure in the authority they claimed, whether for the *raj* or for Congress as national spokesman. Furthermore, neither was assured of widespread support for the strategy of resolution which he planned.

Irwin's strategy was to establish a form of government for India on a consensus generated by rational discussion of constitutional possibilities. It was a brave initiative, given the blatancy of Indian divisions and of the hostility among many British politicians to any radical change in India. It is the more striking considering that it was the first in a long series of conferences which stretched over the next four decades of British disengagement from formal empire. By the 1960s they were almost routine, but in 1930 it was a novel mechanism for considering devolution of power, and a sign of the distance British imperial thinking had moved since 1917.

It was hoped that the solemnity of the London gathering and the insulation of the Indian visitors from some of the pressures of Indian politics would help achieve a consensus over India's future despite Congress refusal to join in consultation. The Conference members accordingly assembled in London late in October 1930. From Britain came a Government delegation of eight which included the Prime Minister; a Conservative group which was fairly flexible in its views on India, whose most active member was Samuel Hoare, and a Liberal group led by Reading. The fifty-eight British Indian delegates were the Viceroy's nominees: men of such eminence that their views carried weight even though they had no formal mandate from the groups they were assumed to represent. They included Liberals such as Sapru, Hindu Communalists and Responsivists, Sikhs, Untouchables, the Madras Justice Party, a Muslim delegation under the Aga Khan, Eurasians, Indian Christians and Europeans. The princes sent sixteen representatives, eight of them nominated by the Standing Committee of the Chamber of

Princes. The princes' unexpected contribution to the conference swung the whole temper and direction of the discussions, liberating it from sterile re-statements of existing positions and claims. It could so easily have been an occasion for just such stonewalling, as many of the participants arrived with prepared positions to defend. The princes' strategy also enabled the minor-ity Labour government to achieve a new policy direction towards India, because it freed MacDonald from the threat of Tory and Liberal opposition in Parliament.

The princes had been jolted into serious conideration of their future in the subcontinent, as individual rulers and as an Order, by two develop-ments—the British pronouncements on Paramountcy in the Butler Com-mission, and the claim for independence voiced in British India, particularly when British Indian politicians were suggesting, as in the Nehru Report, that a free India should inherit the British role in relation to the princely states. For many of the princes some type of federation with British India seemed a sound defence against both threats; particularly a federation in whose creation they had a major voice, and so could contrive safeguards for their autonomy and power over their subjects. They were not united in what they hoped to achieve through a federation. The southern, landlocked, states wished to protect themselves against a strengthened British India, particularly the Nizam of Hyderabad who saw the political, economic, and strategic dangers of encirclement by powerful Hindu provinces. For the western and central states the strategic threat was less real, and federation was appealing more because it seemed to offer a buttress against the opera-tion of British Paramountcy. However, they joined in late 1930 in support of the general idea, and this in turn powerfully influenced the other delegates to the Conference. It got the British off the hook of having to confront an Indian demand for Dominion status; and freed the government's hand by persuading even the Conservative Party in the Commons that with the guarantee of a conservative princely bloc at the centre in any federal India it would be safe to advance beyond Simon's recommendations and to devolve a measure of responsibility to Indians in the central government. The Muslims had long been aware of the advantages to them of the right kind of federation; and they fell in with the idea in London. Finally Sapru began to favour it, because of the promise it offered of Muslim and princely backing for a rapid devolution of some central responsibility to Indians. His hard labour in London largely helped to swing Hindu opinion behind the demand, despite initial hostility to any reversal of the principle of devolu-tion of power to a democratically elected British Indian central govern-ment. Consequently the outcome of the London gathering was more radical than could have been anticipated. On 19 January 1931 Ramsay MacDonald closed the session with the declaration that the British government ac-cepted the principle of the responsibility of the Executive to the Legislature provided that the new All-India Legislature was constituted on a federal basis.

The details of the federation would have to be worked out in future sessions: but it looked as if a very significant breakthrough had occurred. Yet there were ominous undercurrents even then. In the first place, British Indian delegates were still deadlocked on the question of safeguards for communal minorities, despite the peace-making attempts of Jinnah and Sapru. Muslim delegates, pressurized by telegrams from Muslims in India, hardened on the necessity for separate electorates, and at the end of the conference it looked as if communal discord would wreck the whole enterprise. Although a breakdown was avoided then, and the Prime Minister suggested a government 'award' of communal safeguards if Indians persisted in failing to find a solution themselves, it was patent that the Muslims might in future be able to frustrate the federal plan. Furthermore, by the close of the session initial princely enthusiasm for federation was cooling and differences among the princes were more apparent. It was likely that from this quarter, too, there might come a virtual veto on federation if the princes were not convinced that its advantages would greatly outweigh the disadvantages of isolation in a changing situation.[22] Irwin's strategy had developed in ways he had not intended: its potential was now greater, as were the dangers of its failure. So his thinking reverted to Gandhi and Congress, and their inclusion in the establishment of a new consensus, after their year in the role of 'rebels'.

Although the Karachi decision for civil disobedience apparently took Congress into the wilderness, remote from constitutional negotiations, the satyagraha campaign was no barren exercise. It increased the political significance and prestige of Congress as an all-India organization, enabled it to re-forge links with a wide span of Indians operating at different political levels, and increased the leverage of its central leaders, particularly Gandhi, over their countrymen and the British. At the outset few Congressmen had any clear idea of what they hoped to achieve by reverting to non-co-operation. Motilal Nehru assumed that they were working for the collapse of the administration:[23] but for most the new campaign was a method of protest which local men could use as it suited them, without submitting to rigorous discipline, self-sacrifice or irrevocable sundering of links with existing sources of patronage and political power. (Not all Congressmen resigned from the legislatures at the beginning of 1930, for example; and many who did so were very reluctant. Nor did civil disobedience include boycott of schools and courts, or withdrawal from local boards, though Gandhi regretted that Congressmen seemed disposed to spend so much of their energy on getting elected to them.)

Gandhi, however, was clear about the goal of renewed satyagraha. In the long term he hoped to create a new, organic, Indian unity, to build *swaraj*, and to shatter the fear and dependence in his countrymen which were the psychological roots of the *raj*. More immediately he hoped to bring Congress to such a strength and representativeness that it could attend a constitutional conference as the one legitimate national spokesman with no need of the assurance of British support for its demands for which he had bargained late in 1929. Satyagraha had therefore to be designed primarily to strengthen and unite Indians; to influence *them* rather than in a direct way to weaken the administration. A decision for confrontation had seemed the best way to establish a broad Indian unity at the close of 1929. But the precise mode of confrontation posed immense problems for the Mahatma. Somehow a campaign must overcome, or at least not exacerbate, the divisions among Congressmen on tactics and in their local and economic positions. It must defuse violence, while recognizing that most of its exponents would adopt it as a tactic rather than out of commitment to non-violence and the Gandhian vision of the meaning of man. It had to be flexible, given Congressmen's regional needs and priorities, and able to run with little central organization or funding. Moreover it must conciliate communal minorities, and attract the sympathy of onlookers, particularly the Liberals and other Hindus who were in a strategic position between Congress and the *raj*, whose reactions the British noted closely, in their search for allies. Gandhi retired to his *ashram* to meditate on a plan, and on his own moral responsibilities in the event of violence.

Congress had delegated a decision on the ways and means of confrontation to the Working Committee: and in mid-February the Committee met at the Sabarmati *ashram* and decided that Gandhi and his associates who were committed to non-violence should initiate the programme. Gandhi's solution to the problem of confrontation was the surprising decision to attack the government's tax on salt. This could never undermine the *raj* financially as salt produced only about 4 per cent of its revenue. But it was an emotive issue on which a wide spectrum of Indians could combine, and which would lead them away from constitutional bargaining to think in moral terms of their conflict with authority, and to understand *swaraj* as a new quality of life which included their poorest neighbours on whom the tax fell most heavily.[24] In particular Gandhi hoped it might be a basis for communal unity. Limiting both the issue and the participants in the initial stages would also lessen the danger of violence erupting as it had done in 1919 and 1922, wrecking his earlier all-India satyagrahas.

The Salt Satyagraha started with a dramatic long march by Gandhi and a group of picked companions from Sabarmati to the coast at Dandi, 240 miles away, where he proceeded to make salt illegally by boiling sea water. The march was a publicity enterprise of great power as the press followed the party's progress through Gujarat, and as the Mahatma exhorted the crowds who flocked to hear him and the villagers at his daily resting-places, expounding his political vision and urging them to reform their lives into the pattern of true *swaraj*. He became a messianic figure, striding out staff in hand, to lead the confrontation with the British, compelling respect for his fearlessness. A religious aura developed round the march, he and his followers kept alluding to the Christian scriptures, and the sale of Bibles among Ahmedabad Hindus shot up. As he journeyed, a Christ-like figure deliberately challenging established authority, village headmen began to resign in large numbers from their posts of collaboration with the *raj*; and in April Irwin reported to London that in Gujarat 'the personal influence of Gandhi threatens to create a position of real embarrassment to the administration . . . as in some areas he has already achieved a considerable measure of success in undermining the authority of Government.'[25] All over India the Mahatma's march attracted attention and comment: and when the government eventually arrested and interned him in early May every province reported demonstrations in protest. Particularly worrying for the government was the range of 'moderate' men who seemed to be sympathizing with Gandhi. Ten Bombay Legislative Councillors, for example, resigned after the arrest. However, Muslims took little notice: salt had not provided the basis for a communal entente, as Gandhi had hoped. Satyagraha had a marked effect on salt sales and revenue only in Bombay. Elsewhere it was little more than a token gesture. Yet it was a powerful symbolic opening to the new phase of confrontation, encouraging contempt for laws publicly declared to be oppressive by leaders claiming to represent the nation, and proving that unarmed citizens could confront the might of the *raj*. For a government particularly dependent on the maintenance of its prestige, and on the acquiescence and collaboration of its subjects, whose networks of communication were often unreliable, it was a disquieting demonstration of the possibilities of widespread disaffection, and of the Mahatma's public appeal, without benefit of any mass media except the press.

The second phase of confrontation began after Gandhi's internment. Unlike 1920–2 it was not masterminded by the central Congress leadership according to a national plan. PCCs were left to organize it in accordance with Working Committee directions. As the committee's communications with PCCs tended to be suggestions rather than directives, they permitted much flexibility in priorities and timing. The campaign stressed first salt, then boycott of foreign cloth, then non-payment of certain taxes, contravention of forest laws, and disobedience to the Ordinances with which government attempted to control the movement. In allowing provincial politicians so much discretion, it deferred to the divisions among Congressmen on civil disobedience and to the diffuse nature of the alliance under the Congress flag: it also recognized the infinite variety of local issues which could be welded into the campaign, and the different points of vulnerability of local administrations. When officials discussed the best way to combat civil disobedience one experienced Governor rejected the military argument of a crushing blow at the vital centre; for the Working Committee was not 'the real motive and directive force behind the movement. It issues resolutions, but does very little actually in the way of organization or direction.'[26] Government's policy further hampered central control by the Working Committee; as the series of Ordinances was promulgated to knock out the leadership, cripple the organization, and stifle publicity. Correspondence of Working Committee members and PCC Presidents was also censored.

In 1930 civil disobedience developed into a formidable psychological challenge to government, and in places became an actual physical threat to administration. By mid-year all provinces had been affected, Bombay city and Gujarat being the storm centres. In the second half of the year regional variations sharpened; but the government felt the situation was easing, except in Gujarat, and in UP and CP where the movement became rural for the first time. By early 1931 the government had won the battle for control. But it had been an immense strain on the civil service, the police, and the jails. The official estimate was that about 60,000 went through prison in the course of the movement. In mid-November just over 29,000 were actually in jail—most of them were adult, Hindu men, though 2,050 were under 17.[27]

The main all-India manifestations of civil disobedience were the sharp drop in the poll in the September elections to the Assembly and the Provincial Legislatures, most marked in the Hindu urban seats; and the boycott of foreign goods, particularly cloth. Compared with the haphazard campaign a decade earlier, Congress had now refined its methods of enforcing boycott through picketing by numerous groups of 'volunteers', *hartals*, and other forms of social and economic pressure. The economic crisis favoured the campaign. Many businessmen were glad for part of 1930 of an excuse to put off settling their trade accounts in a time of falling prices, though by the end of the year Congress leaders were told firmly that their business supporters were wanting to revert to normal trade. The real strength of civil disobedience, however, was shown in areas where local political campaigns dovetailed with all-India protest, and local men found the 'national' campaign a vehicle for specific and often longstanding issues. Bombay Presidency was the heartland of disaffection and disruption. The Governor wrote of 'more or less overt rebellion' and 'practically a mass movement'.[28] Disloyalty had a band-waggon effect, and any who would have preferred to retain their allegiance to the *raj* either kept silent or were forced to go with the majority. In parts of Gujarat government almost collapsed, while Congress won prestige and the allegiance of the Patidar farmers who had worked with it and Gandhi in their local interests for over a decade. As prices slumped they became willing to embark on a campaign of non-payment of land revenue, and to force the resignation of government officials in their villages by social boycott. Areas of Bombay city also became 'no-go areas' for the police. Pickets, processions, meetings, and the continuing circulation of the illegal Congress bulletin under the nose of the helpless police were all publicly staged demonstrations of Congress power. Those most deeply implicated were locally resident Gujaratis, businessmen, traders and clerks, who were in different ways hard hit by the depression in trade and resulting unemployment. Outside Bombay Presidency the government was not often seriously challenged, an exception being the Bengal district of Midnapore, long notorious for its turbulence, where salt satyagraha was followed by boycott of government servants, attacks on police and magistrates, intimidation of *chaukidars* (watchmen), and refusal to pay the *chaukidari* tax. Midnapore men were not suddenly converted to non-violence or to devotion to Gandhi: then, as in 1920–2, they found a 'national' flag convenient cover for longstanding local hostilities. Elsewhere the tie-up between local concerns and national protest was far looser and temporary. Assam, Punjab, and the South were in general little troubled. Bihar was fairly free of disturbances, unlike its experience in 1920–2, though the attack on the excise proved highly popular, and catastrophic for government revenues. UP and CP were comparatively quiet early in 1930, but then became disturbingly deep centres of rural disaffection. In UP falling prices and landlord pressure made peasant groups responsive to an anti-land tax campaign, and in CP local politicians decided to back disobedience to forest regulations, which threatened nobody's political or social interests but could rally popular support and 'prove' that they were good nationalists rather than power seekers!

Civil disobedience was often little more than a loose alignment of local conflicts. Yet in 1930 it became clearly a national movement in span, if not in drive and intention. The flexible framework of broad conflict with authority was able to find a place for many different levels and styles of political awareness and action. It could mobilize many different groups. The range of people involved suggests how significant a factor civil disobedience was in the development of political awareness and articulation. The hard core of participants in processions, meetings, and overt law-breaking were Hindu townsmen, joined by a considerable number of students, though boycott of government schools and colleges was significantly not part of the programme. Most were literate, many of them in English, and were loosely referred to by contemporaries as 'middle class'. They were the sort of people who for several decades had been in touch with or active in the politics of Congress and a range of voluntary associations, and of government's formal institutions of consultation. Many were prosperous, respected citizens, who could not be dismissed as unemployed agitators. As satyagraha provided a novel mode for integrating diverse and local interests into 'national' politics, a sizeable bloc of participants also came from the more prosperous peasant castes, as in Gujarat and parts of Tamil Nad.

Another development which perturbed moderate politicians and exerted pressure on government was the moral and financial support given to Congress by a range of businessmen. In nearly every Province they poured money into Congress coffers early in the campaign, and participated or at least acquiesced in the boycott of foreign cloth: they acted under economic and social pressure but also from the hope of forcing the *raj* to concede financial control of Indian affairs to Indians. Women were a further new and unexpected source of support. Before 1930 they had barely had a political voice or role, but now they joined actively, taking their place in local Congress organizations as men were arrested, and forming picket lines with Gandhi's particular encouragement, because he felt that non-violent 'persuasion' was peculiarly suited to the female temperament and talents. In November 1930 nearly 360 women were in jail for their part in the campaign.

For all these people satyagraha was an educative and uniting experience, giving them a wider sense of national identity and a new relationship with what had once been assumed to be the legitimate authority of the *raj*. Even though many of them reverted to inactivity or more local politics once satyagraha was over, they were a reservoir for future campaigns and a potential vote-bank for Congress when the franchise was extended. Thus new and stronger linkages were being forged between national and local levels of politics. The great failure of satyagraha, on the other hand, was in relation to Indian Muslims. Driven by the Khilafat issue, they had been a formidable cutting edge of non-co-operation, but now they held aloof from civil disobedience in virtually every part of India. In November 1930 out of the total of 29,000 in prison, only 1,500 were Muslims. Only on the North-West Frontier was civil disobedience in any sense a Muslim campaign, because there it channelled a Pathan movement led by Abdul Ghaffar Khan who was known as the 'Frontier Gandhi'. Despite his devotion to Gandhi and non-violence, though, the Pathan movement pre-dated civil disobedience, and had its own momentum and timing. In other areas where Muslims were majorities or sizeable minorities their refusal to support satyagraha severely weakened it. Even in beleaguered Bombay Presidency, Sind—the Muslim area—was little disturbed, for here the locally influential Pirs threw their weight against it.

Given the large element of local and temporary support civil disobedience attracted, it is hardly surprising that the campaign did not transform Congress into a national party or overcome the disunities and weaknesses against which Gandhi had fought since the end of 1928. Its organization at local level remained sketchy, often *ad hoc*, and frequently immobilized by government harassment. Its finances, though more buoyant than in the late 1920s, were inadequate for a genuinely national campaign, and funds came in erratically and unpredictably from subscriptions, delegates' fees, provincial contributions and hefty individual donations.[29] Most of Congress's money was gathered locally from businessmen, house-to-house, street, and cafe collections, and in some places, Calcutta being a notorious example, from municipal corporations and local boards which levied tolls from traders and contractors. Similarly, it was used locally, with little central control, and the inevitable corollary was the rapid disintegration of local campaigns when provincial funds dried up. By September 1930 many provinces were beginning to run out of money. Those in jail could no longer be given such amenities as oil or soap and volunteers could not be fed or ferried about. The AICC could not make up the short-fall. Yet although the central Congress leadership was not paymaster it was strengthened by civil disobedience. It became less easy for reluctant non-co-operators, as in Bengal, to defy the Working Committee. Congress as a national body became even more important as a political resource which politicians ignored at the peril of their careers. Although it was still essential to have a firm local base, fewer aspirant leaders could 'go it alone' in the 1930s, ignoring all-India resources and appeals. Its enhanced prestige and psychological status gave Congress leverage not only among Indians but over the British as they searched for a wider and more solid span of collaborators in the imperial enterprise. In 1930 the government became increasingly perturbed over Congress's growth in standing in the eyes of ordinary people. As Sapru told Irwin in September:

I have been compelled by personal experience to revise some of my opinions. The Congress has undoubtedly acquired a great hold on popular imaginations. On roadside stations where until a few months ago I could hardly have suspected that people had any politics, I have seen with my own eyes demonstrations and heard with my own ears the usual Congress slogans. The popular feeling is one of intense excitement. It is fed from day to day by continuous and persistent propaganda on the part of the Congressmen—by lectures delivered by their volunteers in running trains and similar other activities. Very few people understand what they say or what they do, but there is no doubt whatever in my mind that there is the most intense distrust of the Government and its professions.[30]

The battle was joined on the issue of legitimacy. In some places Congress seemed to have usurped the role of government, most obviously in Bombay city where Congress demonstrations were regular theatrical assertions of a counter-authority, and in parts of Gujarat. But even in one Bihar district for a short while Indian officials took orders from local Congressmen. Government authority was similarly undermined in the places where its own institutions designed to attract Indian collaboration were used by Congressmen to organize and finance civil disobedience. This was true of some Gujarati municipalities and local boards. Even in the less turbulent south (in Guntur town, for example), the whole machinery of municipal government was put at the service of civil disobedience—not only in fund-raising, but in providing places for Congress meetings, servants to make arrangements, and even municipal lorries to carry volunteers to make illegal salt on the coast.[31] It was understandable why Governors like Sykes from Bombay urged on Delhi the need to ease the physical and psychological strain on those who did remain dependable in the administration, and to prove to them that government would not sacrifice them for political ends.

Equally disturbing to government was the evidence in 1930 that civil disobedience and Gandhi's repute were pushing many Hindu politicians outside Congress to join the campaign or at least to proclaim their sympathy for it and their disquiet at government's suppressive tactics. Genuine feeling was mixed up with the desire to protect their own political credibility among Responsivists and RSS members in Bombay and CP, for example, who joined in. B. S. Moonje and M. S. Aney both spent time in jail, despite their hostility to Congress policy. (The Governor thought this was an electioneering stunt; even if it was it indicated what they thought would appeal to voters!) Liberals, too, felt increasing pressure to sympathize publicly with Congress and Gandhi, as the campaign gathered wide support and they feared government repression would increase that support. Partly to ease Liberal embarrassment and to rally them round government strategy, Irwin was prepared to countenance an attempt by Sapru and Jayakar at mediation between the Congress leaders and the *raj* in mid-1930. It proved abortive because Gandhi was still sensitive to the need to retain the alliance of the younger Nehru: but at least it secured the *raj* against the non-Congressmen's charge of implacable repression.

Congress's changed position in public life was ironically made clearest not in its achievements when civil disobedience was at its peak in mid-1930 but when it ended early in 1931 in a 'truce' which many Congressmen considered a sell-out. By that date Irwin wanted to seize the opportunity of political reform within a federal framework and to involve Congress in the planning lest its hostility should wreck at the outset such an unexpected chance of re-establishing the imperial interest on a new foundation, the like of which might not recur at least for some years. Yet he knew he must not appear to bargain with Congress, because he needed to stiffen the morale of the services and those who had not joined in confrontation. Gandhi for his part knew that the campaign was winding down, that its business backers were anxious to revert to normal trade and relations with government, and that many moderate Congressmen and Nationalist Muslims were anxious for a face-saving end to conflict. Yet he, like Irwin, could not appear too conciliatory: in his case because of the persistent militancy of the section of opinion which Jawaharlal voiced and the particular problems of the Gujarati farmers whose lands had been forfeited for non-payment of revenue. Irwin prepared the way for Congress to reconsider its position by releasing all Working Committee members from jail. At liberty they were at once approached by the returning conference delegates who wanted to protect their work from wreckage on the rocks of Congress non-co-operation. In February Sastri, Jayakar, and Sapru engineered a series of meetings between Gandhi and Irwin, banking on the hope that these two earnest and overtly religious men might so trust each other personally that they could contrive a public agreement. Their hopes were fulfilled in the Gandhi–Irwin Pact of March.

As a result of the Pact Congress agreed to participate in discussion of the constitutional plan conceived in London, whose essentials were Federation, Indian responsibility, but safeguards on matters such as defence and credit for a transitional period. There was little difficulty over agreement on this between the two, even though the new plan did not concede complete independence which Congress had demanded. Gandhi argued in justification of his agreement that the plan might prove a framework for attaining this goal: but Congressmen could now make their position clear at the conference table and could attend from a position of strength rather than weakness (as would have been the case in 1930) as a result of their satyagraha. The danger of a breakdown in the Gandhi–Irwin talks arose over practical matters such as police action during civil disobedience, the right to make salt and picket, and the fate of forfeited lands which had been re-sold. The bargaining on these seemingly secondary issues reflected the need of both men to convince their colleagues and followers that the conflict had not been in vain and that their particular interests were not being sacrificed for an all-India strategy. These sensitive issues also demonstrated the ambiguous interconnections between different levels of political life, particularly for the Congress as it strove to be an all-India movement, but in order to be so had to incorporate a variety of particular interests critical for those who were its main adherents in their own areas. Finally each gave up something, and a package was agreed whereby Congress would withdraw civil disobedience and Government would withdraw the Ordinances. Gandhi compromised by not pressing for an inquiry into police conduct or for the return of forfeited lands to their original owners where these had been sold to third parties. The *raj* agreed to permit peaceful picketing in pursuit of *swadeshi*, and to allow inhabitants of salt-producing areas to collect and make salt for domestic consumption.[32]

The fact that Gandhi and Irwin both had to defend their Pact to those of their colleagues who felt they had given too much away showed that neither had gained outstanding advantage or lost face irretrievably. Government had won peace for its constitutional discussions to go forward, and the prospect of Congress co-operation in finding a new solution to the problem of empire. Congress had gained enormously in prestige and respectability in the much-publicized and prolonged parleys between its main spokesman and the head of the *raj*. It could now justly claim that even government recognized that no major decisions about India's future could be made without Congress participation; it could now be seen as a significant political voice, if not the sole spokesman for the Indian nation.

Yet within twelve months Irwin's strategy of consultation and Gandhi's attempt to forge Indian unity through conflict had both failed. Early in 1932 the Viceroy's term of office was complete and he was replaced by Willingdon, who lacked the personality and temperament to engage in 'heart to heart' encounters with wily saints. Nor did he feel the need to collaborate with Gandhi as a notable who could secure the loyalty of his 'followers', because he was urged by his Home Department and Governors that the vital strategy now was to buttress the services and conciliate those elements of Indian opinion which were prepared to co-operate in forward planning and present administration rather than join in Congress's renewed civil disobedience in January 1932. The Mahatma was jailed on 4 January, dispensable to government rather than being the key to its strategy, having failed both in the months of 'truce' in India and as sole Congress spokesman at the second Round Table Conference in October–December 1931 to unite Indian opinion behind him and firmly establish Congress claims to be the legitimate voice of the nation.

The strategy of renewed conflict was forced on Gandhi when he returned from London, by the particular problems of certain areas—Bengal, UP and the North-West Frontier—where local Congressmen or their allies had become involved in confrontation with the British. But when Gandhi launched an all-India movement to help them he found it had none of the bonding or educative effects of the 1930 movement, which he had been able to start in his own time and way. It never really gathered momentum nor threatened the government, partly because the administration cracked down on it at the outset, and because it rarely fed on local situations in which regional leaders and groups found it a productive strategy. In Gujarat, for example, there was never such widespread rural disaffection as in 1930. Even in UP, where economic conditions had precipitated an explosion of anti-landlord and anti-government agitation late in 1931 and stiffened Jawaharlal's demand for renewed civil disobedience on Gandhi's return, a slight lift of prices and government inquiries into rural distress blunted peasant readiness for confrontation.[33]

Yet Irwin's original strategy of re-establishing a viable imperial connection through consultation was being strangled by increasing hostility within the Conservative party, now a partner in the National Government, and declining Indian enthusiasm. Sympathy for the *raj* among potential Indian collaborators in consultation ebbed as a result of government's repressive measures against Congress and its incarceration of the Mahatma. The outcome was not the great breakthrough which had seemed possible at the time of the Pact, but a battered and ill-liked package of partial reforms. The 1935 Government of India Act was born not of vision and enthusiasm but through tedium and attrition. The increasingly dispiriting processes of hammering out a reform package involved three sessions of the Round Table Conference (although the British tried hard to abandon the third in late 1932), perambulating committees in India investigating such technical problems as franchise and finance, a consultative committee of the Conference working in India, and a discussion by a Joint Committee of both Houses of Parliament in consultation with delegates from India on a White Paper. Finally the bill was debated in Parliament for over a month. It received the royal assent in August 1935.[34]

Its main provisions came into operation on 1 April 1937 and gave the provinces virtual autonomy from Delhi and London (increasing their financial resources to make that autonomy reality), abolishing dyarchy, and putting Indian ministers responsible to the electorate in charge of all branches of provincial government. Ministers' authority was subject to certain safeguards including reserve powers in the hands of provincial Governors, for use in such cases as the protection of minorities and rights of civil servants, or 'the prevention of any grave menace to the peace or tranquillity', of all or part of a province, or the breakdown of the constitution. The franchise, though still based on a property qualification, was greatly enlarged: more than thirty million Indians now had the vote, about one-sixth of the number who would have been enfranchised under universal suffrage. Other parts of the Act envisaged a federation of princely and British India with an elected Council of State and Federal Assembly which would have power over internal affairs, but not on such matters as the army, defence or external affairs (i.e., a form of dyarchy at the centre just when it was ended in the provinces). However before this part of the Act could operate a sufficient number of the States had to accede to the Federation to fill half the seats allotted to them in the Upper House, and to ensure that at least half the total population of all the States was within the Federation. This never happened, and the federal part of the Act remained a paper plan.[35]

Judged by the hopes of the Mahatma and former Viceroy, five weary years of constitutional wrangling and spasmodic conflict between Congress and the *raj* following the Gandhi–Irwin Pact had been a time of failure. Yet in retrospect this phase cannot but seem significant. Some crucial decisions were made and some not made, and it reveals much about the viability of British empire in the subcontinent and about the reality of Indian nationhood. Obviously, the British had been forced to acknowledge that they must be flexible and inventive if they were to retain a political connection with India which would safeguard their changing interests on the subcontinent in the context of international and domestic economic disturbance and reorientation. They had to take account of sharpening political awareness and demand among their Indian subjects just at the time when their primary local representatives, ICS men in the districts, were losing reserves of authority and influence as a result of the 1919 reforms. Few in British public life envisaged a rapid British departure from India, but many henceforth recognized that only a far looser imperial connection and lighter exercise of British power was possible. Any attempt to halt the devolution of power or to use 'suppressive' tactics other than in short bursts had been shown to be politically and economically counter-productive. British officials who had experienced the 1919 constitutional experiment, the Simon Commission débâcle and civil disobedience knew they had to conciliate a widening range of Indian political opinion and to harness it to the processes of government. Even Willingdon's administration, which refused to 'deal' or 'treat' with Gandhi in 1932–3, realized that Ordinance rule and smashing the Congress organization was only a temporary solution. At the turn of 1931–2 Willingdon had unsuccessfully tried to extract from London greater freedom in appointing his Executive Council, partly to enable him to admit more Indians as a counterpoise to the draconian policies adopted to crush civil disobedience. He argued that he could not use the big stick unless he could demonstrate real movement towards more Indian political responsibility. His Home Member similarly argued that though they had to crush civil disobedience it was equally vital to secure swift constitutional reform, because only this would bring contentment to political India.[36]

Given such messages from the men on the spot, only the die-hard wing of the Tory Party led by Churchill and Salisbury, backed by the Rothermere press, argued otherwise. For reasons of ideology and party strategy they belaboured the National Government's attempts to produce a reform package. Churchill in debate on the 1935 Act spoke of British government being the best India had ever had, of 'the undue exaltation of the principle of self-government', and made an emotive yet anachronistic pledge which echoed the Anglicists of 1835 rather than the realities of 1935.

We hope once and for all to kill the idea that the British in India are aliens moving, with many apologies, out of the country as soon as they have been able to set up any kind of governing organism to take their place. We shall try to inculcate this idea . . . that we are there for ever as honoured partners with our Indian fellow subjects whom we invite in all faithfulness to join with us in the highest functions of government for their lasting benefit and for our own.

Yet his opponents in British politics were not radical decolonizers. The great debate about Britain's tie with India was between conservatives, whatever their party label. The 1935 Act with its reliance on a princely bloc in an All-India Federation as a *quid pro quo* for central Indian responsibility was a truly conservative measure—in aim and timing. It was designed to salvage and buttress the empire, not to liquidate it: and it conceded only as much as seemed necessary to prevent destabilizing conflict or administrative paralysis.[37] The Act was a British recognition that continuing empire in India primarily posed a political problem to which political solutions must be found.

The mechanisms of the Act were also profoundly significant for India's future. They decreased London's power over Indian affairs and elevated the authority of the Viceroy as opposed to that of the Secretary of State— a trend which would have been even more marked had the federal provisions come into operation. Moreover through these reforms the British effectively fell back upon Delhi. Within the provinces initiative and influence went largely into Indian hands. This changed the context of Indian politics; increasing the stakes of provincial politics, laying down the access points and ground rules, and inviting Indians to adjust their political styles and their horizontal and vertical linkages with their compatriots to take advantage of the new opportunities. The 1935 Act completed the process begun in 1919, whereby the province became the most important arena or level in political life. It confirmed not only the autonomy of each province, but its unique identity and the power of strongly-based provincial leadership. Consequently it was to affect profoundly the nature of all-India, 'national' leadership and power in the subsequent decade, and after independence, when the provinces were transformed into the component states of the Indian Union.

One resounding success of those years of failed strategies and dashed hopes was the transplantation of modified forms of western political institutions into Indian society. Churchill and his cronies might decry the export of ideas and institutions of self-government, but Indian political opinion claimed representative institutions and an enlarged franchise as a natural right. Given the safeguard of communal representation for minorities, none challenged the legitimacy of western-style democratic institutions in India. They were accepted as appropriate mechanisms for the satisfaction of the needs and aspirations generated by an Asian society, alien in structure and ideology from the society which had produced them though it might be. Deepening Indian commitment to this particular imported political style and framework was partly ideological, the fruit of expanding western education and its implicit values. It was also a tactical response of men who recognized the advantage of using the language and categories of those from whom they wished to extract concessions.

Striking evidence of the magnetism of the new political institutions was the fleeting commitment of Congressmen to civil disobedience. Few saw it in terms of self-purification and striving after truth. For most it was a tactic for temporary use when apparently productive, to be dropped if it involved them in more suffering and frustration than benefit. Consequently as the *raj* cracked down on the renewed campaign, and as it became increasingly clear that greatly extended power would be open to those who positioned themselves to participate in provincial elections and legislative politics, a wide range of Congressmen found Gandhi's perspective and strategies deeply frustrating and politically destructive. From mid-1933 the endeavour to extricate Congress from the sterile politics of confrontation gathered momentum. In many provinces men founded parties for constitutional action: some used the Congress name, but others did not, opening their ranks to non-Congressmen. But there was deep unease and confusion as they realized the importance of a strong appeal and organization which only a revived Congress could guarantee, and the significance of Gandhi as a public figure whose reputation they could not lightly jettison. Senior Congressmen, including some Nationalist Muslims, began to urge Gandhi to free Congress from the civil disobedience programme, though there was no unanimity among them about the best policy to replace it. By March 1934 Gandhi had realized that open discussion was necessary to prevent Congress destroying itself in suppressed frustration and controversy. As he wrote to Dr Ansari, 'My emphatic opinion is that this paralysis of the intelligent[s]ia must be removed. However much therefore I may differ on the Council-Entry programme ... I should welcome a party of Congressmen prosecuting the programme rather than they should be sullen discontented and yet utterly inactive.'[38] Those in search of a new programme decided with Gandhi's blessing to revive the Swaraj Party and to prepare constructively for future constitutional politics, a programme which included contesting the Assembly elections to be held in 1934 under the old constitution in order to use that forum to publicize their views on the White Paper. Internal Congress conflicts threatened even this hesitant change of direction, the issue in contention being control of the new work. Eventually as a result of Gandhi's skill in arranging compromises the Swaraj Party idea was abandoned and Congress itself organized the election preparations through a Congress Parliamentary Board. (In practice most of the work was done by provincial boards.)

So Congressmen extricated themselves from fruitless conflict, without losing the resources of the Congress name and the Mahatma's presence and prestige. In so doing they confirmed the crucial place of the new political institutions in Indian political life, and their belief that the needs of Indian society could be pursued through them. This presaged the increasing integration of many of the different types and styles of politics which had coexisted on the subcontinent for decades, and the channelling of many interests and much political ambition into the new democratic politics. Though it must be remembered that until after independence the less educated and privileged in society were not enfranchised, and they were peripheral at best to the politics of most of those who worked the new provincial institutions, as many found to their cost when Congress took on the role of provincial government rather than being primarily a political movement anxious to cohere as broad a band of allies as possible under its banner. The depth of Indians' commitment to the new political institutions and the sheer length of their experience in managing their techniques was to be one of the firmest foundations of independent India's constitution and comparative stability after 1947—ironically since it is often stated that the hallmark of India's conflict with the *raj* was the reverse of this commitment, namely civil disobedience.

The contribution of the early 1930s to the sense and reality of Indian nationhood is more ambiguous. The disparate nature of civil disobedience suggests that the nationalist movement was built as much on particularist interests and provincial identities as on an upsurge of commitment to a single, free nation. Moreover, the diversity and ambiguity in Indian senses of public identity were shown by the abstention of most Muslims from the conflict. In the constitutional discussions, too, it became obvious that no one group or leader could legitimately claim to speak for an Indian nation.

The princes, for example, who emerged from individual feudal twilights to make a significant combined political appearance on the continental stage in 1930–1, soon lost any initiative or leadership they then had. From mid-1931 divisions among British Indian politicians convinced the princes that they had less reason to fear a strong and united British India, and consequently their interest in federation as a protection waned. Their different priorities re-emerged, and they began to bargain, each for favourable conditions for accession to a federation. Many of them left before the second conference session closed, and only one attended the third session in person. In the words of a British official with long experience of the states, 'Now that the outlook is so gloomy and the chance of agreement between the British Indian parties so remote, the Princes have begun to hope that nothing will become of the Conference, and that they will be able to continue their sheltered existence while Hindus and Muhammadans wage communal war in British India . . . there is not one genuine friend of federation left amongst the Princes.'[39] As divisions on self-protective strategies re-emerged the princes not only lost the political initiative, but damned themselves in the sight of British Indian politicians and of some of their own subjects. This increased the likelihood of eventual confrontation rather than co-operation with Congress.

Yet Congress itself could not justify its claim to speak for one Indian nation. This was made clear in three episodes—in its failure to get the communal minorities to support it, and the resulting British Communal Award in the absence of Indian agreement; in Gandhi's attempt to prevent separate electorates for Untouchables; and in the reaction of Congressmen to the Award as they prepared to re-enter constitutional politics. Gandhi was personally involved in an attempt to reach an agreement with the All-India Muslim Conference in Delhi in April 1931, which claimed separate electorates for Muslims and special weightage in provincial and federal legislatures, the creation of several new Muslim provinces, and the provinces' retention of residual powers in any federation. These negotiations broke down, not least because the Nationalist Muslims opposed separate electorates, and Gandhi could not abandon his allies, because they were the flimsy evidence of non-Hindu allegiance to Congress. He was no more successful in arranging a communal accord in London, and, indeed, generated much frustration and hostility by his attempts. Eventually the Muslims were joined by some smaller minorities including the Sikhs, the Untouchable group led by Dr Ambedkar, and the Anglo-Indians, in a joint demand for separate electorates, fair representation in the public services and in the cabinets of Viceroy and provincial Governors.[40] Deadlock led the London government to make a Communal Award in August 1932, allocating seats through separate electorates to the different communities in each province (Table H). Not the least of the government's concerns was to conciliate Indian Muslims and prevent their joining the anti-imperial movement, or—as seemed more likely—their withdrawal from constitutional discussions if their demands were not met.

The other two major demonstrations of Congress's inability to speak even for all India's Hindus were the direct outcome of the Communal Award. In London Gandhi had talked of resisting with his life the grant of separate electorates to Untouchables; and in March he reiterated this in a letter to the Secretary of State, indicating that even if he was released from jail he would fast to death if the Award granted Untouchables this mark of a political identity separate from other Hindus.[41] British officials and Indian politicians were non-plussed or angry when his decision was made public; and many suspected him of devious motives. Some felt it was a stunt to revive civil disobedience: others considered it blackmail. Undoubtedly he was moved by a mixture of considerations, including a wish to throw his whole weight against a social division he had long considered profoundly false and damaging to Hinduism and destructive of Indian nationhood, a hope of stinging caste Hindu consciences by this dramatic gesture of suffering, and a realization that if this division were written into the new constitution on top of the grant of separate electorates to Muslims, then Indian unity and independence would be harder than ever to achieve. A fast might educate and unite as satyagraha had failed to do: and it was one of the few ways open to him as a prisoner of influencing public life.

Such was the emotional and political pressure his fast exerted on a wide spectrum of Hindus that a distinguished group conferred in Bombay under M.M. Malaviya with leaders of the Untouchables, including Ambedkar. They hammered out a compromise package of proposals which several of

Table H. Communal Award: Allocation of Seats in Lower Houses of Provincial Legislatures

Province	General	Depressed Classes	Representatives from Backward Areas	Sikh	Muhammadan	Indian Christian	Anglo-Indian	European	Commerce and Industry, Mining and Planting, Special	Land-holders, Special	University, Special	Labour, Special	Total
Madras	134 (including 6 women)	18	1	0	29 (including 1 woman)	9 (inc. 1 woman)	2	3	6	6	1	6	215
Bombay (including Sind)	97 (including 5 women)	10	1	0	63 (including 1 woman)	3	2	4	8	3	1	8	200
Bengal	80* (including 2 women)	*	0	0	119 (including 2 women)	2	4 (including 1 woman)	11	19	5	2	8	250
United Provinces	132 (including 4 women)	12	0	0	66 (including 2 women)	2	1	2	3	6	1	3	228
Punjab	43 (including 1 woman)	0	0	32 (including 1 woman)	86 (including 2 women)	2	1	1	1	5	1	3	175
Bihar and Orissa	99 (including 3 women)	7	8	0	42 (including 1 woman)	2	1	2	4	5	1	4	175
Central Provinces (including Berar)	77 (including 3 women)	10	1	0	14	0	1	1	2	3	1	2	112
Assam	44 (including 1 woman)	4	9	0	34	1	0	1	11	0	0	4	108
North-West Frontier Province	9	0	0	3	36	0	0	0	0	2	0	0	50
Bombay (without Sind)	109 (including 5 women)	10	1	0	30 (including 1 woman)	3	2	3	7	2	1	7	175
Sind	19 (including 1 woman)	0	0	0	34 (including 1 woman)	0	0	2	2	2	0	1	60

* As explained in paragraph 9 of the statement, the number of special Depressed Class seats in Bengal—which will not exceed 10—has not yet been fixed. The number of General seats will be 80, less the number of special Depressed Class seats.

Source: East India (Constitutional Reforms), Communal Decision PP, 1931–2, XVIII, Cmd. 4147.

them took by night train to Poona where Gandhi was in jail, having declined a government offer to release him to a private house under certain restrictions. He was by this time growing rapidly weaker, and there was a danger of his imminent mental and physical collapse. But he was able to discuss the proposals with caste Hindus and Untouchables for several days, and the outcome was the Poona Pact. Its essence was the abandonment of separate electorates for Untouchables as offered in the official Award. In their place was to be a system of primary and secondary elections for a certain number of seats reserved for Untouchables, and in the primary elections Untouchables alone would vote. But Ambedkar had managed to drive a hard bargain, despite Hindu pressure and the claims of other Untouchable politicians to represent the Depressed Classes which weakened his hand. He secured the reservation of 148 seats in the provincial legislatures for them, double the number offered in the Communal Award, a guarantee about representation in any federal assembly, and the promise that a sum of money would be earmarked in every provincial budget for Untouchables' education. The Cabinet accepted the provisions of the Poona Pact in place of the corresponding parts of the Award; and when he heard this Gandhi ended his fast. Meanwhile the Bombay conference under Malaviya ratified the Pact and passed a resolution Gandhi had drafted—that henceforth no Hindu should be regarded as Untouchable because of his birth, and that those who had been called Untouchables would have equal access with other Hindus to public wells, roads, schools and other public institutions.

Pacts, however, could not end profound divisions within Hindu society. This Gandhi recognized; and he threw himself into a campaign against Untouchability, which he conducted first from jail and then after his release in a series of major educative and fund-raising tours. Dramatic demonstrations of fraternity across the pollution line followed the Pact and accompanied Gandhi's perambulations, extending to ceremonial meals shared by Untouchables and caste Hindus ('inter-dining'), and the opening of many Hindu temples to Untouchables. Yet it was to take decades to produce real change in Untouchables' status. Furthermore the Pact alienated many caste Hindus, especially in the Punjab and Bengal not primarily because of its ritual implications, but because of the harsh repercussions on their access to seats in the new legislatures. The Punjabis were now asked by Gandhi and Congress to give up eight of their precious seats to Untouchables, whereas under the Award there had been no special provision for Untouchables. Bengali Hindus, their representation already cut savagely by the Award, now had to give up thirty of their seats in place of the probable ten suggested for Untouchables in the Award. It was little wonder that both provincial groups rejected the plans of the all-India Congress leadership and tried to extricate themselves from the provisions of the Pact. Given such Hindu hostility, together with the need to avoid rejecting the Award outright because of the attachment of most Muslims to it, the central Congress leadership was paralysed. It could not afford to wreck what little unity there was among Congressmen in the painful aftermath of civil disobedience, and in June 1934 the Working Committee shelved the problem and declined to accept or reject the Award, claiming that only a constituent assembly could settle the communal problem finally. Its decision that it could not decide was a clear sign of its precarious position as the spokesman of Hindus, let alone as representative of an Indian nation.[42]

The diversity of emerging senses of public and political identity and the crisis of potential nationhood in a plural and deeply regionalized society was even more apparent in the careers of aspirant all-India leaders. What was occurring on the subcontinent was no simple emergence of a nation's movement against its imperial rulers, though this was perhaps inevitably the theme stressed in Indian accounts of political change written at the time and immediatly after independence. Undoubtedly the common framework of the *raj*, and the growing perception that imperial rule was at the heart of many of their perceived problems, drove many into concerted anti-British politics. But India was an immensely complex and segmented society, experiencing a broad range of change at different political levels, the rate, nature, and unevenness of which sharpened at the prospect of the devolution of power. Particularist senses of identity intensified as groups realized the importance of what was being offered and their unequal access to it. Consequently not all political aspiration was channelled into 'nationalist' politics; nor was it clear which public identities would become politically privileged in any new order. In this complex situation different types of leaders emerged. They tried to do different things, had different power bases, and could only be persuaded at particular moments to co-operate across sectional and regional interests to create a movement which was continental in spread if not national in aim. National leadership was therefore peculiarly difficult. Those who tried to fill that role had to show much creativity both in tactics and ideology. They had not only to construct linkages across the continent for unified or co-ordinated political action: they also at a deeper level had to construct a national community and identity by giving Indians a common story about their past, their present, and their future. Some, like Jinnah or Motilal Nehru, who tried to present a national constitutional programme found themselves isolated. Death saved Motilal early in 1931, but Jinnah retired in despair to England, to return as the spokesman for a specifically communal interest which he helped to elevate to the status of a national demand by Muslims not for protection within one Indian nation but for separate nationhood. Others like Sapru retained national repute and leverage by acting as mediators between the British and their more radical compatriots, because both parties needed their services as bridge-builders. Even Gandhi, who came nearest to being a living symbol of Indian nationhood and the one whose widespread popularity most obviously suggests that he was a national leader, not only alienated most Muslims and some Hindus, but experienced great troughs as well as peaks in his actual ability to influence public life and politics. In the complex interplay of British and Indians, and of Indians with each other, his skills as tactician, publicist, ideologue, and arranger of compromises at times gave him a central role and great leverage—as in Congress in 1929–30, early in 1931, or as Congressmen tried to disentangle themselves from confrontation in 1933–4. At other junctures, as at the second Round Table Conference, Gandhi failed utterly to unite Indian opinion behind him and so to exert influence on the British; in that particular context his skills served no useful purpose. Anyone who tried as he did to unite as many Indian interests as possible under a national flag faced immense problems of conciliation and mediation, of integrating actions at different political levels, while attempting to handle urgent issues in the relationship between rulers and ruled. Gandhi's peculiar resilience as a leader lay in his broad perception of his own role and his willingness to withdraw from certain styles or arenas of politics and to concentrate on other constructive work when he felt that he and his methods (particularly satyagraha) were considered useless or were being manipulated by his compatriots. This was quite clear when he withdrew civil disobedience temporarily in 1934, as it had been in his retirement in the 1920s.[43]

iii   The constitutional experiment

For all its limitations the 1935 Act was a major experiment in the devolution of power in a non-white part of Britain's empire. Its imperial framers hoped it would channel the interests and forces in Indian public life through institutions which would protect Britain's diminishing interests on the sub-continent and require from Britain much lighter exercise of imperial control and decreased expenditure of resources; though by the time of its enactment it seemed a battered and much cobbled measure, disliked by most Indian politicians and a significant group of British MPs. Even to contemporaries it seemed a frail buttress for the burdens intended for it. Among the sceptics was Linlithgow, the unlucky Viceroy who had to try to work it. He reported to London in mid-1936:

It is vital that the impetus of the new Statute and the consummation of Provincial Autonomy should carry us straight on into Federation. For indeed there would be grave danger in allowing any prolonged interval of time to elapse between Provincial Autonomy and the final phase. Federation has few enthusiastic friends. The Princes, I believe, for the most part regard it as inevitable but do not welcome it.

Congress hate it, and Provinces will soon, whether as regards their bureaucracies or their public opinion, develop a degree of local patriotism, which would view with easy acquiescence the progressive weakening of central authority, such as would most certainly eventuate if the reconstruction of the Centre is unduly delayed.[44]

The constitutional experiment was to last from the 1937 elections until just after the outbreak of war in 1939. Then Congress withdrew from co-operation in government, leaving the Governors of provinces where Congress had formed ministries to run them under emergency powers. The Government of India also stopped negotiations to bring the princes into a federation. The 1935 Act therefore never solved the crisis of empire on the subcontinent. Yet its operation and failures indicated the way the issues of identity and nationhood might be resolved.

As a buttress of a new kind of empire the constitutional experiment most obviously failed on an all-India scale because a continental federation never developed. The princes were largely responsible for this. By late 1936 it was obvious that princely hostility, evident as the Round Table Conferences proceeded, had now hardened, that some were demanding a high price for accession, and that few really understood the implications of federation. Emissaries went from Delhi to the states to discuss the problem; but London warned Delhi not to press the princes too hard lest they be frightened off, and also because Zetland, the Secretary of State, had to watch the Tory die-hards who might well join hands with worried princes to block the federation. Zetland was right when he reckoned early in 1937 that they were dealing with 'unwilling sellers'; for the princes were now prepared to bargain hard, particularly to protect their fiscal rights. In January 1939 Linlithgow presented them with a final offer which was rejected by a large princely conference in Bombay in June, though in so doing they rejected the terms offered rather than the principle of federation. By the outbreak of war two-fifths of the states had indicated their willingness to accede.

Much controversy surrounds the roles of Linlithgow and Zetland in this prolonged and fruitless interlude. Whatever their relative hesitations or ineptitudes, it is clear that forces and attitudes outside the negotiations were affecting the princes, reinforcing their natural desire to give up as little as possible and suggesting that they might find allies in stubbornness. Tory die-hard hostility to federation and determination to prevent forced princely accession impinged on the princes and constrained Zetland and Linlithgow. Simultaneously communal antipathy increased in British India, and with it Muslim hostility to a potentially Hindu-dominated federation. Even more disturbing to the princes was the novel display of overt antagonism to some of their order when Congressmen backed movements for reform and increasing representative government among the princes' own subjects. Unrest developed in many states, including Mysore, Travancore, Kashmir,

Hyderabad, Jaipur, and Rajkot, after the passage of the 1935 Act, as dissident princely subjects wanted to force reform before any federation occurred and confirmed princely autocracy. In several of these Congressmen intervened directly, or Congress governments declined to use their power against agitations organized in their provinces against neighbouring princely states. Official Congress relations with the All India States Peoples Conference, representing the states' dissidents, were ambivalent in the 1930s. Congress opposed the idea of princely nomination of states' representatives to any federal legislature, and wished to see princely autocracy ended. Yet the established all-India Congress leadership was anxious lest their own unruly Congress members should use states' agitations to build up power bases from which to attack the central Congress leaders, the so-called 'High Command'. Consequently in February 1938 at the Haripura Congress they secured a resolution which attempted to limit Congress intervention in the states and to control those who used the Congress name. Congress pledged itself to the same political, economic, and social freedom for the states and British India, but it could not liberate the states' peoples. It could render moral support, and individual Congressmen could aid the states' struggles. But Congress Committees in the states must submit to the Working Committee's direction and must not use the Congress name. These provisions were more often ignored than observed, however; and Congressmen and the Congress name continued to be associated with attacks on the states, though these were seldom very real threats to princely power.[45]

States' problems were consequently intertwined with the whole issue of Indian national identity. The late 1930s left a legacy of hostility between Congressmen and the princes, and between some princes and their subjects, particularly where there was an added communal dimension, as in Hyderabad where a Muslim Nizam ruled a Hindu state. This boded ill for the peaceful inclusion of the princes in free India. In another, unplanned way the British also left the states unprepared for participation in a free, democratic India. Since the 1919 Reforms and the establishment of the Chamber of Princes in 1921 democratic institutions had begun to take root in British India, but the British had increasingly treated their princely allies as honoured partners (while maintaining the doctrine of Paramountcy), declining to force them into internal reform, though prepared to warn and chide. Because the Paramount Power would not and could not enforce reform, the prospect for the princes when their imperial allies left them to work out their relationship with British Indian Congressmen was bleak indeed. Unreformed they stood little chance of positive participation in a new India.[46]

Despite this long-term failure to provide a federal solution to the imperial problem of ruling the subcontinent, the 1935 Act succeeded as a temporary solution to the problem of governing British India. For two years the British tactic of retreat to the centre, leaving the provinces to run themselves under Indian ministers, paid off spectacularly. (Some have argued that had war not intervened Indian independence would have come more quickly and peacefully as a result of the provinces' experience of working the new constitution. This is speculation which ignores the princes and the minorities. But it reflects the effective working of the provincial provisions of the 1935 Act.) Congressmen had done well in the last Assembly elections under the old constitution (1934), winning 44 of the 88 elected seats. Their greater triumph came in the 1937 elections to the new provincial legislative assemblies, when they won 716 out of 1585 seats, having clear majorities in five provinces—Madras, Bihar, Orissa, CP and UP (See Table I)—the same areas where they had performed best in 1934.[47] Congress was also strong in Bombay, Assam, and the North-West Frontier Province, though a coalition of opponents could outnumber it. In Bengal, Punjab, and Sind it had little prospect of power. At first it seemed that the Congress 'High Command' would refuse to allow these victors to accept office, despite strong pressures from provincial leaders to be allowed to pluck the fruits of power. (When questioned by the AICC early in 1937, thirteen out of eighteen Congress 'provinces' said they wished for office acceptance: feeling was particularly strong where Congressmen had secured a majority.) The central leadership hesitated because it was divided—the established leadership aligned behind Gandhi and favouring parliamentary politics for lack of any other coherent continental strategy, facing the group who ranged themselves alongside Jawaharlal Nehru in a new radicalism which made them loathe the idea of co-operating in a disliked constitution and accepting responsibility when the levers of ultimate power were still in British hands. The Working Committee postponed the issue as long as possible to avoid a split which would weaken Congress; and eventually Gandhi tried to arrange a compromise between the opposing groups by bargaining with the British for limitations on the use of Governors' special powers. The upshot was an informal compromise with the government (in which Congress did most of the climbing down) whereby Congress was assured that Governors would not use their special powers to interfere with normal administration.[48] The provincial part of the 1935 Act was thereafter able to operate throughout British India.

Non-Congress ministries were formed in Bengal, Punjab, Assam, and Sind; and throughout this period the constitution functioned in those areas. Indian ministers governed with little formal intervention by Governors or disagreements with them. Except in the Punjab they were not strong governments, but uneasy coalitions always vulnerable to defeat in the legislature. The strength of the Punjab ministry rested on an almost unique

Table I. *Results of the elections to provincial lower houses, 1937*

(a) In statistical form

Province	Total seats	Seats won by Congress
Madras	215	159
Bihar	152	95
Orissa	60	36
CP	112	71
UP	228	133
Bombay	175	88
Assam	108	35
N-WFP	50	19
Bengal	250	54
Punjab	175	18
Sind	60	8

Source: *Return Showing the Results of Elections in India (1937)*, PP, 1937–8, XXI, Cmd. 5589.

Note: The 'official' Congress historian gives some different figures, but the difference is slight. B. Pattabhi Sitaramayya, *History of the Indian National Congress. Volume II (1935–1947)* (Delhi, 1969, reprint of 1947 edn.), p. 39.

(b) In tabular form (Congress black, non-Congress white)

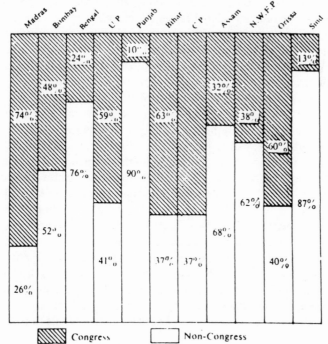

Source: R. Coupland, *Indian Politics 1936–1942* (London, 1943), opp. p. 27.

phenomenon which reflected the province's social and communal structure—a stable cross-communal coalition, the National Unionist Party under Sir Sikander Hyat Khan. It represented the broad agrarian interest of
Punjabi agriculturalists and made one of its prime objectives the preservation of that interest by a series of protective measures such as restrictions on
the alienation of land to non-agriculturalists and limiting money-lenders'
powers.

Congress came to power in Madras, Bombay, CP, UP, Bihar, Orissa, and
the North-West Frontier. British observers believed that the degree of
discipline exercised by the central leadership over provincial Congressmen
who became ministers in fact flouted two key principles of the constitution
of 1935—responsibility and autonomy. Ministers were ultimately answer-
able to the 'High Command' rather than to their electors; and there was a
uniformity throughout Congress governments which undermined the autonomy of each provincial government. Yet they could not deny that both
because of their majorities and their party discipline they formed more
stable governments than in most of the non-Congress provinces. The new
machinery went rapidly into smooth working order, proving more than
adequate to its task, confirming the commitment of an increasingly wide
range of Indian political opinion to this political style. Cabinets functioned;
legislative business was conducted competently and decorously with little
opposition. Furthermore, Congressmen, once in power, proved as willing as
their imperial predecessors to enforce law and order when agrarian, industrial, and communal disorder threatened, using existing weapons and some
new ones. They also engaged in considerable legislative reform, mainly
directed towards agrarian problems and prohibition. Two radical attempts
to alter the land revenue system (in Madras and Orissa) were dropped: but
within the confines of the existing system much was done to protect tenants
(e.g. the comprehensive UP Act XVII of 1939 and Bihar's piecemeal legislation of 1937–9), to relieve peasant indebtedness and to restrain money-
lenders. Prohibition had long been a theme in Congress politics, as well as
one of Gandhi's cherished projects; and Congress ministers were told to
achieve prohibition in three years; despite the financial loss involved and its
inevitable repercussions on the availability of funds for social services,
education and development, unless replacement taxes were levied. Bombay
pushed ahead fastest; but by the time Congress governments resigned in
1939 all had sacrificed considerable excise revenue. Congress governments
backed by large majorities were more prepared than their predecessors to
help Untouchables with legislation and executive measures, particularly in
such matters as temple entry, education, and the removal of civil disabilities. Like non-Congress governments they also spent considerable and
increasing sums on education. Peculiar to Congress provinces, however,
was an additional educational experiment—Basic Education, centred on

crafts and activity rather than book-learning. This owed much to Gandhi's own experiments with education, crafts, and simple living in his successive communities, and also reflected the need to fashion an economical and self-financing educational system as funds from excise dried up.[49]

Many British observers, including officials, were warm in their tribute to the new provincial governments. Linlithgow spoke of 'a distinguished record of public achievement', and Hoare referred in Parliament to the 'great constitutional success' of the constitutional experiment in the provinces. Two Governors of Congress provinces, UP and Madras, on ending their terms of office published articles about their provinces under the 1935 constitution and noted the general efficiency and good will of the new administrations, and their courage in tackling problems possible only for 'popular' governments.[50] Yet it was clear that the actual fabric of administration was tautly stretched by the activities of the new Indian governments and the range of new demands imposed on civil servants as their reform and development policies expanded. Despite fears that European recruitment to the ICS might dry up because of constitutional change, young men were still attracted to India and recruitment boomed in the late 1930s. But the service was undermanned as a result of earlier shortfalls, just at the point when it was required to be physically and politically flexible in response to new demands from Indian politicians and the erosion of its old prestige in Indian eyes. Civil servants' letters home reflected their immense and varied workload, and their curious political position during the constitutional experiment. As one young officer wrote in February 1937, 'The enigma of the ICS at present is that a Conservative would hate having to treat Indians as equals or superiors, and a Labourite would hate being unable to put his political principles into practice, & being the sort of little tin god I am here!' Although there were some instances in the early days of provincial autonomy of Congressmen seeing themselves as a 'parallel government' and of ministers distrusting or interfering with the work of administrators, there was no breakdown in co-operation between the politicians and the executive. Many ICS men came to enjoy good working and social relations with the new Indian politicians and to feel that they still had much in an educative as well as administrative role to give to the creation of a new India. The main problem lay in the burden of work placed on a skeletal service—a situation in which there was no leeway to cope with a major crisis, as Linlithgow noted grimly.[51]

That crisis was to come almost immediately in the shape of world war. It brought the ending of ICS recruitment, the withdrawal of many civilians to active military service, and the collapse of the constitutional experiment in the Congress provinces when the Congress 'High Command' withdrew Congressmen from co-operation in government. The logic behind this apparently destructive decision lay in Congress's nature as a movement of opposition to an imperial regime built out of a loose aggregation of alliances, which had contrived to become also a party of government. Yet this dual role, as well as the diversities among Congressmen and their differing local priorities, imposed almost intolerable strains on party unity: and unity was still crucial if the national endeavour for independence was to be pushed on and Congress was not to lapse into the role of a provincial office-holders' club. Gandhi had avoided fission in 1937 by achieving a formula for office acceptance. In 1939 unity was again achieved by withdrawal from the constitutional experiment. It was a decision made by the central leadership not so much on the principle of refusing assistance in the war or out of real antagonism to the British because war was declared on India's behalf by the Viceroy. Indeed there was no idea that withdrawal from the ministries would mean long-term exile in the constitutional wilderness. Rather, the strains within Congress, and the ambivalence of Congressmen at their role as part of government, threatened major internal disruption. This had to be avoided if Congress was to press home its achievements of the previous two years and capitalize on British wartime difficulties. Temporary self-denial seemed essential if Congress was still to claim to speak for the nation.[52]

The successes and failures of the constitutional experiment illuminate the crisis of national identity within British India, as well as the dimension of that crisis which involved the princes and their subjects. Given the record of Congress as the party of government in large areas of British India, is it historically accurate to assert that by 1939 Congress was indeed becoming an 'alternative *raj*' and a true focus for a sense of national identity? The clash of imperialism and nationalism has proved an attractive interpretation of Indian political development, and indeed was a necessary element in the 'imagining' of India, creating for an aspirant and then independent nation its common, public story. But our material has shown how inadequate this is by itself, although the growth of overt nationalist ideology and agitational politics were a significant part of that development. Among the tangled strands in the skein of political change one which became increasingly visible in the late 1930s was the accretion to Congress of ruling authority. There is considerable truth in the observation of one historian that 'alongside the protracted conflict between Congress and the British . . . there was the no less significant process by which Congress captured the Raj in India from the British by supersession.'[53]

One aspect of this was the public image of Congress among a wide range of Hindus who were politically aware in the sense of perceiving the nature and significance of the changing institutions of politics and government created by the British, and their potential for the exercise of power over the lives of ordinary people. Many of these men and women were literate, at least in a vernacular, and though articulate on political matters were generally not career politicians, party activists or participants in agitational politics. Their influence lay in the ballot box; and in the estimation of their feelings by political activists. Evidence of this significant if amorphous band of Hindu public opinion comes in contemporary comment by neutral observers as well as concerned officials, in letters and memoirs, and increasingly in election results following the extension of the franchise under the 1935 Act. Such sources indicate that by the late 1930s in the eyes of most Hindus Congress was the accepted focus of national identity, the legitimate spokesman of Indian aspirations to the British, and the natural alternative and successor to British rule.[54]

Within this broad spectrum of growing Hindu support for Congress the responses of two groups were particularly marked. Indian businessmen were becoming an increasingly influential force in public life, acutely aware of the way governments could impinge on their activities and their profits. Some were known to support Congress financially. But despite the differences among them and their hesitations about overt hostility to the British and clear support for Congress, it seems that by the late 1930s most realized that Congress was the dominant Indian political group to be dealt with in the future; while their experience of Congress in provincial government confirmed that Congress would not create an environment politically and socially hostile to their interests.[55] It was also noticeable how many educated women were becoming Congress supporters, as their participation in civil disobedience had shown. Often women followed their male relatives in this. But Gandhi's role in encouraging women to become active in public affairs was also a significant incentive: in particular, his use of traditional images of Hindu womanhood, and his insistence on special roles and programmes for women, so that they never lost an image of respectability by coming out into the public sphere. As in the beginnings of women's participation in the world outside the home at the turn of the century, now they still to a large extent both in agitational politics and in their own sociopolitical organizations operated in a predominantly female public space. This, however, limited their participation and influence in nationalist politics, and eventually in the politics of independent India.[56]

This shift and consolidation of much Hindu political sympathy behind Congress can partly be explained by a genuine growth in a sense of Indian national identity fostered by decades of Congress propaganda, the growth of education, and the expansion of literacy. Congress's record of 'sacrifice' in the civil disobedience campaigns, tales of clashes with a brutal police, and the tally of Congressmen's jail sentences all contributed to its heroic image. Gandhi's reputation and association with Congress were also contributory factors. 'Charisma' is undoubtedly a glib explanation for his popularity and public position, since his political influence fluctuated and depended more on the matching of his skills with the conjunctions of circumstances and issues than on any simple mass charismatic appeal. Yet his sincerity, simplicity, and devotion to India at the expense of self, and his location within Hindu traditions of saintly authority exercised a remarkable attraction for many thousands, including those who never actually followed his precepts. Congress reaped the harvest of its ambivalent relationship with the Mahatma; and as the Governor of Madras observed, the slogan which won the day for Congress in the 1937 elections among an electorate which included many illiterates was 'Vote for Gandhi and the yellow box'.[57]

When this public opinion had to be articulated through the ballot box Congress's electioneering machine was vital. Here the experience of agitational politics paid off and Congress was in 1937 the one party which had accumulated skills of mass propaganda and a reservoir of volunteers who took the Congress message into towns and deep into the countryside. Its campaign managers were often highly professional in their approach, and took pains both to organize direct mass appeals to the electorate and to approach significant local men and institutions, caste and community leaders, as possible 'vote banks', tailoring the message to their needs, and on occasion promising substantial considerations in return for votes and assistance. One CP Congress candidate offered a powerful temple trust in Nagpur city, a cut in its rates for electric light. Where Congressmen controlled local boards they used these for electioneering, manipulating taxation and expenditure for example; and organizing municipal employees such as teachers into canvassing networks. Furthermore the Congress manifesto was often modified by local men to suit local conditions, playing up anti-*zamindar* feeling or soothing orthodox Hindu feeling as locally necessary. The distribution of the Congress ticket was also managed in such a way as to field candidates who 'matched' their constituency and could in their own right, by virtue of caste, status or wealth pull in votes. Enormous sums were spent in the 1937 elections, most of the money coming from local rather than provincial or central Congress sources. Each seat contested probably involved expenditure of about Rs. 4,000. This made it imperative for Congress to choose candidates who could largely finance themselves; and in practice it was at district rather than provincial level that the crucial selection decisions were made.

By contrast opposing parties were poorly organized and funded; and had little grasp of the requirements of electioneering in so greatly extended an electorate. Madras's once triumphant Justice Party was a stunned casualty of the new dispensation: as were the two UP landlord parties established in 1934, which foundered as old electioneering techniques relying on the influence of landed gentry failed to deliver a popular vote.[58] In such a situation another cause of Congress's rising prestige was the 'band-waggon effect'. Quite ordinary people could see no viable alternative—either in parties ranged against Congress, or even in the British *raj* itself. The Governor of UP stated this quite bluntly. In the run-up to the 1937 elections Congress went into action not spasmodically but continuously, through their resident workers in every village. Meetings and processions, slogans and flags, the exploitation of grievances, promises which held out the vision of a new heaven and a new earth, stirred the countryside into a ferment such as it had never before experienced. The sense of impending change awakened the villages. The Government, which had in past agitations opposed the Congress with the weight of its authority, now stood inactive. It was too much to expect that the villager would understand the constitutional necessity for this attitude. He felt that the British Raj was weakening, that the Congress Raj was coming, and, as so often happens, threw himself definitely on what seemed to be the winning side.[59]

As the legitimacy of Congress as a potential *raj* increased in Hindu public opinion another dimension of the process developed—among the smaller segment of Hindus who chose to be active in politics, beyond the mere casting of their vote. For them Congress increasingly became the complete and inevitable political environment in which they operated. All their aspirations were channelled into it; as were their hostilities and fears. There seemed little point in pursuing power outside its flexible confines. The past history of those who became Congress candidates in the 1937 elections shows this. Many were not new recruits to this political level, but men who previously had worn other party labels or been independents. This was clear in UP, Bihar and CP, for example. (In Banda district of UP one Congress candidate had previously been a Liberal in the provincial legislature, a Congress Nationalist, and part of an anti-Congress faction in the UP Hindu Sabha!) In Madras after the elections there were 159 'Congress' members of the Legislative Assembly. A hard core of these had for years been asociated with Congress and fifty-five had been to jail in the process. A second group were established politicians who had never identified themselves with political labels. But about one-third of the 'Congress' party in the Assembly had changed allegiances since 1934, and fourteen had actually sat in previous legislatures under other labels. Many of these were in flight from the sinking Justice Party.[60]

Further proof that Congress was becoming the natural arena for Hindu political activists was the very large rise in Congress membership in the late 1930s (See Table J). These 'new' Congressmen were increasingly from the countryside and often from locally dominant agricultural castes. This broadening of Congress's geographical and social base was evident both in the membership, and among those who rose to higher positions in Congress as delegates to sessions or office-holders in the provincial organizations. In UP for example, out of a total of 62,703 members in 1935, 39,000 (62.2 per cent) were 'rural' and 23,703 (37.8 per cent) were 'urban'. By 1938 there were 1,472,456 provincial members: 1,345,781 (91.4 per cent) were 'rural' and 126,675 (8.6 per cent) were 'urban'. A sample of political leaders in West Bengal in the decade after independence showed that half of those born before 1900 were of village origin; while 74 per cent of the younger

Table J. *Congress membership in the late 1930s*

Area	1935–6	1936–7	1937–8	1938–9
Bihar	78,305	104,743	462,787	575,139
Utkal*	6,819	5,760	87,857	197,201
Mahakoshal*	24,527	35,986	85,607	126,554
Nagpur*	8,164	6,961	26,912	44,854
Vidarbha*	7,054	11,692	46,728	78,396
UP	62,703	65,733	993,340	1,472,456
Andhra Pradesh	45,103	50,866	334,030	n.a.
	(late 1935)	(late 1936)	(1938)	
Tamilnad	55,044	65,105	115,971	n.a.
	(late 1935)	(late 1936)	(1938)	
All-India	473,336	635,504	n.a.	4,511,858

Source: Tomlinson, *The Indian National Congress and the Raj*, p. 86; C. J. Baker, *The Politics of South India 1920–1937*, p. 316.

Note: * These are the names of Congress linguistic 'provinces' where these did not coincide with administrative provinces: often these, as in the case of CP, spanned several linguistic areas.

men (born after 1920) came from villages. Considerable numbers of these Bengalis were small landowners. In UP, too, there was by the 1930s a broad band of district Congress leaders who came from reasonably prosperous rural backgrounds, men from small landholding families. The trend towards recruitment of prosperous rural groups, often at the expense of higher castes who had dominated the early Congress, occurred in many other areas. In the south it was clear among the Gounders of Tamil Nad; among Kammas and Reddis in Andhra districts. In the Belgaum district of Bombay Brahmins increasingly lost power in Congress to prosperous non-Brahmins. Brahmins had been Presidents of the District Congress Committee in the 1920s and early 1930s; but from 1936–40 the office was held by a Reddi then a Lingayat.[61]

Recruitment of this broader social group from the countryside into Congress was partly the result of deliberate tactics by Congress leaders who realized the need to forge links with the newly enfranchised and to attract men of local standing who could bring their resources of prestige, money, and followings into the organization. Furthermore, as membership of local and provincial Congress Committees and of local institutions of self-government became more important, aspirants tended to help recruit more Congressmen as supporters in order to ensure their election to such local offices. It was no coincidence that in Andhra, for example, membership of Congress fluctuated in direct proportion to the imminence of elections to the district boards. From the point of view of those who were recruited, involvement in Congress became increasingly attractive. Not only was it a powerful patron as the party of provincial government. There were few alternatives if one had aspirations to power; it was the natural pathway in a political career. Consequently many men who had been active in municipalities, district boards, and co-operatives without needing any party label now linked themselves to Congress, particularly if they aspired to higher political levels. Congress became itself the political arena for most Hindus in the Congress provinces. Power was pursued within it: conflicts were fought out within its ranks rather than by forming parties opposed to it. This occurred even where Hindus were a minority and Congress was not in power in provincial government. Bengali Hindus stayed within Congress, not forming a separate party but expressing their dissidence and hostility to the central leadership within it, as in their support for Subhas Bose's bid for central power against Gandhi and the 'High Command' in 1939. Even the Punjabi Hindus who felt betrayed by the Congress and harried by the cross-communal agrarian party in power increasingly turned to Congress: indeed they had no viable alternative.[62] This gave Congress the character of a whole complex or system of parties rather than of a single political party. This 'umbrella' function of Congress (as it has been called) was to last well into the politics of independent India.

The nature of Congress posed formidable leadership problems. Each component group had its bosses, each provincial organization its leaders, and these levels of leadership had somehow to be persuaded or coerced to work together, under the over-arching guidance of the 'High Command', the key members of the Working Committee which was nominated by the President. The difficulties of all-India leadership were compounded by the dual nature of Congress: it was both provincial party of government or opposition, attending to the bread and butter issues of administration and people's ordinary lives, and yet still an all-India movement and mouthpiece of national aspiration for full control of India's political system and destiny. After 1934 Congressmen rejected Gandhi's radical (some thought 'unpolitical') plan for a national constructive policy and the reformation of Congress into a body of dedicated, spiritual leaders. In its place, and for lack of any more compelling continental strategy once civil disobedience had proved unproductive, the major all-India leaders pursued legislative and ministerial politics—a course bound not to cement a heroic national unity but to underline provincial interests, harden provincial identities and exacerbate internal Congress disputes over policy details, particularly in such sensitive areas as social and land reform. The tension between Congress as inclusive national movement and Congress as government became very clear when Congress provincial governments formulated labour legislation, or, as in Bihar, turned their backs on and indeed helped to quash potentially radical peasant movements. The most disadvantaged in society were, ironically, driven even further to the edges of Congress political thinking by the party's very success in the 1937 elections. The legitimacy Congress gained as India's representative from the limited range of the enfranchised meant that the leaders saw little need to engage in broader and radical politicization in town or countryside in order to gain power and the status of national spokesmen.[63]

Between the end of civil disobedience and Congress ministers' departure from the provincial corridors of power there were certain specific sources of division within Congress. Regional groups with provincial priorities campaigned to go their own ways. Factions split Congress at continental, provincial, and local levels. Such splits and alignments were not particularly new in character: Tilak and Gokhale would have recognized them. But the changed political role of Congress and the actual power available within its ranks and through control of its machinery now gave them greater political significance. The other marked change in the later 1930s was the development of more overtly ideological splits, or at least of social and political ideals which were used to bond factional groups and to belabour established leaderships at provincial and all-India level.

The most important sign of this was the emergence in 1934 of the Congress Socialist Party (CSP). Radical political and social ideals had been developing in the previous decade among the student generation, many of whom had looked to Nehru as their spokesman and influence on the more pragmatic all-India leaders. Gandhi—an idealist and a socialist *sui generis*—had kept this segment of opinion in touch with Congress through his sensitive handling of the young Nehru. Mahatma and young firebrand had worked together from mutual affection and esteem, as well as the recognition that each needed the other for the fruition of their different ideals. But at times their relationship was fraught with mutual incomprehension. Now, in 1934, disillusioned by the failure of civil disobedience and the paltry results of Gandhi's plans for grass-roots reconstruction of national life, and by the tame policy of constitutional politics which now replaced conflict, a group of those who had been in jail during civil disobedience formed the CSP, as a more formal mechanism for challenging the established leaders, and spreading a message of more radical political, economic, and social reform. In J. P. Narayan's words, 'Gandhism has played its part. It cannot carry us further and hence we must march and be guided by the ideology of socialism.'[64] Narayan was one of the CSP leaders, with Asok Mehta, A. Patwardhan, Yusuf Meherally and M. R. Masani. They had no single or clear ideology, but drew variously on a *melange* of Marxism, European socialism, and British Labour Party ideals, leavened with the experience of civil disobedience. Nehru was sympathetic to their hopes and fears, but too sensitively pragmatic to the particular conditions of Indian society and conscious that India's overriding priority must be unity in face of the *raj* to join them. The CSP challenge to the Congress establishment was couched in fierce propaganda; but this seldom succeeded in achieving anything except annoyance and verbal disruption. But the Socialists also attempted to infiltrate provincial Congress organizations; and to build up power based outside the Congress to put pressure on it, through their alliance with states' politicians and particularly their mobilization of provincial peasant groups in Kisan Sabhas.[65] In this they had considerable success, though they achieved little in the way of all-India organization either among peasants or industrial workers.

In the face of such divisions, the all-India leadership adopted various tactics to keep Congress as united and inclusive as possible. Shelving or postponing awkward issues (as over the Communal Award or office acceptance) and arranging face-saving compromises had long been standard practice. Many ambiguities and diversities of opinion were tolerated, and on a wide range of organizational matters, such as candidate selection, the central leadership deliberately delegated power to provincial and local leaders, and if controversy erupted often refused to be formally involved. More rarely the 'High Command' was prepared to battle for the enforcement of its priorities when fundamental leadership or policy questions were at stake. CP's Congress Chief Minister, N. B. Khare, was disciplined when as a local faction leader he attempted to reconstruct his ministry to the detriment of Congress unity and credibility in the province. The Working Committee forced Khare to resign as Chief Minister and then expelled him from Congress: but only after central leaders had tried to smooth matters over within the local Congress. The Socialist challenge to the established leadership and its pragmatically inclusive ideology was equally firmly dealt with—by resolutions at the 1938 Haripura session preventing Congressmen building up extra-mural power bases in Kisan Sabhas and states' organizations; and supremely in 1939 by the Working Committee's refusal to co-operate with Bose when he was elected President of Congress for a second term in a deliberate bid to challenge the existing 'High Command' and to alter the basic stance of Congress towards the constitution.[66]

The intricacies of internal Congress politics consumed the time and energies of many Congressmen; so, too, can they divert the historian. Their significance lies partly in the training they gave participants in a new political professionalism; and their contribution to a fund of experience of political management, the arts and crafts of opposition, of compromise and of conciliation. This in turn helped the stable functioning of India's political system after independence. More importantly the strains, compromises, and crises of the late 1930s indicated the nature of Congress. As a political environment rather than an exclusive party there was a constant and necessary interplay between centre and periphery, between all-India priorities and local needs. The 'High Command' and the local leaders needed each other, because each needed the resources and manpower pertaining to the other's political level if the whole was to function. The irretrievable breakdown of such a relationship of mutual need was a prospect few would countenance; because it would have meant the collapse of the framework which had become central to most Hindus conscious of the implications of the constitutional experiment and its potential for the Congress acquisition of legitimacy as government.

However, in one crucial respect—in its relations with Indian Muslims—Congress failed to acquire legitimacy either as the spokesman for the nation or as an alternative *raj*. Its organizational framework did not become a natural environment for most Muslim political enterprise. The later 1930s saw a serious deterioration in Congress–Muslim relations, at the level of politicians and their organizations. In these years there was the beginning of a shift in the self-perception and political identification of many Muslims outside the small circle of political activists. Yet it is easy to exaggerate this process in the knowledge of the country's later partition on communal lines, and tempting, but erroneous, to assume a permanent breakdown in political co-operation and the development of a mass Muslim sense of national identity based on Islam. At the outbreak of war Muslims were as hostile to continuing British rule as were Hindus; and there was still potential for cross-communal co-operation in politics and the persistence of a common sense of Indian nationhood. But the evidence of a deepening crisis of nationhood within British India is clear.

The 1937 elections showed that despite its claims Congress did not speak for India's Muslims. 482 seats in the provincial legislative assemblies were reserved for Muslims. Congress could not field enough Muslims to contest all these, and fought only 58, winning 26, i.e. 5.4 per cent of all Muslim seats, and 44.8 per cent of those it contested. Most of its successes were in the North-West Frontier—a curious case where Congress popularity went back to civil disobedience and its alliance with the Pathan movement; with a few in Madras and Bihar. No Muslim was returned on the Congress ticket for Muslim constituencies in Bengal, Sind, and Punjab, the main Muslim majority areas, in UP, where Muslims were an influential minority, or in Assam, Bombay, CP, and Orissa. As a Madras newspaper noted, the ballot box indicated that a rift between Hindus and Muslims was deepening and many Muslims now believed that Congress was 'a predominantly Hindu party out to serve the Hindu community'.[67] Consequent on the elections Congress had no part in the governments formed in the Muslim majority provinces. In Bengal a Muslim-dominated coalition took office under Fazl-ul-Haq; and in the next two years the different Muslim groups worked increasingly together. Punjab was governed by the National Unionist Party, in which Congressmen did not participate; and Sind was under a shifting series of Muslim-dominated coalitions.

Between the elections and the outbreak of war the rift between the politicians of both communities widened, feeding on the record of the Congress governments and Muslims' fears for their future. The criticism and accusations hurled by each group further poisoned communal relations in widening circles, whatever the factual foundations of the allegations. 'Myth' developed, in this case Congress persecution of Muslims; and became in its own right part of the political context—both political fact and force. The official Congress line was uniformly conciliatory. It claimed to represent the whole Indian nation, but took care to present itself as the protector of minority interests. In October 1937 the Working Committee stated:

The Congress has solemnly and repeatedly declared its policy in regard to the rights of the minorities in India and has stated that it considers it its duty to protect these rights and ensure the widest possible scope for the development of these minorities and their participation in the fullest measure in the political, economic and cultural life of the nation. The objective of the Congress is an independent and united India where no class or group or majority or minority may exploit another to its own advantage and where all the elements in the nation may co-operate for the common good and the advancement of the people of India.[68]

Yet the Muslim League under M. A. Jinnah increasingly stood forward to dispute the Congress claim. At its 1937 session Jinnah warned that Hindus were already showing that independent India would be for the Hindus; and at the 1938 session he accused Congress of killing any hope of a communal settlement, or even of wanting one—except one whose terms it could dictate. He dismissed the Nationalist Muslims in Congress as misled or moved by ulterior motives, and thundered, 'the Congress leaders may cry as much as they like that Congress is a national body. But I say it is not true. The Congress is nothing but a Hindu body.' Jinnah and Nehru also carried on an acrimonious debate in speeches and correspondence in which Nehru claimed that the only two significant parties in contemporary politics were Congress and the *raj*, representing nationalism and imperialism; while Jinnah argued that Muslim India was a vital and distinct element in the situation which Congress did not represent. In April 1938 he wrote ominously that if Congress would not recognize the Muslim League 'on a footing of complete equality' and negotiate a Hindu–Muslim settlement, then the League would have to depend upon its 'inherent strength' to convince Congress that it must deal with it.[69]

Communal antagonism was also fuelled by Muslim publications reporting on their treatment by Congress provincial governments. These alleged under-representation of minorities in public appointments, unfair treatment of Muslims by Congress Ministers, and deliberate exaltation of Hindu culture, values, and the Hindi language at the expense of Muslim culture

and Urdu. (The most important of these inventories of communal com-
plaint were the 1938 *Report of the Inquiry Committee appointed by the
Council of the All-India Muslim League to inquire into Muslim Grievances
in Congress Provinces*, which was produced under the chairmanship of the
Raja of Pirpur and took his name; and the 1939 indictment, popularly
known by the name of its draughtsman, S. M. Shareef, *Report of the Enquiry Committee appointed by the Working Committee of the Bihar Provincial Muslim League to enquire into some grievances of Muslims in Bihar*.) If
further evidence was needed of Congress's inability to convince Muslims of
its legitimacy as a future national *raj*, and of Muslim politicians' determination to underline this in the minds and emotions of ordinary Muslims, it
came when the Congress Ministries resigned in 1939. Then Jinnah exhorted
Muslims to celebrate 2 December as a day of deliverance from the tyranny,
oppression, and injustice of Congress rule.

Various attempts have been made to locate single and simple causes for
the widening communal gulf. Often such monocausal theories were highly
emotive, not least because in the prelude to and aftermath of partition
Pakistani and Indian politicians and historians needed to generate emotions
of loyalty and solidarity to the two new nations. Understandably Muslims
dedicated to the idea of Muslim separatism have argued that communal
discord and political division were the inevitable result of deepening Muslim awareness of their essential nationhood, based on religion, language,
and culture. Some orthodox Hindus argued similarly from a diametrically
opposite concept of nationhood, bewailing what they saw as the vivisection
of the holy motherland, blaming the more secular Congress leadership for
giving way to illegitimate Muslim claims which had no place for consideration in 'Hindustan'—the land of the Hindus. More Congressmen were
disposed to blame the British for fostering Muslim separatism in a deliberate policy of 'Divide and Rule'. Those like Nehru who looked also at
economic and social causes judged the Muslim League to be the implement
of a 'reactionary' class of landholders determined to maintain their power
in a changing world; and they underplayed the role of religion in the
deepening communal divide, suggesting that the true solution to the problem was the end of a divisive colonialism and a more egalitarian social and
economic policy for independent India. Yet others attempting to be less
emotive and partisan have scrutinized the politics of the 1930s and 1940s,
assessing the policies of Congress and the attitudes of the major leaders, in
the hope of locating some point of breakdown in communal co-operation,
of 'no-return' beyond which the Hindus and Muslims were set on the paths
of inevitable division. (The failure of Congress to form coalition governments with Muslim League politicians in 1937 is a popular candidate for
such a role.)

In all these theories there is some element of truth; though each taken singly is woefully inadequate as an explanation of the complexities of Muslim responses to Congress power and claims. The heart of the problem was the novel experiment of devolving power on an increasingly democratic basis in a plural society where economic and political development had been uneven for many decades. Counting heads to obtain political opinions and consensus had worked in the comparatively homogeneous society to which the British were accustomed and in which they had developed their democratic political theory and practice. It had worked in the white colonies which were their only 'blue print' for their experiment in India—provided that the most obviously different and underdeveloped segments of the population were excluded from the political nation, as in the case of South Africa's non-white peoples. In India it raised an increasingly sharp dilemma for any group which was a permanent minority. Indian Muslims in the 1930s had a clear sense of themselves as a cluster of distinctive provincial groups; and British plans to devolve power had forced them to cooperate across provincial boundaries to contrive all-India plans for the protection of their separate identity. It had often proved hard for Muslims to agree on a continental package because their provincial positions were so different. Now the operation of the 1935 Act forced them to reconsider the most effective mechanisms for their protection as an all-India minority. It was only in that process of reconsideration that they came to a sense of identity as a separate nation rather than as a minority in need of special security.

At the Muslim League session in the winter of 1938 it became evident that the League no longer believed that provincial autonomy as it was operating was an adequate safeguard for Muslim interests. It resolved to authorize its Working Committee to take direct action against the provincial constitution when it considered it necessary. Simultaneously Muslims were withdrawing their support for the federal provisions of the 1935 Act, deeply fearful that Congress on its upsurge of strength would dominate the centre and transform it into a device for Hindu *raj*. All earlier Muslim negotiations had been based on the assumption that the federal centre would be a safeguard for Muslims against that precise eventuality. At the Sind Provincial Muslim League Conference in October 1938 there was talk of two separate federations, one Muslim and one not. The session eventually passed a resolution merely asking the All-India Muslim League 'to review and revise the entire conception of what should be the suitable constitution for India which will secure honourable and legitimate status to them', but the 'them' referred to were, significantly, the Hindus and Muslims, who were called two nations earlier in the resolution. By mid-1939 Zetland, the Secretary of State, was very doubtful whether Muslims would consent to work the federal part of the act.[70]

The rapid disillusionment of Muslims with the provincial and federal aspects of the constitutional experiment clearly requires explanation in terms of the Muslim political arena. Unfortunately we know much less about the details of Muslim politics, political organizations, and the relationships between its leaders and the rank-and-file than we do about Congress. Some elements in the Muslims' perception of their situation are clear, none the less. The dramatic Congress triumphs in the 1937 elections shook Muslims, particularly where they were minorities. They rapidly came to feel that they were victims of Congress 'totalitarianism'. Even though many of their allegations against Congress were ill-founded, Congress certainly claimed a special national status as spokesman for India's diverse peoples. Its claims were furthered in practice by its continental organization and campaign of mass contact, aimed particularly at Muslims after it had been proven by the elections that Congress could not rally a Muslim vote. Not only did Muslim politicians feel that Congress, and more specifically its Nationalist Muslims, were trying to undercut their political base. In some provinces, notably UP, they felt they were squeezed out of a fair share of power by the Congress refusal to construct coalition ministries including League members. Almost certainly little formal negotiation had prepared the way for such coalitions but when the informal offers of co-operation in government came to nothing the breakdown became in its turn a potent part of the political myth that Congress was using its provincial power to exclude Muslims from influence.[71] Other areas of friction were the 'Hindu' aspects of Congress nationalism—the reverence given to Gandhi, the use of a famous Hindu song, *Bande Mataram*, as an unofficial national anthem, and the Basic Education scheme launched by Congress governments which Muslims dubbed as Hindu in tone.

Whatever official Congress policy was towards Muslims a further factor dividing it from Muslims was the leadership's inability to control Congressmen at the level of village and town. Long-standing communal antagonisms were given a new dimension as new avenues of power were opened up. The unsophisticated 'new' Congressmen of the late 1930s were more likely to be aggressively Hindu than leaders at the higher levels of Congress with longer experience of the continental pressures for cross-communal co-operation. In Bihar, for example, Congressmen at District Committee level ignored a provincial Congress decision that Muslims should receive an adequate number of Congress tickets in local board elections. District leaders needed their patronage too much for their own ends to obey higher orders reflective of a broader view of Congress's role. The Governor of UP noted how at local level the growing enthusiasm for Congress *raj* melted easily into a notion of Hindu *raj*, which Muslims gravely resented. Some well educated UP Muslims were deeply disturbed by the new type of Congressman who flocked into the Legislative Assembly and seemed to take over provincial politics. As one remembered decades later, 'I felt extremely uncomfortable.

I could not spot anyone dressed like me, the language spoken around me was not the Urdu which I thought was the language of Lucknow, the cultural metropolis of Uttar Pradesh, and there seemed to be no one within sight worth talking to. I left the assembly building with a feeling of mingled panic and disgust.'[72] In such an atmosphere of rising suspicion it was little wonder that many Muslims came to feel that provincial autonomy and federation could not protect their position against Congress.

Although Congress failed to gain legitimacy in Muslim eyes as the nation's spokesman and potential *raj*, no single Muslim counter-focus existed. There was no ideology, organization or leadership which could weld Muslims into a continental unity. Muslim politics were as disintegrated as they had been for decades, not only between provinces but even within provinces. The All-India Muslim Conference which had served as a focus for Muslim aspirations and plans during the period of constitutional discussions wound itself up before the 1937 elections; and provincial Muslim groups managed the elections without an all-India discipline and programme, despite the last-minute attempts of Jinnah and the Muslim League to create some continental Muslim coherence in the campaign. Local groups were too jealous of their freedom and identity to submit to any but the loosest central co-ordination. The League won 60 per cent of the seats it contested, but only 22.6 per cent of the total seats reserved for Muslims (109/482), receiving just under 5 per cent of the Muslim vote. It did best in Bengal, Bombay, and UP: but in no way could it claim to represent all India's Muslims.

However, two developments in the late 1930s began to change this situation. An organization and a slogan emerged which were potentially integrative forces in Muslim politics—the Muslim League and the idea of Pakistan ('Land of the Pure') as a separate homeland for a nation identified with India's Muslims. Jinnah was the leader behind the revival of the All-India Muslim League, returning to India for this purpose in 1935 after 'retiring' in London in disillusion at the development of Indian politics and communal relations. His return from self-imposed exile later in life and his electrifying effect on Muslim politics bore an ironic resemblance to Gandhi's impact on Congress when he returned as a middle-aged stranger from South Africa. There the likeness ended; for Jinnah was the last person one could have predicted as a 'popular' leader—an aloof, elitist figure with little personal warmth; unlike the Mahatma's radiating concern for the poor and under-privileged, and outgoing personality which so often compelled affection as well as respect.

On his return Jinnah was ill-pleased with the League: it was poor, ill-organized and in his own estimation composed 'mostly of big landlords, title-holders and selfish people who looked to their class and personal interests more than to communal and national interests and who had always been ready to sacrifice them to suit British policies.'[73] His failure to make it a focus for Muslim politics in the 1937 elections and the increasing power of Congress meant that by 1937 all his previous strategies over twenty years to protect Muslim interests and weld them as a secure minority into an Indian nation which could take power from its imperial rulers lay in ruins. In Muslim majority provinces Muslims were divided—as in faction-ridden Sind, for example—and thus weakened in any attempt to force Congress to deal with them as one significant political force. In areas where Muslims were a minority Congress had swept to power. Federation and provincial autonomy with separate electorates, which had seemed adequate safeguards, now looked fragile barriers against Congress dominance. In response to this new situation Jinnah argued that the League must now build itself up as an organization representing Muslims of all provinces and social groups, extending itself geographically and socially so that its inherent strength would force Congress to listen to its views. Only recognition of each other's strength would enable understanding between the two communities on a basis of equality.

The build-up of the League in the late 1930s has not yet been documented with the detail available on the Congress expansion of the later 1930s. It seems to have begun in earnest after the League session in October 1937. Membership fees were drastically reduced (as Congress's had been in 1934), and plans were laid to reshape its provincial and district branches, and to create a council of over 450 members elected by provincial branches. Figures indicating the implementation of these plans and of recruitment are sketchy; but by the end of 1937 over 170 new branches had been established. Madras claimed at the end of 1938 to have 43,920 members; by September 1938 CP had enrolled 23,000; and in 1939 UP districts were each thought by a touring League delegation to have 8–10,000 members. The growth of Muslim League strength in UP was dramatic. But strength in Muslim minority provinces could not give the League the status Jinnah envisaged. So, as significant in the emergence of the League as a focus for Indian politics, was the decision of Muslim political leaders in the Muslim majority areas of Punjab and Bengal to align with the League on all-India questions, though they retained considerable autonomy on provincial matters as a *quid pro quo*; and relations between the two provincial leaders and Jinnah were often acrimonious. At this stage there seems to have been little popular support for the League or grass-roots organization of it in the Muslim majority areas—a fact which weakened Jinnah's hand in dealing with the provincial Muslim leaders.[74]

The other political development which had enormous potential as an integrative force among Muslims was the emerging idea of a separate homeland for a separate Muslim nation.[75] The poet, Iqbal, presiding over the League's 1930 session, had spoken of consolidating the north western

Muslim parts of British India as the final destiny of Indian Muslims from that area. He almost certainly envisaged such a Muslim unit as part of an all-India federation. A group of Indian Muslim students in England contemplated a true partition however; circulating a pamphlet in 1933 which called for Pakistan for the Muslims of north and west India, claiming that they were a distinct nation with a common cultural heritage and a right to this territory by virtue of long residence there. Such ideas found little support among Muslims either at a popular level or among politicians; not least because of the Muslim minorities who would be left in other parts of India, and because the Bengal Muslim majority seemed to have no place in such a venture. Yet by later 1938, as the Sind League Conference had shown, there was a distinct shift in the thinking of some Muslims towards identifying with their co-religionists as a distinct nation. The idea of a specifically Muslim federation as the solution to the threats generated by the constitutional experiment also seemed more attractive. Should this re-shaping of identity and appropriate political and territorial safeguards be refined by Muslim leaders and then unleashed as a stark cry for an Islamic nation's homeland, the response of the *ulema* and ordinary Muslims was unpredictable. Like the cry of 'Islam in danger' which had accompanied the Khilafat agitation twenty years before it might well evoke an emotional and uncontrollable popular outcry. The appeal of the idea and slogan of Pakistan and the organization of the League were by 1939 still limited as actual *focuses* of a new Muslim political unity: but their emergence underlined the fact that the development of multiple political identities in India in the context of rapid political change challenged the very idea of Indian nationhood.

In many conventional histories of twentieth-century India the 1930s seem less important than the climactic years of the Second World War and its aftermath. Yet in the making of India into the first Asian democracy the 1930s were arguably more important. They were the years when many of the forces shaping the India of the later twentieth century were generated. Moreover, despite the trappings of imperial authority the penultimate decade of the British *raj* wrought a weakening and withdrawal of resources. The weakening occurred at the level of Britain's basic interests in India, her ability to protect them, and of the legitimacy recognized in the *raj* by the mass of its subjects. Yet though the imperial regime appeared less the natural government endowed with *izzat*, prestige, no obvious alternative was accepted by all Indians. The vague and pragmatic nationalism of earlier decades, which had been an element in the complex patterns of political change and had helped to weld diverse groups and regions together at certain stages, now proved inadequate, once the replacement of the British *raj* became a real possibility. A crisis deepened on the subcontinent equal to that faced by imperialists in the ebb-tide of power: what constituted nationhood in India and what was the rightful form of government for any emergent nation? The crisis of nationhood was most clearly demonstrated in the 'high politics' of the decade, in relations between the Congress, the princes and the diverse Muslim groups. It was also apparent in the wide gulf between the politics of self-proclaimed 'nationalists' in Congress, and the interests of the underprivileged in town and countryside whom the former so often ignored or on occasion attempted to silence. In the political conflicts generated among Indians and in the linkages left unmade the lineaments of future identities and power became clearer, and the questions in need of resolution starker. The stage was being set and the cast assembled for the denouement of the 1940s. Part of that preparation in the 1930s was the appearance of the human sinews and institutional mechanisms of power in the new Indian state. The influx of influential rural men into Congress during the constitutional experiment showed who would be key figures in the new India. They already found in the 'imported' political institutions of successive constitutional reforms a vital arena for the pursuit of their political interests: in the 1930s a whole new political system was gaining key collaborators. It was of incalculable importance to India's future as a democracy that the new political institutions put down such strong social roots and that politics became increasingly 'integrated'. People who might before have operated in different styles at different levels now chose to articulate their political awareness in this idiom, and to pursue their political interests through its institutions. The 1930s brought not just the spread of democratic practice and ideas, but also more radical consideration of the desirable nature of a future Indian society. Before the appearance of the CSP such radical pondering on the distribution of power and inter-group relationships had tended to be limited to the Gandhians and a few well-read, well-travelled young idealists such as Nehru. However limited the socialism of the later 1930s, however often a mask for factional conflict rather than a true commitment to social change, commitment to the refashioning of India's economy and society on a more egalitarian and secular basis became part of the content and language of politics. Congress and the League both couched their election manifestos in 'progressive' tones; the need to plan and engineer a new society became a widely-held political assumption. So another significant element of the political culture of modern India emerged from the decade in which the legitimacy of imperial rule had been challenged, as had the shape of any successor nation.

CHAPTER VI

India in the 1940s: A Great Divide?

Indian public life in the 1940s was dominated by the Second World War, which affected the subcontinent far more closely and deeply than that of 1914–18, and by the escalation of communal hostilities which cost thousands of lives and resulted in the country's partition when the British withdrew in August 1947. Obviously a case can be made out that the decade was a great dividing line in the Indian experience, and that 1947 marked the end of an era. That year saw the end of the *raj* and the coming of the political independence India's politicians had demanded for over half a century. This had major domestic consequences, but also far-reaching international effects. It heralded the obvious decline of British world influence and the contraction of the British empire, particularly in Africa where colonies lost much of their significance once they were no longer needed as guarantees of the routes to India. India's independence was also a powerful symbol and a practical example to other colonial nationalist movements in the empires of various European nations. 1947 also seems at first sight to be an obvious dividing-line because of the subcontinent's partition into India and a curious two-winged Pakistan in the north-western and north-eastern parts of the former empire; and because of the demolition of the princely order which was older than the *raj* itself and had been so cosseted by the British in their need for allies. Undoubtedly, too, 1947 was a symbol of a brave new world for some Indians. Gandhi was burdened with despair at the shattering of his vision for a new India; but Nehru's famous speech at independence was passionately hopeful, claiming the end had come of 'a period of ill fortune' and that India was about to rediscover her true self.

Long years ago we made a tryst with destiny, and now the time comes when we shall redeem out pledge. . . . At the stroke of the midnight hour, when the world sleeps, India will awake to life and freedom. A moment comes, which comes but rarely in history, when we step out from the old to the new, when an age ends, and when the soul of a nation, long suppressed, finds utterance. It is fitting that at this solemn moment we take the pledge of dedication to the service of India and her people and to the still larger cause of humanity.[1]

Yet this very speech was made at midnight because independence had to occur on an auspicious day for Hindus, and the British had not considered

317

this when they fixed their departure date—a symbol of continuities in Indian life, despite the decade's political upheavals! It can be argued powerfully that there was really far more continuity than change in the 1940s. 1947 is more important to the historian searching for tidy demarcations than a deeply critical point of division in the Indian experience—not just in the realm of traditions, ideas, life-styles and the land's basic economic and social structures and problems, but in government and politics, too. Even the apparently dramatic changes of the 1940s were often the culmination of long-term trends, though some of them were intensified by the war's impact. (The end of the *raj* itself was hardly unexpected, though the actual British exit was more precipitate than anyone could have imagined even six months before it occurred.) Therefore it is more accurate to describe the 1940s as a significant middle passage in a long saga of a people's experience. Consequently this chapter focuses on the continuities as much as the changes, as both were vital in making India into an Asian democracy, and in generating the tensions and contradictions which were to beset its consolidation and operation. This chapter is therefore thematic, not chronological: nor does it give a detailed account of the abortive offers and negotiations which preceded independence, because these seem less important in introducing the real forces making modern India than longer-term trends. For the reader's convenience, a chronological appendix at the end of the chapter sets out the main moves in the tortuous politics of 1939–47 in the context of major changes in British politics and the war situation which impinged on Indian affairs.[2]

The most obvious change on the subcontinent was the end of the British *raj*—the formal transfer of ultimate authority from the British Parliament to an Indian legislature, and the departure of British troops and the majority of Britons in the civilian services. Why did the British choose to resolve their imperial crisis by total exit rather than by techniques similar to those they had used since the Great War? The impact of the Second World War on Britain and on India was obviously crucial in determining the timing of their departure, and in making it essential to solve the imperial crisis— outstanding from the late 1930s—in months rather than years after the war. But the end of formal *raj* can only be understood in relation to the long-term character of the empire. Its precise nature and strength at any particular time was always the end-product of a balance between the basic British interests at stake in India, and the cheapest, most ideologically acceptable methods they could contrive to secure those interests. For nearly two centuries the Indian empire had rested on a fine balance of actual force, whether deployed or in reserve, the attraction of allies within India, and the creation of a public image of prestige and legitimacy in the eyes of its subjects, so that the majority of them acquiesced in its presence as an unquestioned if remote authority in their lives. The degree of force shifted a times, as did the people on whom the British relied as active friends: the interests at stake also changed over time. But an equilibrium was maintained. However, by 1947 the balance of interests and viable modes of control had disintegrated, and the British had no option but to go.

Changing British stakes in India were a significant aspect of this new plunge into disequilibrium. In the last hundred years they had included various kinds of economic profit, expatriates' civil and military careers, and the subcontinent's crucial position in imperial defence. These interests were altering significantly in the decade before the 1939–45 war. (See above, pp. 262–4.) During the Second World War the erosion of British interests in India was dramatically halted. She became a vital source of men, money, and war materials; and a major base for operations in the Middle East and against the invading Japanese in South-East Asia. The army increased in size from 205,058 in October 1939 to 2,251,050 in July 1945. Defence expenditure ran at its highest in 1944–5, when the grand total was Rs. 896.16 crores; over half of which was actually chargeable to India. Between 1941 and 1946 India provided £286.5 million worth of materials for the war, mainly textiles, clothing, and ordnance.[3]

However when the emergency of world war ended the longer-term trends reasserted themselves. Demobilization, a pervading desire to get 'home' after the war, and the contraction of the ICS meant that fewer Britons looked on India as a place for a career. But more significantly, for economic and political reasons Britain could even less than in the 1930s assume that India's economy would balance metropolitan trading books with other parts of the world, or provide a protected market for British goods. Tariff policy had been controlled in India and made subject to the pressures of Indian political opinion before the war. This could not be reversed a decade later; and furthermore, under the terms of the Cripps Offer of 1942 (see below, pp. 327–8) Britain had promised independence after the war. It seemed that the remaining, and still significant, trading and investment connections between the two countries could best be maintained through friendship between equal nations. Some British business firms were selling out to Indian buyers. Many of the successful 'new' British entrepreneurs needed as the context for their operations an administration set on planning and post-war reconstruction: they required no imperial protection and patronage—unlike older, expatriate enterprises. At the level of international exchange transactions India's relationship with Britain had been transformed by her expenditure in the war. It was no longer for Britain a question of ensuring that India paid her debts in sterling. She had now piled up sterling balances in London, and by 1946 Britain owed India more than £1,300 million. Britain's last significant stake in India was imperial defence. Before the war it had become clear that India could no longer be forced to contribute anything more than a strictly limited and agreed amount; and once global conflict ended Britain, as India's debtor, faced the fact that it would be more prudent and effective to base future imperial defence on treaties with a friendly independent state or on Commonwealth co-operation. At that stage the worst thing for British defence interests would be a subcontinent in turmoil, fighting an imperial regime or engaged in internecine conflicts. Rarely did the British openly discuss what India meant to them. But in times of crisis the role of the subcontinent was articulated. Reflecting on the prospects for British interests in 1946, Wavell sent a note to London which concluded that, provided power could be transferred in an orderly manner to a friendly and united India, and arrangements could be made for defence, 'The general conclusion is that on the whole Great Britain should not lose, but on the contrary, may gain in prestige and even in power, by handing over to Indians'; while Britain ought to profit naturally because of her established links with the subcontinent from any expansion in Indian trade and industry.[4] After the war long-term changes in British interests, combined with the Cripps Offer, dictated that a profitable and peaceful connection with India could best be maintained by friendship and treaties with an independent member of the Commonwealth.

Yet this was not the whole picture—as the existence of the Cripps Offer indicated. The situation was more complex than a simple calculation of the cost effectiveness, in maintaining current stakes, of friendship as against control of a reluctant empire. By 1946 it was manifest that the old methods of formal empire were actually unworkable. Before inquiring into the final decay of those older methods of imperial control it must be underlined that the British were never pushed physically out of India by the strength of a mass, nationalist movement: though such claims have been made for Gandhi's final, most famous but most 'un-Gandhian' all-India campaign, the 1942 'Quit India movement'. The Congress leadership decided to embark on 'Quit India' after their rejection of the Cripps Offer earlier that year, not because they felt the country was on the brink of mass revolution or readiness for non-violent resistance to the *raj*, nor because they were assured of sufficiently widespread support to force the British to leave. The prospect of another major conflict with the *raj* was not in fact appealing to many of them. Rather it was a policy which achieved a compromise within the Congress leadership and enabled them to deal as a united body with the interlocking questions which divided them—non-violence as a principle, the possibility of a Japanese invasion if the British remained in India, whether in the *raj*'s hour of crisis to assist the opponents of its imperialism who were also opposed to so much of what the Congress itself stood for, and if not, how to maintain a nationalist movement and a national demand in relation to a *raj* which refused to offer immediate power in such crucial areas as defence to Indians, such was its preoccupation with winning the war.[5]

When the AICC launched the movement in August control of it slipped out of the hands of the Congress leadership far more rapidly than in 1920–1 or 1930–1, because the leaders were promptly jailed and the Congress organization disrupted by swift government reprisals. So the 'Quit India movement' became the enterprise of lower-level leaders and those who, as in Bihar, had been pushed out of power in Congress because of their factional loyalties, left-wing leanings and connections with economic groups such as the Kisans whose demands embarrassed the main leadership. Students also played prominent parts in organizing resistance, particularly in towns. While in some areas there was substantial rural upheaval. There was little co-ordination of the movement (and considerable controversy about the extent to which it had been pre-planned). Each local leadership or group acted on its own authority, issuing its own instructions, forced to work underground and in isolation by government suppression. Not surprisingly the result was often violent, extremely patchy and followed no over-all plan. But its main manifestations were assaults on obvious aspects of and key links in the *raj*'s hold over India, particularly government property and communications. Police stations and post offices, railway stations, track, and rolling-stock were prime targets. (By the end of 1943 332 stations and 945 post offices had been destroyed or severely damaged, and it was virtually impossible to estimate damage to track.) From the *raj*'s point of view this was the worst rebellion it had encountered since 1857, and one which it tried to conceal for reasons of military security: but the worst was over in weeks. The storm-centres had been Bihar, eastern UP, and Bombay. At its height breakdown in communications followed by widespread looting led to local losses of government control. For brief periods whole district administrations collapsed, as in Ballia (UP), while Bengal and Assam were isolated from the rest of India by disturbances and disruption of communications in Bihar. (The Bihar administration resorted to Tiger Moths of the Bihar Flying Club to keep communications open with one of its districts!) [See Table A for detailed evidence of the nature and regional variations of the movement.][6]

Yet very rapidly the British were able to bring 'Quit India' under control. Not only had they a well-prepared plan for immediate incarceration of the Congress leadership and a pre-emptive stike against Congress. Now under pressure of war and with an expanded army on the spot they had both the motivation and the man-power to smash the movement hard, and fast, in a way they could not have contemplated in 1920 or 1930. 'Quit India' was pathetically like a flotilla of rafts colliding with a battleship. Well over fifty battalions of troops were deployed in the early suppression of the movement, and by the end of 1943 troops had fired sixty-eight times inflicting

Table A. *Evidence of the regional incidence of the 'Quit India movement'*

Category	Madras	Bombay	Bengal	United Provinces	Punjab
Government servants (excluding those of the central governments)					
Police					
Number of occasions on which police fired	21	226	63	116	1
Number of casualties inflicted, fatal	39	112	87	207	—
Number of casualties inflicted, non-fatal	86	406	149	458	—
Number of casualties suffered, fatal	—	6	5	16	—
Number of casualties suffered, non-fatal	91	563	180	333	—
Number of defections from police	1	6	6--	2	—
Other government servants					
Number of attacks on other government servants, fatal	—	1	—	3	—
Number of attacks on other government servants, non-fatal	19	50	14	141	—
Number of defections from other government services	—	3	—	9	—
Damage to property (excluding central government property)					
Number of police stations or outposts etc. destroyed or severely damaged	5	46	4	42	—
Number of other government buildings destroyed or severely damaged	50	318	95	45	2
Number of public buildings other than government buildings, e.g., municipal property, schools, hospitals, etc., destroyed or severely damaged	57	152	58	37	4
Number of important private buildings destroyed or severely damaged	11	38	29	3	5
Estimated loss to government	Rs. 225192	945410	171876	363366	1000
Estimated loss to other parties	Rs. 916025	563581	55391	102778	105000
Cases of sabotage					
Number of bomb explosions	17	447	51	60	—
Number of bombs or explosives discovered without damage	35	738	106	157	1
Number of cases of sabotage to roads	32	78	57	84	—
Number of cases in which collective fines imposed	41	73	20	7	—
Amount of collective fines imposed	Rs. 1034359	817950	605503	3176973	—
Number of sentences of whipping inficted	295	17	2	1252	—
Number of arrests made	5859	24416	4818	16796	2501
Number of local authorities superseded under Defence Rule 38B or otherwise	27	19	11	7	—

Source: Home Political File 3/52/43(1); quoted in Hutchins, *India's Revolution*, pp. 230–1.

Bihar	Central Provinces	Assam	North-West Frontier Province	Orissa	Sindh	Delhi	Coorg	Total
96	42	4	1	9	—	22	—	601
166	45	15	3	69	—	20	—	763
508	181	19	13	111	—	10	—	1941
26	8	—	—	1	1	—	—	63
342	256	17	52	26	90	62	—	2012
205	2	—	—	—	—	—	—	216
4	2	—	—	—	—	—	—	10
87	39	—	—	13	—	1	—	364
4	—	—	5	—	—	—	1	22
72	29	4	—	5	—	1	—	208
103	41	64	1	25	—	4	1	749
92	45	66	—	8	2	4	—	525
119	2	61	—	2	1	2	—	273
354720	424840	284582	200	46459	1904	15456	120	2735125
495231	167270	194847	—	33598	2932	370376	245	3007274
8	10	10	1	—	50	—	10	664
218	18	9	1	—	13	11	12	1319
169	7	43	—	4	—	—	—	474
16	3	1	—	—	5	—	7	173
2660765	344595	339487	—	27750	—	—	—	9007382
340	282	—	—	9	—	—	—	2562
16202	8753	2707	2339	2806	3689	90	860	91836
3	35	—	—	5	—	1	—	108

nearly 300 fatal and over 200 non-fatal casualties. Despite temporary losses of control the over-all security of the *raj* was never endangered by the movement. After its destruction the British proved capable of putting Indian politics 'on ice' until the end of the war, not least by the device of locking up the major Congress leaders, and leaving at liberty only those politicians, including 'Moderates' and Muslims, who were disposed to collaborate in the wartime administration or to refrain from disrupting it. Within a year of the August eruptions the Secretary of State could write, 'it looks as if India had never been so quiet politically as it is at this moment.' Not surprisingly this demonstration of imperial power irked a wide range of the politically aware, including those who would never have countenanced or participated in the actions taken in the name of 'Quit India', though they were staunch supporters of eventual Indian independence. One southern politician who had been in Liberal and Congress politics for years said this to the new Viceroy's face in 1944. Wavell reported to London his informant's view that 'the present regime could carry on quite comfortably till the end of the war . . . it was this knowledge and the fear that we should do so which was making the intellectuals so bitter.'[7] Yet 'Quit India' was a lesson the British could not forget: for it demonstrated the frailty of their local administrative structures and warned them of the possible strength of any future Congress-led movement which was well co-ordinated, particularly if it occurred after the war when the *raj* was no longer so well equipped psychologically or materially for ruthless suppression.

Although neither satyagraha nor violent upheaval pushed the British into the Indian Ocean there accumulated during the 1940s indisputable evidence of the weakening of the network of collaboration on which the British had relied for imperial stability and the routine functioning of their administration. Two major strands in the network had been the services, and the politicians who since 1919 had been increasingly incorporated into the formal support structure of the *raj* and by 1939 were far more significant than the great landlords who half a century earlier had been the most valued of British buttresses. Both strands in the network were by 1946 either broken or badly stretched.

The army and police were the *raj*'s main instruments of coercion, and they had always been predominantly manned, though not officered, by Indians. During the war there was no lack of recruits for either service; and very few disaffections even during 'Quit India'. [See Table A. The 'Indian National Army', those Indian soldiers who defected to the Japanese, was a special case. Their disaffection occurred not in India but when they were captured by the Japanese. Many prisoners remained loyal to the British despite pressure and hardship.] The chronic weakness of the police in some areas had long been a source of concern to government. This problem remained unsolved and war exacerbated it because considerable numbers resigned to join the army. Moreover in some places, notably Bihar, there were ominous signs that this combined with declining morale was leading to a breakdown in the *raj*'s intelligence network. The Governor of Bihar admitted that his province's intelligence system was probably 'badly at fault' in failing to report the possibility of severe local disturbances in 1942, and that he had 'had very poor reports of the ordinary constabulary and in some places of the armed police: their hearts are not in the job.'[8] Confused loyalties among officials and a breakdown in intelligence were notorious signs of the end-game of empire, as the Moguls has found out two centuries before.

It was after the war that the loyalty of the police and troops came to be seriously doubted or displayed. In April 1946 some of the Malabar Special Police (crack armed companies) went on strike over conditions of service and pay, though the Madras government suspected political influence at work. Four companies were disbanded and nearly 1,000 men were dismissed. Bihar also experienced a police strike in 1946. By September 1946 Wavell was reporting to London that they could not rely implicitly on the police (or other provincial services) to carry out the orders of a British government. Earlier that year there had been mutinies in the Indian navy, in which politics and service conditions were sources of discontent: again, an occurrence for which the government had practically no warning. But the real threat now to the dependability of the police and troops was not political propaganda from a Congress which acted as a counter focus and possible successor to the *raj*, but the pressure of communal strife. By the close of 1946 Wavell and his advisers believed that the army was still dependable despite escalating communal violence, but that communalism had undermined the loyalty of some of the police.[9]

But how reliable was the ICS, the 'steel-frame' of empire into which Indians had been recruited rapidly in the 1920s and 1930s? Even before the war its capacity to respond to a major crisis had worried the Viceroy. In 1943 Indian recruitment to the ICS was stopped because European recruitment had dried up as Britain mobilized her man-power in the fight for her own survival. As a result of this and secondment to other work in wartime, the ICS was badly understaffed just at the point where it was stretched to limits inconceivable before the war. The economic effects of the conflict and India's contribution to the war effort soon took their toll of the Indian economy, bringing inflation and food shortages. Government became involved in a wide range of new activities, from air-raid precautions and civil defence, to food procurement: and these burdens were laid on the ICS man over and above his ordinary and heavy work load. Late in 1943 Wavell told the Secretary of State that the Governors believed the services were stretched to breaking-point and pointed to the horror of the Bengal famine to warn what could happen when an administration proved incompetent in the face of a major disaster. In July the Governor of CP had painted a vivid picture of an administrative machine stretched beyond its limits by the demands of war; when the basic problem of food supplies consumed the energies of all administrative staff from the Deputy Commissioners downwards, and when the province's 'ICS cadre has been absorbed by the Government of India to an extent which was never dreamt of in the calculation on which the strength of that service is based.'[10]

Of longer term significance than the physical strain on the civilian services, and their spearhead, the ICS, was the fact that by 1940 there were for the first time more Indians than Europeans in the ICS (614 as opposed to 587): at the beginning of 1947 there were 510 Indians and only 429 Europeans. Indians were also by this time in very senior administrative posts. They were known to sympathize with the political aspirations of their compatriots and to want independence as strongly as any Congressman. Naturally, too, they began to wonder what their future would be and to look to Congress as the new locus of authority, despite their understandably ambivalent attitudes to it. Although the loyalty of Indian ICS men was never in doubt, their possible reaction if government decided to crush Congress rather than transfer power to India after the war was a crucial consideration in British appreciation of their options. In December 1946 Wavell told the Cabinet that Indian ICS men could not be expected to carry out 'a firm policy' unless they knew the British would be there for at least a decade afterwards to protect their interests.[11]

By 1946 the British knew their network of Indian allies in their various services was a fast-weakening support and instrument of their rule. The strains of war, the prospect of transferred power, and the communal conflict had eroded efficiency and morale, and now threatened ultimately loyalty to the *raj* itself. Wavell was in no doubt that he was not only presiding over an imperial edifice which must be dismantled or collapse. He was also head of a government whose very mechanisms for daily administration were breaking down. In September he argued that simply on administrative grounds the *raj* could not last more than 18 months; and looking back over 1946 he noted in late October, 'Our time in India is limited and our power to control events almost gone. We have only prestige and previous momentum to trade on and they will not last long.' On the last day of the year he confided to his journal, 'And while the British are still legally and morally responsible for what happens in India, we have lost nearly all power to control events; we are simply running on the momentum of our previous prestige.'[12]

The *raj* had always relied heavily on the 'informal' part of its collaborative network of support—those Indians who were not paid in hard cash to serve it but chose for a variety of reasons to give it informal support, advice, and information, and to guarantee it the backing of their own followers. For thirty years the British had responded to changes in the distribution of power and influence in Indian society and had remodelled their methods of attracting such support, particularly to enlist in new constitutional structures the growing numbers of educated and others aware of the potential of new styles of politics. Now during the early stages of the war this enterprise was severely weakened by the decision of Congress to withdraw from cooperation. Its first step was withdrawal from the provincial ministries late in 1939. But for two years thereafter at local level Congressmen continued to contest local board elections and support the political system by participation in it. Gandhi's 1940–1 civil disobedience campaign, in which individuals spoke against the war, was a holding operation, to demonstrate Congress's claim to status as national spokesman, and to mask the fact that the leadership could contrive no alternative policy and was sitting on the fence rather than split Congress apart. Individual civil disobedience barely inconvenienced the government; and the campaign began to flag early in 1941. Meantime the British were content to administer the former Congress-controlled provinces through their governors exercising their special powers, and to keep the 1935 constitution in operation in those provinces where non-Congress ministries had carried on co-operating.

The real breakdown of co-operation between Congress and government occurred early in 1942. By then the attack on Pearl Harbour and American entry into the war, followed by the fall of Singapore and Rangoon, convinced the Cabinet in London that a new attempt must be made to get Congress collaborating in government and the prosecution of the war which was now reaching India's borders as the Japanese swept north; or at least that an attempt to do so must be seen publicly, to soothe American, British Labour, and Indian Moderate opinion. The result was the mission of Sir Stafford Cripps, Lord Privy Seal and Leader of the Commons, to offer India full Dominion status at the end of the war, or the chance to secede from the Commonwealth and go for total independence, with the proviso that no part of India could be forced to join the new state. In the short term there was to be no constitutional change, but Indians were to be urged to put their full weight into the urgent war effort, and were to be given more places on the Viceroy's Executive Council to facilitate such collaboration. The device failed to weld Congress into the collaborative enterprise, and its rejection by the leadership led to open confrontation with government in 'Quit India'. Much controversy surrounded the mission at the time, and has continued among historians—on the actual terms Cripps was empowered to offer, his conduct of negotiations with Indian leaders, the hostility of the Viceroy and Churchill to his endeavours, the role of Gandhi, and the precise reasons why Congress rejected the offer.[13] It seems from the official records now open that Cripps' brief was never fully clarified before he left London, and that the Cabinet was much divided on the whole matter. It was therefore quite possible for Linlithgow to jerk Churchill into restraining action when he felt that Cripps' discussions and proffered concessions to Congress leaders, together with the intervention of Louis Johnson, a peripatetic envoy of Roosevelt, were imperilling Viceregal powers over his Executive Council. The breakdown with Congress amid consequent accusations of bad faith, was probably the compound of Congress leaders' dislike of the 'opting out' provision in the long-term plan, and their understanding that whatever Cripps might say his political masters had no intention of allowing complete Indianization of the Viceroy's Executive Council, its functioning with collective responsibility like a Cabinet, or Indian control over defence in wartime.

The failure to achieve a formula for wartime co-operation with India's main Hindu political group did not prevent the *raj* from administering India for the rest of the war, with officials where politicians could not be found to work the constitution, or from suppressing 'Quit India'. Yet the Cripps Offer was the point at which the British departure after the war became inevitable. As even Churchill recognized, there could be no retraction of the offer of independence.[14] So, ironically, a hasty and ill-conceived attempt in large part designed to placate opinion outside India as well as to attract Indian politicians' co-operation at one of the war's darkest hours became the charter for India's freedom. The decision was made by a handful of British politicians as a by-product of war, not as a result of any prolonged discussion among India's rulers or the Parliamentary representatives of the British people about ultimate goals and priorities. After the war the attraction of political co-operation was still necessary, but for a different reason. Indian leaders no longer had to be incorporated into the foundations of imperial power, but built into a bridge for India's passage from one *raj* to another. They had to be persuaded to participate in provincial and central government until power could be transferred to legal successors of the British. The politicians, including Congressmen, readily formed provincial governments after the elections of winter 1945–6. When their collaboration was not forthcoming it was not because of hostility to the British but because of communal strife and the tactics of Congress and League in bargaining for position as heirs of empire as in 1945 when Wavell vainly conferred with political leaders at Simla to achieve agreement on the reconstruction of his Executive Council, or in 1946 when he formed an Interim Government. Yet these final years of the *raj* showed conclusively that British rule had lost legitimacy and that among the vast majority of Hindus Congress had become the *raj*'s legitimate successor. Tangible proof came in the 1945–6 elections to the central and provincial legislatures. In the former Congress won 91 per cent of the votes cast in non-Muslim constituencies; and in the latter gained an absolute majority and became the provincial *raj* in eight provinces. The acquiescence of the politically aware (though possibly not of many villagers even at this point) would have been seriously in doubt if the British had displayed any intention of staying in India. This in turn reacted on all those who had been the *raj*'s 'friends' or paid servants, making their position highly ambiguous, and, in the case of the latter, eroding their morale and efficiency. European ICS men sensed that support for them was dropping away, and were aware that increasingly where Congress politicians had gained power their own ability to carry on the administration depended on Congress goodwill and co-operation. The trends evident in the late 1930s was now virtually complete. Wavell was bluntly realistic when landed gentry waited on him, asking what they should do as 'loyalists' and 'friends' of the *raj*. He felt that many of them had actually done little to help the *raj* and were loyal only because they could draw their rents while the British kept order. Now in a series of painful interviews with such he reminded them of the plain facts of political life.

I always feel it is better to be honest and to say that we are going to hand over power; that it is right that we should do so and leave Indians to govern themselves; that while the Congress is not a body one would have chosen as the representatives of the great mass of the Indian people, it is the body that the Indian people have chosen for themselves and we have to do business with the men of their choice.[15]

So far the end of the *raj* has been explained in terms of changing British interests in India and the erosion of older methods of imperial control. Both trends originated far earlier than the 1940s but were intensified by the experience and pressures of war. A final element in the demolition of empire was the subjective one of British commitment to formal rule. It is significant, because by 1946 it had become plain that only a massive injection of men and money over at least two decades could have re-established the *raj* on anything like its old foundations. Even after the crucial Cripps declaration some British politicians concerned with India still envisaged a form of long-term British presence on the subcontinent, to provide unity and defence. R. A. Butler was among them. Amery and Linlithgow, despite their realism about anti-imperial sentiment among Indian politicians, found it hard to envisage an end to the British presence and lamented apparent British loss of a sense of world mission, and were loth to 'lie back and let ourselves be pushed off the map by the Americans.'[16] Churchill was bitterly hostile to Indian aspirations and given to tirades in Cabinet about the maintenance of empire. His ignorance of India, yet the reluctance of his Cabinet colleagues to challenge him, made realistic assessment of the British position and prospects in India, extremely difficult. His priority anyway was winning the war. Implicit in this was keeping the Americans' good will, however. Churchill only deigned to consider India when, as in 1942, a policy shift seemed necessary to serve his main task. He was essentially a maverick in British political thinking; and when war ended, bringing Labour to office, their tradition of sympathy for Indian aspirations, and for Congress in particular, meant there was a chance of a new Cabinet realism on Indian affairs. Despite very real ignorance of India, still, in government circles, it was accepted that Britain must quit—and soon.

It was not just Labour's landslide victory which weakened British politicians' hankering after a modified British presence in India. American hostility to British imperialism was another crucial factor; as it had been during the war when even Churchill felt the need to 'prove' to the Americans that Congress 'recalcitrance' rather than continuing imperial aspirations prevented political advance in India. In a real sense the *raj* was losing international legitimacy, just as its prestige and authority within India were draining away.[17] Furthermore, at 'home', beneath the level of India Office and Cabinet it was increasingly clear that the British public and consequently their Parliamentary representatives had other priorities than keeping up the *raj*. Jobs, coal, electricity, and housing were the political and practical agenda in the immediate post-war period. India had always been a minority interest in British public life; no great body of public opinion now emerged to argue that war-weary and impoverished Britain should send troops and money to hold it against its will in an empire of doubtful value. By late 1946 both Prime Minister and Secretary of State for India recognized that neither international opinion nor their own voters would stand for any reassertion of *raj*, even if there had been the men, money, and administrative machinery with which to do so.[18]

This compound crisis of empire proved amenable to the simple solution of British withdrawal. The crisis of Indian nationhood, on the contrary, deepened as the British made clear their intention to leave, and it became increasingly urgent to decide who constituted the Indian nation which would inherit imperial power. The ingredients of the problem of national identity were becoming clear in the 1930s, most strikingly in relations between British and princely India, and between Congress and British India's minorities. Although the most obvious dimension of the latter was Congress's fraught relations with Muslim groups, there were also the Sikhs' growing fears about their future as a minority in Muslim-dominated Punjab, the unease of linguistic areas and backward castes about their likely position under an Indian government, and the claims of the more militant Hindu nationalists who wanted independent India to be a homeland for 'pure Hinduism' in contrast to the secular concept of nationhood promulgated by Congress.

Although the Muslim dimension of India's deepening crisis of political identity culminated in Pakistan, one should remember that there was no historical 'inevitability' about the 'Great Divide' despite the almost mythic proportions partition gained in the historical self-imagining of post-independent India and Pakistan, and in many historical accounts of the 1940s. Muslims had found cross-communal alliances viable political strategies for decades at different levels of political life, in UP district board politics for example, or at provincial level in the Punjab under the 1919 and 1935 constitutions. As late as 1947 there was serious thought about the viability of a united Bengal where Hindus and Muslims might co-operate as Bengalis rather than seeing their Bengali homeland partitioned. Even some of the Muslim clerisy, notably those of the deeply conservative seminary at Deoband (UP), opposed the idea of Pakistan, believing it would not serve the interests of orthodox Islam, despite the League's claims that it would be a land where Islamic purity would be secure. Clearly although Muslims saw themselves as a distinct religious community, and increasingly as a community whose interests needed political protection as the British devolved power to Indians, they were divided over the nature of that political protection (depending on their local strength and status), and had no common commitment to the idea of religious identity fusing with territorial national identity as found in Europe. Moreover throughout the 1940s it was not at all clear that Muslims in general or their politicians had any clear idea of what Pakistan might mean in practical geographical or constitutional terms—the whole of north-west India (which would include large Hindu and Sikh groups in Punjab), north-west and north-east India, the north-west and east with Bengal and Punjab partitioned, a totally separate state, or a Muslim bloc in a loose continental confederation? H. V. Hodson, a Government of India Reforms Commissioner, touring south and north-east India late in 1941, noted that virtually all Muslim League politicians he met saw Pakistan in the context of a federation with Hindu India, not as a separate successor state. In April 1943 Jinnah specifically advised the League's Working Committee against producing 'a cut and dried scheme for Pakistan' because this would only create division among Muslims. Furthermore, in May 1946 Jinnah for the League offered the visiting Cabinet Mission as a 'minimum demand' the plan for six Muslim provinces (Punjab, North-West Frontier Province, Baluchistan, Sind, Bengal, and Assam) to be a group within a loose continental federation which would deal with foreign affairs and defence, and later accepted the Mission's own plan which would have given Muslim areas their own 'groups' within an Indian federation for certain subjects, and would have avoided any territorial division of the subcontinent.[19] But if 'Pakistan' was neither *inevitable* nor even an unambiguous claim in the 1940s, what made it *possible* was the almost total integration of Indian Muslims' politics for the first time behind the claims of the Muslim League under Jinnah's autocratic leadership. His leadership, the emotive Pakistan claim and the League's organization strenthened it to a degree inconceivable even in 1937—in relation to Indian Muslims (including jealously autonomous provincial groups), to Congress and the British. By 1946 the League had gained legitimacy among Muslims as Congress had among Hindus over a longer period.

The basis of the leverage Jinnah and the League increasingly exerted over the British, and consequently over Congress in negotiations, was the famous Lahore Resolution of the League in March 1940, just days after Congress has called for complete independence and a constituent assembly to frame India's new constitution. Jinnah, presiding at the Lahore session, claimed that Muslims, too, called for India's freedom; but a freedom in which the Muslim nation as one of the major nations on the subcontinent had its own homeland and state and was not subject to government by a permanent Hindu majority. Just what he had in mind is suggested by his article published in the London magazine, *Time and Tide*, in January 1940, where he wrote of a new constitution which would recognize that in India there were two nations which must share the governance of their common motherland. The League rejected the 1935 federation scheme and resolved

that no constitutional plan would be workable in this country or acceptable to the Muslims unless it is designed on the following basic principle, viz., that geographically contiguous units are demarcated into regions which should be so constituted with such territorial readjustments as may be necessary that the areas in which the Muslims are numerically in a majority, as in the north-western and eastern zones of India, should be grouped to constitute 'independent States' in which the constituent units shall be autonomous and sovereign. . . .

Significantly this resolution was not only vague on details but nowhere mentioned 'Pakistan'; and indeed Jinnah later complained that others (Hindus and the British) had foisted that name on the Lahore Resolution. It seems increasingly likely from the evidence of recent scholarship that Jinnah in fact did not want the sort of partition which occurred in 1947. It was not a popular Muslim demand at the time, made little sense to Muslims secure in provincial majorities, and offered nothing to the millions of Muslims scattered as minorities throughout the subcontinent. Furthermore, it made little sense in terms of economics and defence. It probably therefore was designed as a bargaining-counter, vague enough to unite Indian Muslims behind it, in order to achieve recognition for Muslims as a 'nation' and therefore as equal with Congress in negotiations about the future, and possibly in the longer term to situate Muslims as a distinct and autonomous element in a larger all-India federation. This reading of Jinnah's intentions would explain why later he refused to define 'Pakistan' more clearly and seemed prepared to countenance solutions which fell short of absolute partition. It also suggests an underlying continuity in his political career as an all-India politician searching for assured status for Muslims within India, rather than a dramatic and unproven conversion to 'communalism' and religiously based nationalism.[20]

The Viceroy was neither impressed nor unduly perturbed by the Lahore resolution. He commented that it was not a serious claim but a bargaining counter.[21] Despite its ambiguities it became highly significant in negotiations for the post-imperial dispositions of power. There is no evidence that the British encouraged the Pakistan demand as a device to divide Indians so deeply that they could maintain their *raj*. Rather, in war time they could not afford to antagonize Muslims who were valuable recruits to the army, and in particular would not risk disturbing the Punjab—that traditionally great recruiting ground for the Indian army. So they reassured the Muslims that they would not be forced to live under any future government against their will. In the 1940 'August Offer' minorities were told that their views would be given weight in any policy revision, and that power would not be transferred to any system of government whose authority was denied by large and powerful elements in India's national life. The assurance was sharpened by the 1942 Cripps Offer of total post-war independence, when it was categorically stated that no part of India would be forced to join the new state.[22] Henceforth the League and its claim had a powerful blocking veto in any British attempts to contrive means for devolving power and departing. Congress implicitly recognized this when in July–October 1944 Gandhi met and corresponded with Jinnah on the Pakistan issue. This raised the status of the Pakistan idea and of Jinnah as the only Muslim leader Congress felt it necessary to deal with, though their contact proved fruitless in terms of a settlement between Congress and the League. Congress's earlier withdrawal from constitutional co-operation with the British had also contributed to the League's growing stature. By going into the political wilderness via 'Quit India' Congress left Jinnah and the League a clear field, not only to build up local strength unchallenged by Congress counter appeals to the masses, but also to insert their politicians into the formal institutions of political consultation and control by forming provincial governments in Bengal (1943), Sind (1942), Assam, and even the North-West Frontier Province which was the one Congress Muslim stronghold (1943). Only in Punjab did the provincial Muslim leadership pursue an independent line and hold office without the League's name.

Jinnah was perfectly ready to use the leverage Congress and the British had given him, and to exercise his power of veto. For the League he proved a highly skilled spokesman negotiating virtually single-handed with the Congress leardership and the government. [Wavell felt himself utterly checkmated by three elderly politicians and complained to his journal, 'I wonder if we shall ever have any chance of a solution till the three intransigent, obstinate, uncompromising principals are out of the way; Gandhi (just on 75), Jinnah (68), Winston (nearing 70).'[23] Jinnah's steady persistence in pursuing the League's claim to speak for all Muslims wrecked the 1945 Simla Conference convened by Wavell as a post-war move to break the political deadlock between the politicians, and to begin a new phase of co-operation between the political leaders and government. His hope had been to form a far more representative and almost entirely Indian Executive Council under the existing constitution, to defeat Japan, govern India until a new constitution could be achieved, and to make such an ultimate achievement easier. The Conference broke down when Jinnah insisted that the League must nominate all the Muslim members. 'He said that it suited the Congress to come into the scheme for they stood for a united India, and once they came in they would strangle Pakistan. In the circumstances it would not be in the interest of the Muslim League to accept the offer.'[24] A year later, when the Cabinet Mission visited India in the hope of breaking the deadlock and extracting Britain from the uncomfortable role of declining *raj*, Jinnah's negotiating position was even stronger because the results of the elections in the intervening months (see below p. 336) had proved his point that the League was undisputed representative of Indian Muslims. The Mission put forward its own plan for a three-tiered constitution of a federation, groups of provinces which chose to act together for agreed topics, and provinces at the base, after Indian leaders failed to agree upon a plan themselves. It also suggested the formation of an interim Government in Delhi representing the main political organizations of British India. This second enterprise foundered on the rock of Muslim representation, as Jinnah refused to co-operate in any Interim Government unless the League nominated all the Muslim members. This Congress could not concede because it would have undermined its own claim to speak for the nation, including Muslims, and would have denied the representative character of its own Nationalist Muslims. The complex longer term plan for India's future ran into the sand after initial hopes that Congress and League would work it. Nehru as Congress President made it plain that Congress believed that once the Constituent Assembly was in being it would be a sovereign body not bound by the Cabinet Mission plan, particularly on the issue of voluntary grouping by provinces. The League thereupon rejected the plan, because it felt sure that Congress would use its weight of numbers in the Assembly to jettison the safeguards proposed in the plan for the Muslim areas. Simultaneously the League called on Muslims to resort to 'direct action' to achieve Pakistan. The communal breakdown occurred amidst bitter recriminations and accusations by the League of British and Congress bad faith, and triggered a wave of communal violence which only deepened the deadlock.[25]

Although Jinnah and the League could create a negotiating deadlock, in the early stages it was far from obvious that their support among Muslims could give 'Pakistan' content and viability. Detailed evidence is still lacking on the League's support in many areas. But it is abundantly clear that during the 1940s the League 'took off' politically. It increased its hold over Muslims dramatically; and consequently strengthened its hand against Congress and its small group of Nationalist Muslims. The build-up of strength in turn had a 'band-wagon' effect which was evident as early as the closing months of 1941. Muslims in politics feared to appear un-Muslim, or to rend Muslim solidarity which seemed increasingly important as Congress manifestly achieved strength and status among Hindus and claimed immediate independence; and the League increasingly appeared a valuable name and resource at election time.[26] Under Jinnah's guidance the League continued to build up its local organization, to enrol members in large numbers, to train 'Muslim national guards', and to create a publicity network which included trained and paid speakers, production of pamphlets and tracts, and even popular songs performed by professional musicians. In 1942 with the help of a Muslim businessman, M.A.H. Ispahani, Jinnah converted the weekly, *Dawn*, into an English language daily and an invaluable Muslim forum and mouthpiece. Among the crucial groups tied into the League's support and propaganda structure were students as communicators, and businessmen as financial backers and planners for the economic construction of Pakistan. In some provinces such as UP there was also evidence that local Leaguers were deliberately courting *maulvis* and *imams*, local Muslim clergy in touch with the grass roots of Muslim opinion and able to influence it through the mosques and Friday prayers.[27]

However, the League's initial success was in Muslim minority areas where Muslims felt most threatened, first by Congress accession to provincial *raj* in 1937, and then by the spectre of British withdrawal. But if Pakistan was to be viable the League had to win over the Muslim leaders or the Muslim population in the majority provinces, which would eventually become Pakistan. At first the Muslim politicians of these provinces were content to rely on their local majorities which had served them well as the franchise was extended, and they kept Jinnah and the League at a safe distance. But increasingly the realities of the all-India political situation made them recognize the importance of having an all-India political voice in decisions about the future: and this need became the more vital once the war ended and it was clear that the British were set on departure and would no longer be guarantors of Muslim political identity and status on the subcontinent. The very ambiguity of the 'Pakistan' claim enabled a degree of all-India Muslim co-operation behind Jinnah and the League. Moreover, in areas of Muslim numerical dominance the League was gaining support particularly from 1943, at the grass-roots level. By May 1944 the Sind Provincial League claimed 300,000 members—25 per cent of the province's adult Muslim male population actually enrolled in the League. This growth of support, extending even into the countryside, did not reflect any radical new politicization, or a clear understanding of and commitment to a new 'Pakistan'. It was largely the result of the shifting attitudes of influential Muslim religious and landowning notables, particularly the Pirs, who began to recognize that in the changing political situation alliance with the League would buttress their local influence rather than the alliance with the *raj* which had served them well in the century since the British annexation of Sind. When they changed their allegiance, so did their many followers: and 'League' strength was consequently not genuinely new and institutionalized support. By contrast in Bengal the League did manage to build the beginning of a mass organization in some areas, claiming 550,000 members by 1944. Here a significant factor was clearly the division between Muslim peasants and Hindu landlords and moneylenders, and the way agrarian tensions, exacerbated by the war, were stretching the province's socio-economic fabric to breaking-point. The swing to the League in the crucial Muslim majority areas has been most clearly documented and analysed in the Punjab, where the League completely undermined the Unionist Party between 1944 and 1946 and won over the bulk of Muslim politicians. Its success in the Punjab was partly the result of a direct and concerted attempt to appeal to and organize ordinary rural Muslims, appealing not only on the Pakistan issue, but playing on a range of other grievances resulting from the war's deep inroads into the provincial economy. Students worked hard in the vacations to rouse popular support, and were specifically trained to use Islam's appeal. But the League's main strategy was to win the support of élite Muslim groups who would then bring their followers with them. Most significant of these were the landlords and many of the Muslim Pirs who, as in Sind, wielded significantly more influence than mosque-based *ulema*, through their networks of followers. These groups began to desert the Unionist Party in large numbers from 1945, undermining that Party's strength in the Legislature and depriving it of its rural support networks.[28]

This swing began to show in elections. Between 1937 and 1945 the League won 55/77 provincial by-elections in Muslim seats: independent Muslims won 18 and Congress only 4. In the winter elections of 1945–6 the League won all the Muslim seats in the Central Legislative Assembly and 439 of the 494 seats reserved for Muslims in the provincial legislatures. This included a stunning 113/119 in Bengal: and 75 in Punjab, compared with the Unionist Party's 10—whereas in 1937 it had only fielded 7 candidates for the 85 seats and won 2. In Bombay and Madras it won all the Muslim seats contested, and in UP 54/64 Muslim seats. So by early 1946 the League could legitimately claim to speak for virtually all Indian Muslims. Only on the North-West Frontier did the League fail to change its local standing: there many Pathans stuck with their Congress alliance until the imminent departure of the British forced them to consider all-India issues and particularly whether they wished to be part of Hindu dominated India or a Muslim Pakistan. So it seemed for the first time that Muslim politics on the subcontinent were almost completely integrated and channelled into one organization, and that provincial strategies had been laid aside to pursue an all-India claim. However, the content of that claim was still profoundly ambiguous; and as the new state of Pakistan was to find to its cost, support for the League was rarely deeply rooted, and reflected the calculation and strategies of provincial Muslim élites who were concerned more with their own standing and interests than the creation of a new nation state.

However, there was a darker and wilder aspect of the breakdown of political relations between Hindus and Muslims, and the divergence of their political identities, than the canny negotiations of high politics, or the building of political organizations. The political use of religion is a potentially inflammable strategy in any society which has not become deeply secular, the more so at a time of extreme social stress, as in India in the 1940s, when war was straining the economy and the very fabric of society. The overtly 'communal' violence which erupted in terrifying proportions in the last year of the *raj* was totally beyond the politicians' control, though their strategies, accusations, and claims often triggered it. It brought India to the brink of civil war. We know comparatively little about the dynamics of communal violence, for it leaves few records but dead, injured, and frightened people and shattered buildings. Observers could only attempt to assess the relative roles of national and local leadership, of new issues and long-standing antagonisms, of rumour, mass panic and fear, and of roving bands of armed thugs. The first wave started with the 'Great Calcutta Killing' which lasted for nearly a week from 16 August 1946, the day designated for 'direct action' (*hartals*, strikes, rallies, and meetings) by the Muslim League Council. About 4,000 people were killed and an unknown number—possibly up to 15,000—injured, and 100,000 made homeless. Muslim actions triggered the violence but as a minority in the city they were its main victims. The weakness and communalism of the police and the lack of proper intelligence made the situation even graver; and the Governor felt that only the presence of three battalions of British troops 'prevented a complete collapse of the administration'. He was sickened by what he saw and heard of the mob 'bestiality', and told the Viceroy, 'I observed very great damage to property and streets littered with corpses. I can honestly say that parts of the city . . . were as bad as anything I saw when I was with the Guards on the Somme.'[29] Trouble then spread to Noakhali district in East Bengal, where Muslims were the aggressors and Hindus the victims; and to Bihar on a far larger scale, where possibly as many as 7,000 Muslims were butchered. Bombay and UP saw some communal disturbances, but elsewhere there was little trouble. Early in 1947 Punjab became the worst scene of communal tension and at times what amounted to carnage, though disorder was chronic in Calcutta and in parts of Bengal and Bihar. In Punjab the Muslim majority was now fanatically pro-Pakistan, and the problem was compounded by the fears of the Hindu minority and the Sikhs, who became increasingly belligerent as they saw the real possibility of their Sikh homelands in central Punjab being divided in the event of Pakistan. The worst violence in Punjab and Delhi did not occur until the actual time of partition, when train loads of refugees crossed the frontier in each direction and were exposed to hostile gangs from other communities who descended on the passengers and engaged in mass slaughter. As one Delhi Muslim commented of the summer of 1947, the old city where many Muslims lived became a living nightmare of stabbing, where even the main roads were dangerous and few ventured out at night. But even before partition, by the end of July, around 5,000 had been killed in Punjab, mainly in rural areas. At this stage Hindus and Sikhs were the main victims, but they took their revenge in the following months.[30]

As India seemed increasingly ungovernable and in danger of plunging into wide-scale civil war, all the major political groups involved realized that the deadlock must be broken lest all of them lose in disorder and devastation what they had been aiming for—the British an orderly devolution of power to a competent and friendly successor state, Congress rapid independence for a strong and unified polity, and the League the equal status it claimed with Congress in deciding India's future mode of governance to protect Muslims' status and security, symbolized in the idea of 'Pakistan'. Attlee's government sacked Wavell, whom it increasingly (and unfairly) judged as politically incompetent, and sent the flamboyant Earl Mountbatten to do with speed and style what Wavell had failed to achieve. Mountbatten's task was made easier in a sense by the communal violence because it pressed Indian leaders into compromise at last: and also by the fact that he had a far freer hand than his Viceregal predecessor, ensuring his own terms on accepting office. He was particularly insistent that Britain should set a precise time-limit for its *raj* to force the Indian parties into realism. On 20 February Attlee announced Mountbatten's appointment and June 1948 as the latest possible date for British withdrawal. In the event independence came in August 1947. Mountbatten saw within a month of his arrival in India that there could be no rescue-operation on the Cabinet Mission Plan, for even though League and Congress were co-operating by this time in the Interim Government the League's representatives were not participating in the Constituent Assembly. He also realized what Wavell had tried to impress on London for so long, that unless a final solution was rapidly achieved there would be civil war and administrative breakdown. The result of his deliberations with the politicians, his hand-picked staff and the Cabinet in London, was the 3 June Plan for swift British withdrawal and the transfer of power to two successor dominions, India and a 'two-winged' Pakistan in the north west and north east of the subcontinent, the exact boundary being drawn by an independent boundary commission after provincial legislators in Bengal and Punjab had voted on whether their provinces should be partitioned. Voting mechanisms were also provided to register the wishes of the other Muslims majority areas.[31]

The partition of the subcontinent and of two of its major provincial units, Punjab and Bengal, was a bitter resolution of the problem of national identity which had developed in the previous decades. For Jinnah it was the wreckage of his all-India plans, and gave Muslims a 'solution' which left the remaining Muslim minority in India unprotected, divided the major Muslim provinces, and produced not only a 'moth-eaten Pakistan', in Jinnah's words, but one divided by a thousand miles of Indian territory. By treating as a real demand what had almost certainly been a bargaining-counter, and calling his bluff, Congress and the British demolished Jinnah's strategy, which had depended on British willingness to stay on until they had imposed a solution, and Congress's wish to maintain Indian unity. But by early 1947 the British would not and could not adopt such a role and were looking for strong and stable successors. Moreover, the Congress leaders themselves, as Gandhi's political influence receded, had come to feel that freedom for a strong new nation state was their priority, even at the expense of the unity they had so long claimed. Quite when this shift in Congress thinking occurred is unclear; but almost certainly well before Mountbatten launched his plan the main leaders, including Nehru and Patel, backed by some of their business allies such as Birla, had concluded that a Muslim element in a federation with an inevitably weak centre would fatally undermine the strong and unified India which they considered essential if India was to plan its economy and launch its people on a path of modernization. Muslims in Congress such as A. K. Azad were deeply distressed by what they saw as the sacrifice of their co-religionists and the partition of the country in effect by Congress itself.[32] For the inhabitants of the two divided provinces, and Punjab in particular, it meant fear, disruption, violence, and a huge transfer of population, as Muslims and Hindus trekked to the 'safe' side of the border. It is impossible to compute the magnitude of migration and disruption. Possibly a million died; and within a year five and a half million refugees had moved each way across the border of West Pakistan and India, while one and a quarter million moved from East Pakistan to the part of Bengal remaining in India.

The problem of nationhood was thus in part made into an international question. In this guise it has remained with India ever since, flaring at times into open warfare between the two countries. But India also retained a large Muslim minority—over thirty million, near 10 per cent of the population after partition. They were scattered after the major majority areas had become part of Pakistan, but there were still locally significant clusters of Muslims in some areas such as Delhi, UP and Hyderabad in the south, once a princely state. This minority was understandably fearful, and vulnerable to communal violence, despite the possible 'safeguard' of the likelihood of

Pakistani retaliation on Hindus left in Pakistan if Indian Muslims were persecuted. The integration of the Muslims into the new Indian nation remained one of the tasks of India's secular and democratic political system. Despite the 'Great Divide' Congress leaders still had to face the problem they had failed to resolve thus far, and to make their political organization the accepted political environment of Muslims within India's own borders.

Other minorities' apprehensions and aspirations were a further dimension of the problem of national identity, and a continuing part of Indian public life. They were less dramatic than the Muslim dimension because no other group had the numerical weight to force territorial or political concessions in the process of the transfer of power. Yet the unease and demands of many of the subcontinent's groups and areas caused concern to Congress before 1947 and threatened considerable problems of governance thereafter.

The Sikhs were a major case.[33] Clustered in central Punjab they were a substantial provincial minority. But even in the Punjabi heartland they were not a local majority, and in the west Muslims were over 60 per cent of the population while in eastern Punjab Hindus were a comparable majority. Yet the Sikhs had a vivid sense of their distinctiveness as a community, and of the role of political power in maintaining their communal identity and integrity. This sense of separation was fostered by the religious reform movements of the later nineteenth and twentieth centuries (see above, pp. 159 *ff.*, 230) and by their special relationship with the British as a source of valuable military recruits who had their community regiments. The succession of constitutional discussions and reforms as the British sought to devolve power to the provinces confirmed their political identity and claim for particular consideration in the Punjabi and all-India contexts. Special Sikh seats in the Punjab legislature and the Central Legislature were first created under the Montagu–Chelmsford Reforms. In the preparation and aftermath of the Nehru and Simon Reports Sikhs claimed separate political identity, and many of them called for continuing separate electorates: and at the Round Table Conferences in London their representatives pressed for reserved seats and for separate electorates if other minorities were to have them. The Communal Award rejected their demand of 30 per cent of seats in the Punjab legislature and gave them only thirty-two seats, leaving Muslims in a permanent majority. However, despite their separate religious and political identity the Sikhs split politically into numerous groups— 'Moderates', those who joined Congress, and the Akali Dal with a distinctive religious orientation, led by Master Tara Singh, which was itself divided politically. In the later 1930s and early 1940s the Akali Dal was in uneasy relationship with Congress and gradually broke with its former ally. Sikhs could not agree among themselves either on provincial political issues, or on co-operation with the British in the war. The absence of an undisputed leadership had tragic consequences as the British prepared to leave. It bred what Punjab's Governor called 'a kind of competitive intemperance among the Sikh leaders which I have always found it very difficult to deal with.'[34] It also left local Sikh populations outside the control of any central leadership which might have helped curb the violence and carnage which accompanied partition.

In the 1940s the Muslim demand for Pakistan precipitated a crisis for the Sikhs. Increasingly it looked as if Pakistan would mean the partition of the Punjab, with the new border cutting through the Sikh homelands in the centre of the province. Furthermore it would lose the Sikhs their leverage in Punjabi politics as a substantial minority with strategic importance in political coalitions, given the Hindu–Muslim–Sikh balance of the population and political representation. Instead it would, they feared, deliver them into the hands of either a Muslim or a Hindu majority. Under the threat of partition Sikhs drew nearer together politically in concerted opposition to the idea. When in 1944 it looked as if some of the Congress leaders, including Gandhi, would ultimately agree to Pakistan, a meeting of Sikh politicians from all parties gathered in protest and empowered Tara Singh to organize 3 September as a 'protest day'. The new Sikh unity was further displayed in the post-war elections when an all-parties Sikh board was constituted to fight the elections in opposition to Pakistan. The resulting Panthic Party won twenty-two seats, and the Sikh Communists, who were the only Sikhs to support Pakistan, were eliminated. Sikh politicians attempted to deal and negotiate with the British, Congress, and the League in attempts to protect their future when it became clear their British patrons were really going. The latter, though sympathetic, felt they could do little except urge the Sikhs not to make trouble and to use their strategic position as protection, because of their dispersed demographic and geographical position. The Congress leaders were prepared to accept partition as the price of independence and peace; while the League was not willing to compromise over power, as the Unionists with their provincial political orientation had been.

As Sikhs looked about in vain for protectors or allies they turned increasingly to the slogan of 'Azad Punjab', though like 'Pakistan' in its early stages the practicalities of the idea were vague. The idea of a 'free Punjab' where Sikhs would be political masters, or of a 'Sikhistan' (land of the Sikhs), had been mooted by Akali Dal leaders even in the 1930s. By 1946 it was the Akali Dal's declared political objective, and the claim made by Sikh representatives to the Cabinet Mission as an alternative to permanent subjection to either a Hindu or a Muslim majority. Tara Singh, for the Sikhs, said he preferred the future to be within a united India in which Sikhs had bargaining power because of differences between Hindus and Muslims; but if partition occurred he wanted a separate Sikh state with the right to federate with Pakistan or Hindustan. [35] Not surprisingly Sikh politicians were angered and frightened by the Cabinet Mission's own proposals for voting on the future in three 'groups', because Punjabi Sikhs were in the predominantly Muslim Group B (Punjab, North-West Frontier Province, Sind, and Baluchistan), even though the idea of partitioning Punjab appeared to have been rejected. As one of the more moderate Sikh leaders, a member of the provincial government, Baldev Singh, put it, 'The seeds of Pakistan are . . . already there in the Group system and as the Constitution of the Groups and their ultimate disposition is to be decided by force of numbers, the Sikhs cannot but contemplate their future with grave misgivings.'[36]

The demand for political recognition of a distinctive Sikh homeland came to nothing, and Sikh fears were not allayed as the main communal conflict pressed the all-India leadership and the British into the final plan for rapid independence and partition. The result was open Sikh violence against their Muslim neighbours and Muslim refugees leaving India, and large-scale Sikh migration across the border into Indian Punjab. The refugees' future caused administrative problems for India's government for many months after independence. Furthermore, the Sikh claim to be a distinct nation with its own state was renewed almost immediately. As early as September 1947 Mountbatten's Press Attaché was writing of the burgeoning of a Sikh 'nationalism' which would not be satisfied even with an Indian province of Sikhistan. Early in 1948 Tara Singh began to call for a Sikh province where the community would be able to protect its identity, tradition, and culture by self-determination in religious, social, and political affairs.[37] The difference between this demand and the pre-partition call for 'Azad Punjab' was that now it was both viable and cogent. Sikh migration to India had meanwhile produced a Sikh majority in the north-western part of Punjab and thereby removed the argument that there was no Sikh majority area to which political power could be devolved. Furthermore Punjab was now a border province with Pakistan, giving its politicians advantages of bargaining power over a central government anxious to keep its border populations loyal; while it remained as it had been under the British *raj* a highly significant recruiting ground for the Indian army.

The Sikh campaign for regional autonomy continued for nearly two decades to concern a central government bent on welding together a new nation. (It revived in a more extreme form with escalating violence in the 1980s.) Somewhat similar fissiparous tendencies occurred in several linguistic areas, though demands for linguistic states within the Indian Union rarely had the reinforcing religious dimension which made the Sikh demand so powerful. Unease among linguistic minorities who felt educationally and politically disadvantaged had for decades been an aspect of the new perceptions of group identity which developed as the sources and distribution of power shifted in public life (see above, pp. 177–8). Telugu-speakers had demanded an Andhra Province and Oriya-speakers an Orissa free from Bengal, for example, long before the imminent transfer of power. Similar proposals had come from Kannada and Malayalam speakers and reached the Bombay and Madras provincial legislatures in the late 1930s. The British were reluctant to tamper with provincial boundaries after their disastrous attempt to divide Bengal in 1905 unless there were clear administrative grounds. The only two new provinces created between the wars were Sind and Orissa in 1935. Congress, however, implicitly encouraged the idea of redrawing provincial boundaries on linguistic lines by recognizing the principle within its own organization from 1920, and explicitly endorsed the principle in a Working Committe resolution of 1938 and in its 1946 election manifesto. But when Congress came to govern an independent state the principle it could so easily uphold as a movement trying to incorporate as many regions and groups as possible proved a divisive threat. The Dar Commission set up in 1948 to consider the cases of potential provinces of Andhra, Karnataka, Kerala, and Maharashtra rejected the notion of linguistic provinces as an obstacle to the growth of nationalism. So widespread was opposition to this conclusion that Congress set up its own committee of Nehru, Patel, and P. Sitaramayya. They proved almost as hostile under the new pressures of building a nation state.

Taking a broad and practical view . . . we feel that the present is not an opportune time for the formation of new Provinces. It would unmistakably retard the process of consolidation of our gains, dislocate our administrative, economic and financial structure, let loose, while we are still in a formative state, forces of disruption and disintegration, and seriously interfere with the progressive solution of our economic and political difficulties . . .

Yet they conceded that as democrats they might have in the future to accept linguistic redistribution 'if public sentiment is insistent and overwhelming'. Thus they ensured the continuity of yet another problem in the governance of India and another hindrance to the growth of national identity, though their intention was the reverse.[38]

The claims of the Sikhs and linguistic groups could be shelved, if not permanently ingnored. The future of the princely states could not, as their link with British India was the British, and they were going. The fate of these blocks of territory, with their rulers and peoples, who were politically and culturally apart yet geographically inextricable from the rest of the subcontinent was one of the most formidable problems facing both the departing rulers and those who wished to construct and govern an inheriting nation state. Ironically it was tackled seriously very late in the process of imperial withdrawal, and earlier planning for the states' future proved of little use because it had been based on the assumption of a united, federal

India as posited in 1935. The demise of the princely order, like the emergence of Pakistan, has generated historical controversy: particularly over the difficult relations between Mountbatten and the Political Department who had different sympathies and priorities, over the methods used to 'persuade' princes to join an Indian Union, and the long-term intentions of British India's politicians and administrators towards the states, despite their conciliatory moves in the threatened chaos of mid-1947.[39] This complex of questions needs more historical investigation. But for our purposes the crucial point is the continuing problem posed by the states in the 1940s and thereafter. It was not disposed of in 1947, but was deepened by Britain's determination on a hasty withdrawal.

Cripps' Mission and Offer in 1942 marked the final collapse of the federal plan on which the British had pinned their hopes for the whole of India. In the new political situation, with total independence on offer to British India after the war, the princes would be far more vulnerable, and would have to come to terms directly with the politicians of British India, though Cripps assured them that the British would not transfer Paramountcy to any other body, would not force any state to join an independent India, and that they would retain both Paramountcy and their obligations in relation to those states which did not join. The British, however, had been far too successful in their policy of buttressing the states as a conservative counterweight to the escalating demands of British India's politicians. Because they had merely encouraged reform rather than coercing the princes into radical change they had left their client-allies ill-equipped to cope with the new situation. Basically the states were anachronistic political and administrative structures built on ideals fast losing legitimacy. Yet in wartime imperialists needed their loyalty and material contributions too much to force reform. Even after the war British policy-makers assumed that there was a considerable time during which they could chivvy the princes to face the new world realistically. The alternative to this gentle approach was to offer protection if any princes tried to 'go it alone'. This they could not have done, though probably some members of the Political Department would have liked to encourage their 'charges' in such an enterprise. The British in fact lacked the physical resources and would not have wished to embitter their relations with the new India by such a move. Instead they spoke vaguely about fulfilling their treaty obligations. The blunt Wavell felt that they ought to be more open and tough with the princes about their predicament. As he told the Cabinet's India Committee as early as 1945, 'We knew that we could not in certain circumstances implement our formal obligations and the States were well aware of that. He thought that there was everything to be said for frankly warning them that in face of the changes that had taken place there were very definite limits to the extent to which we could honour obligations given in quite different circumstances.'[40]

With justification the princes were becoming increasingly apprehensive. They demonstrated this when the whole Standing Committee of the Chamber of Princes resigned late in 1944 in protest against what they termed the deterioration of their position and disregard of their interests. They were only pacified six months later when Wavell assured them that their relationship with the crown would not be transferred to any other body without their consent, provided they themselves did not unreasonably veto any constitutional changes. Their predicament became really acute when the British made precise proposals for a swift departure. When the Cabinet Mission visited India in 1946 it told the princes bluntly that when independent India came into being the British would no longer be able to exercise Paramountcy and did not intend to keep British troops on the subcontinent for that purpose. Paramountcy would lapse, states would regain all the rights they had surrendered to the crown, and would have to make their own arrangements with the successor authority (or authorities) in British India.[41] Eventually the princes accepted the Cabinet Mission Plan as a basis for further negotiation, and as containing the machinery for independence, and set up a negotiating committee to work with the corresponding committee of the Constituent Assembly. While they were pressurized by their patron's explicit statement of their unprotected future the princes were simultaneously harassed by the belligerent stance of some Congressmen, particularly Nehru, who said publicly that no state could hold out against India once the princes lost British support, and that any state which did not join in the Constituent Assembly would be treated as a hostile state. Under pressure the princes could not agree whether to sit on the fence or plunge into the Constituent Assembly.

Mountbatten's June pronouncement that there were but weeks to independence forced decisions on to the princes. The Viceroy saw this and from then on relied on the new States Department rather than the existing Political Service to conduct relations with the states. Its key men were Vallabhbhai Patel, the Minister, and his chief aide, V.P. Menon, who had long been in government service with particular expertise in the details of constitutional changes. All three men realized both the short time at their disposal to solve the problem of the states' futures, and the thin line between the country and chaos. Together they achieved a policy to 'stop the gap', as Menon put it. Its essence was the states' accession to the new India (or Pakistan) on three fundamentals—Defence, Foreign Affairs, and Communications. Later negotiations could take place with each state on other matters which were covered in the meantime by 'stand-still agreements'. Patel and Menon combined conciliation and toughness (at times amounting to threats and blackmail), and were reinforced by Mountbatten's charm and moral pressure as he threw the weight of his personality and office behind the new policy. By the moment of independence only three states had withstood their efforts and declined to accede. After independence the Hindu ruler of Muslim Kashmir acceded to India rather than Pakistan in circumstances which led to acute international tension between the two countries and counter-accusations which continued for decades. The remaining states, tiny Junagadh and vast Hyderabad, were ultimately subdued by armed actions of dubious legality. Thereafter administrative and political arrangements were made to weld the former states into a uniform all-India structure. Some smaller states were merged into surrounding provinces. Others were grouped to form state unions equivalent to provinces. While eight, including Kashmir, Hyderabad, and Mysore, retained their separate identity. All now were equipped with democratic institutions like those of the provinces of former British India. However, ex-rulers were granted privy purses, some private property, and personal dignities and privileges, including their former titles. In units developed from ex-princely states, as in Rajasthan and Travancore, princes also received a constitutional position of leadership in the new democratic context with the title of *Rajpramukh*. Details varied from state to state, and often the process of integration was smooth and amicable.[42] But the truth was that within a short time after independence the new Government of India was the paramount power on the subcontinent, whatever the pre-independence assurances of the British and of Vallabhbhai Patel himself.

The integration of the states into the new India's political and administrative structures was complex, but at least concrete. More subtle, but equally vital for India's future as a democracy, was the integration of the states' peoples into an all-India political environment, and their political education to value and use the new sources of political power and the novel pathways to power through elections, parties, and legislatures. The task confronting politicians and administrators was to create a political culture and inculcate patterns of activity similar to those which had developed unevenly through the previous century in British India. This is another area where much research still needs to be done. Rajasthan has been studied in depth, and the integration of the former princely subjects into a new political arena as participant citizens explored.[43] There was nothing there like the PCCs and DCCs which became vital organizational units in the provinces of British India and the structure through which most political activity was channelled, but there existed a range of urban protest movements, *Praja Mandals*. They were often tenuously connected, but their leaders were often in touch with Congress in British India. There were also peasant movements, very different in origin and aims, many of which grew out of the social reform movement of the Jat caste. Both types of movement were bases on which a new Rajasthan Congress could draw for support and local leadership, and which provided stepping-stones for local men to move from the political styles and concerns of the princely world to those of a democratic state. Not surprisingly it was the urban-based *Praja Mandals* which first joined as a unit in the All India States Peoples conference and in 1948 became the Rajputana Pradesh Congress Committee. Since then the resulting Rajasthan Congress Party has reflected the segmented character of the older order. But it has adapted to the local environment with its particular past and social structure. It has proved a means of integrating Rajasthan's people into a new democratic order, by drawing in men from small towns and rural areas and catering for the needs of the new recruits to politics within a Congress framework, so channelling their interests through new political institutions and behavioural conventions.

However it was not only groups clearly distinguishable by their minority status or their separate historical development which raised the issue of national identity. Others who were deeply committed to independent India had a very different vision of the essence of Indian nationhood from that of the Congress leadership. To sustain its inclusive nature in a plural society Congress had felt it essential to present the ideal of nationhood in secular terms, the nation's members being bound by common citizenship in a democracy where religious identity should not be a barrier to full participation. Though Gandhi was distressed by the 'unspiritual' basis of Congress politics and ideals of nationhood, he too rejected the idea that India was solely for the Hindu majority and envisaged adherents of all religions pouring their spiritual resources into the new India. Yet this was a difficult sense of nationhood to publicize and for which to generate a genuine loyalty. Even Gandhi had found that support accrued to him because he was seen in 'Hindu' terms, not as the apostle of an inclusive national unity. But there were Hindus who deplored the attitudes of Congress and Gandhi alike. Like the Mahatma, they also had a spiritual, almost mystical, vision of Indian nationhood. The second leader of the RSS expounded this in 1939 in his book *We or Our Nationhood Defined*. Hindustan was to be the land of the Hindus where they could practise their all-prevailing religious tradition without contamination from European or Muslim culture. Any non-Hindus in India 'must learn to respect and hold in reverence Hindu religion, must entertain no idea but those of glorification of the Hindu race and culture', and could only stay in the country 'wholly subordinated to the Hindu nation, claiming nothing, deserving no privileges, far less any preferential treatment'. After independence this vision led Hindu Communalists into bitter diatribes against Pakistan and condemnation of legislative reform of aspects of Hindu society according to secular criteria. But in the early 1940s that main Communalist cry was hostility to the idea of partition and to the Congress leadership who appeared willing to barter away the Hindus' birthright. Partition was 'vivisection' of the Holy Motherland, and Congress leaders, including Gandhi, traitors in their eyes.[44]

It is impossible to enumerate precisely the number of activists in such communal organizations as the Hindu Mahasabha or the RSS, let alone those who formed a penumbra of sympathizers, attracted less by a coherent ideology than by fear of communal violence and hope of some protection from the bands of activists who were given uniforms and para-military training. Support for the Mahasabha and RSS expanded in the 1940s; initially while Congress was politically inoperative and its leadership in jail, leaving a free run for communalist politicians, and later when communal bitterness and violence escalated in the months before and after partition. The RSS always remained strongest in the north where communal tension was sharpest, though efforts were made to extend it in the south at the start of the decade. In contrast to Congress which had been putting down increasingly deep and broad-spreading rural roots, it remained an urban movement, attracting students, lowly placed government servants, some business and professional people, and—predictably—refugees from Pakistan. Communal groups could not hope to challenge Congress as the legitimate successor of the *raj* in most Indians' eyes. But their dangerous potential in public life was demonstrated in January 1948 when a young man who had connections with both Mahasabha and RSS shot Gandhi at one of his regular public prayer meetings in Delhi. A wave of emotional hostility to communal groups engulfed a horrified country. The RSS was banned, while the Mahasabha voluntarily withdrew from political activity.

At the time of Gandhi's assassination it looked as if the force of communalism had struck a grievous blow at the Indian nation at a crucial phase of its consolidation. A desolate Nehru spoke of a light going out of their lives with Gandhi's death, thousands flocked to Delhi to watch with grief and awe the passage of his frail old body to the cremation grounds, and even beyond the subcontinent millions mourned one who had embodied the Indian claim to a new order, who had made non-violence a living political reality, and who had in the previous months by his physical presence in Bengal, Calcutta, and Delhi helped to stem the tide of communal killing.[45] Yet Gandhi martyred proved even more powerful a bond for Indians than he had been when alive, particularly in his last years when he had been isolated from the main stream of Congress politics and weakened by the escalation of Muslim nationalism. He became a national symbol, and in time almost a myth; his name invoked in times of national crisis and disunity, and his career part of the historical picture of their country and their political education received by Indian schoolchildren as future citizens and patriots. But though Gandhi's death cast a slur on the most overt forms of Hindu communalism, communal bodies re-emerged in public life in 1949. The RSS was only permitted because it submitted a new constitution to the government which stated that it was a non-political cultural organization and would preach religious tolerance. Yet militant Hindus' persistent concern to protect the Hindu religious and cultural heritage, and their complaints against 'secularization', have remained a potentially explosive element in public life. To the Congress leadership they proved embarrassing and ambiguous in their implications, for India's new rulers had to walk a tightrope between the Hindus and India's minorities as they tried both to weld a new country and to embark on major social reforms.

When the historian shifts his focus from the most urgent questions of national identity in the 1940s and from the dramas of independence and partition to the mundane business of actually welding and governing the new nation state, continuity rather than striking change is again a dominant motif in India's experience. It is unusual to stress the continuity of the problems facing the old and new government, and the resources at their disposal. But realism about what was little changed, however out of tune with the heady aspirations of Indians in August 1947, is essential for an understanding of the achievements and limitations of India as a democratic state in subsequent decades. The institutions of government, the structure of society, and the fundamental beliefs of most Indians did not change just because the Union Jack was lowered and the last British troops marched to the Gateway of India to board ship in Bombay harbour, or even because a new constitution in 1950 laid down ideals and institutional frameworks which were intended to be a new basis for the nation's public life.

Independence and partition caused a range of very specific problems which India had to solve immediately to aviod chaos. The government confronted them with remarkable speed and success. One was the virtually unprecedented division of the resources of central government between two inheriting authorities, including civil servants, the armed forces and their equipment, and the paraphernalia of government down to office furniture. India had the advantage of being the 'sitting tenant', whereas Pakistan had to construct a new capital city and central government. The other administrative crisis was the influx of refugees in continuing circumstances of communal bitterness and fear. Patel and Nehru were so appalled by the gravity of the situation in Delhi in September 1947 that they consulted Mountbatten, by then Governor-General, and when he proposed an Emergency Committee they asked him to chair it. It dealt with the transport and settlement of refugees, harvesting crops in deserted Punjabi villages, keeping some newspapers and the Delhi telephone service going, bringing government servants to work and burying the dead left on the streets by communal strife. By the end of November its work was done. In UP which faced similar problems because of its communal composition and geographical position the premier, Pandit Pant, a leading Congress politician experienced in government and opposition, saved the province from chaos by exceptionally firm government. Just over half the refugees eventually settled in towns, particularly in UP and the great cities of Delhi and Calcutta. But the ultimate fortunes of these new Indian citizens, their relative prosperity compared with their previous lives, and their contribution to the new country, have been little studied, so sensitive is the topic.

By far the greater range of matters concerning the new government were of far longer standing. Chief among them was the country's economic base and the poverty of so many of her people. Poverty had not left an imperial government unmoved, but given its limited resources and the magnitude of the problem, and its basic rationale, it only took steps to alleviate distress when it seemed so acute as to threaten disorder. The 1939–45 war, for example, had sharply focused government attention on the problem because of its inflationary impact on India.[46] But far more significant than any short-run inflation produced by exceptional circumstances was the grindingly low standard of living of the vast majority, which was unacceptable to a goverment which was committed to a new order for its people and also realized that the low level of income, and consequently of demand and potential investment, was a drag on development in every part of the economy, whether agriculture, industry or the service sector. In 1949 a National Income Committee was established to discover the dimensions of Indian poverty. Its report in 1950/1 showed that average annual income per person was Rs. 260 or $55. Some fell below this level, particularly those engaged in domestic service and in agriculture, where families did not own land from which to feed themselves. A decade later (by which time prices had risen further) 38 per cent of the rural poor lived on less than Rs. 180 a year, or about ten cents a day; and roughly half the urban population earned less than the Rs. 270 which was required in towns to maintain an officially recognized minimum daily intake of calories (2,250). Such poverty where there is little state welfare provision, is of a degree never seen in the west in the late twentieth century. It means almost perpetual hunger, a monotonous and unbalanced diet at the best of times, cramped and squalid housing, perhaps one change of meagre clothes, insufficient bedding to prevent deaths from cold in the northern Indian winter, children's absence from school for lack of clothes or books or the need to earn to feed the family, and no money for doctors or medicines. Poverty and malnutrition produce a vicious spiral of ill-health, vulnerability to infection, and inability to maintain minimum standards of cleanliness and sanitation. Moreover, given the patriarchal nature of Indian society and the high value placed on males for economic and cultural reasons, women are even more disadvantaged than men in conditions of poverty, and have less access to food, medicine, and education.

India's economic problems were not amenable to easy solutions. What progress was made was rapidly swallowed by a rising population, though the upward trend only became a frightening explosion from the 1950s. (In 1951 the population was *c.* 360 million.) In rural areas life went on much as it had for centuries. Much farming was still for subsistence on tiny plots, and only in certain areas did farmers produce for the market and consequently have the profits to invest in even more efficient agriculture. By 1950 agricultural technology was still very limited. A tiny proportion of farmers had tractors or tube wells and less fertilizer was used per acre than in any other country. New equipment, new seed producing sturdier and more abundant crops, secure water supplies, cheaper and accessible credit to the poorer farmers, and redistribution of land were all important ingredients of any reform of the country's agricultural base.

Unlike most African countries at independence in the 1960s India did have a substantial and well-established industrial sector in 1947, with the financial networks to support it. Her involvement in the Second World War encouraged industrial expansion, though much of the increased production was for armaments or was drawn off for other military requirements, and was therefore not available for civilian consumption. For example, all mill production of wool textiles, all factory production of leather and footwear, nearly three-quarters of steel and cement production and over two-fifths of paper production was directed away from the civilian economy. Only certain industries really boomed—steel, chemicals, paper, paint, and cement, for example. But shortages in capital goods and skilled manpower prevented major new industrial ventures, as did government policy of restricting non-food production of consumer goods.[47] A further reflection of wartime industrial growth was the increase in the urban percentage of the population (from nearly 13 per cent in 1941 to just over 16 per cent in 1951). But still in 1950/1 factories produced only 6.5 per cent of the national income, and less than 3 per cent of the labour force was employed in factories and mining, compared with nearly 75 per cent in agriculture.[48] The limited nature of industrial development and its restricted geographical distribution could only be overcome by major investment. That meant the generation of resources in rural as well as industrial sectors of the economy, and their direction into industry, either by market forces or by government through such instruments as taxation and licensing.

Economics always were, and still are, at the root of many of India's social problems. Her resources have long been both absolutely scarce and very unevenly distributed among her peoples. Whole regions are poor, particularly where agriculture is precarious and population density high. Bihar, Orissa, and Rajasthan are at the bottom of the heap; fertile Punjab and parts of western India like Gujarat have a far higher *per capita* income. A National Survey soon after independence showed up the inequalities between families. Fourteen to fifteen million households (22 per cent of rural households) owned no land at all. Just under half of the country's rural households owned 1.5 per cent of India's cultivated land, whereas the remaining half were incomparably better placed, particularly the top 25.5 per cent who owned over 83 per cent of all the cultivated land, in parcels of at least five acres, though some of the holdings of this wealthiest group were well over ten acres.[49] Great distinctions of wealth have also meant uneven access to services such as medical care and education. Provision of doctors, nurses, rural clinics, hospitals, colleges, and schools were an urgent priority for the new government, for despite developments in medicine and education through the century these had not been areas of massive government expenditure, even when they had been handed over to Indian control (see above, pp. 244, 298–9). Educational standards varied from region to region, reflecting each region's past history, its degree of urbanization, and its *per capita* income. In 1951 literacy was still very low, particularly among country women (See Table B). Without improvement here there could be little hope of significant change in attitudes, in the economy, or an end to the deprivation of so many who had no resources of land or skills other than their manual labour.

The social problems generated by uneven access to opportunities in the environment of absolute scarcity which the new government inherited were particularly sharply focused in the plight of certain groups whose deprivation was reinforced by their ritual status in Hindu society. Despite advances in female education and the participation of some women in political life through satyagrahas and the enlarged franchise, the vast majority of women still had no choice over their destinies. Neither the limited movement for social reform nor the ways in which women had participated in politics had challenged the fundamental assumptions and institutions of patriarchal society. Consequently women's marriages were arranged, often in childhood or early adolescence, and from that time tending husband, children, and crops was their lot. Divorce or even separation were neither legal nor sanctioned by society. Restrictions on inheritance and ownership of property curtailed women's chances of a livelihood other than through dependence on men; low educational standards similarly deprived them of a viable alternative by barring their entry into a range of service jobs such as those of secretary, clerk, nurse, or teacher. Hindu ideals of womanhood and ritual prescriptions powerfully reinforced these economic and social restric-

Table B. *Literacy in 1951*

	Men	Women
All areas:	23.54	7.62
Rural areas:	19.02	4.87
Urban areas:	45.05	12.34

Source: Census of India, 1951, quoted in J. N. Sinha, 'India: A Demographic Profile', in S. C. Dube (ed.), *India since Independence. Social Report on India 1947–1972* (New Delhi, 1977), p. 32.

tions. For most Untouchables, too, their deprived and isolated position in Hindu society remained unchanged. Despite Gandhi's campaigns, abject poverty, ritual degradation, and a consequential barring of them from access to resources which might have changed their position, such as land, education or skilled work, all ground them down. The new government recognized the burden of its inheritance in these areas of society and the 1950 constitution stated its commitment to fundamental change and a denial of Hindu conventions which an alien government had not dared to initiate. The Directive Principles laid down in the constitution that the state's duty was 'to promote the welfare of the people by securing and promoting . . . a social order in which justice, social, economic and political, shall inform all the institutions of the national life.' Among the Fundamental Rights laid down as enforceable by the courts were rights of equality, freedom, ownership of property, and protection against exploitation. Accordingly Untouchability was now abolished. But it was clear that further legislation, administrative engineering in society, and economic change would be needed if Untouchables or women were to attain a status reflecting their constitutional rights, or if India was to be the secular state founded on the equality of its citizens which it claimed to be.

Hindu ideas of inequality and ritual status were deeply rooted in the minds of millions. Even the deprived and exploited—in non-Hindu eyes—often subscribed to the ideals which were the rationale of the society in which their roles were so circumscribed. However, economic developments in previous decades had shown that Hindu beliefs and ritual status were in themselves no bar to industrialization, responsiveness to market forces and occupational and geographical mobility. Even caste identities and practices had proved flexible and able to accommodate change, although the social and ritual (as opposed to the public, work) context of people's behaviour was slow to change. Despite the constitution's brave claims and the genuine convictions of many of India's new leaders, traditional identities, values, and patterns of behaviour were so strong that they were a dead weight against social change. Yet the very stability of society in the 1940s was in another way a valuable inheritance for the new regime as it sought to weld and govern the nation state. Its reverse, major economic and social instability, would have generated other dilemmas which might well have detroyed the government and the new state's precarious unity.

Ironically, too, the new Congress governments in Delhi and the former provinces faced political problems of attracting collaboration similar to those of their imperial predecessors, though they had themselves as the main opposition to the *raj* constituted one of its major dilemmas. Like any other government they had to gain allies and reward them with the knowledge that their interests would be considered in the processes of decision-making and government. Now the ground rules for attracting allies were changed, and universal suffrage created a comprehensive framework for soliciting support at all political levels. However, the Congress triumph in the 1946 elections and the legitimacy it had gained among Hindus as the natural heir to the British was not a guarantee of unlimited support from the electorate. Congress governments would have to keep on proving their responsiveness to the needs of those crucial to the functioning of the economy, and to those who by virtue of their economic or social position could act as vote-banks, promising the votes of their caste group, followers, clients or allies. In a land where local identities, interests, and loyalties were still dominant, the political importance of the 'local notable' remained great, though Congress had looked to notables rather different from those who had aided the British *raj*. This process began long before independence, in the relations of Congress with Indian businessmen and the more prosperous peasant farmers enfranchised between the wars, who were welcomed into the party's discussions and institutions. After 1947 it did not hesitate to welcome the support of prominent rural figures who had once been at home in British durbars, and now paid court to the new *raj*: particularly when such landlords or former princes could fund the party or pay for their own election campaigns. But it also had to attract broader and deeper swathes of the population into the party or at least into the polling booths as its supporters. Rarely had it made truly populist appeals before, and the legacy of its past ambivalence towards the demands of the poorest suggested that it was ill-equipped for the task, now made more difficult by the social and economic problems it had inherited and which it was now responsible for solving. Furthermore, its public commitment to equality, freedom from want and exploitation, to a rising standard of living and universal education, and to a creative role for the state, helped to generate rising expectations and to set a new standard by which its performance would be judged.

Just as there was continuity in the problems facing imperial and independent governments in the 1940s there was similarity and continuity in the resources of government—in terms of institutions, personnel, and even ideas. Remarkably little changed after 1947 because the British had relied so heavily on Indians to man their *raj* and devolved so much power before they left, creating structures and traditions which endured because they worked, however fiercely Congress had originally decried them. The main changes occurred at the top of the governmental pyramid with the removal of the Viceroy and Secretary of State, signifying the end of the authority of the British crown and parliament, and India's transformation after a short phase as a Dominion with a Governor-General into an Independent republic freely associatively with the Commonwealth.

The institutions of consultation, decision-making and legislation were laid down in the 1950 constitution drawn up by the Constituent Assembly, which after 1947 became a provisional Parliament.[50] It drew very heavily on the 1935 Government of India Act, taking from it about 250 articles virtually unchanged. Consequently the institutions already operating at provincial level in British India remained. Former provinces became states within the federal union of India. State governmental structure changed little, and is a miniature version of the Union government, each state having its legislative assembly (eight states also have second chambers). Each state has its Chief Minister appointed by the state Governor because he can form a stable ministry and run a government responsible to the legislature. The Governor is appointed by Delhi—by the President in consultation with the ministry in power in the state. At the centre the formal head of state is the President, chosen by a special electoral college representing elected members of state and central legislatures. He in turn appoints the Prime Minister who is normally the leader of the majority in the lower house of Parliament. Parliament consists of the Lok Sabha (lower house) and the Rajya Sabha (upper house), members of the former being elected at least every five years, members of the smaller upper house being Presidential nominees or men elected by the states.

Much of this structure was drawn from India's previous experience under the British, and beyond that from the British tradition of a parliamentary democracy with a head of state exercising a significant but limited constitutional role beside his symbolic and ritual functions. As at Westminster real power rests in the hands of the Prime Minister who must have parliamentary support. India's constitution also lays down the powers of the centre and the states, and the topics shared between them[51]—as had the two previous acts of constitutional reform. Residual power remains with the Union, not the states. By various devices, including the allocation of tax resources, the supreme power of the centre is maintained, though the centre simultaneously needs the states' co-operation in the implementation of policies. (In practice much depends at any time on whether the same party is in power at centre and state level, on the Prime Minister of the day, on the issue at stake, and on the extent to which states co-operate together against the centre.) Both the interplay between different levels of government, and the strong centre, were remarkably reminiscent of the days of the *raj*. Those who had argued for a weak centre, and for decentralization on Gandhian lines were disappointed. Gandhi had never come to terms with the nature and potential of the state in the modern world; and disliking what he saw, he increasingly took flight from the practicalities of politics and so provided no genuine counter focus to those who argued for strong, centralized government. Congress was itself reponsible for this fundamental continuity in the institutions of government and consultation—not just by its stance in the Constituent Assembly, but because of its pre-independence role. By co-operating in the provincial institutions through which the British devolved power, by mobilizing men unversed in the politics appropriate to such arenas and encouraging and educating a widening social range of supporters to value them, it lowered foreign imports on to an indigenous social structure. By helping the reformed structures to strike deep social roots and ensuring that they responded to the needs of local people it made them effective and durable.

Superficial consideration suggests that whatever institutional continuity remained through the decade and beyond, 1947 marked a sharp break in the ideological resources of government. Certainly the primary commitment of the new state to creating a freer, more equal and prosperous society is in strong contrast to the pragmatism of the nineteenth-century *raj* in its heyday, with its implicit rationale of supporting British world-wide interests. Although a belief in the 'white man's burden', his duty to reform the manners and morals of his Asian subjects, was interwoven with material interests in British imperial ideology, lack of men and money accompanied by fear of social upheaval prevented the government from considering radical social and economic reform. However, in the later years of the *raj* the interests it upheld had shifted markedly and far less was at stake for the metropolitan country. Furthermore, as constitutional reforms were instituted so Indian opinion increasingly determined policies, even if the British were nominally still masters. Tariffs and defence expenditure were examples. In some areas of public life Indian legislators also began deliberate reforms; as in the provision of primary education and the partial lifting of some disabilities, such as the ban on temple entry, from Untouchables, by provincial governments using the power devolved on them by the 1935 Act.

The great change in government's perception of its role occurred during the Second World War. The deep and painful impact of the war on the economy and the need to maximize India's contribution to the war effort forced government into unprecedented intervention and planning. It imposed an Excess Profits Tax to reduce purchasing power, in order to control inflation. It regulated the issue of industrial shares, preventing the production of non-essential goods. Ultimately it had to control prices, organize rationing, and involve itself in production, procurement, and distribution of essential items such as food and cloth. It also began to hammer out a coherent plan for post-war reconstruction, which was published in 1944. It stated explicitly the 'need for planning for the whole of India and the exercise of far more initiative by the State than hitherto in matters of social reform and economic development'. Another but independent stream of thought favouring government planning and intervention joined the official one flowing from government necessity. Congress had committed itself to planning from 1938, and a planning committee had worked under Nehru, incorporating such leading businessmen as Purshotamdas Thakurdas, Ambalal Sarabhai and Walchand Hirachand. During the war, though Con-

gress leaders were in jail, many representatives of Indian business continued to work along these lines and in 1944 published what became known as
the Bombay Plan for the development of India's economy and the increasing prosperity of her people. It envisaged raising output in agriculture by
130 per cent, in industry by 500 per cent and in the service sector by 200 per
cent within about fifteen years. Not surprisingly the new government after
independence drew on both these ideological developments and committed
itself to planned economic expansion and social change. In 1950 it established a Planning Commission to advise government on priorities and the
most effective use of the country's resources. But the breakthrough to
government visualizing its role as a creative and directive one had occurred
not at independence but early in the decade, when the British themselves
discarded their old assumptions and threw themselves into a role inconceivable in the 1930s.[52]

A further element of continuity in the ideas behind governmental practice before and after independence needs stressing if one is to understand a
dimension of India's democratic experience which was most powerfully
demonstrated in Mrs Gandhi's 'Emergency Rule' thirty years after independence. Although Congress in opposition had bitterly opposed
government's ability to rule with emergency powers, yet as the party of
government intent on welding a new state it incorporated into the constitution very significant provisions for just such rule after 1947. It permitted the
President to suspend the right to freedom and to constitutional remedies in
situations of national emergency, and also provided for preventive detention of those thought likely to injure society. The family likeness to the *raj*'s
coercive powers was even greater when in the early 1960s a Defence of
India Act provided for the detention of anyone thought likely to prejudice
the defence of India. The old emergency powers of Viceroy and provincial
governors reappeared in those given to the states' governors and the President: both, like their British predecessors, have power to promulgate ordinances. Furthermore, the President can in certain circumstances suspend a
state government and bring the state under Union control—so-called
'President's Rule'. Here is potential for coercion and authoritarian rule as
stern as anything the British had produced.[53]

Even more strikingly than in ideology and institutions, the continuity in
the resources available for governing India is apparent in actual people. Not
only were many of the politicians who came to power at independence
already experienced in government—at provincial level like UP's Pandit
Pant, or in Delhi itself as in Nehru's case. Those who were paid servants and
instruments of government rather than its elected members were initially
employed and trained by the British and remained to serve new masters
without radical re-training or ideological 'reformation'. The vast bulk of
ordinary government officials, the police and the army, had been Indian

throughout the British *raj*. Inheriting such a resource of trained, experienced servants was a valuable legacy in the face of threatened administrative chaos in the north; though a certain number of Muslims in all the services left for service in Pakistan. At partition about 230,000 soldiers were allotted to India: and the number in India's bureaucracy at independence was probably about three million. At the highest levels in the army, police, and civil service there were still a certain number of senior British officials. Half the army officers were British, but a far smaller proportion of the ICS, following deliberate Indianization of the service over the previous decades and the difficulties of European recruitment. At independence there were about ninety more Indians than British in the ICS. Few British people stayed on in the services for long after 1947 and for a short phase there had to be rapid promotion to the higher ranks and emergency recruitment to the lower levels to replace those whose careers suddenly blossomed at the departure of the British. (One Bombay ICS man recruited in 1927 became a Cabinet Secretary to the Government of India in 1946—a staggeringly swift escalation of the promotion ladder!)

However, even with the influx of new army officers and members of the Indian Administrative Service (IAS as the ICS became after independence), traditions and patterns of action in the services created over decades changed little. The traditions bred at Sandhurst among Indians commissioned and trained under the *raj* flourished as the surviving military élite moulded their successors at the Indian Military Academy at Dehra Dun, and by practical example in parade grounds and Officers' Messes in the old British cantonments up and down the country. English remained the medium of recruitment and training, military life-style and social conventions remained; as did a tradition of elegant professionalism and career orientation, and non-involvement in political matters. Indeed such has been the strength of the old ways in the officer corps that it has been the butt of parliamentary criticism as 'un-Indian'. Yet the legacy of an apolitical army has been of great significance in India's very existence as a democracy, in sharp contrast to the experience of newly independent territories in other continents, or in neighbouring Pakistan. More ambiguous for India's political future was the continuity in its police during the transition from colonialism to independence—given the manifest weakness of the police force, its corruption, and its record as an instrument of coercion lacking the trust of the people.

Similarly, the ICS tradition continues in the IAS. It remains an élite and highly paid administrative body, drawn by competitive examination from a small social range, its recruits being sons of professional men, many of them in government service, who could afford an English medium education for their children. New recruits are further shaped by their professional training and apprenticeship in the districts under established officers many of whom were produced by a similar process at the hands of British ICS men. The last officer recruited under the British only retired in 1980. The service maintained not only their tradition of 'general competence' rather than technical expertise, but the cumbersome and often paper-laden procedural rules of their predecessors. It is still the 'steel frame' of Indian governance, despite Nehru's insistence before 1947 that no new order could be built in India while the ICS spirit remained. However, Patel as Home Minister in the Interim Government was well aware that in the turbulent days of 1946–7 the ICS, whatever its previous image in the eyes of Congressmen, was a bastion against chaos and the disintegration of government. He was partly instrumental in persuading other Congressmen that continuity in administration must be maintained. Clearly the service was a source of stability. But its capacity to serve a country where radical change was desired or essential was an open question.[54]

In retrospect the decade seems less the start of a new era or a great divide in the experience of India's people, than a time of continuity or at least of changes shaped by existing trends. India's new rulers had no clean slate on which to draw a new world, and no new instruments with which to create new designs. They bore a paradoxical inheritance—from their imperial predecessors and from their own past as both party of provincial government and leaders of a loosely co-ordinated movement of opposition to the *raj* in the name of a nation, the composition of which was unclear. The context of a stable society, a poor economy, and continuity in the problems and resources of government does much to explain the strengths and weaknesses of India's democracy in operation—both its deep roots and durability, yet its failures to respond to the country's most urgent needs.

Appendix to Chapter VI

Chronology of main events leading to the independence of India and the partition of the subcontinent in August 1947.

1939

September:	Outbreak of war.
18 October:	*Viceroy's Statement on War Aims and the War Effort*: reiterates that goal of British Policy is Dominion Status for India, but that 1935 Act is open to modification at the end of the war, in the light of Indian opinion. Offers association of Indian opinion in war effort through consultative group representing major political parties in British India and the princes.
October:	Resignation of Congress Ministries.
22 December:	Muslim League observes 'Deliverance Day'.

1940

10 January:	Viceroy restates British policy.
19–20 March:	Congress at Ramgarh demands independence and a constituent assembly to frame new constitution. Announces that it plans to embark on civil disobedience.
23 March:	Muslim League at Lahore demands 'Pakistan'.
April:	*Blitzkrieg* begins in western Europe.
May:	Churchill becomes Prime Minister in Britain.
7 August:	Viceroy, Linlithgow, makes *'August Offer'*: offers places to representative Indians in an expanded Executive Council and on a new War Advisory Council. Assures minorities that their views will be given weight in any constitutional changes and that power will not be transferred to any government whose authority is denied by important elements in India; and gives tentative welcome to idea of post-war constituent assembly to frame new constitution.
September:	Congress and Muslim League both reject 'August Offer'.
17 October:	Congress launches individual civil disobedience.

1941

7 December:	Pearl Harbor: America enters war.

1942

15 February:	Fall of Singapore.
22 March–	
12 April:	Mission of Sir Stafford Cripps to India.
29 March:	*Cripps Offer*: elected body after the war to frame new constitution for India; and during war Indian participation in government. Envisages Indian Dominion after the war with power to secede from the Commonwealth (i.e. implication that total independence is possible)—with the proviso that no part of India could be forced to join this Dominion.
April:	Congress and Muslim League reject offer.
8 August:	Congress launches 'Quit India movement' and is declared unlawful organization.

1943

October:	Wavell succeeds Linlithgow as Viceroy.

1944

September:	Failure of Gandhi–Jinnah talks on nature of Pakistan and future of Indian Muslims.

1945

March–June:	Wavell visits London for policy discussions.
7 May:	Surrender of Germany.
14 June:	Wavell makes broadcast announcing plan to reconstitute his Executive council from among Indian politicians and the plan for a conference of Indian leaders to achieve this.
15 June:	Imprisoned Congress leaders released.
June–July:	Simla Conference fails to agree on Wavell's plan for almost entirely Indian Executive Council.
26 July:	Labour Victory in British General Election; Attlee becomes Prime Minister.
14 August:	Surrender of Japan.
December–	
January 1946:	General Elections in India.

1946

January:	Parliamentary Delegation visits India, to give British MPs first-hand evidence about conditions in India.
23 March–	
29 June:	Cabinet Mission visits India.
16 May:	*Cabinet Mission announces its plan*: after failure to achieve

agreed plan among Indian leaders at Simla during their visit they offer their own—an Indian Union of British and princely India, with its executive and legislature, dealing with foreign affairs, defence, and communications only (i.e. a very weak centre to soothe minorities and Muslims in particular, but offering offering an alternative to outright partition of the subcontinent). Residual powers should remain with provinces. Provinces are to be free to form groups with executives and legislatures dealing with topics which groups have decided to take in common. Details of such a three-tiered structure are to be worked out by a constituent assembly. Meanwhile there should be the immediate formation of an Interim Government with the support of the major Indian political parties.

June–July:	Congress and Muslim League both reject Cabinet Mission Plan.
16 August:	Muslims observe 'Direct Action Day'.
16–18 August:	The 'Great Calcutta Killing'.
2 September:	Interim Government formed.
13 October:	Muslim League decides to join Interim Government.
October:	Communal rioting erupts, particularly in Bengal and Bihar.
3–6 December:	Abortive London conference of major Indian leaders.
9 December:	Constituent Assembly meets (without Muslim League members).

1947

February:	Communal violence, particularly in Punjab.
20 February:	Attlee announces British intention of leaving India by June 1948, and that Mountbatten is to succeed Wavell as Viceroy.
22 March:	Mountbatten arrives in India.
3 June:	Mountbatten announces plan of partition of subcontinent into India and Pakistan, and British withdrawal in August.
15 August:	India and Pakistan gain independence.

Note: A more detailed chronology covering 1933–47 is available in Philips & Wainwright (eds.), *The Partition Of India*, pp. 554–83.

CHAPTER VII

Epilogue:
India's Democratic Experience

India's ability to sustain democratic forms of government and politics through the second half of this century is in sharp contrast to the experience of her Asian neighbours, and of most former colonies in Africa. There have been no military bids for power, and even Mrs Gandhi's months of 'Emergency Rule' (which many thought perilously close to dictatorship) were ended by the electors' verdict in 1977. Despite phases of acute domestic strain and violence, the assassination of two Prime Ministers, and a number of armed conflicts with neighbours, she has also remained a stable, independent regional power. It is no wonder that India's democratic experience has fascinated historians and political scientists, not to speak of those western visitors who find in India so much that is familiar yet is obviously different in her political life. This book set out to examine the making of this rare political phenomenon, an Asian democracy. It has investigated its roots in the growth of institutions and new patterns of political behaviour, in the development of Indian ideas, particularly about power, authority and group identity, and in the nature of the society into which democratic forms have been welcomed, despite their alien social and cultural origins. But our study would be incomplete without some consideration of India's continuing experience of democracy since independence, some attempt to understand both its durability and its frailties, and also whether it has accomplished the tasks set for it by the end of colonial rule and the expectation of its peoples. This epilogue is only an introduction to the complexities of modern India's democratic experience. Excellent literature is available on the political system, society, and economy, and the varied experience of different states with the Indian Union: some are suggested at the end of this volume. What follows is a discussion of some important themes as signposts for readers who wish to explore more deeply the lives of a people we have followed for two centuries, from being subjects of a Muslim empire in the process of erosion by long-term change, to becoming citizens of a democratic, secular state caught up in the political and economic turbulence of the late twentieth-century world.

i   Democracy at Work

Definitions of democracy can generate endless discussion. For our purposes it is taken to mean, first, the provision of regular mechanisms for registering the people's wishes about who should govern them and what their policies should be, and for providing a check on the actions of government if it disregards these wishes or deprives the people of such basic rights as freedom of speech and association. Such mechanisms were laid down in the 1950 constitution as the basis of legitimate government. (As noted in Chapter VI, they consisted of a structure of political life in elections to consultative, legislative assemblies, of stated powers for the different sections and agents of government, and of specified rights for the individual citizen. The judiciary was the ultimate remedy for the preservation of the constitution.) Besides this participatory aspect of democracy there is, secondly, the issue of the uses to which the structures of government are put, and whether they promote the expressed wishes of the people. This section of the epilogue deals primarily with the first, participatory aspect; while the later parts deal with the second, though the two are clearly and inevitably inter-connected and react upon each other.

How then have the institutions of democracy 'worked' in India? Elections to state legislatures and the Lok Sabha in Delhi are the obvious starting-point. These have been held regularly and have been no rubber stamp: the people's verdict has produced major and sometimes dramatic results. In 1967 Congress for the first time failed to gain majorities in eight states and had its Lok Sabha majority sliced to 54 per cent from well over 70 per cent in the previous three elections. In 1971 there was a major resurgence of Congress after it had split and the majority within it had followed Nehru's daughter, Indira Gandhi, leaving behind an enfeebled rump known as Congress (O). Indira Gandhi was in turn ousted from power in 1977 after her 'Emergency Rule'—and honoured the election result rather than attempting to reimpose her authoritarian regime by force. Yet the ramshackle alliance of her opponents, the Janata Party, fell apart and failed to attract the electorate in 1980, and Indira's Congress swept back with 67 per cent of Lok Sabha seats compared with 28 per cent in the previous electoral débâcle. In 1989 the electorate gave further proof of its power and sophistication of choice by returning a minority government for the first time to power in Delhi.[1]

The sheer holding of such elections is an extraordinary organizational achievement on the part of the Central Election Commission and the political organizations which seek to mobilize the voters. About two million officials conducted the 1980 elections, and there were about 438,000 polling stations. Because communications are poor, national elections used to take time: nineteen days in 1957, cut to four days in 1977 and two days in 1980.

All citizens aged twenty-one years and over are enfranchised—some 320 millions in 1977 and 354 millions in 1980. The politicians have had to learn to make contact with and appeal to this vast electorate, many of whom are illiterate. All parties have followed similar strategies, particularly that of careful selection of candidates to 'match' each local constituency, taking into account its caste, communal, and economic characteristics. Caste loyalties still help to determine political loyalties. But no political party seeking national status can afford to rely on a single caste appeal. All parties therefore tend to prefer candidates from locally dominant castes which have the numbers and connections to ensure wide support; and, as castes are often factionally divided, this presents few problems. Modern electioneering can, therefore, weaken old group identities. It helps to construct new 'vertical' linkages in society as politicians try to put together a local following. Some overt vote-buying with hard cash still occurs, though this is almost certainly on the decrease as the electorate becomes more aware of its influence. More powerful as appeals are candidates' promises to solve local problems, provide wells, roads, and schools. Until the 1970s most elections were fought in such local terms, and until then the 'linking' in time of state and central elections helped to militate against appeal on nation-wide issues. A change to Lok Sabha elections contested on national issues occurred in 1971, the year of the 'Indira wave' as it became known, when Mrs Gandhi's personality and slogan 'Get rid of poverty' were the core of the Congress campaign. In 1977 and 1980, too, there was really only one basic question at stake—the record of government in the previous months. Increasingly in the 1980s elections became personality rather than genuinely issue-orientated—particularly the personality—and prestige of the members of the Nehru family who led Congress, Indira Gandhi until her assassination in 1984, and then her surviving son, Rajiv, until his murder in 1991. The tendency towards such electoral populism was closely related to the decline of the Congress as an organized party, as we shall subsequently see.

Accusations of bribery and corruption during elections are rife. Court cases on these grounds are favourite tactics of defeated candidates against their successful opponents—as they were in eighteenth-century England. Whatever the facts in particular cases it is clear that elections are exceedingly expensive for politicians; and though there is a limit on what the candidate can spend there is no legal limit placed on his party's expenditure on his behalf. It was estimated in 1971 that Congress spent about Rs. 250 million—Rs. 480,000 per constituency.[2] The money goes on transport for the candidate and his henchmen, on posters, painted slogans, multiplication of carefully chosen and emotive party symbols (see Fig. i), flags, badges, and loud speaker equipment. In the south the DMK, a regional party, has also used the resources of the local and highly popular film industry, its stars and vocalists, to further its cause. Elections are as exciting as marriages and

INDIAN NATIONAL CONGRESS (I)   COMMUNIST PARTY OF INDIA (M)

LOK DAL

BHARATIYA JANATA PARTY

Fig. i. *Examples of Symbols used by National Political Parties in India*

festivals, and can generate interest and tension equal to that experienced in western democracies. The 1977 and 1980 contests were particularly remarkable for the atmosphere they created. Eyewitnesses, including the author, testified to the electric atmosphere as the results began to pour in and were broadcast to eager groups clustered around radios. During the 1991 election campaign Rajiv Gandhi was assassinated: and there was acute fear that the country would be convulsed by violence, such is the intensity of public interest and involvement in the electoral process.

An indicator of the effectiveness of electioneering and of the functioning of the electoral mechanism is voter turn-out (See Table A). By the 1960s the number of the enfranchised actually voting was comparable to that in western democracies. (In 1976, for example, the turn-out in the USA was 54 per cent.) There is little difference between town and country as such in this respect, though education seems to be the most important variable affecting turn-out. Country women vote less than their city sisters: but at each election women's participation has increased. By 1977 55 per cent of elegible women voted, compared with 65.7 per cent of enfranchised men. A further sign of the 'health' of elections is freedom from violence and intimidation. Given the size of the electoral enterprise, Indian elections have been re-

Table A. *Indian Parliamentary Elections*

Year	Electorate (in millions)	Polling stations	Votes polled (in millions)	Turnout (per cent)
1952	173.2	132,560	80.7	46.6
1957	193.7	220,478	91.3	47.1
1962	217.7	238,355	119.9	55.1
1967	250.1	267,555	152.7	61.1
1971	274.1	342,944	151.5	55.3
1977	321.2	373,908	194.3	60.5
1980	355.6	434,442	202.3	56.9
1984	375.8	479,214	238.4	63.4

Source: P. R. Brass, *The Politics of India since Independence* (Cambridge, 1990), p. 90.

markably peaceful. In 1952 and 1957 only a handful of polling stations were disrupted, causing adjournment of the poll, and in 1962 no adjournments were necessary because of breaches of the peace. However, in 1967 and 1971 there was considerable unrest, and numerous but generally unproven allegations of assault, kidnapping and murder. Bihar was badly affected in 1967 and the poll was adjourned in twelve places. In 1971 the worst area was West Bengal because of specific local political conditions, and the army had to patrol the Calcutta streets at election time. 1,027 violent incidents were reported in this state, and 215 deaths in connection with the polls. The national total was 2,291 violent incidents and 244 deaths. The 1989 elections, when there was no equivalent regional turbulence, were marked by violence, however, with more than 100 election-related deaths officially recorded.[3]

Candidates who succeed in the elections proceed to the state legislatures or the Lok Sabha in Delhi. It is notable that MPs and MLAs (Members of Legislative Assemblies) increasingly come from rural backgrounds. In the Lok Sabha, for example, the proportion of lawyers has decreased as a result of the first four general elections from 35 per cent to 30 per cent, 24.5 per cent and 17.5 per cent: and in the corresponding parliaments the number of agriculturalists has risen from 22.4 per cent, through 29.1 per cent and 27.4 per cent to 31.1 per cent. In state legislatures this 'ruralization' is even more marked, in contrast to the earliest post-independence assemblies when the more highly educated, westernized and professional people still had a dominant role. As 80 per cent of Indians are country folk it can be said broadly that their legislators have become somewhat more 'representative'.[4]

The Lok Sabha with its open sessions and committees has a role similar to that of the British House of Commons. It debates and passes legislation, scrutinizes the action of government agencies and personnel, and their use of public funds, and provides a forum for the verbal questioning of the Prime Minister. Its members can, of course, bring down a government if they withdraw their support. The Lok Sabha's conventions are much like British ones, and generally its proceedings have been decorous and orderly. Parliament's debates are well reported in the Press. In the first two decades of its existence it was firmly dominated by large Congress majorities, and for most of that time, too, by the revered figure of India's first Prime Minister, Jawaharlal Nehru. None the less, the small opposition parties were respected and heard, Parliament was a significant arena of political exchange, and a wide range of laws was passed, including major acts of social reform. However, after the death of Nehru and the first generation of Indian parliamentarians, the quality of parliamentary life and the significance of the Lok Sabha in Indian politics deteriorated very greatly. One element in this process was the arrival of new members with little education and no parliamentary experience. This in itself would not have mattered had there been senior party members with the impetus to 'socialize' these new recruits. Indira Gandhi, unlike her father, was increasingly contemptuous of parliament and would not perform this role. Her son, Sanjay, whom she groomed to succeed her (but was killed in an air crash) accentuated this by organizing the election of young cronies who were more prone to violence than the observance of parliamentary forms and courtesies. A further element in the decline of parliament as a working instrument of democracy was the tendency under Indira Gandhi, continued when her other son, Rajiv, succeeded her, to downgrade the Cabinet and with it the influence of elected Ministers, in favour of a 'kitchen cabinet' of selected henchmen and advisors. It was only during the 1975–7 'Emergency' that Parliament became in effect the rubber stamp of an undemocratic government. Many MPs did not attend, the principal opposition party leaders were in jail, and press censorship further crippled parliament as a public watchdog. Although the Janata government brought to power by the electorate after 1977 rescinded much of the structure of authoritarian rule which had been enacted by the pliant parliament, the quality of parliamentary life and the authority of the Lok Sabha have not been restored to their earlier levels. Although the role of leaders in this process has been significant, it is also clear that the Indian parliament, like many other legislatures, has found it increasingly difficult to maintain its role in policy-making, as opposed to that of bureaucrats and specialists, as governmental functions have become more complex. In the Indian case opposition parties have been so unstable and fragmented that they have never built up the expertise to challenge government on policy *details* and provide viable alternatives.

This deterioration in the life of parliamentary institutions is even more pronounced in the state legislatures. Again, an element in this has been the influx of inexperienced local people with no conception of a parliamentary role and little grasp of the policy issues needing discussion. Compounding this is the lack of local party discipline and organization, particularly since Congress lost its local dominance in the late 1960s. State assemblies since that time have often proved incapable of producing stable governments. Loosely patched-up and precarious coalitions, waves of political defections or 'floor-crossing' as MLAs seek office and security are commonplace in state politics, and seriously threaten the status of the MLA as the representative of his constituents.[5] At worst these trends have meant that state governments try to circumvent the legislature by reducing legislative working days and ruling through executive ordinances. In Bihar, for example, legislative days reached a nadir of 33 in 1969. This does not, however, mean that people do not want to become MLAs or that potential constituents are not profoundly interested in their representative in the state capital. The MLA is a highly significant political operator, important to his constituents not so much for his part in debate and the passage of legislation, but for his intervention in administration on their behalf, and his ability to get them jobs, college places or one of the permits to engage in particular businesses which are a troublesome and ubiquitous part of a planned economy. He tends to belong to a wide range of associations—marketing and credit societies, co-operative banks. Some MLAs combine small businesses with landholding. With such a wide rural base and the connections achieved by his multifarious economic and political activities the MLA becomes a significant modern type of patron, and a channel through which villagers are connected to a wider political world. He is both educator and broker as he stands between these political worlds.

Even more disquieting a feature of India's democracy at work than the quality of state legislative life has been the erosion of the 'federal' aspect of the democratic structure by the deliberate intervention of the centre in the politics and government of the states. There have also been a disturbing number of times when state legislatures have been suspended and President's Rule imposed—not because of genuine national emergency or local disorder, but because of conflict between state and centre. Not surprisingly they have been most numerous when different parties are in power in state and Union and the centre feels its authority threatened. The early cases of Kerala (1959) and Uttar Pradesh (1970) were particularly controversial. In Kerala a Communist government controlled the state and retained its majority in the legislature; but the local Congress was behind widespread anti-government agitation and public disorder. The Congress government in Delhi intervened on the debatable ground of breakdown of law and order. Central intervention in Uttar Pradesh was even more overtly partisan for though the local Chief Minister had lost his majority through defections he had not been given the chance to test his support in the legislature, as it was not in session, nor was there any public disorder.[5] This tendency towards intervention in the states by President's Rule and other means has increased, whatever the party in power in Delhi. The Janata government in Delhi in 1977 dismissed the nine Congress governments remaining in the states; and Congress followed its precedent in a mirror-image action when it won general elections in 1980. So the power of the locally elected legislature in the states to provide or deny a majority to the state government has been grievously eroded. Yet a further aspect of this was the weakening of the Congress as a genuine political party, and the persistent interference by Mrs Gandhi and her son in local party matters, often insisting that the Chief Minister in any particular state should be a man of the Prime Minister's choosing and of proven loyalty to him or her, rather than one who commanded local Congress support.[6]

The democratic functioning or malfunctioning of elections and the legislatures manifestly depends heavily on the state of political parties. Their role in India is similar to that of parties in longer established democracies. By organising groups of candidates and legislators round known issues, policies, and leaders they appeal to and mobilize the electorate, giving elections coherence and direction, and making orderly parliamentary business possible. By speaking for particular material interests and social groups, and voicing distinctive ideals, they enable citizens to use the democratic processes more effectively, and so increase the legitimacy of those processes. Furthermore, by organizing support for particular policies before they pass into law, they increase the likelihood that such policies will be enacted in practice. However, in India as in any new democratic polity parties have much more work to do and a vitally creative role in the preservation and strengthening of democracy. Where literacy is low and communications still poor, parties have to work much harder and more ingeniously to contact voters and convince them of the significance of their vote. Where a sense of identity is still strongly connected to village, locality, and caste, and where ties of blood and patronage remain important, parties have to use these primordial linkages and loyalties in the service of democratic politics, and ultimately to transcend them. For example, the controversies which have raged on the role of caste and caste associations in politics suggest that the use of caste names and connections is an important, though sometimes transitional, element in democratic politics and forms a bridge over which people can pass to new political identities and forms of association.[7] Furthermore in India voluntary associations of interest groups such as trade unions are weak by comparison with their counterparts in Europe and America. In the experience of long established democracies labour, trade, business, and civic groups, and bodies representing consumers or rate-players, for example, are an important part of the infrastructure of political life. They are a criss-crossing web of connections through which people articulate their interests and exert pressure on government. In India the absence or weakness of similar associations means that the political parties are particularly important in forging links between people and government. Only if these links are strong and effective, only if government responds to the messages conveyed by them, will people become—and remain—convinced of the legitimacy of the political system because of its proven utility to them. A primary function and characteristic of a democratic polity is to achieve adjustments between the interests of its members: such adjustments can only occur if the interests are heard in the first place.

India's experience of party politics since independence changed fundamentally in 1967 when Congress lost power in many states for the first time though it retained a majority in Delhi. There is neither need nor space in our epilogue for a narrative of politics,[8] but it is important to see the role parties and their fluctuating fortunes have played in the working of democracy. From 1947 to 1967 Congress was the major and totally dominant party. But its dominance was unlike the one-party rule which so often followed independence in other newly independent states and in effect silenced legitimate opposition. Firstly, other parties functioned freely, including Communist parties, several socialist groups, Hindu communal parties and some regional parties such as Tamil Nadu's DMK. Furthermore Congress by its very nature helped to encourage and organize the exchange of opinion and the airing of interests which are central to democratic politics. It was often called an 'umbrella party' or a whole party system within itself, for it contained and allowed free expression of a wide range of political opinions and interests. In its many internal ideological and factional conflicts a bargaining and reconciliation process was at work which produced an all-India consensus based on the articulation of diversity and conflict, not its suppression. Its inclusive quality owed much to its pre-independence role as a welder of a national movement out of disparate groups, and also to the presence at its helm of Jawaharlal Nehru. He combined charm, vision, energy, and a streak of authoritarianism which kept the party together and firmly under the control of its parliamentarians. He was a strong political force until the early 1960s, and neither the party nor the majority of voters could visualize India without him. Another attraction of Congress was its role as government. Aspiring politicians wanted to be where the action was, where careers and patronage were available. As in the late 1930s in the provinces, so in the 1950s in states and Union, men naturally gravitated into it rather than dissipate their energies on the political sidelines.

The sheer length of time Congress and its established leaders held power helped to stabilize the political system: as did their ability to 'manage' the succession to leadership when Nehru died in 1964, successfully coping with what is a critical point in the experience of most 'new' states. Apart from the time factor, Congress's mode of operation also embedded democratic politics firmly into Indian public life. Not only did it provide an ambience for controlled conflict and the emergence of a broad political consensus. Its financial resources and historical image enabled it to mobilize and educate voters. Its deliberate strategies of tailoring itself to each locality, of attracting local 'notables'—from prosperous peasants to ex-landlords and even princes—helped to integrate the politics and power structures of localities into a national democratic system, and to channel old loyalties and patronage ties into new patterns of political behaviour. Furthermore it recruited a new generation of potential activists and continued to give places to men from widening social groups, continuing its pattern of opening its doors to those outside established political élites. No single élite retained dominance in Congress, and in each state and even district Congress adapted, chameleon-like, to local conditions. Such openness and flexibility attracted voters and activists, and contributed to the continuing legitimacy of democratic politics.[9]

However, in 1966 Nehru's successor, Lal Bahadur Shastri, died suddenly after signing a historic truce with Pakistan. The struggle for leadership which ensued eventually broke the party asunder and contributed to its failure at the polls in 1967. From then on the 'umbrella party system' was in ruins, and once the central and state elections were 'delinked' in the 1970s Indian politics became much more open, fragmented, and competitive. In the all-India political arena Congress remained the one party constantly contesting for power, but now no longer always able to win elections. Some all-India parties proved ephemeral and those oppositional coalitions which have wrested power in Delhi could rarely maintain their unity and provide a long-term alternative to Congress government. Each state developed its own distinctive party system. In most Congress was a force to be reckoned with, but there have also developed a wide spectrum of regional or ideologically orientated parties who alone or in coalition have ruled the states, though as we have already noted, they are under constant threat of central intervention.

Given the immensely important role of parties in the functioning of a democratic system, one of the gravest issues facing India in the later twentieth century is precisely the weakness of its parties. Few of the alternatives to Congress have proved disciplined bodies, ideologically coherent, or structured round distinctive policies, and able to organize and retain grassroots support. There are honourable exceptions such as the CPM which has generated a crucial degree of popular organization and support, and proved its coherence and competence as government of West Bengal for many years since 1977. But many regional parties are rent by faction and destablized by defections, and can only build up strength when they have the resources of government to reward their members. Furthermore, Congress itself after it split in 1969 became more a Nehru family patrimony than a functioning political party. Indira Gandhi proceeded to centralize that portion of the old Congress which rallied round her after 1969 and swept to power in the early 1970s. From that point onwards no elections were held within the party organization and she made loyalty to herself the supreme qualification for office and party position in states and the centre, and concentrated decisions in her own hands. Thereby she abandoned older patterns of adjustment and reconciliation. By ousting established local leaders with independent power bases in favour of 'loyal' men she destroyed the local political foundations of state Congress parties. Consequently Congress, though amenable to her, was less able to perform its crucial role of mobilizing support and integrating local interests into national politics.[10] The extent to which Congress had changed from an umbrella party into a family fiefdom was shown by the succession of Rajiv Gandhi, on his mother's assassination in 1984, to the leadership of the party and the Prime Ministership, though he was devoid of political ambition, and had only recently begun to acquire political experience, having been a career civil pilot. Nor did he greatly change the nature of Congress despite apparent intentions early in his time of office to hold intraparty elections and revive the Congress as a genuinely party organization. Interlocked with this erosion of the local bases of the party and the decline of accommodating leadership in preference for autocracy was the development of an all-India populist style of leadership. It was a strategy to win elections in the all-India arena, relying on personal appeal rather than solid organizational support—a strategy at which both Indira and Rajiv proved adept, with their family prestige, their personal charm, and their 'hands-on' approach to electioneering. Yet this style bypassed serious discussion of key policy issues; and further eroded the institutions of party and government on which democracy rests.

Even where political parties function effectively as linkages between government and citizens and in consequence grievances can normally be channelled through an integral part of the democratic system, there can be issues and occasions which provoke dissent too great for party mechanisms to contain it. How often citizens feel they have to express their aspirations and needs by direct demonstrations, and how government reacts, are further indicators of the nature of political life. In India even during the phase of Congress dominance some groups felt ignored and took to the streets in demonstrations, protests, acts of civil disobedience and even of violence. Congress' own patterns of protest under the *raj* had ironically provided education in such action. Among the most serious direct actions have been a Naga tribal rebellion on the north-east frontier (1955–64), and the Communist-inspired attempts at social and political revolution in the late 1960s—the so-called Naxalite movement.[11] Riots also accompanied regional movements for linguistic states in the 1950s, and one Andhra politician fasted to death in 1952 to further the cause of a Telugu-speaking state.

Language riots erupted in the 1960s among southerners in particular, who feared the imposition on them of Hindi as the one national language. Among other groups who fairly regularly take to open protest are students and landless labourers.[12] Among the most serious examples of direct action and violent agitation in the 1980s have been protests against 'reservations' for backward castes, and the devastating breakdown of normal political life in the Punjab as the result of a Sikh terrorist movement, and in Kashmir as Delhi opposes a bitter separatist movement.

Governments have responded to these direct expressions of dissent in varied ways, their responsiveness always hampered by the need to adjust between conflicting demands, as between landed and landless or different groups of language-speakers; and by the poverty of the country which means that often there are just not the goods and facilities with which to satisfy the demands made.[13] Where possible governments manage dissent by organizing potentially vocal interest groups within party structures. Major political parties have all organized trade union wings, for example, and their own peasant fronts. Congress had its variations of these, and also its youth department in an unsuccessful attempt to 'de-politicize' students. In other instances dissenting groups are so powerful and persistent that governments bow to public opinion and change their policies even at the cost of appearing to 'give in' to violence, civil disobedience and a range of unconstitutional actions. The major examples here were the Congress government's ultimate agreement to states' reorganization on linguistic lines in 1956, despite its firm stand immediately after independence; and the retention of English alongside Hindi as one of the official languages of the Union.[14]

A third alternative in the face of overt dissent is overt coercion—the suppression of opinion by the state's monopoly of organized force. Its use is an index of failure to reach an accommodation of interests in public life, and an indicator that the democratic consensus about the polity's goals has broken down. India's government was equipped at the outset with formidable coercive powers, many of which pre-dated independence (See Chapter VI). Since 1947 it has reinforced itself against the Press (Press [Objectionable matter] Act) and against strikers (1958 Maintenance of Essential Services Act and 1954 Industrial Disputes Act). It also increased its powers of detention without trial by the 1962 Defence of India Act and the 1971 Maintenance of Internal Security Act known as MISA. It is also significant that the size and cost of the police has increased markedly. Between 1969 and 1971 central government expenditure on police forces doubled: by 1974 it had increased fifty-two times since a democratic government had taken control of the country from the departing imperialists. Police forces' expansion has not only kept pace with but has outstripped population growth. In 1960 there were *c.* 12 policemen for every 1,000

Indians: by 1971 there were 12.9 police for every 1,000. The trend has continued: and between 1961 and 1981 there was a 93 per cent increase in police numbers whereas the population increase during the same period was 89 per cent. The armed proportion of the ordinary state police has dropped (from about two-fifths in 1960 to about a quarter in 1971); but there has developed a strong central core of armed police including the Central Reserve Police and the Border Security Force housed in barracks and disciplined like soldiers. By the mid-1970s the centrally controlled police probably numbered *c.* 800,000—three-quarters as large a force as the army; and by 1986 the para-military element at the disposal of the centre was 255,000. The total extent of coercion cannot accurately be gauged. But it is a persistent and increasing aspect of public life and relations between government and its citizens. For example, it was the official response to Naxalite violence in Bengal; as it has been to Sikh separatism in the 1980s. Students have often been on the receiving end, as were rail-strikers in 1974 when 6,000 labour leaders were arrested at once, and 30,000 activists in the course of the strike. Amnesty International has estimated that at times there have been fifteen to twenty thousand people in Indian prisons who were not accused of specific criminal acts. Yet further evidence of coercion is the increasing use of the army to maintain civil order. In some cases these were swift operations; but increasingly they have been of such duration that they amount to martial law. Between 1951 and 1970 the army were called in to suppress domestic violence on *c.* 476 occasions: in the eighteen months alone between June 1979 and December 1980 there 64 such occasions. It has been calculated that in 1984 there were at least 40 million Indians living under military rule, mainly in Assam and Punjab.

The fragility of India's democratic order and its ineffectiveness in providing means for the peaceful adjustment of interests between citizens, and between citizens and government, is abundantly clear from the accumulating evidence of citizens' violence and government's deliberate and persistent use of the authoritarian potential in its position. Both are symptoms of a breakdown in the democratic political system. Citizens' violence occurs in different contexts of fear or frustration—in many of the student and peasant agitations and language riots mentioned above, in attacks on Untouchables, and in continuing explosions of communal violence. The level of violence has been increasing since independence, and particularly in the politically confused years after 1967. In the eight largest cities the number of riots (officially defined as involving five or more people) rose from 581 in 1961 to 2,319 in 1970: and cities account for at most 3 per cent of all the country's riots. Between 1953 and 1972 riots have increased more than three-fold, from 20,529 in 1953 to 65,781 in 1972. Particularly disturbing as an indication of the failure of democratic structures to ensure peace between citizens of different religious affiliations and to deepen commitment to the secular nature of political life and India's common national identity is the rising trend of 'communal' violence. (Though it must be remembered that even when violence appears to originate in religious identities and conflicts, often many other issues feed into the situation just as they did before 1947. Economic conflicts are one such issue, as is the deliberate use of religious loyalties by politicians seeking support, often in the absence of party structures.) Until 1964 the annual figures for reported communal violence were in double figures only. Since then they have been at a far higher level, with some particularly bad years (1964–1,070; 1969–519; 1970–521) and some particularly brutal incidents, often involving police violence towards Muslims. In a few days late in 1992 probably 1,000 people were killed India-wide in riots following the storming by Hindu militants of a mosque in Uttar Pradesh built on the reputed birthplace of Ram, and the violence spread to places such as Calcutta and Bombay which had prided themselves on the cosmopolitan and secular nature of their civic life.[15]

As we have noted, successive governments have used their powers of detention and coercion by the police and army with increasing rigour since 1947. But it was not until Mrs Gandhi's 'Emergency Rule' that any government persistently used its authoritarian potential to distort the political system over many months and permanently to curtail democratic rights, rather than to deal with temporary crises such as war or the threatened collapse of the railway network. The origins of the 'Emergency'—in Mrs Gandhi's vision of herself, her frustrations and ambitions, in country-wide opposition, and in the challenge to her position as an MP on grounds of electoral malpractice—have been discussed at length. What is significant for our investigation of the Indian democratic experience is the extraordinary and virtually dictatorial position she was able to achieve so rapidly.[16]

Her clamp-down on opposition was as fierce as anything the British had attempted, even in 1942. Once the pliant President had declared an emergency where internal disturbances were alleged to be threatening India's security, the way was clear for the use of emergency powers. But even *before* that the principal opposition leaders, nearly 700, were arrested under MISA, and electricity supplies to the main Delhi papers were cut off to impose a news black-out. From then on rigid press censorship was imposed, a range of organizations including the RSS was banned, and *c.* 110,000 people imprisoned without trial. Presidential orders were one means of coercion—for example, suspending citizens' rights to seek constitutional protection through the courts. Later a cowed Lok Sabha passed legislation to protect Mrs Gandhi's personal position as an MP since the court case on electoral malpractice had gone against her, and to alter the constitution— particularly to weaken the power of the courts as ultimate protectors of people against government power. For example, the Supreme Court was denied the power of judicial review of amendments to the constitution, and the courts were not permitted to review either a presidential proclamation of an emergency or orders imposed under an emergency. The normal processes of parliamentary debate, of government by Ministers responsible to Parliament, disintegrated, as Mrs Gandhi ruled with the help of picked advisers, her so-called 'kitchen cabinet' in which her son, Sanjay, was an increasingly dominant force. She also seems to have used direct channels of communication with 'loyal' chief ministers in the states. By abandoning established mechanisms for receiving messages of the state of public opinion and for consulting with established local politicians, and by silencing public opposition and press debate, she isolated herself from the harsh realities of public dissent and fear, and probably from the truth about the acts of oppression and destruction of personal liberty and integrity done in the name of her government. Her dramatic fall in 1977 occurred when she attempted to legitimize her position by going to the electorate—an ill-advised strategy demonstrating the collapse of her 'intelligence' as had been the fate of the British and Moguls before her as their regimes crumbled.

Much of this structure of authoritarian government was demolished by Janata after their 1977 electoral landslide. But MISA remains, as does preventive detention. The 'Emergency' has proved conclusively that democratic politics and government can be demolished almost overnight at Union and state level if the government of the day chooses to use its potential and has a pliant President and Parliament.

The working of politics and government at state and national level are not, however, the only evidence of India's experience of democracy. At local level a remarkable institutional innovation has occurred which was not provided for in the constitution but was created as a result of local experimentation in the 1950s with the intention of involving citizens in the decisions and actions necessary for the country's economic and social development. *Panchayati raj*, is the technical name, meaning 'rule by *panchayat*', but it bears little relation to the older *panchayats*, or caste and village councils. It is a three-tiered system of elected committees stretching from village to district. At the base is the *panchayat* of ten to fifteen members who represent one or several villages. Some members are co-opted to represent women and Untouchables. All the *panchayat* chairmen in the area known as the block form the next tier, the *panchayat samiti*, where they are joined by the MLAs and the development officer for that block. The third tier is congruent with the administrative district, and includes all the *samiti* chairmen, the MLAs and MPs from the district. There have been many problems associated with this experiment, including the ambiguous relationship between the elected members and the administration, the financial weakness of the new institutions, and the fact that they tend to become vehicles for prosperous peasants to increase their dominance in rural society and their grip on scarce resources and services; while the token low caste representatives can do little to ensure an equitable spread of development funds and facilities. But it seems indisputable that the new institutions of rural self-government and elections to them have helped to educate the Indian villager politically—to convince him of the value of his vote, and to link him to political parties who play an active role in elections even though this arena of democracy is meant to be party-less. Furthermore they provide a new and valuable political arena for young men and those from aspiring but not dominant village groups and act as a recruitment and training ground for people who go on from village politics to the higher levels in the system and even to state level. *Panchayati raj*, for all its limitations as a mechanism for social and economic development, has become part of the infrastructure of India's democracy.[17]

* * *

In a technical sense India's democratic structures have clearly worked. They have provided mechanisms for citizens to register their responses to government, for debate and legislation, and to some extent for the adjustment of interests between different regional, linguistic, and economic sections of society. The durability of democracy, compared with many other 'new' states' experience of rapid reversion to authoritarian rule, can be explained in terms of India's lengthy experience of working partially democratic structures under the British, of Congress activity under Nehru in constructing a political institution which was accommodative and responsive and in building the new politics on firm social foundations, and of the ideological commitment of both the leadership and a broad swathe of experienced politicians in 1947 to a democratic state. Furthermore, the socially segmented nature of Indian society tended to prevent any India-wide movement of dissent overwhelming the political order; while electoral politics have encouraged leaders to construct alliances across social groups in order to gain power, thus blunting particularist pressures. The regional and federal system of politics has also meant that where localized dissent and disruption has occurred it could in a sense be quarantined and prevented from threatening the centre or other states. It has also been highly significant that politics and administration had for years absorbed some of the most ambitious and intellectually agile, and therefore the armed services tended to attract those more suited to a disciplined, active life than to politics. This was a marked contrast to African states where the limited facilities for education and African participation in administration steered many aspiring young men into the army, creating a great reservoir of men with contacts beyond their village or region with force at their disposal, who were not content to stand on the political sidelines if the politicians appeared inefficient or hopelessly incapable of creating stable government.

India's officer corps by disposition, training, tradition, and a structure of civilian control, has remained apolitical even in times of political turmoil.[18] Furthermore, enough people have gained from the democratic patterns India has developed, and felt that as a result of their operation their inter- ests were secure, to provide a significant band of economic and social support for the political status quo. Among them have been most notably the growing 'middle class' including bureaucrats and politicans whose jobs are created by the political structures, prosperous peasants, whose agricultural incomes are untaxed and who take advantage of govern- ment credit facilities and *panchayati raj*, and businessmen, despite their complaints about government hostility to the private sector, the harass- ments of 'permit *raj*' and labour indiscipline.[19] Although such strategic support may guarantee political stability it can also imprison governments and prevent them from coping with the country's major problems—a hidden cost of democracy to which we will shortly turn.

However, the checks on governmental power are certainly not foolproof though democratic forms have endured. Moreover, the very institutions of state and politics which sustain the practice of democracy show unmistak- able signs of erosion as the twentieth century closes. For example, the courts have provided a bulwark against dictatorial government, and the integrity and independence of India's judiciary has been a remarkable phenomenon, brought about by India's experience under the *raj* when the British not only respected the court system and its functionaries but ap- pointed Indian judges long before they allowed Indian entry into the ICS or army officer corps. However, as the 'Emergency' showed, that check can be weakened by parliamentary legislation if the Lok Sabha is pliant; while the judges' independence depends on the independence of the President, who appoints them.[20] After the 'Emergency' it was the Supreme Court which enabled the Janata government to attack the federal nature of the constitu- tion by dismissing non-Janata state governments. Even the IAS has found itself becoming increasingly politicized as the turbulent politics of the 1970s and beyond led to 'political' transfers and promotions, placing increasing pressure on civil servants to be committed to the government of the day rather than to a service role for the state as a whole by giving competent advice and providing impartial administration.[21] If the highest echelons of the civil service still struggle to maintain impartiality and incorruptibility, the same cannot be said of the police force. Never popular, honest, or well- paid before independence, the police are now more of a liability to democ- racy than a support to it. Police brutality, alignment with powerful rural figures against the underpriviledged, with corrupt politicians, and increas- ingly with the Hindu community against the minorities, is sadly common- place in Indian public life. Moreover, the high incidence of strikes within the alleged internal peace-keeping forces further invites paramilitary or military intervention, and alienates the public from one of the most apparent institutions of civic life.[22]

Perhaps the most serious erosion of the institutions central to democratic life is that we have already noted—affecting India's political parties and particularly the Congress. The checks on governments exercised by legislatures and elections themselves depend in turn for their effectiveness on the operation of a genuine party system, or an accommodating umbrella party. Where parties are weak and faction-ridden the voters have little real choice, are offered populist appeals rather than genuine policies, and legislatures can easily become arenas of chronic instability, producing short-lived and weak governments, or lie open to governmental domination.

At least two developments seem to be following on from this trend in Indian political life. One is the way in which once parties fail the citizens, increasing numbers of them take flight from democratic politics and resort to direct action in pursuit of their interests. It is no coincidence that violent and undemocratic assertion of demands increased as the Congress party disintegrated as a functioning political institution without being replaced by any other as a mechanism for expressing discontent, recruiting the politically aspirant, and enabling government to hear what its citizens are saying.[23] The other development is the apparently growing disillusion among many Indian citizens with the secular state as created in 1947. Indian nationalist leaders such as Nehru and Gandhi had been profoundly aware of the need to create a new public sense of Indianness, of belonging to a nation which respected religious diversity but treated all its citizens as equal. For both of them tolerance and democracy were intertwined as the only way forward for India as a plural society in which all citizens could feel secure. However, such a public sense of inclusive, secular identity was difficult to spread beyond the more highly educated, and in independent India would need constant commitment by the leaders of opinion and the organizers of political life, as millions more citizens with more parochial and narrow loyalties became aware of the implications of public choices and were increasingly themselves significant actors in the political arena. The erosion of Congress as a locally based, inclusive party, generating a political culture of negotiation and accommodation, has seriously weakened the commitment of politicians to the secular definition of Indian identity and the Indian state, and have, from Prime Ministers downwards, encouraged reliance on particularist and particularly communal appeals for support, once the organizational structure for the consolidation of support disintegrated. Furthermore, citizens, disillusioned by politicians, and by the practical results of India's secular democracy, seem increasingly amenable to the appeal of those politicians who deliberately seek to contrive a sense of Hindu identity as the basis both of civil life and of political loyalty.[24] What this could mean for India's integrity and stability is clear if one remembers that in India over 11 per cent of the population are Muslim, and India has the second largest Muslim population of any country in the world, after Indonesia. Indian Muslims who remained after partition have been ill served both by the strategy of partition and by India's democracy. They are generally poor, and underprivileged and underrepresented in politics and in governmental service. For them the presence of an effectively secular state and the evolution of a genuinely inclusive political life are critical—as they are for India as a whole.

ii Responding to major problems

Central to India's democratic experience is the issue of performance. The democratic mechanisms of government and politics may function: but have independent India's governments responded creatively to the country's outstanding problems? Has democratic government, like the institutions of colonial government, been to a significant extent imprisoned by economic and social forces? Has the weakening of so many of the institutions of democracy inhibited the performance of government? Have freedom and democracy enabled India to take control of her destiny at home and abroad and exercise an international influence as Nehru so passionately hoped in August 1947?

a Foreign affairs

Most obviously foreign affairs demanded new initiatives after 1947, when for the first time Indians could choose their foreign policy and patterns of relations with other countries. The thrust of nationalist sentiment demanded that the new rulers should formulate a distinctive international role for the new state, in contrast to two centuries of subservience to British imperial designs. The nature of that role was suggested by Congress's position on foreign affairs before independence, particularly its leaders' ambivalence in the Second World War, in applauding the allied struggle against Fascism, yet demanding that India be free of external influence in her policy formulation. The seeds of Nehru's foreign policy of non-alignment with Eastern or Western blocs were present before 1947. India's strategic position as the gateway to the Indian Ocean confirmed that non-alignment could best preserve her territorial integrity and avoid aggression by either of the superpowers, particularly during the 'Cold War'. However, India's geographical and economic position imposed constraints on her governments' freedom to manoeuvre. Like the *raj* before them they were ever-conscious of Russia and China just beyond their borders, restrained by mountains and the small states of Afghanistan and Tibet. These restraints were far weaker than in the nineteenth century because of the development of air power and road-building technology. Furthermore the shadow of these immense neighbours was darkened over India by the existence after 1947 of two-winged Pakistan on India's immediate land border as a hostile neighbour who might look for allies to north east or north west. Another new dimension of India's international position after independence was her urgent need for foreign aid to finance her economic development until that became self-sustaining. But aid without 'strings' is scarce: and India's rulers would have to devise a strategy for avoiding the exercise of 'neocolonialism' by donor nations.

Three main patterns have dominated India's foreign affairs.[25] One has been the strained relations between India and Pakistan which have erupted into armed conflict on three occasions. The questions at issue stemmed from the circumstances of partition and the division of natural resources between the two states; the most persistent flashpoint being Kashmir, the Muslim state with a Hindu ruler which had acceeded to India in a manner Pakistan refused to accept. In late 1972 the issue was the 'liberation' of the eastern wing of Pakistan from dominance by the western wing, and its birth in bloodshed and bitterness as the independent state of Bangladesh with moral and material support from India. Only in late 1976 did India and truncated Pakistan on her western border renew full diplomatic relations, and open civilian air and rail links between them. Another pattern leading to conflict in 1962 (in which India was humiliated by contrast with her wars against Pakistan) was the deterioration of her relationship with China, which was increasingly a major power in Asia and the world after the 1949 Communist revolution. Nehru had placed his hopes for peace with China on five principles of friendship negotiated in 1955: these included non-aggression and non-interference in each other's internal affairs, as well as respect for each other's sovereignty and territorial integrity. But war broke out over control of disputed areas on India's north-east border. India's armed forces were shown up as woefully unprepared: she was only saved from further humiliation by China's unilateral cease-fire. In the late 1970s relations improved, but India still sees both China and Pakistan as potential threats to her integrity. The third element in India's foreign relations was the ebb and flow of her connections with America and the USSR as she strove not only to defend her own boundaries but to keep superpower conflict out of the South Asian region. Relations with America have deteriorated whenever the White House has given what India considers as undue aid and military assistance to Pakistan, to bolster it as part of America's Asian barrier against the expansion of Communist influence—as in the 1965 Indo-Pakistani conflict and during the Bangladesh crisis; or when the USA renewed its support for Pakistan after the Soviet invasion of Afghanistan in 1979. India's connections with Russia have grown closer, and included provision of aid and arms, as her relations with China deteriorated. India's governments have realized the need to maintain a balance in their responses to America and Russia, recognizing both the economic and strategic dangers of over-dependence on one or the other. The ending of the Cold War and superpower conflict in the last decade of the century will necessitate some rethinking of India's foreign relations, as will the collapse of the USSR as an ally and an arms and aid supplier. India's support for the allied powers during the Gulf War of 1991 was an indication that subtle changes were under way.

As a result of these interlocking patterns India has achieved considerable international standing. Not only has she protected her own borders, with the exception of the 1962 débâcle at the hands of the Chinese. As a member of the British Commonwealth, strategic guardian of the Indian Ocean, the dominant force on the South Asian subcontinent after the Bangladesh war, and as a major voice in wider Asian affairs, she cannot be ignored by other nations, and has achieved considerable room for international initiative and manoeuvre. There has been comparatively little difference in foreign policy between successive Indian governments, and all have received general support from the people on the main shape of foreign relations. This popular consensus and the avoidance of any international defeat since 1962 has in itself been a factor in the stability of the internal political system.

However these achievements have been bought at a price. Her defence capacity and expenditure has risen markedly since the days of the *raj*. By the end of the 1960s the armed forces were five times their peacetime strength in British India; and in the early 1990s her army of 1,100,000 was the third largest in the world, and her total armed forces stood at 1,265,000. In 1992–3 India's defence budget totalled $6.75 billion, this being 15 per cent of the overall budget. (By comparison only 1.5 per cent of national income was spent on military purposes in 1938.) Military expenditure has been primarily on conventional forces. But in 1974 India exploded a nuclear device 'for peaceful purposes' and by the 1990s had a domestically produced intermediate-range ballistic missile. But, like arms, nuclear power is a symbol and guarantee of national status and international strength. India's people have been prepared to accept the expenditure of scarce resources on national integrity and standing and deflection of a significant proportion of their limited wealth from economic development and welfare provision. Each conflict with and victory over Pakistan, for example, led to a wave of support for the government of the day.

A further dimension of India's foreign relations which links both with the issues of national sovereignty and domestic affairs is her need of foreign aid. In the early years of independence her need of aid was substantial; and by the early 1980s she had received a total of $30 billions, most of it in loans whose repayments are a heavy financial burden. The USA was at first the largest donor, providing 45 per cent of all aid between 1947 and 1975, followed by the World Bank, Great Britain, West Germany, the USSR, and Japan. By the mid-1980s the US share of the total was well under 10 per cent while over 50 per cent came from IBRD and IDA. However, as Indian leaders are well aware, receipt of aid means vulnerability to foreign pressure—as in 1965 when America cut back during the crisis with Pakistan, or in 1966 when the IMF and USA insisted on a devaluation of the rupee, or in 1991 when the IMF made emergency financial help dependent on major economic reform.

b   Domestic issues

India's national identity and integrity has not only been an issue in external affairs. Her new rulers faced at independence the task of continuing to weld a nation out of the diverse regions and communities within the country, for the task was only partially performed in the years of political change before the British departure. Such a challenge to the political system and to the politicians was made infinitely more difficult by changing social conditions and attitudes. Since independence India's peoples have had rising expectations of life, as with increasing education and broader experience they perceive the possibilities for change and are far more equipped to articulate their demands than they were as colonial subjects. Furthermore, it is most often to the state that they look for the granting of their wishes and the resolution of their perceived problems. This is partly because the gaining of freedom itself aroused major expectations of independent governments: it is also because in an environment of scarcity it is the state which is the source of so many 'goods' desired—whether jobs, special rights or preferences, allocation of resources, or beneficial tax arrangements. Ironically because the state itself is so important in people's lives (compared with its colonial predecessor) its capacity to manage change, to deal with demands, and to mediate between conflicting interests is central to its legitimacy. So the issue of 'performance' becomes as significant as the presence of democratic institutions for the reality of democracy in India and its meaning for India's peoples. Three themes relating to political performance and the reality of democracy will be highlighted here—the dynamics of particularist movements, the processes of economic development, and the limitations on socio-economic change—to illustrate the constraint on governments and the weaknesses of the democratic order in India as an agent both of stability and of change.

One of the most remarkable features of Indian public life in the last half of this century has been the fact that particularist movements, often rooted in primordial loyalties such as religion, language, or region, have not been weakened, as many predicted they would as a result of economic and political development once India could command her own affairs. India's first leaders viewed with suspicion any particularist movements which appeared divisive, might undermine the authority of the federal centre, or weaken the state's claim to be secular (a crucial element in the integration within the new polity of religious minorities). Government hostility to the demand by linguistic areas for political recognition as state units was a major instance. It only conceded the principle in 1956 after years of bitter controversy and regional pressure. However the cases of Bombay and Punjab remained unresolved by the States Reorganization Act of that year. Both were sensitive areas where two linguistic groups were in dispute, and in both areas prolonged agitation often degenerating into violence occurred before the centre was prepared to concede, and create in the one case Gujarat and Maharashtra (respectively Gujarati and Marathi-speaking), and in the other Punjab and Haryana, where the majorities spoke Punjabi and Hindi. However this concession to a regional and religious sense of particular identity did not weaken the Indian Union. Punjab remained a source of military recruitment, a leader in agricultural development and food production, and a loyal frontier province. The creation of linguistic states certainly confirms linguistic and regional consciousness, and possibly 'provincializes' people's political awareness and activity. But government's reluctant acquiescence in linguistic demands has not undermined the nation, except when the centre has attempted to maintain an unrealistic conception of national unity, coercing discontented elements instead of trusting that unity can be founded on local diversity, and that old loyalties can coexist and even reinforce new ones.

The case of the Punjab is particularly instructive because of the elements of continuity with pre-1947 demands, the religious element combined with linguistic claims, and ultimately the contrast between the handling of the problem in the first two decades of independence compared with the political breakdown which ensued in the state in the 1980s.[26] The cry for 'Punjabi Subha' was both a Sikh demand for a political environment where Sikhs could preserve their religious identity, and the manifestation of anxiety by a linguistic group to guarantee for themselves access to a range of government jobs, by insisting that the state's official language should be their own—an anxiety all too familiar as a result of India's linguistic diversity and uneven educational development. The Sikh demand for a Punjabi-speaking state was articulated by the Akali Dal, which revived its old demands for a Sikh-dominated area in this linguistic guise when the States Reorganization Commission declared that Punjab should be a bilingual state with Hindi and Punjabi as its official languages. However, the Dal did not have the support of all Sikhs: the Harijan or Untouchable Sikhs throughout the state opposed the claim because they feared increased domination by higher caste landowners. Hindus in the state similarly opposed the idea, arguing that it was a device for Sikh hegemony and theocracy. Delhi rejected the idea, too, on the grounds that it threatened both national unity and the secular state. The Akali Dal developed three strategies to break down the government's refusal. It engaged in the normal political mechanisms in an entirely constitutional fashion, using the legislature, public meetings and mass rallies, petitions and deputations to prominent government men. It also at times attempted to work within the Congress party; though this infiltration tactic caused deep divisions in the Dal. Finally the Dal organized a dramatic agitational strategy, reminiscent of the days of Gandhian civil disobedience. Quasi-military formations of Sikhs deliberately sought confrontation with the police and courted arrest. In 1955 *c.* 12,000 were involved; and in the spectacular 1960–1 agitation 26,000 Akalis were arrested according to government, though the Dal estimated 57,000. Furthermore, several prominent religious leaders went on prolonged fast, threatening to fast until death, though they broke their fasts in compromise unlike the Andhra politician who died a decade earlier in pursuit of his linguistic state. This range of pressure alone did not convince the Congress leaders. It took war with Pakistan in 1965 to persuade the Union government to review the 1956 decision. Sikh participation in the army and their now crucial role as a population clustered on the Pakistan frontier were elements in the change of heart, as were parallel and growing demands by the Hindi-speaking area to separate from the Punjabi-speakers. Consequently in 1966 the two states of Punjab and Haryana emerged out of the old Punjab.

The structures and conventions of politics and government had ultimately proved able to channel and resolve tension between government and citizens and between different groups of citizens but only after prolonged struggle including civil disobedience, and only when subjected to the external pressure of war. The sequel to the 1960s just two decades later suggests that by the 1980s the political system had in certain vital respects changed so that it was no longer able to resolve conflict and manage demands without the state resorting to violent coercion. Some important issues were not resolved between the two new states in 1966, such as the status of the capital of Chandigarh. But over and above these, economic and social change in the Punjab, one of India's most prosperous states, combined with religious conflicts internal to the Sikh community to produce a minority Sikh movement of militant violence for the renewal of Sikh purity and identity and also the creation of a specifically Sikh state. It is unclear how much support the main militant leader, Bhindranwale, had among

Sikhs, but his stance undercut the more moderate Sikh politicians who might have renegotiated a compromise with Delhi. But crucial to the failure of political adjustment and the onset both of terrorist violence and government coercion in the 1980s was the way in which the centre, in the person of Indira Gandhi, was prepared to stir up strife among the Sikhs instead of encouraging the moderates, and had no united, effective local Congress party to negotiate with the Sikhs. Here were examples of the decay of the Congress party as a strong local political unit, and the erosion of the federal aspect of politics at the behest of the centre, discussed earlier in this epilogue. They rendered the structures of democratic politics incapable of solving acute problems which were destabilizing the political order and the lives of thousands of Punjabis.[27]

Although the Punjab has been one of the most egregious examples of particularist demands which need management and resolution, others have surfaced in secessionist demands of tribal groups wanting their own states; and in the several 'sons of the soil' movements of native language speakers of particular regions where there are substantial groups of migrants who are seen as having undue influence and access to scarce resources. Assam, Andhra Pradesh, and Bombay have witnessed examples of such movements. These all show how with increasing political and social mobilization demands are directed at the state, because control of state resources are seen as the surest way to buttress a group's identity and security in a changing world. But as these involve conflicts between Indians, and tend to create categories of citizenship locally despite presumed shared all-India citizenship, their peaceful resolution is crucial to the identity and integrity of the Indian nation. Although some have been resolved pragmatically by state action, others have not, a primary reason again being the need of the centre to buttress its power in the states by direct intervention in contrast to the earlier accommodating stance of the centre, in acceptance that Indian identity had to be founded on pluralism and accommodation.[28] The emergence of demands by 'backward castes' for special reservations in the allocation of political and material resources similarly puts acute pressure on the state, and the failure to resolve many of these issues, leading to violence as in Gujarat in the 1980s, suggests yet again the failure of democratic management structures, reflecting the decay of party organization and the centre's resort to populist electoral appeals which cannot guarantee support for admittedly hard political choices.

'Ethnic' and particularist movements are dynamic affairs, using old loyalties, reworking and transforming them for new ends in a changing environment—central to which is increasing expectations in an environment of scarcity and competition. The complexity and force of conflicting demands on the state is thus linked to questions of economic policy and performance. Consequently economic development is inseparable from the problems of national identity and integration, and the accommodation of group interests. But more urgently for the sake of the sheer survival and minimum living standards of millions of Indians, as well as India's international autonomy, the political leadership recognized that the economy was one of its major problems. They inherited a compound of poverty, a traditional agricultural base still largely geared to subsistence, reliance on a precarious climate, and a limited, regionalized growth of industry. This was accompanied after independence by unprecedented population growth; not because of an increase in the birth rate but because the death rate fell, mainly as a result of the control of killer diseases such as smallpox, cholera, and malaria. Population had been growing steadily since the First World War; but it was in the decades after 1951 that the growth became dramatic (See Table B). In the 1990s the population was thought to be nearing 900 million. By 1971 India was the second most populous country in the world (only China was ahead): it had 15 per cent of the world's people but only 2.4 per cent the world's area. Such an explosion strains all the country's resources—food, education, housing, jobs, welfare services, and consumer goods. Furthermore, it is a compounding dilemma because as more mothers and children survive, so the population becomes younger, more people survive into their potentially reproductive years, and more women live through the whole of their fertile span. By 1961 the life expectancy of Indian women was just over forty-six years, and for men forty-seven years. By the early 1980s, life expectancy had risen to over fifty years and by 1991 was over 62. A large proportion of the population are too young to be economically productive and have to be supported by the efforts of the rest. In 1961 just over 41 per cent of Indians were under fifteen, and adding to them the small percentage of those over sixty, nearly 47 per cent of the population was 'dependent'.[29] As life expectancy has risen, so has the number of the aged dependent on the working population; and it has been estimated that by the end of the century there will be 76 million Indians over 60.

Table B. *Population increase, 1941–1981*

Year	Population in Millions	% Increase
1941	318.7	14.22
1951	361.1	13.31
1961	439.2	21.50
1971	547.0	24.57
1981	683.0	24.86

Source: 1941–1971: B. Kuppuswamy, *Population and Society in India* (Bombay, 1975), p. 20.
1981: February 1981 Census reported in *The Times*, March 1981.

In the face of these compound problems India's government decided on a strategy of planning: to raise agricultural and industrial production, and to encourage the limitation of families, not only to satisfy the basic human and social needs of the population at an acceptable level, but to make India industrially self-sufficient and therefore less vulnerable to international economic and political pressure. The strategy was clarified in 1954–6 in Parliament and the Congress party, under the guidance of the Planning Commission which worked very closely with Nehru and owed much to Soviet techniques of planning and models of development. The emphasis was heavily on the role of the public sector, which was to include basic and strategic industries, and public utilities, and was meant to grow absolutely and comparatively at a faster rate than the private sector. Modern industry and mining were to expand in relation to the total economy; and there was to be a shift towards the production of capital rather than consumer goods.[30]

The strategy did not fulfil the expectations of the planners or solve India's economic problems. But before considering its 'failure' it is right to note the remarkable changes which have occurred since 1947. These have been decades when regular visitors from abroad have seen great strides in communications, including the expansion of the metalled road network, regular internal air services, and the growing availability of transistor radios; the expansion of the electricity supply both for agricultural and industrial production and for domestic consumption even in quite remote villages; the growth of towns and a vast range of new industries; the availability of more Indian-produced consumer goods; the mechanization of agriculture in some areas and the dramatic increase in wheat production where new seed has been introduced. Some statistics indicate the scale of economic change. By 1968–9 the national product was over 80 per cent more than in 1951, and *per capita* income had risen by about 30 per cent, despite the rising population. By 1966 the index of industrial production was 160 per cent above its 1951 level. By 1969 there were about 376,000 tube wells in operation compared with $3\frac{1}{2}$ thousand in 1950; and in the two decades after 1951 gross irrigated area increased by 16 million hectares. Mainly as a result of improved yields per acre total crop production increased by 80 per cent in India's first twenty years of independence. India is still predominantly an agricultural country, with 70 per cent of its labour force engaged in agriculture. But business and industry now contribute one-third of the country's income, compared with 5 per cent at independence. In spite of this remarkable record the development plans have not obliterated poverty or led to self-sustaining growth.

Central to this dilemma is the fact that no way has been found of limiting population growth. The age of marriage is an extremely sensitive religious topic among Hindus, as the British had found to their cost. Although the Hindu Marriage Act of 1955 raised the minimum age for girls to fifteen, the law was loosely enforced and child marriage has continued in practice. In 1971 in country districts 13.6 per cent of girls between ten and fourteen years old were married. Government's main strategy to limit population growth has been to encourage research into and provision for family planning. Each five-year plan laid increasing stress on this and allocated larger funds—rising from Rs. 6.5 million in the first plan to a proposed Rs. 5,600 million in the fifth plan. By the end of the 1950s the government favoured all means, including sterilization. The public have been bombarded with the message that two or three children are enough, that small families are happy families; from posters, films, radio, and touring officials. Clinics have been set up to provide planning advice and services; and subsidies provided for the sale of contraceptives in shops. However by the end of the 1960s only just over 3 million people were thought to have taken advantage of the various methods—about 8 per cent of married couples in the reproductive age group.

Vasectomy has understandably proved one of the most popular methods, having the advantages of simplicity, cheapness, and permanence. Between 1952 and mid-1976 about nineteen million men underwent voluntary sterilization, though some were doubtless helped to decide by the incentives given, which at one point included transistor radios! Sanjay Gandhi made mass sterilization to solve the population problem one of his particular enterprises during his mother's 'Emergency'. Pressures amounting to coercion ensued. For example, central government employees with more than three children were not given government housing unless they were sterilized. In some states officials' pay and promotion depended on 'persuading' a quota of men to undergo vasectomy. In 1976–7 in fact the target of $7\frac{1}{2}$ million vasectomies was surpassed. But such was the fear and disgust produced by these tactics that they contributed significantly to Mrs Gandhi's electoral defeat in 1977. They have also made the promotion of family planning infinitely more difficult for succeeding governments. The population growth rate which slowed during the 'Emergency' began to rise under the Janata government.

Most Indians are aware of the possibility and need for family planning, and few would have real religious objections. Yet no government policy is likely to succeed until people are convinced that those children they have will survive. For children are not only of religious significance. They are vital hands in rural households from an early age, and an insurance against their parents' destitution in old age. Furthermore if women are to take on responsibility for contraception they need a higher level of education, more basic health care and advice geared to the needs and possibilities of village life, and a psychological release from dependence on their husbands in all vital decisions. That such a bundle of changes can take place is evident from India's southern state of Kerala; which as a result of distinctive historical, political, and social experiences now has greater life expectancy, lower infant mortality, a lower birth-rate, and greater literacy, particularly for women, than anywhere else in India.[31] Population control is therefore interwoven with provision for education, general health, and social security, all of which in their turn are now stretched to breaking-point as population increases.

Even without the constant erosion of economic gains by the expanding population the succession of five-year plans failed to live up expectations, except for the first (and most limited) one starting in 1951. Percentage increases in national income in the first three plans were projected as 11.2, 25 and 35: the actual percentage increases were 18, 21 and 13. Increases in food-grain production were well below expectations, as was industrial production.[32] Although India by the 1980s was self-sufficient in food, and in certain areas had experienced what came to be known as the 'Green Revolution', it is still devastatingly true that nearly half the population (in varying proportions from state to state) suffers from poverty, malnutrition, or downright hunger. Definitions of poverty are problematic, but in the early 1970s it was estimated that 38 per cent of the rural population and nearly 50 per cent of the urban population lived in virtual destitution.[33] What economic advances have occurred have not helped to equalize society, and gross inequalities persist, despite the official commitment to a socialist pattern of society. There are still major disparities between regions. In 1964–5, for example, Punjab, Maharashtra, Gujarat, and Haryana were the top four states, all having *per capita* incomes of over Rs. 500: Bihar trailed with the lowest figure—Rs. 299. Two decades later those inequalities between regions still persisted, with the same four states towering above the other parts of India, as they draw on their greater industrialization and irrigation. Inequalities between families are also extremely wide. Those belonging to the growing urban middle class (estimated in the 1990s to be about 60–80 million) are doing well, as are those with enough land to exploit the commercial opportunities of agriculture. But despite the problems of reaching accurate statistics it seems evident that landless labour is increasing as are the number of 'marginal' farmers. The census put the percentage of landless agricultural workers in the total work force at 26 in 1971 compared with 17 a decade earlier: while another estimate puts the figure at 37 per cent of the rural work force in 1981 compared with 28 per cent in 1951. The number of 'marginal' farmers is also rising—by 1970–1 nearly 70 per cent of agricultural holdings were under 5 acres, while 15 per cent of all holdings were over 10 acres and accounted for over 60 per cent of cultivated land.[34]

The failure of the country's original economic strategy in terms both of production and redistribution of resources was due to a complex combination of influences—including faulty planning (in particular too great an emphasis on heavy industry and insufficient on consumer goods and agriculture), under-used and badly-managed public enterprises, diversion of vital government funds into defence expenditure as relations with Pakistan worsened, unpredictable supplies of foreign aid, and in 1965–6 a catastrophic drought and two bad harvests. Such a natural calamity had ripple effects beyond the food supply; for it reduced purchasing power and taxable income, and therefore affected private and government investment in industry, as well as demand for industrial products and industrial output. From then onwards economic strategy altered to place greater stress on agricultural output, both to feed India's millions and to provide a buoyant base to the whole economy. This has meant in practice that more resources—seed, fertilizer, and credit—go to those who can best use them, that is the already prospering peasant farmers who produce for the market. Furthermore, in the industrial sector it was clear that the really efficient and productive enterprises were privately owned, and government has had to capitalize on this despite its 'socialist' commitment, and has progressively relaxed controls on a wide range of industries. So governments have been forced to loosen their grip on economic policy and to rely on just those economic groups whose productivity is economically vital but will not transform the existing inequalities in society or bring a swift end to poverty. Nor is this just a cost of a democratic political system in which governments have to attract crucial supporters regularly through elections, and secure the acquiescence of representatives of public opinion in the legislatures on policy decisions. Even Mrs Gandhi's 'Emergency' government at its most dictatorial did not attempt radical economic restructuring because of the social and political as well as economic upheaval that would entail. Rajiv Gandhi's attempts to 'liberalize' the economy were likewise hampered by political opposition and the need to retain an electoral base: and it was only near-bankruptcy in 1991 which made his successors take the plunge into what the Finance Minister called 'measures to unshackle the Indian industrial economy from the cobwebs of unnecessary bureaucratic control'.[35] To what extent this will alter the conditions of the poor is still an urgent and open question.

India's major social problems are often exacerbated if not caused by the scarcity of economic resources or their uneven distribution. The 'drop-out' rate in schools (children are needed for labour by their families) or the chronic unemployment of millions are examples,[36] as are the distribution of land and the Untouchables' position. Although democratic governments have found no solutions to many fundamental social problems, it is proper, as in the case of continuing economic problems, to set them in their context, which is a phase of major change on a scale and at a speed never seen before on the subcontinent and inconceivable in the days of the *raj*.

In the decades since independence there has been a clear loosening of caste restrictions on work and casual social contact, particularly in towns. Towns have grown as industry and business have expanded; and there is now a recognizable urban middle class which commutes daily to professional employment, much as in western conurbations. Urban non-professional workers remain a disparate and disorganized group with little sense of 'working class' identity; not least because of the weak role of the trade unions, and because organized factory labour is a privileged and secure élite of the urban work force and anxious to remain so. There is increasingly a blurring of the urban/rural divide as many villages are now linked by road and economic ties to nearby towns, and villagers may well work in towns if they can find employment, or have close relatives who do. Traditional patron–client ties in villages are breaking down, and though this allows for geographical and occupational mobility it can leave the former service groups without permanent employment or the security of a patron. Education has expanded dramatically. In 1971 the literacy rate was almost 30 per cent (40 per cent for men and 19 per cent for women). According to the 1981 Census these figures had risen to a general literacy rate of 36 per cent (46.9 per cent for men and 24.8 per cent for women)—a striking contrast to the start of the century when male literacy was under 10 per cent and female literacy under 1 per cent. This in turn has enabled far greater occupational mobility and choice, its effect being particularly deep in the lives of those such as lower castes and women who have been educationally deprived in the past.

The institutions of democracy, and the consequent knowledge of public decision-makers that they are acting in accordance with the wishes of India's peoples have enabled governments to make massive investment of public resources in economic development, health, and education. In a totally new way the nation has been able to modify trends, patterns of behaviour, and the distribution of resources which have dominated life on the subcontinent for centuries. But despite the acceleration of change since 1947, despite the government's spending priorities, and despite its commitment to a socialist pattern of society, some of the deepest-rooted inequalities and deprivations remain. Two specific problems demonstrate the dynamics of change and of resistance to change in the later twentieth century.

The unequal distribution of land is one glaring example of the persistence of old inequalities, and even of their intensification. Government has been committed to redistributing land; not only to lessen inequality, but in the hope of reducing the number of landless labourers, and of increasing agricultural productivity by expanding 'marginal' holdings. The first and second five-year plans endorsed the principle of fixing 'ceilings' to agricultural holdings by each individual. It was the states' responsibility to decide on the nature, extent, and timing of legislation to enact the all-India commitment:

predictably their response varied. But from many parts of India comes the same melancholy evidence that 'ceiling legislation' has been slow in passing through state legislatures because of the larger farmers' lobbies and the reluctance of Congress to alienate important supporters, that implementation of legislation has been delayed by challenges in the courts, and that many of those whose holdings would be limited as a result have taken advantage of these delays to protect their holdings by such devices as semi-fictitious donation of land among family members or changing its usage to exploit the legislation's loopholes. Furthermore, the factual evidence and administrative machinery for enforcement of 'ceilings' and the redistribution of resulting freed land often just did not exist.

Nowhere has 'ceiling legislation' produced major change in the social and economic structure of rural life: nor have the problems of rural poverty and landless labour been solved. In Uttar Pradesh, for example, the *zamindars* and *taluqdars* had been the object of Congress hostility for decades, because of their inequitable treatment of their tenants and their role as conservative buttresses of British *raj*. In 1951 legislation was passed to strip them of the bulk of their lands. Some did find their economic and social base collapsing overnight: but many have proved remarkably resilient, not least because of canny preparation for *zamindari* abolition by evasive devices such as those already mentioned. In the state as a whole the percentage of households with large holdings (of 10+ acres) compared with the state average of 3.5 acres was 6.1 before *zamindari* abolition, this privileged group owning nearly 35 per cent of the land. While by the late 1970s this group had risen to 6.25 per cent of households, owning nearly 40 per cent of the land, whereas the average holding had declined to nearly 2.9 acres. In one village, for example, in 1953, ex-landlords of the dominant Thakur caste still owned and cultivated approximately 70 per cent of the land, and the Untouchable labourers experienced virtually no change in their status. 'Ceiling' legislation in the late 1950s proved even less effective as a means of change in the state. As a result less than 0.4 per cent of cultivated land has been redistributed, and much of that is poor land anyway.[37] In neighbouring Bihar 'ceiling legislation' was planned in the late 1950s but shelved because the local Congress party was so divided on the issue that the Congress state government could not muster enough support for the legislation. This gave landlords time to circumvent the legislation which was eventually passed in 1961/2, diluted and so full of loopholes that the opponents of the earlier proposals could find little objectionable in it. Thereafter the government made little attempt to implement its provisions, and the presence of the legislation on the statute book in fact worsened the status of the undertenants who had no occupancy right and were being systematically evicted by the landlords in the 1960s because of the provision for resumption of land from such tenants for 'personal cultivation' over and above the 'ceiling' allowed. It is hardly surprising that tension has been rising in rural society, and that the lower caste tenantry are no longer subservient to the higher castes who not only own most land but have dominated the formal political processes in the state through their participation in Congress before independence and their commanding role in the state government and legislature thereafter.[38]

The problem of implementing laws intended to achieve major social reform when officials and the dominant members of local communities oppose the legislation is apparent in the continuing plight of India's 'Untouchables'. Congress had been morally committed to the abolition of Untouchability since the events surrounding Gandhi's fast in 1932. The constitutional declaration of the end of Untouchability was given teeth in the 1955 Untouchability Offences Act which outlawed the enforcement of disabilities 'on the ground of untouchability'. Law could only deal with public acts in public places, such as refusing to allow Untouchables access to wells, temples, cafes, and footpaths. Even with its limited range it has proved extremely difficult to enforce. It has been challenged in the courts on various grounds; and there are numerous loopholes whereby offenders evade conviction. (For example, the defendant can argue that an act of discrimination was not 'on grounds of untouchability' but for other reasons; or he can claim that the 'offence' occurred on private property.) To take a case to court is expensive for the victim, and there are no central resources to assist him in a test-case or a prolonged lawsuit. Moreover evidence is hard to collect when possible witnesses including the police are often of higher caste or dependent on the higher castes. Even if a prosecution succeeds the penalties tend to be ludicrously light and in no way deterrent.[39] Even if the law was effective in its limited goal of modifying public behaviour it could do little to change fundamental attitudes. As Gandhi recognized decades before, what was needed was a 'change of heart', particularly among the higher castes. Belief in pollution at the hands of an 'Untouchable' remains in India, particularly in rural areas and among women. Urbanization and education are gradually undermining older religious attitudes, but for many Untouchables there is little change in the way they are treated or in the way they see themselves.

The Untouchables' deprived position in society is not just the result of a Hindu understanding of purity and pollution. It is compounded by abject poverty. Consequently government has adopted another strategy for raising their status—so-called 'protective discrimination', which includes providing financial help for higher education, reserved jobs in government service, and continuing special political representation through reserved seats. It has taken at least three decades before enough Untouchables have been educated sufficiently to take advantage of their reserved quotas in the highest levels of government service. The educational drop-out rate among them is still higher than for other castes, and their literacy is lower. (In 1961 only just over 10 per cent of Untouchables were literate compared with the general rate of 24 per cent.) Those who stay the course and receive higher education tend to become an élite, isolated from their caste fellows; and their achieved status does not have a profound effect on that of their caste fellows who remain tied within the conventions and economic pressures of rural society. Until economic opportunities and possibilities of alternative work are available it seems likely that these deprived and still unequal citizens will remain so. Their plight indicates again how inextricable are social and economic problems—for until the unemployment crisis and the issue of land redistribution are resolved there seems little hope for a major improvement in their situation. In an environment of scarcity the weakest go to the wall, whatever the intentions of legislators and reformers.

The particular problems involved in attempts to reform the Untouchables' position and redistribute land more equally demonstrate a significant and far broader dilemma in India's experience of democracy. The strength of economic and social forces, and the persistence of traditional beliefs, have prevented the new democratic political system from responding creatively to some of the country's major problems. Governments after 1947, as before, were the prisoners of those on whom they were forced to rely— officials, taxpayers, key producers of wealth, party activists, and a proportion of the electorate. Such groups are buttresses of democratic institutions as they have developed in India, having learnt to work within and gain from them. Yet they constrain while supporting government; and consequently there are high costs to India from democratic politics and government as there were from imperial rule. To understand the specifically Indian reality within the familiar democratic forms the outsider must study not only the institutions of government and politics but the society in which they have become embedded, paying particular attention to the various patterns of dominance and dependence within it and the ideas and beliefs which are its rationale. These three strands—institutions, ideas, and society—have run through our study of India, and together they begin to explain the roots of this democratic phenomenon in Asia, and both its remarkable durability yet its limited capacity to engineer change.

However, to emphasize vested interests and traditional beliefs is to underestimate the power of political creativity—both in the sense of political ideals and of political organization. One theme of this epilogue has been the weakness and even the atrophy of political parties in India, particularly of the Congress party. Congress never came to terms with the needs and demands of the poorest and least privileged before 1947: the presence of a colonial regime and the nature of 'subaltern' politics meant Congressmen could construct a broad anti-colonial movement and avoid hard decisions about entitlements and distribution of resources. Yet it had the potential to become an all-India organization capable of deepening support, managing conflict and generating a vision and commitment to a secular, democratic state and a more equal society. Ongoing management of interests, and acceptance of change and the need for further changes was vital for India's stability and prosperity. Yet as the Congress organization in the localities disintegrated and the party degenerated into a family fiefdom, it ceased to perform the vital and creative functions necessary if democracy is to manage change. As its top leadership came to rely on populist appeals rather than careful policies reached through consultation and accommodation, so they increasingly were unable to pursue policies crucial to the country's integrity and economic well-being. At a lower level its decay allowed powerful competing groups to hijack politics, often with the assistance of the instruments of government, or with organized gangs of ruffians, to the detriment of those who need the protection and articulation given by and through political organization. Yet this is neither inevitable nor irreversible. At least at state level it has proved possible to achieve stable democratic government which can manage and promote essential change, and can mediate between different groups of citizens, as the CPM regime in West Bengal has shown.[40] Politicians are little loved in India, as the century of independence closes. Yet politicians with vision who can create living party organizations with deeper social roots than just those who have prospered in the new India have a vital role to play in making its democracy a living reality rather than a hollow shell. The Indian polity today faces far greater dilemmas than in the past, as expectations of and demands on the state have multiplied. If it is to face these problems it needs the services of flourishing political institutions lest its leaders rely on the state's powers of coercion and control.

* * *

This study began with the ancient attraction of India to travellers from other continents, first as a remote place of fabled beasts and wealth, then as a more accessible land for plunder and trade. In turn these visitors were replaced by men enthused with European ideas, eager to experiment with social and economic change, and to transform the beliefs and lives of Indians. Later still imperial administrators abandoned such a sanguine enterprise in the face of Indian reality, and settled to the more limited yet profitable task of keeping their *raj* going as the economic and strategic hinge of the British empire. Since independence further waves of foreigners have 'invaded' India, in search of sun, its marvels of art, architecture, and music, the outstanding natural beauty of its mountains and coasts, and the supposed spiritual wealth of its *gurus* as the source of enlightenment to people grown weary of their religious traditions and material values. Yet to all of us, even those who can never visit India, the land, its peoples, and their dilemmas are of great significance. They wrestle as a result of their unique historical experience with issues which are crucial to the world of the later twentieth century—the use of limited natural resources, the relation of human freedom and dignity to economic and political processes, the role of violence in national and international life, the relationship of privileged and underprivileged groups, and the place of politicians with their skills and systems in ordering the life of men and women in community. We cannot ignore India's problems, for many of them are our own.

Notes

CHAPTER I. THE INDIAN SUBCONTINENT: LAND, PEOPLE, AND POWER

1   *Indian Opinion*, 2 October 1909, *The Collected Works of Mahatma Gandhi*, vol. ix (Delhi, 1963), p. 389.
    For a discussion of image-making by Indians and westerners about each other, see M. Singer, *When a Great Tradition Modernizes. An Anthropological Approach to Indian Civilization* (London, 1972), pp. 11–38; U. King, 'Indian Spirituality, Western Materialism: An Image and its Function in the Reinterpretation of Modern Hinduism', *Social Action*, 28, 1 (Jan.–Mar. 1978), pp. 62–86.
2   P. J. Marshall, *East Indian Fortunes. The British in Bengal in the Eighteenth Century* (Oxford, 1976), p. 34. See also P. J. Marshall, *Bengal: The British Bridgehead. Eastern India 1740–1828* (Cambridge, 1987); C. A. Bayly, *Imperial Meridian. The British Empire and the World 1780–1830* (London and New York, 1989).
3   A good introduction to this complex topic is A. T. Embree, 'Landholding in India and British Institutions', in R. E. Frykenberg (ed.), *Land Control and Social Structure in Indian History* (Madison, Milwaukee and London, 1969), pp. 33–52. See also E. Stokes, *The Peasant And The Raj. Studies in agrarian society and peasant rebellion in colonial India* (Cambridge, 1978), pp. 1–3. On the emergence of patrimonial in place of prebendal holdings, see C. A. Bayly, *Imperial Meridian*, pp. 27–9; C. A. Bayly, *Indian Society and the Making of the British Empire* (Cambridge, 1988), pp. 10–11.
4   Such a generalization masks differences between India's different agricultural regions. One regional study indicates pressure on land before the late nineteenth century. See D. Kumar, *Land And Caste In South India. Agricultural labour in the Madras Presidency during the nineteenth century* (Cambridge, 1965).
5   A. Das Gupta, 'The Merchants Of Surat, *c.* 1700–50', in E. Leach and S. N. Mukherjee (eds.), *Elites In South Asia* (Cambridge, 1970), p. 215. The subsequent evidence on Surat comes from H. Furber, *Bombay Presidency in the Mid-Eighteenth Century* (New York, 1965), pp. 7–8. Further case studies are A. Das Gupta, *Malabar In Asian Trade, 1740–1800* (Cambridge, 1967); Marshall, *East Indian Fortunes* and *Bengal: The British Bridgehead*. See also K. N. Chaudhuri, *The Trading World of Asia and the English East India Company, 1660–1760* (Cambridge, 1978).
6   For the financing of hinterland trade see the case study by C. A. Bayly, 'Indian Merchants in a "Traditional" Setting: Benares, 1780–1830', pp. 171–93, in C. Dewey and A. G. Hopkins (eds.), *The Imperial Impact: Studies in the Economic History of Africa and India* (London, 1978).
7   A. Maddison, *Class Structure and Economic Growth. India and Pakistan since the Moghuls* (London, 1971), p. 33.
8   Introductory works on the Muslims and Sikhs are P. Hardy, *The Muslims of British India* (Cambridge, 1972); K. Singh, *A History of The Sikhs*, 2 vols. (Princeton, 1963 and 1966); W. O. Cole and P. S. Sambhi, *The Sikhs. Their Religious Beliefs and Practices* (London, 1978). On South Indian Christians an excellent study is S. B. Bayly, *Saints, Goddesses and*

Kings. Muslims and Christians in South Indian Society, 1700–1900 (Cambridge, 1989). There is no adequate book on northern Christians or indeed on European missionary activity: references to some classic works are to be found in Chapter III, n. 62.

9 See D. G. Mandelbaum, 'Family, *Jati*, Village', chapter 2 of M. Singer and B. S. Cohn (eds.), *Structure and Change in Indian Society* (Chicago, 1968); D. G. Mandelbaum, *Society in India. Volume One. Continuity and Change* (Berkeley, Los Angeles, and London, 1970); G. M. Carstairs, *The Twice-Born. A Study of a Community of High-Caste Hindus* (London, 1957).

10 M. N. Srinivas, 'Mobility in the Caste System', chapter 8 of Singer and Cohn, *Structure and Change*; J. Silverberg (ed.), *Social Mobility In India. An Interdisciplinary Symposium* (The Hague and Paris, 1968). A case study of a caste and its comparatively recent emergence in the eighteenth century is F. F. Conlon, *A Caste in a Changing World. The Chitrapur Saraswat Brahmans, 1700–1935* (Berkeley and Los Angeles, 1977). A major modern work on the caste system as a whole, which has not been without its critics, is L. Dumont, *Homo Hierarchicus. The Caste System and its Implications* (English translation, London, 1970).

11 For an inquiry into recent changes in the Hindu religious experience, including the late nineteenth-century 'invention of Hinduism', see J. M. Brown, *Men And Gods In A Changing World. Some Themes in the Religious Experience of Twentieth-Century Hindus and Christians* (London, 1980). (This study begins with a survey of some of the main features of the Hindu context and way of thinking about religion compared with those within a monotheistic context, which are briefly touched on in this book.)

12 See L. A. Babb, *The Divine Hierarchy: Popular Hinduism in Central India* (New York and London, 1975); D. F. Pocock, *Mind, Body And Wealth. A Study of Belief and Practice in an Indian Village* (Oxford, 1973). A theoretical introduction to the relationship of Great and Little Traditions is Singer, *When a Great Tradition Modernizes*, pp. 39–52.

13 A good introductory discussion of this is D. E. Smith's essay, 'The Political Implications of Asian Religions', in D. E. Smith (ed.), *South Asian Politics And Religion* (Princeton, 1969), pp. 3–20.

14 B. S. Cohn describes three levels of administration in the Banares region in the eighteenth century. I have added the village level at the base: here there was no formal administration, but certainly a mode of regulating affairs, and it, like the other three levels, was a focus or arena of political action. The dividing line between village and Cohn's local level is often blurred, certainly in some areas. See B. S. Cohn, 'The Initial British Impact on India. A Case Study of the Benares Region', *JAS*, vol. xix, no. 4 (August 1960), pp. 418–31; and his 'Structural Change in Indian Rural Society 1596–1885', in R. E. Frykenberg (ed.), *Land Control And Social Structure*, particularly pp. 57–63. See also, R. Ray, 'The Bengal Zamindars: Local Magnates and the state before the Permanent Settlement', *IESHR*, vol. xii, no. 3 (July–Sept. 1975), pp. 263–92. For an overview of the differentiated nature of power in eighteenth-century India see C. A. Bayly, *Indian Society and the Making of the British Empire*, pp. 13–22.

15 For a broad overview of the Mogul empire and its fate see C. A. Bayly, *Imperial Meridian*, chs. 1 and 2. For detailed work on the imperial system see S. P. Blake, 'The Patrimonial-Bureaucratic Empire of the Mughals', *JAS*, vol. xxxix, no. 1 (Nov. 1979), pp. 77–94. This stresses the patrimonial nature of the empire and is a good counter-weight to the more usual description of the imperial administration in terms of a centralized and formal bureaucracy. In this tradition is P. Spear, *India. A Modern History* (Ann Arbor, 1961), and his 'The Mughal *Mansabdari* System', in E. Leach and S. N. Mukherjee (eds.), *Elites In South Asia*, pp. 1–15.

16 'Symposium: Decline of the Mughal Empire' (contributions by M. N. Pearson, J. F.

Richards and P. Hardy), *JAS*, vol. xxxv, no. 2 (Feb. 1976), pp. 221–63.

17 P. J. Marshall, *Problems Of Empire. Britain and India 1757–1813* (London, 1968), pp. 17,118. This book of documents and accompanying text is one of the best introductions to this period from the British angle.

18 Marshall, *East Indian Fortunes*, p. 10. For a delightful discussion of early British life in India see P. Spear, *The Nabobs. A Study of the Social Life of the English in Eighteenth Century India* (London, 1963, Oxford Paperback edition).

19 Marshall, *East Indian Fortunes*, is the main source of this information. See also his 'Economic and Political Expansion: The Case of Oudh', *MAS*, vol. 9, part 4 (October 1975), pp. 465–82.

20 Details of this intricate phase can be found in standard narratives such as Spear, *India. A Modern History*, or S. A. Wolpert, *A New History of India* (2nd edition, New York and Oxford, 1982), or more recently in C. A. Bayly, *Indian Society and the Making of the British Empire*. For a detailed analysis of developments in Bengal, 1740–1828, see Marshall, *Bengal: The British Bridgehead.*

CHAPTER II. THE CONSOLIDATION OF DOMINION: ILLUSION AND REALITY

1 H. Furber, *John Company at Work* (2nd. edn., Cambridge, Mass., 1951).

2 For detailed inquiries into particular phases of British territorial expansion see Marshall, *East Indian Fortunes*, pp. 259–60; Marshall, *MAS*, vol. 9, part 4 (Oct. 1975), pp. 465–82; P. Nightingale, *Trade and Empire In Western India 1784–1806* (Cambridge, 1970); C. A. Bayly, *Indian Society and the Making of the British Empire*, pp. 79–105. (There are good maps of the expansion of British rule in north and south India, pp. 52 and 88.)

3 See Marshall, *East Indian Fortunes* and *Problems Of Empire*, pp. 28, 58–60; B. S. Cohn, 'Recruitment and Training of British Civil Servants in India, 1600–1860', in R. Braibanti (ed.), *Asian Bureaucratic Systems Emergent from the British Imperial Tradition* (Duke, 1966), pp. 94–5.

4 In 1784 there were 60 MPs with Indian interests; 95 in 1802; 103 in 1806; but from 1830–4 the number dropped from 62 to 45. C. H. Philips, *The East India Company 1784–1833* (2nd. edn., Manchester, 1961), p. 299. Details are in Appendix 1.

5 The best introduction to these attempts at Parliamentary control and the tangled politics behind them is Marshall, *Problems Of Empire*, pp. 21–51.

6 For much of what follows see Cohn, 'Recruitment and Training', in Braibanti (ed.), op. cit., pp. 87–140.

7 The influence of British philosophy, particularly Utilitarian doctrines, on land revenue and the forms of government is a complex topic which recurs in this chapter. The most important study of it, which also covers changes in administrative structure, is E. Stokes, *The English Utilitarians And India* (Oxford, 1959).

8 The main local administrative studies available, on which this section draws heavily, are R. E. Frykenberg, *Guntur District 1788–1848. A History of Local Influence and Central Authority in South India* (Oxford, 1965), and his 'Village Strength in South India', in his *Land Control and Social Structure*, pp. 227–47; J. Rosselli, 'Theory And Practice In North India', *IESHR*, vol. viii, no. 2 (June 1971), pp. 134–63; N. Rabitoy, 'System v. Expediency: The Reality of Land Revenue Administration in the Bombay Presidency, 1812–1820', *MAS*, vol. 9, part 4 (Oct. 1975), pp. 529–40.

9 An indication of the power of the Madras *Sheristadar*, or chief Indian revenue officer in the headquarters office, is given in this summary by the Madras Board of Revenue in 1836: Frykenberg, *Guntur District 1788–1848*, p. 76.

'He superintends every department and is the general inspector and controller of accounts. He is usually consulted by the Collector on every question connected with the administration of the revenue and particularly in the annual settlement; and the orders of the Collector for guidance of the subordinate executive Officers are generally passed after discussion with him.'

10 See Marshall, *Problems Of Empire*, Introduction 3, 'Trade and Tribute', pp. 78–101.

11 See Marshall, *Problems Of Empire*, pp. 89–90; and a specialist study, M. Greenberg, *British Trade and The Opening of China 1800–42* (Cambridge, 1951).

12 Quoted in Greenberg, op. cit., pp. 106–7.

13 Some of the main works on land settlement are:
B. H. Baden-Powell, *A Short Account of the Land Revenue and its Administration in British India; with a sketch of the Land Tenures* (2nd. edn., London, 1907); E. Stokes, *The English Utilitarians And India*; S. Gopal, *The Permanent Settlement In Bengal And Its Results* (London, 1949); T. H. Beaglehole, *Thomas Munro And The Development Of Administrative Policy In Madras* (Cambridge, 1966); B. Stein, *Thomas Munro. The Origins of the Colonial State and His Vision of Empire* (Delhi, 1989); D. Kumar, *Land And Caste In South India*; K. Ballhatchet, *Social Policy And Social Change In Western India 1817–1830* (London, 1957); W. C. Neale, *Economic Change in Rural India. Land Tenure and Reform in Uttar Pradesh, 1800–1955* (New Haven and London, 1962); E. Stokes, 'The land-revenue systems of the North-Western Provinces and Bombay Deccan 1830–80: ideology and the official mind', *The Peasant And The Raj*, pp. 90–119.

14 S. Gopal, *The Permanent Settlement In Bengal*, p. 16.

15 D. Kumar, *Land And Caste In South India*, p. 81; Stein, *Thomas Munro*, p. 289. On the variability of *ryotwari* in practice, see Stein, *Thomas Munro*, pp. 340 ff.; D. Ludden, *Peasant History in South India* (Princeton, 1985).

16 Rosselli, *IESHR*, vol. viii, no. 2 (June 1971), pp. 134–63.

17 See articles by M. D. Wainwright, 'Continuity in Mysore', and R. J. Bingle, 'Changing Attitudes to the Indian States, 1820–1850; a study of Oudh, Hyderabad and Jaipur', pp. 165–85, 69–79, C. H. Philips and M. D. Wainwright (eds.), *Indian Society and the Beginnings of Modernisation c. 1830–1850* (London, 1976); also C. A. Bayly, *Indian Society and the Making of the British Empire*, pp. 110–13.

18 Minute of 30. 8. 48, quoted in T. R. Metcalf, *The Aftermath Of Revolt. India, 1857–1870* (Princeton, 1964), pp. 31–2.

19 Quoted in Beaglehole, *Thomas Munro And The Development Of Administrative Policy In Madras*, pp. 116–17.

20 R. E. Frykenberg, 'The Impact of Conversion and Social Reform upon Society in South India during the late Company Period: Questions concerning Hindu–Christian Encounters with special reference to Tinnevelly', Philips and Wainwright (eds.), *Indian Society and the Beginnings of Modernisation*, p. 212. By 'civil religion' Frykenberg means 'a system of ideologies, myths, ceremonies, rituals, and institutions which are encouraged and strengthened by the political authority and power of the state for the very reason that such religion supports the state, reinforcing its legitimacy and enhancing its sway . . .' ibid. p. 211.

21 Bentinck's comment is quoted in Spear; *India*, p. 256. For Marx's analysis of the nature of Indian society and the effects of British rule, see E. Stokes, 'The first century of British rule in India: social revolution or social stagnation?', in Stokes, *The Peasant And The Raj*, pp. 19–25. This essay is an important survey of trends in scholarly understanding of the nature of early British influence.

22 Quoted in F. G. Hutchins, *The Illusion Of Permanence. British Imperialism in India* (Princeton, 1967), p. 10. Chapter 1 of this book and Stokes, *The English Utilitarians And India*, pp. 27–37, are a good introduction to evangelical ideas in the Indian context.

23 Quoted in Stokes, *The English Utilitarians And India*, p. 34.

24 R. J. Moore, 'Imperialism and "Free Trade" Policy in India, 1853–4', *Ec. H. R.*, 2nd Series, vol. xvii, no. 1 (1964), pp. 135–45; A. W. Silver, *Manchester Men And Indian Cotton 1847–1872* (Manchester, 1966); D. Thorner, *Investment in Empire. British Railway and Steam Shipping Enterprise in India 1825–1849* (Philadelphia, 1950).

25 C. A. Bayly, *Indian Society and the Making of the British Empire*, pp. 120–3; E. T. Stokes, 'Bureaucracy and Ideology: Britain and India in the nineteenth century', *TRHS*, 5th series, vol. 30 (1980), pp. 131–56. Hardinge's instructions are quoted in G. D. Bearce, *British Attitudes Towards India 1784–1858* (Oxford, 1961), pp. 202–3: 'If you can keep peace, reduce expense, extend commerce, and strengthen our hold on India by confidence in our justice, kindness, and wisdom, you will be received on your return with acclamation a thousand times louder, and a welcome infinitely more cordial than if you have a dozen victories to boast of, and annex the Punjab to the overgrown empire of India.'

26 Cohn, *JAS*, vol. xix, no. 4 (Aug. 1960), pp. 418–31; E. I. Brodkin, 'Proprietory Mutations and the Mutiny in Rohilkhand', *JAS*, vol. xxviii, no. 4 (Aug. 1969), pp. 667–83.

27 Quoted in Brodkin, op. cit., p. 677. See also for actual change in different areas Ray, *IESHR*, vol. xii, no. 3 (July–Sept. 1975), pp. 263–92; R. Ray, 'Land Transfer and Social Change Under The Permanent Settlement: A Study of Two Localities', *IESHR*, vol. xi, no. 1 (Mar. 1974), pp. 1–45; B. B. Chaudhuri, 'Land Market in Eastern India, 1793–1940 Part II: The Changing Composition of the Landed Society', *IESHR*, vol. xii, no. 2 (Apr.–June 1975), pp. 133–67; Cohn, *JAS*, vol. xix, no. 4 (Aug. 1960), pp. 418–31; Cohn, 'Structural Change in Indian Rural Society 1596–1885', Frykenberg (ed.), *Land Control and Social Structure*, pp. 53–121; Brodkin, *JAS*, vol. xxviii, no. 4 (Aug. 1969), pp. 667–83; Rosselli, *IESHR*, vol. viii, no. 2 (June 1971), pp. 134–63.

28 Some of the reform campaigns against 'abuses' and their difficulties are discussed in K. Ingham, *Reformers In India 1793–1833. An account of the work of Christian Missionaries on behalf of social reform* (Cambridge, 1956); on slavery in south India, see D. Kumar, *Land And Caste In South India*.

29 S. Nurullah and J. P. Naik, *A History of Education In India* (2nd. edn., Bombay, 1951); B. T. McCully, *English Education And The Origins of Indian Nationalism* (Columbia, 1940). An important work almost contemporary with the controversy is C. E. Trevelyan, *On The Education Of The People Of India* (London, 1838).

30 Quoted in McCully, op. cit., p. 69.

31 Quoted in C. H. Heimsath, *Indian Nationalism and Hindu Social Reform* (Princeton, 1964), p. 74.

32 Some key contributions to the academic controversy are in M. D. Morris *et al.* (eds.), *Indian Economy in the Nineteenth Century: A Symposium* (Delhi, 1969). A useful starting point is chapter 3 of Maddison, *Class Structure and Economic Growth*. See also C. A. Bayly, *Indian Society and the Making of the British Empire* and 'The Age of Hiatus: the North Indian Economy and Society', in Philips and Wainwright (eds.), *Indian Society and the Beginnings of Modernisation*, pp. 83–105; and introduction to K. N. Chaudhuri (ed.), *The Economic Development of India under the East India Company 1814–58* (Cambridge, 1971), pp. 1–50. The most detailed and broad-ranging study of a particular area in the early years of British expansion is C. A. Bayly, *Rulers, Townsmen and Bazaars. North Indian society in the age of British expansion, 1770–1870* (Cambridge, 1983).

33 Quoted in Thorner, *Investment In Empire*, p. 152.
    On Dalhousie see S. C. Ghosh, 'The Utilitarianism of Dalhousie and the Material Improvement of India', *MAS*, vol. 12, part 1 (1978), pp. 97–110.

34 On rebellions before 1857 see C. A. Bayly, *Indian Society and the Making of the British Empire*, pp. 169–78.
    This section draws heavily on the research of scholars such as E. Stokes, who have

opened new perspectives on the social and economic background of civil rebellion in 1857. The main sources are listed in the guide to further reading for this chapter. A good introduction to the events and how these have been interpreted is Metcalf, *The Aftermath Of Revolt*, chapter 2.

35 M. R. Gubbins, *An Account of the Mutinies in Oudh, and of The Siege of the Lucknow Residency* (2nd. edn., London, 1858), p. 118.
36 Entry for 3 April 1858, M. Edwardes (ed.), W. H. Russell, *My Indian Mutiny Diary* (London, 1857), p. 119.
37 Gubbins, op. cit., p. 100.
38 H. Lawrence to Canning, 9 May 1857, quoted in Metcalf, *The Aftermath Of Revolt*, p. 48.
39 Entry for 19 November 1858, Edwardes (ed.), Russell's *Mutiny Diary*, p. 229.
40 Report by A. Hume, 18 November 1858, Narrative of Events regarding the Mutiny in India of 1857–58 and the Restoration of Authority, Volume 1, p. 178 (India Office Records).
41 William Edwards, Collector of Budaon, on his personal experiences during the Mutiny, quoted in Brodkin, *JAS*, vol. xxviii, no. 4 (Aug. 1969), p. 667.
42 Entry for 1 February 1858, Edwardes (ed.), Russell's *Mutiny Diary*, p. 16.

CHAPTER III. THE DILEMMAS OF DOMINION

1 C. E. Trevelyan, 1853, quoted in R. J. Moore, *Liberalism and Indian Politics 1872–1922* (London, 1966), p. 7. See also Hutchins, *The Illusion Of Permanence*, pp. 88–91.
2 On the problem of ICS recruitment and training see R. J. Moore, 'The abolition of patrongage in the ICS and the closure of Haileybury College', *HJ*, vol. vii. no. 2 (1964), pp. 246–57; J. M. Compton, 'Open Competition and the ICS, 1854–76', *EHR*, vol. lxxxiii (Apr. 1968), pp. 265–84; B. Spangenberg, 'The problem of recruitment for the Indian Civil Service in the late nineteenth century', *JAS*, vol. xxx, no. 2 (Feb. 1971), pp. 341–60; C. J. Dewey, 'The education of a ruling caste: the Indian Civil Service in the era of competitive examination', *EHR*, lxxxviii (Apr. 1973), pp. 262–85.
  The best single book on the ICS, which has much on the traditions of the service, although its focus is the twentieth century, is D. C. Potter, *India's Political Administrators 1919–1983* (Oxford, 1986).
3 H. Cotton to Curzon, 5 May 1899, quoted in D. Dilks, *Curzon in India. 1. Achievement* (London, 1969), p. 82.
4 A good introduction to the study of white women in the empire is M. Strobel, *European Women and the Second British Empire* (Bloomington and Indianapolis, 1991). See also M. A. Lind, *The Compassionate Memsahibs. Welfare Activities of British Women in India, 1900–1947* (Westport, 1988). A study which highlights the issue of sexual relations in imperial preservation of distance, prestige, and power is K. Ballhatchet, *Race, Sex and Class under the Raj. Imperial Attitudes and Policies and their Critics, 1793–1905* (London, 1980). Apart from the Indian stories and poetry of Kipling other works of fiction which evoke 'the *raj*' and its social world are the novels of P. Scott and J. Masters. See also C. Allen (ed.), *Plain Tales From The Raj. Images of British India in the Twentieth Century* (London, 1975). Evocative books of pictures are C. Allen (ed.), *Raj. A Scrapbook of British India 1877–1947* (London, 1977), and *The Last Empire. Photography in British India, 1855–1911* (London, 1976). See also P. Kanwar, *Imperial Simla. The Political Culture of the Raj* (Delhi, 1990).
5 *India's Contribution to the Great War* (Calcutta, 1923); see also R. Robinson, J. Gallagher and A. Denny, *Africa And The Victorians. The Official Mind of Imperialism* (London, 1965), pp. 11–13.

6 A convenient and lucid introduction to India's economic importance for Britain is B. R. Tomlinson, *The Political Economy Of The Raj 1914–1947. The Economics of Decolonization in India* (London, 1979), pp. 1–6. He draws heavily on S. B. Saul, *Studies in British Overseas Trade 1870–1914* (Liverpool, 1960).

7 See, for example, *The Nineteenth Century*, vol. xiv, no. lxxx (October, 1883), containing discussions provoked by controversy over the Ilbert Bill: E. Baring, 'Recent Events In India', pp. 569–89; and J. Fitzjames Stephen, 'Foundations Of The Government Of India', pp. 541–68. An excellent discussion of the assumptions of later nineteenth-century imperialism is Chapter 1 of Robinson and Gallagher, *Africa And The Victorians*. Important literary studies are A. J. Greenberger, *The British Image Of India. A Study in the Literature of Imperialism 1880–1960* (London, 1969), and B. Parry, *Delusions and Discoveries. Studies on India in the British Imagination 1880–1930* (London, 1972).

8 On changing attitudes to race in nineteenth-century Britain, see P. B. Rich, *Race and Empire in British Politics* (2nd edn., Cambridge, 1990), ch. 1; C. Bolt, *Victorian Attitudes to Race* (London, 1971), and more briefly 'Race and the Victorians', ch. 6 of C. C. Eldridge (ed.), *British Imperialism in the Nineteenth Century* (Basingstoke, 1984), pp. 126–47. See also chapter on 'Concepts of Indian Character', Hutchins, *The Illusion Of Permanence*, pp. 53–78; and Ballhatchet, *Race, Sex and Class under the Raj*.

9 Quoted in Parry, *Delusions and Discoveries*, p. 28.

10 Stephen, *The Nineteenth Century*, vol. xiv, no. lxxx, p. 554. See also Stokes, *The English Utilitarians And India*, chapter 4, for the authoritarian strand in the Utilitarian legacy. Lytton's remarks were in a letter to Salisbury, 11 May 1876, in Lady Balfour (ed.), *Personal and Literary Letters of Robert, First Earl of Lytton. Vol. 2* (London, 1906), p. 20.

11 Ripon to Hartington, 31 December 1881, S. Gopal, *The Viceroyalty Of Lord Ripon 1880–1884* (London, 1953), p. 84.

12 Speech on 30 September 1905, quoted in S. Gopal, *British Policy In India 1858–1905* (Cambridge, 1965), p. 249.

13 See above, p. 83. For policies towards and developments in communications see R. J. Moore, *Sir Charles Wood's Indian Policy 1853–66* (Manchester, 1966), pp. 124 ff.; P. Griffiths, *The British Impact On India* (London, 1952), pp. 420–7; J. M. Hurd, 'Railways', in D. Kumar and M. Desai (eds.), *The Cambridge Economic History of India, Volume 2: c.1757–c.1970* (Cambridge, 1983), pp. 737–61.

14 For a good overview see M. D. Morris, 'The Growth of Large-Scale Industry to 1947', ch. vii of Kumar and Desai (eds.), op. cit., pp. 553 ff.; see also J. Krishnamurty, 'The Occupational Structure', ch. vi, ibid., pp. 533 ff.

15 For internal migration, the growth of cities, and problems of accurate enumeration, see K. Davis, *The Population Of India And Pakistan* (Princeton, New Jersey, 1951), pp. 107–37. The following series for Bombay City is on p. 136.

Year	Percentage of city population born outside the city:
1872	68.9
1881	72.2
1891	75.0
1901	76.6
1911	80.4
1921	84.0

16 See M. D. Morris, *The Emergence Of An Industrial Labor Force In India. A Study of the Bombay Cotton Mills, 1854–1947* (Berkeley and Los Angeles, 1965); K. L. Gillion, *Ahmedabad. A Study in Indian Urban History* (Berkeley and Los Angeles, 1968); R. Das Gupta, 'Factory Labour in Eastern India: Sources of Supply, 1855–1946: Some Prelimi-

nary Findings', *IESHR*, vol. xiii, no. 3 (1976), pp. 277–329; D. Chakrabarty, *Rethinking Working-Class History. Bengal 1890–1940* (Princeton, 1989).

17   A. K. Bagchi, 'European and Indian Entrepreneurship in India, 1900–30', in E. Leach and S. N. Mukherjee (eds.), *Elites In South Asia*, pp. 223–56.

18   J. H. Broomfield, 'The Rural Parvenu. A Report of Research in Progress', *South Asian Review*, vol. vi, no. 3 (Apr. 1973), pp. 181–95.

19   Gillion, *Ahmedabad*, p. 88.

20   On these controversial matters see Tomlinson, *The Political Economy Of The Raj 1914– 1947*, pp. 15–16; P. Harnetty, *Imperialism And Free Trade: Lancashire and India in the Mid-Nineteenth Century* (Manchester, 1972); C. Dewey, 'The End of the Imperialism of Free Trade: The Eclipse of the Lancashire Lobby and the Concession of Fiscal Autonomy to India', Dewey and Hopkins (eds.), *The Imperial Impact*, pp. 35–67; N. Charlesworth, *British Rule and the Indian Economy 1800–1914* (London and Basingstoke, 1982).

21   M. D. Morris, 'Values as an Obstacle to Economic Growth in South Asia: An Historical Survey', *Journal of Economic History*, vol. 27, no. 4 (Dec. 1967), pp. 588–607; M. Singer, 'Industrial Leadership, the Hindu Ethic, and the Spirit of Socialism', in Singer, *When a Great Tradition Modernizes*, pp. 272–380.

22   On irrigation see Griffiths, *The British Impact On India*, pp. 405–14; Davis, *The Population Of India And Pakistan*, p. 40; E. Whitcombe, 'Irrigation', in Kumar and Desai (eds.), op. cit., pp. 677–737, and *Agrarian Conditions In Northern India. Volume 1. The United Provinces under British Rule, 1860–1900* (Berkeley, Los Angeles, and London, 1972), pp. 71 ff.; I. Stone, 'Canal Irrigation and Agrarian Change: The Experience of the Ganges Canal Tract, Muzaffarnagar District (UP), 1840–1900', K. N. Chaudhuri and C. J. Dewey (eds.), *Economy And Society. Essays in Indian Economic and Social History* (Delhi, 1979), pp. 86–112; I. Stone, *Canal Irrigation in British India. Perspectives on Technological Change in a Peasant Economy* (Cambridge, 1984).

23   Davis, op. cit., p. 27 has adjusted the census figures in the light of enumeration technicalities to produce the following population figures:

Year	Estimated Population (in millions):
1871	255.2
1881	257.4
1891	282.1
1901	285.3
1911	303.0
1921	305.7

For a detailed study of population and the determinants of growth rates, see L. and P. Vinaria, 'Population (1757–1947)', ch. v of Kumar and Desai (eds.), op. cit., pp. 463–532.

24   T. G. Kessinger, *Vilyatpur 1848–1968. Social and Economic Change in a North Indian Village* (Berkeley, Los Angeles, and London, 1974), pp. 113–17; Davis, op. cit., p. 207; N. Charlesworth, 'Trends in the Agricultural Performance of an Indian Province: The Bombay Presidency, 1900–1920', Chaudhuri and Dewey (eds.), *Economy And Society*, pp. 113–40; and N. Charlesworth, *Peasants and Imperial Rule. Agriculture and Agrarian Society in the Bombay Presidency, 1850–1935* (Cambridge, 1985).

25   Maddison, *Class Structure and Economic Growth*, pp. 51–2; G. Blyn, *Agricultural Trends in India, 1891–1947: Output, Availability, and Productivity* (Philadelphia, 1966).

26   See the regional surveys (chs. ii and iii) in Kumar and Desai (eds.), op. cit., pp. 36–375. For more local case studies see P. Harnetty, 'Crop Trends in the Central Provinces of India, 1861–1921', *MAS*, vol. 11, part 3 (July 1977), pp. 341–77; Charlesworth, 'Trends in the Agricultural Performance of an Indian Province: The Bombay Presidency, 1900– 1920', Chaudhuri and Dewey (eds.), *Economy And Society*, pp. 113–40 and *Peasants and Imperial Rule*; C. J. Baker, *An Indian Rural Economy 1880–1955. The Tamilnad Country-*

side (Oxford, 1984); Kessinger, op. cit. The Punjab official's comment is quoted in Kessinger, op. cit., p. 104. On the problem of inaccurate statistics see C. Dewey, '*Patwari and Chaukidar*: Subordinate Officials and the Reliability of India's Agricultural Statistics', Dewey and Hopkins (eds.), *The Imperial Impact*, pp. 280–314.

27   On rural credit see Whitcombe, op. cit., pp. 110–18, 161–70; P. J. Musgrave, 'Rural Credit and Rural Society in the United Provinces, 1860–1920', Dewey and Hopkins (eds.), *The Imperial Impact*, pp. 216–32; Charlesworth, *Peasants and Imperial Rule*, pp. 82–94; I. J. Catenach, *Rural Credit in Western India 1875–1930. Rural Credit and the Co-operative Movement in the Bombay Presidency* (Berkeley, Los Angeles and Bombay, 1970).

28   Whitcombe, op. cit.; D. Washbrook, 'Economic Development and Social Stratification in Rural Madras: The "Dry Region", 1878–1929', and N. Charlesworth, 'Rich Peasants and Poor Peasants in Late Nineteenth-Century Maharashtra', Dewey and Hopkins (eds.), *The Imperial Impact*, pp. 68–82, 97–113.

29   Moore, *Sir Charles Wood's Indian Policy 1853–66*, pp. 108–23. A convenient survey of educational policy is pp. 9–18 of *Interim Report of the Indian Statutory Commission (Review of growth of Education in British India by the Auxiliary Committee appointed by the Commission). September, 1929* (London, 1929), Cmd. 3407. (Hereafter referred to as *1929 Interim Report on Education.*) This section on education draws heavily on the above report and on McCully, op. cit.

30   B. B. Misra, *The Indian Middle Classes. Their Growth In Modern Times* (London, 1961), p. 303; A. Seal, *The Emergence Of Indian Nationalism. Competition and Collaboration in the Later Nineteenth Century* (Cambridge, 1968), p. 18.

31   McCully, op. cit., pp. 187–9.

32   Figures for 1912, *1929 Interim Report on Education*, p. 133.

33   McCully, op. cit., pp. 194–5.

34   Metcalf, *The Aftermath Of Revolt*: the simplicity and adequacy of his interpretation is criticized by E. Stokes in a review in *HJ*, vol. 10, no. i (1967), pp. 143–5.

35   Wood to Canning, 8 April 1861, quoted in Metcalf, *The Aftermath Of Revolt*, pp. 297–8. On the Indian army between the Mutiny and 1914, see Part IV of P. Mason, *A Matter of Honour. An account of the Indian army, its officers and men* (London, 1974).

36   S. Bhattacharyya, *Financial Foundations Of The British Raj. Men and Ideas in the post-Mutiny Period of Reconstruction of Indian Public Finance, 1858–1872* (Simla, 1971).

37   See C. A. Bayly, *The Local Roots of Indian Politics. Allahabad 1880–1920* (Oxford, 1975); C. Dobbin, *Urban Leadership in Western India. Politics and Communities in Bombay City 1840–1885* (London, 1972).

38   Baring to Mallet, 25 September 1882, quoted in Seal, *The Emergence Of Indian Nationalism*, p. 156. See also extracts from Government of India resolutions on municipalities (31 August 1864), provincial assignments (14 December 1870) and constitution of local boards (18 May 1882), in C. H. Philips and B. N. Pandey (eds.), *The Evolution Of India And Pakistan 1858 to 1947. Select Documents* (London, 1962), pp. 43–4, 580–3, 50–6.

39   Curzon to Hamilton, 11 June 1901, quoted in Dilks, *Curzon in India. 1*, p. 191. Details of frontier policy are in S. Gopal, *British Policy In India 1858–1905*.

40   Bartle Frere to Sir Charles Wood, 10 April 1861, quoted in Bhattacharyya, *Financial Foundations Of The British Raj*, p. 14.

41   Royal Proclamation, 1 November 1858, Philips and Pandey (eds.), *The Evolution Of India And Pakistan 1858 to 1947*, pp. 10–11. On the Ilbert Bill controversy see S. Gopal, *The Viceroyalty Of Lord Ripon 1880–1884*, pp. 113–66; C. Dobbin, 'The Ilbert Bill: a Study of Anglo-Indian Opinion in India, 1883', *Historical Studies, Australia and New Zealand*, vol. xii, no. 45 (Oct. 1965); M. Sinha, '"Chathams, Pitts, And Gladstones In Petticoats." The Politics of Gender and Race in the Ilbert Bill Controversy, 1883–1884', N. Chaudhuri and M. Strobel (eds.), *Western Women and Imperialism. Complicity and Resistance*

(Bloomington and Indianapolis, 1992), pp. 98–116.

42 Curzon's minutes on military matters, July 1902; Curzon to Salisbury, 21 June 1903; Queen Victoria to Salisbury, 29 May 1898; quoted in Dilks, *Curzon in India. 1*, pp. 211–12, 105, 64.

43 P. Griffiths, *To Guard My People. The History Of The Indian Police* (London and Bombay, 1971), p. 88. This is a standard work on the police. See also D. J. Arnold, 'The Police and Colonial Control in South India, 1890–1947', *Social Scientist*, no. 48 (1976), pp. 3–16, and *Police Power And Colonial Rule. Madras 1859–1947* (Delhi, 1986); P. Robb, 'The ordering of rural India: the policing of nineteenth-century Bengal and Bihar', ch. 8 of D. M. Anderson and D. Killingray (eds.), *Policing The Empire. Government, Authority and Control, 1830–1940* (Manchester and New York, 1991), pp. 126–50.

44 Part I of N. G. Barrier, *Banned. Controversial Literature And Political Control In British India 1907–1947* (Missouri, 1974).

45 30 April 1860, quoted in Metcalf, *The Aftermath Of Revolt*, p. 224. On the Political Service see T. C. Coen, *The Indian Political Service. A Study in Indirect Rule* (London, 1971). On the role of the princes in a new 'feudalism' and the elaboration of imperial ceremonial, see Cohn, 'Representing Authority in Victorian India', Hobsbawm and Ranger (eds.), *The Invention of Tradition*, pp. 179–209.

46 Quoted in M. Maclagen, *'Clemency' Canning* (London, 1962), p. 190. On the Oudh settlement and the British–*taluqdari* alliance see T. R. Metcalf, 'From Raja to Landlord: The Oudh Talukdars, 1850–1870', and 'Social Effects of British Land Policy in Oudh', Frykenberg (ed.), *Land Control and Social Structure in Indian History*, pp. 123–41, 143–62; P. Reeves, *Landlords And Governments In Uttar Pradesh. A study of their relations until zamindari abolition* (Bombay, 1991), particularly chs. 1 & 2.

   On a similar but less elaborate imperial-landlord alliance in Sind, see Ansari, *Sufi Saints And State Power*. A Study of a 'permanent settlement' area in Bihar shows the working of a British alliance with the landed as an instrument of local control, and stresses the importance of the Court of Wards in propping up the landed when necessary: A. A. Yang, *The Limited Raj. Agrarian Relations in Colonial India. Saran District, 1793–1920* (Delhi, 1989), particularly ch. 4.

47 Note by Sir John Hewett, 16 August 1909, quoted in P. J. Musgrave, 'Landlords and Lords of the Land: Estate Management and Social Control in Uttar Pradesh 1860–1920', *MAS*, vol. 6, part 3 (July 1972), p. 260.

48 Quoted in N. G. Barrier, *The Punjab Alienation Of Land Bill Of 1900* (Durham, NC, 1966), p. 37. See also Catanach, *Rural Credit in Western India 1875–1930*, pp. 10–26; N. Charlesworth, 'The Myth of The Deccan Riots of 1875', *MAS*, vol. 6, part 4 (Oct. 1972), pp. 401–21; Metcalf, *The Aftermath Of Revolt*, pp. 174–218.

49 Quoted on p. 376 of N. G. Barrier, 'The Punjab Disturbances of 1907: the response of the British Government in India to Agrarian unrest', *MAS*, vol. i, part 4 (Oct. 1967), pp. 353–83.

50 C. A. Bayly, 'Local Control in Indian Towns—the case of Allahabad 1880–1920', *MAS*, vol. 5, part 1 (1971), pp. 289–311. Canning's comment to Sir Charles Wood on Lucknow, 10 April 1861, is quoted in Maclagen, *'Clemency' Canning*, p. 299.

51 Lytton to Lord George Hamilton, 22 January 1877, quoted in Gopal, *British Policy In India, 1858–1905*, p. 117. Salisbury's letter to Lytton, 9 June 1876, Balfour (ed.), *Personal and Literary Letters of Lytton*, 2, p. 22.

52 Curzon in Parliamentary debate, 28 March 1892, quoted in H. Tinker, 'People and Government in Southern Asia', *TRHS*, 5th Series, vol. ix (1959), pp. 156–7.

53 Seal, *The Emergence Of Indian Nationalism*, pp. 148–53: quotation is from Ripon to Hartington, 31 December 1881, ibid. p. 152.

54 Minto to Morley, 27 February 1907, quoted in Mary, Countess of Minto, *India, Minto and Morley 1905–1910* (London, 1934), p. 104. See also for a survey of this new accomodation

chapter entitled 'The Growth of Indian Nationalism and British Policy in India, 1885–1910', in S. R. Mehrotra, *India And The Commonwealth 1885–1929* (London, 1965).
55 Sir Charles Wood to Sir Bartle Frere, 18 August 1861, Philips and Pandey (eds.), *The Evolution Of India And Pakistan 1858 to 1947*, p. 40.
56 Quoted in S. A. Wolpert, *Morley And India 1906–1910* (Berkeley and Los Angeles, 1967), p. 139. A detailed account of the development of the reforms package is on pp. 129–66.
57 Dufferin to George Allen, editor of *The Pioneer*, 1 January 1887, quoted in Gopal, *British Policy In India, 1858–1905*, p. 160. The best single account of India's diverse Muslim community and Muslim relations with government is Hardy, *The Muslims of British India*. Regional variation in Muslim employment in local administration is clear in the following table: Metcalf, *The Aftermath Of Revolt*, p. 304.

Area:	Percentage of Muslims in population:	Percentage of Muslims in executive and judicial services:
Bengal	31.2	8.5
North-West Provinces and Oudh	13.4	45.1
Punjab	51.3	39.3

58 N. G. Barrier, 'The Punjab Government and Communal Politics, 1870–1908', *JAS*, vol. xxvii, no. 3 (May 1968), pp. 523–39; F. C. R. Robinson, 'Consultation and Control. The United Provinces' government and its allies, 1860–1906', *MAS*, vol. 5, part 4 (Dec. 1971), pp. 313–36; F. C. R. Robinson, *Separatism among Indian Muslims. The politics of the United Provinces' Muslims 1860–1923* (Cambridge, 1974).
59 Wolpert, *Morley And India 1906–1910*, pp. 185–200.
60 These issues are dealt with in Hardy, *The Muslims of British India*, pp. 92–115.
61 A. Basu, *The Growth of Education and Political Development in India, 1898–1920* (Delhi, 1974), pp. 36–9. C. N. Bose's essay read in 1878 is quoted in McCully, op. cit., p. 221, fn. 138. Mazzini was an inspiration to patriotism and concern for humanity to many educated Indians. See the autobiography of the prominent Bengali, Surendranath Banerjea (1848–1925), *A Nation In Making* (Calcutta, 1963; first published, 1925), p. 40.
62 There is no single good history of Christian missions in India. A good introduction to nineteenth-century missionary work is K. S. Latourette, *A History Of The Expansion Of Christianity (Vol. VI). The Great Century In Northern Africa And Asia AD 1800–AD 1914* (London, n.d., c.1945), pp. 65–214. The standard history of the established church is E. Chatterton, *A History Of The Church Of England In India Since the Early Days of the East India Company* (London, 1924). A study of the Christian challenge to caste is D. B. Forrester, *Caste and Christianity. Attitudes and Policies on Caste of Anglo-Saxon Protestant Missions in India* (London and Dublin, 1980).
63 Bipin Chandra Pal (1916), quoted in McCully, op. cit., p. 240. Good discussions of the turmoil in Hindu minds as people grappled with the significance of western influences and the meaning of imperial rule are B. Parekh, *Colonialism, Tradition and Reform. An Analysis of Gandhi's Political Discourse* (New Delhi, Newbury Park, and London, 1989), particularly ch. 2, 'Hindu Responses to British Rule'; and T. Raychaudhuri, *Europe Reconsidered. Perceptions of the West in Nineteenth-Century Bengal* (Delhi, 1988). See also the provocative study by P. Chatterjee, *Nationalist Thought and the Colonial World. A Derivative Discourse?* (London, 1986): he makes the important point that even modes of thinking are profoundly influenced by power relations, and in the Indian case by the intellectual assumptions and discourse of the British, located in post-Enlightenment European thought.
64 Speech by L. M. Ghose, 4 November 1880, reported in *Indian Mirror*, 16 November 1880, McCully, op. cit., pp. 285–6.
65 *Indian Mirror*, 5 March 1884, McCully, op. cit., pp. 243–4.

66 Syed Ahmed Khan to B. Tyabji, 24 January 1888, quoted in Seal, *The Emergence Of Indian Nationalism*, p. 334. A good introduction to the turmoil in Muslim thinking on the meaning of being a Muslim in late nineteenth-century India is A. Ahmad, *Islamic Modernism In India And Pakistan 1857–1964* (London, 1967). See also F. Shaikh, *Community and Consensus in Islam. Muslim Representation in Colonial India, 1860–1947* (Cambridge, 1989).

67 K. W. Jones, 'Religious identity and the Indian Census', in N. G. Barrier (ed.), *The Census in British India. New Perspectives* (Delhi, 1981), pp. 73–101. More generally on the census and changing Indian notions of identity, see B. S. Cohn, 'The Census, Social Structure and Objectification in South Asia', in B. S. Cohn, *An Anthropologist among the Historians and Other Essays* (paperback edn., Delhi, 1990), pp. 224–54.

68 The best introduction to this range of problems is C. H. Heimsath, *Indian Nationalism and Hindu Social Reform*. Autobiographical reminiscences of one reformer who married a twenty-four-year old widow in 1893 and suffered much consequent social ostracism are D. K. Karve, 'My Life Story', in D. D. Karve, *The New Brahmans. Five Maharashtrian Families* (Berkeley, Los Angeles and Cambridge, 1963), pp. 17–57.

69 See D. Engals, 'The Age of Consent Act of 1891: Colonial Ideology in Bengal', *SAR*, vol. iii, no. 2 (Nov. 1983), pp. 107–34; M. Sinha, 'The Age of Consent Act: The ideal of masculinity and colonial ideology in nineteenth century Bengal', in T. K. Stewart (ed.), *Shaping Bengali Worlds, Public and Private* (Asian Studies Centre, Michigan State University, 1989; South Asian Series Occasional papers No. 37), pp. 99–111.

70 On the extent and limitations of change in women's lives, see M. Borthwick, *The Changing Role of Women in Bengal 1849–1905* (Princeton, 1984); G. Pearson, 'The Female Intelligentsia in a Segregated Society—Bombay. A Case Study', in M. Allen and S. N. Mukherjee (eds.), *Women in India and Nepal* (Canberra, 1982; ANU Monographs on South Asia, no. 8), pp. 136–54; P. Chatterjee, 'The Nationalist Resolution of the Women's Question', in K. Sangri and S. Vaid (eds.), *Recasting Women. Essays in Colonial History* (New Delhi, 1989), pp. 233–53.

71 See L. Mani, 'Contentious Traditions: The Debate on *Sati* in Colonial India', in Sangri and Vaid (eds.), op. cit., pp. 88–126.

72 K. W. Jones, *Socio-Religious Reform Movements in British India* (Cambridge, 1989) is now the best survey and analysis, and includes Hindu, Sikh, and Muslim movements. It replaces an old classic work, J. N. Farquhar, *Modern Religious Movements In India* (New Delhi, 1977; first published 1914).

On Hindu movements discussed here see also Heimsath, op. cit.; part iv of J. R. McLane, *Indian Nationalism And the Early Congress* (Princeton, 1977); K. W. Jones, *Arya Dharm. Hindu Consciousness in 19th-Century Punjab* (Berkeley, Los Angeles, and London, 1976); C. R. Pangbourn, 'The Ramakrishna Math and Mission: A Case Study of a Revitalizing Movement', W. G. Neevel, 'The Transformation of Sri Ramakrishna' in B. L. Smith (ed.), *Hinduism. New Essays in the History of Religions* (Leiden, 1976), pp. 98–119, 53–97.

Two good books on Muslim self-questioning and identity are D. Lelyveld, *Aligarh's First Generation. Muslim Solidarity in British India* (Princeton, 1978); B. D. Metcalf, *Islamic Revival in British India* (Princeton, 1982).

73 *Census of India, 1911. Volume V. Bengal, Bihar And Orissa And Sikkim. Part 1. Report* (Calcutta, 1913), p. 440.

74 *Census of India, 1921. Volume VII. Bihar And Orissa. Part 1. Report* (Patna, 1923), pp. 236–7. See also L. I. and S. H. Rudolph, *The Modernity Of Tradition. Political Development in India* (Chicago and London, 1967), pp. 29–64.

75 Barrier, *MAS*, vol. 1, part 4 (October 1967), pp. 353–83.

76 Ramachandra Guha, 'Forestry and Social Protest in British Kumaon, *c.*1893–1921', in

Ranajit Guha (ed.), *Subaltern Studies IV. Writings on South Asian History and Society* (Delhi, 1985), pp. 54–100; Ramachandra Guha, *The Unquiet Woods. Ecological Change and Peasant Resistance in the Himalaya* (Paperback edn., New Delhi, 1991).

77 D. Washbrook, 'Country Politics: Madras 1880–1930', J. Gallagher, G. Johnson, and A. Seal (eds.), *Locality, Province and Nation. Essays on Indian Politics 1870–1940* (Cambridge, 1973), pp. 155–211. See also C. Baker, 'Temples and Political Development', C. J. Baker and D. A. Washbrook (eds.), *South India: Political Institutions and Political Change 1880–1940* (Delhi, 1975), pp. 69–97.

78 Musgrave, *MAS*, vol. 6, part 3 (July 1972), pp. 257–75. See also a study of an estate in Bihar, S. Henningham, *A Great Estate and its Landlords in Colonial India: Darbhanga 1860–1942* (Delhi, 1990).

79 Seal, *The Emergence Of Indian Nationalism*, pp. 194–226; Rajat Ray, *Urban Roots of Indian Nationalism. Pressure Groups and Conflicts in Calcutta City Politics, 1875–1939* (New Delhi, 1979), pp. 11–50.

80 D. E. Wacha, quoted in Seal, *The Emergence Of Indian Nationalism*, p. 231. See also C. Dobbin, 'Competing Elites in Bombay City Politics in the Mid-Nineteenth Century (1852–83)', Leach and Mukherjee (eds.), *Elites In South Asia*, pp. 79–94.

81 G. Johnson, 'Chitpavan Brahmins and Politics in Western India in the Late Nineteenth and Early Twentieth Centuries', Leach and Mukherjee (eds.), *Elites In South Asia*, pp. 95–118; G. Johnson, *Provincial Politics and Indian Nationalism. Bombay and the Indian National Congress 1880–1915* (Cambridge, 1973).

82 Bayly, *The Local Roots of Indian Politics*, pp. 99–121.

83 H. A. Gould, 'The Emergence of Modern Indian Politics: Political Development in Faizabad, Part I: 1884–1935', *Journal of Commonwealth and Comparative Politics*, vol. xxi, no. 1 (Mar. 1974), p. 27; F. C. R. Robinson, 'Municipal Government and Muslim Separatism in the United Provinces 1883 to 1916', Gallagher, Johnson and Seal (eds.), *Locality, Province and Nation*, pp. 69–121.

84 F. G. Bailey, *Politics And Social Change. Orissa In 1959* (Bombay, 1963), pp. 161–5; J. G. Leonard, 'Politics And Social Change In South India: A Study Of The Andhra Movement', *Journal of Commonwealth Political Studies*, vol. v, no. 1 (Mar. 1967), pp. 60–77.

85 G. Johnson, 'Partition, Agitation and Congress: Bengal 1904 to 1908', Gallagher, Johnson and Seal (eds.), *Locality, Province and Nation*, pp. 213–68, particularly pp. 251–7; McLane, *Indian Nationalism And The Early Congress*, pp. 343–57.

86 R. O'Hanlon, *Caste, Conflict and Ideology. Mahatma Jotirao Phule and Low Caste Protest in Nineteenth-Century India* (Cambridge, 1985).

87 UP Muslims' experience is traced in Robinson, *Separatism among Indian Muslims*; on the sharpening of communal tensions and new movements in Punjab see K. W. Jones, 'Communalism in the Punjab. The Arya Samaj Contribution', *JAS*, vol. xxviii, no. 1 (Nov. 1968), pp. 39–54.

88 Johnson, 'Partition, Agitation and Congress: Bengal 1904 to 1908', Gallagher, Johnson, and Seal (eds.), *Locality, Province and Nation*, pp. 213–68; J.R. McLane, 'The Decision to Partition Bengal in 1905', *IESHR*, vol. ii, no. 3 (July 1965), pp. 221–31.

89 On the emergence, development, and history of the early Congress see Seal, *The Emergence Of Indian Nationalism*, pp. 245–97; McLane, *Indian Nationalism And the Early Congress*; Johnson, *Provincial Politics and Indian Nationalism*.

90 *The Virat*, 30 April 1917, quoted in A. Husain, *Fazl-i-Husain. A Political Biography* (Bombay, 1946), p. 82. On 1 November 1915 D. E. Wacha, a Bombay politician, wrote to Sir James Meston, Lt.-Governor of UP, about public life in UP: 'My countrymen in the backward provinces have got to learn the fundamental essentials of public life and even of organization and procedure,' IOL, Meston Papers, Mss. EUR. F. 136 (4).

91 See chapters 5 and 6 of Bayly, *The Local Roots of Indian Politics*.

92 The 'moderate'/'extremist' split, the personalities, and issues involved, are discussed in Johnson, *Provincial Politics and Indian Nationalism*; and R. K. Ray, 'Moderates, Extremists, and Revolutionaries: Bengal, 1900–1908', in R. Sisson and S. Wolpert (eds.), *Congress and Indian Nationalism: The Pre-Independence Phase* (Berkeley, 1988), pp. 62–89. The main 1906 Congress resolutions and Tilak's 'New Party' speech on 2 January 1907 are in Philips and Pandey (eds.), *The Evolution Of India And Pakistan 1858 to 1947*, pp. 159–60, 161–3.

93 *Aligarh Institute Gazette*, 4 February 1888, quoted in Johnson, *Provincial Politics and Indian Nationalism*, p. 26, fn. 3. Details of the Muslim break from the early Congress are in Seal, *The Emergence Of Indian Nationalism*, pp. 298–340. See also Shaikh, *Community and Consensus in Islam*, particularly chs. 1–4.

94 Hardy, *The Muslims of British India*, pp. 164–7; Robinson, *Separatism among Indian Muslims*, pp. 133–74.

CHAPTER IV. WAR AND THE SEARCH FOR A NEW ORDER

1 *Land Revenue Administration Report, Part ii, of the Bombay Presidency, Including Sind, For The Year 1917–18* (Bombay, 1919), p. 6. For surveys of the economic effects of the war see *India's Contribution to the Great War; India in 1919* (Calcutta, 1920); B. R. Tomlinson, 'India and the British Empire, 1880–1935', *IESHR*, vol. xii, no. 4 (Oct.–Dec. 1975), pp. 337–80; K. G. Saini, 'The Economic Aspects of India's Participation in the First World War', D. C. Ellinwood and S. D. Pradhan (eds.), *India And World War I* (New Delhi, 1978), pp. 141–76; J. M. Brown, 'War and the Colonial Relationship: Britain, India and the War of 1914–18', M. R. D. Foot (ed.) *War And Society. Historical Essays in honour and memory of J. R. Western 1928–1971* (London, 1973), pp. 85–106, reprinted in Ellinwood and Pradhan (eds.), op. cit., pp. 19–47.

2 30 September/2 October 1918, internal political situration report, Bombay, NAI, Home Poll., Deposit, October 1918, No. 32. Delhi was again the seat of the Government of India; the capital was transferred from Calcutta for political reasons connected with the reunification of Bengal in 1911. The British then built a new city alongside the old Mogul capital, known as New Delhi.

3 Hardinge to V. Chirol, 19 November 1914, Cambridge UL, Hardinge Mss. (93).

4 *Report of the Thirtieth Indian National Congress held at Bombay on the 27th, 28th and 29th December 1915* (Bombay, 1916), p. 117.

5 Speech on 23 March 1917, *Speeches and Writings of Pandit Madan Mohan Malaviya* (Madras, 1919), p. 129. Resolution at 1916 Congress on self-government, *Report of the Thirty-first Indian National Congress held at Lucknow on the 26th, 28th, 29th, and 30th December, 1916* (Allahabad, 1917), p. 70.

6 H. F. Owen, 'Towards Nation-Wide Agitation And Organization: The Home Rule Leagues, 1915–18', D. A. Low (ed.), *Soundings in Modern South Asian History* (London, 1968), pp. 159–95; J. M. Brown, *Gandhi's Rise To Power. Indian Politics 1915–1922* (Cambridge, 1972), pp. 26–8.

7 For the terms of the Lucknow Pact see Philips and Pandey (eds.), *The Evolution Of India And Pakistan 1858 to 1947*, pp. 171–3. The background of Pan-Islamic sentiment and Indian politics is discussed in Hardy, *The Muslims of British India*, pp. 175–88; Robinson, *Separatism among Indian Muslims*, pp. 175–256; Brown, *Gandhi's Rise To Power*, pp. 30–2, 136–40; H. F. Owen, 'Negotiating the Lucknow Pact', *JAS*, vol. xxxi, no. 3 (May 1972), pp. 561–87. An illuminating study of the particular problems of the Bengal Muslims is J. H. Broomfield, 'The Forgotten Majority: The Bengal Muslims And September 1918', Low (ed.), *Soundings in Modern South Asian History*, pp. 196–224.

8 Sir James Meston to Viceroy, Lord Chelmsford, 11 January 1917, IOL, Chelmsford

Papers, Mss. EUR. E. 264 (18); Hardinge to G. B. Allen, 19 August 1915, Hardinge Mss. (94). An analysis of the degree to which the war *actually* weakened the *raj* is J. M. Brown, 'War and the Colonial Relationship', Foot (ed.), op. cit., pp. 85–106.

9   N. G. Barrier, 'Ruling India: Coercion and Propaganda in British India during the First World War', Ellinwood and Pradhan (eds.), *India And World War I*, pp. 75–108; Barrier, *Banned*, pp. 66–76.

10 E. S. Montagu to Chelmsford, 10 October 1918, Mss. EUR. E. 264 (4). On the deliberations leading to the Rowlatt Committee and subsequent legislation, J. M. Brown, *Gandhi's Rise To Power*, pp. 160–3; P. G. Robb, *The Government Of India And Reform. Policies towards Politics and the Constitution* (Oxford, 1976), pp. 147–63.

11 Hardinge to Crewe, 4 July 1912, Crewe to Hardinge, 18 July 1912, Hardinge Mss. (118); Hardinge to Sir Walter Lawrence, 29 July 1915, Hardinge Mss. (94).

12 Montagu Declaration, 20 August 1917, Philips and Pandey (eds.), *The Evolution Of India And Pakistan 1858 to 1947*, pp. 264–5. On the decision-making process behind the Declaration see Robb, op. cit., pp. 53–85.

13 Details in *Report of the Indian Statutory Commission, Vol. 1*, Cmd. 3568 (London, 1930) (Simon Commission). The making of the 1919 Act is traced in Robb, op. cit. pp. 86–116. Lengthy extracts from the 1919 Act are in Philips and Pandey (eds.), op. cit., pp. 273–82.

14 See R. A. Huttenback, *Gandhi in South Africa. British Imperialism and the Indian Question, 1860–1914* (Ithaca and London, 1971); M. Swan, *Gandhi. The South African Experience* (Johannesburg, 1985); J. M. Brown, *Gandhi. Prisoner of Hope* (New Haven and London, 1989), particularly chs. 2 and 3.

15 M. K. Gandhi, *An Autobiography. The Story of My Experiments with Truth* (1966 edn., London), p. xiii. Important studies of the strands in Gandhi's thinking are A. L. Basham, 'Traditional influences on the thought of Mahatma Gandhi', R. Kumar (ed.), *Essays On Gandhian Politics. The Rowlatt Satyagraha of 1919* (Oxford, 1971), pp. 17–42; S. N. Hay, 'Jain influences on Gandhi's early thought', S. Ray (ed.), *Gandhi, India, and the World* (Melbourne, 1970), pp. 29–38. The most helpful books on Gandhi's thought are R. N. Iyer, *The Moral and Political Thought of Mahatma Gandhi* (New York, 1973); M. Chatterjee, *Gandhi's Religious Thought* (London and Basingstoke, 1983); B. K. Parekh, *Colonialism, Tradition and Reform*, and *Gandhi's Political Philosophy. A Critical Examination* (London and Basingstoke, 1989).

16 H. Spodek, 'On the Origins of Gandhi's Political Methodology: The Heritage of Kathiawad and Gujarat', *JAS*, vol. xxx, no. 2 (Feb. 1971), pp. 361–72.

17 Gandhi's relationship to Hindu tradition is a complex issue. See J. M. Brown, *Men And Gods In A Changing World*, pp. 105–6, 135–6, 140–1, and the references given there; Parekh, *Colonialism, Tradition and Reform*; Chatterjee, *Gandhi's Religious Thought*.

18 J. Nehru, *An Autobiography* (London, 1941 reprint; first published 1936), p. 76; *Young India*, 26 January 1921, *CW*, vol. xix, pp. 277–8. *Hind Swaraj* is available in *CW*, vol. x, pp. 6–68.

19 'I admit it is because of my faith in the British people that I can advise as I am doing. I believe that, though this nation has done India much harm, it is to our advantage to retain connection with it. Their virtues seem to me to outweigh their vices . . . As their partners, there is much we can receive and much that we can give and our connection with them based on that relationship is likely to benefit the world. If such was not my faith and if I thought it desirable to become absolutely independent of that nation, I would not only not advise co-operation but would on the contrary ask the people to beware, advising them to rebel, and paying the penalty for doing so. We are not in a position today to stand on our own feet unaided and alone. I believe that our good lies in becoming and remaining equal partners in the Empire . . .' 22 June 1918, recruiting leaflet by Gandhi, *CW*, vol. xiv, p. 442. For Gandhi's attitude to the British and his war work see J. M. Brown, *Gandhi's Rise To Power*, pp. 14–15, 147–8; P. M. H. Van den Dungen, 'Gandhi in 1919: loyalist or rebel?',

R. Kumar (ed.), *Essays On Gandhian Politics*, pp. 43–63.

20 Gandhi, *An Autobiography*, pp. 420, xii.

21 Gandhi to S. Schlesin, 2 June 1919, *CW*, vol. xv, p. 341.

22 Gandhi to M. Ali, 18 November 1918, ibid. pp. 63–4.

23 Gandhi to C. F. Andrews, 25 February 1919, ibid., p. 104. On the Rowlatt Satyagraha see J. M. Brown, *Gandhi's Rise To Power*, pp. 163–89; R. Kumar (ed.), *Essays On Gandhian Politics*.

24 *Young India*, 22 September 1920, *CW*, vol. xviii, pp. 270–3. Lord Reading, the Viceroy, interviewed Gandhi on 13/14 May 1921 and reported by telegram to the Secretary of State on 14 May, 'All I could gather was that when Indians had regained their self-respect and had pursued a policy of non-co-operation with the Government and had refrained from violence they would have attained Swaraj.' IOL, Reading Papers, Mss. EUR. E. 238 (10).

25 *Young India*, 28 July 1920, *CW*, vol. xviii, p. 89; *Young India*, 9 June 1920, *CW*, vol. xvii, p. 483.

26 'It is a distinct departure from the even tenor of my life for me to belong to an organization that is purely and frankly political . . . I felt that if I was accepted by the League as I was, I should be wrong in not identifying myself with an organization that I could utilize for the advancement of the causes in which I had specialized and of the methods which experience has shown me are attended with quicker and better results than those that are usually adopted.' *Young India*, 28 April 1920, *CW*, vol. xvii, pp. 347–9.

27 J. M. Brown, *Gandhi's Rise To Power*, pp. 250–306; J. H. Broomfield, 'The Non-Cooperation Decision Of 1920: A Crisis In Bengal Politics', Low (ed.), *Soundings in Modern South Asian History*, pp. 225–60; R. Gordon, 'Non-cooperation and Council Entry, 1919 to 1920', Gallagher, Johnson and Seal (eds.), *Locality, Province and Nation*, pp. 123–53.

28 Note by S. P. O'Donnell, 14 January 1921, Home Poll, Deposit, January 1921, No. 3 and K.–W.

29 D. A. Low, 'The Government of India and the first non-co-operation movement, 1920–1922', R. Kumar (ed.), *Essays On Gandhian Politics*, pp. 298–323.

30 J. M. Brown, *Gandhi's Rise To Power*, pp. 284–8; *Return Showing the Results of Elections In India* (London, 1921), Cmd. 1261.

31 On the all-India and local manifestations of non-co-operation see J. M. Brown, op. cit., pp. 309–43; C. Baker, 'Non-cooperation in South India', Baker and Washbrook (eds.), *South India*, pp. 98–149; P. D. Reeves, 'The Politics of Order. "Anti-Non-Co-operation" in the United Provinces, 1921', *JAS*, vol. xxv, no. 2 (Feb. 1966), pp. 261–74; W. F. Crawley, 'Kisan Sabhas and Agrarian Revolt in the United Provinces 1920 to 1921', *MAS*, vol. 5, part 2 (Apr. 1971), pp. 95–109; G. Pandey, 'Peasant Revolt and Indian Nationalism: The Peasant Movement in Awadh, 1919–1922', Guha (ed.), *Subaltern Studies I*, pp. 143–97; S. Sarkar, 'The Conditions and Nature of Subaltern Militancy: Bengal from Swadeshi to Non-Co-operation, c. 1905–22', Guha (ed.), *Subaltern Studies III*, pp. 271–320; R. Guha, 'Forestry and Social Protest in British Kumaon, c. 1893–1921', *Subaltern Studies IV*, pp. 54–100.

    An important study of how Gandhi was understood and 'imagined' in one locality is S. Amin, 'Gandhi as Mahatma: Gorakhpur District, Eastern UP, 1921–2', Guha (ed.), *Subaltern Studies III*, pp. 2–61.

32 On Congress organization and finances see J. M. Brown, op. cit., pp. 297–300, 320–2; C. Baker, 'Non-cooperation in South India', Baker and Washbrook (eds.), *South India*, pp. 130–1, 136; G. Pandey, *The Ascendancy of the Congress in Uttar Pradesh 1926–34. A Study in Imperfect Mobilization* (Delhi, 1978), pp. 54–8; G. Krishna, 'The Development of the Indian National Congress as a Mass Organization, 1918–1923', *JAS*, vol. xxv, no. 3 (May 1966), pp. 413–30.

33 For a Bengali description of this see S. C. Bose, *The Indian Struggle 1920–1942* (New

York, 1964), pp. 67–8.

34 *Justice,* 9 April 1921, E. F. Irschick, *Politics And Social Conflict In South India. The Non-Brahman Movement and Tamil Separatism, 1916–1929* (Berkeley and Los Angeles, 1969), pp. 186–7. This reported also the 'marks of deification' accorded to Gandhi on a visit to Madras, including hymns, coconuts broken and camphor burnt in front of him, and the offering of holy water in a silver basin.

35 *Navayuga,* 16 April 1921, quoted in J. M. Brown, *Gandhi's Rise To Power,* p. 329.

36 S. Gopal, *The Viceroyalty Of Lord Irwin 1926–1931* (Oxford, 1957), p. 15.

37 M. to J. Nehru, 30 March 1927, Nehru Memorial Museum and Library (NMML), J. Nehru Papers, part 1, vol. lxix.

38 For Gandhi's stock-taking of the contemporary situation and his activities see J. M. Brown, *Gandhi and Civil Disobedience. The Mahatma in Indian Politics 1928–34* (Cambridge, 1977), pp. 14–28.
Gandhi was quite clear about his detached role, telling a Calcutta politician in 1928, 'I am biding my time and you will find me leading the country in the field of politics when the country is ready. I have no false modesty about me. I am undoubtedly a politician in my own way, and I have a scheme for the country's freedom. But my time is not yet and may never come to me in this life. If it does not, I shall not shed a single tear. We are all in the hands of God. I shall therefore await His guidance.' Gandhi to Dr. B. C. Roy, 1 May 1928, *CW,* vol. xxxvi, p. 287.

39 D. E. U. Baker, 'The Break-Down of Nationalist Unity and the Formation of the Swaraj Parties, India, 1922 to 1924', G. C. Bolton and H. F. Owen (eds.), *University Studies in History,* vol. v, no. 4 (1970), pp. 85–113; G. A. Heeger, 'The Growth of the Congress Movement in Punjab, 1920–1940', *JAS,* vol. xxxii, no. 1 (Nov. 1972), pp. 39–51.

40 The importance and texture of provincial life is shown in the regional studies indicated in the suggestions for reading.
This book has for one of its themes the problem of making linkages between the different political worlds in India. For two essays which tackle this problem from different angles, see A. Seal, 'Imperialism and Nationalism in India', Gallagher, Johnson and Seal (eds.), *Locality, Province and Nation,* pp. 1–27; D. Hardiman, 'The Indian "Faction": A Political Theory Examined', Guha (ed.), *Subaltern Studies I,* pp. 198–231.

41 R. Gordon, 'The Hindu Mahasabha and the Indian National Congress, 1915 to 1926', *MAS,* vol. 9, part 2 (1975), pp. 145–203.

42 On Muslim politics in the 1920s and the role of the Punjabi Muslims, see D. Page, *Prelude To Partition. The Indian Muslims and the Imperial System of Control 1920–1932* (Karachi, 1987); and A. Jalal and A. Seal, 'Alternative to Partition: Muslim Politics between the Wars', C. Baker, G. Johnson, and A. Seal (eds.), *Power, Profit and Politics; Essays on Imperialism, Nationalism and Change in Twentieth-Century India* (Cambridge, 1981), pp. 415–54.

43 See V. N. Datta and B. E. Cleghorn (eds.), *A Nationalist Muslim and Indian Politics. Being the Selected Correspondence of the late Dr. Syed Mahmud* (Delhi, 1974); M. Hasan (ed.), *Muslims And The Congress: Select Correspondence of Dr. M. A. Ansari 1912–1935* (Delhi, 1979); Page, *Prelude to Partition.*

44 J. M. Brown, *Gandhi and Civil Disobedience,* pp. 10–11, 24. On the local breakdowns of communal harmony see Hardy, *The Muslims of British India,* pp. 201–9; M. Hasan, *Nationalism And Communal Politics In India, 1916–1928* (Delhi, 1979), pp. 185–262. A study of 'communal' riots in one area is S. Das, *Communal Riots in Bengal 1905–1947* (Delhi, 1991). Two broad-ranging studies of the meaning and construction of 'communalism' are G. Pandy, *The Construction of Communalism in Colonial North India* (Delhi, 1990); and S. B. Freitag, *Collective Action and Community. Public Arenas and the Emergence of Communalism in North India* (Berkeley, Los Angeles, and Oxford, 1989).

45 See the example of one provincial Congess: Pandey, *The Ascendancy of the Congress in Uttar Pradesh 1926–34.*

46 On the world of the industrial worker, his loyalties, strategies, and leaders, see Chakrabarty, *Rethinking Working Class History* (on Bengal); R. Chandarvarkar, 'Workers' politics and the Mill Districts in Bombay between the Wars', Baker, Johnson, and Seal (eds.), *Power, Profit and Politics*, pp. 603–47, and 'Workers' Resistance and the Rationalization of Work in Bombay between the Wars', D. Haynes and G. Prakash (eds.), *Contesting Power. Resistance and Everyday Social Relations in South Asia* (Delhi, 1991), pp. 109–44.

47 On 'left-wing' movements and ideas, see the essays in B. R. Nanda (ed.), *Socialism in India* (Delhi, 1972).

48 M. to J. Nehru, 14 April 1927, J. Nehru Papers, part 1, vol. lxix. See also Chatterjee, *Nationalist Thought and the Colonial World*; and 'Gandhi and the Critique of Civil Society', Guha (ed.), *Subaltern Studies III*, pp. 153–95.

49 At the end of the decade the visiting British Commission paid the following tribute: 'Members of the Statutory Commission had the privilege of attending several debates in more than one province. We were much struck by the good attendance of members in the Chamber, by the high level of courteous speech, and by the respect shown to the Chair. The public galleries were well filled, and the proceedings were obviously followed with much interest. The provincial councils owe much to their Presidents. There have been striking instances in the provinces of the impartiality of elected presidents previously belonging to a party in opposition to Government.' *Simon Commission, Vol. I*, p. 216. This volume contains valuable evidence of the working of the reformed constitution. See also report by a British academic, R. Coupland, *The Indian Problem 1833–1935* (London, 1942), pp. 69–72, 76–9; and the book by an Indian using the pseudonymn 'Kerala Putra', *The Working of Dyarchy in India 1919–1928* (Bombay, 1928).

50 Sir Henry Wheeler, Governor of Bihar and Orissa, to Lord Irwin, 22 April 1926, IOL, Papers of the Earl of Halifax (Lord Irwin), Mss. EUR. C. 152 (20).

51 On the problems inherent in working the reforms, see the report of the committee chaired by Sir Alexander Muddiman, and the minority report signed by four of the Indian members: *Report of the Reforms Enquiry Committee, 1924, Appointed by the Government of India and Connected Papers* (London, 1925), Cmd. 2360.

52 W. L. Richter and B. Ramusack, "The Chamber and the Consultation: Changing Forms of Princely Association in India', *JAS*, vol. xxxiv, no. 3 (May 1975), pp. 755–76. See also R. J. Moore, *The Crisis Of Indian Unity 1917–1940* (Oxford, 1974), pp. 25–33.

53 Extracts from the correspondence between the Nizam and the Viceroy (1925–6), the princes' legal arguments to the Butler Committee, and the Committee's report are in Philips and Pandey (eds.), *The Evolution Of India And Pakistan 1858 to 1947*, pp. 428–33.

54 C. Dewey, 'The Government of India's 'New Industrial Policy', 1900–1925: Formation and Failure', Chaudhuri and Dewey (eds.), *Economy And Society*, pp. 215–57.

55 One ex-Governor of the Punjab gave as evidence of his informal political work sixteen volumes recording interviews he had given, and the state of his digestion after numerous meals in the homes of Punjabi landholders. The strains of governing India under the 1919 constitution are discussed in J. M. Brown, 'Imperial Facade: some constraints upon and contradictions in the British position in India, 1919–35', *TRHS*, 5th Series, vol. xxvi (1976), pp. 35–52. See also on the 'political work' of ICS men, Potter, *India's Political Administrators 1919–1983*, pp. 35–56.

56 T. H. Beaglehole, 'From Rulers to Servants: The ICS and the British Demission of Power in India', *MAS*, vol. 11, part 2 (Apr. 1977), pp. 237–55; D. C. Potter, 'Manpower Shortage and the End of Colonialism. The Case of the Indian Civil Service', *MAS*, vol. 7, part 1 (Jan. 1973), pp. 47–73; and *India's Political Administrators 1919–1983*.

   On the circumstances of the Lee Commission, see A. Ewing, 'The Indian Civil Service

1919–1924: Service Discontent and the Response in London and in Delhi', *MAS*, vol. 18, part 1 (1984), pp. 33–53. An investigation of the changing role of the ICS man in the districts after the 1919 reforms is S. Epstein, 'British Officers in Decline: The Erosion of British Authority in the Bombay Countryside, 1919 to 1947', *MAS*, vol. 16, part 3 (1982), pp. 493–518.

57 This final section draws substantially on Tomlinson, *IESHR*, vol. xii, no. 4 (Oct.–Dec. 1975), pp. 337–80; Tomlinson, *The Political Economy Of the Raj 1914–1947*.

The rupee's exchange value is a complex question: it impinges on financial technicalities and wider economic policy. See Tomlinson, *The Political Economy Of The Raj 1914–1947*, and B. R. Tomlinson, 'Monetary Policy and Economic Development: The Rupee Ratio Question 1921–1927', Chaudhuri and Dewey (eds.), *Economy And Society*, pp. 197–211.

58 On the extent of westernization, its meaning in the Indian context, and Indian ambivalence towards western values, see chapter 2, 'Westernization', in M. N. Srinivas, *Social Change In Modern India* (Berkeley and Los Angeles, 1966). See also the autobiographical account of one Indian family, P. Tandon, *Punjabi Century 1857–1947* (London, 1963); and E. M. Forster's novel, *A Passage to India* (London, 1924).

CHAPTER V. A CRITICAL DECADE: INDIA—EMPIRE OR NATION?

1 Davis, *The Population Of India And Pakistan*, pp. 27–8, 36, 21, 207. Different regions fared differently, and land distribution patterns in each village depended on types of inheritance and the strength or division of joint families. In one Punjab village from 1934 there was a marked decline in the size of farms, in direct relation to a rise in population. Kessinger, *Vilyatpur 1848–1968*, pp. 116–17. In Gujarat the average holding of 9.5 acres at the end of the nineteenth century had decreased to 6 acres in 1942–3: H. Fukazawa, 'Agrarian Relations: Western India', Kumar and Desai (eds.), op. cit., p. 199. On population, see also L. and P. Vinaria, 'Population (1757–1947)', ibid., pp. 463–532.

2 Davis, op. cit., pp. 127–8; K. Davis, 'Social and Demographic Aspects of Economic Development in India', S. Kuznets, W. E. Moore, and J. J. Spengler (eds.), *Economic Growth: Brazil, India, Japan* (Durham, NC, 1955), p. 271.

3 The percentage of the male work force engaged in cultivation, agriculture, livestock rearing, hunting, fishing etc. was 71.7 in 1901; 73.8 in 1911; 74.6 in 1921; 74.2 in 1931; 73.2 in 1951. Table 2, J. Krishnamurty, 'The Distribution of the Indian Working Force, 1901–1951', Chaudhuri and Dewey (eds.), *Economy And Society*, p. 264. See also Krishnamurty's essay, 'The Occupational Structure', Kumar and Desai (eds.), op. cit., pp. 533–50.

4 Variations in the fortunes of different industries are suggested in these figures for production:

Production in selected industries (1925=100)

	1931	1937
Cotton	111	152
Jute	81	90
Sugar	128	584
Iron and Steel	84	133
Paper	119	168
Cement	121	222
Coal	92	103

Source: V. Anstey, *The Economic Development of India* (4th edn., London, 1952), p. 519. See also chapter 2, Tomlinson, *The Political Economy Of The Raj 1914–1947*; chapter 16,

D. R. Gadgil, *The Industrial Evolution Of India In Recent Times 1860–1939* (5th edn., Delhi, 1971); R. K. Ray, *Industrialization In India. Growth and Conflict in the Private Corporate Sector 1914–47* (Delhi, 1979); M. D. Morris, 'The Growth of Large-Scale Industry to 1947', Kumar and Desai (eds.), op. cit., pp. 553–676.

5 On the complex question of foreign and Indian capital see chapter 2, Tomlinson, *The Political Economy Of The Raj 1914–1947*; B. R. Tomlinson, 'Foreign Private Investment in India 1920–1950', *MAS*, vol. 12, part 4 (Oct. 1978), pp. 655–77; B. R. Tomlinson, 'Colonial Firms and the Decline of Colonialism in Eastern India 1914–1947', pp. 455–86 of Baker, Johnson, and Seal (eds.), *Power, Profit and Politics*; Ray, *Industrialization In India* (particularly chapter 2); A. K. Bagchi, *Private Investment In India 1900–1939* (Cambridge, 1972). See also C. Markovits, *Indian Business and Nationalist Politics 1931–39. The Indigenous Capitalist Class and the Rise of the Congress Party* (Cambridge, 1985).

6 C. J. Baker, 'Debt and the Depression in Madras, 1929–1936', Dewey and Hopkins (eds.), *The Imperial Impact*, pp. 233–42; Tomlinson, *The Political Economy Of the Raj 1914–1947*, pp. 34–5, 43; G. Pandey, *The Ascendancy Of The Congress In Uttar Pradesh 1926–34*, pp. 162–5.

7 *Expenditure from government funds on education* (in Rs. lakhs)

1921–2	...	9,02
1926–7	...	11,93
1930–1	...	13,61
1931–2	...	12,46
1932–3	...	11,35
1933–4	...	11,47
1934–5	...	11,59
1935–6	...	11,84
1936–7	...	12,36

Source: Nurullah and Naik, *A History Of Education In India*, p. 619.

8 Ibid. p. 716.
For a survey of education under dyarchy, 1921–37, see chapter 11, ibid.

9 In one UP village when missionaries attempted to help Untouchables enter the District Board School in the late 1920s the parents of higher caste removed their children from classes. In neighbouring villages Untouchable children attended for a while, then withdrew. W. and C. Wiser, *Behind Mud Walls 1930–1960* (Berkeley and Los Angeles, 1969), pp. 55–8. In another UP village Untouchables from the Chamar caste attended the local primary school with other children from the late 1930s; though even in the early 1950s they were given no part in school dramas. B. S. Cohn, 'The Changing Status of a Depressed Caste', M. Marriott (ed.), *Village India. Studies in the Little Community* (paperback edn., Chicago and London, 1969), p. 63.

10 For the simultaneous decline of the Thakur *panchayat* and the increasing authority of the elders of the Untouchable Chamars, who were aspiring to higher status, occurring in the same UP village, see Cohn, ibid. pp. 68–9.

11 On caste *sabhas* see above, Chapter III, p. 168. For a theoretical discussion of the propriety of using 'caste' to describe groups, their identities and behaviours outside the setting of ritual-economic relationships of interdependence within a hierarchical structure, see E. R. Leach, 'Introduction: What Should We Mean by Caste?', E. R. Leach (ed.), *Aspects of Caste in South India, Ceylon and North-West Pakistan* (Cambridge, 1971), pp. 1–10.

12 See Chapter 2, Tomlinson, *The Political Economy Of The Raj 1914–1947*, on the changing role of India in the world economy.

% *Share of British goods in India's imports, 1913–1938*

	1913–14	1928–9	1938–9
Cotton piece-goods	94	79	32
Iron and Steel	78	56	50
Other metal manufactures	46	34	34
Hardware and cutlery	56	26	29
Electrical machinery	79	66	57
General machinery	92	76	57
Railway locomotives and carriages	95	88	61
Motor vehicles	66	15	30
Chemicals	75	59	57

Source: Tomlinson, loc. cit., p. 47.

13 For this agreement and the actual expenditure of Britain and India on war measures, 1939–45, see Tomlinson, loc. cit., pp. 92–3; B. R. Tomlinson, 'India and the British Empire, 1935–1947', *IESHR*, vol. xiii, no. 3 (July–Sept. 1976), pp. 332–8.

14 Further details of events and negotiations are most readily available in Moore, *The Crisis Of Indian Unity 1917–1940*; Page, *Prelude To Partition*, pp. 162–74; and J. M. Brown, *Gandhi and Civil Disobedience*. (The latter is a detailed study of Gandhi's role in Indian politics, 1928–34.)

15 On diverse Muslim responses to the Nehru Report see Hasan, *Nationalism And Communal Politics In India, 1916–1928*, pp. 280–305; Moore, op. cit., pp. 38–9; Page, op. cit., pp. 174 ff. Primary evidence on the All Parties Muslim Conference is in K. K. Aziz (ed.), *The All India Muslim Conference 1928–1935, A Documentary Record* (Karachi, 1972). The role of the 'Nationalist Muslims' who aligned with Congress is well illustrated in the correspondence of M. A. Ansari and Syed Mahmud: see Hasan (ed.), *Muslims And The Congress*, and Datta and Cleghorn (eds.), *A Nationalist Muslim And Indian Politics*; see also M. Hasan, ' "Congress Muslims", and Indian Nationalism: Dilemma and Decline, 1928–1934', J. Masselos (ed.), *Struggling and Ruling. The Indian National Congress 1885–1985* (London, 1987), pp. 102–20. Jinnah is studied in H. Bolitho, *Jinnah. Creator of Pakistan* (London, 1954); and in K. B. Sayeed, 'The Personality of Jinnah and his Political Strategy', in C. H. Philips and M. D. Wainwright (eds.), *The Partition Of India. Policies and Perspectives 1935–1947* (London, 1970), pp. 276–293. An important study from the perspective of the Muslim majority in Punjab is A. Jalal and A. Seal, 'Alternative to Partition: Muslim Politics between the Wars', Baker, Johnson, and Seal (eds.), *Power, Profit and Politics*, pp. 415–54.

16 24 May 1929, Diary of B. S. Moonje, Microfilm, NMML, New Delhi; J. M. Brown, *Gandhi and Civil Disobedience*, pp. 49–53.

17 See above, Chapter 4, n. 38. For Gandhi's activities between Non-co-operation and 1929, see Brown, *Gandhi. Prisoner of Hope*, pp. 176–213.

18 For the Bardoli campaign and its significance for Gandhi, see Brown, *Gandhi and Civil Disobedience*, pp. 49–53, *Gandhi. Prisoner of Hope*, pp. 219–21. The official Gandhian version of the campaign is M. Desai, *The Story of Bardoli* (reprint of 1929 edn., Ahmedabad, 1957). On Bardoli in the context of Gujarati politics, see A. Bhatt, 'Caste and Political Mobilisation in a Gujarat District', in R. Kothari (ed.), *Caste in Indian Politics* (New Delhi, 1970), pp. 299–339; S. J. M. Epstein, *The Earthy Soil. Bombay Peasants and the Indian Nationalist Movement 1919–1947* (Delhi, 1988), particularly chapter 2.

19 Peel to Irwin, 17 January 1929, Mss. EUR. C. 152 (6). On government policy towards civil disobedience see D. A. Low, ' "Civil Martial Law": The Government of India and the Civil Disobedience Movements, 1930–34', in D. A. Low (ed.), *Congress And The Raj. Facets of the Indian Struggle 1917–47* (London, 1977), pp. 165–98.

20 For a very detailed analysis of the genesis of the Irwin Declaration, the campaign against it in England and debates on it in Parliament, see Moore, *The Crisis Of Indian Unity 1917–1940*, pp. 51–94. The suggestion that Irwin was attempting to delude Indians by a clever use of words is made in G. Peele, 'A Note on the Irwin Declaration', *The Journal of Imperial and Commonwealth History*, vol. i, no. 3 (May 1973), pp. 331–7. The Declaration is quoted extensively in Philips and Pandey (eds.), *The Evolution Of India And Pakistan 1858 to 1947*, pp. 286–7.

21 Congress's Independence resolution, 31 December 1929, ibid. p. 237.

22 On the first Round Table Conference see Moore, *The Crisis Of Indian Unity 1917–1940*, pp. 103–64; Page, *Prelude to Partition*, pp. 220–9; on the wider problem of federation R. J. Moore, 'The Making of India's Paper Federation, 1927–35', in Philips and Wainwright (eds.), *The Partition Of India*, pp. 54–78. In the latter Moore makes clear his fundamental doubts that federation could ever have solved the problem of India's future as a united, independent state, given the differing priorities and fundamental aims of those who were nonetheless prepared to consider it in 1930–1.

23 M. Nehru to Vithalbhai Patel, 12 June 1930, NMML, M. Nehru Papers, File P.6.

24 Gandhi's concern to fill out the meaning of independence was clear in January when he proposed '11 Points' to Irwin, satisfaction on which would enable Congress to participate in the conference. These included the abolition of the salt tax, prohibition, and reduction of land revenue. Many Congressmen were bewildered and angry at this unilateral offer which seemed so remote from the constitutional demand for independence. The '11 Points' demonstrated Gandhi's priorities, and his awareness of the need to make independence both a moral issue and as widely appealing as possible. J. M. Brown, *Gandhi and Civil Disobedience*, pp. 92–3.

25 Irwin to Wedgwood Benn, 24 April 1930, Mss. EUR. C. 152 (6).

26 Sir Malcolm Hailey to Irwin, 25 June 1930, Home Poll., 1930, File No. 257/111.

27 Viceroy to Secretary of State, telegram, 3 February 1931, Mss. EUR. C. 152 (11); November jail figures, Home Poll., 1931, File No. 23/26. A detailed survey of civil disobedience is in J. M. Brown, *Gandhi and Civil Disobedience*, pp. 99–152.

28 Sir Frederick Sykes to Irwin, 21 May and 20 June 1930, IOL, Sykes Papers, Mss. EUR. F. 150 (2).

29 Some donations were direct gifts to Gandhi: in 1930 Motilal gave him Rs. 2 lakhs, and the great business magnate, G. D. Birla, gave him a munificent gift rumoured at between Rs. 1 and 5 lakhs.

30 Sapru to Irwin, 19 September 1930, Mss. EUR. C. 152 (25).

31 Enc. in Sykes to Irwin, 22 April 1930, Mss. EUR. C. 152 (24); J. Masselos, 'Audiences, Actors and Congress Dramas: Crowd events in Bombay City in 1930', Masselos (ed.), op. cit., pp. 71–85; Epstein, *The Earthy Soil*, chapter 3; C. J. Baker, *The Politics of South India 1920–1937* (Cambridge, 1976), pp. 216–17; G. McDonald, 'Unity on Trial: Congress in Bihar, 1929–39', Low (ed.), *Congress And The Raj*, pp. 295–6.

32 Terms of Pact, 5 March 1931, *India in 1930–31* (Calcutta, 1932), pp. 655–9; extracts are quoted in Philips and Pandey (eds.), *The Evolution Of India And Pakistan 1858 to 1947*, pp. 241–2.

33 The pressures leading to the renewal of civil disobedience, and details of the second campaign are discussed in J. M. Brown, *Gandhi and Civil Disobedience*, pp. 263–304.

34 These processes can be followed in Moore, 'The Making of India's Paper Federation, 1927–35', Philips and Wainwright (eds.), *The Partition Of India*, pp. 54–78, or at greater length in Moore, *The Crisis Of Indian Unity 1917–1940*, pp. 208–317.

35 The act is described in detail in Coupland, *The Indian Problem 1833–1935*, pp. 132–41; large extracts of the act are in Philips and Pandey (eds.), *The Evolution Of India And Pakistan 1858 to 1947*, pp. 320–34. On the details of minority representation see below in

this chapter in the discussion of the 1932 Communal Award.

36 Willingdon to Hoare, 30 November 1931, IOL, Templewood Papers, Mss. EUR. E. 240 (5); H. Haig to E. Miéville, 13 April 1932, IOL, Haig Papers, Mss. EUR. F. 115 (1).

37 Winston Churchill's speech in House of Commons, 11 February 1935, Philips and Pandey (eds.), op. cit., pp. 315–17. The debate within an essentially conservative British political ambience is discussed in D. A. Low, 'Sequence in the Demission of Power', D. A. Low, *Lion Rampant. Essays in the Study of British Imperialism* (London, 1973), pp. 167–8.

38 Gandhi to M. A. Ansari, 18 March 1934, Home Poll., 1934, File No. 3/6. On this process of extrication from civil disobedience, see J. M. Brown, *Gandhi and Civil Disobedience*, pp. 360–77.

39 Memo by Sir Reginald Glancy, 29 October 1931, quoted in Moore, *The Crisis Of Indian Unity 1917–1940*, p. 231.

40 Philips and Pandey (eds.), op. cit., pp. 298–301. Gandhi's failures to arrange a compromise in India and London are discussed in J. M. Brown, *Gandhi and Civil Disobedience*, pp. 221–3, 245–50.

41 Gandhi to Hoare, 11 March 1932, Mss. EUR. E. 240 (16). On the fast and subsequent pact, see J. M. Brown, *Gandhi and Civil Disobedience*, pp. 313–23; and R. Kumar, 'Gandhi, Ambedkar and the Poona Pact, 1932', Masselos (ed.), op. cit., pp. 87–101.

42 On the particular problems of local Hindu minorities and their hostility to the central leadership of the Congress with its all-India priorities, see J. Gallagher, 'Congress in Decline: Bengal, 1930 to 1939', Gallagher, Johnson and Seal (eds.), *Locality, Province and Nation*, pp. 269–325; and Heeger, *JAS*, vol. xxxii, no. 1 (Nov. 1972), pp. 39–51.

43 See J. M. Brown, 'The role of a national leader: Gandhi, Congress and civil disobedience, 1929–34', Low (ed.), *Congress And The Raj*, pp. 133–64; and more generally in *Gandhi. Prisoner of Hope*.

44 Linlithgow to Zetland, 15 June 1936, J. Glendevon, *The Viceroy at Bay, Lord Linlithgow in India 1936–1943* (London, 1971), p. 30. This is an account of Linlithgow by his son: a more objective, brief study covering the period of the constitutional experiment is R. J. Moore, 'British Policy and the Indian Problem,1936–40', Philips and Wainwright (eds.), *The Partition Of India*, pp. 79–94.

45 B. R. Tomlinson, *The Indian National Congress and the Raj, 1929–1942. The Penultimate Phase* (London, 1976), pp. 118–22; I. Copland, 'Congress Paternalism: The "High Command" and the struggle for freedom in princely India, c. 1920–1940', Masselos (ed.), op. cit., pp. 121–40; B. N. Ramusack, 'Congress and the People's Movement in Princely India: Ambivalence in Strategy and Organization', R. Sisson and S. Wolpert (eds.), *Congress and Indian Nationalism. The Pre-Independence Phase* (Berkeley and Los Angeles, 1988), pp. 377–403. Mysore was one of the main states where agitation occurred with active help from Congressmen from British India: see J. Manor, 'Gandhian Politics and the Challenge to Princely Authority in Mysore, 1936–47', Low (ed.), *Congress And The Raj*, pp. 405–33. For the failure of a satyagraha against Rajkot state, in which Gandhi was personally involved, see J. R. Wood, 'Rajkot. Indian Nationalism in the Princely Context: the Rajkot Satyagraha of 1938–9', R. Jeffrey (ed.), *People, Princes And Paramount Power. Society and Politics in the Indian Princely States* (Delhi, 1978), pp 240–74.

46 J. Manor, 'The Demise of the Princely Order: A Reassesment', Jeffrey (ed.), op. cit., pp. 306–28.

47 *Return Showing the Results of Elections in India (1937)*, PP, 1937–8, xxi, Cmd. 5589; *Return Showing the Results of the General Election to the Legislative Assembly in India 1934*, PP, 1934–5, xvi, Cmd. 4939.

48 On the issue of 'office-acceptance' and the internal politics of Congress see Tomlinson, *The Indian National Congress and the Raj*, pp. 59–64. Nehru's role is studied in B. R.

Nanda, 'Nehru, the Indian National Congress and the Partition of India, 1935–47', Philips and Wainwright (eds.), *The Partition Of India*, pp. 148–87.

49 See R. Coupland, *Indian Politics 1936–1942* (London, 1943), chapters III–XV on the working of provincial self-government. On Basic Education see Brown, *Gandhi. Prisoner of Hope*, pp. 302–3.

50 Coupland, *Indian Politics 1936–1942*, p. 157; Sir Harry Haig, 'The United Provinces And The New Constitution', *Asiatic Review*, xxxvi (July 1940), pp. 423–34; Lord Erskine, 'Madras And the New Constitution', *Asiatic Review*, xxxvii (Jan. 1941), pp. 12–22.

51 In 1938 Linlithgow noted, 'Seeing as I do in growing measure the shortage of really competent men of sufficient seniority and experience to hold high and important posts and the almost entire absence of men who are not overworked, I cannot but feel uneasy at the position which will confront us if we are faced with a sudden and prolonged crisis . . . one cannot improvise policemen or civil servants of 20 years service, more particularly for work in the districts. Nor is there any source on which we can hope to call for men on any scale that would be of the least value to us.' Glendevon, op. cit., p. 92. The earlier quotation from a new ICS man's letter home, 16 February 1937, is from W. H. Saumarez Smith, *A Young Man's Country. Letters of a Subdivisional Officer of the Indian Civil Service 1936–1937* (Salisbury, 1977), p. 58. See also Beaglehole, *MAS*, vol. 11, part 2 (April 1977), pp. 237–55; R. Hunt and J. Harrison, *The District Officer in India 1930–1947* (London, 1980); Potter, *India's Political Administrators*; Epstein, *MAS*, vol. 16, part 3 (1982), pp. 493–518.

52 Tomlinson, *The Indian National Congress and the Raj*, p. 111; J. H. Voigt, 'Co-operation or confrontation? War and Congress politics 1939–42', Low (ed.), *Congress And The Raj*, pp. 349–374.

53 D. A. Low, 'Introduction: The Climactic Years 1917–47', Low (ed.), *Congress And The Raj*, p. 14.

54 One of the few studies of this broad band of Hindu public opinion is P. Spear, 'A Third Force in India 1920–47: A Study in Political Analysis', Philips and Wainwright (eds.), *The Partition Of India*, pp. 490–503. Congress popularity among voters in the Hindu majority provinces is evident in the 1937 election results: see above, Chapter 5, Table I. Congress percentage of the votes cast was approximately as follows: Madras: 65 per cent; Bihar: 75 percent; Bengal: 25 per cent; CP: 61 per cent; Bombay: 56 per cent; UP: 65 per cent; Punjab: 13 per cent; Sind: 12 per cent; Sitaramayya, op. cit., p. 39.

55 See Markovits, *Indian Business and Nationalist Politics 1931–39*; C. Markovits, 'Congress Policy Towards Business in the Pre-Independence Era', Sisson and Wolpert (eds.), op. cit., pp. 250–68, and 'Indian Business and the Congress Provincial Governments 1937–39', Baker, Johnson, and Seal (eds.), *Power, Profit and Politics*, pp. 487–526.

56 See G. Forbes, 'The Indian Women's Movement: A Struggle for Women's Rights or National Liberation?', G. Minault (ed.), *The Extended Family. Women and Political Participation in India and Pakistan* (Delhi, 1981), pp. 49–82; G. Forbes, 'The Politics of Respectability: Indian Women and the Indian National Congress', D. A. Low (ed.), *The Indian National Congress. Centenary Hindsights* (Delhi, 1988), pp. 54–97.

57 Erskine, *Asiatic Review*, xxxvii (Jan, 1941), p. 21.

58 On the 1937 elections and the campaigns of different parties, see Tomlinson, *The Indian National Congress and the Raj*, pp. 71–85; C. J. Baker, *The Politics of South India 1920–1937*, pp. 299–312; P. D. Reeves, 'Landlords and Party Politics in the United Provinces, 1934–7', Low (ed.), *Soundings in Modern South Asian History*, pp. 261–93.

59 Haig, *Asiatic Review*, xxxvi (July 1940), pp. 424–5.

60 Tomlinson, *The Indian National Congress and the Raj*, pp. 76–81; C. J. Baker, *The Politics of South India 1920–1937*, pp. 313–14.

61 L. Brennan, 'From One Raj to Another: Congress Politics in Rohilkhand, 1930–50', Low

(ed.), *Congress And The Raj*, p. 480; Pandey, *The Ascendancy of the Congress in Uttar Pradesh 1926–34*, pp. 51–4; M. Weiner, 'Changing Patterns of Political Leadership in West Bengal', *Pacific Affairs*, vol. xxxii, no. 3 (September 1959), pp. 277–87; M. Weiner, *Party Building In A New Nation. The Indian National Congress* (Chicago, 1967); D. Arnold, 'The Gounders and the Congress: Political Recruitment in South India, 1920–1937', *South Asia*, no. 4 (Oct. 1974), pp. 1–20. See also S. A. Kochanek, *The Congress Party Of India. The Dynamics Of One-Party Democracy* (Princeton, 1968), Part III.

62 The development of Congress into a total political environment is the main theme of Tomlinson, *The Indian National Congress and the* Raj. On the Hindus of Bengal and Punjab see Gallagher, 'Congress in Decline: Bengal, 1930–1939', Gallagher, Johnson, and Seal (eds.), *Locality, Province and Nation*, pp. 269–325; Heeger, *JAS*, vol. xxxii, no. 1 (Nov. 1972), pp. 39–51.

63 V. Damodaran, *Broken Promises. Popular Protest, Indian Nationalism and the Congress Party in Bihar, 1935–1946* (Delhi, 1992), particularly chapter 2; D. A. Low, 'Congress and "Mass Contacts", 1936–1937: Ideology, Interests, and Conflict over the Basis of Party Representation', Sisson and Wolpert (eds.), op. cit., pp. 134–58; Markovits, 'Indian Business and the Congress Provincial Governments 1937–39', Baker, Johnson, and Seal (eds.), *Power, Profit and Politics*, pp. 511–16.

64 Quoted in B. R. Nanda, 'Socialism In India, 1919–1939: A Retrospect', Nanda (ed.), *Socialism in India*, p. 12. On the CSP see also Tomlinson, *The Indian National Congress and the* Raj, e.g. pp. 50–5. See also J. M. Brown, 'Nehru's Relations with Gandhi', M. Israel (ed.), *Nehru and the Twentieth Century* (Toronto, 1991), pp. 84–107.

65 In Bihar, for example, socialist ideals and Kisan Sabhas were the natural idiom and refuge of disgruntled Congressmen. The campaign among the peasantry led to considerable social and political strife and became a serious challenge to the provincial Congress Ministry. Withdrawal from office was a release from this deepening conflict. G. McDonald, 'Unity on Trial: Congress in Bihar, 1929–39', Low (ed,), *Congress And The* Raj, particularly pp. 302–11; Damodaran, *Broken Promises*, chapter 2.

66 On the crises of authority in Congress see Tomlinson, *The Indian National Congress and the* Raj, particularly chapter 4; D. Taylor, 'The Crisis of Authority in the Indian National Congress, 1936–1939', B. N. Pandey (ed.), *Leadership In South Asia* (New Delhi, 1977), pp. 321–40.

67 *Madras Mail*, quoted in *Star of India*, 12 March 1937, Z. H. Zaidi, 'Aspects of the Development of Muslim League Policy, 1937–47', Philips and Wainwright (eds.), *The Partition Of India*, p. 253.

68 Quoted in Coupland, *Indian Politics 1936–1942*, pp. 181–2.

69 Jinnah to J. Nehru, 12 April 1938, Philips and Pandey (eds.), op. cit., p. 350; Jinnah's presidential address to Muslim League, December 1938, ibid. p. 351.

70 Hardy, *The Muslims of British India*, p. 229; original and modified resolutions at Sind Provincial League Conference are quoted in S. R. Mehrotra, 'The Congress and the Partition of India', Philips and Wainwright (eds.), *The Partition Of India*, pp. 206–7.

71 On the question of provincial coalitions see Tomlinson, *The Indian National Congress and the* Raj, pp. 103–4; Mehrotra, 'The Congress and the Partition of India', Philips and Wainwright (eds.), *The Partition Of India*, pp. 195–9; Nanda, 'Nehru, the Indian National Congress and the Partition of India, 1935–47', ibid. pp. 155–7.

72 M. Mujeeb, 'The Partition of India in Retrospect', ibid. pp. 410–11.

73 Nanda, 'Nehru, the Indian National Congress and the Partition of India, 1935–47', ibid. p. 154. On the relationship of Jinnah and the League to provincial Muslim leaderships, see Jalal and Seal, 'Alternative to Partition', Baker, Johnson and Seal (eds.), *Power, Profit and Politics*, pp. 415–54.

74 Zaidi, 'Aspects of the Development of Muslim League Policy, 1937–47', Philips and

Wainwright (eds.), *The Partition Of India*, pp. 245–75; A. Jalal, *The Sole Spokesman. Jinnah, the Muslim League and the Demand for Pakistan* (Cambridge, 1985), pp. 13–44.
75 Shaikh, *Community and Consensus in Islam*, pp. 200–7.

CHAPTER VI. INDIA IN THE 1940s: A GREAT DIVIDE?

1   14 August 1947, speech by Jawaharlal Nehru, B. N. Pandey (ed.), *The Indian Nationalist Movement, 1885–1947* (London, 1979), p. 219.
2   Chronological accounts and details can be found in such general works as Spear, *India. A Modern History*, or H. V. Hodson, *The Great Divide. Britain–India–Pakistan* (London, 1969). For Wavell's Viceroyalty, 1943–7, a most illuminating and readable primary source is P. Moon (ed.), *Wavell. The Viceroy's Journal* (London, 1973).
3   For India's contribution to the war and the disruptions to her economy because of the war, see Tomlinson, *IESHR*, vol. xiii, no. 3 (July–Sept. 1976), pp. 338–41; Tomlinson, *The Political Economy Of the Raj*, pp. 92–103; J. M. Brown's entry on India in I. Dear and M.R.D. Foot (eds.), *Companion to the Second World War* (Oxford, forthcoming).
4   Note appended to letter from Wavell to Pethick-Lawrence, 13 July 1946, N. Mansergh (ed.), *The Transfer Of Power 1942–7*, vol. xiii (London, 1979), pp. 50–2. See also Tomlinson's analysis in the works cited in fn. 3. A useful general book on the international and domestic contexts of Britain's decolonization is J. Darwin, *Britain and Decolonisation. The Retreat from Empire in the Post-War World* (Basingstoke and London, 1988), particularly chapters 1–3.
5   Voigt, 'Co-operation or confrontation? War and Congress politics 1939–42', Low (ed.), *Congress And The Raj*, pp. 349–74; J. H. Voigt, *India in the Second World War* (New Delhi, 1987); Brown, *Gandhi. Prisoner of Hope*, chapter 9; Tomlinson, *The Indian National Congress and the Raj*, chapter 5.
6   There is no single good study of the 'Quit India movement'. A summary of events from an all-India perspective is F. G. Hutchins, *India's Revolution. Gandhi and the Quit India Movement* (Cambridge, Mass., 1973), chapter 9. Analyses of why popular upheavals occurred in particular regions are Epstein, *The Earthy Soil*, chapter 4; M. Harcourt, 'Kisan Populism and Revolution in Rural India: The 1942 Disturbaces in Bihar and East United Provinces', Low (ed.), *Congress And The Raj*, pp. 315–48; S. Henningham, 'Quit India in Bihar and the Eastern United Provinces: The Dual Revolt', Guha (ed.), *Subaltern Studies II*, pp. 130–79; Damodaran, *Broken Promises*, chapter 4.
     On the experience of one Indian ICS officer in UP during 'Quit India' and the collapse of administration in Ballia district, see N. B. Bonarjee, *Under Two Masters* (Calcutta, 1970), pp. 186–204; see also Hunt and Harrison, *The District Officer in India 1930–1947*, pp. 200–5.
7   Wavell to Amery, 25 February 1944, Amery to Linlithgow, 28 June 1943, N. Mansergh (ed.), *The Transfer Of Power 1942–7*, vol. iv (London, 1973), pp. 760–1, 36.
8   Sir T. Stewart to Linlithgow, 22 August 1942, N. Mansergh (ed.), *The Transfer Of Power 1942–7*, vol. ii (London, 1971), pp. 789–91. See also evidence cited in Harcourt, 'Kisan Populism and Revolution in Rural India', Low (ed.), *Congress And The Raj*, pp. 342–3; Damodaran, op. cit., pp. 235–6.
9   Entry for 31 December 1946, Moon (ed.), *Wavell. The Viceroy's Journal*, p. 402; Wavell's 'Breakdown Plan', September 1946, Mansergh (ed.), *The Transfer Of Power 1942–7*, vol. viii, p. 456; D. Arnold, 'The Armed Police and Colonial Rule in South India, 1914–1947', *MAS*, vol. 11, part 1 (Feb. 1977), p. 124; and D. Arnold, 'Police power and the demise of British rule in India, 1930–47', D. M. Anderson and D. Killingray (eds.), *Policing and*

Decolonisation. Politics, Nationalism and the Police, 1917–65 (Manchester and New York), pp. 42–61.

10 Note enclosed in letter from Sir H. Twynam to Linlithgow, 26 July 1943; Wavell to Amery, 24 November 1943; Mansergh (ed.), *The Transfer Of Power 1942–7*, vol. iv, pp. 123, 493. See also 'The Impact of War', Hunt and Harrison, op. cit., chapter 11.

11 On the loyalties of Indian members of the ICS, see Potter, *MAS*, vol. 7, part 1 (Jan. 1973), pp. 67–71 and *India's Political Administrators*, chapter 3; M. and T. Zinkin, 'Impressions, 1938–47', Philips and Wainwright (eds.), *The Partition Of India*, p. 547; Minutes of India and Burma Committee of the Cabinet, 11 December 1946, N. Mansergh (ed.), *The Transfer Of Power 1942–7*, vol. ix (London, 1980), p. 334.

12 Wavell's 'Breakdown Plan', September 1946, Mansergh (ed.), *The Transfer Of Power 1942–7*, vol. viii, p. 455; Moon (ed.), *Wavell. The Viceroy's Journal*, pp. 368, 402. The decreasing efficiency of administration in the provinces is confirmed in Bonarjee, *Under Two Masters*, chapter 12.

13 On the Cripps Mission see R. J. Moore, *Churchill, Cripps, And India, 1939–1945* (Oxford, 1979), particularly chapters 3–5; R. J. Moore, 'The Mystery Of The Cripps Mission', *Journal of Commonwealth Political Studies*, vol. xi, no. 3 (1973), pp. 195–212; E. Stokes, 'Cripps In India' (Review Article), *Historical Journal*, vol. 14, no. 2 (June 1971), pp. 427–34.

14 R. J. Moore, 'The Problem of Freedom with Unity: London's India Policy, 1917–47', Low (ed.), *Congress And The Raj*, pp. 391–6.

15 Entry for 12 August 1946, Moon (ed.), *Wavell. The Viceroy's Journal*, p. 333. See also Wavell's appreciation of the political situation, December 1945, ibid. pp. 196–7; Zinkin, 'Impressions, 1938–47', Philips and Wainwright (eds.), *The Partition Of India*, pp. 546–53; Potter, *India's Political Administrators*, pp. 135–7.

16 Linlithgow to Amery, 15 April 1943, Amery to Linlithgow, 31 March 1943, N. Mansergh (ed.), *The Transfer Of Power 1942–7*, vol. iii (London, 1971) , pp. 889–90, 820–1.

17 British politicians constantly referred to the need to placate American opinion over India. One of the most forthright expressions of this came in a minute by the (Australian) Governor of Bengal, 'I don't think it is an exaggeration to say that we have to weigh in the balance good Anglo-American relations—or a neat and tidy Indian settlement. If we are obliged to remain in India for another 10 years, ill-disposed Americans will use this as a very heavy stick to beat us with—and this will poison Anglo-American relations—which is the most important matter in prospect in the post-war world. Personally, I would rather get out of India tomorrow than risk the damage to Anglo-American relations that would inevitably be entailed by any long drawn out negotiations for a settlement of the Indian problem.' Minute by R. G. Casey, 17 August 1944, ibid. vol. iv, p. 1208.

18 Undated notes by Attlee, early November 1946, Pethick-Lawrence to Wavell, 25 November 1946, ibid. vol. ix, pp. 68, 174. A detailed account of the Attlee government's policy towards India is R. J. Moore, *Escape From Empire. The Attlee Government and the Indian Problem* (Oxford, 1983).

19 Jinnah to Pethick-Lawrence with enclosure, 12 May 1946, N Mansergh (ed.), *The Transfer Of Power 1942–7*, vol. viii (London, 1977), pp. 516–17; note on Muslim League meetings, 24–26 April 1943, ibid. vol. iii, p. 922; note by H. V. Hodson on his tour of Madras, Orissa, Assam, Bengal, and Bihar, 8 November–7 December 1941, N. Mansergh (ed.), *The Transfer Of Power 1942–7*, vol. i (London, 1970), p. 66.

20 Extracts from Jinnah's presidential speech and the Pakistan Resolution, Muslim League meeting, Lahore, 22–4 March 1940, Philips and Pandey (ed.), *The Evolution Of India And Pakistan 1858 to 1947*, pp. 353–5. Jinnah's January 1940 article is quoted in G. Rizvi, *Linlithgow And India. A Study of British Policy and the Political Impasse in India, 1936–43* (London, 1978), p. 116.

For the radical reassessment of Jinnah's politics now possible as a result of the availability to scholars of the Jinnah and Muslim League papers, see Jalal, *The Sole Spokesman*; and review article by A. Roy, 'The High Politics of India's Partition: The Revisionist Perspective', *MAS*, vol. 24, part 2 (1990), pp. 385–415.

21 'I do not attach too much importance to Jinnah's demands . . . I would judge myself that his attitude at the moment is that, as the Congress are putting forward a preposterous claim which they know is incapable of acceptance, he equally will put forward just as extreme a claim.' Linlithgow to Zetland, 25 March 1940, quoted in Moore, 'British Policy and the Indian Problem, 1936–40', Philips and Wainwright (eds.), *The Partition Of India*, p. 93.

22 Extracts of 8 August 1940 and Cripps' 1942 Offers, Philips and Pandey (eds.), op. cit., pp. 370–3.

23 Entry for 11 July 1944, Moon (ed.), *Wavell. The Viceroy's Journal*, p. 79.

24 Minutes of final meeting of Simla Conference, 14 July 1945, N. Mansergh (ed.), *The Transfer Of Power 1942–7*, vol. v (London, 1974), p. 1245, text of Wavell's broadcast announcing Simla Conference and its aims, 14 June 1945, ibid. pp. 1122–4.

25 Two resolutions of Muslim League Council, Bombay, 29 July 1946, ibid. vol. viii, pp. 135–9. Volumes vii and viii of *The Transfer of Power* documents contain the record of the complex details of the schemes proposed and the various objections and accusations made. See chronological appendix to this chapter, pp. 361–2, for an outline of the Cabinet Mission Plan.

26 Note by H. V. Hodson on his tour of Madras, Orissa, Assam, Bengal, and Bihar, 8 November–7 December 1941, Mansergh (ed.), *The Transfer Of Power 1942–7*, vol. i, p. 66.

27 Governor of UP to Wavell, 29 August 1946, ibid. vol. viii, pp. 342–3; Zaidi, 'Aspects of the Development of Muslim League Policy, 1937–47', Philips and Wainwright (eds.), *The Partition Of India*, particularly, pp. 267–71.

28 See I. Talbot, *Provincial Politics and the Pakistan Movement. The Growth of the Muslim League in North-West and North-East India 1937–47* (Karachi, 1988); D. A. Low (ed.), *The Political Inheritance of Pakistan* (Basingstoke and London, 1991). On Sind see Ansari, *Sufi Saints and State Power*, pp. 118–28. On the Punjab see I. A. Talbot, 'The 1946 Punjab Elections', *MAS*, vol. 14, part 1 (Feb. 1980), pp. 65–91; D. Gilmartin, 'Religious Leadership and the Pakistan Movement in the Punjab', *MAS*, vol. 13, part 3 (July 1979), pp. 485–517.

29 Governor of Bengal to Wavell, 22 August 1946, Mansergh (ed.), *The Transfer Of Power 1942–7*, vol. viii, pp. 293–303.

30 I. H. Qureshi, 'A Case Study of the Social Relations Between the Muslims and the Hindus, 1935–47', Philips and Wainwright (eds.), *The Partition Of India*, pp. 360–8; M. D. Wainwright, 'Keeping the Peace in India, 1946–7: the Role of Lieut.-General Sir Francis Tuker in Eastern Command', ibid. pp. 127–47; Hodson, *The Great Divide*. Eye-witness accounts of the violence are F. Tuker, *While Memory Serves* (London, 1950); P. Moon, *Divide and Quit* (Berkeley and Los Angeles, 1962).

   Recent attempts to analyse the mechanics of violent outbreaks are Das, *Communal Riots in Bengal 1905–1947*; Damodaran, *Broken Promises*, chapter 6; S. Bose, *Agrarian Bengal. Economy, Social Structure and Politics, 1919–1947* (Cambridge, 1986), pp. 223–32.

31 Attlee's statement in Parliament on the transfer of power, 20 February 1947; 3 June 1947 plan for the immediate transfer of power; Philips and Pandey (eds.), *The Evolution Of India And Pakistan 1858 to 1947*, pp. 391–3, 397–402.

32 See Roy's review article, *MAS*, vol. 24, part 2 (1990), pp. 385–415; also the complete version of A. K. Azad, *India Wins Freedom* (London, 1988).

33 See K. Singh, *A History Of The Sikhs. Volume 2: 1839–1964*; B. R. Nayar, 'Sikh Separat-

ism in the Punjab', D. E. Smith (ed.), *South Asian Politics And Religion*, pp. 150–75; S. Oren, 'The Sikhs, Congress, and the Unionists in British Punjab, 1937–1945', *MAS*, vol. 8, part 3 (July 1974), pp. 397–418.

34 Sir E. Jenkins to Wavell, 27 May 1946, Mansergh (ed.), *The Transfer Of Power 1942–7*, vol. vii, p. 712.

35 The record of Sikh delegates' discussions with the Cabinet Mission and Wavell, 5 April 1946, ibid. pp. 138–43. Resolution of the Akali Dal, 22 March 1946, *Tribune*, 23 March 1946, quoted in Singh, op. cit., vol. 2, p. 259, fn. 5.

36 Baldev Singh to Pethick-Lawrence, 4 June 1946, Mansergh (ed.), op. cit., vol. vii, pp. 797–8; See also Tara Singh to Pethick-Lawrence, 25 May 1946, ibid. pp. 696–7, and Resolution of Sikh Panthic Conference, 10 June 1946, ibid. pp. 858–9.

37 Diary of A. Campbell-Johnson, 23 September 1947, A. Campbell-Johnson, *Mission With Mountbatten* (London, 1951), pp. 204–5; Tara Singh's statements, February 1948, quoted in Nayar, 'Sikh Separatism in the Punjab', D. E. Smith (ed.), *South Asian Politics And Religion*, p. 153.

38 M. Windmiller, 'Linguistic Regionalism in India', *Pacific Affairs*, vol. xxvii, no. 4 (Dec. 1954), pp. 291–318.

39 See J. Manor, 'The Demise of the Princely Order. A Reassessment', W. L. Richter, 'Traditional Rulers in Post-Traditional Societies: The Princes of India and Pakistan', Jeffrey (ed.), *People, Princes And Paramount Power*, pp. 306–28, 329–54; V. P. Menon, *The Story of the Integration of The Indian States* (Madras, 1961 edn.); C. Corfield, *The Princely India I Knew. From Reading To Mountbatten* (Madras, 1975); C. Corfield, 'Some Thoughts on British Policy and the Indian States, 1935–47', E. W. R. Lumby, 'British Policy Towards the Indian States, 1940–7', Philips and Wainwright (eds.), *The Partition Of India*, pp. 527–34, 95–103.

40 Minutes of meeting of Burma Committee of Cabinet, 11 September 1945, at which Wavell was present, N. Mansergh (ed.), *The Transfer Of Power 1942–7*, vol. vi (London, 1976), p. 253.

41 Cabinet Mission Memorandum on States' Treaties and Paramountcy, 12 May 1946, ibid. vol. vii, pp. 522–4.

42 See, for example, the creation of Rajasthan in western India out of the former Rajputana States, which was completed in 1949. R. Sisson, *The Congress Party In Rajasthan. Political Integration and Institution-Building in an Indian State* (Berkeley, Los Angeles and London, 1972), particularly pp. 104–11.

43 ibid. See also J. Manor, *Political Change In An Indian State. Mysore 1917–1955* (New Delhi, 1977).

44 Statement by President of Hindu Mahasabha, January 1945, Philips and Pandey (eds.), *The Evolution Of India And Pakistan 1858 to 1947*, p. 369. Golwalkar's book is quoted at length in J. A. Curran, *Militant Hinduism In Indian Politics. A Study of the RSS* (New York, 1951).

45 See D. G. Dalton, 'Gandhi During Partition: a Case Study in the Nature of Satyagraha', Philips and Wainwright (eds.), *The Partition Of India*, pp. 222–44. On the last months of Gandhi's life see Brown, *Gandhi. Prisoner of Hope*, chapter 10.

46 *Movement of Prices, 1939–44.*
(August 1939 = 100)

Dec. (Year)	Rice	Wheat	Cotton manufactures	Kerosene
1941	172	212	196	140
1942	218	232	414	194
1943	951	330	501	201
1944	333	381	285	175

Quoted in Tomlinson, *The Political Economy Of the The Raj*, p. 94. Inflation resulted from expansion of the money supply to pay for the war effort when cash could not be shipped to India from Britain to pay for her contribution to defence expenditure, combined with a diminishing supply of consumer goods to civilians as imports fell and Indian products were syphoned off to meet military needs.

The fragility of life on the subcontinent was devastatingly displayed in the Bengal famine of 1943–4: see P. R. Greenough, *Prosperity And Misery in Modern Bengal. The Famine of 1943–1944* (New York and Oxford, 1982).

47 For the impact of the war on India's economy see Tomlinson, *The Political Economy Of The Raj*, pp. 92–103.

48 W. Malenbaum, *Modern India's Economy. Two Decades of Planned Growth* (Columbus, 1971), particularly chapter 2, 'The Economy At Independence'.

49 Table showing distribution of land ownership in 1953, Maddison, *Class Structure and Economic Growth*, p. 106.

50 A good introduction to the Constitution and the political structure is R. L. Hardgrave, *India. Government and Politics in a Developing Nation* (3rd edn., New York, 1980), pp. 47–86, 101–4. Detailed analysis of the constituent Assembly and the constitution is in G. Austin, *The Indian Constitution: Cornerstone Of A Nation* (New York, 1966).

51 The centre has exclusive authority over such obviously national affairs as defence, foreign relations, currency, and income tax. It shares with the states law, social and economic planning. States control public order, police, welfare, health, education, local government, industry, agriculture, and land revenue. In any conflict Union law prevails. The centre can also create new states, alter state boundaries, and even abolish a state.

52 On the official and unofficial commitments to government intervention and planning see Tomlinson, *The Political Economy Of The Raj*, pp. 97–100; K. N. Chaudhuri, 'Economic Problems and Indian Independence', Philips and Wainwright (eds.), *The Partition Of India*, pp. 310–12; C. Baker, 'Colonial Rule and the Internal Economy in Twentieth-Century Madras', Baker, Johnson and Seal (eds.), *Power, Profit and Politics*, particularly pp. 590–8 (this is a local examination of government involvement in a provincial economy).

53 This area of continuity is explored by R. E. Frykenberg, 'The Last Emergency of the Raj', in H. C. Hart (ed.), *Indira Gandhi's India. A Political System Reappraised* (Boulder, Colorado, 1976), pp. 37–66.

54 On the structure of the public services see Hardgrave, *India*, pp. 69–76; Potter, *India's Political Administrators*: see pp. 146–9 for Patel's role in securing the service's position.

CHAPTER VII. EPILOGUE: INDIA'S DEMOCRATIC EXPERIENCE

1 State elections were originally held simultaneously with Lok Sabha elections: they were 'de-linked' in 1972 and thereafter held separately. Details of results in state and Union elections are in Hardgrave, *India*, pp. 204–9, xv–xvii.

2 Kuldip Nayar's estimate in *The Statesman*, 9 March 1971, W. H. Morris-Jones, 'India Elects for Change—and Stability', *Asian Survey*, vol. 11 (Aug. 1971), pp. 723–4.

3 B. Venkataraman and D. Venugopal, 'Public Order', Dube (ed.), *India since Independence*, pp. 468–70; A. Kohli (ed.), *India's Democracy. An Analysis of Changing State-Society Relations* (Princeton, 1990 edn.), p. 330.

4 R. Kothari, *Politics in India* (Boston, 1970), p. 205; Weiner, *Pacific Affairs*, vol. xxxii, no. 3 (Sept. 1959), pp. 277–87; Kochanek, *The Congress Party Of India*, chapter xv, 'The Composition of the Parliamentary Wing', pp. 370–404; D. B. Forrester, 'State Legislators in Madras', *JCPS*, vol. vii (1969), pp. 36–57.

5 Between 1967 and *c*. 1972 15% of MLAs (3,500) 'floor-crossed': several hundred were rewarded with office. For the case of Haryana state see A. H. Hanson and J. Douglas,

India's Democracy (London, 1972), p. 109. After the 1971 Lok Sabha elections many state politicians hastily made their peace with the new party of central government, and non-Congress state governments began to fall although there had not been state elections: see Morris-Jones, *Asian Survey*, vol. 11 (Aug. 1971), pp. 738–9.

On the 'decline' of parliamentary life, see L. I. and S. H. Rudolph, *In Pursuit of Lakshmi. The Political Economy of the Indian State* (Chicago and London, 1987), pp. 95–8.

6 On the centre's interference with the installation of state governments and the choice of Chief Minister, see Hanson and Douglas, op. cit., pp. 47, 121–3; Rudolph and Rudolph, *In Pursuit of Lakshmi*, pp. 98–102; P. R. Brass, *The Politics of India since Independence* (Cambridge, 1990), pp. 99–107.

7 See Kothari, *Politics in India*, chapter VI, 'Social Infrastructure', pp. 224–49; Rudolph, *The Modernity Of Tradition*. (The Rudolphs' work is concerned with the elements in tradition which help mediate between old and new in Indian political development. Part I examines how caste has helped Indians to work democratic forms.)

8 The best introduction is chapter 6, 'Parties and Politics', Hardgrave, *India*, pp. 148–98. (His suggestions for further reading, ibid. pp. 196–8, include case studies of particular parties.) See also Brass, *The Politics of India since Independence*; J. Manor, 'Parties and the Party System', chapter 2 of Kohli (ed.), *India's Democracy*.

9 'Élite circulation', as political scientists call the process of continually changing patterns of recruitment into politics, is discussed in D. B. Rosenthal, 'Deurbanization, Elite Displacement, and Political Change in India', *Comparative Politics*, no. 2 (Jan. 1970), pp. 169–201. The best analysis of Congress adaptation to the needs and social structure of different areas is Weiner, *Party Building In A New Nation*. A fascinating example of Congress flexibility is in UP, where Congress and some of the landlords, now stripped of much of their land, have made their peace; because the party needed to tap landlord influence and money, while the landlords wanted honour and prestige in the new order to replace the protection and privilege the British had once accorded them. See T. R. Metcalf, 'Landlords Without Land: The UP Zamindars Today', *Pacific Affairs*, vol. xl, nos. 1 and 2 (Spring and Summer 1967), pp. 5–18.

10 S. A. Kochanek, 'Mrs. Gandhi's Pyramid: The New Congress', Hart (ed.), *Indira Gandhi's India*, pp. 93–124; Rudolph and Rudolph, *In Pursuit of Lakshmi*, pp. 132–58.

11 The Naxalite violence originated in and was named after an area in West Bengal where a tribal group attempted to seize land and set up a people's administration. It lasted fifty days but was copied elsewhere, and in 1969 spread to Calcutta. Only a section of Indian Communists sympathized with this strategy. Most have been prepared to function within the democratic framework and to form state governments where they have opportunity, as in Kerala and West Bengal.

12 Student agitations have been an increasing phenomenon from the mid-1960s, on a range of political and academic issues, in part reflective of students' economic problems, discontent over teaching methods, and fears of unemployment. An indication of their spread are the totals for student agitations: 1,801 (1964–5), 1,732 (1965–6), 3,073 (1966–7), 2,941 (1967–8), 2,606 (1968–9), 3,326 (1969–70). Agrarian protests on rights to land, harvesting and sharing of produce ran at 402 (1967), 833 (1968), 1,236 (1969), 2,953 (1970): West Bengal, Bihar, UP, Andhra Pradesh, Rajasthan and Kerala have been the worst affected states. Venkataraman and Venugopal, 'Public Order', Dube (ed.), *India since Independence*, pp. 462–8.

13 An excellent study dealing with the early years after independence is M. Weiner, *The Politics Of Scarcity. Public Pressure and Political Response in India* (Chicago, 1962).

14 On language and politics see Hardgrave, *India*, pp. 95–100; W. H. Morris-Jones, 'Language and Region Within the Indian Union', P. Mason (ed.), *India and Ceylon: Unity and*

Diversity. A Symposium (London, 1967), pp. 51–66; Brass, *The Politics of India since Independence*, chapter 5.

15 Venkataraman and Venugopal, 'Public Order', Dube (ed.), *India since Independence*, pp. 453, 473–7; table of incidents of communal violence, 1954–82, Brass, *The Politics of India since Independence*, p. 198.

16 The best introductions are Hardgrave, *India*, pp. 164–72; and the essays in Hart (ed.), *Indira Gandhi's India*.

17 Hardgrave, *India*, pp. 105–9; Hanson and Douglas, *India's Democracy*, pp. 184–207; Brass, *The Politics of India since Independence*, pp. 119–21.

18 On the army's apolitical stance, with particular reference to the 'Emergency', see S. P. Cohen, 'The Military', Hart (ed.), *Indira Gandhi's India*, pp. 207–39; and S. P. Cohen, 'The Military and Indian Democracy', Kohli (ed.), *India's Democracy*, pp. 99–143.

19 See S. A. Kochanek, *Business and Politics in India* (Berkeley, 1974); Rudolph and Rudolph, *In Pursuit of Lakshmi*.

20 Hardgrave, *India*, pp. 76–9.

21 On the IAS (successor to the ICS) see Potter, *India's Political Administrators*, chapter 6; Rudolph and Rudolph, *In Pursuit of Lakshmi*, pp. 74–83.

22 On the police see Rudolph and Rudolph, *In Pursuit of Lakshmi*, pp. 91–5; a table of police strikes is in Kohli (ed.), *India's Democracy*, p. 127.

23 This is one of the main themes of A. Kohli, *Democracy and Discontent. India's growing crisis of governability* (Cambridge, 1990).

24 Much of this section reflects the author's attempt to understand the violence which erupted in India at the end of 1992, and the broad spectrum of support evident then for the Hindu understanding of the Indian state and nation put forward by the BJP. This was in stark contrast to the failure of earlier Hindu parties to achieve a broad basis of support: see B. Graham, *Hindu Nationalism And Indian Politics. The Origins and Development of the Bharatiya Jana Sangh* (Cambridge, 1990). On the use of Hindu themes by Indira and Rajiv Gandhi, see J. Manor, chapter 2 of Kohli (ed.), *India's Democracy*, pp. 80–2.

25 A good introduction to India's foreign affairs, including a guide to detailed reading, is Hardgrave, *India*, pp. 236–58. See also R. W. Bradnock, *India's Foreign Policy since 1971* (London, 1990).

26 Nayar, 'Sikh Separatism in the Punjab', Smith (ed.), *South Asian Politics And Religion*, pp. 150–75; B. R. Nayar, *Minority Politics In The Punjab* (Princeton, 1966); B. R. Nayar, 'Punjab', M. Weiner (ed.), *State Politics In India* (Princeton, 1968), particularly pp. 449–56.

27 On the Punjab in the 1980s see R. Jeffrey, *What's Happening To India? Punjab, Ethnic Conflict, Mrs. Gandhi's Death and the Test for Federalism* (Basingstoke and London, 1986); Brass, *The Politics of India since Independence*, pp 170–4; P. R. Brass, 'The Punjab Crisis and the Unity of India', chapter 5, Kohli (ed.), *India's Democracy*; Kohli, *Democracy and Discontent*, chapter 12.

28 See Brass, *The Politics of India since Independence*, pp. 222–41; M. Weiner, *Sons Of The Soil. Migration and Ethnic Conflict in India* (Princeton, 1978).

29 An excellent, brief introduction to the population question is B. Kuppuswamy, *Population and Society in India* (Bombay, 1975).

30 On India's economic strategy as shown in her five-year plans, and the adoption by Parliament in 1954 of the goal of a 'socialist pattern of society', see Maddison, *Class Structure and Economic Growth*, pp. 111 ff.; Malenbaum, *Modern India's Economy*, pp. 47–58. A good overview of plans and economic performance is A. Vaidyanathan, 'The Indian Economy since Independence (1947–70)', Kumar and Desai (eds.), op. cit., pp. 947–94.

31 On Kerala see R. Jeffrey, *Politics, Women and Well-Being: How Kerala became a 'Model'*

(Basingstoke and London, 1992).

32 Malenbaum, op. cit., pp. 134 ff.; P. S. Jha, 'Economic Development: Failure of a Strategy', Dube (ed.), op. cit., pp. 485–509. A major discussion of India's economic dilemmas is F. R. Frankel, *India's Political Economy, 1947–1977. The Gradual Revolution* (Princeton, 1978).

33 For a discussion of poverty see Brass, *The Politics of India since Independence*, pp. 266–9; and on the extent and limits of the 'Green Revolution', ibid., pp. 286–94.

34 Frankel, op. cit., pp. 493, 495; Maddison, op. cit., p. 129; F. C. R. Robinson (ed.), *The Cambridge Encyclopedia of India, Pakistan . . .* (Cambridge, 1989), pp. 271–3. See also the discussion 'Capitalist Agriculture and Rural Well-Being', M. Weiner, *The Indian Paradox. Essays in Indian Politics* (New Delhi, Newbury Park, and London, 1989), chapter 4.

35 Statement by India's Finance Minister, 24 July 1991; on Rajiv Gandhi's abortive attempts at liberalization see Kohli, *Democracy and Discontent*, chapter 11.

36 In 1978 the Planning Commission estimated that 20.6 millions were unemployed; over three-quarters of these in country areas. The problem of educated unemployment is growing particularly acute, and is an element in student unrest. Educational 'drop-out' as children are needed in the home has scarcely eased since independence. By the early 1970s only 40 per cent of children initially enrolled in primary school reach Class V, and only 25 per cent reach Class VIII, i.e. are educated into their early teens. Hardgrave, *India*, p. 92; J. P. Naik, 'Education', Dube (ed.), op. cit., pp. 240–62.

37 On UP see Metcalf, *Pacific Affairs*, vol. xl, nos. 1 and 2 (Spring and Summer 1967), pp. 5–18; Cohn, 'The Changing Status of a Depressed Caste', Marriott (ed.), *Village India*, pp. 53–77; R. S. Newell, 'Ideology and Realities: Land Redistribution in Uttar Pradesh', *Pacific Affairs*, vol. 45, no. 2 (Summer 1972), pp. 220–39; Reeves, *Landlords and Governments in Uttar Pradesh*, pp. 321–5.

38 F. T. Jannuzi, *Agrarian Crisis in India. The Case of Bihar* (Austin and London, 1974). This evidence relates back to the problem experienced by the Congress leadership in relation to the CSP in the late 1930s, and the explosion of violence in Bihar in 1942 in the 'Quit India' campaign.

39 M. Galanter, 'The Abolition of Disabilities—Untouchability and the Law', J. M. Mahar (ed.), *The Untouchables in Contemporary India* (Tucson, 1972), pp. 227–314. This whole collection of essays is a most important review of the Untouchables' position.

40 See A. Kohli, *The State and Poverty in India. The Politics of Reform* (Cambridge, 1987), particularly chapter 3 on West Bengal under the CPM government.

Suggestions for Further Reading

CHAPTER I

(A) GENERAL

B. S. Cohn, *India: The Social Anthropology of a Civilization*, Prentice Hall, Inc., Englewood Cliffs, New Jersey, 1971
F. Robinson (ed.), *The Cambridge Encyclopedia of India, Pakistan, Bangladesh, Sri Lanka, Nepal, Bhutan and the Maldives*, Cambridge, 1989
P. Spear, *India. A Modern History*, University of Michigan Press, Ann Arbor, 1961
S. A. Wolpert, *A New History of India*, OUP, New York, 1977; 2nd edition, OUP, New York and Oxford, 1982
A. Maddison, *Class Structure and Economic Growth. India and Pakistan since the Moghuls*, George Allen & Unwin Ltd., London, 1971 (particularly ch. 2)

(B) RELIGION AND SOCIETY

C. Maloney, *Peoples of South Asia*, New York, 1974
P. Hardy, *The Muslims of British India*, Cambridge, CUP, 1972
S. B. Bayly, *Saints, Goddesses and Kings. Muslims and Christians in South Indian Society, 1700–1900*, Cambridge, 1989
W. O. Cole and P. S. Sambhi, *The Sikhs. Their Religious Beliefs and Practices*, Routledge and Kegan Paul, London, 1978
K̈. Singh, *A History of the Sikhs*, 2 vols., Princeton University Press, Princeton, 1963 and 1966
K. M. Sen, *Hinduism*, Harmondsworth, 1961
R. C. Zaehner, *Hinduism*, Oxford, 1962
N. C. Chaudhuri, *Hinduism*, Chatto and Windus, London, 1979
L. A. Babb, *The Divine Hierarchy: Popular Hinduism in Central India*, New York and London, 1975
D. L. Eck, *Darsan. Seeing the Divine Image in India*, Chambersburg, 1981
D. L. Eck, *Banares. City of Light*, London, 1983
M. R. Anand, *Untouchable*, Indian paperback edn., Delhi, 1970
Hazari, *Untouchable. The Autobiography of an Indian Outcaste*, Praeger, New York and London, 1969
J. M. Freeman, *Untouchable. An Indian Life History*, London, 1979

(C) VILLAGE STUDIES

T. G. Kessinger, *Vilyatpur 1848–1968*, California, 1974
M. N. Srinivas, *The Remembered Village*, OUP, Delhi, 1976
W. H. and C. V. Wiser, *Behind Mud Walls 1930–1960*, Berkeley and Los Angeles, 1969

(D) THE MOGULS

C. A. Bayly, *Imperial Meridian. The British Empire and the World 1780–1830*, London and New York, 1989
C. A. Bayly, *Indian Society and the Making of the British Empire*, Cambridge, 1988
S. P. Blake, 'The Patrimonial–Bureaucratic Empire of the Mughals', *JAS*, vol. xxxix, no. 1 (Nov. 1979), 77–94
J. F. Richards, *Mughal Administration in Golconda*, Oxford, 1975
'Symposium: Decline of the Mughal Empire', *JAS*, vol. xxxv, no. 2 (Feb. 1976), 221–63
K. N. Chaudhuri, *Trade and Civilisation in the Indian Ocean. An Economic History from the Rise of Islam to 1750*, Cambridge, 1985

(E) THE ENGLISH INTEREST

P. J. Marshall, *Problems of Empire. Britain and India 1757–1813*, London, 1968
P. J. Marshall, *East Indian Fortunes. The British in Bengal in the Eighteenth Century*, Oxford, 1976
P. J. Marshall, *Bengal: The British Bridgehead. Eastern India 1740–1828*, Cambridge, 1987
K. N. Chaudhuri, *The Trading World of Asia and the English East India Company, 1660–1760*, Cambridge, 1978
P. Spear, *The Nabobs. A Study of the Social Life of the English in Eighteenth Century India*, London, 1963. Oxford Paperback edn.
H. Dodwell, *Dupleix And Clive. The Beginning of Empire* (Classic narrative first published in 1920. Republished London, 1967)
M. Bence-Jones, *Clive of India*, Constable, London, 1974 (very readable)
H. Furber, *John Company at Work*, Cambridge, Mass., 1948, 2nd edition, 1951 (Classic discussion of English economic activity, but concentrates more on later eighteenth century)

CHAPTER II

(A) EXPANSION AND STABILIZATION OF DOMINION

H. Furber, *John Company at Work*, 2nd edition, Cambridge, Mass., 1951
P. J. Marshall, *Problems Of Empire. Britain and India 1757–1813*, London, 1968

P. J. Marshall, *East Indian Fortunes. The British in Bengal in the Eighteenth Century*, Oxford, 1976

P. Nightingale, *Trade And Empire In Western India 1784–1806*, Cambridge, 1970

B. S. Cohn, 'Recruitment and Training of British Civil Servants in India, 1600–1860', in R. Braibanti (ed.), *Asian Bureaucratic Systems Emergent from the British Imperial Tradition*, Duke University Press, 1966

R. E. Frykenberg, *Guntur Distict, 1788–1848: A History of Local Influence and Central Authority in South Asia*, Oxford, 1965

C. A. Bayly, *Indian Society and the Making of the British Empire*, Cambridge, 1988

(B) BUTTRESSES OF DOMINION

P. J. Marshall, *Problems Of Empire. Britain and India 1757–1813*, London, 1968

M. Greenberg, *British Trade and The Opening of China 1800–42*, Cambridge, 1951

E. Stokes, *The English Utilitarians And India*, Oxford, 1959

S. Gopal, *The Permanent Settlement In Bengal And Its Results*, London, 1949

T. H. Beaglehole, *Thomas Munro And The Development of Administrative Policy, In Madras*, Cambridge, 1966

B. Stein, *Thomas Munro. The Origins of the Colonial State and His Vision of Empire*, Delhi, 1989

W. C. Neale, *Economic Change in Rural India. Land Tenure and Reform in Uttar Pradesh, 1800–1955*, New Haven and London, 1962

C. H. Philips and M. D. Wainwright (eds.), *Indian Society and the Beginnings of Modernisation c. 1830–1850*, SOAS, London, 1976

S. F. D. Ansari, *Sufi Saints and State Power. The* Pirs *Of Sind, 1843–1947*, Cambridge, 1991 (ch. 2 describes the construction of a 'neo-durbari' style of political alliance with the religious and land-owning élite peculiar to Sind)

B. S. Cohn, 'Representing Authority in Victorian India', in E. Hobsbawm and T. O. Ranger (eds.), *The Invention of Tradition*, Cambridge, 1983, pp. 165–209

(C) CHANGE AND CONTINUITY

E. Stokes, *The English Utilitarians And India*, Oxford, 1959

E. Stokes, *The Peasant And The Raj. Studies in agrarian history and peasant rebellion in colonial India* (particularly ch. 1), Cambridge, 1978

D. Kumar, *Land And Caste In South India. Agricultural labour in the Madras Presidency during the nineteenth century*, Cambridge, 1965

D. Ludden, *Peasant History in South India*, Princeton, 1985

K. Ballhatchet, *Social Policy And Social Change In Western India 1817–1830*, London, 1957

B. S. Cohn, 'Structural Change In Indian Rural Society 1596–1885', in R. E. Frykenberg (ed.), *Land Control And Social Structure In Indian History*, Madison and London, 1969

K. Ingham, *Reformers In India 1793–1833. An account of the work of Christian*

Missionaries on behalf of social reform, Cambridge, 1956

D. B. Forrester, *Caste and Christianity. Attitudes and Policies on Caste of Anglo-Saxon Protestant Missions in India*, London and Dublin, 1980

E. D. Potts, *British Baptist Missionaries in India, 1793–1837. The History of Serampore and its Missions*, Cambridge, 1967

M. A. Laird, *Missionaries and Education in Bengal, 1793–1837*, Oxford, 1972

B. T. McCully, *English Education And The Origins Of Indian Nationalism*, Columbia, 1940

M. D. Morris *et al.* (ed.), *Indian Economy in the Nineteenth Century: A Symposium*, Delhi, 1969

C. H. Philips and M. D. Wainwright (eds.), *Indian Society and the Beginnings of Modernisation c. 1830–1850*, SOAS, London, 1976

A. Maddison, *Class Structure and Economic Growth. India and Pakistan since the Moghuls* (ch. III), London, 1971

K. N. Chaudhuri (ed.), *The Economic Development of India under the East India Company 1814–58* (Introduction), Cambridge, 1971

C. A. Bayly, *Indian Society and the Making of the British Empire*, Cambridge, 1988

C. A. Bayly, *Rulers, Townsmen and Bazaars. North Indian socicety in the age of British Expansion 1770–1870*, Cambridge, 1983

D. Kumar and M. Desai (eds.), *The Cambridge Economic History of India, Volume 2, c. 1757–c. 1970*, Cambridge 1983, Parts I and II

(D) FURTHER READING ON THE MUTINY

GENERAL STUDIES AND NARRATIVE

T. R. Metcalf, *The Aftermath Of Revolt. India, 1857–1870*, Princeton, 1964 (ch. 2)

C. A. Bayly, *Indian Society and the Making of the British Empire*, Cambridge, 1988, pp. 169–94

M. Maclagan, *'Clemency' Canning*, London, 1962

J. A. B. Palmer, *The Mutiny Outbreak At Meerut In 1857*, Cambridge, 1966

A. T. Embree (ed.), *1857 In India. Mutiny or War of Independence?* (Problems in Asian Civilizations Series) Boston, 1963

M. Edwardes, *A Season In Hell. The Defence Of The Lucknow Residency*, London, 1973

DETAILED REGIONAL STUDIES

E. Stokes, *The Peasant And The Raj. Studies in agrarian society and peasant rebellion in colonial India*, Cambridge, 1978 (chs. 5–8)

E. T. Stokes (ed. C. A. Bayly), *The Peasant Armed: The Indian Revolt of 1857*, Oxford, 1986

E. I. Brodkin, 'Proprietary Mutations and the Mutiny in Rohilkhand', *JAS*, vol. xxviii, no. 4 (Aug. 1969), pp. 667–83

E. I. Brodkin, 'The Struggle for Succession: Rebels and Loyalists in the Indian Mutiny of 1857', *MAS*, vol. 6, part 3 (July 1972), pp. 227–90
W. C. Neale, *Economic Change in Rural India. Land Tenure and Reform in Uttar Pradesh, 1800–1955*, Newhaven and London, 1962
R. Mukherjee, *Awadh In Revolt. A Study of Popular Resistance*, New Delhi, 1984

SOME PRIMARY SOURCES

M. Edwardes (ed.), W. H. Russell, *My Indian Mutiny Diary*, London, 1957
M. R. Gubbins, *An Account of the Mutinies In Oudh, and of The Siege of the Lucknow Residency*, 2nd edition, London, 1858
J. Lunt (ed.), *From Sepoy to Subedar being the Life and Adventures of Subedar Sita Ram, a Native Officer of the Bengal Army written and related by himself*, 1st English edition, 1873; London, 1970

CHAPTER III

(A) PRIMARY SOURCES

C. H. Philips and B. N. Pandey (eds.), *The Evolution Of India And Pakistan 1858 to 1947. Select Documents*, London, 1962
B. N. Pandey (ed.), *The Indian Nationalist Movement, 1885–1947. Select Documents*, London, 1979
S. Banerjea, *A Nation In Making*, first published 1925: Calcutta, 1963
M. Gilbert, *Servant of India*, London, 1966
Hardinge, *My Indian Years 1910–1916*, London, 1948
Minto, Mary Countess of, *India, Minto and Morley 1905–1910*, London, 1934

(B) INDIAN POLITICS

J. Masselos, *Nationalism on the Indian Subcontinent. An Introductory History*, Melbourne, 1972
J. McLane, *Indian Nationalism And The Early Congress*, Princeton, 1977
A. Seal, *The Emergence Of Indian Nationalism. Competition and Collaboration in the Later Nineteenth Century*, Cambridge, 1968
J. Gallagher, G. Johnson and A. Seal (eds.), *Locality, Province and Nation. Essays on Indian Politics 1870–1940*, Cambridge, 1973
Rajat Ray, *Urban Roots of Indian Nationalism. Pressure Groups and Conflict of Interests in Calcutta City Politics, 1875–1939*, New Delhi, 1979
C. Dobbin, *Urban Leadership in Western India. Politics and Communities in Bombay City 1840–1855*, London, 1972
G. Johnson, *Provincial Politics and Indian Nationalism. Bombay and the Indian National Congress 1880 to 1915*, Cambridge, 1973

D. A. Washbrook, *The Emergence of Provincial Politics. The Madras Presidency 1870–1920*, Cambridge, 1976

C. A.Bayly, *The Local Roots of Indian Politics. Allahabad 1880–1920*, Oxford, 1975

F. C. R. Robinson, *Separatism among Indian Muslims. The Politics of the United Provinces' Muslims 1860–1923*, Cambridge, 1974

P. Hardy, *The Muslims of British India*, Cambridge, 1972

K. W. Jones, 'Communalism in the Punjab. The Arya Samaj Contribution', *JAS*, vol. xxviii, no. 1 (November 1968), pp. 39–54

Ranajit Guha (ed.), *Subaltern Studies. Writings on South Asian History and Society* (Delhi, 1982–). These are not arranged chronologically, and each volume contains a wide variety of material illuminating 'subalternity' and 'subaltern' modes of action, using 'subaltern' in the Gramscian sense.

(c) INDIAN IDEAS

B. T. McCully, *English Education And The Origins Of Indian Nationalism*, Columbia, 1940

T. Raychaudhuri, *Europe Reconsidered. Perceptions of the West in Nineteenth-Century Bengal*, Delhi, 1988

C.H. Heimsath, *Indian Nationalism and Hindu Social Reform*, Princeton. 1964

K. W. Jones, *Socio-Religious Reform Movements in British India*, Cambridge, 1989

K.W. Jones, *Arya Dharm. Hindu Consciousness In 19th-Century Punjab*, Berkeley, Los Angeles and London, 1976

B. Chandra, 'Indian Nationalists & the Drain, 1880–1905', *IESHR*, vol. ii no. 2 (Apr. 1965), pp. 103–44

B. Chandra, *The Rise and Growth of Economic Nationalism in India: Economic Policies of Indian National Leadership, 1880–1905*, New Delhi, 1966

I. Klein, 'Indian Nationalism and Anti-Industrialization: The Roots of Gandhian Economics', *South Asia*, 3 (1973–4), pp. 93–104

A. Ahmad, *Islamic Modernism In India And Pakistan 1857–1964*, London, 1967

F. Shaikh, *Community and Consensus in Islam. Muslim Representation in Colonial India, 1860–1947*, Cambridge, 1989

R. O'Hanlon, *Caste, Conflict and Ideology. Mahatma Jotirao Phule and Low Caste Protest in Nineteenth-Century Western India*, Cambridge, 1985

(d) BRITISH POLICY

S. Gopal, *British Policy In India 1858–1905*, Cambridge, 1965

S. Gopal, *The Viceroyalty Of Lord Ripon 1880–1884*, London, 1953

R.J. Moore, *Liberalism and Indian Politics 1872–1922*, London, 1966

D. Dilks, *Curzon in India. 1. Achievement*, London, 1969

D. Dilks, *Curzon in India. 2. Frustration*, London, 1970.

K. Rose, *Curzon: A Most Superior Person*, London, 1969

S. R. Wasti, *Lord Minto and the Indian Nationalist Movement 1905 to 1910*, Oxford, 1964

S.A. Wolpert, *Morley And India 1906–1910*, Berkeley and Los Angeles, 1967

N.G. Barrier, *Banned. Controversial Literature And Political Control In British India 1907–1947*, Missouri, 1974

D.J. Arnold, *Police Power And Colonial Rule. Madras 1859–1947*, Delhi, 1986

P. D. Reeves, *Landlords And Governments In Uttar Pradesh. A Study of their Relations until Zamindari Abolition*, Bombay, 1991

B.R. Tomlinson, 'India and the British Empire, 1880–1935', *IESHR*, vol. xii, no. 4 (Oct.–Dec. 1975), pp. 341–80

F.G. Hutchins, *The Illusion Of Permanence. British Imperialism in India*, Princeton, 1967

(E) ECONOMY AND SOCIETY

D. Kumar and M. Desai (eds.), *The Cambridge Economic History of India, Volume 2: c. 1757–c. 1970*, Cambridge, 1983

A.Maddison, *Class Structure and Economic Growth. India and Pakistan since the Mughals*, London, 1971

P. Griffiths, *The British Impact On India*, London, 1952

B.B. Misra, *The Indian Middle Classes. Their Growth In Modern Times*, London, 1961

B.S. Cohn, *India: The Social Anthropology Of A Civilization*, Englewood Cliffs, 1971

A. K. Bagchi, 'European and Indian Entrepreneurship in India, 1900–30', in E. Leach and S. N. Mukherjee (eds.), *Elites In South Asia*, Cambridge, 1970

M. D. Morris *et al.* (eds.), *Indian Economy in the Nineteenth Century: A Symposium*, Delhi, 1969

M. D. Morris, *The Emergence Of An Industrial Labor Force In India. A Study of the Bombay Cotton Mills, 1854–1947*, Berkeley and Los Angeles, 1965

K. L. Gillion, *Ahmedabad. A Study in Indian Urban History*, Berkeley and Los Angeles, 1968

D. Chakrabarty, *Rethinking Working-Class History. Bengal 1870–1940*, Princeton, 1989

T. G. Kessinger, *Vilyatpur 1848–1968. Social and Economic Change in a North Indian Village*, Berkeley and Los Angeles, 1974

N. Charlesworth, *Peasants and Imperial Rule. Agriculture and Agrarian Society in the Bombay Presidency, 1850–1935*, Cambridge, 1985

C. J. Baker, *An Indian Rural Economy 1880–1955. The Tamilnad Countryside*, Oxford, 1984

I. Stone, *Canal Irrigation in British India. Perspectives on Technological Change in a Peasant Economy*, Cambridge, 1984

E. Whitcombe, *Agrarian Conditions In Northern India. Volume I. The United Provinces under British Rule, 1860–1900*, Berkeley, Los Angeles and London, 1972

I. J. Catanach, *Rural Credit in Western India 1875–1930. Rural Credit and the Cooperative Movement in the Bombay Presidency*, Berkeley, Los Angeles and Bombay, 1970

G. Blyn, *Agricultural Trends in India, 1891–1947: Output, Availability, and Produc-*

tivity, Philadelphia, 1966

P. Harnetty, 'Crop Trends in the Central Provinces of India, 1861–1921', *MAS*, vol. 11, part 3 (July 1979), pp. 341–77

C. J. Dewey and A. G. Hopkins (eds.), *The Imperial Impact. Studies in the Economic History of Africa and India*, London, 1978

K. N. Chaudhuri and C. J. Dewey (eds.), *Economy And Society. Essays in Indian Economic and Social History*, Delhi, 1979

C. A. Bayly, *Rulers, Townsmen and Bazaars. North Indian Society in the Age of British Expansion, 1770–1870*, Cambridge, 1983

T. A. Timberg, *The Marwaris: From Traders to Industrialists*, New Delhi, 1978

B. R. Tomlinson, *The Political Economy Of The Raj 1914–1947. The Economics of Decolonization in India*, London, 1979

CHAPTER IV

(A) SOURCE MATERIAL

C. H. Philips and B. N. Pandey (eds.), *The Evolution Of India And Pakistan 1858 to 1947. Select Documents*, London, 1962

B. N. Pandey (ed.), *The Indian Nationalist Movement, 1885–1947. Select Documents*, London, 1979

E. S. Montagu, *An Indian Diary*, London, 1930

M. K. Gandhi, *An Autobiography. The Story of my Experiments with Truth*, paperback edn., London, 1966

R. Iyer (ed.), *The Moral and Political Writings of Mahatma Gandhi* (3 vols.), Oxford, 1986–7

J. Nehru, *An Autobiography*, London, 1936

S. C. Bose, *The Indian Struggle 1920–1942*, New York, 1964

S. Banerjea, *A Nation in Making*, first pub. 1925: Calcutta, 1963

V. N. Datta and B. E. Cleghorn (eds.), *A Nationalist Muslim and Indian Politics. Being the Selected Correspondence of the late Dr. Syed Mahmud*, Delhi, 1974

M. Hasan (ed.), *Muslims And The Congress: Select Correspondence of Dr. M. A. Ansari 1921–1935*, Delhi, 1979

T. N. Jagadisan (ed.), *Letters of the Right Honourable V. S. Srinivasa Sastri*, 2nd edn., Bombay, 1963

(B) THE CATALYST OF WAR

D. C. Ellinwood and S. D. Pradhan (eds.), *India And World War I*, New Delhi, 1978

P. G. Robb, *The Government Of India And Reform. Policies towards Politics and the Constitution*, Oxford, 1976

B. R. Tomlinson, 'India and the British Empire, 1880–1935', *IESHR*, vol. xii, no. 4 (Oct.–Dec. 1975), pp. 337–80

F. C. R. Robinson, *Separation among Indian Muslims. The politics of the United Provinces' Muslims 1860–1923*, Cambridge, 1974

P. Hardy, *The Muslims of British India*, Cambridge, 1972

S. R. Mehrotra, 'The Politics behind the Montagu Declaration of 1917', in C. H. Philips (ed.), *Politics And Society In India*, London, 1963

D. A. Low (ed.), *Soundings in Modern South Asian History*, London, 1968

H. F. Owen, 'Negotiating the Lucknow Pact', *JAS*, vol. xxxi, no. 3 (May 1972), pp. 561–87

(C) GANDHI

P. Moon, *Gandhi and Modern India*, London, 1968

A. Copley, *Gandhi. Against the Tide* (Historical Association Studies), Oxford, 1987

B. Parekh, *Colonialism, Tradition and Reform. An Analysis of Gandhi's Political Discourse*, New Delhi, Newbury Park, and London, 1989

B. Parekh, *Gandhi's Political Philosophy. A Critical Analysis*, London and Basingstoke, 1989

M. Chatterjee, *Gandhi's Religious Thought*, London and Basingstoke, 1983

L. I. and S. H. Rudolph, *The Modernity Of Tradition. Political Development in India*, Chicago and London, 1967

R. N. Iyer, *The Moral And Political Thought Of Mahatma Gandhi*, New York, 1973

J. Masselos, *Nationalism on the Indian Subcontinent. An Introductory History*, Melbourne, 1972

R. A. Huttenback, *Gandhi in South Africa. British Imperialism and the Indian Question, 1860–1914*, Ithaca and London, 1971

M. Swan, *Gandhi. The South African Experience*, Johannesburg, 1985

J. M. Brown, *Gandhi. Prisoner of Hope*, New Haven and London, 1989

J. M. Brown, *Gandhi's Rise To Power. Indian Politics 1915–1922*, Cambridge, 1972

R. Kumar (ed.), *Essays On Gandhian Politics. The Rowlatt Satyagraha of 1919*, Oxford, 1971

G. Minault, *The Khilafat Movement: Religious Symbolism and Political Mobilization in India*, New York, 1982

S. Amin, 'Gandhi as Mahatma: Gorakhpur District, Eastern UP, 1921–2', R. Guha (ed.), *Subaltern Studies III. Writings on South Asian History and Society*, Delhi, 1984, pp. 1–61

G. Krishna, 'The Development of the Indian National Congress as a Mass Organization, 1918–1923', *JAS*, vol. xxv, no. 3 (May 1966), pp. 413–30

C Baker, *'Non-cooperation in South India'*, in C. J. Baker and D. A. Washbrook (eds.), *South India, Political Institutions and Political Change 1880–1940*, Delhi 1975, pp. 98–149

(D) THE 1920s

R. J. Moore, *The Crisis Of Indian Unity 1917–1940*, Oxford, 1974

J. M. Brown, *Gandhi and Civil Disobedience. The Mahatma in Indian Politics 1928–34*, Cambridge, 1977

S. Gopal, *The Viceroyalty Of Lord Irwin 1926–1931*, Oxford, 1957

S. Gopal, *Jawaharlal Nehru. A Biography. Volume I 1889–1947*, London, 1975

D. Keer, *Veer Savarkar*, 2nd edn., Bombay, 1966

J. A. Curran, *Militant Hinduism In Indian Politics. A History Of The R. S. S.*, New York, 1951

R. Gordon, 'The Hindu Mahasabha and the Indian National Congress, 1915 to 1926', *MAS*, vol. 9, part 2 (April 1975), pp. 145–203

B. R. Nanda (ed.), *Socialism in India*, Delhi, 1972

D. E. U. Baker, 'The Break-Down of Nationalist Unity and the Formation of the Swaraj Parties, India, 1922 to 1924', G. C. Bolton and H. F. Owen (eds.), *University Studies in History*, vol. v, no. 4 (1970), pp. 85–113

M. Hasan, *Nationalism And Communal Politics In India, 1916–1928*, Delhi, 1979

D. Page, *Prelude To Partition. The Indian Muslims and the Imperial System of Control 1920–1932*, Karachi, 1987

V. P. Menon, *The Story of the Integration of the Indian States*, Second edn., Delhi, 1961

R. Jeffrey (ed.), *People, Princes And Paramount Power. Society and Politics in the Princely States*, Delhi, 1978

B. Ramusack, *The Princes of India in the Twilight of Empire: Dissolution of a Patron–Client System, 1914–1939*, Columbus, 1978

S. R. Ashton, *British Policy Towards The Indian States 1905–1938*, London and Dublin, 1982

D. C. Potter, *India's Political Administrators 1919–1983*, Oxford, 1986

D. C. Potter, 'Manpower Shortage and the End of Colonialism. The Case of the Indian Civil Service', *MAS*, vol. 7, part 1 (Jan. 1973), pp. 47–73

T. H. Beaglehole, 'From Rulers to Servants: The I. C. S. and the British Demission of Power in India', *MAS*, vol. 11, part 2 (April 1977), pp. 237–55

A. Ewing, 'The Indian Civil Service 1919–1924: Service Discontent and the Response in London and in Delhi', *MAS*, vol. 18, part 1 (1984), pp. 33–53

S. Epstein, 'British Officers in Decline: The Erosion of British Authority in the Bombay Countryside, 1919 to 1947', *MAS*, vol. 16, part 3 (1982), pp. 493–518

B. R. Tomlinson, 'India and the British Empire, 1880–1935', *IESHR*, vol. xii, no. 4 (Oct.–Dec. 1975), pp. 337–80

B. R. Tomlinson, *The Political Economy Of The Raj 1914–1947. The Economics of Decolonization in India*, London, 1979

C. Baker, G. Johnson and A. Seal (eds.), *Power, Profit and Politics: Essays on Imperialism, Nationalism and Change in Twentieth-Century India*, Cambridge, 1981

(E) REGIONAL STUDIES

J. H. Broomfield, *Elite Conflict in a Plural Society: Twentieth-Century Bengal*, Berkeley and Los Angeles, 1968

D. Chakrabarty, *Rethinking Working-Class History. Bengal 1890–1940*, Princeton, 1989

G. A. Heeger, 'The Growth of the Congress Movement in Punjab, 1920–1940', *JAS*, vol. xxxii, no. 1 (Nov. 1972), pp. 39–51

G. Pandey, *The Ascendancy Of The Congress In Uttar Pradesh 1926–34. A Study in Imperfect Mobilization*, Delhi, 1978

P. Reeves, *Landlords and Governments in Uttar Pradesh. A Study of their Relations until Zamindari Abolition*, Bombay, 1991

D. Hardiman, *Peasant Nationalists of Gujarat. Kheda District 1917–1934*, Delhi, 1981

S. J. M. Epstein, *The Earthy Soil. Bombay Peasants and the Indian Nationalist Movement 1919–1947*, Delhi, 1988

S. F. D. Ansari, *Sufi Saints and State Power. The* pirs *of Sind, 1843–1947*, Cambridge, 1992

D. E. U. Baker, *Changing Political Leadership in an Indian Province: The Central Provinces and Berar 1919–1939*, Delhi, 1979

D. Arnold, *The Congress In Tamilnad. Nationalist Politics in South India, 1919–1937*, London and Dublin, 1977

C. J. Baker, *The Politics of South India 1920–1937*, Cambridge, 1977

J. Manor, *Political Change In An Indian State. Mysore 1917–1955*, New Delhi, 1977

K. McPherson, 'The Social Background and Politics of the Muslims of Tamil Nad, 1901–1937', *IESHR*, vol. vi, no. 4 (Dec. 1969), pp. 381–402

E. F. Irschick, *Politics And Social Conflict In South India. The Non-Brahman Movement and Tamil Separatism, 1916–1929*, Berkeley and Los Angeles, 1969

A. D. D. Gordon, *Businessmen and Politics. Rising Nationalism and a Modernising Economy in Bombay, 1918–1933*, New Delhi, 1978

CHAPTER V

(A) SOURCE MATERIAL

C. H. Philips and B. N. Pandey (eds.), *The Evolution Of India And Pakistan 1858 to 1947. Select Documents*, London, 1962

B. N. Pandey (ed.), *The Indian Nationalist Movement, 1885–1947. Select Documents*, London, 1979

K. K. Aziz (ed.), *The All India Muslim Conference 1928–1935. A Documentary Record*, Karachi, 1972

J. Nehru, *An Autobiography*, London, 1936

S. C. Bose, *The Indian Struggle 1920–1942*, New York, 1964

T. N. Jagadisan (ed.), *Letters of the Right Honourable V. S. Srinivasa Sastri*, 2nd edn., Bombay, 1963

B. E. Cleghorn and V. N. Datta (eds.), *A Nationalist Muslim and Indian Politics. Being the Selected Correspondence of the late Dr. Syed Mahmud*, Delhi, 1974

M. Hasan (ed.), *Muslims And The Congress: Select Correspondence of Dr. M. A. Ansari 1912–1935*, Delhi, 1979

Halifax (Lord Irwin), *Fulness of Days*, London, 1957

Zetland, *'Essayez'*, London, 1956

W. H. Saumarez Smith, *A Young Man's Country. Letters of a Subdivisional Officer of the Indian Civil Service 1936–1937*, Salisbury, 1977

F. Moraes, *Witness to an Era. India 1920 to the present day*, London, 1973

(B) GENERAL

J. M. Brown, *Gandhi. Prisoner of Hope*, New Haven and London, 1989

S. Gopal, *Jawaharlal Nehru. A Biography. Volume I 1889–1947*, London, 1975

H. Bolitho, *Jinnah. Creator of Pakistan*, London, 1954

A. Jalal and A. Seal, 'Alternative to Partition: Muslim Politics between the Wars', C. Baker, G. Johnson, and A. Seal (eds.), *Power, Profit and Politics: Essays on Imperialism, Nationalism and Change in Twentieth-Century India*, Cambridge, 1981, pp. 415–54.

A. Jalal, *The Sole Spokesman. Jinnah, the Muslim League and the Demand for Pakistan*, Cambridge, 1985

K. B. Sayeed, 'The Personality of Jinnah and his Political Strategy', pp. 276–93 of C. H. Philips and M. D. Wainwright (eds.), *The Partition Of India. Policies and Perspectives 1935–1947*, London, 1970

R. J. Moore, *The Crisis Of Indian Unity 1917–1940*, Oxford, 1974

D. A. Low (ed.), *Congress And The Raj. Facets of the Indian Struggle 1917–47*, London, 1977

R. Sisson and S. Wolpert (eds.), *Congress and Indian Nationalism. The Pre-Independence Phase*, Berkeley and Los Angeles, 1988

J. Masselos (ed.), *Struggling and Ruling. The Indian National Congress 1885–1985*, London, 1987

C. H. Philips and M. D. Wainwright (eds.), *The Partition Of India. Policies and Perspectives 1935–1947*, London, 1970

B. R. Tomlinson, *The Indian National Congress and the* Raj*, 1929–1942. The Penultimate Phase*, London, 1976

B. R. Nanda (ed.), *Socialism in India*, Delhi, 1972

J. P. Haithcox, *Communism And Nationalism In India. M. N. Roy and Comintern Policy 1920–1939*, Princeton, 1971

G. D. Overstreet and M. Windmiller, *Communism in India*, Berkeley and Los Angeles, 1959

P. Hardy, *The Muslims of British India*, Cambridge, 1972

D. Page, *Prelude to Partition. The Indian Muslims and the Imperial System of Control 1920–1932*, Karachi, 1987

F. Shaikh, *Community and Consensus in Islam. Muslim Representation in Colonial India, 1860–1947*, Cambridge, 1989

A. Inder Singh, *The Origins of the Partition of India 1936–1947*, Delhi, 1987

K. B. Sayeed, *Pakistan The Formative Phase 1857–1948* (2nd edn.), London, 1968

R. Symonds, *The Making Of Pakistan*, London, 1949

C. Markovits, *Indian Business and Nationalist Politics 1931–39. The Indigenous Capitalist Class and the Rise of the Congress Party*, Cambridge, 1985

M. Weiner, *Party Building In A New Nation. The Indian National Congress*, Chicago, 1967

V. P. Menon, *The Story of the Integration of the Indian States*, London, 1956

B. Ramusack, *The Princes of India in the Twilight of Empire: Dissolution of a Patron–Client System, 1914–1939*, Columbus, 1978

S. R. Ashton, *British Policy Towards the Indian States, 1905–1939*, London, 1982

R. Jeffrey (ed.), *People, Princes and Paramount Power. Society and Politics in the Indian Princely States*, Delhi, 1978

B. N. Pandey (ed.), *Leadership In South Asia*, New Delhi, 1977

C. Baker, G. Johnson and A. Seal (eds.), *Power, Profit and Politics: Essays on Imperialism, Nationalism and Change in Twentieth-Century India*, Cambridge, 1981

R. Hunt and J. Harrison, *The District Officer in India 1930–1947*, London, 1980

D. C. Potter, *India's Political Administrators 1919–1983*, Oxford, 1986

S. Epstein, 'British Officers in Decline: The Erosion of British Authority in the Bombay Countryside, 1919 to 1947', *MAS*, vol. 16, no. 3 (1982), pp. 493–518

(c) ECONOMIC AND SOCIAL TRENDS

B. R. Tomlinson, *The Political Economy Of The Raj 1914–1947. The Economics of Decolonization in India*, London, 1979

D. Kumar and M. Desai (eds.), *The Cambridge Economic History of India. Volume 2: c. 1757–c. 1970*, Cambridge, 1983

A. K. Bagchi, *Private Investment In India 1900–1939*, Cambridge, 1972

R. K. Ray, *Industrialization In India. Growth and Conflict in the Private Corporate Sector 1914–47*, Delhi, 1979

J. Krishnamurty, 'The Distribution of the Indian Working Force, 1901–1951', pp. 258–76 of K. N. Chaudhuri and C. J. Dewey (eds.), *Economy And Society. Essays in Indian Economic and Social History*, Delhi, 1979

C. J. Baker, 'Debt and the Depression in Madras, 1929–1936', pp. 233–42 of C. Dewey and A. G. Hopkins (eds.), *The Imperial Impact: Studies in the Economic History of Africa and India*, London, 1978

K. Davis, *The Population Of India And Pakistan*, Princeton, 1951

K. Davis, 'Social and Demographic Aspects of Economic Development in India', pp. 263–315 of S. Kuznets, W. E. Moore and J. J. Spengler (eds.), *Economic Growth: Brazil, India, Japan*, Durham, N. C., 1955

T. G. Kessinger, *Vilyatpur 1848–1968. Social and Economic Change in a North Indian Village*, Berkeley, Los Angeles and London, 1974

C. J. Baker, *An Indian Rural Economy 1880–1955. The Tamilnad Countryside*, Oxford, 1984

W. and C. Wiser, *Behind Mud Walls 1930–1960*, Berkeley and Los Angeles, 1969

S. Nurullah and J. P. Naik, *A History Of Education In India* (2nd edn.), Bombay, 1951

(d) REGIONAL STUDIES

J. Gallagher, 'Congress in Decline: Bengal, 1930 to 1939', pp. 269–325 of J. Gallagher, G. Johnson and A. Seal (eds.), *Locality, Province and Nation. Essays on Indian Politics 1870–1940*, Cambridge, 1973

L. A. Gordon, *Bengal: The Nationalist Movement 1876–1940*, New York and London, 1974

J. H. Broomfield, *Elite Conflict in a Plural Society: Twentieth-Century Bengal,*

Berkeley and Los Angeles, 1968

D. Chakrabarty, *Rethinking Working-Class History. Bengal 1890–1940*, Princeton, 1989

G. Pandey, *The Ascendancy Of The Congress In Uttar Pradesh 1926–34. A Study in Imperfect Mobilization*, Delhi, 1978

H. A. Gould, 'The Emergence of Modern Indian Politics: Political Development in Faizabad Part I: 1884–1935', *Journal of Commonwealth and Comparative Politics*, xxi, 1 (Mar. 1974), pp. 20–41

H. A. Gould, 'The Emergence of Modern Indian Politics: Political Development in Faizabad Part II: 1935 to Independence', *Journal of Commonwealth and Comparative Politics*, xxi, 2 (July 1974), pp. 157–88

P. D. Reeves, *Landlords and Governments in Uttar Pradesh. A Study of their Relations until Zamindari Abolition*, Bombay, 1991

V. Damodaran, *Broken Promises. Popular Protest, Indian Nationalism and the Congress Party in Bihar, 1935–1946*, Delhi, 1992

G. A. Heeger, 'The Growth of the Congress Movement in Punjab, 1920–1940', *JAS*, xxxii, 1 (Nov. 1972), pp. 397–451

S. Oren, 'The Sikhs, Congress, and the Unionists in British Punjab, 1937–1945', *MAS*, vol. 8, part 3 (July, 1974), pp. 397–418

S. F. D. Ansari, *Sufi Saints and State Power. The pirs of Sind, 1843–1947*, Cambridge, 1992

D. Hardiman, *Peasant Nationalists of Gujarat. Kheda District 1917–1934*, Delhi, 1981

S. J. M. Epstein, *The Earthy Soil. Bombay Peasants and the Indian Nationalist Movement 1919–1947*, Delhi, 1988

A. D. Gordon, *Businessmen And Politics: Rising Nationalism and a Modernizing Economy in Bombay, 1918–1933*, New Delhi, 1978

D. E. U. Baker, *Changing Political Leadership in an Indian Province: The Central Provinces and Berar 1919–1939*, Delhi, 1979

D. Arnold, *The Congress In Tamilnad. Nationalist Politics in South India, 1919–1937*, London and Dublin, 1977

C. J. Baker, *The Politics of South India 1920–1937*, Cambridge, 1976

See also the regional studies relating to this period on Gujarat, Bombay City, Andhra, UP, CP and Berar, Tamilnad, Bihar, Mysore, Travancore, and Rohilkhand (UP), in D. A. Low (ed.), *Congress And The Raj. Facets of the Indian Struggle 1917–47*, London, 1977

(E) CHRONOLOGICALLY LIMITED STUDIES

1. *1929–34*:

S. Gopal, *The Viceroyalty Of Lord Irwin 1926–1931*, Oxford, 1957

J. M. Brown, *Gandhi and Civil Disobedience. The Mahatma in Indian Politics 1928–34*, Cambridge, 1977

R. J. Moore, 'The Making of India's Paper Federation, 1927–35', pp. 54–78 of C. H. Philips and M. D. Wainwright (eds.), *The Partition Of India. Policies and Perspec-*

tives 1935–47, London, 1970

S. C. Ghosh, 'Decision Making and Power in the British Conservative Party: A Case Study of the Indian Problem, 1929–34', *Political Studies*, xiii (1965), pp. 198–212

E. Zelliot, 'Gandhi and Ambedkar: A Study in Leadership', pp. 69–95 of J. Michael Mahar (ed.), *The Untouchables in Contemporary India*, Tucson, 1972

2. *1935–40:*

J. Glendevon, *The Viceroy at Bay. Lord Linlithgow in India 1936–1943*, London, 1971

R. J. Moore, 'British Policy and the Indian Problem, 1936–40', pp. 79–94 of C. H. Philips and M. D. Wainwright (eds.), *The Partition of India. Policies and Perspectives 1935–1947*, London, 1970

R. Coupland, *Indian Politics 1936–1942*, London, 1943

S. R. Mehrotra, 'The Congress and the Partition of India', pp. 188–221 of C. H. Philips and M. D. Wainwright (eds.), *The Partition Of India. Policies and Perspectives 1935–1947*, London, 1970

B. R. Nanda, 'Nehru, the Indian National Congress and the Partition of India, 1935–47', ibid., pp. 148–87

Z. H. Zaidi, 'Aspects of the Development of Muslim League Policy, 1937–47', ibid., pp. 245–75

J. P. Haithcox, 'Left Wing Unity and the Indian Nationalist Movement: M. N. Roy and the Congress Socialist Party', *MAS*, vol. 3, part 1 (Jan. 1969), pp. 17–56

CHAPTER VI

(A) SOURCE MATERIAL

C. H. Philips and B. N. Pandey (eds.), *The Evolution Of India And Pakistan 1858 to 1947. Select Documents*, London, 1962

B. N. Pandey (ed.), *The Indian Nationalist Movement, 1885–1947. Select Documents*, London, 1979

B. E. Cleghorn and V. N. Datta (eds.), *A Nationalist Muslim and Indian Politics. Being the Selected Correspondence of the late Dr. Syed Mahmud*, Delhi, 1974

A. K. Azad, *India Wins Freedom*, complete version, London, 1988

F. Moraes, *Witness to an Era. India 1920 to the present day*, London, 1973

N. B. Bonarjee, *Under Two Masters*, Calcutta, 1970

P. Moon (ed.), *Wavell. The Viceroy's Journal*, London, 1973

F. Tuker, *While Memory Serves*, London, 1950

C. Corfield, *The Princely India I Knew. From Reading to Mountbatten*, Madras, 1975

A. Campbell-Johnson, *Mission With Mountbatten*, London, 1951

(B) COLLECTIONS OF ESSAYS

C. H. Philips and M. D. Wainwright (eds.), *The Partition Of India. Policies and Perspectives 1935–1947*, London, 1970

D. A. Low (ed.), *Congress And the Raj. Facets of the Indian Struggle 1917–47*,

London, 1977

D. A. Low, *Eclipse of Empire*, Cambridge, 1991 (particularly chapters 3 and 4)

R. Sisson and S. Wolpert (eds.), *Congress and Indian Nationalism. The Pre-Independence Phase*, Berkeley and Los Angeles, 1988

D. A. Low (ed.), *The Political Inheritance of Pakistan*, Basingstoke and London, 1991

R. Jeffrey (ed.), *People, Princes And Paramount Power. Society and Politics in the Indian Princely States*, Delhi, 1978

H. C. Hart (ed.), *Indira Gandhi's India. A Political System Reappraised*, Boulder, Colorado, 1976

C. Baker, G. Johnson and A. Seal (eds.), *Power, Profit and Politics: Essays on Imperialism, Nationalism and Change in Twentieth-Century India*, Cambridge, 1981

(C) GENERAL WORKS

H. V. Hodson, *The Great Divide. Britain–India–Pakistan*, London, 1969

P. Hardy, *The Muslims of British India*, Cambridge, 1972

J. Masselos, *Nationalism on the Indian Subcontinent*, Melbourne, 1972

J. Glendevon, *The Viceroy at Bay. Lord Linlithgow in India 1936–1943*, London, 1971

J. H. Voigt, *India in the Second World War*, New Delhi, 1987

V. P. Menon, *The Transfer Of Power In India*, Bombay edn., 1968

(D) PARTICULAR STUDIES

K. Singh, *A History Of The Sikhs. Volume 2: 1839–1964*, Princeton, 1966

B. R. Nayar, *Minority Politics In The Punjab*, Princeton, 1966

B. R. Nayar, 'Sikh Separatism in the Punjab', pp. 150–75 of D. E. Smith (ed.), *South Asian Politics And Religion*, Princeton, 1969

S. Oren, 'The Sikhs, Congress, and the Unionists in British Punjab, 1937–1945', *MAS*, vol. 8, no. 3 (July 1974), pp. 397–418

G. A. Heeger, 'The Growth of the Congress Movement in Punjab, 1920–1940', *JAS*, vol. xxxii, no. 1 (Nov. 1972), pp. 39–51

I. A. Talbot, 'The 1946 Punjab Elections', *MAS*, vol. 14, part 1 (1980), pp. 65–91

D. Gilmartin, 'Religious Leadership And The Pakistan Movement in the Punjab', *MAS*, vol. 13, part 3 (July 1979), pp. 485–517

I. Talbot, *Provincial Politics And The Pakistan Movement. The Growth of the Muslim League in North-West and North-East India 1937–47*, Karachi, 1988

S. F. D. Ansari, *Sufi Saints and State Power. The pirs of Sind, 1843–1947*, Cambridge, 1992

F. Shaikh, *Community And Consensus In Islam. Muslim Representation in Colonial India 1860–1947*, Cambridge, 1985

A. Jalal, *The Sole Spokesman. Jinnah, the Muslim League and the Demand for Pakistan*, Cambridge, 1985

S. Das, *Communal Riots in Bengal 1905–1947*, Delhi, 1991

P. Moon, *Divide and Quit*, Berkeley and Los Angeles, 1962

R. J. Moore, *Churchill, Cripps, And India, 1939–1945*, Oxford, 1979

R. J. Moore, *Escape From Empire. The Attlee Government and the Indian Problem*, Oxford, 1983

V. P. Menon, *The Story of the Integration of the Indian States*, Madras edn., 1961

F. G. Hutchins, *India's Revolution. Gandhi and the Quit India Movement*, Cambridge, Mass., 1973

B. R. Tomlinson, *The Indian National Congress and the* Raj*, 1929–1942. The Penultimate Phase*, London, 1976

B. R. Tomlinson, *The Political Economy Of The Raj 1914–1947. The Economics of Decolonization in India*, London, 1979

D. C. Potter, 'Manpower Shortage and the End of Colonialism. The Case of the Indian Civil Service', *MAS*, vol. 7, part 1 (Jan. 1973), pp. 47–73

D. C. Potter, *India's Political Administrators 1919–1983*, Oxford, 1986

R. Hunt and J. Harrison, *The District Officer in India 1930–1947*, London, 1980

R. Ray, *Industrialization In India. Growth and Conflict in the Private Corporate Sector 1914–47*, Delhi, 1979

M. Windmiller, 'Linguistic Regionalism in India', *Pacific Affairs*, vol. xxvii, no. 4 (Dec. 1954), pp. 291–318

R. Sisson, *The Congress Party In Rajasthan. Political Integration and Institution-Building in an Indian State*, Berkeley, Los Angeles, and London, 1972

J. Manor, *Political Change In An Indian State. Mysore 1917–1955*, New Delhi, 1977

V. Damodaran, *Broken Promises. Popular Protest, Indian Nationalism and the Congress Party in Bihar 1935–1946*, Delhi, 1992

S. J. M. Epstein, *The Earthy Soil. Bombay Peasants and the Indian Nationalist Movement 1919–1947*, Delhi, 1988

S. A. Kochanek, *The Congress Party Of India. The Dynamics Of One-Party Democracy*, Princeton, 1968

R. L. Hardgrave, *India. Government and Politics in a Developing Nation*, 3rd edn., New York, 1980

H. Bolitho, *Jinnah. Creator of Pakistan*, London, 1954

S. Gopal, *Jawaharlal Nehru. A Biography. Volume 1 1889–1947*, London, 1975

J. M. Brown, *Gandhi. Prisoner of Hope*, New Haven and London, 1989

P. Greenough, *Prosperity And Misery In Modern Bengal. The Famine of 1943–1944*, New York and Oxford, 1982

S. Bose, *Agrarian Bengal. Economy, Social Structure and Politics, 1919–1947*, Cambridge, 1986

C. J. Baker, *An Indian Rural Economy 1880–1955. The Tamilnad Countryside*, Oxford, 1984

CHAPTER VII

(A) GENERAL INTRODUCTIONS

S. A. Kochanek, 'India', in R. N. Kearney (ed.), *Politics and Modernization in South and Southeast Asia*, New York, 1975

R. L. Hardgrave, *India. Government and Politics in a Developing Nation*, 4th edn., San Diego, 1986

W. H. Morris-Jones, *The Government and Politics of India*, 3rd edn., Huntingdon, 1987

R. Kothari, *Politics in India*, Boston, 1970

A. H. Hanson and J. Douglas, *India's Democracy*, London, 1972

P. R. Brass, *The Politics of India since Independence*, Cambridge, 1990

D. E. Smith (ed.), *South Asian Politics And Religion*, Princeton, 1969

D. E. Smith, *India as a Secular State*, Princeton, 1963

A. T. Embree, *Utopias in Conflict. Religion and Nationalism in Modern India*, Berkeley, Los Angeles and Oxford, 1990

H. Tinker, 'Structure of the British Imperial Heritage', in R. Braibanti (ed.), *Asian Bureaucratic Systems Emergent from the British Imperial Tradition*, Duke University Press, 1966

D. C. Potter, 'Bureaucratic Change in India', in Braibanti (ed.) ibid.

(B) POLITICAL STUDIES

S. A. Kochanek, *The Congress Party Of India: The Dynamics Of One-Party Democracy*, Princeton, 1968

S. A. Kochanek, *Business and Politics in India*, Berkeley, 1974

M. Weiner, *Party Building In A New Nation. The Indian National Congress*, Chicago, 1967

M. Weiner, *The Politics Of Scarcity. Public Pressure and Political Response in India*, Chicago, 1962

M. Weiner, *State Politics In India*, Princeton, 1968

M. Weiner (ed. A. Varshney), *The Indian Paradox. Essays in Indian Politics*, New Delhi, Newbury Park, and London, 1989

A. Kohli, *Democracy and Discontent. India's growing crisis of governability*, Cambridge, 1990

A. Kohli (ed.), *India's Democracy. An Analysis of Changing State–Society Relations*, Princeton, 1990

H. C. Hart (ed.), *A Political System Reappraised*, Boulder, Colorado, 1976

R. L. Park and I. Tinker (eds.), *Leadership and Political Institutions in India*, Princeton, 1959

D. H. Bayley, *The Police and Political Development in India*, Princeton, 1969

D. C. Potter, *India's Political Administrators 1919–1983*, Oxford, 1986

R. W. Jones, *Urban Politics in India. Area, Power, and Policy in a Penetrated System*, Berkeley, Los Angeles and London, 1974

D. B. Rosenthal, *The Limited Elite: Politics and Government in Two Indian Cities*, Chicago and London, 1970

D. B. Rosenthal (ed.), *The City in Indian Politics*, Faridabad, 1976

H. Crouch, *Trade Unions and Politics in India*, Bombay, 1966

L. I. and S. H. Rudolph, *The Modernity Of Tradition. Political Development in India*, Chicago and London, 1967

L. I. and S. H. Rudolph, *In Pursuit of Lakshmi. The Political Economy of the Indian*

State, Chicago and London, 1987

R. W. Bradnock, *India's Foreign Policy since 1971*, London, 1990

(C) SOCIAL, ECONOMIC AND RELIGIOUS STUDIES

D. Kumar and M. Desai (eds.), *The Cambridge Economic History Of India. Volume 2: c.1757–c.1970*, Cambridge, 1983 (chapter XIII)

S. C. Dube (ed.), *India since Independence. Social report on India 1947–1972*, New Delhi, 1977

B. Kuppuswamy, *Population and Society in India*, Bombay, 1975

R. H. Cassen, *India: Population, Economy, Society*, London and Basingstoke, 1978

A. Maddison, *Class Structure and Economic Growth. India and Pakistan since the Mughuls*, London, 1971

W. Malenbaum, *Modern India's Economy. Two Decades of Planned Growth*, Columbus, 1971

F. R. Frankel, *India's Political Economy, 1947–1977. The Gradual Revolution*, Princeton, 1978

F. T. Jannuzi, *Agrarian Crisis in India. The Case of Bihar*, Austin and London, 1974

A. Kohli, *The State And Poverty In India. The Politics of Reform*, Cambridge, 1987

W. and C. Wiser, *Behind Mud Walls 1930–1960*, Berkeley and Los Angeles, 1969

M. Marriott (ed.), *Village India. Studies in the Little Community*, paperback edition, Chicago and London, 1969

M. N. Srinivas, *Social Change in Modern India*, Berkeley and Los Angeles, 1966

J. M. Mahar (ed.), *The Untouchables in Contemporary India*, Tucson, 1972

M. Holmström, *South Indian Factory Workers. Their life and their world*, Cambridge, 1976

M. Holmström, *Industry And Inequality. The social anthropology of Indian labour*, Cambridge, 1984

P. Ashby, *Modern Trends in Hinduism*, New York and London, 1974

L. A. Babb, *The Divine Hierarchy: Popular Hinduism in Central India*, New York and London, 1975

P. Brent, *Godmen of India*, London, 1972

J. M. Brown, *Men And Gods In A Changing World. Some Themes in the Religious Experience of Twentieth-Century Hindus and Christians*, London, 1980

(D) BIOGRAPHIES AND AUTOBIOGRAPHIES

S. Gopal, *Jawaharlal Nehru. A Biography. Volume 2: 1947–1956*, London, 1979 and *Volume 3: 1956–1964*, London, 1984

D. Moraes, *Mrs. Gandhi*, London, 1980

F. Moraes, *Witness to an Era. India 1920 to the present day*, London, 1973

N. B. Bonarjee, *Under Two Masters*, Calcutta, 1970

M. Tyler, *My Years in an Indian Prison*, Penguin edition, 1978

S. Hobson, *Family Web. A Story of India*, London, 1978

J. M. Freeman, *Untouchable. An Indian Life History*, London, 1979

INDEX